Library of Shakespearean Biography and Criticism

I. PRIMARY REFERENCE WORKS ON SHAKESPEARE

II. CRITICISM AND INTERPRETATION

    A. Textual Treatises, Commentaries
    B. Treatment of Specal Subjects
    C. Dramatic and Literary Art in Shakespeare

III. SHAKESPEARE AND HIS TIME

    A. General Treatises. Biography
    B. The Age of Shakespeare
    C. Authorship

Series III, Part A

SHAKESPEARE: A PORTRAIT RESTORED

The Frontispiece to *The Works of William Shakespeare, revised and corrected by Nicholas Rowe* (1709), the first critical edition of Shakespeare.

Library of Shakespearean Biography and Criticism

SHAKESPEARE:
A PORTRAIT RESTORED

by

CLARA LONGWORTH DE CHAMBRUN

BOOKS FOR LIBRARIES PRESS
FREEPORT, NEW YORK

First published 1957 by Hollis & Carter, Ltd.

Reprinted 1970 by arrangement with The Bodley Head

STANDARD BOOK NUMBER:
8369-5251-0

LIBRARY OF CONGRESS CATALOG CARD NUMBER:
77-109642

PRINTED IN THE UNITED STATES OF AMERICA

PUBLISHER'S NOTE

Shakespeare : A Portrait Restored is the translation made by Clara Long-worth, Countess de Chambrun, of her *Shakespeare Retrouvé*, published in France in 1947. The Countess de Chambrun obtained her Doctorate from the University of Paris in 1921 with a thesis on Giovanni Florio, who revealed the masterpieces of the Italian Renaissance to Shakespeare. She was considered in France as one of the great authorities on Elizabethan times, to the study of which she devoted the greater part of her life.

She gathered a collection of rare sixteenth- and seventeenth-century volumes in her own library in Paris, and when these sources were insufficient, she completed her documentation at the Folger Library in Washington, at Shakespeare's birthplace in Stratford, at the Bodleian Library in Oxford, or at the British Museum and the Record Office in London. The more untrodden the path, the more enthusiastically did she pursue her researches.

The Countess de Chambrun published over a score of books, most of which were devoted to her favourite subject. She considered that *Shakespeare : A Portrait Restored*, her last volume, summed up her life's work. The text that she herself revised before her death in 1954 contains several passages written especially for French readers—the preamble, for example. We are publishing her text in its entirety, since we are certain that English readers will observe with satisfaction the fervour of overseas admirers of our national poet, and they will agree with Professor J. B. Harrison " that new notions about Shakespeare, especially when unfamiliar and perhaps disturbing, should be received with an open mind ".

CONTENTS

PREAMBLE

SHAKESPEARE'S ENGLAND UNDER THE ELIZABETHAN STATUTES

THE more new volumes about Shakespeare flood the book market —the more the poet of nature and the human heart seems to elude readers bent on discovering his real personality. And yet the living image drawn by his first biographers : Fuller, Fulman and Aubrey, was handed down intact to the nineteenth century by Rowe, Langbaine and Malone.

At this point, however, the portrait became blurred and befogged in the thick mists of vain controversy. If the praiseworthy industry of the late Sir Sidney Lee, Sir E. K. Chambers and Professor Dover Wilson has succeeded in throwing much light on the existing documents, it has not, I believe, completely restored the original colours. A whole troop of eager iconoclasts rushed in to undermine the work of scholarly predecessors, followed by a host of uncritical enthusiasts. Some, having evolved a personal theory as to how, why and when the dramatist came to write, even went so far in support of an idea as to alter, suppress, or mutilate existing documents, no doubt self-convinced that they did so with the highest motives.

Thus someone thought fit to efface from a Bodleian manuscript John Aubrey's account of Shakespeare's intrigue with an Oxford innkeeper's wife—though in his sonnets the poet himself made full confession of the affair—and contemporary pamphleteers embroidered and enlarged on the scandal it created. Another destroyed the original draft of John Shakespeare's testament, presumably for no better reason than that it gave evidence of Roman Catholic proclivities. Others for more unfathomable reasons eliminated from Sir William D'Avenant's papers an autograph letter from King James addressed to William Shakespeare which probably accompanied his nomination as chief of His Majesties Players still exhibited in the Public Record Office.

In recent days, however, the evidence which has come to light confirms the old traditions and reminiscences repeated by the poet's immediate successors. The Scottish History Publications and those of the Dugdale, Camden and Catholic Record Societies (not to speak of hitherto unpublished discoveries among the state archives) have brought to light new documents which fully substantiate the findings of other days.

Shakespeare's work, like that of any author whose writings glow with feeling and emotion, cannot be fully understood apart from the public events of his day. His inspiration bears the indelible imprint of heredity and education and also shows trace of the many inhibitions which prevented his parents and brethren from drawing free breath and exposed them to constant perils and vexations. Their loyalty to the ancient faith, and refusal to attend the religious service " as by law established ", kept them in difficulty, for each omission to attend Protestant service was heavily fined. When the new legislation began to be enforced in Stratford, young William saw the Vicar of Holy Trinity and three masters of the Grammar School driven into exile to escape punishment under the new penal code. Two of his neighbours, Robert Dibdale of Shottery and William Hartley of Rowington, were hanged, drawn and quartered in London.

This atmosphere is essential to recreate if we would know anything about the poet's youthful sympathies. Although certain events throw a sombre shadow over his early days they also explain his conduct and help us to understand his character. In his case persecution did not warp his mind nor engender hatred and malice, as too often happens. On the contrary it led to tolerance and charity. It also underlines the constant appeal for liberty, justice and clemency perceptible in all his work.

The great Statute Book of Elizabeth should be read as preface to any study of Shakespeare's life and work. It explains the material difficulties of his family, so prosperous in his early youth, the mystery of his marriage, his disputes with local authority, his flight from Stratford, his choice of a protector in London, his espousal of the Essex cause and the joy with which his muse welcomed the advent of James Stuart.

The death of Mary Tudor on November 17th, 1558 was followed the very same evening by that of the Archbishop of Canterbury, Reginald Pole. The young Princess Elizabeth found herself in a precarious position as to the legality of her succession to the English throne. She had been declared a bastard by the king her father, and the high ecclesiastical authority which should have effaced the stigma and recognized her rights no longer existed. However, she was consecrated on January 15th at Westminster Abbey during a High Mass at which the Bishop of Carlisle [1] officiated and registered her solemn oath that she would protect the Catholic faith throughout her reign.

But, though Elizabeth herself had decided leanings toward the ancient faith—she always maintained that bishops should not marry, and she continued to have tapers and crucifixes in her private chapel—her ministers, and the exigencies of the situation, determined otherwise, and the Privy Council prepared without delay to establish by force a reformed religion among a people of whom only a fraction can have been convinced supporters of it. In the early months of 1559, after a year of difficulties and uncertainty, two measures were passed which were to alter radically the life of every English citizen. *The Act of Supremacy* decreed that whatever man or woman by word or writing acknowledged the spiritual authority of the Pope or refused to recognize the Queen as supreme governor in ecclesiastical as well

---

[1] It should have been the Archbishop of York who presided on this solemn occasion but, having heard that among other novelties the litanies were to be sung in English, the chancellor preferred to remain absent.

as temporal affairs would be liable to heavy penalties. *The Act of Uniformity* went further. In this, sanctions were decreed against all persons who professed a faith or entertained ideas contrary to those set forth in the Prayer Book of 1559. Attendance at the Church as by law established became obligatory and the celebration of Mass anywhere or at any time was strictly forbidden throughout the entire realm. An oath of allegiance was to be demanded from every ecclesiastic, magistrate, judge or mayor, also from any person in the pay of the Crown. When it is remembered that the government which ordained these measures represented only a small percentage of the population which it ruled with a rod of iron, the audacity of such a measure seems astonishing.

The Act of Uniformity was passed at the third reading by a bare majority of three votes in the House of Lords. We find Sir Simonds d'Ewes recording in the official minutes of this initial session this commentary : [1]

There may still be observed the obstinacy and boldness of the Popish Bishops who opposed all things that tended but to the least reformation of Idolatry and Superstition or abolishing the usurped authority of the Bishop of Rome.

The dissenting voices were those of the Archbishop of York, the Bishops of London, Ely, Worcester, Llandaff, Exeter, Chester, Coventry and Carlisle, who were joined by eight peers led by Viscount Montague, the only layman in the House of Lords with enough courage to denounce the Acts as unjust, unreasonable and untrue, and who added that no greater tyranny can be conceived than to compel a man under penalty of death to swear to that which his conscience believes to be false.

Among other consequences, this legislation introduced three new words into the English language : Papists were those who recognized the spiritual authority of Rome ; Recusants those who refused to take the oath of allegiance ; Pursuivants was the name given to the whole band of spies and informers attracted by the rewards offered by Richard Topcliffe, head of the Queen's secret service, commissioned to supervise and chastise.

The Act of Supremacy only applied to the Roman Catholics while that of Uniformity was couched in terms which appeared threatening to the many Protestant sects who refused to bow before the rubric of the Prayer Book as drawn up by Cranmer ; but the Non-conformists were for the most part left in peace for another thirty years. The Catholic problem was the only one with which the legislator of 1559 was prepared to deal.

Even much later, when an attempt was made to repress the extremely widespread and vociferous new sect founded by Robert Brown of Cambridge, and when one of the members of Parliament, Mr. Dalton, seconded by Dr. Lewin, demanded that the Brownists should be treated with the same severity as the Papist recusants, Sir Walter Raleigh himself answered :

In my concern, the Brownists are worthy to be uprooted and thrown out of the commonwealth : but what danger would grow to ourselves it were fit to

[1] *The Journal of the House of Lords*, London, 1595, p. 30.

consider. . . . I am sorry for it, I am afraid there is near twenty thousand of them (Brownists) in England, and when they be gone who shall maintain their wives and children. . . . Touching the explanation of a branch of the Statutes made for reducing loyal subjects to their due obedience it is only for such as are of the Romish Religion.[1]

The government agreed with Raleigh. In the instructions given to inquisitors, it was explicitly forbidden to " disquiet anyone on the subject of doctrine or conscience " ; the three points upon which the examiners were to insist were clearly enumerated : loyalty to the queen, opinion on papal supremacy and the maintenance of religious colleges.

During the period which preceded the application of the acts passed by parliament the Council could hope that the fourteen intractable bishops would consent to swim with the tide in their own interests. This calculation proved false. The Bishop of Llandaff was the only one amongst his brethren to conform. The others were summarily dismissed. At the same time twelve archdeacons, ten deans, forty-seven prebendaries, fifteen heads of colleges or universities, and many other lesser churchmen said farewell to their duties.

Many incumbents refused to submit in the first year ; those who offered to fill their vacancies were often without instruction or aptitude for the ministry. What they sought was simply a livelihood. Most did not even know how to make use of the new Prayer Book ; as for their flocks, they were incapable of responding aright. The country folk in general remained faithful to their old clergy and gave a lukewarm welcome to the pastor who came to take possession of the priest's house, brought wife and children with him, prayed and preached without a book and ascended the pulpit in garments which bore no sign of a religious vocation.

Sir Roger Dyos, the old Stratford vicar who baptized Shakespeare's elder sister, was the first priest to be removed from his cure and sent into exile. In order to obtain payment of his last emoluments, he was constrained to initiate a lawsuit.[2]

Shakespeare, in *The Merry Wives of Windsor*, draws the portrait of a preacher as ignorant as pretentious which the archives of the diocese of Worcester show not to have been exaggerated. Questioned as to his competence for the ministry of Charlecote, near Stratford, Richard Southam replied in 1565 :

I have taken no degree of school, neither in Oxford nor Cambridge, I have no licence to preach neither am I any preacher. . . . I know not any that doth

---

[1] It is interesting to find in *Twelfth Night* an allusion to the turbulent Brownist sect made by Sir Andrew Aguecheek, " I had as lief be a Brownist as a Politician " (Act III, Sc. 2). In the same play when the austere Malvolio is described as a Puritan Sir Andrew remarks, " If I thought that, I'ld beat him like a dog " (Act II, Sc. 3).

[2] The municipal account books of Stratford record that there was paid to Sir Roger Dyos, in 1576, thirteen pounds, seventeen shillings and sixpence for arrears, with cost of wax to seal it, and a box to bear the same.

challenge the gift of the vicarage within my parish but my good patron and master Sir Thomas Lucy,[1] knight, the true patron thereof.[2]

The Council, however, was determined to continue the work begun by parliament. In 1563 a new law, *Act for the Better Assurance of Royal Power* (5 Elizabeth, c. 1) reinforced the legislation of 1559 in giving it retroactive effect. The oath could now be exacted from anyone having held a public position or who was about to do so. Priests, schoolmasters, barristers and members of the House of Commons were liable. For once again the central power seemed decided to proceed gradually in the application of the law. This new act was the precursor of more severe measures ; vexations of every kind grew in number, though as yet there was no recourse to capital punishment. The government had need of money rather than blood to establish its prestige ; the extortion of fines from the Catholics who were still rich seemed a good means of obtaining it.

A fine of twelve pence per person had been decreed as the penalty for individuals who did not attend regular church service at least once a month, but to hear Mass cost the worshipper a hundred marks. Two witnesses were sufficient to prove the infringement of this rule, and the denouncer was awarded a third of the fine. Thus cupidity played as important a part as sectarian prejudice, and in a great number of cases personal spite still more so.

In order not to be constantly harassed certain families came to terms with the authorities. In consideration of a fine of forty pounds per annum, they were spared from molestation. Sir Thomas Gerard for example, imprisoned in the Tower, was invited to buy his family's immunity by means of a " voluntary gift ". In response : " He humbly submitteth himself to her Majesty's pleasure but is not able to offer any great sums offering his own person to serve her Highness in any place in the world. If he shall not be admitted thereto then he offereth with very good will thirty pounds a year which is a fourth part of the small portion remaining now left to maintain himself and his poor children."

Evidently this amount was not judged sufficient for the name of his wife, Dame Elisabeth Gerard, heads the list of recusants resident in Middlesex " now dispersed into other countries ".

Considerable sums were thus levied on Catholic citizens. The Crown also benefited from Peter's Pence, which the papal legate, Horatio Palavicini, deposited in the coffers of the Royal Treasury instead of taking what he had raised back to Italy. The wits of the time said of this foreign opportunist :

> This is Horatio Palavicene
> Who robbed the Pope to pay the Queen.

When the Crown under Henry VIII seized the goods of the regular clergy and distributed the wealth of the monasteries to favourites, the country

---

[1] Sir Thomas Lucy was always the implacable enemy of the Shakespeares, as will be seen in the following chapters.

[2] *Shakespeare's Marriage and Departure from Stratford*, J. W. Gray (London, 1905), p. 265.

folk bitterly regretted the departure of the monks. They, at least, spent their money on their own acres—the monastery was an open market for the neighbouring farmers. Its hospitality was taken for granted and the unfortunate frequently found relief from their suffering within its walls—quite different was the management of these estates when they were handed over to courtiers and noblemen who spent their income in London and often enclosed extensive grounds, for hunting or sheep breeding, thus depriving the farmer of small means of the commons where he used to graze his cows. But now it was the law of the land which threatened the goods and liberties of her own children. Indignation would have been greater if the countryside had understood the meaning of the acts which affirmed the royal power. In Warwickshire in particular, where the Catholic element predominated, the ancient habits were strongly rooted; and at Stratford, when orders were given to whitewash the frescoes of the ancient chapel of Holy Cross, to smash the statues, to sell surplices, vestments and chasubles, the townsmen must have begun at last to comprehend that this was the end of the religious customs of old England.

That the poet's family should refuse to submit was quite natural. In this part of the country resistance against the establishment of the Anglican Church remained very stubborn. Even today manors with hidden chapels, and ingenious secret hiding places for sheltering the priest and baffling the pursuivants, bear witness to their owners' passive resistance to the new ideas. The Earl of Leicester, the County Lieutenant, complained of the arrogance of the Papists and of the fact that the royal authority was constantly flouted. The Anglican bishop on his part apologized for not having succeeded in imposing his authority over this region " where some are attracted by Puritan innovations " and others remain rooted in their obstinacy.

Elsewhere discontent showed itself in violence. In the north near the borders of Scotland, an actual rebellion took place in 1569. More than four thousand malcontents led by six hundred horsemen followed the cross, occupied Durham and began to move southwards. But the leadership was indecisive, and, attacked by the armies of Warwick and Sussex, the rebels were obliged to disperse. The leaders fled into Scotland, while severe measures were taken against their followers. Eight hundred of the demonstrators were executed with Thomas Plumtrie,[1] the priest who acted as their chaplain.[2]

Until 1581 the laws of the new penal code were directed especially against churchmen and high officials, but from this date, every new edict, proclamation or injunction made the existence of the ordinary citizen more precarious. The statute commonly called the *Act of Persuasion* [3] declared it high treason

---

[1] Executed at Durham, January 1573.

[2] The reprisals which followed the Northern Rebellion caused the definite rupture between London and the Holy See. The Queen of England was excommunicated by Bull of the Pope (Feb. 1570) and in response to this action Elizabeth issued the Anti-Papal Act (13 Elizabeth, cc. 1, 2).

[3] 23 Elizabeth, c. 1, *Act to keep The Queen's Majesty's other subjects in their due Obedience.*

to be reconciled to the Roman Catholic Church.   Four years later, in 1585, the other *Act against Jesuits, Seminary Priests and suchlike Disobedient Persons* [1] made the presence in England of any Catholic priest a case of treason.   A royal proclamation of October 18th, 1591, invited the whole nation to seek out recusants.   Finally in 1593, the *Acte against Popishe Recusantes* [2] completed the measures intended to establish solidly the state religion and root out Catholicism.   Thus, in 1603 when Elizabeth was called to her final account, the statutes which bear her name had caused nearly two hundred of her subjects to die for their faith.[3]   These included tradesmen, workmen, farmers, artisans, priests, knights, gentlemen, earls, dukes and ladies of quality, without mentioning the Queen of Scots !   More than thirty thousand English citizens were obliged to fly the country or died in prison.   The concentration camp of Wisbeach castle is sadly notorious.   The list of proscribed persons included five hundred doctors of theology, five hundred and thirty priests, eighteen doctors of law and three hundred and twenty-six gentlemen of note.   Thus England was deprived of many men and women who represented the intellectual flower of the country.

While this pressure was being made to force minds into submission, the legislator attempted to dry up the spring of independent thought by attacking the freedom of the press.   Among the injunctions of Her Majesty which were promulgated as a corollary to the edicts of 1559, was one forbidding the printing of any book or document of any sort or nature or in any language, the ideas of which were not in conformity with the spirit of the official Prayer Book.   No work, brochure or book was permitted to appear unless licensed by Her Majesty, six of her Privy Council, or certain dignitaries of the Church.

Editions of Latin and Greek classics were exempt from these arbitrary measures, but bookselling in all its ramifications was affected by this surveillance which became more strict as time went on.

In 1566 the Star Chamber had issued an Ordinance for the reform of divers disorders in the printing and publication of books.   Heavy fines and imprisonment had been imposed on those who published or brought into the country any book contrary to the form and intention of the statutes, laws or injunctions decreed by royal authority.   Later a series of proclamations enforced the Ordinance of 1566.   Catholic books were included among the works which were pronounced seditious.

The punishments already imposed on the printing and importation of unauthorized books were extended to those who sold, stitched or bound them.   With the exception of a single press at Oxford and another at Cambridge, the establishment of any printing press outside London was forbidden in 1586.   Luckily for culture in the time of Elizabeth, this Draconian law was often evaded.   Clandestine Papist literature filled the far corners of many London back shops where volumes printed at Douai,

---

[1] 27 Elizabeth, c. 2.   [2] 35 Elizabeth, c. 2.
[3] Not counting those executed after the Northern Rebellion.

Rheims or Antwerp were piled up. Their sale often exceeded that of authorized books. It is even interesting to note that the first mention of Shakespeare as a man of letters is made by a certain jealous critic who accuses the author of *Hamlet* of spending hours at a time examining and turning over proscribed literature imported from Douai.[1]

While the Queen's government was thus organizing a fight to the finish against Catholicism, a great Englishman, little known today but whose work was remarkable, succeeded in gathering together on foreign soil the elements of a literary and spiritual revival.

Before the accession of Elizabeth, William Allen appeared to be destined for a brilliant career, and had for some time been principal of St. Mary's Hall, Oxford, when the death of Mary put a sudden end to his hopes and turned his activities towards a new vocation.

He conceived the idea of founding a college overseas where exiled youths could continue and finish their studies. He established schools first at Louvain, then at Malines and Douai, where he founded a seminary for the education of priests. When political agitation in the Low Countries threatened Douai, teachers and classes were divided between Rheims and Rome. Subsidiary colleges were later founded at Valladolid and Lisbon.

Shakespeare in an early comedy, *The Taming of the Shrew*, when introducing two young men reputed for their acquirements, described one of them as having come from the newly established college.

> I do present you with a man of mine,
> Cunning in music and the mathematics.

> Freely I give unto you this young scholar
> That hath been long studying at Rheims,
> As cunning in Greek, Latin and other languages
> As the other in music and mathematics.
> *(Taming of the Shrew*, Act II, Sc. I)

At Rheims the aim was to give men of the world a fully humanistic education, while in the seminary stern discipline prepared those entering holy orders for the rough road which they were to travel.

The Queen's ministers, especially Walsingham, realized that the Anglican clergy, poorly educated and devoid of aptitude for making sermons, would be no match for graduates from the overseas college. They then had recourse to a new policy and declared, like Shakespeare's Julius Caesar, that men who read and think too much constitute a grave danger to the State. The " Cardinal's men "—as they were called—were represented as conspirators meriting arrest under the Act of Persuasion.

This edict indeed was at first applicable only to the missionary priests from Rheims. It is never difficult to make Englishmen believe that compatriots living abroad are suspicious characters, even when their exile is compulsory, but that the former parish priest had become a traitor because

---

[1] Preface to *Menaphon* by Robert Green, 1589. See Chapter XIII.

he had been deprived of his pulpit and emoluments was an idea which time alone could make clear. Moreover, the ministers thought the best thing to do was to deal first with those who were studying on the other side of the channel.

They hastened to distribute tracts describing the evil designs of the seminary and schools of Cardinal Allen. A pamphlet entitled *The English Romayne Life* (Anthony Munday, London, 1582) is an example of this kind of literature. Their propaganda announced that a whole army of priests was ready to invade England and to put the inhabitants to fire and sword. These false rumours had the desired effect : even the Catholics trembled at the thought of such a landing.

The truth was quite otherwise. The number of missionaries was comparatively small, and their purpose exclusively religious. They were under strict orders to avoid even talking of politics. Campion himself landed at Dover on June 25th, 1580. His fame as writer and preacher was already considerable among those in high place ; it also penetrated to distant villages and manor houses. For months on end the young apostle's burning words revived the dying flame in the heart of England, while his fellow missionaries did the like from north to south, from east to west. Printed declarations of faith from those mysterious presses which Walsingham, with all the means at his disposal, was never able to discover, were distributed. One of these tracts was found two hundred years later in Shakespeare's house, hidden in the roofing, as though to avoid seizure.

After six months, the reward offered by Richard Topcliffe, head of the secret police, attracted pursuivants sixty strong who burst into the manor of Lyford where Campion was preaching his last sermon. Transferred to London with a paper crown on his head bearing the inscription " Campion, the seditious Jesuit ", he was thrown into such a narrow cell that during four days he could neither lie down nor stand up. From there he was brought to Leicester's Palace and told to keep his promise of discussing theology before the Queen. He found Elizabeth enthroned among her Privy Counsellors, and the Earl of Leicester close beside her. No more on this dramatic occasion nor later, when under torture, he was made to argue with clever university men, did he give up one of his deep convictions. Then Lord Hunsdon, the Queen's cousin, declared that it would be easier to tear the heart out of this man than to succeed in extracting one word contrary to his conscience, and the ministers realized that it was vain to struggle against the flame of such a spirit ; the only remedy was to extinguish it.

Campion was hanged on October 1st, 1581, with seven of his missionaries mostly captured in Warwickshire, among them Thomas Cottam, brother of John Cottam, late teacher at Stratford Grammar School, where young Will Shakespeare had just terminated his schooling.[1]

In this little town, more than elsewhere, the recusants had good reason

---

[1] *A Briefe Historie of the glorious Martyrdom of XII Reverend Priests* (Cardinal Allen, 1582).

to tremble.   The lieutenant of their county was none other than Leicester, the most influential man of the Queen's entourage, and a reformer little inclined to mercy.   Whether he was in residence in his princely domain of Kenilworth or whether his duties kept him in London or with the army in Flanders, the weight of his dreaded hand was always feared.   He felt the more irritated against Catholics and Jesuits as he held them responsible for the famous political satire, *Leicester's Commonwealth* which had made him notorious throughout England and even over the entire Continent.   It was vain for the authorities to track down these volumes printed on clandestine presses ;   they reappeared in the form of manuscripts.[1]

" The author of this book must be a devil incarnate to have imagined such infamies ", exclaimed the Queen, when she took up her pen to order the destruction of the volumes and the punishment of their owners.[2]

It is difficult to reconcile the wisdom and judgement which Elizabeth's historians recognize in her with her partiality for her favourite.   Even when the Council, at Burleigh's instigation, vetoed this alliance, the Queen never renounced either her plan nor yet her love.

Leicester was born in 1533, the fifth son of the Duke of Northumberland and was, with his father, his brother, Guildford and his sister-in-law, Lady Jane Grey, condemned to death for having proclaimed the latter sovereign of England instead of Mary Tudor.   But so well did he know how to pay court to King Philip, that, instead of mounting the scaffold like his father and sister-in-law, he was nominated keeper of Windsor Castle ;   and when Queen Mary and her consort wished to communicate with the Princess Elizabeth, then under guard at Woodstock or at Hatfield, they enlisted his services.   Endowed with great physical presence and entirely unscrupulous, he gained from the first moment a complete ascendancy over the future Queen of England.   The position of chief equerry which she entrusted to him after her coronation facilitated this domination.   He ended by never leaving her, rode at her side, stood near her throne, controlled access to her boudoir, and captured the ear of the Council.   With his brother Ambrose, Lord of Warwick Castle, he monopolized erstwhile church property in the whole region.   To many sinecures was added that of Chancellor of Oxford University.

Leicester's two principal agents almost excelled their master.   In London, Richard Topcliffe, chief pursuivant and member of the Commission against the Jesuits, persuaded the Queen to authorize him, contrary to the law of the realm, to install a private torture chamber in his own house ;   in Warwickshire his right hand man, Sir Thomas Lucy, of whom Shakespeare has left us the

---

[1] One sample was evidently in the hands of Shakespeare and still exists at Alnwick Castle.   See Chapter XI.

A French translation was published in 1585 under the title : *Discours de la vie abominable, ruses, trahisons, impostures . . . desquelles a usé le mylord de Leicester.*

A Latin version also appeared at Naples the same year : *Flores-Lacestrial.*   Three editions in English were reprinted in 1641 ;   two others in 1706 ;   another finally in 1721, this last entitled : *The Perfect Picture of a favourite.*

[2] Letter to the Cheshire magistrates of June 20th, 1585.

portrait, became a veritable scourge to the neighbourhood and acted, as will be shown, the part of evil genius toward the poet's father and his kin.

A curious and unpleasing personality was that of Sir Thomas ; he put his Puritan convictions in his pocket under Mary Tudor, soliciting her favour so sedulously that his fortunes waxed enough to permit the renovation and enlargement of his beautiful manor house separated from Stratford by two bends of the Avon. When Elizabeth came to the throne there was no more faithful supporter of the Anglican Church once it was solidly established. By the time his building was completed, the ground plan had assumed the shape of a capital E, still pointed out to visitors as a graceful compliment to the new Protestant sovereign. Elizabeth honoured the owner by stopping there to take refreshment on her way to the Kenilworth festivities. He showed equal address in making his personal interest harmonize with each political current, thus accumulating for himself all the functions and emoluments worth striving for. Successively recruiting officer, Justice of the Peace, Keeper of the county archives (*custos rotulorum*) member of parliament for Gloucestershire and High Sheriff with jurisdiction over both counties. Finally President of a commission " To put down abuses in Religion " he denounced eleven priests and brought to the scaffold eight who failed to escape detection. The name of Master John Shakespeare figures twice on his list of Catholic recusants in Stratford and he was personally responsible for the death of Edward Arden of Park Hall and three members of his family, near relatives of Mary Arden, the poet's mother.

Sir Thomas Lucy's doings will be examined and detailed each and every time they appear to have influenced the life or the work of William Shakespeare.

CHAPTER I

YOUTH AT STRATFORD

Shakespeare's parents—Birth of the poet—Stratford and its customs—Prosperity of Shakespeare's family; the poet's father becomes mayor of the town—He encourages the players—Celebrations at Kenilworth—William Shakespeare at school—His masters—His books—His standard of education—His handwriting —His companions—Sports and pastimes—Youthful memories—Difficulties and disappointments

DURING the third or fourth year of " Lord Philip and Lady Mary's reign ", the marriage of John Shakespeare and Mary Arden was solemnized in the little parish church of Aston Cantlow. This wedding happily united two well-known Warwickshire families.

The ancestors of John Shakespeare had fought at Hastings for William the Conqueror and he could establish descent from three generations of freeholders. The surname [1] often figures on the registers of the Guild of Knowle, a religious foundation to which only the aristocracy of the county could belong. His wife had greater claims to distinction. The Ardens traced their ancestry to before the Norman conquest. Robert, Mary's father, had the status of an esquire while John Shakespeare aspired only to that of gentleman. Both families had considerable property. Four years later John shared with his brother Henry their father's legacy, that is to say, Snitterfield farm just outside Stratford with its dependencies, and the beautiful meadow of Ingon. [2] Mary Arden brought still more to the family. [3]

---

[1] The name Shakespeare was widespread in England after the Norman conquest; the original seems to have been Sacespée, which is still to be met with in Calvados. The derivations of the name are spelt in many different ways, from Shakespeare to Chacsper. In Warwickshire there is Shakelaunce, Briselaunce, Breakspear, and Lycelaunce, the corruption of the Norman names having been made sometimes by assonance, sometimes by translation.

[2] John Shakespeare was named executor of his father Richard's property, by the decision of the court of February 10th, 1561 : Testamenta Vetusta Vigorniensia. *Worcester Probate Registry.*

[3] The will of Robert Arden, registered at Worcester, December 16th, 1556, begins thus :

In the name of God, Amen. The twenty-third day of November of the year of Our Lord 1556, and in the third and fourth year of the reign of our Sovereign Lord Philip and of Lady Mary, King and Queen, I, Robert Arden of Wilmcote of the parish of Aston Cauntlow, suffering in body but in perfect memory, I make this last testament in the following form :

Primo : I leave my soul to all-powerful God and to Our Blessed Lady Saint Mary and to all the heavenly host, and my body to be buried in the cemetery of St. John the Baptist at Aston above-named. . . . I leave to my youngest daughter Mary, all my

[OVER

She possessed in her own right the domain of Asbies with its tall dovecote at Wilmcote, the envy of less fortunate neighbours.

The young couple immediately established themselves in the centre of Stratford on Henley Street.[1] Their gardens and orchards stretched as far as the banks of the Avon, where the river flows wide and placid before entering the mill. It was in this dwelling, half country manor, half town house, that William Shakespeare spent his childhood. On the ground floor was the glover's workshop, a large kitchen whose windows overlooked the street, and a room giving access to the garden. The floor above was divided into four rooms.[2]

The house was situated between the forge of the blacksmith Richard Hornby and the tailor's shop of William Wedgewood. The very spot is recalled in *King John* when the poet describes the arrival of a royal messenger :

> I saw a smith stand with his hammer, thus,
> The whilst his iron did on the anvil cool,
> With open mouth swallowing a tailor's news ;
> Who, with his shears and measure in his hand,
> Standing on slippers—which his nimble haste
> Had falsely thrust upon contrary feet—
> Told of a many thousand warlike French.[3]

The first years of John Shakespeare's marriage to Mary Arden were saddened by the loss of two daughters : however, the birth on April 23rd, 1564, of a sturdy boy, William, baptized three days after at the font of Holy Trinity,[4] the old collegiate church, heralded a period of prosperity when fortune seemed to smile on the young couple. Five children were born after William : Gilbert (1566), Joanne (1569), Anne (1571), Richard (1574) and finally, in 1580, Edmund, who, like his elder brother, was later to become an actor. Thanks to the archives of Stratford, preserved in Shakespeare's

---

domain of Wilmcote named Asbyes, together with the sown and tilled land as it lies, plus six pounds, thirteen shillings and fourpence in money which should be paid before the sharing of my goods.

The inventory which accompanies this will reveals that Robert Arden possessed, besides the usual furnishings of a large farm, valued at a hundred pounds, fourteen painted canvases which adorned the chief room and the great hall.

[1] John Shakespeare had acquired this house on October 2nd, 1556 (*Corp. Records Mis. Dic.* vol. vii, no. 40).

[2] Shakespeare's birthplace was restored in the mid nineteenth century. The roof was slightly lifted and pinions added. This house was at one time divided into two parts. It is certain that John Shakespeare was the proprietor of the whole building from 1575 and probably from the day when he went to live there in 1556.

[3] Act IV, Sc. 2.

[4] Extract from the register of the parish church of Holy Trinity :

26 April, 1564, Baptism Gulielmus filius Johannes Shakspere.
13 October, 1566, Baptism Gilbertus filius Johannis Shakspere.
15 April, 1569, Baptism Jone the daughter of John Shakspere.
28 September, 1571, Baptism Anna filia magistri Shakspere.
11 March, 1574, Baptism Richard Sonne to Mr. John Shakspeer.
3 May, 1580, Baptism Edmund sonne to Mr. John Shakespere.

birthplace,[1] it is easy to trace the family history, to witness each step of its rise and establish the reasons for its decline.

" Labour and Industry " was the motto of this locality, a kind of miniature corporate state whose usages and customs were derived from the religious guild of St. John, and where idleness was looked upon as a major vice. A market was held every Thursday at the High Cross which stood at the north end of Bridge Street. Royal proclamations were read and sermons sometimes preached there. The stocks, pillory and whipping-post were set near by so that the ears of those undergoing punishment might also be edified. In Rother Street, salt meat, raw hides, butter, cheese and skeins of yarn were sold. Thrice yearly on fair days, the butchers of the region set up their stalls in the High Street, paying for this privilege eightpence an ell for the space they occupied. There was a local association authorized by the municipality to make soap and tallow ; but among the tailors, weavers, skinners, collar and shoemakers, bakers, pewterers, brewers, grocers, mercers, carpenters and painters, no trade mark was more in honour than that of the wool merchants whose crest adorned John Shakespeare's stained-glass window, a sign of his superiority over the neighbours whose casements consisted merely of transparent parchment stretched over wooden frames.[2]

The wool men were very powerful in this county where sheep farming was gradually replacing arable farming : the two local landowners, John Clopton, descendant of Sir Hugh, the philanthropist to whom Stratford owes the fine bridge of fourteen arches over the Avon, and Sir Thomas Lucy, that severe magistrate, were both members of the Woolmen's Guild.

As long as the town councillors were able to resist the reforms which Elizabeth's ministers were about to impose on England, Stratford lived just inside the regulations and tried to reconcile the new exigencies with the traditions of the ancient Guild of the Holy Cross. As in the Middle Ages, the dead were considered as much as the living ; four special priests prayed for the deceased in the old chapel ; the Guild had funds for the poor, almshouses for the aged ; orphans were generously assisted, and no litigation could be undertaken without the mayor's consent. The community was responsible for policing the town and for the management of the school. Women were admitted as members of the guild under the curious name of " Soestryn ",[3] and had their privileges and duties also, since the name of Mary Shakespeare with those of two other women is mentioned on a list of jurors.

In 1557, John Shakespeare exercised the functions of taster, an important occupation in a place where ale was the habitual drink. He was often called upon to settle differences or to make a valuation of goods. His liberality

---

[1] Halliwell Phillips published in a folio volume the Stratford archives from the thirteenth to the eighteenth century. The chief events in which William Shakespeare took part were collected by Malone and more recently by J. W. Gray, *Shakespeare's Marriage and Departure from Stratford.*

[2] Samuel Ireland, *Picturesque Views of the Upper or Warwickshire Avon* (London, 1795).

[3] Soestryn : old form of Sisters (Murray).

is attested by the entries found in the archives.   There are registered gifts to the poor, an advance of several pounds to a farmer of the neighbouring hamlet of Shottery, Richard Hathaway, whose daughter Anne was to become his daughter-in-law, a security of ten pounds in favour of his brother Henry, and another to the same amount for the benefit of his neighbour, Michael Pryce.[1]

On July 4th, 1565, he was nominated alderman, and fulfilled the functions of chamberlain ; then on September 4th, 1570, succeeding the haberdasher, Adrian Quinney, he was elected mayor, or " bailiff ".   Finally he attained the summit of his career as " caput aldermani " [2] which entitled him to wear an ample fur-lined robe and to be preceded by the ceremonial mace when attending court as magistrate.

John Shakespeare was zealous in his duties as mayor.   He was energetic during the visitations of the plague which like the ancient Minotaur yearly carried off a seventh of the population.   During these unhappy days the Council, to avoid infection, held its sittings, not in the Town Hall, but in the orchards and gardens of the neighbourhood.

That John Shakespeare at the time of his prosperity was a methodical and businesslike man is indisputable ; the municipal accounts, which he scrupulously supervised for many years, are countersigned with finely-drawn compasses, trademark of the Glovemakers' Guild which he had adopted as his personal sign manual.   Indeed he sold the gloves he made to a numerous array of customers.   Why should not the burgesses of Stratford give their patronage to such an important man who, besides his municipal functions, was in a position to supply the community with wood from his forests, hay from his meadows, and the various Guilds with the skins and fleeces of his sheep and cattle ?   How much the Henley Street household was interested in the glove trade may be seen in the writings of John's son.   He was familiar with glove making in all the stages of manufacture.   Often he uses technical terms in mentioning the special tools which his father continually had in hand.   To describe the beard of one of his characters he finds a homely comparison :   " Like a glover's paring-knife." [3]   This rounded instrument represents exactly the cut of beard which was fashionable at the time.

John Shakespeare seems to have set much store by the recognition of gentility.   He had applied to the herald's college around 1576 for permission to display a coat of arms.   He might have cited his services to the parish

---

[1] Extract from the registers showing the advances paid by John Shakespeare :
" Aug. 30, 1564,
        At a Hall holldyn in oure garden the 30 daye of auguste anno 1564. . . . Moneye paid towardes the releffe of the poore . . . John shacksper xijd."
        " 6 Sept.   Towards the releyff of those that he visited John Shacksper VId.
    July 1565.   Peyd to Shakspeyr for the rest of an old debt £3 2s. 7d.
    Chamberlain's accounts to Michaelmas 1565."
        For the security in favour of Henry Shakespeare and of Pryce, see Court of Records 1587 and Controlment Roll, Mich. Term, 29 Eliz. K.B. 29/223 mm. 44.
[2] The highest distinction attainable by a citizen of Stratford.
[3] The Merry Wives of Windsor, Act 1, Sc. 4.

in support of this claim, but he preferred to recall those of his ancestor who served Henry VII, and his alliance with the heiress of Robert Arden. John Shakespeare could not have asked for this honour if he had not possessed the outward signs of wealth to support it—at least two servants, and the means of cutting a good figure, that is to say of keeping open house. Twenty years later, the heralds at arms recognized the justice of his demand and granted John Shakespeare and his posterity an expressive or punning coat of arms [1]—a falcon brandishing a spear with the proud device : " Non sans droit."

No sooner had he become mayor than John Shakespeare began to encourage stage representations. If the play was considered suitable by the town council, the actors were authorized to produce their show in public in the yard of one of the inns, the Bear, the Swan or the Falcon. The town was festively decorated on these occasions and the young people welcomed the procession at the bridge end. Every company of players wore the arms of its recognized patron. The servants of the earls of Worcester, Leicester, Nottingham, and even those of the Queen were successively admired. [2]

Dressed in satin and lace, the players advanced along Bridge Street ; the trumpeter in scarlet cloth embroidered with gold, wheeled his horse about, whilst the drummer beat his drum at a run holding on to his stirrup-leather. A mule or a sturdy horse followed the troupe carrying the stage properties and other baggage. Any young man who could obtain from a councillor the favour of a place was allowed to witness what was called the " Mayor's show ".

Among other entertainments was the " Cradle of Security ", an old " morality " in which Envy, Sloth and Lust were shown leading their followers to the Last Judgement in a sea of flame. These pastimes were favoured by the ancient Church, which considered them practical commentaries on the catechism.

An old Stratford priest after explaining the articles of faith concluded his sermon by inviting his congregation to go to the Coventry play, " The Mystery of the Holy Sacrament ". " If you do not believe what I say, go to Coventry ; there you will see every one of the twelve articles of our Faith in flesh and blood, to the great profit of your understanding."

Indeed the neighbouring town of Coventry was celebrated for the spectacles presented in its market place and possessed in its monastery-school a veritable nursery for actors. From every corner of England people came to see the Corpus Christi play.

---

[1] Or on a bend sable, a spear of the first steeled argent and for his crest or cognizance a falcon, with wings displayed argent standing on a wreath of his colours, supporting a spear or, steeled as aforesaid set upon a helmet with mantels and tassels.

[2] Visits of companies of players to Stratford are recorded as follows : the troupe patronized by the Earl of Leicester in 1573 and 1577 ; the Earl of Warwick's company in 1576, 1577, 1581, 1582 ; the players of Lord Strange and the Countess of Essex in 1579 ; 1580, Lord Derby's company ; in 1581 and 1583, that of Lord Berkeley and the players of Lord Chandos ; in 1584, the companies of the Earls of Oxford, Warwick and Essex.

At Stratford pageants were frequently given. " The Procession of Saint George and the Dragon " took place at Whitsuntide ; [1] " The Pantomime of Robin and Marion " was the rule for May 1st. Morris dances, wooden horses and greased poles enlivened these festivities and figure among the diversions so often mentioned in Shakespeare's plays.[2]

A dozen visits can be counted between 1568 and 1584 of players sponsored by different notables. But none of these approached the famous celebrations at Kenilworth in July, 1575, which John Shakespeare must have attended officially and whose extraordinary magnificence dazzled the imagination of his son William, then twelve years of age. The Queen was present for nineteen days at Kenilworth Castle, where the preparations, it was said, had cost the powerful favourite Robert Dudley, Earl of Leicester, sixty thousand pounds. Never before had England witnessed such splendour.

Between the main tower and the postern gate of Kenilworth an artificial lake had been made, over which engineers had constructed a bridge so that the Queen could admire the water pageant and fireworks as she rode towards the castle. Fairies, witches, magicians and goddesses all had their place. A band of water-nymphs riding on dolphins greeted the arrival of Cynthia in song, whilst Arion, holding a harp, made his court to Phoebe from the back of a sea monster. Armed with the symbolic club of the Leicester blazon, the doorkeeper, disguised as Hercules, led a bear in chains, so that, the keys of the castle were offered to the Queen by the living symbols of Robert Dudley's crest. Then mythology gave place to legend : Merlin the Enchanter, Vivian the Sorceress and Fay Morgana left their floating island, and on bended knee renounced their magic powers in favour of a queen more admirable than King Arthur.[3]

A troupe of actors, the first to receive letters patent, took part in these festivities under the direction of James Burbage, pioneer in theatrical art, who built in London the first permanent theatre. It was there that William Shakespeare was to start his famous career with James Burbage's son, Richard, the celebrated tragedian, who created all the great Shakespearean rôles from Romeo to King Lear.

It is scarcely necessary to recall the traces left by the Kenilworth pageants in Shakespeare's theatrical work. For the inhabitants of the county the rejoicings seemed to presage the betrothal of Elizabeth to the most ambitious

---

[1] . . . At Pentecost,
When all our pageants of delight were played
Our youth got me to play the woman's part . . .
. . . 'twas Ariadne, passioning
For Theseus' perjury and unjust flight.
        The Two Gentlemen of Verona, Act IV, Sc. 4.
[2] The Puritan régime put a stop to all these plays and rejoicings. But William Shakespeare was able to see and doubtless to take part in them until his sixteenth year.
[3] " Kenilworth Festivities comprising Laneham's Description of the Pageantry and Gascoigne's Masques represented before Queen Elizabeth at Kenilworth Castle : Anno 1575." John Merridew, Warwick and Leamington (MDCCXXV).

of her subjects.[1] Leicester himself certainly believed that the celebrations had this significance. Fifteen years later when Shakespeare presented *A Midsummer Night's Dream*, he well knew that he would capture the attention of his audience and also flatter the Sovereign by recalling these entertainments and at the same time the disillusion which followed them. Elizabeth had granted herself a monopoly of the name and attributes of the goddess Diana ; hence Oberon, king of the fairies,[2] having described the songs of the mermaid on the dolphin's back, and recalled the fireworks, continues his description thus :

> That very time I saw, but thou couldst not,
> Flying between the cold moon and the earth
> Cupid all armed : a certain aim he took
> At a fair vestal throned by the west,
> And loos'd his love-shaft smartly from his bow,
> As it should pierce a hundred thousand hearts ;
> But I might see young Cupid's fiery shaft
> Quench'd in the chaste beams of the watery moon,
> And the imperial votaress passed on,
> In maiden meditation, fancy-free.[3]

It was on the school bench that the future actor-poet learned the essential elements of his education ; these were not negligible, for the humble town where he lived enjoyed the reputation of an intellectual centre.

Stratford had benefited from the generosity of an enlightened philanthropist, Sir Hugh Clopton, already mentioned. This patron had restored the local grammar school and had founded scholarships at Oxford and Cambridge for its best pupils. Learning was so highly thought of in Stratford during Shakespeare's youth, that the " magister " of the little town was paid twenty pounds a year, a salary superior to that of an Eton master.[4] The grammar school was free to all sons of notable citizens. The masters had to be university graduates. Those who undertook Shakespeare's education, paid by his father as treasurer of the baileywick, were, successively, John Acton, Walter Roche, Simon Hunt, Thomas Jenkins, and John Cottam. It has been said that the portrait of Sir Hugh Evans in *The Merry Wives of Windsor* with his characteristic Welsh accent was drawn from Thomas Jenkins. Probably the scene where a boy named Will recites his Latin

---

[1] Three times Leicester hoped to realize his scheme to marry the queen : the first time in 1559 after the tragic death of his first wife, Amy Robsart, a death so opportune that public opinion suspected the royal favourite of being responsible ; then in 1574, when he sought a divorce from his second wife, Lady Douglas Sheffield, on condition of an annual payment of seven hundred pounds ; finally in 1578, when he influenced the queen against marriage with the brother of the French king.

[2] Huon de Bordeaux presented for the first time the character of Oberon, king of the fairies. The text, rendered accessible to the English by the translation of Lord Berners, appeared in 1534, and suggested to Shakespeare the name and character of his Oberon.

[3] *A Midsummer Night's Dream*, Act II, Sc. 1.

[4] C. C. Stopes, *Shakespeare's Environment*, p. 55.

lesson before his mother and an admiring friend was written from personal recollections.[1]

Shakespeare himself has given us a portrait of the lad with " shining morning face, creeping like snail, unwillingly to school ", in *As You Like It*.[2]

At seven years old the prospective pupil was supposed to be sufficiently instructed by his parents to be able to read and write, at least well enough to prepare his lessons without help. The father then brought his son to the schoolmaster who ascertained by preliminary questioning whether the little William, Henry or Richard was capable of beginning the study of Latin. Then the candidate listened to a reading of the rules of the school, and consented to submit to punishment whenever he failed in his scholastic duties. On payment of the modest sum of fourpence his name was entered in the register.

A contemporary publication on *How to bring up children and youth*[3] permits the reconstruction hour by hour of the school day.

Every child had to begin his morning with prayers, to wash his face, comb his hair, greet his parents, collect his books, and shoulder his satchel before starting for school. The bell rang at a quarter to six in summer, and an hour later in winter. On the last stroke the pupil was supposed to be in class.

Young Shakespeare was one of the privileged. He lived close by ; a few steps in Henley Street, a few more in Chapel Street, and at the corner of Chapel Lane stood the square stone tower the gate of which opened on the school yard. The classroom itself was on the first floor. About thirty desks were lined up in order at that time and they are there still. Everyone said " Good morning " to the master, then lessons began with choral singing. The morning session, with a short break, lasted until eleven o'clock. The pupil must then return home and help with the housework. The children were responsible for laying the table with cloth, plates, wooden bowls and knives. The bread was cut on the board without scattering crumbs. Four large receptacles were placed at each corner of the table to hold the scraps of the meal. The eldest son, who had the privilege of drawing the ale from its cask, poured it into a large jug and said grace ; then, before sitting down he carved the meat and helped his parents.

After dinner the boys returned to school at one o'clock and remained until five, with fifteen minutes' recreation ; Thursday and Saturday afternoons were devoted to the games and competitions of which the youth of that day was so fond. Shakespeare recalls many times in his writings how he played at marbles, bowls, top spinning, hoop rolling, blind man's buff, hide and seek, swimming, sliding on the frozen ponds ; there are also many allusions to the training of falcons, at that time a useful science.

When an " obstinate and ungovernable " pupil needed to be subdued, the schoolmaster was authorized to choose four boys known for good

---

[1] *The Merry Wives of Windsor*, Act IV, Sc. I.   [2] Act II, Sc. 6.
[3] F. Seager, *The Schoole of vertue and the Book of good Nourture for chyldren and youth* (1557).

character, serious disposition and muscular strength. The young justiciaries seized their unhappy schoolmate by his arms and legs so as to " dispose him conveniently " on one of the desks ; they were recommended to abstain from threats, oaths or insults. It was for the master to apply the sharp blows or " jerks " with the rod of birch or willow. Moral advice completed the punishment. " God has sanctified the rod, thus it must be used as the instrument of God."

Of the five masters who directed the Stratford school at the time William Shakespeare attended it, three were obliged to leave because of their faith. The first, John Acton, disappeared after the Christmas term of 1571 with the old priest Hilman, obliged to fly when severe repression followed the revolt of the Duke of Norfolk. Walter Roche replaced him, but did not stay long, having decided to abandon teaching in order to set up at Stratford as a barrister.

The register of the Bishop of Worcester shows that a certain Simon Hunt, who had recently received the Degree of Bachelor of Arts at Oxford was nominated to succeed Roche.[1] Hunt was of superior quality. He began his duties in 1571, and remained at the head of the school for four years although his Catholicism made his task difficult. After the Massacre of Saint Bartholomew, a band of Puritans invaded the classroom breaking windows and woodwork. The master took up a collection among his pupils and brought a sufficient sum to the town council to pay the carpenter for three days' work. Thus the damage was repaired without scandal. Hunt baffled his enemies for several years, but had to give in at midsummer, 1575. His ability may be computed by his subsequent career. When he left the grammar school he set out for the seminary of Rheims ; thence he went to Rome where he succeeded Father Robert Parsons as grand Penitentiary when this celebrated Jesuit left with Campion for their mission to England.

The incumbency of Simon Hunt's successor at the grammar school was by no means brilliant. If it is indeed the portrait of Thomas Jenkins which Shakespeare has given us in the character of the Puritan magister of *The Merry Wives of Windsor*, evidently this Jenkins was far from possessing a powerful brain ; what is certain is that he accepted, in the middle of the school year, the sum of six pounds to hand over his duties to a competent master of the old type, John Cottam, lately come from Oxford. Cottam's term was short, but for other reasons. The execution of his eldest brother, who was martyred at Tyburn with Campion, caused fresh suspicions to fall on the Papist leanings of the Stratford school, and he was obliged to disappear. But just at that time William's days as a pupil came to an end. The great school of life was to continue and complete the efforts of his masters.

It is easy to ascertain the standard of education reached on leaving the grammar school ; the textbooks used therein are well known. The *Sententiae*

---

[1] " XXIX die ejusdem mensis, anno predicto emanavit licencia Simoni Hunt in artibus bacch. docendi litteras instruendi pueros in Schola grammaticali in villa de Stratford super Avon."

pueriles, the grammar of William Lyly and Thomas Wilson's *Arte of Rhetorike* were among the manuals used.   They contained commentaries on numerous passages of Seneca, Terence, Cicero, Virgil, Plautus and Horace.

> O ! 'tis a verse in Horace ; I knew it well :
> I read it in grammar long ago.[1]

Shakespeare quotes Lyly's " Grammar " at least ten times in his plays. His two pedants in *Love's Labour's Lost* knew many a passage from *Familiares colloquendi formulae in usum scolarum concinnatae*, a work studied by the advanced pupils of the school.   Among the school books another must be mentioned, the *Bucolica* of Mantuanus, a Latinist beloved of the Renaissance, whose work was considered more appropriate to youth than the *Bucolics* of Virgil.

> Ah ! good old Mantuan . . . who understandeth thee
> Not, loves thee not.[2]

exclaims Holofernes in *Love's Labour's Lost*.

Shakespeare frequently borrowed from the *Aeneid*, but the Latin author of his choice, his model, and constant inspiration was Ovid (Publius Ovidius Naso).   " And why indeed Naso, but for smelling out the odoriferous flowers of fancy."[3]

Shakespeare owes to the *Metamorphoses* his knowledge of mythology. The *Amores* inspired the epigraph of his first volume of poetry.   His *Venus and Adonis* is almost a transposition of Ovid, although at the same time a work of great originality ; his *Rape of Lucrece* closely follows the *Fasti*.   Was not Ovid of all Latin poets the one whose turn of wit was most likely to please in a country just awakening to the influence of the Renaissance ?

Shakespeare was recognized as the English Ovid by Francis Meres as early as 1598 [4] and it is noteworthy that numerous rival poets with Puritan leanings reproached the author of *Venus and Adonis* for his over-sensuous pen influenced by " the lascivious Ovid ".

His literary debt to Plutarch is almost as great.   The *Lives of Illustrious Men* provided historical material for *Julius Caesar, Antony and Cleopatra, Timon of Athens* and *Coriolanus*.   In reading Plutarch, an author much appreciated in England through the remarkable translation of Sir Thomas North, he found a reflection of the Renaissance as well as a picture of antiquity, for the English volume follows almost word for word the celebrated version of Amyot.[5]

The scholar of the grammar school had within easy reach an authority on his own country.   Raphael Holinshed, an historian of rare quality, lived at Packwood in the immediate vicinity of Stratford, and this could not but

---

[1] *Titus Andronicus*, Act IV, Sc. 2.   [2] *Love's Labour's Lost*, Act IV, Sc. 2.
[3] *Love's Labour's Lost*, Act IV, Sc. 2.
[4] *Palladis Tamia* (Francis Meres, Master of Arts of both Universities, 1598).
[5] *The Lives of the noble Graecians and Romanes*, translated out of Greek by James Amyot and out of French into English by Thomas North (Thomas Vautrollier, 1579).

encourage masters and pupils to study the *Chronicles of England, Ireland and Scotland*, whence the dramatist derived the historical background for *King Lear, Cymbeline, Macbeth, King John*, the *Henrys V, VI* and *VIII, Richard II*, and *Richard III*.

Shakespeare found in the monumental work of Holinshed not only subjects but sometimes whole passages and even pages. It is curious to observe how such an original and personal writer who altered other material to his own liking, followed Holinshed with such fidelity. The fact is easily explained. In 1577, when the great work of this historian appeared, Shakespeare was on the point of finishing his studies. In the small community around Stratford, the presence of a scholar of the calibre of Holinshed, then living close to Christopher Shakespeare, the poet's cousin, must have created great interest among educated people in the town.

In his childhood, he was naturally familiar with the tales of the Round Table, the ballads of Robin Hood, the History of the Nine Worthies, the poetry of Chaucer and Gower. To this reading must be added that of the Bible to which school children were obliged to listen in church every Sunday morning and evening.

Shakespeare quotes sacred texts more than any other author of his day— at least two hundred times—but appears to have preferred the narrative and dramatic [1] passages rather than those of a mystical nature. After the year 1582, he had at hand the English translation of the New Testament by Gregory Martin published at Rheims by order of the Seminary. Many similarities indicate that this Catholic version was known to him. In speaking, for example, of the parable of the sower in St. Matthew's Gospel, he uses the word " cockle " instead of " tares ". This word " cockle " is only to be found in the text of the Rheims translation.

" Allons, allons, sowed cockle reapes no corn ", says Biron in *Love's Labour's Lost ;* [2] and in *Coriolanus* also :

> The cockle of rebellion, insolence, sedition
> Which we ourselves have plough'd for, sow'd and scatter'd.[3]

The Protestant bibles, known as " breeches " or " bishops' " make use of the word " tares " which Shakespeare never employs.

Much later, in London, Giovanni Florio introduced him to the Italian works which influenced his first manner of writing, then to the French philosophical thought that gave a new orientation to his genius.

The study of French was in favour at Stratford. Shakespeare shows in his first plays some knowledge of the language. His childhood friend young William Combe published soon after leaving school a translation of a French work,[4] and another schoolfellow, Richard Field, the tanner's son, as soon as he reached London entered the house of Vautrollier, a printer from Rouen

---

[1] He was particularly impressed by the story of Cain, the treachery of Judas and the parable of the Prodigal Son.

[2] *Love's Labour's Lost*, Act IV, Sc. 3.   [3] Act III, Sc. 1.

[4] William Combe wrote his name also in a law book : " C'est le livre de Gulihelme Combe."

who specialized in learned works, and employed six Frenchmen and one
Dutchman in his business. Thomas Quinney, yet another Stratford
neighbour, was acquainted with the work of Octavien de Saint-Gelais,[1] the
papal notary of Angoulême, since in the account book which he kept for
the municipality he inscribed this epigraph :

> Bienheureux est celuy qui pour devenir sage
> Qui par le mal d'aultruy fait son apprentissage.

His brother George was, according to Dr. Hall,[2] " very expert in foreign
languages ". All this shows that the middle-class townsmen did not lack
general culture.

It shows also that a boy with grammar school training possessed what
could be called a good education. The poet was evidently one of the
school's best pupils, for an actor of his company told the biographer Aubrey [3]
that he had taught Latin in the country. Certainly in such a large class,
the master would make use of the cleverest boy to help him as monitor.
Shakespeare's desk is exceptionally large ; it is more like that of a master.
It was brought to his birthplace at the beginning of the nineteenth century.
The lid, covered with inscriptions cut with a knife, has several times been
planed, but there remains a space protected by the hinges where three words
are cut with a penknife in characters, the approximate date of which is
certain. They belong to the end of the sixteenth century. The inscription
recalls perhaps a moment when the monitor of the grammar school felt
discouraged : *Nulla emolumenta laborum* (no reward for work).

The schools of Warwickshire, like most of those in the provinces, continued to teach the ancient script with its straight or gothic letters. All his
life, Shakespeare practised this handwriting described as " rustic " by his
contemporaries of London where only the " roman " hand was esteemed.
Hamlet tells us that, in order to conform to the new fashion, he tried to
unlearn the straight characters [4] which were termed " vulgar ". Luckily
for the Prince of Denmark, as for the author of *Hamlet*, Queen Elizabeth
also wrote after the old style ; in a letter to Catherine de Medici she apologizes for not using the " roman characters ", hoping that her " gross handwriting would not blush with shame at finding itself in such august hands ".
But archaism does not imply ignorance on the part of either the Queen of
England or the Stratford schoolboy.

If one judges by the specimens of writing left by pupils of the grammar
school, discipline must have been strict in that institution. At first sight
it is difficult to distinguish the handwriting of Quinney the tradesman from

---

[1] *Séjour d'honneur*, par Octavien de Saint-Gelais (Paris, Anthoyne Verard, 1519).

[2] Dr. Hall married Shakespeare's daughter.

[3] Brief lives chiefly of contemporaries set down by John Aubrey between the years
1669 and 1694, edited by Andrew Clark (Oxford, 1898).

[4] I once did hold it, as our statists do,
A baseness to write fair, and laboured much
How to forget that learning . . .
Hamlet, Act v, Sc. 2.

that of the lawyer Francis Collins, who drew up the will of his schoolfellow Shakespeare ; that of Collins, at first sight, strongly resembles the writing of the testator himself. However, a close study of the letters reveals the difference between the two. That of the actor-poet is recognizable by its mobility, its vigour and the habit of elongating certain letters or filling in empty spaces between words with useless lines or dots. The script in the play of *Sir Thomas More* [1] is flowing, even hurried, as if the writer were always short of time ; in contrast, his signatures, full or abbreviated, are authoritative : that in Florio's translation of Montaigne shows considerable application.

A close comradeship linked Shakespeare to the young men of his age, his fellow pupils who lived in Stratford or its immediate neighbourhood. Two childhood friends, Richard Field and Thomas Quinney, have already been mentioned. Another intimate, Hamlet Saddler, and his wife Judith should also be remembered. They it was who gave their unusual names to Shakespeare's twins born in 1585. Another school mate, Francis Collins, left Stratford to become a barrister at Warwick but returned towards the end of his life to his native town, where he died as secretary to the mayor.

Mention must be made of the faithful friend Thomas Russell who belonged to the recusant aristocracy. He found Shakespeare again in the literary and theatrical circles of London, frequented the Harringtons, the Digges, and, like the poet, returned to the scene of his childhood before ending his days.

Young Trussel too must not be forgotten ; he lived near Stratford, in the fine manor of Billesley, known for its beautiful library whose panelling conceals a secret room where the priest could hide on the arrival of the pursuivants. According to tradition, Shakespeare often went to Billesley and this was natural since Trussel and he were first cousins, their mothers being sisters. Poetry linked them also. At the time Shakespeare wrote *The Rape of Lucrece* his comrade produced the *Rape of the Beautiful Helen*, a flattering imitation of his more gifted contemporary.

John Trussel was a remarkable prose writer, and shared with Samuel Daniel and Francis Bacon in the authorship of a History of England [2] dedicated to Queen Anne of Denmark. Daniel dealt with Saxon times as far as Edward III ; Trussel wrote the continuation, and described with great originality the whole period so dear to Shakespeare, namely, the struggles between York and Lancaster, and the times of Richard II and Richard III. His nervous and vigorous style is extremely vivid, and the reader cannot fail to notice that he is inspired by Shakespeare's dramas in his descriptions of historical personages.

Trussel also composed a poem in honour of Robert Dover, founder of

[1] See Chapter IV.

[2] *The Collection of the History of England with a continuation unto the reign of Henry the Seventh* by John Trussel (London, printed by F. Leach for Benjamin Tooke at the Ship in St. Paul's (5th edn., 1685)).

the games and sports which took place on the Cotswold Hills [1] near Stratford·
His name is included in this volume among those of half-a-dozen of Shakespeare's associates including Drayton and Ben Jonson, who had given their
patronage to these Olympic games. This same Trussel succeeded twice in
publishing the poetry of the young Jesuit Robert Southwell, without the
intervention of the censor. He finished his career as town clerk of the city
of Winchester, and in this capacity officially received Queen Henrietta Maria.

Shakespeare's will proves his fidelity to life-long friends. Many schoolmates or childhood neighbours are mentioned beside the actors of his
company, Heminge, Condell and Burbage as beneficiaries, witnesses or
executors. Francis Collins received thirteen pounds, Thomas Russell five
pounds, Hamlet Saddler and William Reynolds each a gold ring ; the same
tokens went to Anthony Nash (whose son later married the granddaughter
of the poet) and to Thomas Tyler. As for Thomas Combe, he inherited
the gentleman's sword which Shakespeare valued so highly.

To these friends from Stratford and round about must be added the
names of those who for reasons of conscience finished their education on the
Continent and returned with a new vocation, but without thereby breaking
the ties which bound them to their native heath. Most of Shakespeare's
biographers quote a letter written in Latin in which young Richard Quinney,
pupil of the grammar school, asks his father to bring back from London two
books, one for himself, the other for his younger brother Thomas—he who
was to marry Shakespeare's younger daughter Judith. Another letter is
perhaps more worthy of attention. It was written by a schoolfellow of the
name of Dibdale, and was brought home by Thomas Cottam, brother of the
Stratford schoolmaster, who was then still at his post. It is dated from
the Seminary at Rheims, and addressed to the Dibdale family, who were
near neighbours of Anne Hathaway, whom Shakespeare married two years
later.

Aftere most humble and dutyfull wyse welbeloved parents, I have me com-
mended unto you desyeringe of you, your dayly blessing. trusting in god that you
are also in healthe and my brothers and systeres. the cause of my wryting unto
you ys, to lett you understand that I am in healthe commending unto you my
espeaciall friend Mr Cottame who hathe bene unto me the to-halfe of my lyfe
I cannot sufficiently commend unto you hys loving kyndnesse showed and bestowed
uppon me. Wherefore I beseech you to take consayle of hyme in matters of great
wayt. I have sente unto you sertaine tokens to be devided amonges you a gylted
crucifixe and medall unto my Father and the payre of bedes unto my sister Jonne
the other payre of bedes unto my mother the sylver Romayne peyce of coyne
unto my sister Agnes and the other peyce of French coyne unto my brother
Rtchard. The two stringe of graynes to be devyded amongest you I have
sent unto my brother John Pace the peice of Frenche coyne wrapped by yt
selfe Thus breifly I ceasse to troble you any Farther Desyringe Almyghty God

---

[1] *Annalia Dubrensia upon the yeerely celebration of Mr. Robert Dover's Olimpick Games
upon the Cotswold Hill*, written by Michael Drayton, Esq., John Trussel, gent., Wm. Basse,
Captain Menese, Thomas Heywood, Ben Jonson (London, 1634).

to preserve you in long lyffe and prosperity and send us a mery meting   Fare you well the fourth day of June Frome Reines youre obedyent sone Robert Dibdall.[1]

The friendship of the three families : Shakespeare, Hathaway and Dibdale is attested by contemporary writings and acknowledgements of mutual debts. Two securities signed by John Shakespeare show that he had come to the rescue of Richard Hathaway.   Now this same Hathaway acknowledges in his will that he owes forty shillings to his neighbour John Pace,[2] the same John Pace mentioned in the above letter.

Dibdale's career, although short, left traces in three contemporary documents.

He made the acquaintance of the celebrated preacher John Foxe, who claimed to have exorcised a young barrister " violently possessed of Satan ". In fact, according to one account of the affair, Satan actually left his victim only when Dibdale practised the exorcisms in which he excelled.[3]

The second reference is found in the Record Office.   It is a denunciation of the young priest's father, who, by means of the carrier Greenwood, despatched to Newgate prison " a loaf of bread, two cheeses and seven shillings in money ".[4]

Finally, Stowe's *Chronicle* relates that on October 8th, 1586, " John Lowe, J. Adams and R. Dibdale, already condemned for high treason, having been made priests by the authority of the Bishop of Rome, were drawn to Tyburn and there hanged."

Three other young men of the county, William Hartley, John Ingram and William Freeman, left England for the college of Cardinal Allen, and enlisted among Campion's followers.   When their mission brought them again to England, the Stratford neighbours anxiously followed their itinerary and learned their tragic end.

> How many a holy and obsequious tear
> Hath dear religious love stolen from mine eye,
> As interest of the dead,[5]

says the poet, showing among other things that he was far from disapproving post mortem tributes.

Hartley,[6] denounced by Sir Thomas Lucy, was hanged over the door of

---

[1] This manuscript is preserved in the Public Record Office (S.P. Dom Eliz. fol. 179, no. 4).

[2] Richard Hathaway's will is published by J. W. Gray, *Shakespeare's Marriage and Departure from Stratford*, p. 121.   Extracts are given in the following chapter.

[3] *History of the Persecution of England* (Diego de Ypez, vol. 1, Chap. XIII).   " Very marvellous things were established during the exorcisms of Mister Dibdale, priest [recently martyred] in the house of a certain catholic [Lord Vaux], things far exceeding the forces of human nature."

[4] This carrier did the journey between Stratford and London twice a week.

[5] Sonnet 31.

[6] " The fifth of October John Weldon and William Hartley, made priests at Paris and remaining here contrary to the statute, were hanged, the one at the Miles end the other nigh the Theator " (Middlesex County Records, vols. i and ii).

A True Report of the inditement, arraignment, conviction, condemnation, and Execution of John Weldon, William Hartley, and Robert Sutton ; who suffered for high Treason, in severall places about the Citie of London, on Saturday the fifth of October, Anno 1588.   (Imprinted at London by Richard Jones, 1588.)

the theatre where Shakespeare was then playing, Ingram [1] at London Bridge. William Freeman,[2] arrested near Stratford and judged by the owner of Charlecote who for the nonce included his brother Timothy Lucy in the jury, suffered the same fate at Warwick on August 13th, 1594.

The Established Church was also represented among Will's friends. John Thornborough, nominated chaplain to the Queen about 1585, and later Bishop of Bristol and Worcester, was mentioned by Doctor Forman [3] as one of the worst poachers of the district.

He was more often seen at schooles of dancing and fence than among the learned and above all loved to steal game in private parks.

Later Thornborough, grown wiser, published a pamphlet advocating the union of the English and Scottish Crowns.[4] He obtained treatment for his rheumatism from Doctor Hall, the poet's son-in-law.[5]

This whole generation was, like the preceding one, devoted to hunting, races and open-air sports. A certain Robert Dover, mentioned above, instituted on the Cotswold Hills annual Olympic games in which nobility and commoners took part, coming from a radius of forty miles. The games included jumping, wrestling, hand-to-hand fighting, wielding the lance, and greyhound racing. " How does your fallow greyhound, sir ? I heard say he was outrun on Cotsall ", says Abraham Slender, who appears to be a caricature of Sir Thomas Lucy's nephew, in *The Merry Wives of Windsor*.[6] But the real sport of this Forest of Arden was hunting, in which great and

---

[1] John Ingram of New College, Oxford, executed at the entrance of London Bridge, 26th July, 1593.

[2] William Freeman of Magdalen College, Oxford, exercised his vocation of priest for five years in the neighbourhood of Stratford.

[3] Doctor Simon Forman, a curious personality of the time, half scholar, half charlatan, well known among the ladies of the court for his illicit practice of medicine. A single example of his work on the *Bases of Longitude* printed by Thomas Dawson, in 1591, is preserved at the Bodleian, but his manuscript entitled *Booke of Playes*, where an account is given of three Shakespearian plays (*Macbeth, Winter's Tale*, and *Cymbeline*), was not published until 1836. About the same time the Camden Society undertook the publication of his journal and his notes on his medical practice between 1596 and 1607 which were kept in the Ashmolean collection under the numbers 202 and 892 respectively. The revelations of his private life and those of some of the court ladies were judged by the editor (J. Halliwell Phillips) to be so immoral and indecent that the book was withdrawn from the press, and only sixteen copies remain.

Forman played the part of go-between for some of the young libertines of Oxford, notably for Robert Pinkney of St. Mary's College and John Thornborough of Magdalen College.

[4] " *A Discourse plainly proving the evident utilitie and urgent neccessitie of the desired happie Union of the two famous Kingdomes of England and Scotland : by way of answer to certaine objections against the same* " (London, Richard Field, 1604).

[5] Like many recusants, John Hall thought it prudent to leave England after the Arden-Somerville affair. It is not known whether he obtained his medical diplomas at Paris, Avignon or Montpellier. He returned to Stratford after Elizabeth's death and married, in 1607, Susanna, Shakespeare's eldest daughter. He was then thirty-two. A good doctor, he had a large practice, of both Protestant and Catholic patients. His book on " notable cures " is filled with interesting observations. There is further mention of him in Chapter XVI.

[6] Act I, Sc. 1.

humble were eager to take part. The prologue of *The Taming of the Shrew* brings the reader to the very domain where Shakespeare's mother was brought up. The characters are the local men and women of his time under their real names, like Marion Hackett, the stout hostess of the Wilmcote Inn, her servant Cicely, the village drunkard, Christopher Sly. We are witness at the return of the pack after a day's coursing.

The dialogue between the young Nimrod and his huntsman [1] shows the author's familiarity with technical terms.

Lord:	Huntsman, I charge thee, tender well my hounds :
	Brach Merriman, the poor cur is emboss'd,
	And couple Clowder with the deep-mouth'd brach.
	Saw'st thou not, boy, how Silver made it good
	At the hedge-corner in the coldest fault ?
	I would not lose the dog for twenty pound.
First Hunt.:	Why, Bellman is as good as he, my lord ;
	He cried upon it at the merest loss,
	And twice to-day pick'd out the dullest scent :
	Trust me, I take him for the better dog.
Lord:	Thou art a fool : if Echo were as fleet,
	I would esteem him worth a dozen such.
	But sup them well, and look unto them all :
	Tomorrow I intend to hunt again.[2]

In this same prologue, Shakespeare describes so vividly the arrival of a troupe of travelling players, that the reader imagines himself transported to Stratford at the time when Leicester's " servants " must have turned his mind towards the theatre.

An echo is to be found, too, of more tragic incidents which had occurred in the town and were retold to the children in the inglenook.

An allusion in *Romeo and Juliet* recalls the sad death of a Stratford child. In 1564 an epidemic raged in the neighbourhood and a young girl who was thought to be dead was buried hurriedly. When the family vault was opened later for the coffin of another victim, the body of the unfortunate girl was found with her shroud thrown off ; she had vainly battered at the door of the vault. Juliet, before venturing alive into the tomb of her ancestors, uttered a cry of horror reminiscent of the nightmare which must have haunted the poet.[3]

> Shall I not then be stifled in the vault,
> To whose foul mouth no healthsome air breathes in,
> And there die strangled ere my Romeo comes ? . . .
> Or if I wake, shall I not be distraught,
> Environed with all these hideous fears,

[1] This Nimrod appears to have been Grey Bridges, nicknamed King of the Cotswolds because of the retinue he kept at Sudely Castle.

[2] *The Taming of the Shrew*, Induction.

[3] C. C. Stopes, *Shakespeare's Warwickshire Contemporaries* (Shakespeare Head Press, Stratford, 1907), p. 217.

And madly play with my forefather's joints,
And pluck the mangled Tybalt from his shroud ?
And, in this rage, with some great kinsman's bone,
As with a club, dash out my desperate brains ? [1]

The other dramatic episode which stirred Stratford was the subject of a coroner's inquest.[2] It took place in February 1580. A girl with the significant name of Katherine Hamlett was drowned in the Avon, at a spot where the roots of an immense willow dammed the current and made a deep pool in the river bed. The jury was inclined to believe that it was a case of suicide. Katherine's family, asking Christian burial, claimed that death was accidental, and that Katherine had slipped when leaning over the bank to moisten her flowers.[3] The mystery which envelops the mournful end of Katherine Hamlett, surrounds too the death of Ophelia. It is understandable that Shakespeare, then sixteen years old, should have been impressed by such an occurrence, and that he drew from memory and imagination the poetic description spoken by Queen Gertrude :

There is a willow grows aslant a brook,
That shows his hoar leaves in the glassy stream ;
There with fantastic garlands did she come
Of crow-flowers, nettles, daisies and long purples,
That liberal shepherds give a grosser name,
But our cold maids do dead men's fingers call them :
There on the pendent boughs her coronet weeds
Clambering to hang, an envious sliver broke,
When down her weedy trophies and herself
Fell in the weeping brook
Her clothes spread wide
And mermaid like a while they bore her up . . .[4]

The death of Katherine Hamlett seems to have suggested not only this passage, but also the lugubrious conversation of the gravediggers about the right of a suicide to rest in consecrated ground. The words of the gravediggers evidently reflect the very terms used at the coroner's inquest.

The manner in which Shakespeare treats this episode is characteristic of his method, which consists in enlivening dry facts [5] by his own vivid impressions. The town of his birth, its countryside, its inhabitants, the fields, hills and forests of the Shire appear continually in his poetry, and it is this recourse to things seen and experienced which makes his work so alive and so human.

[1] *Romeo and Juliet*, Act IV, Sc. 3.
[2] Edgar I. Fripp, *Shakespeare, Man and Artist*, p. 146. See also Archives of Alveston.
[3] The inquest went on for eight weeks and resulted in the conclusion that the dead was " per infortunium et non aliter nec allio modo ad mortem suam devenit ", but a page of the register which would have helped to finally unravel the mystery, has been torn out.
[4] *Hamlet*, Act IV, Sc. 7.
[5] The " Danish Chronicle " of Saxo Grammaticus, and the tragic history of Belleforest, whence Shakespeare drew the story of his tragedy, are both silent about the death of the girl who wrested Amleth's secret from him.

At the age of fourteen, the future was full of promise for the young Stratfordian ; he had the right, like any good pupil of the grammar school, to benefit by one of the scholarships which the generosity of Sir Hugh Clopton had made available to the students of the town. The gates of the University of Oxford were open to many of them. The scholarship given to one of the Quinney brothers, for example, might have gone to Will Shakespeare. But at the time when most well-to-do young men are free to decide on their future career, troubles came upon young Will and his relatives. Misfortune descended upon this family hitherto so prosperous, and, as will be seen in the following chapter, it was not at the university that the future dramatist completed his education, but in the rough school of life.

CHAPTER II

HARD TIMES

Fortune no longer favours the Shakespeares—Troubles in Warwickshire—John Shakespeare retires from public life—His spiritual testament—Distress of his family ; his son William becomes the breadwinner—He marries Anne Hathaway —Circumstances of this marriage—Their home in Henley Street—Birth of their three children.

IF Warwickshire was amongst the last of the midland counties where the consequences of Queen Elizabeth's statutes were felt, it may be said that in Stratford and the small neighbouring localities passive resistance showed its most obstinate character. In this corporate town with its old and deeply rooted traditions, the political and religious dissensions appeared only when the Royal authority was firmly established, when the "commissioners" appointed by the government had realized their power and when Sir Thomas Lucy, the local sheriff, felt himself duly covered by legal texts and by Leicester, his lord and master.

But once engaged the conflict never ceased, causing to the Shakespeares constant difficulties and perils. It is easy to follow each stage of their social and financial decline, dating from 1578, in the municipal account book. There we read that John Shakespeare was to be exempted from the weekly tax of sixpence payable by every member of the borough council until his removal from the council itself.

But it was not until the ruling powers appointed Sir Thomas Lucy High Sheriff of Warwickshire and conferred upon him full powers to deal with recusants as he saw fit, that the spirit of rebellion flared up and continued burning. Soon Leicester's lieutenant felt that the time was ripe for the application of the process of forfeiture to the recalcitrant.

One of the first to suffer from the new régime of fines and spoliation was certainly John Shakespeare. If we are to believe official records from 1578 on, the ex-Bailiff was in ever growing financial straits. That year, he joined with his wife Mary to mortgage her estate of Asbies at Wilmcote [1] for the sum of forty pounds. This evidently was a heart-breaking decision for both. But, under the terms of the agreement, they expected to recover the

---

[1] These possessions comprised : " Duobus mesuagiis, duobus gardinis, quinquaginta acris terrae, duobus acris prati, quatuor acris pasturae et communia pasturae pro omni modis averiis." And elsewhere : " septuaginta acris terrae, sex acris prati, decem acris pasturae et communia pasturae pro omni. modis averiis." Feet of Fines Mich. 20 Eliz. and Easter 21 Eliz. Warr.

cherished property the following year ; for the holder of the mortgage was Edmund Lambert, brother-in-law to Mary Shakespeare through his marriage with Joan Arden her half-sister, and he had promised to abandon his rights on the estate if the following year, on Michaelmas day, John Shakespeare would present himself at Barton-on-the-Heath with the forty pounds.[1] No interest was stipulated ; in lieu of this, Lambert was to benefit by all the proceeds of the farm during the twelve months of his incumbency.

That same year John Shakespeare was unable to pay his portion (six shillings and fourpence) for the arming and upkeep of six additional soldiers, three pikemen, two billmen and an archer for the municipal police. He also failed to pay the weekly tax for the poor of the parish.

The year following, his name reappears on the list of those who remained in debt for the purchase of arms. He was also fined for not having declared his mortgage on the Asbies property.[2]

In 1580, having acquired forty pounds from the sale of part of his Snitterfield farm, he went to Barton-on-the-Heath to recover his wife's beloved acres ; but only met with Lambert's refusal of his offer on the pretext that John had too many other debts.[3]

Nor were John Shakespeare's troubles merely financial. On April 4th, 1579, he lost his eight-year-old daughter Anne, whose brother William had just attained his fourteenth year. The municipal register records that eightpence was paid " for the bell and pall of Mr. Shakspeare's dawter ".[4]

Political troubles pursued the unfortunate Alderman of Stratford. Although apparently he avoided seeing his name mixed up with the Mytton-Snitterfield affair, it took place on his own ground and his brother Henry did not escape responsibility. Together with Richard Brookes he headed a faction of Catholic partisans who seized and held the Mytton tithe-barn, and, armed with harquebuses, sustained a regular siege with such vigour that their numerous adversaries from Warwick failed to rout them though backed by the Stratford billmen, halberdiers and archers ; it was only when the assailants started to burn down the wooden building that the defenders gave up.[5]

A document recently brought to light by the Dugdale Society shows that shortly after the Mytton riot another uprising of greater importance took place (1580) when John himself was far from alone in delinquency. His name figures at the head of a long list of gentleman-landowners from Stratford summoned to hold themselves at the disposition of the Westminster Courts of Justice between June 3rd and 22nd, 1580. This trial brought together one hundred and forty recusants of the adjacent counties, all men belonging to the ancient faith who were accused of disturbing the peace of the realm. John Shakespeare did not appear, and had to pay the heavy penalty of forty pounds, twenty for his absence and twenty for not having

[1] Halliwell Phillips, *Outlines*, vol. ii, p. 15.   [2] Stratford Accounts.
[3] Public Record Office. Feet of Fines Easter 22 Eliz. Warr.
[4] Chamberlain's Accounts Council Book A.
[5] *Black Book of Warwick*, p. 467.

presented John Audley of Nottingham, according to his guarantee. On the same day, Audley himself was sentenced to pay forty pounds for his own absence and ten for that of John Shakespeare. In the same affair, the lawyer Thomas Cooley was obliged to pay ten pounds for not having been able to produce John Shakespeare before the judges. These fines were in fact turned over to the Crown ; the receipt of the money paid by Councillor Shakespeare is recorded in a state document. In order to realize the considerable value of these sums, it suffices to recall that forty pounds had been the purchase price of the large house in Henley Street with its orchard and dependencies.[1]

These recusant disorders may well be explained by a renewed hope that the Sovereign was on the point of abandoning the councillors whom she had hitherto followed so faithfully. It was generally believed that the project then in negotiation of a marriage with the future King of France [2] would put an end to Catholic persecutions. The project seemed to be succeeding, but it aroused indignant Protestant opposition. A pamphlet, published in London, cost the ears of its author, John Stubbs, who had dared to publish :

his discovery of a Gaping Gulf whereunto England is like to be swallowed by another French marriage, if the Lord forbid not the banns by letting her Majesty see the sin and punishment thereof ; [3]

and in Warwickshire, Leicester and his brother Ambrose Dudley openly proclaimed that " the project was intolerable " and that it would not be accomplished without bloodshed and " broken heads ". They were not mistaken ; the unrest in London spread to the provinces. At Stratford there was great agitation ; municipal registers mention numerous scenes of disorder. These days were full of anxiety and danger for John Shakespeare.

For a long period John was conspicuous by his absence from council meetings at the Town Hall ; on one occasion only he came to vote for an old friend John Saddler proposed for the office of mayor as being " the man the most apt to fill this office ", and in 1586 we read rather sadly on the official record that Alderman Shakespeare is no longer member of the company :

For that Mr. Wheler dothe desire to be put out of the Company and Mr. Shakespear dothe not come to the Halles when they be warned nor hath done of long time.[4]

Such negligence on the part of a man who had previously been scrupulous

---

[1] Coram Rege Roll, Fines and Cemerciaments m. 7th Trinity term 22 Eliz.

[2] Hercule François, younger son of Catherine de Medicis, had inherited the pretentions of his brother Henry III who, when he was Duke of Anjou, had aspired to the hand of Elizabeth. The suit of the young Duke of Alençon had been ably prepared by his ambassador, Simier ; and when the duke arrived, the queen really appeared to be interested in him. After two months of beating about the bush, she announced to Walsingham and Leicester that she had decided to marry the French prince. Rings were exchanged, the affianced couple solemnly embraced, and when the Duke of Alençon (escorted by Leicester, Sidney, Lord Hunsdon and Sir John Morris) rode away to be governor of Brabant, the Queen pranced at his side as far as Canterbury and bade him the weeping farewell of a true betrothed.

[3] *Black Book of Warwick.*   [4] Stratford Council Book.

in the exercise of his function, proud of his standing and his furred gown, is not surprising when it is remembered that at every session of the Council the oath of allegiance could be exacted. Doubtless he who was wise enough to lie low might hope that the storm would blow over, but after the arrival of Father Parsons, Edmund Campion and their missionaries, Catholics at home found themselves under much closer surveillance.

In the manor houses of the neighbourhood there still remain some fifteen clandestine altars and hiding places which bear witness to the owners' fear of the sheriff and desire to satisfy conscience. " Little John " Owen, a carpenter who specialized in this sort of work, went from manor to manor, and farm to farm with his bag of tools. According to the writings of Father Gerard he saved hundreds of lives, before he succumbed himself at the Tower of London in 1606 under question, without having revealed the scenes of his exploits.

A very curious document witnesses the distress of John Shakespeare's mind in these troublous times. Less than two centuries after his death, a tiler replacing the old tiles of the Henley Street house, found between the joists and the beams five tiny pages sewn together with pack thread. Every paragraph began with John Shakespeare's name. Thanks to the intervention of the Stratford vicar, who had them copied at once by John Jordan, they were sent to London to Edmund Malone, the best paleographer and Shakespearian commentator of the day. Malone, much interested, had no doubt as to their authenticity, but could not explain how the poet's father had come to sign such a strange document. The style was florid in the manner of the Italian Renaissance, and the handwriting seemed to him to be of a later period than the signature. Halliwell Phillips in 1865, Sir Sidney Lee in 1890, and J. R. Harries later, exercised their irony on this document : " recent fabrication ", says the first, " work of an eighteenth century forger ", says the second, " absurd gibberish, hidden like a mouse behind the wainscot ", affirms the third. But time and scholarly research have finally confirmed the value of these pages.[1]

In 1923, Herbert Thurston, S.J., whilst working at the British Museum, found a little work printed in the city of Mexico, where the signatory, a certain Juan Phelipe Hernandez, had used the same terms as John Shakespeare.

This Spanish text is entitled :

Testament or last will of the soul made in good health to assure the Christian against the temptations of the devil in the hour of death, recommended by Saint Charles Borromeo, Cardinal of Saint-Praxedis and Archbishop of Milan.[2]

[1] In an article published in May 1882, in the review *The Month*, Father Thurston offers evidence that it would have been impossible for a Protestant to have falsified the text in question. Thirty years later, in the November 1911 number of the same publication, he was in a position to establish the authenticity of the document by comparing it to a similar text in Spanish.

[2] *The Month* Oct. 1923. Testamente o Ultima voluntad del Alma hecho in Salud para asseguarasse el christiano de las tentacione del Demonia, en la hora de la muerte ; Ordenado por San Carlos Borromeo, Cardinal de Santa Praxedis y Arcopispo de Milan.

Guided by this clue, Father Thurston found the original Italian model in the *Life of Alexander Sauli*,[1] where the profession of faith approved by Charles Borromeo is given *in extenso*. This same version was published at Baraduz in the Swiss Romansch dialect. A Spanish manuscript identical with the Mexican example also exists; it is signed by Maria Theresa Cardenas. An earlier French version of the sixteenth century may be consulted at the Bibliothèque Nationale.[2]

Before leaving Rome for England, Campion's missionaries went to Milan to receive final instructions. Amongst other tracts distributed to them was a formula for a spiritual testament drawn up to reassure the believer who feared to face death without the help of religion. Naturally this formula was composed in an ecclesiastical style. As for the letters and spelling whose modernity surprised Malone, these belong to a writer more learned and progressive than the old English yeoman, for all missionaries who graduated from Cardinal Allen's seminary were endowed with a superior education.

The testator, who spells his name Jhon Shakespear, declares his wish to receive, before death, the sacrament of extreme unction; he affirms his confidence in the mercy of God and founds his hope of salvation—not on his own merits—but on the sacrifice of his Redeemer; he declares himself ready to endure any bodily pains which may be inflicted upon him and those of his death as well; he forgives all who have done him wrong, expresses gratitude for past mercies and concludes by invoking divine aid so that he may never be tempted to efface or alter any portion of the testament which he signs.

The comparison of certain paragraphs of this two thousand word document, rendered tedious by frequent repetitions, with the corresponding paragraphs of the French or Italian texts suffices to convey its general character and give evidence of its authenticity. Even the errors of those who discovered and transcribed the original document confirm rather than diminish its value. Both Jordan and Malone made flagrant mistakes in deciphering paragraph IV, because of their ignorance of liturgical terms. They were puzzled by the word "gusting", in the sentence where the testator asks forgiveness for his sins committed by sight, hearing, smell, speech and "gusting". Jordan read "justing", and Malone "feeling". Their Protestant training had not taught them that the priest when anointing the lips of the dying, pronounces the formula: "Quidquid per *gustum* et locutionem deliquisti"—words naturally familiar to the old John Shakespeare.[3] His son William employs the verb to gust in the same sense four times:

---

[1] F. Bianchi, *Vita del Beato Alessandro Sauli* (Bologna, 1838).

[2] This French version is entitled: "Ordonnance de la dernière volonté de l'âme, en forme de testament, composée par ce grand serviteur di Dieu, sainct Charles-Borromée (Bibliothèque Nationale, K 5207). For the English text, see *Shakespeare Rediscovered* by the present author (Scribner's, London and New York, 1938).

[3] Whatever sin thou hast committed through speech or through taste.

" The gust he hath in quarrelling " (*Twelfth Night*, Act I, Sc. 3).
" Sin's extremest gust " (*Timon of Athens*, Act III, Sc. 5).
" When I shall gust it last " (*The Winter's Tale*, Act I, Sc. 2).
" Mine eye well knows what with his gust is 'greeing " (Sonnet 114).

It may be interesting to compare paragraph IV of John Shakespeare's Spiritual Testament with the corresponding passage of the French text :

Paragraph IV :
Item : I John Shakespeare doe protest that I will also passe out of this life armed with the last sacrament of extreme unction, the which, if through any let or hindrance, I should not then be able to have I doe now also for that time demand and crave the same ; beseeching His Divine Majesty that He will be pleased to anoynt my senses both internall and externall with the sacred oyle of His infinite mercy and to pardon all my sins committed by seeing, speaking, *gusting*, smelling, hearing, touching or by any other way whatsoever.

Paragraphe IV :
Je proteste vouloir passer de cette vie armé du dernier sacrement de l'extrême-onction ; et, arrivant par quelque empeschement que je ne puisse le recevoir semblablement, dès maintenant et pour lors, je le demande et désire priant la divine Majesté de daigner oindre tous mes sens tant intérieurs qu' extérieurs avec l'huile de son infinie miséricorde et me pardonner tous mes peschés que j'ay commis par mes yeux, ma langue, mon goust, mon odorat, mon ouye, mon attouchement et en quelque autre manière que ce soit.

The Italian version is noteworthy because it precedes the will found in Stratford by several years, and permits the detection of another error made by those who first deciphered the English text. Jordan and Malone were intrigued by the words " sharp-cutting razor " in paragraph XIII. Jordan thought it should read : " charge in a censor ". Malone abandoned the attempt to explain it, after having written in vain to the vicar of Stratford to ask him to elucidate this unusual expression.[1] However, the words " sharp-cutting razor " were simply a reminiscence of the hymn " Vexilla Regis " : " quo vulneratus insuper mucrone diro lanceae " (wounded by a sharp-cutting lance).[2]

It appears from this study that Jordan, far from meriting Sir Sidney

---

[1] Letter from Edmund Malone to Dr. Davenport (October 21st, 1789).

[2] Paragraph XIII. Item : I Jhon Shakespear doe by this my will and testament bequeath my soul as soon as it shall be delivered and loosened from the prison of my body to be entombed in the swet and amorous coffin of the side of Jesus Christ, and that in this life-giving sepulchre it may rest and live perpetually enclosed in that eternal habitation of repose, there to bless for ever and ever that direful iron of a launce which like a " charge in a censor " (sharp cutting razor) forms so sweet and pleasant a monument within the sacred breast of my Lord and Saviour.

Paragraph XIII : Voglio e lascio che l'anima mia, subito sciolta da questo carcere terreno, sia sepolta nell'amorosa caverna del costato di Gesù Cristo, nella quale vivifica sepoltura giaccia e viva perpetuamente confinata in quella requie e riposa, col benedire mille volte quel ferro della lancia che a guisa di scalpello pungente fece un monumento cosi dolce nell'amato petto del mio Signore,

Lee's accusation of "forger", comes through this test as a zealous and sincere searcher but without sufficient learning to understand the full import of the document with which he was dealing.

Paragraph X of this will was one which also puzzled commentators. Father Thurston himself, to whom a large part of the preceding study is due, was astonished [1] to find John Shakespeare asking Saint Winifred to remain near him and be present at the hour of his death.

Here it is the Spanish text which sheds the necessary light on the subject. In this formula a space marked N.N. is left blank for the signatory to insert the name of the saint of his choice.[2] The former mayor expressed his personal preference in naming Winifred, the young saint massacred by Danish invaders while protecting her convent, who was especially venerated in the midland counties. One of Campion's missionaries, Edward Old-corne,[3] who for seventeen years baffled pursuit in Warwickshire, declares that he owed the cure of a serious illness to a relic of Saint Winifred owned by one of the families that gave him refuge in Stratford.

Briefly, this moving testament truly reflects the sentiments which might be expected over the signature of John Shakespeare. It shows the moral turmoil in which the former mayor of Stratford lived in the year 1582.

Was it Campion himself, James Thomson, William Hartley, Edward Oldcorne, or another, who brought the profession of faith into the now famous house in Henley Street ? It is of small importance. Once signed, the document became, after the Act of Persuasion, highly compromising and it is not strange that it should have been hidden beneath the roof the moment a search was feared. We can only regret that a text of such historical value should, once it was found, have been made away with by those who lightly declared it to be a forgery.

In these distressful years, the spectre of hunger more than once threatened the Shakespeare home, formerly so prosperous. No more dreams of honours and armorial bearings ; no longer any question of a university degree for the eldest son. Will had to earn his living and take his share in the expenses of the house where, since the birth of his young brother Edmund in 1580, there was another mouth to feed.[4]

---

[1] *The Month* (June, 1911) and *Dublin Review* (October-December, 1923).

[2] Item, quiero, y desseo summamente, y con toda piedad ruego, que esta mi ultima voluntad, sea Protectora la gloriosa siempre Virgen Maria, refugio y Abogada de los pecca-dores a la qual especialmente, demas de los otros santos y santas, mis devotos, que son (N.N.) invoco, y llamo, que se hallen presentes à la hora de mi muerte ; y ruego à su Uni-genito Hijo, que reciva me espiritu en paz.

[3] Challoner, *Memoirs of Missionary Priests* as well secular as regular and other Catholics of both sexes, that have suffered death in England on religious accounts, from the year of our lord 1577 to 1684 (pp. 289-291).

[4] The situation of the Henley Street family grew steadily worse ; even in 1589, when William joined with his parents to back their plea for the recovery of their ancestral acres, the plaintiff's description of their status tells the whole story " of small wealthe and very few friends and allegiance in said county ", whereas their adversary John Lambert " is of good wealth and abilitie and is well friended and allied ".

It was probably to his neighbour, Thomas Giles, established as butcher in Sheep Street, or perhaps to Ralph Cawdrey in Bridge Street, that John Shakespeare offered Will's services. The families of Giles, Cawdrey and Shakespeare [1] were already linked by the skin and leather trade. Their religion also brought them together. But it must not be supposed that this temporary employment as butcher's apprentice was the profession to which young Shakespeare was especially drawn. According to one of his first biographers, John Aubrey, " when he kill'd a Calf, he would do it in a *high style*, & make a Speech ". Bravado, no doubt, for in Henry VI the sacrifice of an innocent beast is described with remarkable feeling.

> And as the butcher takes away a calf
> And binds the wretch and beats it when it strays,
> Beating it to the bloody slaughter house,
> Even so remorseless have they borne him hence ;
> And as his dam runs lowing up and down,
> Looking the way her harmless young one went,
> And can do naught but wail her darling's loss.[2]

Scarcely had he passed his eighteenth year when the future poet added responsibilities of his own to the difficulties of his family. In the autumn of 1582, he married Anne Hathaway, daughter of a farmer in the neighbouring hamlet of Shottery. Her cottage, covered with climbing roses and set in a bower of green, possessed a deliciously romantic appearance which it retains today.[3] Sixteen years later, when more favoured by fortune, he entered into negotiations to buy back this property dear to him since the days of his courtship.[4] In 1610, he helped his brother-in-law acquire it, so that it eventually became a family possession.[5]

Richard Hathaway's family had not long been established in the county, but they could boast of arms gained at the battle of Agincourt—three arrow heads surmounted by a hunting horn with silver scallops and tassels—while the Shakespeares' falcon with outspread wings was then only a hope. The sums twice lent to Anne's father by John Shakespeare attest the bonds of friendship which united them, and the generous legacy left by Lady Barnard, granddaughter of the poet, to her five nieces, Judith, Joan, Rose, Elizabeth and Susanna Hathaway show that, at the third generation, their good relations still continued. There is another indication of sympathy :

---

[1] Ralph Cawdrey had been mayor of Stratford before Shakespeare. Giles had joined forces with Shakespeare to save their neighbour Michael Pryce when the latter was prosecuted for felony.

[2] *Henry VI*, Part II, Act, III, Sc. I.

[3] This country house inspired the Arcadian setting of *As You Like It*. Shakespeare substituted grey southern olives for the silver willows to give an exotic atmosphere.

[4] In a letter dated January 24th, 1598, Abraham Sturley, former mayor of Stratford, writes : " Our fellow citizen, Master Shakespeare wishes to lay out some money to acquire a few acres at Shottery."

[5] Fripp, p. 496.

Bartholomew, brother of Anne, asked to be buried in Stratford parish church, beside his sister and his illustrious brother-in-law.[1]

It is possible to read enough between the lines of her father's will to obtain an impression of the environment in which the wife of the poet grew up. Richard Hathaway, yeoman-proprietor of Hewlands, the fine estate situated at Shottery, was twice married. He had three children by his first wife: Anne, Bartholomew and Catherine, the last born seven years after her elder sister. These three children lived under the same roof as the numerous family of their step-mother. Anne or Agnes Hathaway—the names are interchangeable—and her sister Catherine, were to "enter into possession of their marriage portion on the day of their wedding". This formula indicates that their father Richard had, before his death, given his consent to their betrothal.

Like every good Catholic of the time, Richard Hathaway begins his will thus:

I bequeath my soul to the hands of Almighty God, my maker, and by faith in the merits and passion of his son Jesus Christ, I believe and hope to be saved, and my body to the earth from whence it came in christian burial of the parish church of old Stratford. (P.C.C. Tirwhite 31 at Somerset House.)

Then he stipulates that his son Bartholomew is to have the management of his agricultural estate, but only as regards the sowings, and that the general upkeep should be the responsibility of his wife Joan. He counts on his son to be the support and comfort of his brothers and sisters, but adds—a significant detail—that if, later, his wife refuses to accept Bartholomew as manager of the farm, she is at liberty to buy the house and land for the sum of forty pounds in legal tender.

The situation of the children of his first marriage rapidly became intolerable, since three months after the decease of his father Bartholomew left the farm, married Isabel Hancocke, and transported himself to the nearby village of Tysoe. Anne, for her part, was obliged to quit Shottery and await her approaching marriage day among her own mother's family, at Temple Grafton, which explains why the poet's wife is described in the diocesan register as living at Temple Grafton and not at Shottery.

Tradition has it that the marriage of William and Anne was celebrated

---

[1] A letter addressed to the author by Margaret Anne Hathaway (March 19th, 1939) confirms the conclusions of this book on the religious beliefs of Shakespeare's wife, and adds that before coming to settle at Shottery, Anne's family, hereditary archers of the Forest of Dean, were known as " Papist ". The writer thinks that Richard Hathaway's move was motivated by the necessity of flying from the dangers of the new penal code. Saint-Briavals is, without doubt, the cradle of all those bearing the name Hathaway or Hatheway. Tradition affirms that their ancestors were there before the Norman conquest. Hathaways formed part of the body of archers who won the battle of Agincourt and, for this reason, they carry three arrow heads on their escutcheon. The name naturally means Heath way. The first mention in the archives is of Artur, father of Nigel, whose son William became constable of the castle of Saint-Briavals in 1287. Some of his descendants allied themselves to the families of Winter, Throckmorton and Baynham. Miss Hathaway observes that her father still carries as coat of arms the arrowheads surmounted by a hunting horn, and that her family still professes the faith of Rome.

at Luddington, the parish which included Temple Grafton, where the old priest Sir John Frith was denounced by the authorities as not very reliable in religion but very skilful in curing ailing falcons. Whether it was this priest, forced to fly as a recusant shortly afterwards, or Hugh Hall, chaplain of the Arden family, or one of those—eleven in number [1]—denounced by Sir Thomas Lucy as hidden in the county and clandestinely celebrating masses, marriages and baptisms according to the Papist rite, does not matter : what is certain is that the permission which made the marriage valid was given by regular authority, that is to say by John Whitgift, Bishop of Worcester, under whose jurisdiction fell the parishioners of Stratford and its environs.

On November 27th, 1582, the marriage licence was granted but the entry in the bishop's registers bears no specification of the date or place of the ceremony.

eodem die similis emanavit licencia inter Wm. Shakespere et Annam Whately de Temple Grafton. [2]

The next day another very strange document was demanded of William Shakespeare ; it was no longer a question of the licence, the price of which varied at that time between three and ten shillings, but of an agreement drawn up in the presence of a notary by which the young husband guaranteed to furnish the sum of forty pounds, for which the sureties were Fulke Sandells,

---

[1] One Hales a very old massing priest who married John Wise gentleman, to his late wife and married Thomas Higginson of Birkswell to his wife now living (it is vehemently supposed with masses). And is commonly resorted to at Mrs. Brookesby's in Tamworth and other places in the county of Warwick. This Hales hath christened divers children in the popish order.

One William Brookes a seditious seminary priest sometime servant of Campion the jesuit traitor, and in the Tower with him.

One Bernard Hartely suspected to be a priest, wore Lady Giffard's livery coat, but what hath become of him presenters know not.

One Barloe an old priest and great persuader of others to Papistry.

One Humphrey Hawes alias Mosely an obstinate papist and old massing priest now in Warwick Gaol. One Mountford Scott a Jesuit Seminary and now hanged as it is thought. These two resorted often to places in Warwickshire where they have done great hurt.

One Henry Sydnall a willful recusant thought to be a priest. He is a vagrant now and cannot be found.

One Sir Robert Whateley an old massing priest but hardly to be found.

One Sir John Appletree a seminary priest and fugitive, within three years past at the house of one Thomas Oldnall, but where he is they know not.

One George Cocke alias Cawdrey.

One Palmer thought to have been a priest from beyond the sea and to have had authority from Rome ir Rheims to reconcile.

Signed by Thomas Lucy, and his nine fellow commissioners.

S.P. Dom. Eliz. Vol. 243, no. 76.

[2] The error of the clerk who wrote Anne's name as " Whately " instead of " Hathaway " need not cause surprise, as he was in the habit of spelling phonetically. One finds in the same register that John Baker has obtained authorization to marry " Joan Baker " instead of " Joan Barbar " ; for " Bradley " he has " Darby ", and " Elcott " is recorded as " Edgcock ". However, the identity of Anne Hathaway with the woman whom Shakespeare married is completely established by the legacy to her from her father's old shepherd, and also by the legacy of the poet's granddaughter to her numerous Hathaway cousins.

Anne's father's executor, and John Richardson, one of the old farmers of Shottery. The agreement, after enumerating in detail the diverse causes of nullity in marriage, stipulates that : the

said William do upon his own proper cost and expense defend and save harmless the right reverend Father in God, Lord John, Bishop of Worcester, and his officers for licensing them, the said William and Anne, to be married together.

There must have been a serious reason to make John Whitgift, Bishop of Worcester, protect himself thus in a diocese where his predecessors, Bullingham and Grindall, were in the habit of closing their eyes to numerous irregularities and of whose members many remained faithful to the old religion.

That this marriage united two Catholic families is certain.[1] It also goes without saying that it was celebrated by a priest, and the fact that the registration of the licence carries neither date nor indication of the place of the past or future ceremony is sufficient proof that it was privately solemnized and not in conformity with the rubric of Elizabeth's Prayer Book. If the bishop wished to protect himself from official reproaches or legal proceedings, he could only have had in mind the displeasure of the highest authorities. The amount of forty pounds is the measure of his fears. Three weeks later the sum demanded for similar authorizations was raised to a hundred pounds, a prohibitive figure for those of moderate fortune.

Since the activities of Campion's missionaries, the bishops and clergy of the Established Church were compelled to act prudently. The Bishop of Worcester may have had wind of the death sentence passed on James Thompson, who was led through the city of York in chains to impress the crowd, and whose execution had been fixed for November 27th, 1582,[2] the very day the marriage licence was granted to Shakespeare.

As this licence was issued about seven months before the birth of Susanna, the poet's first daughter, several commentators have thought that an early ceremony was necessary to protect the reputation of the future mother. This is a pure supposition of which no trace appears in the local gossip, and which cannot seriously be maintained. Here again the considerable amount of the security demanded clearly shows that the Bishop of Worcester was safeguarding himself against the possible displeasure, not of parents, but of the higher authorities.

In every case where the entries in the diocesan registers do not specify the name of the church, the Catholic ritual was followed. The licence then appeared not as an authorization but as a regularization of marriage. The union of Francis Throckmorton with Anne Sutton, indubitably Catholic, was entered on the Worcester register as " allowed to take place in any church

---

[1] Alone among the English critics, James William Gray has devoted to this problem of Shakespeare's marriage a wide and serious study, but this heavy volume has long ago been cast aside, and those who quote it today forget its conclusion : that the marriage was solemnized according to the old rites.

[2] *Memoirs of Missionary Priests* (Challoner, 1778).

chapel or oratory in the county and celebrated by any fit priest ". Further-more, the fact that a licence bore no indication of church nor of the officiating clergyman's name is generally accepted as proof of a ceremony between Catholics. Many marriages of this kind left no official trace ; the families of the old faith contented themselves with a private rite and found it wiser to forgo a public declaration. Thus the marriage of Joan, sister of the poet, to William Hart, is not found on any register. In the case of Anne Hathaway a licence was necessary to permit her to enter legally into possession of her small dowry.

What more natural for Shakespeare, inclined to dramatize personal experience, than to have behaved like his own characters ? Romeo and Juliet were blessed by Friar Laurence : the marriage of Sebastian and Olivia took place in a neighbouring oratory : the wedding of Claudio and Hero was blessed in the church at Messina, that of Petruchio and Katherine in the church at Padua. The poet never conceived that true love could exist between two persons of high station without being sanctified by a religious ceremony. The definition of marriage pronounced by the priest in *Twelfth Night* is that of the writer, who insists on the divine and indissol-uble character of the sacrament.

> A contract of eternal bond of love,
> Confirm'd by mutual joinder of your hands,
> Attested by the holy close of lips,
> Strengthen'd by interchangement of your rings ;
> And all the ceremony of this compact
> Seal'd in my function, by my testimony.[1]

In *Romeo and Juliet*, Friar Laurence welcomes the young couple with these words : [2]

> So smile the heaven upon this holy act,
> That after-hours with sorrow chide us not.

and Romeo answers :

> Amen, amen ! . . .
> Do thou but close our hands with holy words,
> Then love-devouring death do what he dare . . .

Prospero, the wisest and most thoughtful of Shakespeare's characters, warns the lovers against transports of passion before the sacred ceremonies are accomplished, otherwise :

> No sweet aspersion shall the heavens let fall
> To make this contract grow ; but barren hate,
> Sour-eyed disdain and discord shall bestrew
> The union of your bed with weeds so loathly
> That you shall hate it both.

---

[1] *Twelfth Night*, Act v, Sc. 1.   [2] *Romeo and Juliet*, Act ii, Sc. 5.

Prince Ferdinand thus admonished, replies :

> . . . the murkiest den,
> The most opportune place, the strongest suggestion
> Our worser genius can, shall never melt
> Mine honour into lust, to take away
> The edge of that day's celebration.[1]

The author never allows himself to stray into facile irony about marriage. On the contrary, he speaks of its holy joys, within " the sacred bond of board and bed ".

Shakespeare considers that the sacrifices inseparable from the marriage state elevate and purify those whom it unites. It is love that softens the Shrew more than Petruchio's switch. Even the terrible Lady Macbeth adores her husband, the excess of her ambitious affection lures her to crime ; and as for the other households described by Shakespeare, Hotspur and Lady Percy, Brutus and Portia, Coriolanus and Virgilia all love and respect one another. Three random quotations illustrate how the marriage yoke can be assumed with a cheerful heart.

> I lov'd the maid I married ; never man
> Sigh'd truer breath ; . . .
> Than when I first my wedded mistress saw
> Bestride my threshold.[2]

> . . . O let me clip ye
> In arms as sound as when I woo'd, in heart
> As merry as when our nuptial day was done,
> And tapers burn'd to bedward.[3]

> . . . But I will be
> A bridegroom in my death, and run into't
> As to a lover's bed . . .[4]

Never has an author described the tender passion with a touch purer or more intense than Shakespeare. Even in his great drama of illicit love, *Antony and Cleopatra*, the tragic denouement finishes with the Queen of Egypt's confession that after so many ardent kisses, the last, sanctified by misfortune, confers immortal grandeur on her love.

> . . . Husband, I come :
> Now to that name my courage prove my title !

In Shakespeare's works, priests are represented quite otherwise than in the plays of his contemporaries. There is no offhand jesting at their expense. They behave with grave sincerity, fully conscious of their high vocation, like Campion, Dibdale, Cottam, Freeman, Ingram, Hartley and the secular priest, Hugh Hall. In *Much Ado About Nothing*, it is Friar Francis who resolves the problem of the drama ; the calumniated bride is saved through

---

[1] *The Tempest*, Act IV, Sc. 1.   [2] *Coriolanus*, Act IV, Sc. 5.
[3] *Coriolanus*, Act I, Sc. 6.   [4] *Antony and Cleopatra*, Act IV, Sc. 12.

his intervention, and the marriage, interrupted by a tragic mistake, happily concludes the comedy.

When Shakespeare sketches a Protestant minister, the features are very different. His pastor in *The Merry Wives of Windsor* is full of goodwill, inclined to conciliation and desirous of promoting peace amongst his neighbours ; but, apart from these laudable qualities, Sir Hugh Evans appears as vain, quarrelsome, indiscreet, and completely devoid of the dignity appropriate to his cloth.[1]

As for the reasons which determined Shakespeare's marriage to Anne Hathaway, these seem self-evident. Certainly financial interest was not the motive of this union, since the bridegroom was obliged to work for his living. The dowry of the bride amounted to exactly six pounds, thirteen shillings and eightpence. If ever there was one,[2] this was a love-match. Anne represented for William the " queen of curds and cream ", a mixture of grace and competence like the Perdita whom he makes us see presiding over the pastoral feast in *The Winter's Tale*.[3] Is there anything surprising in a young man of mature nature and highly developed mind who chooses for his life companion a woman whose character and intelligence were already formed ? A Juliet of fifteen years would hardly have been a fit mate ; English country girls rarely reach the height of their charm before the twenties.

More than any of his fellow dramatists, Shakespeare assigns a predominant place to women and to love. His heroines differ essentially from the other heroines of literature by the gifts of personality and intelligence with which he endows them. They are generous, courageous, loyal and inflexible on questions of honour.

Shakespeare saw the beloved one, not as a toy, but as a goddess of the home ; on first acquaintance with love he placed the object of love far above himself, and his last works are proof that he kept intact the ideal of his youth. Years later he was enslaved by an illicit attachment, which took possession of him and annihilated resistance, but he found therein small satisfaction and much anguish, which he sang in incomparable tones of despair. Apart from the twenty-seven sonnets addressed to the " Dark Lady ", his poetry is a hymn to the strong and wholesome love which he had known in his

---

[1] In *Love's Labour's Lost*, Sir Nathaniel, the Protestant pastor, is as ridiculous as the pedant Holofernes and the braggart Armado.

[2] O most potential love ! vow, bond, nor space,
In thee hath neither sting, knot nor confine,
For thou art all, and all things else are thine.
When thou impressest, what are precepts worth
Of stele example ? When thou wilt inflame,
How coldly those impediments stand forth
Of wealth, of filial fear, law, kindred, fame !
Love's aims are peace, 'gainst rule, 'gainst sense, 'gainst shame,
And sweetens, in the suffering pangs it bears,
The aloes of all forces, shocks, and fears.

Lover's Complaint.

[3] Act IV, Sc. 3.

adolescence, and whose image remained adorable. It would be rash to pretend that the woman who gave him his three children still possessed the charm he had seen in his country sweetheart, but certain it is that after a life of bitter trials and astounding successes, he returned to his wife and children, and that thenceforward his work expressed the serenity of moral calm after storm.

The reasons which determined Anne to take William Shakespeare as her husband are more easily imaginable.

He was " handsome and well-shaped ", says John Aubrey. His nature was open and generous, according to Ben Jonson. " His demeanor no lesse civill than he excelent in the qualitie he professes . . . his uprightness of dealing . . . argues his honesty," declares Chettle in 1592. Our " Friend and fellow ", he is called by John Heminge and Henry Condell. All these qualities were evident at the time of his courtship.

Arched eyebrows strongly overshadowed his hazel eyes ; the straight nose was finely chiselled ; the mouth, with its lines showing sensibility, passion and strength of will, was not yet hidden by the moustache and more or less trimmed beard shown in the " Chandos " and " Flower " portraits and the Droeshout engraving. The lips contrasted in their mobility with a high forehead framed in auburn hair.[1]

Relative tranquillity awaited the young couple at home in Henley Street. Children were not lacking in the house. Edmund, Will's youngest brother, was scarcely three years old when Susanna the cherished daughter of the poet was born on May 26th, 1583.[2] Two years later Anne Shakespeare gave birth to twins, a boy and a girl. The registers of the old parish church mention the baptisms on February 2nd, 1585, of Hamlet [3] and Judith, son and daughter of William Shakespeare.

The two Sadlers were chosen as god-parents and gave their unusual christian names to the infants. The Sadlers throughout life [4] remained linked to the poet and will reappear at his death bed.

The presence of John Shakespeare and his wife Mary at this difficult time must have produced an atmosphere of depression. Mary Shakespeare

---

[1] There are four portraits probably made directly from life. The " Chandos " canvas of the National Portrait Gallery, is ascribed to Richard Burbage, who was throughout life the fellow actor of the man whose face he has tried to immortalize. The " Flower " portrait was probably painted a little later and may have been used for the engraving published in the folio of 1623. The original has not the mistakes in drawing of the engraving. The latter, however, was declared to be a good likeness by Ben Jonson who knew Shakespeare intimately. As for the tomb bust which is more than mediocre, this serves to check feature by feature the resemblance of the three portraits. A magnificent terra cotta bust exists, the work of François Roubaillac, pupil of Coysevox, which used to be in the Memorial Theatre and is now in the Garrick Club ; the sculptor was as near Shakespeare's character and likeness as Houdon to his model when he executed the fine marble bust of Molière.

[2] May 26, 1583, Baptism Susanna daughter to William Shakespeare, Paris Register.

[3] February 2, 1585, Baptisms. Hamnet and Judith, sonne and daughter to William Shakespeare. *Idem.* (Hamlet is spelled Hamnet, and even sometimes Hamlett, as in Shakespeare's will.)

[4] Hamnet Sadler had married the daughter of Thomas Staunton.

with her old-world principles was in constant revolt against the new order from which all the Catholic élite suffered. Her Arden blood certainly boiled on hearing of the vexations and death sentences meted out to her co-religionists ; the ex-mayor, disappointed and ruined, could only bitterly remember the days of his past glory. It has been suggested that the name of Edmund, given to his youngest child, was chosen in homage to Edmund Campion, just returned to revive the old faith in England. From the testamentary formula signed by the old man one is tempted to believe that remorse was mingled with regrets. As a member of the local council he had had his share of responsibility. He had witnessed the rising tide of the Reformation without, perhaps, attempting as he should have done, to stem the current. Had he not allowed the frescoes of the Guild Chapel, [1] so dear to the Stratford inhabitants, to be obliterated by a thick layer of whitewash ? These had portrayed Adam and Eve beneath the tree of knowledge under the eye of the insidious serpent, and, below, the last judgement where the flames of hell soar between the damned and the elect. Even the great mural painting of the murder of Thomas à Becket had disappeared beneath the work of the iconoclasts along with Saint Helena's discovery of the true Cross.

It was difficult for the ex-mayor to believe that a national Saint like Becket—venerated during four centuries by English pilgrims who crowded to the altar at Canterbury which had witnessed his murder—should have become a seditious priest disloyal to the Crown and traitor to his Sovereign simply because Parliament had so decided. A man of the temper of John Shakespeare could not bring himself to think that Mass celebrated with so much piety as a sacred duty towards the dead members of the guild was the manifestation of " blasphemous fables and dangerous deceits ", as the articles of faith of the new Anglican Church had declared it.

In short, the discontent and misery of the elder generation and the perpetual caterwauling of babies filled the atmosphere of the Henley Street home with perturbation and it is not surprising if the future poet should often have sought in the nearby forest, that peace which was lacking at home.

If he ventured beyond the paternal acres perhaps he was not led merely by the fascination of the melancholy boughs. A more imperious need directed his steps and his arrows, that of adding a few roebuck, hares or rabbits to the family's usual scanty fare ; such morsels were perhaps all the more appreciated because taken from the common enemy, the tyrannical and jealous lord of the manor, Sir Thomas Lucy. On his side, if the knight were to prosecute young Will and succeed in magnifying the disorders of which he was guilty into crimes against the security of the State, he would be entitled to seize the Snitterfield farm, a fine property, conveniently situated close to Fulbrook Park.

[1] Recently these frescoes have been partially uncovered.

CHAPTER III

ENFORCED DEPARTURE

Sir Thomas Lucy and the Arden-Somerville affair—The poaching incident—
Shakespeare's flight from Stratford—Situation of the family after his departure.

SIX months after the birth of his daughter Susanna, William Shakespeare, like all the members of his family, was stirred by a tragic
episode. His near neighbour, John Somerville, proprietor of the
manor of Edreston, was condemned to death for an alleged plot against the
Queen, and his accomplices were sought in Stratford and its neighbourhood.

Somerville, scarcely older than Shakespeare, already was father of two
children ; he had married Margaret Arden, daughter of the squire of Park
Hall, and cousin of the Shakespeares of Henley Street.

On graduating from Hart Hall, Oxford, he found every liberal career
closed to those of his faith ; travel was prohibited, even short journeys were
limited in extent ; the vigilance of the local authority forbade the sons of
Catholics any activity or ambition. He ill resigned himself to the mono-
tonous life of a gentleman farmer, and soon fell into melancholia. Disturbed
by his sudden fits of violence, his family kept him under close surveillance
but he succeeded in baffling their care.

With the cunning of madness, feigning sleep, he escaped on Friday,
October 25th, 1583, terrorized the stable lad and ordered him to saddle two
horses. Scantily clothed, penniless, armed with two unloaded pistols, a
dagger at his belt, he rode off in the direction of London, promising himself
to remonstrate with the Queen, whom he considered " a viper ". The
groom abandoned him near the village of Aynho-on-the-Hill, where he was
arrested and taken to Oxford, then to London, almost without food but under
a strong escort.[1]

The Privy Council insisted on the gravity of the threats uttered against
the Queen although the guards who reported them declared that their prisoner
had lost his reason. He was condemned to be hanged as a traitor, and Sir
Thomas Lucy was ordered to seek out his accomplices. The Sheriff lost
no time in arresting Elizabeth Somerville, the prisoner's sister, and his wife,
Margaret ; then he went personally to arrest the Ardens of Park Hall.
Edward Arden, his wife Mary, his brother Francis and the priest Hugh Hall,
their chaplain, were apprehended. The priest was beloved in the whole

---

[1] Twelve men and twelve horses were necessary to accomplish this task which brought
thirteen pounds, seven shillings to John d'Oilley for " the trouble which he had given himself
in the service of Her Majesty ". (Accounts of the Treasurer of the Chamber, 1583.)

region, where he had passed more than thirteen years, specializing, apart from his religious vocation, in the cultivation of orchards and in the art of designing those formal gardens of which Shakespeare writes with evident pleasure. What is known of Father Hall suggests that he was the model for Friar Laurence in *Romeo and Juliet*, so well versed in the study of horticulture and medicinal plants. Hugh Hall possessed a house at Idlicote, within a mile of Stratford. It was there that he gave shelter to Somerville's mother, who went mad while the tragedy was taking place in London.

Sir Francis Throckmorton, the chief Catholic landowner of the county, was arraigned in his turn, and " a vast plot woven against the safety of the State " was publicly announced.

The meagre evidence in this famous case, a veritable parody of justice, is contained in a collection of secret documents.[1] A parchment to which is attached the great seal of Elizabeth, signifying the death warrant, contains the names of four condemned persons : Edward Arden, John Somerville and the priest Hugh Hall were to be hanged, and Mary Arden was condemned to be burned alive " for the crime of high treason against the queen " ; these details are inscribed in the margin of the document.

When Edward Arden appeared alone on the scaffold at Smithfield, the prisoners' friends waited in agony of mind to know the fate of his companions, only to learn that John Somerville had been strangled in his cell by way of avoiding the anger of the crowd at the sight of a madman brought to execution. His prosecutor, Thomas Wilkes, admitted in his report that the condemned youth was indeed a maniac.

I perceive that it will be alleged in his excuse to save him from the danger of the law, that he hath been since midsummer affected with a frantic humour. . . . True it is that three or four days before he departed from his house, his mind was greatly troubled. in somuch that he could not sleep. . . . It is confessed by Joyce Hill that Elizabeth Somerville brought the book to her brother, who after reading thereof was much perplexed in mind, and that the book was conveyed again by her.[2]

In looking further Wilkes discovered to his satisfaction that Margaret Somerville was a " very perverse and malitious Papist " who had been in France " as was proved by a letter written from St. Omer in August three months ago before returning to this realm ".

But the case did not conclude there. The Council, wishing at all hazards to establish proofs of a long-hatched plot, called upon the Stratford authorities to bestir themselves, and discover other culprits. They were especially ordered to trace the volume which had driven Somerville to madness.[3]

---

[1] Baga de Secretis Pouch 45 mm. 9, 10.

[2] Thomas Wilkes' report is to be found in full among the *S.P. Dom. Eliz.* vol. 163, no. 55. It is addressed to the " Lord Treasurer and Secretary " from Charlecote on November 7, 1583.

[3] The little devotional book entitled " A Booke of Prayers and Meditations, Fourteen in number written in Spanish by F. Louis de Granada, and translated into English by Michael Hopkins " (Paris, 1582). It contained nothing dangerous or subversive, but certain passages of lofty philosophy suggest that the author of *Hamlet* was acquainted with it.

But those who were on the spot avowed the futility of efforts to comply with the authorities' request.   The suspects had hidden all compromising objects and the proscribed priests had disappeared as if by magic.   Search weary, Thomas Wilkes, Topcliffe's zealous agent, working under Lucy's orders, complained that all his researches in Charlecote had come to nought.   In his secret document Wilkes thus reports to Walsingham :

. . . Albeit we cannot with all travail here attain to the depth of this treason which in my simple opinion, will reach to more papists, than Summerfeild and Hall the priest, as by further examination had of them two will most aptly be discovered : Yet I doubt not but your honour will judge that this one argument will be of no small efficacy to touch them, which is, that in all the houses of the papists where we have made search, although most of them are knowen to be very notorious papists.   We have not founde either bookes lctters or any show of popery by beades crosses or other trumperies that might draw them into suspicion : which hath been prevented by conveying away from their houses all such things, immediately upon the rumour of the apprehension of Somerville.[1]

Thoroughly discouraged by his failure to discover more culprits in the Stratford region, Wilkes suggested to the London Council that as they had the ringleaders of the plot conveniently at hand in the Tower they should obtain matter from their own mouths, a euphemistic invitation to extort confessions under torture.

I have thought good nevertheless to signify unto your honour that unless you can make Somerville, Arden, Hall the priest, Somerville's wife, and his sister, to speak directly to those things which you desire to have discovered, that it will not be possible for us here to find out more than is found already, for that the papists in this county generally do work upon the advantage of clearing their houses of all shows of suspicion and therefore unless you can charge them with matter from the mounth of your prisoners look not to wring anything from them by finding of matter suspicious in their houses.[2]

In London the Council's activity redoubled and was concentrated on the person of Hugh Hall considered as chief instigator of this " terrible crime ".

Thomas Wilkes and Thomas Morton drew up the attainder on the last day of December, 1583 ;[3] here is the gist of this document containing the priest's answers to the accusations of plotting with Francis Throckmorton, making conversions, etc. . . .

For reconciling says that he has no authority so to do, for he thinks that it requires episcopal sanction.

Has only heard confessions but of such as were in the Catholic church already.

He has had no familiarity with Francis Throckmorton since seven or eight years and does not remember to have seen him these four or five years.   With Mr. John Talbot, Sir John Throckmorton, Lord Windesor, Mr. Sheldon he hath

---

[1] See *Shakespeare's Warwickshire Contemporaries*, C. C. Stopes (Shakespeare Head Press), pp. 85-110.   [2] Ibid.
[3] S.P. Dom. Eliz. vol. 164, no. 77.

most commonly conversed and sometimes said mass ; but held no conference of state these thirteen past only of religion ; with Sir Thomas Cornwallis and Sir Thomas Kidson he held no conference but of Orchards and gardens.

In Warwickshire he had not conversed with others than Edward Arden but denies that he was ever present at any mariage with a mass.

These declarations Hall signed with a trembling hand.

Francis Throckmorton, that unhappy young man of adventurous and chivalrous disposition, was questioned at the same time as Hugh Hall. On being removed from the rack, he confessed under further torture, that he had carried letters to the Queen of Scots.[1]

He was executed shortly after Edward Arden ; but of the priest Hugh Hall, there was no further mention. His name is not included in the official lists of those executed. Amongst the archives of the Tower, however, certain entries in the gaoler's account book show that small sums were disbursed for " heating and candles " supposedly for the unhappy prisoner. Suddenly all records concerning Hugh Hall cease without explanation. But it was an open secret that the warders officially prolonged the life of those who died under question—on their registers at least—thus suppressing a cause of scandal and augmenting the petty profits to be derived from the sale of the personal effects and clothing which had belonged to the captives in the Tower.

This famous case, although today forgotten, stirred not only Stratford and Warwickshire, but all England. The treatment inflicted upon Somerville, considered by friends, family and guards to be mentally deficient and certainly incapable of the least conspiracy, aroused, above all, compassion. The sentence passed on Edward Arden, model of the traditional virtues of a country gentleman, encountered universal reprobation. Burleigh thought it prudent to cover the Council's action by a pamphlet entitled :

The execution of Justice in England for maintenaunce of publique and Christian peace against certeine stirrers of sedition, and adherents to the traytors and enemies of the Realme, without any persecution of them for questions of Religion, as is falsely reported and published by the fosterers of their treasons.

This publication is dated December 17th, 1583, three days before Somerville's death, but Burleigh proceeded thus :

Those who falsely pretend that certain persons who have already suffered for their treasons are martyrs for their religion should add to the pope's calendar of martyrs, the name of a furious young man of Warwickshire by name Somerville, who of late was discovered and taken on his way coming with a full intent to have killed Her Majesty.

---

[1] The order to torture Francis Throckmorton for the second time is consigned in the hand of Walsingham himself with this cynical remark : " I have seen as resolute men as Throckmorton stoop, notwithstanding the great shew he hath made of Roman resolution. I suppose the grief of the last torture will suffice without any extremity of racking, to make him more conformable than he hath hitherto shewed himself." (S.P. Dom. Eliz. vol. 163, no. 65).

To this specious argument, Cardinal Allen replied by :

A true, sincere and modest Defence of English Catholics that suffer for their faith both at home and abroad against a false and slanderous libel intituled The Execution of Justice in England.

Allen seems to have had the last word ; though the index of Burleigh's political papers [1] lists a chapter entitled " The Arden Somerville Affair ", all reference to this case is suppressed. Evidently those responsible, finding public opinion hostile, thought it opportune to say no more about the pretended Warwickshire plot.

The Arden-Somerville affair put Sir Thomas Lucy in the first rank of Richard Topcliffe's agents. He received official thanks for the zeal he displayed in the pursuit of notable recusants, the list of whom he continually augmented.

If Stratford's former mayor found means of taking refuge from the storm, his son William was less successful. A fervent disciple of Saint Hubert, he had already attracted the lightnings of local justice. There are few traces of Shakespeare as butcher ; on the other hand, concerning Shakespeare the poacher numerous instances are cited.

The tradition of young Will's hunting adventures is based on five reliable documents ; among these the manuscript notes of William Fulman, deposited in Corpus Christi library in 1690, though little known are most important.

William Fulman, a learned historian and impassioned collector, devoted himself for half a century to assembling and annotating all sorts of documents and correspondence. His collection comprises twenty-seven volumes. [2] After his death, his collaborator and friend, the scholar Richard Davies, completed his works, and presented them to Corpus Christi College, Oxford.

On the first page, devoted to Shakespeare, can be read in Fulman's fine and meticulous writing : " Shakespeare was born at Stratford-on-Avon in Warwickshire, about 1563-1564 ", then the rapid and straggling hand or Davies adds :

Much given to all unluckiness in stealing venison and rabbits particularly from Sir Lucy who had him oft whipt and sometimes imprisoned and at last made him fly his native country to his great advancement. But his revenge was so great that he is his Justice Clod-pate and calls him a great man and yt in allusion to his name bore three louses rampant for his arms.

Rowe, in his *Works of William Shakespeare* [3] where he utilizes the information collected at Stratford by the actor Betterton, writes :

He had, by a Misfortune common enough to young Fellows, fallen into ill Company ; and amongst them, some that made a frequent practice of Deer-

---

[1] *Burleigh Papers*, edited by Martin, 1759.
[2] Fulman died in 1688 at Meysey Hampton, not far from Stratford. See Chapter XX.
[3] *The Works of William Shakespeare ;* in six volumes adorned with cuts. Revised and corrected, with an account of the life and writing of the author by N. Rowe, Esq., London, printed for Jacob Tonson, MDCCIX.

stealing, engag'd him with them more than once in robbing a Park that belong'd to Sir Thomas Lucy of Cherlecot, near Stratford. For this he was prosecuted by that Gentleman, as he thought, somewhat too severely ; and in order to revenge that ill usage, he made a Ballad upon him. And tho' this, probably the first Essay of his Poetry, be lost, yet it is said to have been so very bitter, that it redoubled the Prosecution against him to that degree, that he was oblig'd to leave his Business and Family in Warwickshire, for some time, and shelter himself in London.

Rowe further states that in *The Merry Wives of Windsor*, Shakespeare, among other extravagances, makes Falstaff a poacher to give him the opportunity of putting his own persecutor on the stage under the name of Justice Shallow.

Hence the two early biographers, Davies and Rowe, although drawing their information from different sources, agree in declaring that Shakespeare quarrelled with Sir Thomas Lucy over the poaching incident, that he was forced to leave Stratford on this account, and that in *The Merry Wives of Windsor* he caricatured his tormentor as Justice Shallow.

Twenty years after Rowe's publication, William Oldys,[1] to whom we owe so many vivid pictures saved from oblivion, repeated the poaching story which he obtained from the Duke of Buckingham, and even quotes the first stanza of the ballad which Rowe knew by hearsay only. The Duke had his information from Sir William Davenant, the poet's godson :

There was a very aged gentleman living in the neighbourhood of Stratford (where he died fifty years since) who had not only heard, from several old people in that town, of Shakespeare's transgression, but could remember the first stanza of that bitter ballad, which, repeating to one of his acquaintance, he preserved it in writing ; and here it is, neither better nor worse, but faithfully transcribed from the copy which his relation very courteously communicated to me.

> A parliemente member, a justice of peace,
> At home a poor scare-crowe at London an asse,
> If lowsie is Lucy, as some volke miscalle it,
> Then Lucy is lowsie, whatever befall it :
> He thinks himself great,
> Yet an asse in his state,
> We allow by his eares but with asses to mate.
> If Lucy is lowsie, as some volke miscalle it,
> Sing Oh Lowsie Lucy whatever befall it.

Other pens have taken up the story. Bishop Warburton remarks in 1747 : [2]

This ballad was not the only shaft which he let fly against his persecutor, whose anger drove him to the extreme end of ruin where he was forced to a very low degree of drudgery for a support.

---

[1] Manuscript quoted by E. K. Chambers, *William Shakespeare*, vol. ii, p. 279.
[2] Preface to his edition of Shakespeare's Works.

In 1767, Edward Capell, the editor,[1] tells us in his notes on *The Merry Wives of Windsor* that according to the statements of the old people of Stratford, the ballad hung on the gates of the park exasperated Sir Thomas Lucy to such an extent that he sought help from the law and ordered the delinquent to be prosecuted.

Capell quotes the first verse of the ballad with unimportant variations, adding that the local inhabitants pronounced " Lowsie like Lucy ".

Between 1780 and 1800, John Jordan [2] claimed to have found the whole text of the satirical verses in a chest of drawers which had belonged to Miss Dorothy Wheeler of Shottery, descendant of the councillor friend of Shakespeare. Criticism justly discredits these six supplementary verses. Admitting that they were not composed by Shakespeare, and merely based on oral tradition, they are none the less interesting as having been written a century before any biographer had seriously examined Sir Thomas Lucy's political career ; [3] for they show that the people of Stratford considered the member of parliament not only vain, ridiculous and foolish, but at the same time a dangerous and cruel personage.

At the beginning of the nineteenth century, Sir Thomas Lucy's descendants still remembered details of the poaching incident and even knew the very spot where it took place.

Sir Walter Scott writes in his diary, April 8th, 1828,[4] when with his daughter Anne he had undertaken a pilgrimage to Warwickshire in order to collect data for his novel *Kenilworth:*

Learning from Washington Irving that the house of Sir Thomas Lucy, the Justice of the Peace who rendered Warwickshire too hot for Shakespeare and drove him to London, was still extant, we went in quest of it.

Charlecote is in high preservation and inhabited by Mr. Lucy, descendant of the worshipful Sir Thomas. . . . While we were surveying the antlered old hall with its painted glass windows, and family pictures, Mr. Lucy came to welcome us in person. . . . He told me the park from which Shakespeare stole the buck was not that which surrounds Charlecote, but belonged to a mansion at some distance where Sir Thomas Lucy resided at the time of the trespass. . . . This visit gave me great pleasure ; it really brought Justice Shallow freshly before my eyes. The luces in his arms which do become an old coat well were not more plainly portrayed in his own armorials in the Hall window, than was his person in my mind's eye.

Walter Scott was well informed about the region where the incident took place. The estate which links the Shakespeares' farms and meadows to the Lucy property, Fulbrook by name, was seized in March 1585, through

---

[1] Edward Capell, *Notes and various readings to Shakespeare* (3 vols., 1783).
[2] John Jordan, *Original memoirs and historical accounts of the families of Shakespeare and Hart* (Olograph MSS. 1790, printed 1865).
[3] Sir Thomas Lucy's life is incorporated in *Shakespeare's Warwickshire Contemporaries* by C. C. Stopes (Shakespeare Head Press, 1907).
[4] *The Journal of Sir Walter Scott*, from the original manuscript at Abbotsford (Harper Brothers, 1890), p. 155.

a procedure which even to the time was considered scandalous. Dugdale, in his *Warwickshire Antiquities* observes that :

In first Queen Marie as I have elsewhere shewed, The Queen passed it (Fulbrook) unto Sir Francis Englefield to hold in capite : Since which it has come to the Lucies of Cherlcote the last Sir Thomas having renewed the park and by the addition of Hampton woods thereto, enlarged it much.[1]

Samuel Ireland corroborates the poaching story, describes Fulbrook Castle and adds :

The adjoining park, which had been antiently in the possession of Sir Francis Englefield, was, in the time of our immortal Shakspeare, in that of the Lucys, who had been long settled in the neighbouring village of Charlecot. It was in this park our bard is said to have been, in a youthful frolic, engaged in stealing deer. . . .[2]

What historians do not mention is the procedure by which the domain of Fulbrook passed from the philanthropic hands of Sir Francis Englefield to those of Sir Thomas Lucy, so that the good people of Stratford were deprived of one of their favourite hunting grounds.[3] From the time of Mary Tudor, the Warwickshire member of parliament was Sir Francis Englefield, who held a high position in the royal household. When, like so many other Catholics, he chose exile, he was replaced in his position by Leicester. Nevertheless, in order to dispossess him of his estates, it was necessary to declare him a traitor. Before the passage of the act against recusants, Sir Thomas obtained a special edict (December 17th, 1584) which assured him the enjoyment of " Fulbrook ".[4]

One month before Sir Thomas had been again returned as knight of the shire to parliament. He was energetic in promoting the Bill against the Jesuits and Seminary Priests and more energetic still against Dr. Parry, the solitary member who had the courage to speak against its tyrannical spirit.

When Dr. Parry's parliamentary immunity was removed, Sir Thomas Lucy took the affair into his own hands. He addressed a petition to the Queen asking that a " new and exemplary punishment " should be invented for such a serious case. His petition was as follows :

Forasmuch as that villainous traitor Parry was a member of this house in the time of some of his most monstrous, horrible and traiterous conspiracies that her Majesty vouchsafe to give licence to this house to proceed to the devising

---

[1] Dugdale, *Antiquities of Warwickshire* (1654), p. 509.

[2] Samuel Ireland, *Picturesque Views on the Upper, or Warwickshire Avon* (London, 1795), pp. 152 *et seq.*

[3] According to the ancient laws of venery : " Every animal found in its wild state may be killed and no proprietorship may be claimed before the death of the beast." In the eyes of the Stratford sportsmen, it was not an offence to hunt in the Fulbrook woods but an ancient right which the dispossession of Englefield in favour of Sir Thomas Lucy could not abrogate.

[4] A Bill for the assurance of certain landes to Sir Thomas Lucy was, upon second reading, committed to Mr. Digley, Mr. Barker and others. (Simonds d'Ewes, p. 340.)

and making of some law for his execution after his conviction as may be thought fittest for his so extraordinary and most horrible kind of treason.

The execution of Parry took place on March 4th at the Palace of Westminster in the presence of members of parliament, the victim protesting to the end that his confession of a " plot " had been extracted from him under torture.[1]

Satisfied at having won his case, Sir Thomas Lucy hastened back to Warwickshire. He left his colleague Barker to defend the projected law which he cherished " on the protection of grain and game ", reached Charlecote to take possession of Fulbrook, the domain he had so much coveted, and surrounded the forest house with palisades to affirm his rights.[2]

The date of the poaching incident, cause of Will Shakespeare's departure from Stratford, can therefore be fixed as 1585, and early in March, that is to say, shortly after the birth of his twins.

Touching the incident itself, the poet recalls it on two occasions, as his first biographers have noticed ; these evocations are especially interesting in that they permit us to observe one of the secrets of Shakespeare's art, with its fine delicacy and moderation. How well he knew how to put aside sterile spite in favour of the different but powerful weapon of ridicule ; with this he overwhelmed his former persecutor ! He took good care to avoid presenting Lucy as a cruel pursuivant, knowing that the censor would never authorize a direct and political attack. He retained only his chief characteristics : obstinacy, egoism and boastfulness, demonstrating thus that stupidity can be as harmful as vice.[3]

The first public function exercised by Lucy was that of recruiting officer for Warwickshire, and it is thus that Shakespeare introduces Justice Shallow in the Second Part of *Henry IV*. He shows him enlisting for military service the most unsuitable persons. As he presents his sickly and pitiful candidates to Falstaff, who is charged with raising a troop, he hardly listens to the protests of the young men who have no taste for fighting, being only interested in proving how " wild " he was in his youth. So ridiculous is he that no sooner has Shallow departed than the astute Falstaff breaks out into a long description of the master of Charlecote :

Lord, Lord ! how subject we old men are to this vice of lying. This same starved justice hath done nothing but prate to me of the wildness of his youth and the feats he hath done about Turnbull Street ; and every third word a lie, duer paid to the hearer than the Turk's tribute. I do remember him at Clement's Inn like a man made after supper of a cheese-paring : when a' was naked he was

[1] Baga de Secretis Pouch 46, February 25th, 1585.

[2] In this park a building still exists known as " Daisy Hill ", which was once the hunting lodge where, according to tradition, Shakespeare was imprisoned. (Samuel Ireland, *Picturesque Views on the Warwickshire Avon* (London, 1795).)

[3] In comparing the career of Sir Thomas Lucy with the portraits Shakespeare has made of him, first in the Second Part of *Henry IV*, then in *The Merry Wives of Windsor*, the resemblance is seen to be striking. His Justice Shallow is certainly the pusillanimous tyrant who spread terror in Stratford and all the neighbourhood ; he has the same duties, speech, opportunism, coat of arms, and small stature as his original.

for all the world like a forked radish, with a head fantastically carved upon it with a knife : a' was so forlorn that his dimensions to any thick sight were invincible : a' was the very genius of famine ; yet lecherous as a monkey. . . . And now is this Vice's dagger become a squire, and talks as familiarly of John of Gaunt as if he had been sworn brother to him ; and I'll be sworn a' never saw him but once in the Tilt-yard, and then he burst his head for crowding among the marshal's men. . . . And now he has land and beefs. Well, I will be acquainted with him, if I return ; and it shall go hard but I will make him a philosopher's two stones to me. If the young dace be a bait for the old pike, I see no reason in the law of nature but I may snap at him.[1]

Falstaff concludes his jeering description by an allusion to the arms of Sir Thomas Lucy : the " luce ", origin of Lucy, is a little pike found in the waters of the Avon. As is well known, three luces ornamented the Lucy blazon.

The master of Charlecote had no university education, his rusticity of language appears in all his correspondence, particularly in the revealing missive addressed to the Earl of Leicester, asking that the judges in an archery competition should cede their position in favour of his own game-keeper :

Right Honourable and singular good lorde, pleaseth it youar honor to be advertised that according to youar lordships request and my one promise, though I send my servaunt Burnell it with a lively fear that he will not be hable to doo yor Worshipp the sarvice his good hart wad desire and such as myself wad wish. By occasion of longe illness his strength is much decayed, and shluting therby hindered. Your Lordshipp must take hede in making off yor matches that Burnell be not overmarked for that at this instante he is hable to shute no farr ground (which if youar lordshipp foresee I do not mistrust but he will be able to shute with the best). . . .[2]

It was therefore natural that Shakespeare should describe his Justice Shallow commenting feelingly on the death of a champion archer :

Jesu ! Jesu ! dead ! a' drew a good bow ; and dead ! a' shot a fine shoot : John of Gaunt loved him well, and betted much money on his head. Dead ! a' would have clapped i' the clout at twelve score : and carried you a forehand shaft a fourteen and fourteen and a half, that it would have done a man's heart good to see.

Death, as the Psalmist saith, is certain to all ; all shall die.[3]

This pious reflection is characteristic of Thomas Lucy, who had been instructed in the Protestant religion by the famous author of the *Book of Martyrs*,[4] John Foxe, who had not hesitated to practise Catholicism under Mary Tudor but who hastened to join the Established Church under Elizabeth. The mentality of this opportunist is revealed in the Justice's interjections. He first swears by " Jesus ", elsewhere by " the Mass ", or by

---

[1] The Second Part of *Henry IV*, Act III, Sc. 2.
[2] Marquis of Bath's Papers at Longleat. See 3rd Rep. Hist. MSS. Com. 1872, p. 200b.
[3] Ibid.   [4] *Acts and Monuments or Book of Martyrs* (1563).

" the cross ", and then, as though to make amends for his faults, the Puritan appears, and he swears only by " yea and nay ".

Lucy, as is known, was proud of his cattle and jealous of his harvests. Shallow does not neglect to find out the price of a pair of bullocks and twenty sheep at Stamford fair ; he stops the wages of a servant who has lost a sack of flour, and recommends his farmer to plant more red wheat on the high land.[1]

More characteristic still is the fatuity shown by the same Shallow in *The Merry Wives of Windsor*, where Shakespeare, conforming to Elizabeth's wish to see how the old reprobate of *Henry IV* would behave as a lover, gives his humour free rein. He recalls the incident of which he himself was the hero and victim, and makes Falstaff an impenitent poacher and Shallow an absurd Justice.

This time the spectator cannot mistake Lucy. Shallow appears as " custos rotulorum ", Justice of the Peace, functions fulfilled by Thomas Lucy at the moment of the young Will's arrest, and Falstaff is introduced as the chief of the band which dared to penetrate into the hunting lodge of Sir Thomas.

Persuade me not, says Shallow I will make a Star Chamber matter of it ; if he were twenty Sir John Falstaffs, he shall not abuse Robert Shallow Esquire.

And when Falstaff is introduced and interpolates the Justice flippantly with :

How Master Shallow you'll complain of me to the King ?
the knight indignantly replies :

You have beaten my men, killed my deer and broke open my lodge ; the Council shall hear of it ; it is a riot.

Not only do these words characterize Sir Thomas, they also recall the famous ballad hung on the gates of Charlecote.

> He said twas a riot
> His men had been beat
> His venison stole
> And clandestinely ate.

Was Shakespeare actually imprisoned in Warwick gaol as Richard Davies supposes, or was it to avoid this that he fled from home ? There is no means of knowing. One thing is certain, however, namely, that between March and July, 1586,[2] he left Stratford ; left his parents, brothers and sisters, his wife, scarcely up from her confinement, his twins Hamlet and Judith and his eldest child Susanna, who was to become the joy of his middle age—a whole family who needed his support, in order to seek his fortune in London.

---

[1] The Second Part of *Henry IV*, Act v, Sc. 1.
[2] The new year began on March 25th.

The anguish of this decision is echoed many times in the poet's work, especially in *Romeo* and *Richard II*.

When the Friar Laurence learns that the prince's order has transformed the sentence of death into exile, Romeo exclaims :

> Ha ! banishment ! be merciful, say ' death ' . . .
> There is no world without Verona walls,
> But purgatory, torture, hell itself.
> > . . . ' Banished ! '
> O friar ! the damned use that word in hell.
> Howlings attend it : how hast thou the heart,
> Being a divine, a ghostly confessor,
> A sin-absolver, and my friend profess'd,
> To mangle me with that word ' banished ' ? . . .
> Wert thou as young as I, Juliet thy love,
>   An hour but married, . . .
> Doting like me, and like me banished,
> Then mightst thou speak, then mightst thou tear thy hair,
> And fall upon the ground, as I do now,
> Taking the measure of an unmade grave.[1]

And Bolingbroke laments his banishment in these terms :

> Nay, rather, every tedious stride I make
> Will but remember me what a deal of world
> I wander from the jewels that I love.
> Must I not serve a long apprenticehood
> To foreign passages, and in the end,
> Having my freedom, boast of nothing else
> But that I was a journeyman to grief ? [2]

William's enforced departure did nothing to improve the precarious position of his family. The affairs of his uncle, the Snitterfield yeoman, were going hardly better than those of his father. Henry Shakespeare seems to have had a dark and violent character. He was obliged to pay a fine for having " fought until blood was drawn " with the second husband of Margaret Arden, and also for " Having disturbed the peace of the Queen ".[3] He vigorously refused to wear the cloth cap prescribed by statute for men of his class, and was declared contumacious.[4] In 1586, he was imprisoned in Warwick prison,[5] and ten pounds borrowed from Nicholas Lane, which his brother John was obliged to pay for his freedom, contributed to the embarrassments of the elder Shakespeare.[6]

---

[1] *Romeo and Juliet*, Act III, Sc. 3.　　　　[2] *Richard II*, Act I, Sc. 3.

[3] Halliwell Phillips, *Outlines*, vol. ii, p. 209.

[4] *Idem.* p. 211. (This sentence was inflicted on December 25th, 1583.)

[5] " Stratford Court of Records ", where Henricus Shaksper is mentioned as Frater dicti Johannis.

[6] Henry Shakespeare's life ended very tragically. He died quite alone at home, without friends or servants, his wife being absent for the day ; it was a neighbour, William Meads, who, on the pretext of recovering a legitimate debt, pillaged the house, broke open the coffers, and stole clothing, then went to the stable whence he took a mare, hay and oats. Margaret Shakespeare died six weeks later, after returning to find her house devastated.

Indeed money difficulties were added to other vexations in Henley Street. The bailiffs who came to make a seizure were told that there were no more goods to be taken.[1]

Finally, as already mentioned, the town records of 1586 contained this interesting notice :

At thys hall Willm Smythe and Richard Cowrte are chosen to be aldermen in the places of John Wheler and John Shaxspere, for that Mr. Wheler doth desyre to be put owt of the Companye, and Mr. Shaxspere dothe not come to the halles when they be warned nor hathe not done of longe tyme.

The best way to avoid taking an oath was to abstain from appearing at official meetings ; but it should be remarked that this return to private life did not protect the former mayor from prosecution or even arrest.

In spite of his numerous entanglements with the law, John Shakespeare never lost the confidence of his old friends nor the esteem of his former fellows on the council. He is to be found during these perilous years now fighting his persecutors, now taking part in town affairs, where his experience earned him the respect of the various guilds, since he remained wool merchant, glover, hide seller and also disposed of wood and other products of his farm.

In 1586, he still appears to have avoided the prison which yawned for a large number of his friends, such as William Reynolds, George Badger, Nicholas Barnhurst, George Bardolph, and William Bayneton, all recusants. Imprudently he came to the rescue of a friend, Michael Pryce, imprisoned in Coventry gaol. Accompanied by his neighbour, Giles, of Henley Street, he rode to the distant town and, in return for a ten pound bail, obtained the freedom of the Stratford coppersmith. However, this sum of money was never repaid, for Pryce, accused of felony, fled, well knowing the fate reserved to those of his religion if found guilty.

On April 29th, 1587, John Shakespeare contested before several courts the legality of a complaint against him, and protected himself with a habeas corpus, maintaining that the queen's bench was alone competent in this case.

He appeared at the Hilary assizes in 1589, but it is probable that no sentence was pronounced against him. The same year, at the repeated request of Nicholas Lane, he was summoned to return the ten pounds which he had borrowed from Lane on his brother's account. He was arrested and imprisoned, but was liberated by a neighbour, Master Richard Hill, a well-to-do mercer, of Catholic faith.

Again arrested for an unknown reason, he was defended by the same William Courte who had taken his place in the municipal council. July 24th, 1591, he is mentioned with two of his friends as appraiser of the goods of Rafe Shaw and, August 21st of the same year, he drew up the inventory of the property of the tanner Henry Field of Bridge Street, father of the Richard who, three years later, was to publish William Shakespeare's first poem.

[1] Sidney Lee, *Life of Shakespeare* (London, 1899), p. 11.

Nevertheless, recusants were continually in danger. Thomas Lucy was on the watch. Secret agents searched all the villages and parishes of Warwickshire, observing those who refused to attend the services of the Established Church. Two lists of recalcitrants signed by Lucy and seven commissioners [1] were prepared, one between March and April, 1591, and the other in September of the same year. The first was deposited at Warwick Castle and the second in the London Record Office ; they are almost identical, but the September list contains in the margin certain modifications concerning the persons inscribed in the spring list.

The recusants are thus listed in this document. Fifteen important persons come first who paid their fines by the month such as : Mistress Jeffreys, widow of the former mayor, Mistress Wheler, Thomas Reynolds and his wife, William Clopton and his wife, the Cawdrey family, etc. Then, grouped in a large bracket, are nine well-known citizens among whom John Shakespeare is the third. A rubric mentions them as not coming to church for fear of being arrested for debt. They are Master John Wheler, his son, Master John Shakespeare, Master Nicholas Barnhurst, Thomas James, alias Gyles, William Baynton, Richard Harrington, William Fluellen, George Bardolfe. [2] Finally six persons are mentioned together who are excused by reason of age or infirmity.

Some sort of collusion must have been established among the people of Stratford, for they acquitted themselves very badly in the rôle of informer. A veritable passive resistance organized itself around the former municipal officers, still respected and even sometimes protected by the agents. Barnhurst, already a councillor, later became mayor of the town. For the rest, the embarrassment of the secret agents is reflected in the vague formula in which they took refuge when inscribing the names of those denounced on their list : " It is said that these last nine come not to church from fear of process for dete."[3]

Sir Thomas Lucy, however, maintained his uncompromising attitude. An official report dated April 1593 shows him continuing to spread terror among his neighbours. At this time, a search was made by his orders at Coughton Court " where Mistress Arden, wife of the traitor Arden that was executed doth dwell at this present ". To this report of the lord of Charlecote the council in London replied with an order of arrest :

It would seem by your letter to Mr. Topcliffe there was resistance offered at such time as you did search the house ; and that they of the household then did not carry themselves with that dutiful course and obedience they ought to do, and that divers superstitious things and furniture for Mass were there found. And it was confessed that a Seminary priest was harboured there who was conveyed out of the way or lieth hid in some secret place.

---

[1] The signatures are Thomas Lucy, John Harrington, Foulke Grevyle, H. Goodyere, Thomas Leigh, Th. Fisher, Edw. Holte, Edw. Dabridgecourt.

[2] George Bardolfe is sometimes written Bardell, sometimes Bardoll. It is noticeable that Shakespeare in his *Henry IV* spells this name in three different ways.

[3] S.P. Dom. Eliz. vol. 243, no. 76.

We have thought good to require you to commit to prison as well the said Mrs. Arden as the rest of her servants to be proceeded with all according to the qualities of their offences which we refer to your discretion.[1]

This cousin of Mary Shakespeare, having escaped the stake, remained in prison until the accession of King James.

But from 1593, date of Will's first successes in London, John Shakespeare and his family were able to look forward to better days. The death of Leicester (1588) led to the rise of a new favourite, who in his turn won Elizabeth's heart. Robert Devereux, Earl of Essex, whose mother had married Leicester, was of quite a different temper. He did not share the political and religious narrowness of his step-father, but had a wide tolerance, and in London early became the patron of art and letters. He soon became Master of the Horse, and it was not long before he succeeded to the positions of Leicester and of Walsingham who died in 1590. For a time at least, even old Burleigh feared for his own influence with the Queen.

It was among the Essex clan that the fugitive from Stratford found his first sympathizers. At the beginning of the last decade of the sixteenth century, Will Shakespeare not only had his foot upon the ladder, but was able to use his influence to avert the danger which threatened his father.

In 1596 when the new Bishop of Worcester, Thomas Bilson, prepared in his turn a list of the recusants in the diocese, he did not mention the old mayor of Stratford.[2] He retains, however, a large number of those who figured in the lists of 1591, including John Wheler the former deputy to Shakespeare who had left the council at the same time. Another sign of improvement was the granting in 1596 of John Shakespeare's long standing demand for the right to bear a coat of arms.

We have a verbal picture of seventy-year-old John, thanks to the memory of one of the Mennes' brothers [3] who was brought as a child to his shop. He recalled how the glover—" a merry cheekd old man "—spoke of his then famous son:

Will was a good honest fellow, but he durst have crackt a jeast with him at any time.[4]

As for the master of Charlecote, he tirelessly pursued his activities. If the Shakespeares were no longer under his lash, there were many others whom he could attain. The Council congratulated him for his part in the conviction of Edward Abingdon, whom he discovered in spite of the secret chambers of Hindlip Hall and brought to the scaffold.

He came often to Stratford to preside over a commission for the punish-

---

[1] Acts of the Privy Counsel, 1593.
[2] The Bishop of Worcester complains of the fact that two hundred notable recusants with their servants, and many vagabonds, are scattered in the forty parishes of his diocese. A hundred and thirty families of gentlemen, of whom several are very rich and powerfully connected, and about five hundred of " those of meaner sort " are also mentioned.
[3] John Mennes or Menese, author of one of the poems published in the *Olympic Games* of the Cotswolds.
[4] " Manuscript of Thomas Plume, archdeacon of Rochester " (Library at Maldon, Essex).

ment of loiterers on the ale house bench; and yet, when he went to town, he expected to receive spice, wine and beer. According to the municipal accounts it was above all wine and sugar—rare at this time—which Sir Thomas especially enjoyed in these libations. The high price [1] of the drink consumed at a series of banquets given in his honour at the time of the village levies contrasts with the modest sums spent on the purchase of bread. Here we cannot help remembering Prince Hal's joking reproach to Falstaff for the prodigious quantity of sweet sack which he had consumed to one halfpenny worth of bread.

In 1595, Sir Thomas was again lucky in finding the hiding-place of a priest, William Freeman, [2] whom he caused to be hanged at Warwick. This seminarist had been sheltered by a rich widow, " Dame Heath ". Thomas Lucy immediately accused her of " giving assistance to a priest " ; this permitted him to seize her manor with its park.

Several months later, his wife, Lady Joyce Lucy, died. The epitaph which he inscribed on her tomb—answer to widespread gossip concerning misunderstandings—is worthy of his pen ; a revealing document certainly. It is as though the Justice of the Peace in treating these lines like a business document wished to certify that he had indeed served as model for Justice Shallow in *Henry IV* and in *The Merry Wives of Windsor*.

Here entombed lyeth the Lady Joyce Lucy the wife of Sir Thomas Lucy of Cherlcote, in the county of Warwick Knight. . . . Who departed out of this wretched world to her heavenly kingdome, the tenth day of February, in the year of our Lord God 1595 and of her age lx and three : All the time of her life a true and faithfull servant of her good God, never detected any crime or vice ; in religion most sound ; in love to her husband most faithfull and true ; in friendship most constant ; To what in trust was committed to her most secret ; In wisdome excelling ; in governing of her house and bringing up of youth in the feare of God that did converse with her, most rare and singular. A great maintainer of hospitality ; greatly esteemed of her betters ; misliked of none unlesse of the envious. When all is spoken that can be said, a woman so furnished and garnished with vertue as not to be bettered, and hardly to be equalled by any. As she lived most vertuously, so she died most godly. Set down by him that best did know what hath been written to be true.   Thomas Lucy. [3]

Lucy himself died on July 7th, 1600, one year before John Shakespeare. [4]

[1] Item for wine and sugar when Sir Fowlke . . . Sir John Harrington and Sir Thomas Lucy gave charge for the muskets. 4 shillings 3 pence. Item for wine and sugar when Sir Thomas did take view of new men to be trained after the first were set forth . . .
Summa Totalis, 17 shillings, 3 pence . . . one penny for bread.
[2] The jury which sentenced Freeman included Timothy, Sir Thomas Lucy's brother. *Unpublished documents relating to the English Martyrs, 1584-1603*, Catholic Record Society, vol. v, pp. 345-360.
[3] Dugdale, *Antiquities of Warwickshire*, 1657.
[4] Charlotte Carmichael Stopes, in her remarkable study of Shakespeare's contemporaries, has devoted numerous pages to the Lucy family, but after a review of the foregoing events, she arrives at this unexpected conclusion :
" There is nothing which indicates that Thomas Lucy was not loyal in his actions and conscientious in his intentions when obeying the government represented by Leicester. We must make some concessions to the customs and circumstances of the times and to the blindness of religious and partisan passion."   [OVER

3*

He lies beneath the marble effigy of Charlecote chapel. Nobody proposed to write his epitaph. William Shakespeare, whom he had caused to fly from Stratford, was the only one to render him immortal.

After collecting all the known facts about the poaching incident, and recalling the grievances of the Shakespeare family against Thomas Lucy, the conclusion is reached that the incidents noted by the poet's early biographers and evoked by his own pen are truly part of the history of his youth, and serve to illuminate the mysterious aspects of what are generally called " the lost years ".

Throughout sixty years of indefatigable work, C. C. Stopes has made the most important researches on Shakespeare and his circle. But she has brought very partial commentaries to bear on the texts which she has discovered. She could not avoid the consequences of a passion for Shakespeare ; she suffered to think that the poet could have possessed any human weakness, and rejected the idea that he was once a poacher. She could not admit that Sir Thomas Lucy had disliked—much less persecuted—a young man of such distinguished talent.

CHAPTER IV

AMONG THE LONDONERS

Shakespeare on arriving in London encounters many difficulties—Hostility of the literary and theatrical world—He modernizes old plays and writes with Dekker, Munday and Heywood—The censored drama of *Sir Thomas More*—*Titus Andronicus, Arden of Feversham*—Shakespeare and Marlowe—*Henry VI*—First sketch for *Hamlet*—Freed from his collaborators, he is attacked by his rivals—The historical drama of *The Life and Death of King John*—First comedies : *Comedy of Errors, The Taming of the Shrew, A Midsummer Night's Dream, Love's Labour's Lost*—The theatres of Shoreditch—Shakespeare takes **rank** among the best dramatists.

THE young Stratfordian's entry into London was far from triumphal. John Dowdall,[1] Nicholas Rowe,[2] and Bishop Warburton [3] are in agreement concerning the material difficulties Shakespeare encountered in his quest for a means of livelihood. The first described him as a " serviture ", the second as " received in the company then in being in a very mean rank " and the third qualifies his work as painful " drudgery ".

The poet's godson Sir William d'Avenant gave more precise information to Betterton, who repeated it to Pope :

When he came to London he was without money and friends, and being a stranger knew not to whom to apply nor by what means to support himself.

At that time, coaches, not being in use and as gentlemen were accustomed to ride to the play house, Shakespeare, driven to the last necessity, went to the Playhouse door, picked up a little money by taking care of the gentlemen's horses who came to the play ; he became eminent even in that profession and was taken notice of for his diligence and skill. He had soon more business than he himself could manage, and at last hired boys under him who were known as " Shakespear's boys " : some of the players accidentally conversing with him found him so

---

[1] In 1693, John Dowdall wrote his impressions of Stratford where he heard from the lips of the octogenarian sexton some facts bearing on Shakespeare's youth.

[2] Nicholas Rowe (1674-1718), playwright and poet laureate, published in 1709 the first complete edition of Shakespeare's works, preceded by a biography and accompanied by an excellent criticism. Of himself, he said that he left the dramatic art, of which he was so fond, to recommend to the world the best of poets, being careful to free his texts from injustices due to printing errors.

[3] William Warburton (1698-1779), Bishop of Gloucester, eminent man of letters, published in 1747 a complete edition of the works of Shakespeare ; it was the ninth since Shakespeare's death. This edition benefited by the emendations of Pope, Theobald, and Hanmer.

acute and master of so fine a conversation that they were struck therewith and recommended him to the house.[1]

Doubtless this was the origin of Robert Greene's insult " rude groom " thrown at the poet ; for Greene claimed that the drama should be a monopoly of university men. That Shakespeare should have been obliged to hold horses for his livelihood need not cause surprise. James Burbage, proprietor of the Theatre, was also owner of a livery stable, a lucky combination since the two enterprises were closely linked. The spectator who arrived on horseback was thus ensured of finding at the door a groom only too happy to take charge of his mount.

This Burbage was not unknown to young Shakespeare, who had admired the spectacles at Kenilworth ; it was Burbage who had produced the theatrical part of those famous celebrations. A carpenter by trade, Burbage had built in London (1577) a large hall for the accommodation of actors who, until then, had been obliged to content themselves with the precarious stages of inn yards, or public buildings. It was upon this new stage called the Theatre that his son Richard later shone in principal parts with Shakespeare as fellow actor. Soon the enterprising proprietor constructed other theatres. When the Stratford youth arrived in London, the " Curtain " had already risen at Shoreditch on the outskirts of the city, and the " Rose ", on the other side of the Thames, was opening its doors. Edmund Malone recalls a stage tradition that Shakespeare's first task was that of Prompters' attendant or call boy.[2]

The theatres, however, were open only three days a week at that time and the modest remuneration of a lad was insufficient to provide for a man in the great city. Without doubt William Shakespeare had other work which earned him the second contemptuous epithet of " Johannes Factotum " from the same hostile faction of which Greene was the chief.

Malone suggests that Shakespeare worked as clerk in a lawyer's office, which would explain the frequent use of legal terms in his sonnets and plays. It would also explain his being referred to as " Noverint ". Two other commentators, equally conscientious, William Blades [3] and William Jaggard,[4] have devoted studies to proving that Shakespeare's work implies a quasi-professional knowledge of the printer's craft. Many passages, it is true, are remarkable for the competence shown by the author in legal procedure or typography. If Shakespeare did in fact practise these two professions, his initiators and masters are easily found.

Two of the families closest to the Shakespeares at Stratford—the Combes and the Fields—were represented in London at this time.

---

[1] William d'Avenant, literary executor of Shakespeare's theatrical enterprise, when the stage was in eclipse under Cromwell's rule, reunited the scattered remnants of the old " Globe " company, in an endeavour to perpetuate the tradition which he learned from Taylor and Lowen, two actors and friends of Shakespeare.

[2] E. K. Chambers, vol. ii, p. 296.

[3] William Blades, *Shakespeare and Typography* (London, 1872).

[4] William Jaggard, *Shakespeare once a printer and bookman* (Stratford, 1933).

William Combe [1] and Richard Field had already made their way in the great city. The former was entered at the bar since 1578, the other was finishing his apprenticeship with the learned printer, Thomas Vautrollier. That Shakespeare should have directed his steps towards these old pupils of the grammar school would have been quite natural. In the Middle Temple, the newcomer with his ready pen could have made himself useful as a clerk while observing everything which occurred in the tortuous paths of legal procedure. [2] William Combe's brother left in his will five pounds to William Shakespeare [3] who in his turn bequeathed his gentleman's sword to Thomas Combe, the barrister's nephew. Thomas himself, Will's schoolfellow, went to London and published at Richard Field's establishment a volume translated from the French, [4] *The Theatre of Fine Devices*. If Shakespeare earned a few pence with William Combe, he later returned them a hundred fold, since it was from him and his brother John that he acquired in 1602 " 107 acres of arable land " at Stratford, for which he paid the considerable sum of three hundred and twenty pounds.

In the house where Richard Field was concluding his apprenticeship, the future poet must have felt quite at home. His childhood friend was about to take over the enterprise [5] which had furnished the class books in use at Stratford, and elsewhere throughout England. The two schoolmates were at one on many subjects : not however about religion. Whilst the one felt drawn towards Catholic circles, the other belonged to a printing house of Calvinistic tendency. But when far from home divergencies of opinion diminish, and the boyhood friends evidently renewed their youthful intimacy.

The master of the establishment, Thomas Vautrollier, whose motto " Anchora Spei " Shakespeare knew, came from Rouen. Early in Elizabeth's reign, he had made an exceptional place for himself in the Printers' Guild, being a remarkable technician and a cultivated and honest man, of sound taste and upright judgement. Enjoying official favour, he had obtained in 1554, besides his licence as printer, a ten-year monopoly of certain books of scholarship and even music. [6] He was permitted to engage

[1] At the Stratford museum there is a law book which used to belong to this Combe, in which he has written in French and Latin : " C'est le livre de Gulihelme Combe. Admissus fui in medium templum anno dni 1571 festo Sti Michaelis." He was admitted to the bar on February 9th, 1578, according to the Temple records where he always retained his lodging.

[2] William Rushton and J. Murray, *Shakespeare's Legal Acquirements* (1859).

[3] John Combe's will was signed on January 28th, 1613, one year before his death.

[4] Richard ffeild Entred for his copie a booke intituled *The Theater of fyne Devises conteyninge an hundred morall Emblemes* translated out of French by Thomas Combe aucthorised under the hand of Master Michaell Morgetrode vj.d ; May ixth, 1593 (Stationers Registers).

[5] The corporation registers on August 19th, 1579, declare that Richard Feyld, son of Henry Feyld of Stratford-on-Avon, was to serve as apprentice for six years with Thomas Vautrollier to learn the art of printing.

[6] Vautrollier was authorized to print manuals and collections for choirmasters. Byrd and Tallis had obtained letters patent for songs and music for the lute and virginal. *Cantionae Sacrae* figures on the printers' registers, beside an introduction to music by Paul de la Motte.

without molestation six foreign workmen: French, Dutch and others.[1]

Unfortunately in publishing the audacious works of Giordano Bruno, he fell into disgrace and had to depart from London suddenly. He thus left the foremost English publishing house under his wife's direction, and that of his young Stratford assistant. He himself founded a press in Edinburgh where King James brought out *The Essayes of a Prentis* [2] and two translations of Du Bartas. Vautrollier returned to London and died shortly afterwards (1587).

As in romantic stories, the enterprising young man from Warwickshire became before the year was out the husband of Jacauline, Vautrollier's widow, and, in 1590, head of the publishing house, an extraordinary feat in view of his youth and the rules of the guild. The number of master printers being limited to twenty-two, each vacancy had to be filled with the consent of the keepers of the Stationers' Registers and the approval of the Archbishop of Canterbury. It was only by inheritance or by marriage with the daughter or widow of a deceased member that anyone could enter the corporation. Richard Field's star was to lead him to the summit of success; before long he became the head of the Honourable Stationers' Company.

With Field, Shakespeare could have found not only employment as proof reader or typographer, but also material to supplement his education and enlarge his outlook. A glance at the list of volumes issued from these presses shows that a curious reader had books enough to fill his mind for a lifetime without leaving the premises.[3]

When Richard Field assumed the direction of the printing house, the number of volumes in foreign languages grew still larger.[4] In 1592, he was joined by his young brother, Jaspar, who, following his example, became an

---

[1] The royal seal was attached to this licence addressed to "Our well-loved subject, Thomas Vautrollier, typographus Londoniensis, in claustro vulgo Blackfriars comorans".

[2] *The Essayes of a Prentise in the Divine art of poesie*, by the King. A book intituled *The Furies* translated by James the Sixte, King of Scotland, together with the *Lepanto* of the same King.

[3] Vautrollier had published among other books, the works of Calvin, Luther and Théodore de Bèze: a "Summary" of Saint Augustine; The *New Testament ;* the *Dialectics of Petrus Ramus* ; the new editions of Ovid and Plutarch ; *An essay on French verbs : the easiest and most perfect Manner of learning the French language ; a Paraphrase of the psalms of David ; the Garden of the virtues and good manners ; the Life of Admiral Coligny ; the French Littleton ; Campo di Fiore or Singing in four languages to aide those who wish to learn latin, French and English, but especially Italian ; Treatise on melancholy and the strange effects which it produces on our brains and bodies*, by Timothy Bright, and *the Christian Hand*. There was even a *Method of teaching English, French and Italian writing to those who wish to become secretaries.*

[4] Among these were : *le Vray Agnus Dei pour désarmer le peuple francois* ecrit pour le Roy très chrétien, Henry III, Roy de France ; *Vray Discours sur la defaicte du duc d'Aumalle et sieur de Batigny avec leurs troupes par le Duc de Longue Ville et austres seigneurs ; Lettres d'un gentilhomme de Beusse aux bourgeois de Paris ; Lettre du Roy de Navarre à Monsieur d'Orléans du 22 Mai 1589, à Banquenay ; Diversi propositi morali politici e economici*, Petrucchio Obaldino, and a translation of *Orlando furioso* by Sir John Harrington. The list of Field's French publications finishes with *l'Histoire du règne d'Elizabeth*, from the Latin work by Camden. The volume of Field's became the *editio princeps* of this work, as Camden only later obtained authorization to publish his History in England.

apprentice.[1] Another Field, a London cousin, entered Shakespeare's company. This Nathan Field later wrote a play which had some vogue,[2] and which contains an allusion to Falstaff. Field also took up the defence of the theatre against the Puritan preachers.

When Shakespeare was at last able to follow his true vocation and place his fertile imagination, histrionic sense, and inspired pen at the service of the theatre, dramatic art was still in its infancy ; the qualities of finesse, moderation and taste which later made his reputation, were not those which helped him at the beginning of his career. On the contrary, the public at this time demanded strong emotions, hearty laughs and flowing tears. The plays, though mostly mediocre, were frequently written by university men, such as Robert Greene, George Peele, and John Lyly, who tended to be vain of their education and looked down upon the unlettered professional actors. A bitter jealousy also separated the two factions of players. James Burbage and his son Richard had the audacity to pit themselves against Philip Henslowe and his son-in-law, Edward Alleyn. When Shakespeare entered the fray on the side of the Burbages, it was Henslowe and Alleyn [3] who laid down the law.

Henslowe was an able impressario. He collected works for the stage, and distributed them among the different companies. In his pay he maintained needy writers some of whom began to show real promise in dramatic composition ; among these were Nashe, Heywood, and Dekker ; but he invariably kept the best plays for his own actors—the Admiral's company, whose usual theatre was the " Rose ". The rest he distributed to the players patronized by the Earl of Derby, the Earl of Essex, or Lord Pembroke. These companies acted at the " Curtain " or " The Theatre ".

The " Rose " had the good fortune to present two great successes ; *The Spanish Tragedy* attributed to Thomas Kyd, a dark drama of deferred vengeance, dominated by a ghost, in which practically all the characters meet with a bloody end. The other was *Tamburlaine*, which left an indelible trace on literature of this kind and made famous its young author, Christopher Marlowe.

A cobbler's son who had been educated at King's School, Canterbury, and had obtained the title of Master of Arts at Cambridge, Marlowe had only to read the stories of the Spaniard Pedro Maxia, and the Florentine Perondinus, to find other subjects than Caesars and Alexanders, and be transported in imagination far beyond the contemporary theatre. Instead of the long and dull scenes of Lodge and Peele, the childish rhymes of the ancient morality plays, he substituted a succession of rapid tableaux enriched by a rhythm now resounding and sonorous like the roll of a drum, now ornamented with a passionate lyricism of which he alone possessed the secret.

---

[1] " 7 February 1592. Jasper Feild son of Henry Feild of Stratford uppon Aven in the county of Warwick Tanner hath put himself an Apprentice to Richard Feild citizen and Staconer of London for seven yeres from the date herof."

[2] *Amends for Ladies* (Nathan Field, 1618. Stationer's Register).

[3] The tragedian Edward Alleyn accumulated a considerable fortune, and was able, at the end of his career, to present Dulwich College with a handsome endowment.

His drama is a series of atrocious episodes selected from the life of the fourteenth-century Tartar shepherd. Two scenes are characteristic : one where the victorious Tamburlaine orders a banquet to be served while his victim, Bajazet, dying of hunger in a cage, must content himself with a few mouthfuls fallen from the conqueror's sword, and the other where the oriental magnate, whip in hand, addresses a pair of kings harnessed to his chariot :

> Holla, ye pamper'd jades of Asia !
> What, can ye draw but twenty miles a day.[1]

Edward Alleyn, worthy interpreter of this monstrous and extravagant character, created the rôle and enhanced it by his forceful declamation.

The play enjoyed immense success. Those who had seen the first part of *Tamburlaine* returned to the theatre for the second. This drama consisted of ten acts and required two performances. There could be no resistance by the wits in face of such applause. The pedants were obliged to fall in step, and before 1589 " Marlowe was the god of the theatre, and Edward Alleyn was his prophet ". In spite of their faults, they had brought to the English theatre a life and vehemence hitherto unknown.

A success equal to that of *Tamburlaine* but more legitimate was accorded to the *Tragicall History of Doctor Faustus*, taken from the medieval legend. *The Jew of Malta* had the same success.

Whatever Marlowe in his thirst for riches and pleasure did not dare to say directly to the public he put into the mouths of his heroes, who revolt not only against the dogma of the Established Church but against the very essence of Christianity. Thus this despiser of every law divine and human baffled the vigilance of the censor and obtained the applause of the crowd, who never suspected that Marlowe's principal characters were modelled from Marlowe himself.

The London theatre would also have witnessed the sanguinary scenes of the Massacre of St. Bartholomew, if the fierce realism of *The Massacre at Paris* [2] had not offended the French ambassador, who caused its suppression on the pretext that state secrets had been violated.

Marlowe expressed his opinions with dangerous boldness. He declared that the book of Genesis was scientifically impossible and claimed that Moses was a charlatan, that the apostles, with the exception of Saint Paul, lacked literary style, and that he could write a much better gospel himself. He went even further and imprudently declared :

---

[1] Tamburlaine the Great, Who, from a Scythian Shephearde by his rare and woonderful Conquests, became the most puissant and mightye Monarq And (for his tyranny and terrour in Warre) was tearmed the Scourge of God. Devided into two Tragicall Discourses, as they were sundrie times shewed upon Stages in the Citie of London. By the Right Honorable the Lord Admyrall his servauntes. Now first, and newlie published London Printed by Richard Jones : at the signe of the Rose and Crowne 1590.

[2] The Massacre at Paris : With the Death of the Duke of Guise, As it was plaide by the right honourable the Lord high Admirall his Servants. Written by Christopher Marlowe (Contemporary edition).

if there be any God or good religion, then it is in the Papists, because the service of God is performed with more ceremonies, as elevation of the mass, organs, singing men, *shaven crowns*, etc. . . . . all protestants are hypocritical Asses.[1]

A warrant had been issued for his arrest when a knife—perhaps in the government's service—cut short his extraordinary career.

Such was the author who was to influence the tender-hearted young poet from Warwickshire ; but before joining Marlowe and collaborating with this master of the hour, Shakespeare had before him a long road beset with difficulties.

The sort of work to which he was subjected when he took up pen in the shadow of anonymity is revealed by a manuscript buried in the Harleian collection until 1844.[2] These precious pages show Shakespeare labouring at the task of writing a play as one of a team. It was an historical drama in praise of Sir Thomas More, Henry VIII's Chancellor, as famous for his civic virtues and his martyrdom in defence of his faith as for his *Utopia*.[3] The play remained in the portfolios of Edmund Tilney, master of the peace, who never authorized its printing, much less its representation.[4]

The manuscript is written in several different hands ; it is thought that one is Thomas Dekker's who had a ready pen, another Thomas Heywood's, lifelong friend of Shakespeare, and perhaps Anthony Munday's,[5] a prolific but second-rate author, quoted by Meres as " being the best for plots ".

The most difficult scene to write, because of its politico-religious problem, is in Shakespeare's own hand, and earned this comment from the censor : " Suppress the riot and the causes thereof, at your risk and peril." Shakespeare had dealt with the episode where Sir Thomas More, thanks to his sympathetic eloquence, saved the life of some unfortunate French and Flemish workers threatened by the crowd, who held them responsible for the rise in the price of food.

The reasons for the banning of this work are evident. The praises of this great Catholic, executed for upholding his faith, were not likely to please Henry VIII's daughter, any more than the memory of a riot provoked by famine was to the taste of her ministers. It was a particularly delicate subject, and if the play never saw the light, modern commentators should not complain too much, since the oblivion to which it was consigned is the

---

[1] Marloes blasphemies as sent to her Highness. A note contayninge the opinion of one Christofer Marlye concerninge his damnable opinions, judgment of Religion and Scorne of God's worde. Endorsed Richard Bame, Harleian MSS. 6853.

[2] *The Booke of Sir Thomas Moore.* Harley manuscript 7368. The title is written back to front on the vellum cover of the manuscript.

[3] Printed in Antwerp in 1516, in Paris in 1516 and in Basle in 1518. It is the last mentioned edition which contains woodcuts by Holbein.

[4] This document was copied and studied by Alexander Dyce in 1844. Thirty years later, Richard Simpson, in an article entitled : " Are there any autograph manuscripts of Shakespeare ? " recognizes the hand of the dramatist in one entire scene. Quite recently, H. W. Pollard and five famous specialists have corroborated Simpson's conclusions, basing them on historical, critical, philological and graphological analysis.

[5] Anthony Munday (1553-1633) collaborated in eighteen plays, of which four survive. He was a notorious anti-Catholic who placed his pen at the service of Topcliffe, chief of the secret police, to denounce Father Campion.

reason for its preservation in the original draft among Tilney's papers. The drama in its entirety need not be discussed later; what is interesting is that here are a hundred and twenty-seven lines written by Shakespeare and already bearing the stamp of his genius.

Closely following the text of the historian Holinshed, Shakespeare describes with fervour these popular demonstrations and More, the London Sheriff, who appeased them. He shifts the reader's sympathy from the fury of the rioters to the man who mastered them by sheer force of just and reasonable argument. Here the style and even the words of *Coriolanus* and *Julius Caesar* are foreshadowed. More's pleading in favour of the foreigners and his warning against the crowd's excesses suggest passages in *Coriolanus*. Without laws, affirms More, " men, like ravenous fishes would feed on one another "; and Coriolanus proclaims that " without the Senate to control them, the Roman plebs would feed on one another ". The shouts of the rioters are identical in the scene in *More* and in that where Mark Antony addresses the crowd: " Friends, Romans, countrymen ! " cries Antony, and in *More* the harangue begins : " Friends, Masters, fellow-citizens ! "

More employs the metaphor of the hunting dog who, suddenly let loose, leaps on his prey : " You'll hold the majesty of law in liom to slip him like a hound ? " A passage which may well be compared with this in *Coriolanus* : " Holding Corioli in the name of Rome even like a fawning grey hound in the leash to let him slip at will."

From the viewpoint of vocabulary, Shakespeare's contribution to the drama of Sir Thomas More is equally interesting : " in ruff of your opinion clothed ", " stale custom ", " unreverent knees ", " self-reason ", " self-right " are expressions dear to the poet and which he alone employed. The word " shark " used as a verb (" would shark on you ") is a peculiarity only found otherwise in *Hamlet*.

The manuscript of More justifies this description of the author's copy given by his fellow-actors :

His mind and hand went together and what he thought he uttered with that easiness that we have scarce received from him a blot in his papers.

In this period when Shakespeare was cutting, adapting and rewriting old plays, *Titus Andronicus* must be placed,[1] a play which surpasses *The Spanish Tragedy* and *Tamburlaine* in horrific invention, and whose success was tremendous both on the stage and in print. It holds the first place among the tragedies of the folio of 1623.[2] Has anyone ever imagined a more

---

[1] According to Dryden *Pericles* belongs to this period. Nicholas Rowe, who quotes Dryden, believes that the greatest part of the play was not written by Shakespeare (see Chapter XVII).

[2] *The Most Lamentable Romaine Tragedie of Titus Andronicus* As it was Plaide by the Right Honourable the Earle of Darbie, Earle of Pembrooke, and Earle of Sussex their Servants. London, Printed by John Danter, and are to be sold by Edward White and Thomas Millington, at the little North doore of Paules at the signe of the Gunne, 1594.

The immense popularity of this melodrama is shown by six other quarto editions besides the folio edition of 1623 : 1595, 1600, 1602, 1611, 1624, 1626. An illustration, probably by Henry Peacham, representing Queen Tamora asking forgiveness of her sons on their way to the place of execution, gives some idea of the costumes of the period.

abandoned villain than the liberated slave Aaron with a heart as black as his face ? His mistress Tamora, though she has achieved the imperial throne, still seeks her pleasure in the arms of her barbaric lover. Shakespeare has obviously sacrificed taste to fashion, but when he can free himself from this sanguinary plot, he becomes once more the poet of Avon. Tamora's invitation to Aaron to abandon hunting and seek refuge from the heat on a mossy bank is a return to his native countryside and is a foretaste of a verse in *Adonis*.

> —Wherefore look'st thou sad,
> When every thing doth make a gleeful boast ?
> The birds chant melody on every bush,
> The snake lies rolled in the cheerful sun,
> The green leaves quiver with the cooling wind,
> And make a chequer'd shadow on the ground.
> Under the sweet shade, Aaron, let us sit,
> And, whilst the babbling echo mocks the hounds,
> Replying shrilly to the well-tun'd horns,
> As if a double hunt were heard at once,
> Let us sit down, and mark their yelping noise.[1]

Some gleams of humanity relieve the horrible descriptions. The scene where Andronicus, worn out and half mad after the loss of his children, reproaches his grandson for killing flies, telling him that they also may have parents capable of suffering, has a daring Shakespearian touch.

There is another melodrama very popular at that time which appeared in quarto (1592) under the title: *The Lamentable and True Tragedy of Mr. Arden of Feversham in Kent. . . .*[2] The play has no author's name, but many commentators see traces of an expert pen. In this drama, in which divine judgement strikes a man who has enriched himself from church property, there is a scene between the guilty wife and her lover which shows a knowledge of feminine psychology rare at that time. Shakespeare's talent was great enough to write the dialogue where the well-bred woman and the low-born lover reproach one another. The conflict of class hatred and irresistible physical attraction is described with master hand. Another fact suggests that Shakespeare was no stranger to the play. Holinshed in his chronicles, where the dramatist frequently delved for his subject matter, devotes seven long columns to the details of this horrible murder, and the author of the play, whoever he was, follows them scrupulously ; it is certainly true that Shakespeare knew all about this tragic episode which had cost the life of one of his distant kinsmen.

At all events, after three years of constant labour he had left his mark on the theatrical repertoire. If there still remained many obstacles to

---

[1] *Titus Andronicus*, Act II, Sc. 3.

[2] *The Lamentable and True Tragedy of Mr. Arden of Feversham in Kent*, who was most wickedly murdered by the meanes of his disloyall and wanton wife, who, for the love she bore to one Mosbie, hyred two desperate ruffians Blackwill and Shakbag to kill him. Wherein is shewed great malice and dissimulation of a wicked woman, the unsatiable desire and filthie lust and the shameful end of all murderers. Imprinted at London for Edward White dwelling at the little North door of Paul's church at the signe of the Gun. 1592.

surmount, and some self-appointed critics chose to ignore or disparage an author who had never sat on a university bench, a man of Marlowe's quality was willing, after his triumphs, to master petty professional jealousies and seek in his own interest to associate with the new talent.

He was not ignorant of the fact that it was his magnificent gift of poetry rather than a true aptitude for dramatic writing which had made the success of *Tamburlaine, Faust,* and *The Jew of Malta.* He had succeeded in increasing the prestige of the theatre in the domain of literature without writing a play of the highest order. He had never been able to bring to life a heroine who spoke as from a woman's heart.

Shakespeare, on the contrary, had shown his facility in dramatic composition and his ability by an intuitive sympathy to create living feminine characters. Already in *Titus Andronicus,* Lavinia, the Roman wife, and Tamora, the barbarian empress, are contrasted with subtlety, sympathy and insight.

Collaboration between Marlowe and Shakespeare was sure to benefit both. The successful author could hope to see his future plays profit by a new technique, and Shakespeare, for his part, would enjoy reflected glory from the magician of the moment. His admiration for Marlowe as an artist is, moreover, indisputable. Though he practically never gave praise to contemporary poets, he makes frequent allusion in his work to Marlowe; in one of the sonnets he speaks of him as a superior spirit, comparing his rival's poetry to a great ship in full sail, while his own resembles a daring barque tossed on the waves.[1] It is possible to distinguish in *Edward II, Edward III,* and especially in *Henry VI,* the portions which belong to each. *Edward II* [2] is the work of Marlowe, but the hand of Shakespeare has had a considerable share, I believe. *Edward III* was played and published entirely anonymously, but this does not prevent the recognition of passages attributable to Marlowe, Shakespeare and, some think, Peele. *Henry VI* now forms an integral part of Shakespeare's theatrical work; Marlowe's contribution, although evident, was not sufficient for the editors to acknowledge his authorship.

In *Edward II,* Marlowe, according to the most penetrating of critics, Emile Legouis, subjected himself to a new discipline:

There are in this play, real dramatic qualities which scarcely existed in Marlowe's previous ones. The declamation is more restrained, the tirades shorter; the blank verse less tense, the dialogue more like human speech—Better constructed than his other plays, free from his usual extravagances, it comes nearer to life and closer to the normal drama.

The alteration noticed by Professor Legouis is due, according to him, to the assistance given by Shakespeare and his restraining influence on Marlowe's

---

[1] Sonnet 80. Scholars are not agreed about the identity of the poet referred to, but the description of his poetry seems to fit Marlowe best.

[2] *The Troublesome Raigne and lamentable death of Edward the second, King of England with the tragicall fall of proud Mortimer*—as it was publiquely acted by the right Honorable the Earle of Pembrooke his servantes. Written by Chri. Marlow Gent. (London, 1598). Subsequent editions appeared in 1612 and 1622.

impetuous flights. Many reminiscences of *Edward II* occur in a play which belongs to Shakespeare alone : *Richard II*. In both cases it is the historian Holinshed who provides the plot and the material is similarly treated by a process which is Shakespeare's own. Having alienated the spectators' sympathy from a sovereign who has proved unworthy of it, he enlists their pity for agonies of such magnitude as to obliterate faults and weaknesses.

The Reign of Edward III [1] is an amalgam of two styles. Marlowe's sonorous verse sounds often in the warlike parts ; certain lyric passages also betray the pen which wrote *Hero and Leander*. But the struggle between duty and honour, passion and virtue looks like Shakespeare's work, and the conversation between the enamoured king and the Countess of Salisbury bears his stamp. His hand in the play appears in a more positive form when he introduces an entire line which is repeated word for word from one of the sonnets :

Lillies that fester smell far worse than weeds.[2]

The powerful drama of *Henry VI* is a bloodthirsty trilogy whose leitmotiv is war ; foreign war, civil war, war between two branches of one family, the houses of York and Lancaster.

The first part transports the spectator to French soil and shows the defeat of the armies of young King Henry VI and the prowess of Talbot, the heroic captain whose bravery is the centre of interest, and whose death while trying to save his son provides the tragic crisis.[3]

It had an unprecedented success. Patriotic Englishmen rejoiced at the heroic speeches and the fitting representation of English kings and warriors. Thomas Nashe, in spite of his satirical pen, was ecstatic :

How would it have joyd brave Talbot (the terror of the French) to thinke that after he had lyne two hundred yeare in his Toomb, he should triumph againe on the Stage, and have his bones new embalmed with the teares of ten thousand spectators at least, (at severall times) who in the Tragedian that represents his person, imagine they behold him fresh bleeding.[4]

The first part of *Henry VI* was not published until the folio of 1623. The second part, however, appeared in quarto a few years after the first performance with this long descriptive title :

The First Part of the Contention betwixt the two famous houses Yorke and Lancaster with the death of the Good Duke Humphrey : and the banishment and death of the Duke of Suffolk and the tragicall end of the proud Cardinall of Winchester with the Notable Rebellion of Jack Cade and the Duke of Yorkes first

---

[1] *The Raigne of King Edward the Third :* as it has bin sundrie times plaied about the Cittie of London, printed for Cuthbert Burby, 1596.
[2] Sonnet 84.
[3] Though this episode of the Hundred Years' War cannot be pleasant to the French, Shakespeare succeeds in entering into the mentality of a patriotic French Prince. He endows the " Dauphin " with a noble character and gives him these prophetic words :
"No longer on Saint Denis will we cry
But Joan la Pucelle shall be France's saint."
[4] Thomas Nashe, *Pierce Penilesse his supplication to the Devell* (London, 1592), p. 26.

claime unto the crown. Printed for Thomas Creed for Thomas Millington and are to be sold at his shop under St. Peter's church. (1594.)

In *The Second Part of Henry VI*, Shakespeare's share is larger. Characteristically striking is the scene where the guilty cardinal, tortured by remorse after the murder of Duke Humphrey, is visited and prayed for by the king. The reader who is familiar with the pages of *Julius Caesar*, *Coriolanus*, and *More* which describe the unstable emotions of the crowd and the violence of popular revolutions, cannot for a moment doubt that the same author has also written the description of Jack Cade's bloody rebellion.

On the other hand, Marlowe is perhaps alone responsible for the scene of Suffolk's murder. The Latin quotations and mythological allusions, and above all the violence of the language are reminiscent of *Faustus* and *Tamburlaine*.

The Third Part of Henry VI was produced under this title :

The True Tragedie of Richard Duke of Yorke and the death of Good King Henrie the Sixt : with the whole contention betweene the two houses, Lancaster and Yorke ; as it was sundrie times acted by the Right Honorable Earle of Pembroke his servauntes.[1]

The title describes the play. With all its faults, exaggerations and bombast, it seems to be the work of Shakespeare alone, then aged twenty-five. In it he makes great use of the *Chronicles* of his former neighbour at Packwood, Raphael Holinshed, closely following his character descriptions and suggestions of motivation.

In illustration we may cite the two accounts of the birth of King Richard III, whom both authors regard as a striking example of physical deformity indicating moral turpitude. Holinshed thus describes and comments on the birth of the hunchbacked monster :

It is for truth reported, that the Duchesse his mother hadde so much adoe in hir travaile, that she could not be delivered of hym uncut, and that he cam into the world with the feete forward, as me be borne outward, and (as the same runneth) also not untoothed, whether men of hatred report above the truth, or else that nature changed hir course in his beginning, which in the course of life many things unnaturally committed.[2]

Shakespeare puts almost the same words into the mouth of Richard himself :

> For often have I heard my mother say
> I came into the world with my legs forward ;
> Had I not reason think ye to make haste
> And seek their ruin that usurped our right ?
> The mid-wife wondered and the women cried
> " O Jesus bless us, he is born with teeth "
> And so I was ; which plainly signified
> That I would snarl and bite and play the dog.
> Then since the heavens have shaped my body so
> Let hell make crook'd my mind to answer it.[3]

---

[1] Printed in London by P. S. for Thomas Millington, 1595.
[2] *Holinshead's Chronicles*, vol. ii, p. 1357.
[3] *The Third Part of King Henry VI*, Act v. Sc. 6.

Shakespeare claims the authorship of this trilogy in spite of all its faults and imperfections.   Later, when concluding the stirring history of *Henry V* he reminds his audience in the epilogue [1] that the same author and the same troupe had presented a few years before the story of his son.   It is therefore difficult to contest the authenticity of *Henry VI* since author, actors and editors agree in ascribing these three plays to the Stratford dramatist.

Henry VI achieved a success almost equal to that of *Tamburlaine* and *The Jew of Malta*.   From Henslowe's diary we know that during the month of January, 1593, *Henry VI* brought in the sum of two pounds one shilling ; *Titus Andronicus*, one pound ten shillings ; *Friar Bacon* (by Robert Greene), one pound ; *The Jew of Malta*, three pounds ; *Tamburlaine*, one pound sixteen shillings ; and *Jeronymo* (by Kyd), one pound two shillings.

Next year the provincial tour was naturally less fruitful ; the receipts reached ten shillings for *The Jew of Malta ;* twelve shillings for *Titus Andronicus ;* for *Hamlet* eight shillings, and for *The Taming of the Shrew*, nine shillings.[2]

That *Hamlet, Prince of Denmark,* should be found in such company is not astonishing, for this first version, called *Hamlet's Revenge*, was doubtless closer to the melodrama dear to the age than to the psychological tragedy famous today in every country.   Thomas Lodge alludes to the former version when he describes :

a particular fiend who looks as pale as the vizard of the ghost which cries so miserably at the theatre—like an oyster-wife : Hamlet Revenge.

It is again to this version that Thomas Nashe refers in his preface to Robert Greene's *Menaphon*, when he expresses scorn for the author.

It is a common practise now-a-days amongst a sort of shifting companions that run through every art and thrive by none, to leave the trade of Noverint, whereto they were born and busy themselves with the endeavours of Art that could scarcely latinize their neck-verse if they should need.   Yet English Seneca read by candle-light yields many good sentences as " Blod is a beggar ", etc. And if you speak him fair on a frosty morning he will afford you whole Hamlets, I should say handfuls of tragical speeches.[3]

On page 46 of his pamphlet which appeared in 1592, entitled *A*

---

[1] Henry the Sixth, in infant bands crowned King
Of France and England did this king succeed ;
Whose state so many had the managing
That they lost France and made his England bleed
Which oft our stage hath shown . . .

[2] In the name of God Amen. Begininge at Newington my lord Admiralle his men my Lorde Chamberlen men As Followethe 1594 :
    . . . heaster & asheweras viij.s . . . the Jewe of Malta x.s
    . . . andronicous xij.s . . . cutlacke xj.s . . . Bellenedon xvij.s
    . . . Hamlet viij.s . . . the tamynge of Ashrowe ix.s
                Henslowe's Diary MSS. Dulwich College (vol. i, p. 17).

[3] See also Chapter XIII.

Groat'sworth of witte bought with a million of repentance,[1] Greene attacked those concerned with *Henry VI*, and warns his companions against :

Those puppets that spake from our mouths, those antics garnished in our colours. . . . Yes trust them not ; for there is an upstart crow beautified with our feathers, that with his *Tygers hart wrapt in a Players hyde* supposes that he is as well able to bombast out a blank verse as the best of you : And being an absolute *Johannes Factotum*, is in his own conceit the only Shake-scene in a country. . . . It is pity men of such rare wits, should be subject to the pleasure of such rude grooms.

That Shakespeare was the object of this diatribe is beyond doubt. " Shake-scene " is a direct allusion to his name and the phrase " with his tiger's heart wrapped in a player's hide " parodies the celebrated passage of *Henry VI*. " A tiger's heart wrapp'd in a woman's hide."

Greene's invectives, and gibes of " Jack-of-all-trades ", " noverint " (petty clerk) and " groom " are understandable. The blow which threatened the headquarters of letters was aimed by a vulgar player who, six years before, was holding horses at the theatre door ! This man from the country could now boast of successes not only in arranging plays of the old repertory, but with subjects of his own choice, in a blank verse of individual style, and with a delicate touch hitherto unknown. At the same time he possessed an intuitive knowledge of what would please both gallery and groundlings.

In his case, the profession of player, instead of detracting from, enhanced his qualities as dramatist. The comedian after all is better placed than an other to gain experience of the spectator's reaction ; he knows which are the telling words, the striking gestures, and the humour which provokes laughter.

In fact, Greene's libel was so badly received that Henry Chettle, his editor, thought it prudent to excuse himself publicly for having printed it. He did not wish to retract what had been said about Marlowe, but in his *Kind heart's Dream* made honourable amends for the views concerning Shakespeare.

About three moneths since died M. Robert Greene, leaving many papers in sundry Booke sellers hands, among other his *Groats-worth of wit*, in which a letter written to divers play-makers, is offensively by one or two of them taken. . . . With neither of them that take offence was I acquainted, and with one of them I care not if I never be. The other, whome at that time I did not so much spare, as since I wish I had. . . . I am as sory, as if the originall fault had beene my fault, because my selfe have seene his demeanor no lesse civill than he exelent in the qualitie he professes : Besides divers of worship have reported, his uprightnes of dealing, which argues his honesty, and his facetious grace in writting, that aprooves his Art.

This apology of Chettle's made in December 1592 shows that Shake-speare had already thrown off the tutelage of the old school. He had gone much further and had fought Henslowe's rival company on their own ground.

[1] London, Imprinted for William Wright, 1592.

These were presenting *The Troublesome Raigne of King John*,[1] inspired by a gross drama written by Bishop John Bale,[2] which was full of scenes of monastic debauchery of the type described by Boccaccio, and of attacks on Papal authority. Success appeared a foregone conclusion. The support of Elizabeth's government was assured for any representation of this sort, in full conformity with the spirit of the recent statutes. In presenting John Lackland and his nephew the bastard Faulconbridge, pillagers of monasteries, and despisers of the Church of Rome, as national heroes and worthy forerunners of Henry VIII, they hoped to rally Protestant opinion.

Shakespeare's *Life and Death of King John*[3] is, as has been justly observed, the reply of moderation and good taste to the vulgar entertainment presented by Henslowe's company. His attempt did not lack boldness, nor did he hesitate to take the episodes staged by his rivals and to treat them in an entirely different manner.

The puppet characters of *The Troublesome Raigne of King John* became under Shakespeare's pen convincing personalities capable of influencing and dominating events. Depicted with vivid realism, we are shown the duplicity of John Lackland, the clever diplomacy of Philippe Auguste, the chivalrous temper of the Dauphin, the indomitable spirit of Eleanor of Aquitaine, the modest charm of Blanche de Castille and the maternal anguish of Constance abandoned and betrayed, driven step by step to madness by the treatment of young Prince Arthur. She stands like a statue of despair at the feet of which all ambitions are shattered. These characters are dominated by the papal legate, whose single-minded desire is to make a lasting peace between Christian nations. It is he who provokes wars and brings them to an end. And what wars!! Historical truth gives way to dramatic effect. The fourteen years' struggle between France and England is reduced by Shakespeare to four months; gunpowder and cannon thunder on the battlefields a century before their invention. In order to make Prince Arthur a more pathetic figure, several years are taken off his age, but at the

[1] *The Troublesome Reign of John King of England*, with the discovery of King Richard Cordelions Base sone (vulgarly named, the Bastard Fawconbridge) also the death of King John at Swinstead Abbey. As it was (sundry times) publikely acted by The Queenes Majesties Players in the honourable Cittie of London. (Imprinted at London for Sampson Clarke and are to be sold at his shop on the back side of the Royal Exchange, 1591.)

[2] Bishop Bale's single manuscript has been printed in facsimile by the Malone Society. The manuscript, formerly in the Duke of Devonshire's library, is now preserved in California at the Henry Huntington Library. The series of dialogues to which Bale has given the title of *King John* scarcely deserves to be called a dramatic work. The principal character is England herself in the rôle of a desolate widow, who denounces the authors of all her woes : the priests, the monks, the cardinals and above all the Pope, helped on by allegorical characters such as Sedition, Treason, and Hypocrisy. The text is everywhere vulgar and obscure, but the hero, King John, is shown as irresponsible, magnanimous and infallible ; the infallibility devolved by divine right to Henry VIII a second Joshua, the leader of his people to the Promised Land of evangelical truth, of which John only had a vision.

[3] There is not a quarto edition of this play ; it seems to have been printed first in the folio of 1623.

It should be pointed out that two quarto editions of *The Troublesome Raigne of King John* were published in 1611 and 1622, wrongly carrying on the frontispiece : " Written by W. Sh."

final reckoning it is Rome's representative who has the last word, without the spectators being able to guess which among these principal characters has the author's sympathy, so objective is the presentation of the interests at stake.   Even the bastard Faulconbridge, the great soldier and mouthpiece of the insular Englishman who fears and despises every foreign idea or influence, cannot claim to be the play's hero.

Whilst the *Troublesome Raigne of King John* finishes with these words :

> If England's peers and people join in one,
> Nor pope, not France, nor Spain, can do them wrong.

Shakespeare concludes his drama more moderately :

> . . . Nought shall make us rue
> If England to itself do rest but true.

King John, in usurping a crown which was Prince Arthur's by right and in denying England's traditions, was for Shakespeare the sole cause of his country's misfortunes.   One cannot but admire the boldness and subtlety which created such a drama in opposition to the official version given by a rival company.

The author's courage on this occasion was all the more praiseworthy because he himself could not have felt reassured about his future.   Executions were taking place not far away.   William Deane and William Gunter had been hanged in the immediate vicinity of "the Curtain".   William Hartley of Rowington, denounced by Sir Thomas Lucy to the London authorities, was hanged before the very theatre where Shakespeare was playing.   The laws of the realm were felt even in his own family ;   his father's name had been placed on a list of suspects.

Beside these serious preoccupations his company was subjected to annoyances of every sort.   The servants of Lord Strange represented lawlessness in the eyes of authority.   The Lord Mayor was always holding up before them the obedient conduct of the Lord Admiral's men.   These respected regulations, whilst the first, when their theatre had been ordered to close, had once hastened to the "Cross-Keys" to give a forbidden show.[1]

However, with characteristic optimism, wishing perhaps to escape in thought from melancholy reflection, Shakespeare deserted the tragic muse to pay court to Thalia, and turned from historical drama to romantic idylls, from farce to fairy tales.   His first four comic works introduced a quite new manner of writing, which England had never known before and in which he showed an astonishing mastery.

The Comedy of Errors, The Taming of the Shrew, A Midsummer Night's Dream, and *Love's Labour's Lost*, precursors of numerous successes in comedy, light, fantastic or mundane, belong to this period when the poet was refining his talent.   These plays have a surprising poetical and pastoral freshness. The confined life of a great city had not effaced the country boy's nostalgia for dewy fields and forests, or the memory of the good folk of Stratford who

---

[1] See Harte to Burleigh, November 6th, 1589.   Lansdowne MSS. 60-47.

enjoyed telling old stories of a country rich in legends round their fireside bowl of punch.

The Comedy of Errors[1] is borrowed from the *Menaechmi* of Plautus whose exaggerated situations Shakespeare carried still further.

An allusion to Henry of Navarre's enterprise to conquer the throne of France serves to assign a date prior to 1591 to this play. In *The Comedy of Errors* Aristotle's rules of unity are observed; it seems that Shakespeare, following his classical model, wished to show his erudite opponents that he was capable of harmonizing the conventions of Latin comedy with romantic magniloquence. But beside this respect for his predecessors, what contempt for historical accuracy! What a cult of anachronism! Before the threshold of the temple of Diana, the author erects a Christian convent. The charitable abbess welcomes outlaws and gives them sanctuary. There is talk of " the sad place of execution " in the ditches behind the convent; this and other allusions show that Shakespeare intentionally evoked recent events which had taken place on the very spot where his theatre stood. It should be remembered that this building was situated in the grounds of the disaffected convent of Holywell, proof to what extent the author was seeking to interest the Elizabethan audience by allusions to topical events.[2]

The Taming of the Shrew,[3] a farce based upon an earlier and coarser play, is abounding in action to which Shakespeare has added a profound psychological study. He brings to life the burlesque nonentities of his model; and, with his subtle insight into the thoughts and characters of women, gives us a shrew elevated by love to sentiment and charity.

A prologue, more interesting to us than the play itself, explains and excuses the extravagance of the action. Shakespeare brings the spectator to the village of Wilmcote, his mother's home, and places him near the inn so familiar to his youth. On a bench before the door an incorrigible drunkard sleeps so soundly that the hostess and her maid cannot wake him. Drunkard, hostess, and servant appear under their real names, Christopher Slye, Marion and Cicely Hackett. The return from the hunt—that of Sudely Castle— swells the number of those trying to revive Sly the tinker.

The huntsman proposes to play a trick on the drunkard,[4] and the arrival of some strolling players—those who annually toured the neighbourhood of Stratford—assist in the success of the practical joke. They agree to act

---

[1] *The Comedy of Errors* first appeared in the folio of 1623.

[2] Professor T. W. Baldwin, in an article entitled " Shakespeare adapts a hanging " (Princeton University Press), has established that the scenes of *The Comedy of Errors* where Ageon the Syracusan merchant is led to his death are a reminder of the execution of Hartley the priest denounced by the government, and hanged at the Holywell theatre door on October 5th, 1588.

[3] *The Taming of the Shrew* appeared in its present form in the folio of 1623 and was never printed in quarto. A comedy with the title " A Pleasant Conceited Historie, called the taming of a Shrew. As it was sundry times acted by the Right honorable the Earle of Pembrook his servants." (London, Peter Short and sold by Cuthbert Busby, 1594) so much resembles the folio play, that it must be considered a sketch later modified and improved by Shakespeare.

[4] This story is taken from " Heuterus " (Rerum Burgundicarum libri). It is told as an incident in the life of Duke Philip of Burgundy.

a farce which will completely confuse Sly's mind, and make him forget his own identity.   This comedy appears far-fetched when read, but, played by actors capable of giving it the rapid tempo it demands, is always convincing and successful.

The mixture of fantasy and vulgar realism is characteristic of Shakespeare at this period.   He makes use, for the first time, of the play within a play, a procedure which must have proved effective, as he later employs it often, notably in *Love's Labour's Lost*, which he wrote shortly after the *Shrew*.

In *A Midsummer Night's Dream* [1] folk-lore and fairy-tale are combined. [2] The title, moreover, excuses anachronisms and absurdities for, while dreaming, no one is bound to respect either logic or history.   The wood near Athens where the play is set has nothing Greek about it ; the artisans, weaver, tailor, tinker and joiner obviously belong to the Guilds of Warwickshire.   Theseus himself, a gentleman equally addicted to literature and sport, resembles Sidney or Essex far more than a demi-god of ancient Greece. It has been said that the idea of this play first came to Shakespeare one June night in the village of Grendon-Underwoods whose charming inn, which bears its sign of the " Ship ", marks the first stage on the journey from Stratford to London.   There he found a townsman who inspired the clownish character of Nick Bottom the weaver, hero of the strange events brought about by Puck during that fantastic night.

The backward glances at the Kenilworth festivities where Essex's mother had conquered Leicester's heart and caused him to abandon his ambitious project of marriage with the queen, are so delicately handled that they can be taken both as complimentary to the triumphant Lady Leicester, or as homage to Elizabeth, " the fair vestal throned by the west " insensible to Cupid's shafts.

This comedy, many times corrected and altered, was printed in 1600, and again in 1609.   No division into acts or scenes is made in either of these quarto editions, but stage directions are given ; two among these deserve notice : by way of avoiding ridicule when making their exit, it is recommended that Titania and Bottom should continue to sleep between the acts ; secondly we read that " Tawyer enters with a trumpet to announce the approach of Theseus and Hippolyta ".

The poetic and sentimental character of this diaphanous fairy play makes it much appreciated.   It was often acted at Elizabeth's court on festive

---

[1] The request for entry in the registers is written in these terms : 1600, 8 Octobris, Thomas Fyssher Entred for his copie under the handes of Master Rodes and the Wardens. A booke called A mydsommer night's Dreame.   The publication of the first quarto edition followed normally under the title : A Midsommer nights dreame.   As it hath beene sundry times publickely acted, by the Right honourable, the Lord Chamberlaine his servants. Written by William Shakespeare.   Imprinted at London, for Thomas Fisher, and are to be soulde at his shoppe, at the signe of the White Hart, in Fleetestreete, 1600.

[2] " E. K.", Spenser's collaborator, associates elves and fairies with Catholic superstition. Such stories are propagated by " bald Friers and knavish shavelings " who keep the people in ignorance " least being once acquainted with the truth of things, they would in tyme smell out the untruth of theyr packed pelfe and Massepenie religion ".   Note to the Sixth Eclogue of *The Shephearde's Calender.*

occasions, especially when important marriages were celebrated. It is said to have been played in 1589 to celebrate that of Essex with Sir Philip Sidney's widow, in 1594 for the marriage of Sir Thomas Heneage with Lady Southampton, and in 1595 for the wedding of Lord Stanley and Elizabeth Vere. In 1604, it was revived in the presence of King James, when a correspondent wrote from court : " We have had a play of Robin Goodfellow ." Later it was also presented as " The Joyous and Witty Humours of Bottom the Weaver ".

Love's Labour's Lost [1] is the author's first essay in pure comedy. The perpetual conflict between university erudition and innate talent is treated with consummate wit ; and from this point of view the play appears a direct answer to Robert Greene and the critics of his school of thought. Every form of pedantry is represented : Armado, the " fantastical Spaniard " with his elaborate figured language ; Nathaniel the preacher, trying vainly to compete with him ; Holofernes, the schoolmaster who amuses the audience by his affectation of superiority and his lectures on rhetoric, grammar and the Tuscan tongue. This caricature of Giovanni Florio, the Earl of Southampton's tutor, was especially appreciated, as the actor who played the part was probably dressed and made up to resemble the Italian pedagogue and apostle of continental culture, who was a well-known figure in London at the time. The thesis that natural gifts at least in the theatre may be more than a match for learned erudition is upheld and developed with remarkable cleverness.

> Study is like the heaven's glorious sun,
> That will not be deep-searched with saucy looks ;
> Small have continual plodders ever won,
> Save base authority from other's books.
> These earthly godfathers of heaven's lights
> That give a name to every fixed star,
> Have no more profit of their shining nights
> Than those that walk and wot not what they are.
> Too much to know is to know nought but fame ;
> And every godfather can give a name.

Though the rhyming dialogue of the play sparkles with puns and witty conceits, the plot is simple. Navarre's courtship of the French princess, like those of his followers Biron, Dumaine, and Longueville, is brought to a sudden halt by the death of the Princess' father, so that when the deputation bids farewell, Biron remarks sadly :

> Our wooing doth not ende like an old play ;
> Jack hath not Jill.

[1] The comedy was published in quarto in 1598, with the title : " *A Pleasant Conceited Comedie called Love's labors lost*, As it was presented before Her Highnes this last Christmas. Newly corrected and augmented by W. Shakespere. Imprinted at London by W. W. (William White,) for Cuthbert Burby."

A second quarto edition was printed in 1607, by John Smethwicke, with the mention that Her Majesty's servants had played it at Blackfriars and at the " Globe " and that it was written by William Shakespeare. Two other editions followed in 1623 and 1631.

Contrariwise in *A Midsummer Night's Dream* Shakespeare makes Puck say before its happy ending :

> Jack shall have Jill
> Nought shall go ill
> The man shall have his mare again,
> And all shall be well.

thus indicating that these two comedies were closely linked in the poet's thought.

Shakespeare wrote this play shortly after the alliance had been concluded with Henry IV, when the interest of all was turned towards France. He placed the action of his comedy in the little court of Nérac and named his characters Longueville, Biron, and Dumaine after the personages mentioned in the treaty. That of La Motte, ambassador to London seems to have suggested the name " Moth " for the title page. Shakespeare's characters had nothing in common with their French namesakes, but he gave the London audiences the impression of witnessing an entertainment with a thoroughly French atmosphere.

When later the comedy was re-arranged, another country was to the fore ; thanks to new commercial treaties, the public began to be interested in Muscovy ; hence the introduction of a troupe of Russian dancers with their strange costumes and rich furs, was much enjoyed. The famous horse belonging to the trainer Banks, chief equerry to the Earl of Leicester, which guessed the age of members of the audience, gave the cube root of numbers, and climbed St. Paul's steeple, was one of the attractions of the moment, and is mentioned in the play. Other allusions are made to such transitory things that they have become incomprehensible. This explains the immense vogue of this comedy which was constantly kept up to date and revived in the author's life-time. It now appears more out of date than Shakespeare's other comedies and is seldom played by modern theatrical directors.

The playhouses which witnessed the birth of Shakespeare's comic muse were situated, as we have said, on the grounds of Holywell, a former Benedictine convent. It derived its name from a spring whose waters gushed out near the brick cloister wall which separated the domain from the park of the Rutlands. In the middle of these gardens and orchards, the enterprising James Burbage had raised his high wooden building like a fort whose towers and donjons rose from a sea of green.[1]

The little village of Shoreditch and its theatre did not yet belong to London, but the short cut still called Curtain Road [2] which pedestrians took from Bishopsgate over Finsbury fields to reach the Theatre more

---

[1] After having described the Benedictine enclosure, the historian John Stowe writes about the theatres : Not far away two houses were built and opened to the public for the recreative representation of comedies, tragedies and historical dramas : the one is named " The Curtain ", the other " The Theatre ", the two buildings are erected in the fields. John Stowe (*Survey of London*, vol. ii, p. 73).

[2] At the present time, the exact site of the " Theatre " is occupied by a school which has taken its name from the old path : " Curtain Road Elementary School."

quickly, was soon frequented by a large public curious to witness the dramatic joustings at the " Theatre " or at the " Curtain ".   For it was a veritable battle in which Lord Strange's men and Shakespeare their accredited author were engaged with the redoubtable Henslowe, supported by his " twin stars ", the famous clown, Will Tarleton, and the no less famous Edward Alleyn.

However, a change had recently taken place.   Richard Burbage's talent asserted itself more and more ; William Kempe, according to some, possessed greater wit than Tarleton who was getting old.   Lord Strange's actors were beginning to feel at home in the varied repertory which Shakespeare had written for them, and the numerous scribes in Henslowe's pay, were not of sufficient stature to bar Shakespeare's progress.   His most formidable rivals gradually disappeared.   Thomas Lodge, fleeing from the new anti-Papal edicts, had in 1591 already departed for Brazil with Cavendish. Robert Greene died in 1592 ; Thomas Kyd disappeared in 1593, the same year that Marlowe was murdered.   Ben Jonson had not yet entered the arena.   Thus, after eight years of indefatigable labour, the " rude groom " was able to establish himself in Cheapside, not far from the Burbages ; half way between the mansion of the Rutlands and that of the great patron Southampton.

CHAPTER V

LYRIC POETRY

Venus and Adonis—Circumstances of its publication ; its success—*Lucrece*—Shakespeare finds a powerful patron in the Earl of Southampton to whom both poems are dedicated—Influence of this protector on his career.

ON the 18th day of April, 1593, Shakespeare asked and received a printing licence for a poem entitled *Venus and Adonis*, a subject treated with a freshness, an innate sense of natural beauty and a technical mastery of prosody which raised him from the still despised category of playwright to the level of Sidney and Spenser.

Francis Meres, Master of Arts both at Oxford and Cambridge declared :

The sweete wittie soule of Ovid lives in mellifluous and hony-tongued Shakespeare, witnes his *Venus and Adonis*, his *Lucrece*, his sugred Sonnets among his private friends . . . the Muses would speake with Shakespears fine filed phrase, if they would speake English.[1]

The undergraduates of St. John's College, Cambridge, took up this event in a comic show, *The Return from Parnassus*, in which the actors, after declaiming a few lines of *Venus and Adonis*, comment upon their new idol :

Oh sweet Mr. Shakespeare !   I'll have his picture in my study at the court,

exclaims the man of fashion, and his friend later says :

Let this duncified worlde esteeme of Spencer and Chaucer, I'le worshipp sweet Mr. Shakspeare, and to honoure him will lay his *Venus and Adonis* under my pillowe, as wee reade of one (I doe not well remember his name, but I am sure he was a kinge) slept with Homer under his bed's heade.[2]

Shakespeare chose the six-line stanza for this poem, a form praised by Richard Puttenham " as very pleasant to the ear " in his treatise *The Art of English Poetry*, which was printed several years previously by Richard Field from Stratford, the same who now₁ undertook to print *Venus and Adonis*.

Chaucer, Lodge, Marlowe, Drayton and Spenser had already touched

---

[1] Francis Meres, *Palladis Tamia*, p. 281 (1598). At the time Francis Meres brought out his *Palladis Tamia*, a good many of Shakespeare's sonnets were circulating among the poet's familiar friends.

[2] *The Pilgrimage to Parnasseus With The Two Parts of The Return from Parnassus*. Three Comedies performed in St. John's College, Cambridge (Oxford, Clarendon Press, 1886).

on the subject of *Adonis* ; even Robert Greene had produced a few curious verses in which French alternates with English in a little work *Never too late* :

> Sweet *Adon'* darst not glaunce thine eye
> *N'oseres vous, mon bel amy,*
> Upon thy *Venus* that must die,
> *Je vous en prie*, pitie me :
> *N'oseres vous, mon bel, mon bel,*
> *N'oseres vous, mon bel amy.*

Shakespeare's narrative poem owes nothing to these English predecessors. Ovid and his *Metamorphoses* was its sole inspiration. A few suggestions were borrowed from Book IV ; from the Eighth he took the description of Calydon's boar ; from the Tenth the episode of Adonis ; but instead of depicting a youthful victim of love, breaking away unwillingly from the arms of Venus to follow the chase, he represents Adonis as full of modesty, even scandalized by the shameless advances of the goddess. This was his usual method of treating the classics, transforming but never translating them. If he found inspiration at their spring, he turned the stream in new directions, towards fresh meadows adorned by his own imagination. His borrowed subjects took on new scent and colour. His thought remained personal ; the atmosphere and the countryside which he created recall the fields and woods of his native shire. As in *Titus Andronicus*, the soft atmosphere, the gradual fusion of day into night are uniquely Shakespearean ; the hour of the day can be guessed from the cadence of his verse : the radiant morning, the weight of noonday, the lengthening shadows, and finally the mystery of evening.

The hundred and twenty-eight verses of *Venus and Adonis* include narrative, dialogue, monologue, apostrophe and elegy. Everything there is to say upon love, beauty, chastity, pity and death, seems here to have been said. About fifty lines are devoted to a description of hunting, wherein every line reveals the strange paradox of the poetic hunter, torn between the ardour of the chase and an immense pity for its victims.

It is impossible to give an idea of the audacity and verve of this extra-ordinary poem, or say whether its qualities derived most from classic times, the Middle Ages, or the Renaissance, whose efflorescence it so completely displays. Botticelli's Venus is there, shaking her golden tresses in the morning zephyrs, St. Francis preaching to the birds and St. Jerome instructing the lion upon eternal truths.

Here it is Adonis' beauty which conquers the king of beasts. The lion hides in the bushes so that his tossing mane will not frighten the charming youth whom he loves to contemplate. Again Adonis' superhuman beauty makes the fishes spread their golden gills to form a mirror when he looks at his shadow in the brook. These are such fantastic conceits that the reader wonders whether they touch the sublime or the ridiculous ! Even to ask this question is to give its answer : the poem is a work of genius and it was

recognized as such immediately on its appearance.   Twelve editions confirmed its brilliant success in the poet's lifetime.

It is natural that Shakespeare's dramatic works should have taken precedence in popular esteem over his lyrical poems, which nevertheless contain
the quintessence of his talent.   It seems strange that *Venus and Adonis* has
been practically ignored by modern men of letters since George Wyndham. [1]
From the concert of praises which welcomed this first poem of Shakespeare's,
posterity seems to remember only the hostile voices of a few contemporaries
whose opinion is of little consequence.

Thomas Middleton, in a comedy oddly named *A Mad World my Masters*, [2]
introduces a jealous husband who exclaims :

I have conveyed away all her wanton pamplets as *Hero and Leander* and *Venus
and Adonis ;* O, two luscious marrow-bone pies for a married young wife.

John Robinson, a paid informer, managed to engage himself as doorkeeper of the English convent at Lisbon where three cousins of Lord
Southampton had taken the veil ; in his published report he asserts that :

these ladies, although making parade of chastity, poverty and obedience possess
licentious books and when the confessor feels merrily disposed after supper, it is
usual for him to read from *Venus and Adonis* or the *Jests of George Peele*, as there
are few idle pamphlets printed in England that are not to be found in this house. [3]

Some critics protested against this new sort of appeal to sensuality,
holding that the beauty of the versification made the volume all the more
insidious.   One writer regrets that so much talent should be expended in
describing the foolish languishment of love ; [4] and even Davies of Hereford
though far from inimical to Shakespeare, deplores in rhyme that his rival
had wasted eternal lines on " Lewd Venus " and had done it so skilfully that
ladies hitherto modest shut themselves up with the book and gave themselves
over to licentious speculation. [5]

The dedication of *Venus and Adonis* broke with the long tradition which
demanded a poet should approach the high and mighty personage whose
patronage he seeks with a certain ceremony :

To the Right Honorable Henrie Wriothesly,
Earle of Southampton and Baron of Titchfield.

Right Honorable, I know not how I shall offend in dedicating my unpolisht
lines to your Lordship, nor how the world will censure me for choosing so strong
a proppe to support so weake a burthen, onely if your Honour seeme but pleased,

---

[1] George Wyndham, the Victorian commentator who specialized in the study of
Shakespeare's lyrical works, declared that *Venus and Adonis* was worthy to take its place
among the world's masterpieces, and that it was one of the incomprehensible whims of
literary criticism that this poem should be never quoted and scarcely even known.   George
Wyndham, *The Poems of Shakespeare* (Methuen, London, 1898).

[2] *Thos. Middleton's Works*, ed. Dyce, 1840, vol. ii.

[3] Thomas Robinson, *The Anatomie of the English Nunnery at Lisbon* (2nd edn., 1623).

[4] *The Return from Parnassus*, Act i, Sc. i.

[5] *The Scourge of Folly* (John Davies of Hereford, *c.* 1611).

I account my selfe highlie praysed, and vow to take advantage of all idle houres, till I have honoured you with some graver labour. But if the first heyre of my invention prove deformed, I shall be sory it had so noble a god-father ; and never after eare so barren a land, for feare it yeeld me still so bad a harvest, I leave it to your Honourable survey, and Your Honor to your hearts content, which I wish may always answere your owne wish, and the worlds hopefull expectation.

Your Honors in all dutie

William Shakespeare.

The substance of this dedication is repeated in the twenty-sixth Sonnet. Shakespeare shows humility and a consciousness of his own inexperience, but the epigraph chosen to introduce *Venus and Adonis* leaves no doubt that the author knew that his inspiration came from Parnassus.

Let base conceited wits admire vile things ;
Fair Phoebus, lead me to the Muses springs.[1]

This poem, judged indecent by laymen, was licensed by the Archbishop of Canterbury himself. The stationers' Register dated April 18th, 1593, contains this notice :

1593 XVIII Aprili Richard Feild Entred for his copie under thandes of the Archbisshop of Canterbury and Mr Stirrop, a book intituled *Venus and Adonis* (VI dos.).[2]

Was this pure routine ? Or was it for love of art, or because of the powerful influence of Southampton, or simply to encourage a young author to whom he had already rendered a service of a different kind, that the Archbishop gave his " imprimatur " ? John Whitgift, before his elevation to the see of Canterbury, had been the Bishop of Worcester who granted licence for the marriage of Will Shakespeare and Anne Hathaway, celebrated as we have seen according to the old rite.[3] That he had a weakness for belles-lettres is certain ; that he was inclined to favour Catholic poetry is shown by the fact that two years previously he authorized the publication of *Mary Magdalen's Funerall Tears*, by the young priest Robert Southwell.[4] John Stowe the historian who in 1600 dedicated his *Flores Historiarum* (Annals) to the Primate saying that it was on account of :

that prelate's great love and entire affection to all good letters in general and to antiquities in particular.[5]

[1] Ovid, *Amores*, Book I, Elegy XV.

" Vilia miretur vulgus ; mini flavus Apollo
Pocula Castalia plena ministret aqua."

The above translation was made by Christopher Marlowe.

[2] June 25th, 1594, Richard Field passed his rights to Mr. Harrison Senior, and at the assembly of the Stationers' Guild, Mr. Harrison's rights in this publication were recognized.

[3] See Chapter II.

[4] 8 novembris [1591]

Master Cawood Entred for his copie under the hand of the Lord Archbishop of Canterbury A booke entituled *Mary Magdalens funerall Teares*.

[5] The last edition of Stowe's annals published during his lifetime is again dedicated to Archbishop Whitgift. See *Surrey of London and Westminster*, by John Stowe (London, MDCLIV), p. v.

While exercising his prerogative of "censor censorum" in favour of Shakespeare and Southwell, the Archbishop of Canterbury gave not only proof of independent character, but of literary intuition, since a success at least equal to that earned by the poet awaited the prose of the Jesuit priest.

Scarcely a year after the triumph of *Venus and Adonis*, Shakespeare honoured his patron with a new poetic homage, and in 1594 dedicated to him *The Rape of Lucrece*. This poem, twice as long as *Venus and Adonis*, contains two hundred and forty stanzas.[1]

Shakespeare, in his artistry, doubtless decided that the form of prosody adopted for *Adonis* was unsuitable to such an agonizing story; for *Lucrece* he employed the "heroic, dignified and solemn" seven-lined verse used by Guillaume de Machaut, the old French poet, and by Chaucer in his *Troilus and Creseyde*, obeying again the precepts of Richard Puttenham who had declared this form "suitable to the most poignant effects".

The story of Lucrece had already been told by Chaucer in the *Legende of good women*, and many ballad-makers had repeated it. But the real source of *Lucrece*, as of *Venus and Adonis*, is again Ovid. This time the second book of the *Fasti* provided the argument. In his *Adonis*, Shakespeare attempted to urge Henry Wriothesley to a worldly marriage; in his *Rape of Lucrece*, he warns him against the strength of an unlawful passion. The second poem is in essential contrast to the first.

The reader of *Venus and Adonis* has the landscape and characters objectively before his eyes. The action unfolds itself visually, the words suggest physical gestures and movements, the whole takes place amid the light and shadows of woodland glades. *Lucrece*, on the other hand, is a tragedy of internal emotion, reflecting the blackness of an ill-omened passion and the moral distress of the victim. Night envelops the scene; the atmosphere is charged with fear. The creaking door hinges and hoarse distant voices can scarcely be heard. The torch tightly grasped in Tarquin's hand illuminates only his own sinister features and renders the surrounding darkness blacker still. The poet seems afraid to reach the end of his own story. To explain such an improbable crime, he is obliged to enter in spite of himself into the troubled soul of his character.

Tarquin, like Macbeth and all Shakespeare's criminals, is conscious of the horror of his act. He has scarcely crossed the ante-chamber, strewn with reeds according to the Stratford custom, and raised the grinding latch of the room where Lucrece is asleep, when he is seized with terror. Parting the curtains of her bed, he gazes at the chaste wife of Collatinus. She appears like a monument of virtue. "Her fair hand of perfect white show'd like an April daisy on the grass." "Her eyes, like marigolds, had sheath'd their light, and canopied in darkness sweetly lay, till they might open to adorn the day."

Unlike *Adonis*, this fearful drama rarely gives place to descriptions of beauty; but with what felicity Shakespeare seizes on each opportunity that

---

[1] 9 Maij [1594] Master Harrishon Senior—Entred for his copie under the hand of master Cawood Warden, a booke intituled *the Ravyshement of Lucrece*—vjd.

is offered for picturesque language !   The tapestry on the wall of this Elizabethan house depicts an episode in the siege of Troy, and immediately the
poet devotes eight pages to a description of this work of art, perhaps one
of the great Flemish tapestries he had marvelled at in Southampton's
residence.

If the narration is rather slow, the precious images which enhance it
enthrall the reader.   All are reminiscences of the country life lived by the
poet in Warwickshire—the high tide which washes against the arches of
Stratford bridge, the inexperienced swimmer drowned in the Avon, the bark
torn away from the tree struck by lightning.   Sinister country sounds—the
lugubrious cry of the screech owl, the squeal of the night prowling weasel,
the knell pealing from the parish church—anachronism rarely bothered
Shakespeare—prepare the reader for the drama to come.   Tarquin stealing
towards his victim is likened to an ugly toad beside a crystal clear spring, a
greedy snake wriggling up to a swallow's nest ; Lucrece in her vain defence
to a mouse in a cat's merciless claws, a bird trembling at the sound of the
falcon's bells, or struggling in the fowler's net, a wild duck helpless against
the north wind, a deer pierced by the arrow, a pale swan beginning the " sad
dirge of her certain ending ".

Eloquent and unforeseen as the imprecations of Venus are the apostrophes
heaped by Lucrece on Night, Opportunity and Time.   Shakespeare was
always haunted by this theme—ten years later when he wrote *Macbeth* he
remembered " Tarquin's ravishing strides " and he saw him like " a ghost "
moving " towards his design ".

The poem [1] certainly satisfied its author ; he adopted a confident tone
when presenting it to the Earl of Southampton.   A comparison between the
dedication of the *Rape of Lucrece* and that of *Venus and Adonis* indicates that
a definite stage had been reached in the relation of patron and poet.   The
one realized that the exceptional talent he had discovered would add lustre
to his own name ; the other knew himself worthy of such high patronage.

To the Right Honourable, Henry Wriothesley,
Earle of Southhampton and Baron of Titchfield

The love I dedicate to your Lordship is without end : wherof this Pamphlet
without beginning is but a superfluous Moity.   The warrant I have of your
Honourable disposition, not the worth of my untutored Lines makes it assured
of acceptance.   What I have done is yours, what I have to doe is yours, being
part in all I have, devoted yours.   Were my worth greater, my duety would shew
greater, meanetime, as it is, it is bound to your Lordship ; To whom I wish long
life still lengthened with all happinesse.

Your Lordships in all duety
William Shakespeare

In London, Oxford and Cambridge the wits discussed the success of

---

[1] It is probable that *The Rape of Lucrece* was spoken in the theatre, and given as an
interlude by one of the actors of the company, since Michael Drayton, in a poem which
he dedicated to " the Chaste Mathilda ", in 1594, refers to a theatrical presentation of
Shakespeare's *Lucrece*.

Shakespeare's second poem.   Poet and patron each had their part in the
concert of praise.   Two of the most assiduous writers close to Southampton,
Gervase Markham and Richard Barnefield, took this opportunity of
offering their tribute ; the first declared that the most victorious of pens
had been crowned by " this brilliant lamp of virtue ", " this glorious Laurel
of the Muses' hill ".[1]

The latter expressed himself thus :

> And Shakespear thou, whose hony-flowing Vaine,
> (Pleasing the World) thy Praises doth obtaine.
> Whose Venus, and whose Lucrece (sweete, and chaste)
> Thy Name in fames immortall Booke have plac't.
> Live ever you, at least in Fame live ever :
> Well may the Bodys dye, but Fame dies never.[2]

The opinion of the learned Gabriel Harvey is more important :

The younger sort takes much delight in *Venus and Adonis* of Shakespeare,
but his *Lucrece* and his tragedy of Hamlet Prince of Denmark have it in them to
please the wiser sort.[3]

John Weever, forgetting his habitual jealousy, publicly congratulates and
encourages Shakespeare to give the world other lyric masterpieces :

> Honie tong'd Shakespeare, when I saw thine issue
> I swore Apollo got them and none other . . .
> Rose-checkt Adonis with his amber tresses
> Faire fire-hot Venus charming him to love her.
> Chaste Lucretia virgin-like her dresses,
> Prowd lust-stung Tarquine seeking still to prove her. . . .[4]

Michael Drayton, the poet from Hartshill near Stratford also contributed
his offering :

> Lucrece, of whom proud Rome hath bosted long
> Lately reviv'd to live another age,
> And here arriv'd to tell of Tarquin's wrong
> Her chaste deniall and the Tyrant's rage
> Acting her passions on our stately stage.[5]

Shakespeare's success aroused the emulation of many other writers.
Even more were those who solicited the honour of Lord Southampton's
patronage.   Thomas Nashe, in a small work entitled *Choice of Valentines*,

[1] " Thou glorious Laurell of the Muses hill,
        Whose eyes doth crowne the most victorious pen,
        Bright Lampe of Vertue, in whose sacred skill,
        Lives all the blisse of eares—inchaunting men."
Preface to the *Tragedie of Sir Richard Grinvile Knight*, James Roberts (London, 1595).
    [2] *Poems in Divers Humours* (1598), p. E2v.
    [3] Manuscript note in the margin of a book of Chaucer's poetry, edited by Speght (1598).
The date of the note itself is uncertain.
    [4] John Weever, *Epigrammes in the oldest cut and newest fashion* (1599).
    [5] *The Legend of Mathilda* (1594).

wrote impertinently to Shakespeare's admirer, seeking to excuse his lascivious verses :

> Ne blame my verse of loose unchastitie
> For painting forth the things that hidden are,
> Since all men acte what I in speech declare
> Onelie induced by varietie. . . .
>
> Yett Ovids wanton Muse did not offend.
> He is the fountaine whence my streames doe flowe.
> Forgive me if I speake as I was taught.

Sarcasm, however, did not help his case. Nashe's poem with its flattering dedication remains in manuscript at the Inner Temple Library. He was more fortunate in prose, for Southampton agreed to sponsor his *Jack Wilton*.[1]

Among other writers seeking the Earl of Southampton's patronage were Barneby Barnes, Henry Constable, Bartholomew Griffin, George Peele, George Wither, Richard Barnefield, Samuel Daniel, Mathias Gwinn, Arthur Pryce, William Pettie and George Chapman. Several doubtless succeeded in attracting the benevolent attention of the young Maecenas. Shakespeare, with his usual candour, did not hesitate to complain at being neglected in favour of inferior talents :

> You to your beauteous blessings add a curse,
> Being fond on praise, which makes your praises worse.[2]

Then in a more dignified tone :

> . . . Thine eyes, that taught the dumb on high to sing
> And heavy ignorance aloft to fly,
> Have added feathers to the learned's wing,
> And given grace a double majesty.
> Yet be most proud of that which I compile,
> Whose influence is thine and born of thee ;
> In others' works thou doth but mend the style,
> And arts with thy sweet graces, graced be ;
> But thou art all my art and dost advance
> As high as learning my rude ignorance.[3]

The literary homage offered by Shakespeare to his patron did not cease with the two poems published by Field. One hundred and twenty-seven sonnets assure this friend favoured by " beauty, birth, wealth and wit " [4] of the immortality of his name.

The critic Meres mentions them in 1598, and a certain number were published a year later ; the complete series, however, did not appear until 1609. The volume containing them is accompanied by another dramatical-lyric poem, the *Lover's complaint*, of which the Earl of Southampton is again the hero.

---

[1] Thomas Nashe, *The Unfortunate Traveller, or the Life of Jack Wilton*, printed by T. Scarlet for C. Burby (London, 1594). The Stationers' Register carries this entry : " John Wolf Entred for his copie under the handes of the [Arch]Bishop of Canterburie and the Wardens, A booke intituled the unfortunate Traveller."

[2] Sonnet 84. [3] Sonnet 78. [4] Sonnet 37.

The interest of this nobleman in his special poet showed itself in other encouragement. He guided him in the choice of subjects, directed his inspiration, and came materially to his assistance, as we are told by Nicholas Rowe :

There is one Instance so singular in the Magnificence of this Patron of Shake-spear's, that if I had not been assur'd that the Story was handed down by Sir William d'Avenant, who was proably very well acquainted with his affairs, I should not have ventur'd to have inserted, that my Lord Southampton, at one time, gave him a thousand Pounds, to enable him to go through with a Purchase which he heard he had a mind to.[1]

It was, probably thanks to this liberality that Shakespeare became the owner of a large part of the shares in his company, and thus obtained a controlling voice in its affairs.

Who was this Henry Wriothesley, Earl of Southampton, baron of Titch-field whom Shakespeare recognized as his only patron ? In 1594 when *Lucrece* appeared, the young lord had just reached his majority and was ready to play a brilliant part in both the military world and that of letters. His portrait was drawn by the poet in the young Greek whom Venus mourned :

> Describe Adonis and his counterfeit
> Is poorly imitated after you.[2]

He was born in the shadow of a prison. His father, second Earl of Southampton, a supporter of Mary Stuart, had been implicated in the northern insurrection in which so many lost their lives. Although allowed to rejoin his wife at the time of the birth of their only son (October 6th, 1573), he did not again leave the Tower except under close surveillance until death came to him in 1581. His heir was then eight years old and passed under the wardship of the Crown ; but Burleigh's vigilance did not succeed in winning the youth away from the Catholic faith.[3]

Young Southampton's mother was daughter of Anthony Browne, Viscount Montague, already mentioned as the only member of the House of Lords possessing sufficient firmness to declare the new statutes unreason-able and unjust. Montague won respect by his courageous personality and his well-known patriotism. The Queen accorded him a grateful admiration before which every attack of her ministers failed. The fact was that Mon-tague could boast of having played a leading part at the time of the Armada's threatened invasion. Differentiating questions of doctrine from national duty, he equipped, at his own expense, his whole household for training at

---

[1] Nicholas Rowe, *The Works of Mr. William Shakespeare* (Tonson, London, 1709), p. 9.
[2] Sonnet 53.
[3] In a letter addressed to the Earl of Leicester, October 25th, 1581, Lady Southampton assures him that she is not responsible for having prevented her son from attending the services of the Established Church. It is also known that a Matthew Saunder, faithful friend of the Southampton family, closely supervised the religious instruction given to young Henry. (C. M. Stopes, *Henry, Third Earl of Southampton*, p. 517.)

Tilbury camp. The company was commanded by his son, his son-in-law and his grandson. None of the Queen's Protestant subjects had rendered such services. His loyalty earned him personal immunity and a position above the law.

At Montague House, Jesuits passing through London found shelter and protection. The Queen came with great pomp to Cowdray, his castle in the country [1] and stayed there ten days in August, 1592. Theatrical and other entertainments enlivened this sojourn, and as the first official payment made to Kemp, Burbage and Shakespeare was countersigned by the owner's daughter, Lady Southampton, there are grounds for believing that some of Shakespeare's plays were acted during the royal visit.

Heir to a great English territorial fortune, Henry Wriothesley was admitted in 1585 to St. John's College, Cambridge, which he left four years later with the title of Master of Arts. [2] A Latin dissertation in strong angular handwriting reveals the principal preoccupation of his life. Its subject is the attraction of fame, and ends with these words :

Facile igitur videri potest quod omnes ad studium virtutis incitantur spe gloriae.

thus corroborating what the historian Camden later said of him :

He adorned the nobility of his high lineage with the ornaments of learning and military science in order to place them at the service of his country. [3]

In London he took possession of Holborn House, a palatial residence, which occupied the site of the present British Museum. In the town which bears his name, he owned the beautiful mansion, Bull House, where in September 1591 he entertained the Queen on an official visit, but it was the Abbey of Titchfield a few miles from Southampton, transformed by his grandfather Thomas Wriothesley, chancellor of Henry VIII, which was his favourite residence. His possessions included the vast domain of Beaulieu, and manors, farms and houses scattered over the villages of Itchell, Westratton, Micheldever and Titchfield. In order better to manage all these estates, he entered Gray's Inn to study law.

On December 28th, 1594, the *Comedy of Errors* was played at Gray's Inn. Can this privilege given to Shakespeare be attributed to Henry Wriothesley's influence ? Mrs. C. Carmichael Stopes always believed so. What is certain is that the play did not please the majority of the students and that Bacon was asked to write a device " to restore the honor of Gray's Inn " lost on the Night of Errors. [4]

It is to be noted, however, that at the time when Southampton's law studies were beginning, a drama took place which left a profound impression

---

[1] H. Wilaert, *History of an Old Catholic Mission* (Cowdray : London, 1928).

[2] Reg. Acad. Cantab. Henricus Wriothesley Comes Southampton cooptatus in ordinem Magistrorum in artibus per gratiam June 6, 1589. St. John's College. University Register.

[3] *Camden's Britannia*, p. 179 (1607).

[4] C. C. Stopes, *Shakespeare's Environment* (London, 1918, C. Bell & Sons Ltd.), pp. 156 and 294.

4*

on his own life and on the career of his favourite poet.   A clandestine mass had just been said at the house of Swithin Wells, his teacher of rhetoric and Italian, who lodged in the grounds of Gray's Inn, when the pursuivants burst in and arrested the mistress of the house, three priests and those who had been present at the celebration.   Two of them, Wells [1] himself and a young priest named Gennings, were hanged outside Gray's Inn in front of Mr. Wells' own door.   There are several accounts of this episode and a curious contemporary engraving representing a group of halberdiers arresting Mrs. Wells, elegantly dressed, and a young priest vested in a chasuble, with this inscription :

Cum veteri peragit missae pia sacra sodali Infestat turbam turba profana piam.

The shock was so sudden that Southampton immediately left London and, under his own sail, reached France with the intention of joining the contingents which, under the command of Essex, were to swell the army of Henry IV. [2]

From Dieppe, Southampton wrote an enthusiastic letter offering his services to him whose " success rivalled his greatness of mind ", but Essex dared not undertake such a responsibility and thought the best course was to order the fugitive to return immediately and keep secret both letter and escapade.

The crafty Burleigh for his part, thought it prudent to exercise discreet supervision over this independent young man.   He appointed, to replace Swithin Wells as his master in French and Italian, a tried Protestant, Giovanni Florio, who agreed to work in the pay of the minister as well as the pupil, and keep the Council informed of what passed among that family of suspected recusants.

---

[1] Swithin Wells is described by his confessor, Father Stanney, as an enthusiastic sportsman and a " courteous gentleman, brave, generous and steadfastly professed the Catholic faith " (because of his eloquence and mastery of the tongues).   He took for wife a virtuous woman who was condemned with him, but who suffered a long martyrdom in prison. (Challoner, Pollen's edn., p. 591.)   Questioned by Judge Young, Mr. Wells affirmed that he had not known that mass was being said at his house to which the judge answered " although he had not been present at the banquet he should taste the sauce ". . . . On the way to execution and perceiving by chance an old friend he could not forget his pleasant ways and greeted him thus : " Goodbye dear friend, goodbye falconry, the chase and all our old past sports.   I am pledged to a better road. . . ."   At the scaffold, far from wishing for delay, he said to Mr. Topcliffe : " make haste, you should be ashamed to allow an old man to stay so long in the cold in his shirt."   (John Genning's relation of the life and death of Mr. Wells.)

" Three priests from the Seminaries to wit : Edmund Gennings, Polidar Plasden and Eustice White were hanged with four other persons for having sheltered and aided them." (Stow's Chronicles, December 10th, 1591.)

[2] Later, Southampton interceded with Sir Robert Cecil to save an old aunt of his :
" My Lord,
I had much rather do your lordship service than be so often troublesome to you.   Yet must I now of necessity renew and old suit in behalf of my poor aunt Katherin Cornwallis, who by your favour has hitherto lived free from trouble for her recusancy, but now by malice is likely to be indicted if you interpose not to help her, I can say no more for her then I have already done.   She is an old woman that lives without scandal." (Hist. MSS. Com. Salisbury MSS., vol. 18, p. 304.)

Burleigh also made every effort to secure the official betrothal of this favourite of fortune, arbiter of elegance, patron of art and the theatre, to his granddaughter Elizabeth Vere, whose guardian he was. The ambitious and worldly Lady Southampton supported the project, and Lord Montague salved his conscience with the thought that the union would give his grandson an opportunity to exert a salutary influence in the world of politics whose doors would be opened to him by this alliance.

The young man himself was the only one to appear recalcitrant. His romantic heart would not consent to a political marriage ; from year to year he pleaded for delays, and at his majority was obliged to pay the sum of five thousand crowns for " breach of contract ", the first example of a fine imposed by English justice in this sort of case.[1] On her side, Elizabeth Vere, accepted another suitor, William Stanley, sixth Earl of Derby, whom she married on January 27th, 1595.

Lord Southampton made use of his recovered freedom, to realize the dream of military glory he was to pursue throughout life. He immediately enlisted with the forces of Essex, who had been appointed commander of the fleet and leader of an expedition against Spain. Southampton won distinction at the capture of Cadiz, and it was on board the *Garland* loaded with the spoils of the defeated enemy that he received the accolade from his admiral. Thus the friendship between those two adventurous spirits was sealed, and henceforward Henry, third Earl of Southampton—like Essex— belongs to history.

Whatever his aspirations and dreams, his fortune or his tragic misfortune, it is Shakespeare who becomes his confidant and interpreter. We can trace conjecturally the reflection of Wriothesley's interests in Shakespeare's plays. Should Henry Wriothesley bury himself in the study of law, the language of the poet is filled with legal terms. Is he dreaming of serving the King of France ? Shakespeare's comedies transport the spectator to Nérac or the Louvre. When his taste turns to the stories of Cinthio and Boccaccio, Shakespeare finds new inspiration from Italian subjects taken from the *Novelle*. When Montaigne's Essays appeared in England, translated by Florio, Shakespeare was the first to rally to the new fashion, and utilize the writings of the French humanist. Southampton's father had risked his life for the Stuart cause, of which the author of *Macbeth* was a firm supporter ; and, later, when his patron threw himself into the great colonial enterprise of the Virginia Company, and became its secretary, equipping ships to link the mother country to the young colonies, it was the wreck of the barque *Sea Adventure* on the Bermudan shore which provided the subject of the *Tempest*, the poet's last creation in the domain of magic and fantasy.

Moreover, if Shakespeare's work permits us to appreciate Southampton, in his turn, Southampton often helps the understanding of Shakespeare's texts. The life of this great nobleman throws light on certain passages which appear obscure. In the hundred and fifth Sonnet for example, when

[1] Letter of Henry Garnet, 1594. Foley, *Records of the English Province of the Society of Jesus*, vol. iv, p. 49.

the poet declares that his songs and praises are dedicated " To one, of one, still such, and ever so ", the puzzled commentators have thought there is a misprint. However, the phrase alludes to the heraldic device of Henry Wriothesley : " Ung partout, tout par ung ", and the sonnet is thus a variation on the theme of the Southampton coat of arms.[1]

At a time when the descriptive anagram was in vogue, " Stamp of Honour ", was frequently used to designate Henry Wriothesley and the epithet " virtuous " often accompanies his name. He was so prominent a figure in the public eye that both official and private records allow us to follow his career step by step ; he has himself left an ample correspondence about his domestic, colonial and political affairs. All these documents corroborate the favourable opinion which his friends and his poet held of him. Shakespeare's admiration for his young patron was justified and the eulogies lavished upon him were perfectly sincere. The Stratford poet was rightly appreciated by those who knew him best for his upright judgement, ripe wisdom and knowledge of the human heart,[2] certainly not as a base flatterer, or as one unable to distinguish between a romantic hero and a worldly dilettante.

[1] " Let not my love be call'd idolatrie,
   Nor my beloved like an Idoll show.
   Since all alike my songs and praises be
   To one of one, still such and ever so."   (Sonnet 105)
   Another poet, William Pettie, interpolates this same motto in old French between his verses to the praise of Southampton, revealing once again the identity of the man to whom Shakespeare addressed his poems.
[2] Cf. Shakespeare's epitaph, which reads : Judicio Pylium. Genio Socratem. Arte Maronem. Terra tegit. Populus maeret, Olympus habet. See Chapter XX.

CHAPTER VI

SHAKESPEARE'S AUTOBIOGRAPHY : THE SONNETS

Date of composition and order of presentation—The series addressed to Southampton—Shakespeare draws his own portrait—He describes his rivals and bids
his patron adieu—The series addressed to the " Dark Lady "—*A Lover's Complaint*—*The Passionate Pilgrim* and other poems—Dedication of the original
edition of the Sonnets—Circumstances attending Thorpe's publication.

LIKE Dante and Petrarch, Shakespeare in a series of exquisite lyric
poems opened his heart and revealed his personality. The hundred
and fifty-four sonnets collected in one volume by the editor, Thomas
Thorpe, constitute a veritable sentimental autobiography of the poet,
indispensable to the study of his character and works.

These poems seem to have been written sometimes from day to day,
sometimes at long intervals, and addressed to the Earl of Southampton to
whom Shakespeare, when he dedicated the *Rape of Lucrece*, promised to
consecrate all his idle hours.

They were the pride of him who inspired them, to such an extent that
they were soon circulating in manuscript form among the literary satellites
whose " Sun " was Southampton.[1] Shakespeare himself, perfectly conscious
of their value, relied on them to establish the fame of his patron. However,
when the moment of their collected publication arrived, the editor more
than once modified their logical and chronological order, to conceal from
" vulgar " eyes the episode of the quarrel which temporarily separated the
poet and his friend. Thus a dozen sonnets which celebrate a reconciliation
appear in the collection before those describing the misunderstanding which
caused the rupture.

Now that Southampton's character and activities are better known and
that Shakespeare's life is no longer a mystery, it is easy to discover the precise
moment when certain of these verses were written. For example, all those
whose object was to exhort Southampton, then aged seventeen, to a marriage
of ambition, can be assigned to the summer of 1590. The correspondence
between Burleigh, Sir Thomas Stanhope, Lord Montague and Lady
Southampton herself leaves no doubt of the pressure exercised by these
guardians on the recalcitrant heir to persuade him to wed Elizabeth Vere,
granddaughter and ward of the Lord Treasurer.[2]

[1] John Benson who re-edited the Sonnets in 1640 declares that Shakespeare in his
lifetime attributed to these poems as much merit as to his dramatic works in spite of the
latter's greater celebrity.

[2] Carmichael Stopes, *The Life of Henry, Third Earl of Southampton*, pp. 36-39.

It is equally possible to date Sonnet 26 in June 1593, since it is a replica in verse of the dedication of *Venus and Adonis*. The sonnet probably served as an envoy to a presentation copy of the poem about to leave Field's press.

Sonnet 104 may be assigned to October 6th, 1594, since Shakespeare declares therein that he has already known Southampton three years ; it is even probable that it was written in honour of the young nobleman's coming of age.

> To me, fair friend, you never can be old,
> For as you were when first your eye I ey'd,
> Such seems your beauty still.   Three winters cold
> Have from the forests shook three summers' pride,
> Three beauteous springs to yellow autumn turn'd
> In process of the seasons have I seen,
> Three April perfumes in three hot Junes burn'd,
> Since first I saw you fresh, which yet are green . . .

Sonnet 107, written much later, celebrates Southampton's liberation from the Tower ; these fine lines therefore can be dated April 10th, 1603, when he regained freedom after three years' captivity.   Similarly Sonnet 125, containing a reference to the coronation of James I must have been written about April 26th of the same year.

It is known, on the other hand, that the episode of the " dark lady ", the enchantress who sowed discord between poet and protector, took place before 1594, date of the calumnious publication, *Willobie his Avisa*, where the whole story is laid bare.[1]   This is a guide to the date of composition of the series addressed to the Dark Mistress.

It is possible, therefore, to regroup these sonnets in the logical and chronological order of their composition.   A single dramatic poem is thus obtained which is, in spite of repetitions, the romance of friendship, jealousy and love as the poet lived it, but which he hesitated to publish before 1609 for fear of offending certain susceptibilities.   To ignore the sonnets is to neglect the best of Shakespeare's poetry, the quintessence of his genius ; it is like closing an open door to the understanding of his private feelings and thoughts ; not to know their history is to leave out of account a first hand commentary on his life and work.

The series begins with a hymn to disinterested friendship.   Shakespeare starts by painting the portrait of the generous friend who, by his high position at court, in town and in the world of letters, smoothed the path of success for his poet after his arrival in London, penniless, earning his living with difficulty in a subordinate capacity at the theatre until his young patron made him known to all.

Shakespeare affirms that he owes no duty towards this protector.   To discharge his debt there was but one way, that of giving to him immortality by his pen.   He wishes also that this rare being possessed of every quality of heart and mind, should leave the world richer on his departure than when he entered it.

[1] Cf. [p. 108 ff. of this chapter].

The first twenty sonnets are an eloquent appeal to the young lord, bereft of his father, to marry and found a family.   To endanger such a precious, heritage constitutes a crime towards man, almost an impiety towards God, the very theme on which Venus elaborated in advising Adonis to listen to the appeal of prolific nature.   Here it is treated a score of times, but always in a new way which does not tire the reader ; certainly a literary *tour de force*.   The gist of these sonnets is as follows :

Were you but only able to defeat death and remain for ever on earth !   Dear friend, when your terrestrial journey is finished, you will belong to earth no longer. Prepare against this fatal end by handing on your fair image to another ; thus your rare beauty of which you are but the trustee will live on.   None save a prodigal allows a fine building to fall into ruin when foresight can preserve it despite of winter storms and the cold hand of death.   You who had a father, let a son of yours one day boast of his.   Why do you not wage war on that blood-thirsty tyrant Time more efficaciously than by means of my vain rhymes ?   Many a fair maid like an untilled garden would at a word grow you living flowers that would be a better resemblance than your painted portrait.   By giving yourself away you thus preserve yourself through a living likeness done by your own hand.

Who in days to come will believe that my muse speaks true ?   How can verse ever show the brilliance of your eyes, or number all your gifts and graces will they not exclaim " Surely this poet lies, never did such heavenly aspect shine on a mortal face ".   So my poor papers yellowed with time will find themselves despised like loquacious old men whose speech contains more verbosity than truth or like old songs or antique fables be contemptuously cast aside untrue.

More than thirty canvasses, miniatures and engravings are still extant to show the kind of beauty the poet admired in Henry Wriothesley.[1]   The firm regular features of his oval face were illuminated by brilliant blue eyes " twin suns " which sparkled with wit and enthusiasm or moistened sympathetically when a woeful tale was poetically told.   His delicately-coloured complexion was framed in a mass of fair hair which fell in modish " love-locks " to his shoulders.   Whether he was clad in armour or decked in silk and velvet, good taste was always in evidence.   With his height and graceful mien he attracted admiration from all, while his fine voice and excellent diction enhanced the poetry he read.   He loved sports and hunting and was an enthusiastic tennis player.

His striking likeness to his mother, mentioned by Shakespeare, is confirmed by a glance at two of the canvasses in the Welbeck Abbey collection, where his features seem literally to have been traced on those of Lady Southampton.

> Thou art thy mother's glass, and she in thee
> Calls back the lovely April of her prime.   (Sonnet 3)

When the poet looks in his glass, it is to see autumn reflected there.   His

[1] Two portraits are by Van Somer, three by Mireveldt, one by Marcus Gheeraerts, one by Van Dyck, one by Mytens ; several are unsigned.   The miniatures are by Peter and Isaac Oliver and the celebrated Hilliard.   Shakespeare must have possessed one of the latter as he mentions it three times.   In Sonnet 47, he describes his pleasure at being able to gaze at his friend's portrait, though far away from him.

image, in striking contrast to his patron's, seems " beated and chopt with tanned antiquity " (Sonnet 62).   There were hardly ten years between their ages, but Shakespeare at thirty suffered from over-work and lack of sleep :

> How can I then return in happy plight,
> That am debarr'd the benefit of rest ?
> When day's oppression is not eas'd by night . . .   (Sonnet 28)

His forehead whence the chestnut hair had receded contributed to this appearance of premature age :

> That time of year thou mayst in me behold
> When yellow leaves, or none, or few, do hang
> Upon those boughs which shake against the cold,
> Bare ruin'd choirs, where late the sweet birds sang . . .
>
> (Sonnet 73)

The character of the author emerges from his sonnets as distinctly as his physical appearance.   He was a man of sure judgement, eminently healthy in mind and body.   His moral qualities were in no way inferior to his intelligence.   He was generous, even magnanimous ; meanness and hatred were unknown to him until he met them in others.   His self-esteem was balanced by acute sensibility, and his sympathetic intuition grasped the point of view of others and often made it his own.   His faculty of detachment from self, a quality required by every great actor, permitted Shakespeare the author to enter into the mind and behaviour of the character he was studying or creating.

He was of his age in that he did not question class inequality and living conditions, and could without loss of self respect admire a being of quite another class.   His only means of reaching the level of his generous friend was by dedicating to him all his devotion and talent.   Finally, the dominating characteristic of his nature was perfect sincerity, perceptible in his art and manifest throughout life.   In the sonnets particularly, he boasts of this straightforward simplicity, contrasting it with the artificiality of his rivals. He refused to be drawn into the fashion of employing " new-found methods " and " compounds strange ", insisting that his best art consisted in " dressing old words new " (Sonnet 76).

His impatience with pedantry is often stressed, but his bitterest writing is reserved for hypocrisy, affectation and duplicity.   For the author of the *Sonnets* as for *Hamlet*, to " outstrip the modesty of nature " is a crime in life as in art.   Shakespeare disliked make-up, and the horror which he openly expresses of false hair at a time when the sovereign's wardrobe contained sixty blonde wigs, must have appeared daring.

> Before these bastard signs of fair were born,
> Or durst inhabit on a living brow ;
> Before the golden tresses of the dead,
> The right of sepulchres were shorn away,
> To live a second life on second head ;
> Ere Beauty's dead fleece made another gay.   (Sonnet 68)

In the *Merchant of Venice* and *Timon of Athens* the same thought is expressed in plainer terms.

To think that Shakespeare underestimated his own value or possessed a servile spirit would be a grave mistake ; but he did refuse to be judged by inferior critics.

> No, I am that I am, and they that level
> At my abuses reckon up their own :
> I may be straight, though they themselves be bevel ;
> By their rank thoughts my deeds must not be shown.   (Sonnet 121)

Like Hamlet, he saw great possibilities of success in the theatrical profession ; he suffered, however, from the discredit attached to it and often regretted that the exigencies of the theatre were sometimes incompatible with his ideal of dramatic art.   Regretfully he recalls some of his stage appearances.

> Alas ! 'tis true I have gone here and there,
> And made myself a motley to the view,
> Gor'd mine own thoughts, sold cheap what is most dear,
> Made old offences of affections new . . .   (Sonnet 110)

This sentiment pervades the sonnet in which he apologizes for his actor's profession.

> O, for my sake do you with Fortune chide,
> The guilty goddess of my harmful deeds
> That did not better for my life provide
> Than public means which public manners breeds.
> Thence comes it that my name receives a brand,
> And almost thence my nature is subdued
> To what it works in, like the dyer's hand.   (Sonnet 111)

The discredit which attached to the player's calling in Shakespeare's time was a source of anxiety.   The law classified them among vagabonds and beggars ; if they did not enjoy the protection of a powerful nobleman, stage players found themselves denied Christian burial so that their remains were likely to fall under the anatomist's scalpel.   The seventy-fourth sonnet shows how the poet was haunted by the thought of becoming after death

> The coward conquest of a wretche's knife.

Hamlet's horror at the profanation of cemeteries, the gravediggers' discussion, the argument between the priest and Laertes before Ophelia's burial, bear witness to the value attached by Shakespeare to burial according to Christian rites—the inscription on the tombstone in Stratford church beneath which he rests, is another reflection of this intimate feeling.

> Blest be the man that spares these stones
> And curst be he that moves my bones.

But Shakespeare found consolation for the worries caused by his profession as actor, and for many others, in the protective friendship of Lord Southampton.

> When, in disgrace with fortune and men's eyes,
> I all alone beweep my outcast state,
> And trouble deaf heaven with my bootless cries,
> And look upon myself, and curse my fate,
> Wishing me like to one more rich in hope,
> Featured like him, like him with friends possessed,
> Desiring this man's art and that man's scope
> With what I most enjoy contented least ;
> Yet in these thoughts myself almost despising
> Haply I think on thee, and then my state, ·
> Like to the lark at brink of day arising
> From sullen earth, Sings at Heaven's gate . . .   (Sonnet 29)

Since these poems shed so much light on the tastes, inclinations and qualities of the author, may they not also reveal certain of his weaknesses ? Those who search in Shakespeare's plays for a principal defect or master passion notice that amongst all the emotions of the human heart so masterfully treated, there is one which he seems to know in every aspect :

> The green-eyed monster who doth make the meat it feeds on.[1]

His contemporary, Robert Southwell, declared : " No man is able to describe a passion which he has not himself felt." If this be true, the writer of the Sonnets knew the very depths of jealousy and wounded pride. He is angry when inferior writers are preferred to him ; he suffers at finding that his profession puts him in an inferior class, where he is apt to be cold shouldered by persons of quality. The poet could not resist contrasting the sincerity of his own muse with the base flattery which inspired his competitors.

Sixteen sonnets dealing with rival poets are evidence of the jealous unrest he was unable to hide from his patron.

> You to your beauteous blessings add a curse,
> Being fond on praise, which makes your praises worse.   (Sonnet 84)

And elsewhere :

> I think good thoughts, while others write good words,
> And, like unletter'd clerk, still cry " Amen "
> To every hymn that able spirit affords,
> In polish'd form of well-refined pen.   (Sonnet 85)

And again :

> O ! learn to read what silent love hath writ :
> To hear with eyes belongs to love's fine wit.   (Sonnet 23)

When Shakespeare takes up arms against his rivals, those to whom he

---

[1] *Othello*, Act III, Sc. 3.

refers are generally recognizable. Gwinn, Barnefield and Barnes are not spared, but there was a better-known poet whom he designates more clearly than the others. This was George Chapman,[1] who overloaded his writings with astronomical comparisons and employed a rather artificial and " conceited " style.

> So is it not with me as with that Muse
> Stirr'd by a painted beauty to his verse,
> Who heaven itself for ornament doth use
> And every fair with his fair doth rehearse,
> Making a couplement of proud compare. . . .
> O ! let me, true in love, but truly write,
> And then believe me, my love is as fair
> As any mother's child, though not so bright
> As those gold candles fix'd in heaven's air :
> Let them say more that like of hear-say well,
> I will not praise that purpose not to sell.   (Sonnet 21)

It was Chapman's name, which prompted Shakespeare to write the last line of this sonnet. The allusion was obvious to those acquainted with *Love's Labour's Lost*, where it is said :

> Beauty is bought by judgment of the eye,
> Not utter'd by base sale of chapman's tongues.

The same author is again an object of irony in *Troilus and Cressida :*

> Fair Diomed, you do as chapmen do
> Dispraise the thing that you desire to buy
> But we in silence hold this virtue well
> We'll but commend what we intend to sell.

Beside the jealousy of Chapman and other poets, a sincere admiration for one of them transpires ; he whom Shakespeare likens to a " Ship of tall building and of goodly pride " compared to his own " saucy bark " (Sonnet 80).

Several traits indicate that this writer, " by spirits taught to write above a mortal pitch " [2] was Christopher Marlowe. If this is so, these sonnets must have been written before *Venus and Adonis* emerged from the press of Richard Field.

Shakespeare makes frequent allusion to his provincial tours in another series of sonnets no less important. During these absences from London, the author found himself again in the smiling landscape of the midland counties, but he was sad at heart, and his horse too seems conscious of the weight of his depression, for the horse's " groan " under the spur

> . . . doth put this in my mind
> My grief lies onward and my joy behind.[3]

---

[1] Author of *Amorous Zodiac, Shadow of Night*, besides his translation of Homer.
[2] Perhaps an allusion to the practice of black magic, of which Marlowe was accused.
[3] Sonnet 50.

Yet, on his return, the anticipated welcome lacked enthusiasm. Young Harry listened absent-mindedly to his poet ; though he granted audience, the appointed hour was forgotten. Two bitter sonnets ironically compare the value of time as it affects a favourite of fortune and a poor actor-poet. The good pleasure of the one excuses caprices. The other must not complain though he sees the hands of the clock vainly turning.

> I am to wait, though waiting so be hell,
> Not blame your pleasure, be it ill or well. (Sonnet 58)

Had slander been at work during his absence ? Was the master of Holborn House beginning to regret the favours heaped on this mere player ? Were there other deeper causes of misunderstanding ? [1]

Shakespeare took a painful decision. Better disappear than seem importunate. He must resolutely avoid the paths frequented by the young Earl. No longer would he pronounce the name which had been so dear for fear of bringing discredit upon it. [2] Like an advocate he would plead the cause of Southampton against Shakespeare and lay the wrongs done by his ex-friend to his own account.

Here his expressions must not be taken too literally ; if he accuses himself, he knows quite well that his patron is the guilty one. Twenty-three sonnets express his disillusionment. The same thought is developed in entirely different forms without repetition. From the point of view of art and language, this sequence, intensely tragic and eternally human, is one of the most beautiful of the collection. Perhaps the masterpiece is the seventy-first in which each line seems to ring the knell of dying friendship.

> No longer mourn for me when I am dead
> Than you shall hear the surly sullen bell
> Give warning to the world that I am fled
> From this vile world, with vilest worms to dwell :
> Nay, if you read this line, remember not
> The hand that writ it ; for I love you so,
> That I in your sweet thought would be forgot,
> If thinking on me then should make you woe.
> O ! if,—I say, you look upon this verse,
> When I perhaps compounded am with clay,
> Do not so much as my poor name rehearse,
> But let your love even with my life decay ;
> Lest the wise world should look into your moan.
> And mock you with me after I am gone.

---

[1] Six sonnets interpolated arbitrarily in the collection spoil the continuity of the author's thought, and bewilder the reader who does not perceive the link attaching them to the whole. However, grouped together, these poems show the cause of the misunderstanding between Shakespeare and Southampton. The handsome young man had seduced the poet's mistress, and the drama which estranged the friends finds its epilogue in the twenty-seven sonnets addressed to the " dark lady ".

[2] Sonnet 49.

The last stage in disenchantment is reached when the poet realizes that the moment has come to bid his friend a long adieu :

> Farewell ! thou art too dear for my possessing,
> And like enough thou know'st thy estimate.   (Sonnet 87)

But one of the noblest traits of Shakespeare's character—strange mixture of pride and abnegation—was fidelity to a high conception of friendship. The moment he learned that Southampton on his side had suffered from their long separation, he again approached his former benefactor.   Knowing that his friend had felt the same loneliness, he brought him, unreservedly " the humble salve which wounded bosom fits " (Sonnet 120) and returned to his " better self ", thus permitting the sonnet story to conclude on a note of serenity.   The series of poems addressed to Southampton cannot better be brought to close than by this one :

> Not marble, nor the gilded monuments
> Of princes, shall outlive this powerful rime ;
> But you shall shine more bright in these contents
> Than unswept stone, besmear'd with sluttish time.
> When wasteful war shall statues overturn
> And broils root out the work of masonry,
> Nor Mars his sword nor war's quick fire shall burn
> The living record of your memory.
> 'Gainst death and all oblivious enmity
> Shall you pace forth ; your praise shall still find room
> Even in the eyes of all posterity
> That wear this world out to the ending doom.
> So, till the judgment that yourself arise,
> You live in this, and dwell in lover's eyes.   (Sonnet 55)

In the original edition of Thomas Thorpe, the series addressed to the so-called " dark lady " is separated from the preceding series by a space, thus showing that the editor knew perfectly well that they were distinct from those addressed to Southampton.   The whole tone is essentially different.   When Shakespeare praised or blamed his patron, he never allowed himself to speak as an equal.   But here, the object of his lines is someone of his own social status, and it is vain when trying to identify the dark enchantress, to look for her, as certain commentators have done and do among the ladies in the Queen's service.[1]

According to Shakespeare she was middle-class, dark, married, a con-firmed coquette, an excellent musician, and highly gifted as a " conver-sationalist ".   There is no mystery here ; the poet's contemporaries

---

[1] Professor Tyler and George Bernard Shaw have tried to identify the " dark lady " with Mary Fytton.   The liaison of this lady-in-waiting with Henry Herbert, Earl of Pem-broke brought about her banishment from the court.   Now, two of the sonnets addressed to the " dark lady " were published before this scandal.   The gay and pretty Mary Fytton was fair with grey eyes, whilst the author of the sonnets declares that his mistress was married, and was a brunette with black eyes.   Two other suggestions have been made : Penelope Devereux, Lady Rich, and Jacqueline Field, the printer's wife.   These deserve even less consideration, as no serious evidence supports them.

entertained no illusions as to the identity of the " bad angel " to whom the last twenty-seven sonnets are addressed.

The first mention of Shakespeare as a dramatist is due to an envious attack on the part of a jealous rival, Robert Greene ; here again the first reference to the author of the poems and sonnets springs from a pen dipped in gall.   Scarcely had the *Rape of Lucrece* appeared than a libel without literary merit was published under the title *Willobie his Avisa*.   It was dated from Oxford and signed with the pseudonym Hadrian Dorell.   This parody, a mixture of prose and verse, is primarily a venomous attack on the wife of an Oxford innkeeper.   The perfect spouse is a rare bird (rara Avis or Avisa), but the author is careful to say that a contrary meaning must be given to his epithets.   Beneath the exterior of a Lucrece the reader at once recognizes the wanton.

Let Lucres-Avis be thy name,[1]

Avis or Avisa has for a lover an actor whose initials are W.S., and, so that no doubt can be left as to his identity, the author adds that William Shakespeare had lately depicted the rape of poor Lucrece.

Avisa's house is indicated no less clearly : " See yonder house where hangs the badge of England's saint."

This probably refers to the " Inn of the Golden Cross ", kept, it is said, by John Davenant, a very grave and discreet citizen yet an admirer and lover of plays and actors and especially of Master Shakespeare.[2]

The author of the slanderous pamphlet shows a swarm of admirers paying assiduous court to the beautiful hostess of the inn as she presides over her counter.   Then the noble Harry W., appears.   He is conquered at first sight of Avisa, and takes his love so tragically that he begins to pine, until his friend the player W. S., who has undergone the same torments, counsels him with the wisdom born of experience.   Here we have the situation, and the very characters of the drama enacted in the sonnets.   The anonymous author does not conceal the identity of " Harry W.", any more than that of the other persons concerned.   Among his intimate friends, Southampton was always known as Harry, and his surname, it is unnecessary to recall, was Wriothesley.   The conversation assigned to him in the inn is also characteristic of his personality, " Harry W." quotes on all occasions proverbs belonging to the collection just brought out by his new Italian master, Giovanni Florio ; many figure in Shakespeare's plays.[3]

The censor naturally ordered the suppression of *Willobie his Avisa ;* but in 1596, a second edition of this parody of the sonnets was circulating at court and in the city.

[1] *Willobie his Avisa* or the true picture of a modest maid and a chaste and constant wife. (Imprinted at London by John Windet, 1594.)

[2] The records are confusing and make it difficult to tell precisely when and for how long Davenant was at the " Golden Cross "—or the house adjoining it. (Cf. Chambers, *William Shakespeare*, I, pp. 572 ff.)   But Davenant's connection with the place is certain, and his relations with Shakespeare emphasized by the Seventeenth-century writers.

[3] *Florios Second Fruits—yelding six thousand Italian Proverbs* (1591, London, printed for Thomas Woodcock dwelling at the Black Beare).

The historian Anthony Wood echoes the scandal, which for years was a subject of gossip at Oxford. He describes the hostess of the " Golden Cross " as " a very beautiful woman of good wit and conversation very agreeable ; in which she was imitated by none of her children but by this William . . ."

John Aubrey goes a step further in calumny :

Mr. William Shakespeare was wont to goe into Warwickshire once a yeare, and did commonly in his journey lye at this house in Oxon. where he was exceedingly respected. I have heard parson Robert say that Mr. W. Shakespeare haz given him a hundred kisses. Now Sir William would sometimes, when he was pleasant over a glasse of wine with his most intimate friends—e.g. Sam. Butler author of *Hudibras*, etc.—say, that it seemed to him that he writt with the very spirit that Shakespeare, and seemed contented enough to be thought his son. He would tell them the story as above, in which way his mother had a very light report. . . .[1]

The manuscript collection containing the notes written by William Fulman on the poaching incident discussed earlier, include also a set of verses in which the poet William Davenant is ridiculed for having changed the spelling of his name, and by the addition of an apostrophe made it more distinguished, thus claiming descent from an ancient Norman family.

" Useless ", adds the writer ironically, " everybody knows that d'Avonant comes from Avon ; this river is the cradle of his muse." [2]

Hence, watchful contemporaries and biographers in pursuit of old gossip agree in linking Shakespeare's name with that of the fascinating hostess of the " Golden Cross ". It is further known that Southampton and his poet stayed at Oxford in the autumn of 1592 ; the former, accompanied as usual by Giovanni Florio, displayed his brilliant person in the Royal retinue,[3] while the second had come with his company to enliven the official entertainments with some comedies. Elizabeth entered Oxford on September 22nd and lodged at Christ Church. The anonymous parody of the sonnets naturally presented the persons who were at that time in the city of learning ; and, as the dramatic representations took place in the courtyard of the " Golden Cross ", it is evident that John Davenant's wife was not far away.

The series of sonnets addressed to the " dark lady ", twenty-seven in number, is printed in logical order, with the exception of the last two dealing with the Waters of Bath which should be read first. Doubtless Thorpe the editor wished to veil the story of betrayed love about which contemporaries had chattered considerably and whose personages were still in the public eye at the time of publication.

[1] John Aubrey, *Brief Lives*, p. 204.

[2] Walter Scott, so well versed in contemporary manuscripts, also identifies Mistress Davenant with Shakespeare's mistress.

[3] The university records state that at the banquet given September 23rd, 1592, at Magdalen college, Southampton was seated between Admiral Lord Howard, patron of Edward Alleyn's company, and Lord Strange, patron of Burbage's and Shakespeare's company. A month previously he had received the title of Master of Arts from the same college.

It was at Bath that the actor-poet on tour met his evil genius.   According to the classic formula, he declared that the spring had gushed, warm and beneficial ever since young Eros had cooled his arrows there.   But alas, the waters which had the reputation of healing so many human ills did nothing to cure the pains of his heart.

> —The bath for my help lies
> Where Cupid got new fire, my mistress' eyes.   (Sonnet 153)

A description then follows of the tender black eyes which have put on mourning to weep for their owner's cruelty.

> Thine eyes I love, and they, as pitying we,
> Knowing thy heart torments me with disdain,
> Have put on black, and loving mourners be,
> Looking with pretty ruth upon my pain.
> And truly not the morning sun of heaven
> Better becomes the grey cheeks of the east,
> Nor that full star that ushers in the even,
> Doth half that glory to the sober west,
> As those two mourning eyes become thy face.   (Sonnet 132)

The poet recalls, however, that in olden days dark women could not pretend to possess beauty.   Shakespeare admits also that the reputation enjoyed by this dark Circe was far from being exemplary.   He confesses besides that he enjoys to be taken for younger than his years.

> When my love swears that she is made of truth,
> I do believe her, though I know she lies,
> That she might think me some untutor'd youth,
> Unlearned in the world's false subtleties.
> Thus vainly thinking that she thinks me young,
> Although she knows my days are past the best,
> Simply I credit her false-speaking tongue :
> On both sides thus is simple truth supprest.
> But wherefore says she not she is unjust ?
> And wherefore say not I that I am old ?
> O ! love's best habit is in seeming trust,
> And age in love loves not to have years told. . . .   (Sonnet 138)

Still in a playful tone, Shakespeare taxes his mistress on her obstinate " Willfulness ", a characteristic trait of the innkeeper's beautiful wife in *Willobie his Avisa*.   This stubbornness permits of a long series of puns on the poet's name.   Every imaginable word play on the two " Wills ", that of the lady, and that of her lover, is presented in two consecutive sonnets :

> . . . Thou being rich in will add to thy will
> One Will of mine to make thy large will more.   (Sonnet 135)

and again :

> Make but my name thy love and love that still
> And then thou lov'st me, for my name is Will.   (Sonnet 136)

After this assertion, does it not seem childish to attribute these sonnets to Francis Bacon, Roger Manners (Lord Rutland) or Edward Vere (Earl of Oxford), the candidates whom the anti-Stratfordian theorists wish to substitute for Will Shakespeare ? [1]

Two sonnets, one of which had already appeared in the collection of the *Passionate Pilgrim*, show the part played by music in this love affair. The poet's dramatic work also demonstrates how sensible he was to musical harmony—one of the rare points where he disagreed with Southampton—" insensible to the concord of sweet sounds ". When Shakespeare describes his " dark lady " seated at her virginals the reader feels the powerful enchantment which she had for him.

> How oft, when thou, my music, music play'st,
> Upon that blessed wood whose motion sounds
> With thy sweet fingers, when thou gently sway'st
> The wiry concord that mine ear confounds,
> Do I envy those jacks that nimble leap
> To kiss the tender inward of thy hand,
> Whilst my poor lips, which should that harvest reap,
> At the wood's boldness by thee blushing stand !
> To be so tickl'd they would change their state
> And situation with those dancing chips,
> O'er whom thy fingers walk with gentle gait,
> Making dead wood more bless'd than living lips.
>   Since saucy jacks so happy are in this,
>   Give them thy fingers, me thy lips to kiss.   (Sonnet 128)

Sentimental verse soon gave place to cruel reality. The heartless mistress deceived not only a trusting husband but a still more blind lover, a treachery all the more painful to the poet because it was his own dearest friend, that " better self " to whom he owed everything, who was now his favoured rival. He then pours out recriminations against the dark beauty, a complexion which seems to him the sign of a corrupt soul.

Nevertheless while deploring his weakness, his senses are still captivated ; his heart is dominated by the proud will of his mistress, but his reason acknowledges his own blindness.

> In faith, I do not love thee with mine eyes,
> For they in thee a thousand errors note ;
> But 'tis my heart that loves what they despise,
> Who, in despite of view is pleas'd to dote.
> Nor are mine ears with thy tongue's tone delighted ;

---

[1] (i) The Baconian paradox dates from 1856. *The Philosophy of the Plays unfolded . . .*, by Delia Bacon, was the point of departure of a long controversy. (ii) The claim of Rutland (Roger Manners) originates in *Lord Rutland est Shakespeare* (C. Demblon, 1913). (iii) The argument in favour of Oxford (Edward Vere, Earl of Oxford) was put forward by C. Palmer in 1920, and B. M. Ward in 1928 : *Shakespeare identified as Edward Vere 17th Earl of Oxford*, and *The Seventeenth Earl of Oxford* (London, Murray). Another English thesis, developed in France by Abel Lefranc, maintains that the sixth Earl of Derby wrote the works of Shakespeare.

> Nor tender feeling, to base touches prone.
> Nor taste nor smell desire to be invited
> To any sensual feast with thee alone ;
> But my five wits, nor my five senses can
> Dissuade one foolish heart from serving thee,
> Who leaves unsway'd the likeness of a man,
> Thy proud heart's slave and vassal wretch to be :
>   Only my plague thus far I count my gain
>   That she that makes me sin, awards me pain.   (Sonnet 141)

Love's torments were never lamented in more poignant and sincere fashion than in the twelve sonnets where the author describes his moral distress.   The bond of marriage was for Shakespeare a sacred tie.   To neglect the companion of his youth for a woman less pure, and perhaps less beautiful than his Anne, was a major crime ; it seemed to him entirely logical that " She who made him sin awards only ' pain ' ".   He deplores the sensual passion which fails to embellish human love with a spiritual aura and drowns disillusion in shame.   Having shown with unaccustomed brutality of language (Sonnet 129) the abyss into which those fall who allow themselves to be led by base passions, the poet breaks away from the flesh, renounces his sinful love and accuses the carnal instincts of being the sole obstacle between man and his obedience to the divine will.

> Poor soul, the centre of my sinful earth,
> Pressed by these rebel powers that thee array,
> Why dost thou pine within and suffer dearth,
> Painting thy outward walls so costly gay ?
> Why so large cost, having so short a lease,
> Dost thou upon thy fading mansion spend ?
> Shall worms, inheritors of this excess,
> Eat up thy charge ?   Is this thy body's end ?
> Then, soul, live thou upon thy servant's loss,
> And let that pine to aggravate thy store ;
> Buy terms divine in selling hours of dross ;
> Within be fed, without be rich no more :
>   So shalt thou feed on Death, that feeds on men,
>   And Death once dead, there's no more dying then.   (Sonnet 146)

The twenty-seven sonnets to the " dark lady ", in which the influence of Robert Southwell's religious poetry is perceptible, especially in the last verses, conclude on this lofty theme.

The main ideas which emerge from this series are the development of the soul by self-denial, the purification of the heart by suffering, and the elevation of the mind by its victory over the flesh, ideals which are all taught by the Christian religion.   The author's self-portrait is not that of a saint —far from it—but of an honest man long accustomed to trouble and knowing above all, how to forgive.

Sir Sidney Lee, and I. P. Fripp, with singular lack of psychology, maintain that if the " dark lady " had any influence on Shakespeare's life and work, this influence was weak and temporary. They seem to have forgotten *Antony and Cleopatra*, the drama in which the poet has recreated the same feminine character already described in the sonnets. Antony's unbridled passion, which destroyed empires, does not differ in essence from the fatal flame which had ravaged the poet's own heart, and made him the " wretched vassal " of a woman whom his reason condemned as cruel, deceitful and unscrupulous.[1]   When Antony bewails his weakness, he uses the stinging words already employed by the poet in his great lyric work.

In the original edition of Thomas Thorpe, Shakespeare's sonnets occupy sixty-two pages ; the twelve that follow and complete the volume contain a poem of forty-eight stanzas entitled *A Lover's Complaint*, where the name of William Shakespeare is repeated as author.[2]

The first group of twenty sonnets, as has already been observed, was written on a single theme ; they formed an eloquent appeal in favour of marriage, and Shakespeare points out that his patron has a large choice. Among the bevy of beauties grouped around him not one but would have been pleased at his selection.

A Lover's Complaint deals with one of them ; its aim is to persuade the young lord that the heroine is worthy to be his wife. This time, the poet's arguments prevailed ; the union he so strongly advocated soon took place.

The Complaint shows Shakespeare himself in guise of a shepherd familiar with court life. He lends a sympathetic ear to the griefs of a forsaken damsel with a view to describing them to his fickle friend. A knotty staff in hand, he approaches the river bank where the weeping girl is seated, and invokes his age and knowledge of the world as an encouragement to her to confide her troubles.

> A thousand favours from a maund she drew
> Of amber, crystal and of beaded jet,
> Which one by one she in a river threw,
> Upon whose weeping margent she was set :
> Like usury applying wet to wet,
> Or monarch's hands that let not bounty fall
> Where want cries " some ", but where excess begs all.
>
> Of folded schedules had she many a one,
> Which she perus'd, sigh'd, tore, and gave the flood,
> Crack'd many a ring of posied gold and bone,
> Bidding them find their sepulchres in mud.

---

[1] See the end of Chapter XVII for an analysis of *Antony and Cleopatra*.

[2] The first French translation of the poem under the title *les Plaintes d'une amoureuse* was made by Francois-Victor Hugo, and was published in the *Revue de Paris*, November 15th, 1856, preceded by these lines :

" The authenticity of this work is not in doubt. Published for the first time by the editor, Thomas Thorpe, in the same volume as the *Sonnets*, it appeared in 1609 with this signature : William Shakespeare. Although dated 1609, this poem seems to us to have been composed much earlier ; it is, we think, of Shakespeare's first manner, and should be assigned like the Sonnets themselves, to the period of the poet's life, when he still felt perhaps in spite of himself, the powerful influence of Italian literature."

Her description of her lover exactly recalls what Shakespeare said of
Adonis :

> Well could he ride, and often men would say
> " That horse his mettle from his rider takes :
> Proud of subjection, noble by the sway,
> What rounds, what bounds, what course, what stop he makes ! "

The rider's detailed portrait is given so that no contemporary could fail
to recognize Henry Wriothesley, Earl of Southampton.

Chestnut hair, cheeks as delicately coloured as a young girl's, and yet
a face full of energy. Often when angry, his eyes would appear to throw
off sparks. As yet his chin was covered only with a light down, soft as
velvet, and his friends discussed whether he appeared to greater advantage
shaven or unshaven. Tall, strong and of graceful figure, his qualities were
as beauteous as his form. Who could turn a deaf ear to his persuasive
arguments ? He held sway over young and old, over men and women.
Many procured his picture to feast their eyes upon. He possessed such
charm and power that at a single feigned tear, the reserve of the unhappy
heroine had melted.

The abandoned girl is as easily identified as is her lover, for this affair
caused many tongues to wag. The worldly and political correspondence
despatched by the indefatigable Rowland White to Sir Henry Sidney,
minister in Flushing, and Governor of the Cinque-Ports, is full of the
supposed scandal.

I heare my Lord Southampton, goes with Mr Secretary to France, . . .
which cours of his, doth extremely grieve his Mistris, that passes her Tyme in
weeping and lamenting.[1]

And again :

I hard of some unkindnes shuld be between (Earl of Southampton) and his
Mistres, occasioned by some Report of Mr. Ambrose Willoughbye. . . . I see
(Earl of Southampton) full of Discontentments.[2]

In February 1597, the same correspondent, moved to sympathy, writes :

Lord Southampton is much troubled at her Majesties straungest usage of
hym. Some Body hath plaied unfrendly Partes with hym. Mr Secretary hath
procured hym Licence to travell. His faire Mistress doth wash her fairest Face
with to many Teares.[3]

" Authorisation to travel " on the continent with ten servants and eight
horses would, at another time, have pleased the young man, permitting him
—as it did—to meet his friends the Danvers in Paris, and perhaps make in
their company the journey beyond the Alps of which he dreamed. However,
it was evidently thought preferable to keep the amorous lord within sight,

---

[1] Roland White to Sidney, January 14th, 1597. Sidney Papers.
[2] *Ibid.* January 19, 1597, p. 82.
[3] *Ibid.* February 1st, 1597. Sidney Papers.

and Robert Cecil, who hastened to France in order to conduct the negotiations which preceded and followed the Treaty of Vervins, retained
Southampton as his private secretary.

Once in Paris, Southampton became extremely friendly with the Duc
de Rohan and Marshal de Biron. The King of France affectionately embraced this friend of Essex, and talked with him of grave affairs of State. In
the eyes of Henry IV and also of Elizabeth, Spain was the common enemy,
but the interests of France and England were sufficiently divergent to prolong
the preliminary conferences. In order to pass the time, the negotiators
hunted and played tennis together ; the stakes must have reached considerable sums, since one of the Queen's many spies wrote from Paris, September
22nd, 1598, to the Earl of Essex's secretary :

I implore you, Sir, to communicate this news to your Lord Earl that is friend
of the Earl of Southampton, who is at present in Paris, is about to ruin himself
if he is not removed from France in a few days. He stakes two, three and four
thousand crowns at games. Marshal de Biron won three thousand crowns from
him in a few days, and everyone laughs at him, so much that the Earl of Essex
would do a good turn to the said Earl by summoning him home at once ; Otherwise
he will lose all his money and reputation in France and England alike for which
I should be sorry, knowing that my Lord, the Earl, loves him dearly.[1]

The agent must have been well informed, for in a personal letter to the
Earl of Essex the unhappy gambler declared himself immobilized in Paris
for lack of funds. And yet an imperious duty recalled him to London.
His clandestine marriage could no longer be concealed. Miss Vernon had
left court on the pretext of illness, and had taken refuge at Essex house with
the exquisite Penelope Devereux, Lady Rich,[2] who had been the " Stella "
of Sir Philip Sidney's famous sonnet sequence ; she offered to look after
her young cousin, whilst gossip ran rife in London. As for Southampton,
he left Paris without asking permission or even taking leave of his superiors,
and having decided to make known the secret marriage solemnized by his
chaplain, Mr. Wright the previous year, rejoined his young wife.[3] A letter
to Robert Cecil explains his situation, and shows at the same time how
little the young bridegroom understood the gravity of such an admission,
wounding to Elizabeth's pride, and punishable under the statutes.

Unfortunately Elizabeth learned the news from one of her secret agents,
before receiving her minister's communication. She was too upset to
attend chapel and spent the whole morning storming at the ladies and
gentlemen of the court, and threatening the young couple with direst
punishments.[4]

---

[1] *Hist. MSS. Com. Hatfield*, pt. VIII, pp. 358-359.

[2] Walter Devereux, *Lives and Letters of the Devereux, Earls of Essex*, 1540-1646 (Murray,
London, 1853). Lady Rich became the godmother of the child born early in November
1598.

[3] *Ibid.*

[4] See " Letter from John Chamberlain to Dudley Carlton ", *Shakespeare's Sonnet story*
(Arthur Acheson, London, 1922), p. 389.

After threatening to send all those who knew about the affair to the Tower, she contented herself with relegating Southampton to the Fleet prison. Neither he nor his wife were received at court after this incident. The following year the Earl of Southampton took part in the Irish expedition organized by his cousin Essex, viceroy and commander-in-chief, who placed him at the head of the cavalry.

If *A Lover's Complaint* is one more proof of Shakespeare's affectionate interest in his noble friend, it shows also that the poet did not lack character or courage in thus taking his stand against the royal wish : he must have realized what a storm would break when the marriage became known. Some commentators see in Sonnet 116—a pearl of the collection—a reference to Southampton's marriage with Elizabeth Vernon ; it is often quoted to illustrate the triumph of constancy over difficulties.

Let me not to the marriage of true minds admit impediments. . . .

This lovely sonnet stands isolated in Thomas Thorpe's book, being linked neither to the one which precedes, nor to those which follow it. Placed as it is among the sonnets addressed to Southampton, it appears certainly to be an allusion to his marriage which had encountered so many obstacles and hindrances.

The young pair were at last happy in this union advised and engineered by the poet. Both belonged to old Catholic families ; both found themselves in a world hostile to their belief, in which the object of their admiration was none other than Essex. For a quarter of a century, their marriage was looked upon as the type of perfect mutual understanding. In the midst of trials of the worst kind, peril, separation and adversity, Lady Southampton always referred to her husband as " dear lord and only joy of my existence ", and would try to " make him merry " by recounting " the latest adventure of his friend, Sir John Falstaff," thus showing that Shakespeare was remembered in their domestic conversation.

In 1599, the names of Shakespeare and Southampton were irrevocably linked at court and among men of letters. Curiosity as to the writings of the one, anxiety about the doings of the other had been so whetted, that the small volume launched by William Jaggard with the title *The Passionate Pilgrim* [1] by William Shakespeare was certain to obtain success.

Francis Meres, justly esteemed for his gifts as critic, had lately drawn attention to the excellence of Shakespeare's lyric poetry, which he ranked with that of Sidney and Spenser. Meres praised the poetic quality not only of *Venus and Adonis* and *Lucrece*, but hinted that many sonnets by the same author, which were circulating among his friends, were no less remarkable.

Jaggard's minute volume was a disappointment ; he had succeeded in

---

[1] *The Passionate Pilgrime* by W. Shakespeare. At London Printed for W. Jaggard, and are to be sold by W. Leake at the Greyhound in Paules Churchyard. The second edition, of which the single copy is undated, concludes like the third (1612), with these words : " Where unto is newly added two Love Epistles, the first from Paris to Hellen and Hellen's answere back againe to Paris ". (Printed by W. Jaggard, 1612.)

procuring only two of the unpublished sonnets belonging to the series addressed to the " dark lady ", which he printed at the beginning of his book. This was sufficient to cause a sensation, for the two poems provided the key to the story of jealousy contained in their entirety in the volume later published by Thorpe :

> Two loves I have of comfort and despair
> Which like two spirits do suggest me still :
> The better angel is a man right fair,
> The worser spirit a woman colour'd ill.
>
> (Sonnet 144.)

Jaggard's little collection contains besides these sonnets three short poems which do not in any way belong to the autobiographical series, but were written for *Love's Labour's Lost*.

Four sonnets follow, a tentative sketch of *Venus and Adonis*, probably rejected when the author adopted the more simple six-line stanza for this poem. Then come some verses on feminine fickleness, on the incompatibility of youth and age, a sonnet on the respective merits of music and poetry, and finally the exquisite " Good-night ", a little masterpiece in five stanzas.

The second part of the volume, separated from the first by a different title, *Sonnets to Sundry Notes of Music* contains divers poems of doubtful authenticity, which the editor does not attribute specifically to Shakespeare.

The author of the sonnets does not appear to have been displeased when Jaggard published his small collection ; but the case was different a few years later when the same editor undertook a second, then a third reprint, accompanied by an alluring title page :

The Passionate Pilgrime Or Certaine Amorous Sonnets, betweene Venus and Adonis, . . . By W. Shakespeare. Where-unto is newly added two Love-Epistles, the first from Paris to Hellen, and Hellens answere backe againe to Paris.

This time the verses chosen by Jaggard to increase the weight and the price of his collection were neither unpublished nor by Shakespeare. The two letters were written by Thomas Heywood and already published in *Troia Britannica*. However, Jaggard was taken to task by Heywood, who, in the *Apology for Actors*, printed in 1612, complained of the theft of his work, and mentioned also Shakespeare's annoyance, adding that the author of the sonnets :

much offended with Mr. Jaggard [1] that presumed to make so bold with his name, to do himself right hath since published them in his owne name.

---

[1] " I must necessarily insert a manifest injury done me in that work, by taking the two Epistles of *Paris* to *Helen* and *Helen* to *Paris*, and printing them in a lesse volume, under the name of another, which may put the world in opinion I might steale them from him ; and hee to doe himselfe right, hath since published them in his owne name : but as I must acknowledge my lines not worthy of his patronage, under whom he hath publisht them, so the Author I know much offended with Mr. *Jaggard* that (altogether unknowne to him) presumed to make so bold with his name." (*Apology for Actors*, Thomas Heywood, 1612.)

This testimony is certainly exact. Thomas Heywood collaborated with Shakespeare from the very beginning, and remained close to him throughout life, never ceasing to praise the literary gifts of his Stratford friend.

The actor-poet made no protest in 1599 against the publication of some examples of his lyric poetry, but he seriously objected when verses which were not his were assigned to him and, in 1609, as we shall see, he gave his consent and approval to the volume containing his one hundred and fifty-four sonnets which Thomas Thorpe brought out with a dedication to Southampton.

It was in fact, in the spring of 1609 that the printing licence was obtained, and a few months later the sonnets appeared on two booksellers' stalls. Neither the author nor the patron were in London at the time.　Shakespeare, having left the stage to lead the quiet life of a country landowner, visited the capital only to present the plays which he had engaged to provide for the Globe, the Blackfriars or Court festivities ; Lord Southampton appointed governor of the Isle of Wight, lived either in Carisbrooke Castle, or at Titchfield Abbey near Southampton.　But in London there was a veritable literary agent in the person of Sir William Hervey, an habitué of the printing world who was not indifferent to the success of this publishing enterprise. In 1598 this Hervey married the dowager Countess of Southampton and became, when she died in 1607, her sole legatee ; he then naturally assumed the task of presenting Shakespeare's poems without reviving unpleasant comment.　With this end in view he thought it advisable to modify the chronological order of the sonnets, whilst preserving the text of each.　By disarranging their order, the guiding thread which would have revealed the inner story of betrayed love was cut out and the public could not suspect the poet's illicit love affair nor his rivalry with his patron.

The dedication of the sonnets confirms that there was an understanding, not to say collusion between William Hervey, the possessor of at least part of the manuscript, Shakespeare, the author who had many times declared that he relied on these poems to glorify the man who inspired them, and the publisher Thorpe, who claims to be " well-intentioned " in launching the work.

Official permission to print the poems having been granted, and the usual fee of sixpence paid, the little volume was entered in the Stationers' register in the following terms :

Thomas Thorpe entred for his copie under thandes of Master Wilson and Master Lowndes Warden.　A Booke called Shakespeare's Sonnettes, VId.

The title page reads :

Shake-Speares Sonnets　Never before imprinted　At London by G. Eld for T. T. and are to be solde by John Wright dwelling at Christ Church gate 1609

Another bookseller, William Aspley obtained the right to sell half of the first edition.

This title is followed by a dedicatory page of careful composition, which has given rise to innumerable controversies since the second half of the nineteenth century.[1] The text is rendered obscure by the fact that all punctuation is absent; the full stop separating each word is purely ornamental:

TO. THE. ONLIE BEGETTER. OF.
THESE. INSUING. SONNETS.
MR. W.H. ALL. HAPPINESSE.
AND. THAT. ETERNITIE.
PROMISED.
BY.
OUR. EVER-LIVING. POET.
WISHETH.
THE. WELL-WISHING.
ADVENTURER. IN.
SETTING.
FORTH.
T.T.

In clearer terms the dedication should be read:

Mr. W. H. wishes all happiness and that eternity promised by our ever-living poet, to the only begetter of these ensuing sonnets.

After the space which follows, the editor, Thomas Thorpe, declares himself " The well-wishing adventurer in setting forth ", and signs himself " T.T."

The initials of William Hervey (Mr. W.H.) had already appeared in the dedication of another volume of poetry, set up by the same printer, George Eld. This dedication greatly resembles that of the Sonnets: the same words, the same typographic composition, the same form of thought: It is addressed to an old tutor of the Southampton family who had supervised the religious instruction of young Harry and his sister Mary, later Lady Arundel. The book, *A Four-Foulde Meditation*,[2] had been written in

---

[1] This controversy has been prolonged because the majority of editors have reproduced this dedicatory page with their own punctuation, sometimes making " Mr. W.H." the indirect object, instead of the subject of " Wisheth ". From the moment this personage became the source of inspiration and not the man who was presenting the *Sonnets*, the most unrealistic speculations have been put forward. For some " W.H." was a young actor, Willy Hughes, although such a person never existed in the profession; for others " W.H." represented the initials of William Himself.

[2] A Foure-Fould
Meditation,
Of the foure last things:
Houre of Death
Day of Judgment
Paines of Hell
Joys of Heaven
Shewing the estate of the Elect and Reprobate
Composed in a Divine Poeme
by R.S. the author of S. Peter's complaint
Imprinted at London By G. Eld. 1606.

collaboration by two prisoners in the Tower, Sir Philip Arundel [1] and the martyr-poet Robert Southwell, who, before his arrest and tragic end at Tyburn, had been confessor to the Arundel and Southampton families.

The dedication of the *Meditations* is thus worded :

> To the Right Worshipfull and
> Vertuous Gentleman, Mathew
> Saunders Esquire.
> W.H. wisheth, with long life, a prosperous
> achievement of his good desires.
>
> .   .   .   .
>
> Your Worships unfained affectionate
>
> W.H. [2]

The identity of William Hervey was well known to those who bought Southwell's book. His initials in the dedication of Shakespeare's Sonnets were a guarantee to the reader that this time he was not in possession of an unauthorized publication such as that of W. Jaggard. We have seen that according to the will of his wife, Lady Southampton, William Hervey was empowered to act as sole legatee and *in loco parentis* for her son and daughter. [3]

No person was in a better position to obtain at the same time Robert Southwell's *Meditations* and Shakespeare's *Sonnets*. He already had in hand the manuscript of the *Meditations*, and it is easy to detect the real feeling which prompted his dedicatory epistle to the worthy tutor of a family which he had himself entered. The death of his wife removed the last obstacle to the publication of the *Sonnets*. Lady Southampton might have disliked the idea of reviving a former scandal in which her " dear Harry " had been involved. But her demise in 1607, gave William Hervey carte blanche for

---

[1] Philip, Earl of Arundel (1557-95), husband of Anne Dacre, converted to Catholicism by Campion and condemned to death in 1589, passed his last days in the Tower. He succeeded in communicating with Robert Southwell by means of a dog, which, according to the jailer, went from one cell to another " to beg or send a blessing ". In fact, the good animal carried the rough sketch of the " Fourefould Meditation " in which Arundel's style and Southwell's emendations can be recognized. After the execution of Southwell and the death of Arundel, these verses naturally came into the possession of the Arundel and Southampton families.

[2] *The Fourefould Meditation*, of which one single copy was discovered in 1874 by Charles Edmonds, was published in the Isham collection with the help of the finder. Edmonds had already published other facsimiles of hitherto unknown editions of Marlowe and Shakespeare. Sir Sidney Lee, who had produced the theory that the initials " W.H." in the Sonnet dedication were those of William Hall, an obscure member of the Stationers' Company, was much disconcerted when he learned of Edmonds' discovery. It was indeed, hardly possible that Hall, an unknown publisher, should have had in his hands the manuscript of the Sonnets ; it was still more improbable that he should have had the unpublished text of the *Meditations*, when he had specialized in the publication of Protestant polemics.

[3] Dudley Carleton, always on the look-out for court news, declares when announcing the death of the old Countess of Southampton, that she left the most showy part of her possessions to her son, and the most considerable part to her husband. This will indicates her constant wish to maintain the prestige and dignity of the name which she always kept, and at the same time to improve the circumstances of her husband, William Hervey.

disposing of her personal effects, and he was not the man to let slip an opportunity of publishing the work of two such popular writers.[1]

The question may be asked: Why does " Mr." precede the initials " W.H." in the dedication of the *Sonnets* when in that of the *Meditations*, " W.H." alone appears ? The answer is simple ; in the first case it is the editor, Thomas Thorpe who signs the page and invokes the authority of William Hervey, whom by courtesy he calls " Master ". In the second it is William Hervey himself who signs the dedication of the *Meditations ;* he therefore quite properly uses no prefix.

In view of the important part played by William Hervey in Elizabeth's as in James's reign, it is surprising that his character and personality have left so few traces : a secret report on political activity in the Low Countries, addressed to the Queen from Lisbon where he was a prisoner and signed only with his initials, a personal letter to Robert Cecil concerning a reception held in honour of King James, and a lengthy will, are the only writings left by the third and last husband of Lady Southampton. This paucity of personal documents can be logically explained. His long letter to the Queen ends with this suggestive request : " May it please your Majesty to make a salamander of these my papers ", a reminder that no recusant catholic wished to incriminate himself by any writing. A man of letters and of taste, Hervey had long been a familiar in Southampton's home, before becoming an inmate. He had commanded the flagship *Garland* in the campaign against Spain during which his future stepson won his first laurels. He served with him in Ireland under Essex. In peace time, his taste drew him to literature. He was Sir Thomas Bodley's assistant in the foundation of the famous library to which Shakespeare's patron contributed a hundred pounds. A supporter of the Stuarts, he was created Lord Hervey of Kidbrooke by James I, and, thanks to his friendship with the Clopton family, was a frequent visitor to the neighbourhood of Stratford. He was therefore most suitably placed to act as link between author and printer when the day came to publish the *Sonnets*. He might perhaps be reproached for not having read the proofs more carefully, but such criticism is of little weight compared with the debt which posterity owes him.

Eleven copies of the original edition of the *Sonnets* are still in existence. The British Museum possesses those named *Grenville* and *Bright*. The Bodleian owns the *Caldecott* and the volume which belonged to Edmund Malone, in which this eminent scholar had bound together the *Sonnets, Venus and Adonis, Lucrece, Hamlet, Love's Labour's Lost, Pericles* and *A Yorkshire Tragedy*. The John Rylands Library boasts of a fine examplar— the Folger of Washington possesses three. The others belong to private persons in England and America.

Manuscript copies of certain sonnets continued to circulate after, as before Thorpe's publication. The eighth sonnet is incorporated in an album

---

[1] The author of the *Sonnets* has himself admitted that he had parted with his manuscript. He excuses this in sonnet 122, by saying that he needed no adjunct to remember what was indelibly graven on his mind tablets.

at the British Museum ; it bears a pseudo-latin title : *In Laudem Musice et opprobrium contempori eiusdem.* Similarly numbers 71 and 32, so intimately linked in thought, appear side by side in a collection acquired by J. Marsden Perry from Halliwell Phillipps. All these transcriptions show slight variations in spelling and punctuation, which lead to the belief that they were made from a different copy from that used by Thorpe.

One of the first biographers of Shakespeare and the second editor of his works, Nicholas Rowe, apologizes in his edition of 1709, for not giving more numerous details of the life of the poet, adding that the character of the man is best seen in his writings.

The search for an author's personality from his dramatic work alone is liable to lead to strange paradoxes. Which character of the vast repertoire should be considered as interpreter of the author's thoughts and feelings ? When Iago and Falstaff discourse on the need of money and the futility of a sound reputation, was Shakespeare giving his opinion on the education of youth ? When he puts into the mouth of the tedious Polonius, the long and banal observations, notorious for their mediocrity, was it his intention to describe his ideal of a statesman ? Surely not. And yet, there have been teachers who quote passages spoken by Iago and Falstaff as expressions of true wisdom, and a prime minister once chose as the " finest examples of noble idealism " the prosaic pronouncements of Ophelia's father.

In order not to wander aimlessly in the labyrinth of a work as varied as Shakespeare's, the explorer is obliged to seek a guiding clue to enable him to distinguish between impersonal ideas on the one hand, and the expression of the author's own thought on the other. Wordsworth in his sonnet in praise of this form of verse rightly says :

With this key, Shakespeare unlocked his heart.

The *Sonnets,* taken as a whole, constitute a human document of inestimable value : the sentimental history of the greatest of poets. Apart from the romance which they unfold, many single poems are masterpieces in themselves. But once in possession of the key to this " Song of Songs ", when the three actors who play their parts in it are known, when the setting in which they appear is made familiar to the reader and when many of the spectators have also been identified, then the whole drama plays itself out before the reader's eyes.

CHAPTER VII

SHAKESPEARE'S STAGE CRAFT

Members of the company—Burbage—Shakespeare—Kempe—The other actors
—Administration and shareholders—Theatres—Stage, properties and costumes—
Shakespearian methods.

IF Shakespeare quickly arrived at the summit of success and retained
a position there throughout his life, this was because his talents were
essentially theatrical. Experienced as dramatist, actor and producer,
he exploited all the resources of the profession, guided like Molière by his
knowledge of the psychology of his audience. Instead of being astonished
that a mere actor could have written masterpieces, it would be more logical
to wonder if he could have created them in any other situation.

At the beginning of his career in London, he felt more at home among
theatrical folk than among the university intellectuals who claimed a monopoly of play-writing. His fellow-actors recognized him as a born leader,
capable of bringing their art to perfection, a good friend, full of sensibility and understanding.

The company he entered and never left played under three different
names, according to the patron of the moment. First they were " Lord
Strange's Men ". When this patron died, the company passed under the
aegis of Henry Carey, Lord Hunsdon and the actors were known as the
" Lord Chamberlain's Servants ", and this name remained when George
Carey succeeded his father. With the accession of James I, the company
was officially recognized, obtained a virtual monopoly of theatrical production, and the members were then known as the " King's Players ".

It was in the Shoreditch Theatre that the troupe began its activities.
Shakespeare, Richard Burbage and William Sly succeeded in attracting to
them William Kempe, Thomas Pope and George Bryan [1] who had belonged
to " Lord Leicester's Servants " ; later Augustin Phillips and Henry Condell,
members of the Lord Admiral's company, and John Hemings,[2] from the

---

[1] These three actors accompanied Leicester on his unlucky mission to the Low Countries.
With five others, they passed three months in the service of Frederick II, King of Denmark.
Kempe is mentioned in contemporary correspondence as " Don Gulielmo " and " Will,
Lord Leicester's jesting player ".

[2] Sonne and heire of George Heminge of Draytwich in the countye of Worcester Gent.
of long tyme servant to Queen Elizabeth of happie memory, also to King James her Royal
successor and to King Charles his Sonne. (E. K. Chambers, *The Elizabethan Stage*, vol. ii,
p. 321.)

Queen's, joined this nucleus.   Some fifteen more players, the principal being
John Lowin, Joseph Taylor, Alexander Cook, Samuel Gilburne and
William Cowley were soon added.[1] With the exception of Kempe, all
remained faithful to the company and died in harness.

From its earliest days, a corporate spirit reigned in this homogeneous
association, a veritable school of dramatic art where the player of each
principal rôle recruited and instructed his understudy.   Thus Shakespeare
taught John Lowin and Joseph Taylor ; Burbage, Nicholas Tooley and
William Ostler ; Kempe initiated Richard Cowley and Robert Armin ;
Augustin Phillips handed on his theatrical and musical knowledge to Samuel
Gilburne ; Heminge passed the torch to John Rice.   These apprentices
were evidently well chosen, since Lowin [2] achieved great success as Morose
in *The Silent Woman* and as the hero of *Volpone,* while Taylor [3] was un-
rivalled in the part of the valet Mosca.   The sharp-tongued Marston went
so far as to say that these actors were " too good " for Jonson's plays.

If Shakespeare did not play the leading parts in the company of which
he was the moving spirit, it was evidently because Richard Burbage seemed
cut out for rôles such as Romeo, Bassanio, or Henry V.   This actor interpreted the characters of heroes and lovers with so much warmth, that he
frequently reduced his fellow-players to tears on the stage.   One day, when
he threw himself into Ophelia's grave, a spectator jumped to his feet to
prevent a real calamity.

He was one year older than Shakespeare,[4] but looked younger ; he had
a perfect stage presence for heroic parts.   An anecdote often repeated after
1590 proves his strong character and determination to defend his father's
interests against officialdom.   Two men appeared with an order from court,
claiming " one part " of the theatrical receipts ; Burbage received them
broom in hand.   He told the story thus : " I gave them their part with the

---

[1] Here is the list of principal actors as it was given in 1623 by the two seniors : William
Shakespeare, Richard Burbage, John Hemminge, Augustine Phillips, William Kempe,
Thomas Poope, George Bryan, Henry Condall, William Slye, Richard Cowley, John Lowin,
Samuel Gross, Alexander Cook, Samuel Gilburne, Robert Armin, William Ostler, Nathan
Field, John Underwood, Nicholas Tooley, William Ecclestone, Joseph Taylor, Robert
Benfield, Robert Goughe, Richard Robinson, John Shancke, John Rice.

[2] Betterton, the theatrical star of the Restoration period, boasted of having been instructed
by Taylor in the rôle of Hamlet, and by Lowin in that of Henry VIII : Hamlet, being performed by Mr. Betterton, Sir William (having seen Mr. Taylor of the Blackfriars company
act it, who, being instructed by the author Mr. Shakespeare) taught Mr. Betterton in every
particle of it, which, by his exact performance of it, gained him esteem and reputation.
. . . The part of the King Henry the VIII, " was so right and justly done by Mr. Betterton,
he being Instructed in it by Sir William, who had it from Old Mr. Lowen, that had his
Instructions from Mr. Shakespear himself, that I dare and will aver, none can, or will come
near him in this Age." (John Downes, *Roscius Anglicanus or An Historical Review of the
Stage,* 1606-1706 (1711), p. 24.)

[3] E. K. Chambers, *The Elizabethan Stage,* vol. ii, pp. 345-346.

[4] The records of the baptism of Richard Burbage and his brother Cuthbert have recently
been discovered in the register of the parish of Saint-Stephen-Colemen ; it was Mr. J. H.
Morrisson who was lucky enough to be able to announce his find in 1931, thus putting an
end to long discussion : " Christenynge of Richard Burdbidge the sonne of James Burdbidge
the XXVIII (28) of Maye 1562. Christenynge of Cutbart Burbidge the child of James
Burbidge the 15 of June anno ut supra (1565).

handle, and they fled without asking for the rest." [1]   On another occasion he pulled the nose of a busybody who tried to intervene and declared himself ready to defy anyone who dared meddle with the business of his father's theatre, even the Lord Admiral himself.

His personal charm explained the love at first sight of Juliet and Rosalind, and made plausible in *Richard III* the immediate conquest of the widow of the Prince of Wales by his murderer.   Burbage was so well known as interpreter of *Richard III*, that a guide, showing the bishop of Oxford over the battlefield of Bosworth, told his astonished auditor : " It was here that Burbage offered his Kingdom for a horse ", and, " It was here that Burbage was killed ".[2]

Another anecdote gathered from the diary of a London student confirms to what extent the tragedian's personality was identified with that of King Richard III.   One day it happened that Shakespeare was at the house of a woman for whose favours the two friends were rivals, when Richard Burbage knocked at the door shouting : " Open in the name of King Richard ! " Shakespeare replied : " William the Conqueror always precedes Richard ! " [3]

Shakespeare perhaps sometimes felt a certain bitterness at the prestige enjoyed by his leading man, and in this passage of *Richard II* he may be referring to his own experience :

> As in a theatre, the eyes of men,
> After a well-graced actor leaves the stage
> Are idly bent on him that enters next
> Thinking his prattle to be tedious ;
> Even so, or with much more contempt, men's eyes
> Did scowl on gentle Richard—
> No joyful tongue gave him his welcome home.
>   (*Richard II*, Act v, Sc. 2)

Whatever may have been his feelings of rivalry as an actor, Shakespeare the dramatist never neglected an opportunity of turning the tragedian's popularity to account.   When Burbage was no longer able to create the illusion of youth necessary for the part of Hamlet, Shakespeare did not hesitate to increase the age of the Prince to suit that of his interpreter.   It was because Burbage had become stout, and short of breath and was obliged to interrupt the duel scene to wipe his streaming brow, that Gertrude offers him her handkerchief with a remark which is difficult to explain if one is ignorant of these facts.

His star continued brilliant even in its decline ; nobody dared come forward to replace him as long as he illumined the stage.   In 1618 when at last he died, the Lord Chamberlain, although blasé in theatrical matters

---

[1] E. K. Chambers, *The Elizabethan Stage*, vol. ii, p. 307.

[2] For when he would have said, King Richard died
And called, a horse, a horse ! he Burbage cried !
       Poems of Richard Corbet, Bishop of Oxford and Norwich.

[3] John Manningham's Diary (Harleian MSS. 5353).

because of his office, declared that it was impossible for him to see any new tragic actor in the rôles Burbage had created without shedding tears.

This player is mentioned in Shakespeare's will on an equal footing with Heminge and Condell. If he did not collaborate with these senior members of the company in editing the folio of 1623, it was because death had intervened. Two epitaphs were proposed for his tomb. The first laments that " a world disappeared with him " and enumerates his great impersonations ; [1] the other is as theatrical as it is laconic ; it consists of two words : " Exit Burbage."

Shakespeare's histrionic gifts were of another kind. Nature had not designed him for a " juvenile lead ". His noble bearing, his maturity, even his premature baldness, marked him for kingly parts or those of " reverend seniors ". In his own plays he is said to have played the Ghost in *Hamlet*, a part which, according to Rowe, he acted with consummate art. Many spectators must consider the murdered king merely a secondary character in the play, but if the text of *Hamlet* is read attentively, or better, if one has had the privilege of seeing the rôle of the ghost well played, it is impossible not to be struck by its possibilities. Rigid in his armour, without gestures and almost motionless, the actor must, solely by the inflection of his voice, give the impression of remoteness from earthly affairs, inspire fear and arouse pity merely by telling the story of the murder, denouncing the murderer, and appealing for mercy on a guilty wife ; to be, in short, both terrible and tender, austere and human. [2]

In Ben Jonson's comedy, *Every Man in His Humour*, Shakespeare undertook the creation of the amusing character of Knowell senior. If the rôle of the murdered King of Denmark requires austere dignity, restrained passion and great delicacy, that of Knowell calls for very different qualities. It is a character of pure comedy, demanding humour and satirical subtlety

---

[1] A Funeral Elegye on ye Death of the famous actor Richard Burbedge who died on Saturday in Lent the 13 of march 1618 :

> He's gone and with him what a world is dead
> Which he revived, to be revived so,
> No more. Young Hamlet, old Hieronimo,
> King Lear, the grieved Moor and more beside
> That lived in him have now forever died.

> Oft have I seen him leap into a grave
> Suiting the person that he seemed to have
> Of a sad lover with so true an eye
> That then I would have sworn he meant to die
> Oft have I seen him play his part in jeast
> So lively that spectators and the rest
> Of his sad crew whilst he but seemed to bleed
> Amazed thought even he had died indeed.

Manuscript formerly belonging to Henry Huth, printed in the *Gentleman's Magazine* of June 1825.

[2] When the company were reduced in number for provincial tours, the actor who played the ghost was free early and had then to take the part of the First Player ; this may explain why Hamlet exclaims at the arrival of the strolling players : " O, my old friend ! Thy face is valanced since I saw thee last : comest then to beard me in Denmark ? " Shakespeare probably reappeared the second time without make-up.

and is, one might say, a precursor of Molière's Philinte or Chrysale. In the tragedy of *Sejanus*, Shakespeare played the Emperor Tiberius ; his name precedes that of Burbage on the list given by Jonson of the actors in his tragedy.

Two texts suggest that the author himself occasionally played the part of Falstaff ; none but a first-rate actor would have dared to undertake this overwhelming rôle.[1]

Shakespeare admits that he sometimes arrayed himself as a jester :

> Alas ! 'tis true, I have gone here and there
> And made myself a motley to the view. (Sonnet 110)

Tradition has it that he played Touchstone in *As You Like It*, the clown whose lively and philosophical art contrasted with the buffoonery practised by Kempe. This in no way invalidates the testimony of Gilbert Shakespeare who said that he saw Will act the part of Adam the old gardener in this same play, since the two characters are never on the stage simultaneously.

To sum up, Shakespeare the actor possessed a talent versatile enough to interpret the most diverse characters, excluding youthful rôles. Furthermore, his contemporaries have not omitted to underline the qualities which he displayed before the spectator.

Henry Chettle declares, as we have seen,

Because my selfe have seene his demeanor no lesse civill than he excelent in the qualitie he professes : Besides divers of worship have reported, his uprightnes of dealing, which argues his honesty, and his facetious grace in writting, that aprooves his Art.

Michael Drayton asserted that his comic vein was as felicitous as his tragic rages were powerful. Christopher Beeston, historian of the stage, claimed that he was superior to his rival Ben Jonson ; and Jonson himself, when the death of the poet put an end to any rivalry wrote :

> —All the Muses still were in their prime
> When, like Apollo, he came forth to warm
> Our ears, or like a Mercury to charm—— [2]

Finally, in an epigram published in 1610 and addressed " to our English Terence, Mr. Will Shakespeare ", John Davies of Hereford declares :

> Some say (good Will) which I, in sport, do sing
> Had'st thou not plaid some Kingly parts in sport,
> Thou hadst bin a companion for a King :
> And, beene a King among the meaner sort.
> Some others raile ; but, raile as they thinke fit,
> Thou hast no rayling, but, a raigning Wit : . . .[3]

[1] Sir Tobie Mathew, whose correspondence so well reflects the spirit of the times, remarks when quoting a passage from Falstaff's part : " As our excellent author Sir John Falstaff used to say." And Lady Southampton, in a letter to her husband, tells him a story about his " friend Sir John Falstaff ". An old theatrical tradition names Heminge as interpreter of this character.

[2] *Ode to the memory of my beloved, the author* (dedicatory pages, Folio 1623).

[3] *The Scourge of Folly*, p. 76.

The same John Davies remarked in 1603 that Shakespeare's poetry and Burbage's painting redeemed the opprobrium hitherto attached to their profession, and showed the possibility of being at the same time actor and gentleman. Burbage was indeed a painter in his odd moments. One of his canvases is preserved in the Dulwich Museum, and the portrait of Shakespeare which belonged to the Duke of Chandos, now at the National Gallery, is generally attributed to his brush. At a tournament in 1613 the Earl of Rutland appeared carrying a shield richly ornamented with his coat of arms and a motto specially composed for the occasion. The verse was Shakespeare's and the painting Burbage's, as shown in the account book of the steward of Belvoir castle.[1]

When Shakespeare, in Sonnet 110 laments the demands of the public, and the bad taste of his age, when he admits he is prisoner of his profession, and often obliged to debase his art, no doubt he had in mind William Kempe who had lately gathered the laurels of the famous Tarleton.

This great comic actor Kempe was one of those elements with which Shakespeare had to reckon. Kempe was, moreover, admirably seconded by Richard Cowley, as pale, tall and thin as he himself was muscular and thick set. It was Kempe who undertook the rôles of Nick Bottom, Peter in *Romeo and Juliet*, the first grave-digger in *Hamlet*, Lancelot Gobbo, Launce in the *Two Gentlemen of Verona*, and Sir Toby Belch. Cowley took those of the second grave-digger, old Gobbo, cousin Slender and Sir Andrew Aguecheek. The third comic parts seem to have been given to Thomas Pope.

An indefatigable dancer, Kempe undertook the journey from London to Norwich without abandoning the rhythmic step of the Morris dance. In this exploit which lasted nine days, he was followed by a large crowd and official timekeepers. On his triumphant arrival, he was given the freedom of the city, and received an annual pension in memory of his astonishing prowess. His pamphlet *Kempe's Nine Daies Wonder* written in a lively and impulsive style as a reply to the attacks of Protestant preachers, and addressed to his beautiful pupil Miss Fytton, is full of literary allusions and witticisms, showing that Shakespeare's fellow-actor, who, by definition, was not the most learned in the company, could plume himself on being no ignoramus. It is understandable that faced with such a popular figure, Shakespeare felt obliged to write large comic rôles for his buffoon. Willynilly he had always to make a place and a large place even in his tragedies for William Kempe, who was a partner in the theatre's administration. This talented acrobat boasted of a heart as light as his heels. The public acclaimed him ; his mere entrance on the stage sufficed to convulse the audience. If he did not appear, to dance his famous jig and proceed to a long clowning act, the whole pit felt they had not been given their money's worth.

Kempe added to his rôles a quantity of asides, funny or coarse, adorned his speeches with numerous tricks of sleight of hand, or intentional clumsiness, for he was an excellent conjuror and acrobat.

---

[1] See Chapter XIX.

If there is a play in which his style would seem quite out of place, it is *Hamlet* ; yet William Kempe had his rôle in it, and his partner, Richard Cowley also.   It is to Shakespeare's credit that he was able to give his two clowns command of the stage in the most moving scene of the tragedy without interrupting the harmony of the whole.   More than this, the grave-diggers lugubrious but humorous dialogue provokes a poignant effect by its contrast with Hamlet s musings on Yorick's skull, an effect which never fails to impress the spectator.   What a sensation must have been produced in those days when the scene, written by the great master of tragedy, was acted by a comedian of the capacity of William Kempe !

Shakespeare would not have had so much to complain of if his clown, intoxicated with success, were not continually departing from the lines which had been written for him.   But nothing could restrain him when he felt in an animated mood.   Hamlet's recommendations to the players about to act the " murder of Gonzago " repeat what Shakespeare, author and stage manager, must have often said in vain to his irrepressible comedian.

> *Hamlet (to Players)*
> And doe you heare ?   Let not your Clowne speake
> More then is set downe, there be of them I can tell you
> That will laugh themselves, to set on some
> Quantitie of barren spectators to laugh with them,
> Albeit there is some necessary point in the Play
> Then to be observed : O t'is vile, and shewes
> A pittiful ambition in the foole that useth it.
> And then you have some agen that keeps one sute
> Of jeasts, as a man is knowne by one sute of
> Apparell, and Gentlemen quotes his jeasts downe
> In their tables, before they come to the play, as thus :
> Cannot you stay till I eate my porrige ? and, you owe me
> A quarters wages : and, my coate wants a cullison :
> And, your beere is sowre : and, blabbering with his lips,
> And thus keeping in his cinkapase of jeasts,
> When, God knows, the warme Clowne cannot make a jest
> Unlesse by chance, as the blinde man catcheth a hare : [1]

Whether it was because of the severe criticisms of the author, or because success turned his head, or because he hoped to triumph more surely in the rival camp, the fact remains that at the turn of the century, when the political storm began to rumble, Kempe left his comrades, sold his shares in the company, and offered his services to Henslowe.

This defection, the first suffered by Shakespeare's troop, did not benefit the famous clown.   He died in poverty (November 1603), after having borrowed twenty shillings from his new patron.   However, as long as Kempe counted as one of the servants of Lord Strange or of the Lord Chamberlain, he drew a share of the benefits, on the same footing as Shakespeare and

---

[1] *Hamlet* (1603), Quarto, f. F.2.

Burbage. The first payment of which an official account has been kept, is thus set down :

To William Kempe, William Shakespeare and Richard Burbage, servants of the Lord Chamberlain, and on the order of the Council of the fifteenth day of March 1594, for two comedies or interludes presented by them before Her Majesty in the season of this last Christmas, to wit Saint Stephen's day and the Innocent's day . . . twelve pounds, six shillings, eight pence ; and as a gratuity from Her Majesty : six pounds, thirteen shillings, four pence. . . .[1]

The two senior actors Heminge and Condell, whose names are always linked for posterity, were the pillars of the company. Together they raised a lasting monument of affectionate gratitude, the first complete edition of the works of their " friend and fellow " Shakespeare. They shared the responsibilities of the company's administration, and appeared on the stage in the most important parts after those reserved for Burbage. They probably played Montague and Capulet in *Romeo*, the two Dukes in *As You Like It*, Horatio and Polonius in *Hamlet*, the doge and Brabantio in *Othello*. Condell achieved a personal success as Polonius. Neither limited himself to Shakespearian plays. They successfully interpreted Jonson, Dekker and Webster and the memory of their triumphs lasted until the reign of Charles I, for. after having figured in James's funeral procession, it was they who received from his son's hands the letters patent renewing the licence of the royal theatre. John Heminge died on October 9th, 1630 : Condell had died three years earlier.

The direction of the company then fell to John Lowin and Joseph Taylor, who saw the theatre in eclipse during the harsh Protectorate of Cromwell, and contributed to its renaissance after the Restoration of the Stuarts.

The Dulwich and Ashmolean museums possess precious iconographic documents revealing the characters of three members of the company : these are the portraits of William Slye, John Lowin and Nathan Field.

Slye's face is full of character and intelligence ; his hair is shown red like Judas's, as tradition ordained for the villain's rôle. His features appear mobile, his expressive eyes seem to hesitate between sarcasm and deceit. An excellent actor without a shadow of doubt, and one of the most useful, he was well equipped to play Claudius, Tybalt, Iago, Edmund, or King John. In private life he remained consistent : he was almost the only actor of the troupe with no wife or children, and he entrusted his last wishes to two notorious courtesans.

John Lowin was of another sort. Shakespeare's understudy obviously desired to imitate the great man as closely as possible. His picture painted in 1640 shows him at the age of sixty-three in a suit of black velvet. Hair, moustache, and underlip tuft are cut like Shakespeare's in the folio engraving.

---

[1] Pipe Office Roll, declared accounts. Shakespeare's company, the Lord Chamberlain's men, gave thirty-two performances at Elizabeth's court, while the Lord Admiral's men only appeared twenty times, and all the other companies put together only thirteen times in the same interval of time.

The face with its serious expression, is framed in a fine starched muslin collar, also reminiscent of the Droeshout portrait. The cravat is adorned with four little bunches of small pearls. The last survivor of Shakespeare's old troop, it was Lowin who continued the tradition, and told those who cared to listen the fascinating story of his fellow actors—up to the year 1669, for he attained the ripe age of ninety-one.

The third portrait is that of Nathan Field, a late-comer to the company. Together with William Ostler, he deserted the " Children of the Chapel " about 1604, preferring to join their more famous rivals. His costume of embroidered cambric, his pretty face, imaginative and sensitive, his wide open eyes, ready to sparkle or to soften into tears, all indicate the actor capable of assuming feminine rôles. When, however, it was a question of defending his profession, he did so passionately. To a preacher named Thomas Sutton who forbade him the sacraments he replied :

You have so laboured . . . to banish me from mine own parish church, that my conscience cannot be quiet within me. . . . pardon me sir, if . . . in patience and humbleness of spirit I expostulate a little with you.

You waded very low with hatred against us when you ransacked Hell to find the register . . . wherein our souls are written *damned*. You might more easily *have found our names written in the Book of Life.* and herein is my faith the stronger, because in God's whole volume, which I have studied as my best part, I find not any trade of life except conjurers, sorcerers and witches (*Ipso facto*) Damned, nay not expressly spoken against, but only the abuses and bad uses of them, and in that point I defend not ours, nor should have disagreed with you, if you had only struck at the corrupt branches, and not laid your axe to the root of the tree.[1]

Kempe's desertion was not a misfortune for Shakespeare, as it allowed him to treat the rôle of the clown in a new and original fashion. His successor, Robert Armin had nothing in common with the " athletic buffoon". He was a delicate, even sickly intellectual who struck a pathetic and ironic note instead of perpetually raising crude laughter. With him, Shakespeare's clowns changed their aspect to become an essential element in the development of the plot. The faithful companion of Lear's vicissitudes is a striking example.

The feminine parts were naturally reserved for the youngest players. In this employment, Robert Gough, Alexander Cooke and George Bryan were replaced by William Ostler, Nathan Field and Edmund Shakespeare, who in their turn played the parts of Juliet, Portia, Rosalind and their confidantes. Thanks to them, Shakespeare overcame the difficulty caused by the English convention forbidding women on the stage.[2] If Thomas Nashe

[1] S.P. Dom. fac. I, vol. 89, no. 105.

[2] In a report to Bishop Laud, the Protestant Thomas Brand, thus gives an account of the first women who had the audacity to appear on the stage of the Blackfriars theatre in 1629 :

" Glad I am to say that they were hissed, hooted and pippin pelted from the stage so that I do not think that they will soon be ready to try the same again." *Annals of the English Stage from Thomas Betterton to Edmund Kean.* (Dr. Doran, London, 1887.)

is to be believed, the absence of the feminine element, not only had no detrimental effect on the drama, but actually improved it.

Our players are not as the players beyond sea, a sort of squirting baudie Comedians, that have whores and common Curtizens to playe womens partes, and forbeare no immodest speech, or unchast action that may procure laughter, but our Sceane is more statelye furnisht than ever it was in the time of Roscius, our representations honourable, and full of gallant resolution, not consisting like theirs of Pantaloun, a Whore, and a Zanie, but of Emperours, Kings and Princes : Whole true Tragedies (Sophocleo Cothurno) they do vaunt.[1]

Although the parts of shepherdesses, wives, queens and princesses were necessarily reserved for the youngest actors, the youth trained to imitate the bearing, gestures and mien of a gracious beauty was in possession of an ephemeral art which he would soon be obliged to hand over to a beardless boy who still had a treble voice and small stature. With all due respect to Nashe, the English convention constituted a difficulty for the dramatist. But it took some time before the public grew accustomed to seeing women on the stage.[2] Thomas Jordan, presenting his wife before the footlights apologized for this innovation in a prologue :

> Must we in England wicked deem
> What earns in France both glory and esteem ?

However able the interpreter, it was difficult for him to maintain the gestures, voice and attitude of a young girl throughout five acts, and to assist and relieve him. Shakespeare introduced the device of disguise, which, perhaps, he abused : Viola, Rosalind, Jessica, Imogen and Julia, could not fail to feel more at ease in breeches. When Portia returns to Belmont in the darkness, she feels obliged to excuse her over-deep voice with a jest :

> He knows me, as the blind man knows the cuckoo,
> By the bad voice. . . .

In the second version of *Hamlet*, the prince, after having welcomed the players, addresses the actor who takes the part of the queen :

What my young lady and mistress ! By'r lady, your ladyship is nearer heaven than when I saw you last, by the altitude of a chopine. Pray God, your voice, like a piece of uncurrent gold, be not crackt within the ring.

He might have added : " Pray God also that your beard does not grow too quickly ! " for there is a story that at a performance of *Henry VIII* before the king and his court the audience waited so long for the play to begin that the king would have lost patience had not the clown given proof of inspiration by turning the ill humour of his majesty and his courtiers into laughter :

Pardon, Sire, a thousand pardons ! but our good queen Katherine has not yet finished shaving !

---

[1] *Pierce Penilesse his Supplication to the Divell*, 1592, p. 27.
[2] Women were admitted on the English stage in 1661.

The names of the actors who permitted Shakespeare to introduce music into his plays are shown in various documents : The manager Phillips specialized in this art, assisted by his friend Samuel Gilburne. James Sands was also his pupil ; and from one of the stage directions of the 1600 Quarto, we learn that Jack Wilson sang the charming madrigal in *Much Ado About Nothing* as the page Balthasar.[1] In *A Midsummer Night's Dream* he had another opportunity of displaying the voice which made him celebrated in the time of Charles I.[2]

Open-hearted gaiety, cordial understanding and solidarity were dominant qualities in Shakespeare's company. The actors, more middle-class than bohemian, prided themselves on being good and respectable fathers of families. Burbage and his wife, Winifred, had eight children : Heminge was proud of his marriage with the widow of the celebrated actor Knell. In 1611, he baptized his twelfth child. His daughter Thomasine[3] chose as her husband William Ostler from her father's company, the same Ostler of whom Davies said :

> If thou play'st thy dying part as well
> As thy stage parts, thou hast no part in Hell.

Robert Gough married Elizabeth Phillips, the manager's daughter, and, like his fellows Cooke and Cowley, raised four children.

The majority of these men had an ample income if one may judge from their London residences. The four houses occupied by Shakespeare before he acquired his beautiful mansion at Blackfriars testify to an ever increasing fortune. Condell, besides two properties in the centre of town, possessed a country house at Fulham beside the river ; Phillips had one at Mortlake.

The notaries' deeds and the actors' wills demonstrate that their families' welfare and the desire to help their colleagues, were a constant preoccupation. At least four of them were church wardens of their parish ; John Rice left the stage after Shakespeare's death, to become ordained in the Church of England. Henry Condell, who appears to have been the real man of business of the company, was chosen as executor by three of the actors, Tooley, Cooke and Underwood ; he himself asked a similar service of his friend Heminge,[4] and his widow Elizabeth Condell turned to John Lowin.

The will of Augustine Phillips resembles all those of his fellow-actors

---

[1] E. F. Rimvault, *Biblioteca Madrigaliana* Boston (1875).

[2] The city records of Lincoln describe how because of a Sunday performance of the *Midsummer Night's Dream* Mr. Wilson was condemned to sit in the pillory his feet in chains wearing an asse's head before an armful of hay, a placard attached to his chest explaining that he had dared to take the part of Bottom in a play given on the Lord's day in the presence of a select audience which was also fined.

[3] This same Thomasine obtained a hundred and fifty pounds in damages from Sir Walter Raleigh's son who had insulted her. (E. K. Chambers, *The Elizabethan Stage*, vol. ii, p. 323.)

[4] Heminge and Condell, who died within three years of each other, ask in their wills, to be buried at the church of St. Mary the Virgin, at night and in Christian manner. The latter is an indication, if not proof, that they wished to have Catholic absolution.

including that of Shakespeare. He chose as executors, Heminge, Burbage and Slye who each received from the testator a silver cup worth five pounds. Shakespeare and Condell were both left a thirty shilling gold piece. His three pupils were better treated. Christopher Beeston [1] received forty shillings ; Samuel Gilburne the same sum and a coat of mouse-grey velvet, a doublet of white taffeta, a suit of black taffeta, a purple cloak, a sword, a poignard, a viol and a double-bass ; James Sands, forty shillings, a guitar, a drum and a lute. Five pounds were to be distributed between the employees of the troupe. All these legacies, among which the poor of his own village were not forgotten, did not prevent the manager from leaving his widow and children very comfortably off.

The administrative complement of the theatre consisted of three technicians, the stage-manager, the wardrobe master and the prompter, who were all, in case of need, able to play subordinate parts on the stage, for in this crew nobody was idle.

Only one woman, and she was already middle-aged, seems to have had a permanent situation in the company. The widow Elizabeth Wheaton, former servant of Henry Condell was installed at the receipt of custom and lodged at the theatre where she occupied the post of doorkeeper, in summer at the " Globe ", in winter at " Blackfriars ".[2]

The eight principal shareholders were Burbage, Shakespeare, Kempe, Bryan, Pope, Phillips, Heminge and Condell. They possessed unequal and variable numbers of shares or part shares. Those who had none, watched and waited their chance to acquire some.[3]

Ben Jonson in *Poetaster*, one of the most biting of his satires, mocks at the actors and their wish to share in the receipts. Heminge, easily recognizable, is named " Seven shares and a half ", and a so-called impresario, Captain Tucca, proposes, when founding a company, that the actors should pay for their costumes and demands for himself two shares in return for his " countenance ".[4] Even Hamlet laughingly claims the right of being a shareholder in the itinerant troupe for which he has just written a scene, and Horatio retorts that half a share would be sufficient reward.[5]

These shares were independent of the interests which the actors could

[1] Christopher Baston, nicknamed the " Living Chronicle of the stage " provided the biographer John Aubrey with very valuable information.

[2] One reads in Henry Condell's will that he bequests to an old servant, Elizabeth Wheaton a mourning dress, forty shillings in money, desiring that during her lifetime she will continue in the place which she occupies and that she will exercise the same privileges which she at present enjoys in the houses of the " Blackfriars " in London, and the " Globe " on Bankside.

Condell died in 1635, and, eight years later, Elizabeth Condell, his widow, confirmed his wishes with regard to Mistress Wheaton, by adding a feather bed, two pairs of sheets, two blankets, two aprons and a silver cup with ten pounds for the education of her daughter.

[3] It was Robert Armin who acquired Kempe's shares.

[4] *Poetaster*, Act III, Sc. 1.

[5] Hamlet : Would not this, sir, and a forest of feathers, if the rest of my fortunes turne Turke with me, with provinciall Roses on my raz'd shoes, get me a fellowship in a cry of players ?

Horatio : Halfe a share.   (*Hamlet*, second version, 1605.)

have in the theatre itself, for the management of the company was the tenant of the theatre. Shakespeare held shares both in his company and in the theatre. The annual income received by an important shareholder would be about one hundred and fifty pounds. Consequently in prosperous times, Shakespeare, who enjoyed the revenues of the " Globe " and the " Black-friars ", earned from this double enterprise a sum of about three hundred pounds exclusive of the payments for court performances, always well rewarded.

In the capacity of author, he received from four to six pounds for each original or adapted play provided for the company.[1] In this way, according to Sir Sidney Lee, he increased his annual income by perhaps twenty pounds. When it is remembered that the author of *The Merry Wives of Windsor* speaks of a man with three hundred a year as rich,[2] it is apparent that Shakespeare could not complain of lack of financial success.

Yet many bitter disappointments awaited the pioneers of this new art in their theatrical enterprises. Attracting the public was a relatively simple thing, but to carry on an unequal struggle against hatred and prejudice, encountering the severity of regulations and injunctions, was more difficult.

A lucky star guided Shakespeare at the outset of his career to James Burbage, proprietor of the " Theatre " where, at this time, the servants of Lord Strange were playing. Fifty yards away stood a little sister theatre, the " Curtain ", built against the ancient ramparts, whose name is connected, in the history of literature, with performances of *Romeo and Juliet*. This playhouse also belonged to Burbage, and was reserved for more refined plays. Zealous reformers viewed these first cradles of dramatic art with suspicion. Besides attacking the morality of plays and players, they knew that this art was directly descended from the mystery and morality plays of the old church, and they suspected a sinister connection between the playhouses and the proscribed faith. Anthony Munday describes the theatrical district as frequented by two proscribed priests who, sometimes in their patron's livery, sometimes disguised as fine gentlemen or in any garb best suited to their purpose, came to say mass and hear confession before or after the performance.[3]

The Lord Mayor of London complains of them in these terms :

They are the ordinary places for vagrant persons, masterless men, thieves, horse-stealers, whoremongers, cozeners, coney catchers, contrivers of treason, and other idle and dangerous persons to meet together and to make their matches to the great displeasure of Almighty God and the hurt and annoyance of her majestie's

---

[1] Quoting Oldys as authority, Malone asserts that Shakespeare only received five pounds for his *Hamlet*.

" Five pounds was, moreover, a good average purchase price for a play. Ben Jonson was much laughed at after the sensational success of his *Humours*, for trying to obtain the price of ten pounds for his own works."

[2]   O what a world of vile ill-favour'd faults
       Looks handsome in three hundred pounds a year !
                              (*The Merry Wives of Windsor*, Act III, Sc. 4)

[3] Anthony Munday, *Discovery of Campion*.

people, which cannot be prevented nor discovered by the governors of the city
for that they are out of the city's jurisdiction.[1]

The Harleian collection of manuscripts contains this report to Walsingham.

The daily abuse of Stage plays is such an offence to the Godly, and so great
a hindrance to the gospel, as the Papists do exceedingly rejoice at the blemish
thereof and not without cause ; for every day in the week the player's bills are
set up in sundry places of the city. . . .

The trumpets sound to the stages, wherat the wicked faction laughs for joy
while the godly weep for sorrow. Woe is me ! The play houses are pestered
when churches are naked ; at the one it is not possible to get a place at the other
void seats are plenty.

In spite of hostility from puritans, public authorities and officials, the
successes of Shakespeare's company at the " Theatre " and at the " Curtain "
became firmly established. It held its own against its formidable rivals,
though Philip Henslowe and his company at the " Rose " were never
disturbed.

Whether it was that Shakespeare and his fellows felt themselves insecure
at Shoreditch, or whether they took into account the increasing favour of the
more cultivated part of their audience, the fact remains that in either 1595
or 1596 they determined to build another playhouse in the centre of London,
near the palace of Westminster. Between them they raised the necessary
capital, and acquired a site next to the ancient monastery of Blackfriars.
This secularized monastery had become a residential quarter. There they
built a convenient stage in a building attractive and almost private in appearance.

Alas, no sooner was the work finished, than their right to use the site
for theatrical purposes was abruptly refused by a more powerful authority
than that of the Lord Mayor and his henchmen. The Prime Minister, Lord
Burleigh himself, favourably received a protest made by certain neighbours
against the presence of players in the vicinity of their residences.

If the theatre was so prejudicial to the morality of the neighbourhood, it
is difficult to understand why permission to occupy the Blackfriars site was
refused to Shakespeare and his companions, but granted without difficulty
to a rival company, the Children of the Chapel Royal, who did not hesitate
to present burlesque and satirical plays, with brilliant success, and whom
the Queen and her ladies-in-waiting encouraged by their presence.

Probably its novelty played a part in the vogue of the " Blackfriars "
theatre,[2] and it is easy to understand why Shakespeare in alluding to the
success of the " Children of the Chapel ", in his 1603 version of *Hamlet*,
expresses himself with some bitterness.

---

[1] Report of the Lord Mayor to the Privy Council. See E. K. Chambers, *Elizabethan
Stage*, vol. iv, p. 322.
[2] In Ben Jonson's *Poetaster*, the bully complains that he can nowhere find on the stage
" a good, bawdy play ", because only " Humours, Revels and Satires " are given. (*Poetaster*,
Act III, Sc. I.)

When the arrival of the itinerant players at Elsinore is announced, Hamlet asks to which company they belong ; to this Rosencrantz answers :

Rosencrantz : My Lord, the Tragedians of the city—those that you took delight to see so often.
Hamlet : How comes it that they travel ? Do they grow rusty ?
Rosencrantz : No, my lord, their reputation holds as it was wont.
Hamlet : How then ?
Rosencrantz : I' faith, my lord, noveltie carries it away, for the principal publike audience that came to them are turned to private players and to the humour of children.
Hamlet : I do not greatly wonder of it, for those that would make mops and moes at my uncle, when my father lived, now give a hundred, two hundred pounds for his picture.

Of all the theatrical companies, Shakespeare's was the most suspected of disaffection towards the régime.[1] It had been said in 1592 that an old priest hunted by the pursuivants had disguised himself in the livery of the company, and followed the actors on one of their provincial tours ; [2] it was also said that the Lord Chamberlain had offered a ransom of a thousand pounds to save the life of John Ingram a Catholic missionary ; [3] Shakespeare's opponents criticized the subject and treatment of each play as designed to please Catholics like Southampton, Arundell, Catesby and Cornwallis who might see in the rising author the mouthpiece for their ideas. Therefore, to allow the company to take possession of a building adjacent to the residence of the Fortescue family, related to the Earl of Southampton, and denounced by the neighbours as " concealing priests and enemies of Her Majesty's decisions ", might appear dangerous to the Queen's secret service agents.

The Fortescue house possessed, according to an official report, several entrance doors, underground passages and a labyrinth of corridors giving access to the banks of the river.[4]

Shakespeare and his fellows, therefore, were forced to try their luck on the other bank of the river in Southwark. There they bought ground not far from the Bear garden ; but, while awaiting the building of the future " Globe ", they were obliged to live by expedients. At the end of the season of 1596 they rented the " Swan Theatre ", lately built by Francis Langley. At last, a year later they inaugurated the " Globe " which they were to make famous with the patriotic spectacle of *Henry V*. When, in 1609, after an interminable lawsuit they regained possession of the beautiful " Blackfriars ", their dreams were finally realized. They now had at their

---

[1] Cf. Anthony Munday, *Discovery of Campion.*

[2] The following is found on a list of recusants to be watched : " Ane old preeste ; and a greate perswader of others to Papistrye ; resorted mutche to Meysham in Darbyesheere and divers places in Warwicksheere ; And that he usethe to Travaile in a Blewe Cote ; with the Eagle, and childe on his Sleeve." (S.P. Dom. Eliz., vol. 243, No. 76.)

[3] Before his execution, Father Ingram thanked the Lord Chamberlain for his offer of a thousand crowns made for the ransom of his life (*English Martyrs*, p. 284).

[4] See Chambers, *William Shakespeare*, vol. ii, pp. 154-169 on the " Gatehouse of Black Friars ".

disposal two theatres, the " Globe ", capable of accommodating a large number of spectators, and the " Blackfriars ", which though less spacious was more suitable for the entertainments sought by those of court circles.

The time when a poster sufficed to indicate the scene of action was long past, but the stage properties were still rudimentary compared to the opulence of the English theatre after the Restoration.

Many of the weaknesses in Shakespeare's dramatic works are due neither to lack of taste nor of art, but to the exigencies of the theatre itself. They are explained and excused by technical difficulties.

The " Globe " on the bankside like its Shoreditch predecessor had a high octagonal tower. It had that famous wooden O, its balconies and boxes. The stage itself, where the performance took place, was about eight yards wide and ten deep. It projected in a blunted point far into the pit. The players were separated from the audience by a low wooden balustrade. Behind this space or proscenium stood a two-storey edifice giving on to the external wall of the building and flanked by two handsome columns which framed the scene. On the lower storey there was probably a kind of alcove or recess opening directly on to the stage. The upper storey formed a balcony adaptable to divers uses. The forepart of the stage was the principal place of action. It could represent a market, a courtyard, forest or garden. The latter was suggested by regularly clipped hedges and a fountain ; a wood consisted of a few bushes and rocks. In the alcove a couch, table, chairs and candlesticks gave the impression of a bedroom. A bar and benches constituted a trial scene ; an altar or a tomb placed the action in a church ; a gallows and chains a prison. A shop was recognized by a furnished counter. A throne and some stools transported the spectator to the court of Denmark or France or to Venice according to the indication of the coat of arms.

Thanks to this arrangement of the stage the producer could show a triple scene. The second storey may have been used for Juliet's balcony and for the battlements whence Richard II parleyed with Bolingbroke who, from the proscenium, besieged the castle ; or again for the high tower from which Prince Arthur threw himself in his vain attempt to escape. A trapdoor in this upper landing permitted the descent from above of goddesses and fairies, or as in the *Jew of Malta*, the fall of Barrabas into a caldron.

The recess could be transversally divided thus making it possible to produce two simultaneous scenes. For instance, in another of Marlowe's tragedies the audience could see the Duc de Guise attacked by his murderers, while the King of France enthroned in the neighbouring room remains ignorant of the drama enacted so close to him.

However the absence of curtain or screen, and the shape itself of the proscenium which extended into the midst of the spectators created a major difficulty for the dramatist. It was impossible to prepare a tableau vivant on the main stage. The action was necessarily regulated by entrances and exits : these were effected through two doors at the right and left of the pillars supporting the background structure. These doors gave access to the green-room where the company dressed, before entering at the call of the assistant prompter. A placard or " platt ", hung in the green room, showed the progress of the play.

When everyone was at his post, three trumpet blasts from a high turret where floated the special banner of the troupe, announced the beginning of the performance.

The action could not be interrupted, as in our day, by blackouts. One of the great pre-occupations of the dramatist, was to provide in the text itself an excuse for the removal of bodies of the slain, and to avoid the ridiculous sight of a " dead " actor getting up and walking off, or being compelled to lie supine until the last of the audience had departed. Hamlet, accordingly, interrupts the conversation with his mother to drag his victim Polonius off the stage, on the pretext of hiding the body. In the final scene, Hamlet himself, hoisted on the shoulders of Fortinbras' soldiers, is carried off the stage to the sound of funeral trumpet, fife and drum, a procedure inevitably repeated at the end of every tragedy : Antony, Cleopatra, Cassius, Brutus, Coriolanus and Lear disappear in the same way. There was another major annoyance for the actors : a privilege granted to certain wits and notabilities authorized them on payment of one shilling, to place their stool on the proscenium from which they judged the merits of the spectacle with due solemnity. Needless to say, this practice was most unpleasing to the rest of the audience whose heads were on a level with the feet of the privileged worldlings.

The satirical Dekker in his amusing A.B.C. addressed to the theatrical snob and entitled the *Gul's Hornebook* gives the would-be dandy of those days precisely the same advice found two generations later in Molière's *Les Fâcheux*. The ambitious spectator should make his entry through the green-room, jostle the players and the Prologue trembling with stage-fright, force himself on to the stage shilling in one hand stool in the other, and struggle to the front of the platform in spite of protests and catcalls. Once firmly ensconced he will gain everybody's respect by showing his disdain for the author by laughing scornfully at the most tragic or tender scenes. Should the author be sufficiently impressed by so much grandeur he will doubtless be ready to offer a dedication or at least a sonnet to so exalted a personage.

In the pit, the audience remained standing. It is true that they only paid one penny for such uncomfortable places. There were boxes and seats around the semi-circular arena.

Quite different conditions prevailed when performances were given at Essex House, at the Savoy, and above all twice a year at court, where splendid festivals which included spectacular effects were organized. A special body —the Revels Office—engaged the actors and chose the programmes for Westminster, Richmond or Greenwich, according to the place chosen by Her Majesty as her residence. John Carow, a scene-painter claimed the sum of fourteen pounds, twelve shillings for stage properties delivered on the occasion of court entertainments.

Six houses in canvas, mounted and painted according to the requirements of each of the plays inscribed in the programme for the year ; a chariot fourteen feet long by eight wide, a mountain with rocks, a fountain for Apollo and his nine muses, a castle with pillars, frieze and roof of gold, the portico ornamented with the arms of France and England.

The dramatist, however, possessed one means of impressing the spectators and allowing them to distinguish the characters, kings, soldiers, courtiers, great ladies and commoners, by creating an atmosphere appropriate to their lives and actions.   The costumes were extremely rich and beautiful ; velvet, lace, satin and cloth of gold aroused the envy of impoverished wits,[1] and provided targets for the anathemas of puritan preachers ; but they permitted the actors to impersonate with suitable pomp the high and powerful persons whom they represented.   This luxury [2] was the only material card in Shakespeare's hand for creating that verisimilitude necessary for the appreciation of the drama.   Apart from this, he had to rely on his knowledge of his craft, manifestly superior to that of his colleagues, and on the talent of his actors.

Surmounting all difficulties of dramatic production, Shakespeare succeeded by art alone in making up for everything lacking to create illusion among his spectators.   On bare boards, supported by creaking trestles, in the yard of an inn, on the primitive stages of the " Curtain ", the " Theatre " or the " Globe ", he succeeded in producing that poetic impression of reality which replaces realism.   He understood that without the artifice of scenery, it is the magic of ideas and the music of words which charms the spectator. The language he puts into the mouths of his monarchs is sufficient to metamorphose the simple player into a man of note.   Whether he transports the action to the French court, to a Venetian palace, or the castle of Elsinore, his characters express themselves in such a fashion that the audience almost believe they are listening to a king of Navarre, a magnifico of the doge's suite, or a friend of the prince of Denmark.

The poet's imagination and the harmony of his verse lend to his landscapes a poetic life which replaces the local colour sometimes abused today.   Titania, the fairy queen, is as convincing as the French princess or the great lady of Illyria.   Shakespeare in animating his characters has developed a personal art with its own rules and procedure.   The method must have been a good

---

[1] England affords those glorious vagabonds
  That carried earst their fardels on their backes
  Coursers to ride on through the gazing streets
  Sooping it in their glaring satten sutes
  And pages to attend their masterships. . . .
        (*Return from Parnassus*, 2nd Part, Act v, Sc. 1)

[2] Thomas Platter, a traveller from Basle who was in England from September 18th to October 20th, 1599, notes :

The comedians are most expensively and elegantly apparelled, since it is customary in England, when distinguished gentlemen or Knights die, for nearly the finest of their clothes to be made over and given to their servants, and as it is not proper for them to wear such clothes but only to imitate them, they give them to the comedians to purchase for a small sum. (Translated from the German by E. K. Chambers, *The Elizabethan Stage*, vol. ii, p. 365.)

one, as his plays have been acclaimed by the public ever since they were written. Despite his contempt for the conventional unities of classic tragedy, and the confusion prevailing in many of his plays, he achieved works of an emotional unity which is peculiar to him alone. His method is symphonic. Each play is a practical demonstration of the multiple effects of a single passion : the drama is woven of several intrigues in juxtaposition, all connected with the climax by the one emotion which acts as *leit-motif*. Thus *Othello* is not merely the tragedy of conjugal jealousy ; the relations of Cassio and Iago reveal the intensity of professional envy ; the courtesan Bianca is jealous of Cassio ; the behaviour of the Venetian Senate to the condottière emphasises political enmity ; Roderigo is envious of the wealth of his superiors, and Iago plays as cleverly on his foolish comrade's weakness as on his master's passion. These various, almost pathological studies of jealousy frame and accentuate Othello's anguish : it is the balance and the art with which the different sub-plots dovetail into the main story, which make this play a masterpiece.

Shakespeare uses this theme again in *Cymbeline* and the *Winter's Tale*, without, however, enlisting for the husband of the gentle Imogen or the suspicious consort of Hermione, the pity perhaps due to their sufferings.

In *King Lear*, vanity spurred on by adroit flattery is shown as stronger than paternal love. The king and his counsellor Gloucester, blinded by selfishness, are led to commit equal injustice. Their eyes are finally opened by the generous devotion of their respective victims, Cordelia and Edgar.

Every scene in *The Merchant of Venice* jingles with the sound of gold and ducats. The whole plot, including the most romantic passages, turns on the greed for material possessions.

Hamlet is the tragedy of doubt, and its reflex, suspicion. Suffering from the same complaint, each of the characters is borne on, but in a different fashion, to his or her fatal destiny.

In *Romeo and Juliet*, the impression of unity of sentiment is obtained by a more subtle procedure. The tragic end of the lovers whose exquisite idyll is ruined by the feud which has for generations disturbed the peace of Verona, far from envenoming discord between the factions, becomes— sublime paradox—the cause of reconciliation. Over the open tomb, Capulet and Montague clasp hands and bury with their children their ancient quarrels.

Julius Caesar, *Coriolanus*, and *Cleopatra* exemplify the deadly clash of political interests, the brutal lust for power and class hatred. But it is not only amid the settings of antiquity that Shakespeare composes his great symphony on the theme of ambition. The dramas inspired by the history of his own country, from *King John* to *Henry VIII*, provide him with magnificent opportunities, while playing on the whole range of this universal passion, to chastise the murderer, to condemn treachery, and to exalt pure patriotism.

CHAPTER VIII

THE POET'S WORLD

Holborn House and the Savoy with their lords and ladies—Essex House : Ambassadors and statesmen—Bohemia—London Taverns and their frequenters—Greene, Lodge, Markham, Peele, Nashe, Warner, Harvey, Bacon, Raleigh, Munday the informer—Ben Jonson, his imprisonment, his conversion—Fletcher—Drayton—Daniel—Spenser.

SHAKESPEARE could not cross the threshold of Holborn House, the London residence of Lord Southampton, without a feeling of confidence, for here, at least, his person was in safety and his art highly honoured. The extent of this sumptuous domain may be imagined from the fact that its site is now occupied by the British Museum. The gallery at Wellbeck which now houses the collections of tapestries, pictures and objects of art belonging to the Southampton family gives an impression of what the furnishings and decorations of Holborn House must have been in those days when thirty servants were at the beck of his young Lordship. There it was that Shakespeare found in the person of Henry Wriothesley the admirer and friend proud to present this new star to his guests and relatives. Lady Southampton, daughter of Viscount Montague, set her seal of approval on the artistic tastes of her son, for it may be remembered that the first official payment made to Shakespeare, Burbage and Kempe of which there is official record, bears her countersign. Lady Southampton could not fail to appreciate the fact that Shakespeare, in his *Sonnets* and the *Lover's Complaint*, had pressed her son to marry the person she had elected. She received the Stratford poet and introduced him to the London élite, to her own daughter, Lady Arundel, and to her inseparable friends, Lady Leicester,[1] Lady Rich, the Countess of Northumberland, her two cousins, Catherine and Elizabeth Fortescue, famed for their beauty, and finally to the sweet and gracious Elizabeth Vernon, who was to become her daughter-in-law. These ladies were such as to inspire the plays of an author who possessed an insight into feminine psychology, and who lent to his living models the vivid colours of his imagination. The style of the letters addressed by Elizabeth

[1] Letitia Knollys, daughter of Anne Boleyn's elder sister, consequently first cousin of Queen Elizabeth, who reproached her for the passion she inspired in the Earl of Leicester to whom she was secretly married. She adored her son Essex, called him her sweet Robin and identified herself with his cause. She survived her daughter Penelope Devereux and lived to be ninety-four.

Vernon to her young husband closely resembles the expressions used by Shakespeare's passionate heroines : Ophelia, Desdemona and Imogen ; all reflect her personality. In creating Portia, Rosalind and Beatrice, those ladies who remained witty even when in love and brave enough to defy convention, the dramatist thought no doubt, of Lady Penelope Devereux, Sydney's mistress, and his " Stella ". Victim of an enforced marriage, her passionate affection for Sir Charles Blount, devoted partisan of her brother made her abandon all to share his lot.

The men of this circle were equally brilliant. It was there that Shakespeare met Sir William Cornwallis, the talented amateur who was the first to attempt a translation of Montaigne's Essays, Sir John Harrington [1] who did the same for Ariosto, Sir Anthony Copley [2] whose religious poetry contrasted with an adventurous life. Hugh Holland [3] also a poet and even famous at the time, but known today only by the elegiac ode which prefaces the dramatic works of his friend Shakespeare. This remark applies equally to Leonard Digges [4] and to James Mabbe [5] whose names have come down to us from the stanzas which appear in the first pages of the folio edition of the plays.

In this company of recusants more or less in hiding were Sir Joycelyn and Sir Charles Percy,[6] brothers of the Earl of Northumberland, Henry

---

[1] Sir John Harrington (1561-1612). This godson of the Queen was noted for his wit and culture, also for his enthusiastic partisanship for Essex. On returning from the Irish campaign he was about to throw himself into the insurrection when checked by an order from the Queen : " Tell my witty nephew to go home quickly and stay there for this is hardly the moment to play the fool away from home." J. E. Neale, *Queen Elizabeth*, p. 378.

[2] Sir Anthony Copley (1561-1612). Denounced by Topcliffe as " The most dangerous young man among us ". At the age of fifteen he escaped with his cousin Robert Southwell, studied at Rheims, served in Flanders and, on returning, was imprisoned in the Tower. After a visit to the Holy Sepulchre he died in Rome. His poetry possesses as much sincere piety as martial dash.

[3] Hugh Holland (1563-1633) pupil and biographer of William Camden ; fellow of Trinity College, Cambridge. Undertook a pilgrimage to the Holy Sepulchre ; on his return to England paid two hundred pounds for religious immunity ; among his elegies the best are his sonnets on Shakespeare and on Prince Henry, who died in 1612. L. I. Guiney, *Recusant Poets* (London, 1938), p. 378.

[4] Leonard Digges (1588-1635), according to Anthony à Wood, " A great Master of the English language, a perfect understander of the French and Spanish, a good Poet and no mean Orator. . . . Several verses of his Composition I have seen printed in the beginning of various authors, particularly those before Shakespeares works, which shew him to have been an eminent Poet of his time. . . . Studied at the overseas college, died and was buried in the Chapel at University College, Oxford, now destroyed." (*Athenae Oxoniensis*, 1691, vol. i, p. 520.)

His mother took as her second husband Sir Thomas Russell executor of Shakespeare's will. *Athenae Oxoniensis*, 1691, vol. i, p. 520.

[5] James Mabbe (1572-1642), judged by Anthony à Wood as " a learned man, good orator and facetious wit. He had been at the overseas college and became lay pre-bendary (Rom. Cath.) in Wells Cathedral, translated from Spanish into English under the name of Don Diego Puedeser, that is James May-be." A reprint of his *Spanish Lady* which deals with adventures in the London recusant world by Cervantes, 1640. Mabbe also translated the Celestina and a book of religious contemplations.

[6] The elegant Sir Charles Percy wrote from his manor of Dumbleton, near Stratford, where he complained of the lack of political news, that his ignorance was comparable " to that of Justice Shallow and of his colleague, Justice Silence ".

Constable [1] the lawyer-poet, Sir Henry Neville, ambassador for Essex in Paris, Thomas Russell, [2] rich landowner near Stratford, Thomas Lodge, who abandoned letters, to practise medicine in London, and Theodore Diodati [3] who combined the two vocations, without counting the swarm of poets and rhymsters, with or without talent, who saw in the person of Harry Wriothesley a son of Apollo, ready to crown with laurels and, better, to receive at his hospitable board both writers and actors.

Holborn was not the only mansion where Shakespeare was assured of cordial welcome. At Leicester's old residence, lately become Essex House, the young Earl of Essex kept open house from 1588. Leicester at his death disinherited the son he had by Lady Douglass Sheffield, his second wife, and left his most sumptuous armour, his two best horses, his residence in London, his jewelled garter to his beloved stepson, the Earl of Essex, assured that in using them the family prestige would be enhanced. Nor was he mistaken. Barely four months sufficed for Robert Devereux, returned from Flanders, to succeed to the honours formerly bestowed upon Leicester. He found himself appointed Knight of the Garter, Master of Horse, Minister of State, and occupied in Elizabeth's heart, the place left vacant by his stepfather. With lightning celerity, Raleigh was supplanted and old Burleigh was forced to acknowledge defeat.

A spirit of youth and charm took possession of the court. Recusants drew a breath of relief at the sight of the increasing influence of a spirited, broad-minded, and highly cultured nobleman whose tolerance and foresight contrasted with ministerial narrow-mindedness. Everyone repeated his name like a lucky omen ; courtiers looked forward to a series of festivities. The young Earl's affection for the " fairie " queen was sincere, at least in the beginning. Apart from the intoxication of personal success, he enjoyed her conversation and company. The Sovereign, when not in a crabbed mood, did not lack brilliance nor originality. Under the spell of this new passion she became sympathetic and attentive, a legendary godmother. The court whispered ; visiting strangers noted the number of hours passed by the new favourite in the royal apartments where, it was said, the two played

---

[1] Henry Constable (1562-1613) addressed some sonnets to Essex, whom he served as political agent on the continent, to Penelope Devereux and King James. Implicated in the Essex plot, he was fined a large sum after three years of captivity in the Tower. Constable died in exile in Liège.

[2] Sir Thomas Russell (1570-1634) on his marriage to the rich widow of Sir Dudley Digges, placed this Catholic fortune where it could not be seized. Many recusants thus avoided the draconian laws of the time. The beautiful house of Alderminster, not far from Stratford, principal residence of the family after 1600, and where the sons lived, is described in a recent work of Leslie Hotson. Many documents on this close friend and executor of Shakespeare's will are published for the first time. (See, " I William Shakespeare do appoint Thomas Russell Esq., . . ." Leslie Hotson, London, Jonathan Cape, 1937.)

[3] Theodore Diodati (1560-1617) native of Lucca, came to settle in London with the Duke of Bedford. He was chosen, according to his compatriot Giovanni Florio, " to adorn and instruct the mind so noble and promising of Sir John Harrington whose tutor he became ". His deeds conformed to his name, and he was considered a true " gift of God " by the grammarian. He has left a name in the world of letters as in that of medicine. His son Charles was the friend and confidant of Milton.

cards and chess until the grey dawn grew rosy. The birds would already be singing when Essex returned home.

He was spirited enough to show jealousy of that " rogue Raleigh ", and provoked the handsome Charles Blount to a duel for daring to appear in public wearing a favour of the Queen's on his sleeve. Elizabeth, flattered at the idea that her beauty was still capable of causing rivalry and bloodshed summoned the two valiant knights before her in order to effect a reconciliation. There was continual revelling, until Essex, disgusted, suddenly left for the army.

Meanwhile his house had become the meeting place of the most brilliant representatives of the literary and political world, at home and abroad. The entertainments included successful plays by the Lord Chamberlain's company performed again in private. Shakespeare's debt to the influence of these surroundings is inestimable. If Essex never made use of the privilege of conferring his badge on a London troupe, this was due to the fact that Leicester's former actors, Kempe, Pope and Bryan, had already joined forces, under Lord Strange's patronage, with men of greater talent, to wit, William Shakespeare and Richard Burbage. These players were more in accord with Essex's refined taste, and romantic ideas than were their rivals. He took the company under his protection, and applauded its repertory from *A Midsummer Night's Dream*, played on the occasion of his marriage with Sir Philip Sidney's widow, to *Twelfth Night*, given at his palace when he received the foreign ambassadors in 1600. But his personal preference went to the drama of *Richard II*.

Shakespeare was not the only one to see in Essex an enlightened patron of art. In 1589, Edmund Spenser addressed to him a complimentary sonnet.[1] In 1591 he dedicated the *Teares of the Muses* to the sister and wife of the favourite. Then in 1596, he took up residence at Essex House where he wrote his *Prothalamion ;* in this poem he apostrophizes the Earl " issuing like Radiant vesper " from his palace at the head of an imposing retinue, as " noble Peer, Great England's glory, and the World's wide wonder ", " Faire branch of Honor, flower of Chevalrie ".

> Joy have thou of thy noble victorie,
> And endlesse happinesse of thine owne name
> That promiseth the same :
> That through thy prowesse and victorious armes,
> Thy country may be freed from forraine harmes :
> And great Elisaes glorious name may ring
> Through all the world, fil'd with thy wide Alarmes.[2]

It was in these cultured surroundings that Shakespeare could not fail to meet many foreign statesmen, for Essex House soon became the centre

---

[1] This sonnet is to be found at the beginning of *The Faerie Queene* (Ponsonby, London, 1589).

[2] *Prothalamion* (lines 152-8).

of the new political thought ; war against Spain was there advocated, and a close alliance with Henry IV of France. In this virtual annex of the Foreign Office, presided over by Anthony Bacon and Sir Henry Wotton, every effort was made to maintain harmonious relations with the courts of Europe.

Anthony Bacon, afflicted with gout, lodged at Essex House to be near his work, which consisted in dealing with a vast correspondence. He employed five secretaries—Ben Jonson was one—to keep it up to date. His brother, Francis,[1] after leaving Gray's Inn, also came to offer his services to the rising sun. He even took part in the amateur masques at which the Queen was a guest. Those who attribute Shakespeare's works to Francis Bacon, should study the play which the latter presented in November 1595. In this literary effort, pedantry vies with poor taste. The Queen, after having contemplated the weighty spectacle " hastened to go to her sleep ", declaring that, " if she had known in advance the manner in which they would speak of her person, she would have abstained from coming ".[2]

The scenario of the *Conference of Pleasure* is entirely written in Bacon's hand, together with a poem by the same pen ; both show the future chancellor in the light, not as capable of creating Shakespeare's works, but rather as an ambitious amateur wishing to shine in a sphere for which he was not fitted.

Under the same roof Antonio Pérez,[3] Lamothe Fénelon, de Maisse,[4] de Thumeri,[5] Hercule de Rohan [6] and the duc de Bracchiano, were often gathered, enabling thus Shakespeare to keep in touch with continental affairs. He was also given the opportunity to acquaint himself sufficiently with foreign names, and events, to give the impression that the action of his foreign plays really took place outside England.

[1] Anthony Bacon, son of chancellor Nicholas Bacon and of his second wife, Anne Cook, was born in 1558, his brother, Francis in 1561. They studied together, left Cambridge in 1573, and went abroad. Francis stayed five years and returned to read law at Gray's Inn, while Anthony entered Walsingham's Intelligence Service in 1592, and later found employment with the Earl of Essex to whom he remained faithful.

[2] Bacon's scenario—*Conference of Pleasure* is thus described in a manuscript at Lambeth : " The persons to be three : one dressed like a Hermit or Philosopher, representing Contemplation ; the second like a captain, represents Fame ; the third, like a councillor of state, representing Experience." Frank G. Burgoine, *Facsimile of Northumberland Manuscript* (Longmans Green & Co., 1904).

[3] Antonio Pérez, Minister of Spain and private secretary to the king, had the temerity to supplant Philip II in the heart of the Princess of Éboli. Denounced to the Inquisition, he escaped after having killed his informer and reached England where he received a warm welcome. He became such a close friend of Francis Bacon that Lady Bacon wrote to her elder son, Anthony, protesting against this too great intimacy of his brother Francis. (See *The Life of Essex*, by G. B. Harrison, p. 81.) Pérez died in Paris in 1611, leaving several works ; cf. *Obras y Relaciones*, printed at Geneva, in 1631.

[4] André Hurault, Lord of Maisse was charged with the difficult mission of ascertaining whether Queen Elizabeth was ready to negotiate peace with Spain or upon what condition she wished to continue the war. His diary of this mission has been published in English (Nonesuch Press, 1931). At the end of these negotiations Maisse continued an authority on Anglo-French questions ; he was the man most responsible for the commercial treaty between the two countries, signed after the treaty of Vervins. He died in 1607.

[5] Maisse's successor in London.   [6] Henry IV's special envoy to Essex.

If Shakespeare frequented the mansions of the great, and even Whitehall Palace, if he incurred Marston's reproach of being a " sponge ", he was also denounced and stigmatized by Joseph Hall for having like the "wicked Rabelays ", described drinking bouts. He would hardly have been a man of his time, and never able to create Falstaff and his merry companions, had he not, like his fellow actors and writers, frequented the London taverns. There everyone met on an equal footing. Courtiers, lawyers, authors and soldiers mixed in care-free fashion. The atmosphere was conducive to emulation ; friends and rivals fraternized or argued, while the philosopher observed the conduct of his contemporaries. It was easy to find a congenial tavern ; these were everywhere.[1] " The Mitre ", and " The Mermaid ", whose proprietor William Johnson was sufficiently close to Shakespeare to figure with the three friends whom the poet called upon when signing the document concerning the mortgage of the " Blackfriars "[2] theatre, were the most famous taverns from Tudor to Stuart times. " The Red Bull " and the " Cross-Keys " possessed large halls often hired by the players when public theatres were not available.

" The Mermaid ", inaugurated in 1450, possessed, besides the entrance in Cheapside, two other doors, one opening in Bread Street, the other on Friday Street.

The roof of this two-storey wooden building sloped steeply, leaving room in an embrasure for its celebrated sign. From the latticed windows of the rough plastered rooms, rose the musty smell of wines, clouds of smoke, curses, shouts and laughter. The principal room was reached through a narrow door on which were improvized drawings and scribbled rhymes. " Oh ! this door ! It let in the whole sixteenth century and closed upon immortals ! "[3]

All the clever and witty men of the day, entered that low-ceilinged room where the Warwickshire conspirators, the poetic Catesby, the rash Copley and the adventurous Ambrose Rookwood met Guy Fawkes and his followers.

Shakespeare's friend Thomas Heywood, looking back on the generation he outlived and which he loved to recall, described the familiarity bordering

---

[1] " The King's Head " with its sign, the portrait of Henry VIII, dominated Chancery Lane. " The Monkey on Horseback ", " The Hole in the Wall ", " The Man in the Moon " competed with houses with more commonplace names, like the " White Bear ", the " Bear in Chains " and the " White Horse ". " The Rose " was famous for the quality of its Bordeaux and Rhenish wines. " The Fleece " was preferred by the military. It was at the " Boar's Head " that Shakespeare set the comic scenes of his *Henry IV*. The Jews, in their yellow caps, sheltered in the " Biblical Tavern ". " The Dog " was a refuge for unemployed intellectuals, and it was there that Ben Jonson, having left " The Mermaid ", " The Mitre " and " The Devil ", came in his old age and decline to make it the centre of his twilight kingdom.

[2] The parchment is signed as follows : Betweene William Shakespeare of Stratford upon Avon in the countie of Warwick, gentleman, William Jonson, citizen and vintner of London, John Jackson and John Hemyng of London gentleman and Henry Walker Citizen and Minstrell of London. *The Plays of William Shakespeare*, J. J. Tournessein MCM (vol. i, p. 81).

[3] George Duval, *Londres, au temps de Shakespeare* (Flammarion, Paris).

on disrespect which incites the English to remember their celebrities by a
nickname : Marlowe was known as *Kit*, Beaumont as *Frank* and

> Mellifluous *Shake-speare*, whose inchanting *Quill*
> Commanded Mirth or Passion, was but *Will*.
> And famous *Jonson*, though his learned Pen
> Be dipt in Castaly, is still but *Ben*.

Fletcher, Webster and all their namesakes, although far from commonplace,
are today no more than " Jacks " ; [1] and Heywood concluded with the
confession that he felt flattered when addressed as " Tom ".

It was at " The Mermaid " that Robert Greene for a time reigned supreme
among his university clique which included Lodge, Markham, Peele and
Lyly. Nashe, the young Juvenal, let loose his satirical shafts while the
timid Drayton drank his pint of small beer in a solitary corner and dreamed
of the beautiful Idea of whom he sang without daring to approach. Marlowe
was glad enough to welcome as skilful a collaborator as the Swan of Avon
when he himself was not engaged in long speculations with Heywood on the
practice of black magic.

A game much in fashion among the poets [2] consisted in suggesting a
subject and choosing an appropriate metre upon which each must improvise
a line or two.[3] The winner was he who returned the ball the quickest.
One of the best hands at these competitions was certainly Sir Walter Raleigh,
Captain of the Palace Guard, who belonged to the group of free thinkers, and
leaned elbow on table beside Marlowe, Royden or Chapman. When he
entered " The Mermaid ", smoking his long silver pipe, a large pearl hanging
from his left ear, every eye was fixed upon this conspicuous figure. Taller
by a head than any other of the Queen's servants he could go nowhere
unobserved. His success with Her Majesty, who had shown her favour by
granting him a place in the Privy Council, was well known. His voyages
to the Americas, his wild speculations in Ireland, his projects for Guiana
lent authority to his talk pronounced with a strong Devonshire accent ;
moreover, nobody would have dared to contradict such a swashbuckler,
whose duels had become countless. The circle of drinkers considered it a
privilege to take a puff of the pipe he willingly passed round, for he had his
reasons for wishing to popularize the use of the West Indian herb, nicotina.

With the entrance of Walter Warner, native of Leicestershire, science
took a large part in the smoking room discourse. This little doctor, mathe-
matician and philosopher, published [4] Harriott's *Algebra logarithm tables*, a

---

[1] Heywood, *Hierarchie of Blessed Angels*, 1635, p. 206.

[2] In one of his sonnets, Shakespeare admits his defeat in this game. When his turn
came to provide a rhyme, he remained silent, struck dumb at seeing Lord Southampton
whisper to one of his perplexed rivals :
> " But when your countenance fill'd up his line,
> Then lack'd I matter ; that enfeebled mine."

[3] Several of these impromptus have been published and attributed either to Raleigh
and Shakespeare or to Barnefield and Shakespeare. It seems probable that these were
some of the improvised compositions where each author had his part.

[4] *Aubrey's Lives* (p. 291).

treatise on optics and other works, for which more ambitious men received reward and credit.   He himself only wrote one book *Artis Analyticae Praxis* (1631).   This curious personage hid his deformed left hand in a long sleeve, with the other he took a frog from his pocket to demonstrate that the heart-beats could only be explained by circulation of the blood, a discovery attributed to Doctor William Harvey, another habitué of " The Mermaid ". John Aubrey, who wrote the biography of both men, wished, doubtless to settle this matter when he declared that Warner's experiments formed the founda-tion of this great discovery the honour of which went to Harvey about twenty years after.   The latter made himself conspicuous in the tavern for his advanced ideas and libertine talk.   He asserted that man was but a mis-chievous gorilla : as for woman, Turkey was the only country wise enough to keep her in her proper place, behind the bars of a seraglio ; of Bacon, his illustrious patient, he said openly that he wrote about morals " like a lord chancellor ", denied him the right to pose as a philosopher and added that it was of his affectations that he would like to cure him ; he also pointed out that his eyes, extremely bright and tinged with yellow, resembled those of a viper.   An early eugenist, Harvey opposed marriages of convenience, maintaining that the children born of these " unions of armorial bearings and wealth " were deformed and rickety.   " It is the instinct known as love which should lead to marriage " quoth he—a theory which might have astonished many hearers, though it certainly did not shock Shakespeare. As for the doctrine which made Harvey [1] celebrated, it was certainly accepted by the author of *Love's Labour's Lost, King John, Coriolanus* and *Hamlet*, long before Molière upheld it.   King John speaks of the " Blood thickened by melancholy " :

> Or if that surly spirit, melancholy
> Had baked thy blood, and made it heavy-thick
> Which else runs tickling up and down thy veins
> Making that idiot, laughter, keep men's eyes. . . .
>   (*King John*, Act III, Sc. 3)

Biron alludes to : " The nimble spirits in the arteries . . .".[2]

---

[1] William Harvey (1575-1657), born at Folkestone went to Canterbury grammar school, matriculated at Caius College, then to Padua to attend the courses of Fabricius.   It was in his lectures on anatomy which he taught from 1607 at St. Bartholomew's Hospital that he put forward his theories, but he refrained from publishing his treatise before reflecting carefully upon it and establishing it upon many experiments.   His *Exercitatio anatomica de motu cordis et sanguinis in animalibus* was dedicated to King Charles and appeared in Frankfort in 1628.   The controversy with Riolanus which he undertook at the Sorbonne was conducted with admirable discretion and courtesy.   Harvey followed his king t battle in the Cotswolds, and saved Prince Charles who promised him much gratitude.   The learned doctor left a large fortune to the College of Physicians, where in 1652, his statu was placed with an inscription establishing the value of his researches.   Aubrey, his bio-grapher, remarks that Harvey was one of the rare scholars who lived long enough to see his doctrine accepted by all the universities of the world, but adds that his numerous clientele abandoned him the day he began to discuss his theory of the circulation of the blood in public.   *Aubrey's Lives*, p. 295.
[2] *Love's Labour's Lost*, Act II, Sc. 2.

Coriolanus's wise friend is still more explicit when the function of the stomach is described in distributing food :

> I send it through the rivers of the blood
> Even to the court, the heart, the seat of the brain,
> And through the cranks and offices of man
> The strongest nerves and small inferior veins
> Whereby they live. . . .
>
> *(Coriolanus, Act I, Sc. 1)*

In *Hamlet*, the ghost describes the effect of poison, enemy of man's blood :

> . . . Swift as quicksilver it courses through
> The natural gates and alleys of the body ;
> And with a sudden vigour it doth posset
> And curd like eager droppings into milk
> The thin and wholesome blood. . . .
>
> *(Hamlet, Act I, Sc. 5)*

However, the presence of great doctors and well-known healers did not always assure good health or lengthen life among the frequenters of the taverns.   It was not advisable to linger too long there if one wished to attain old, or even middle age.   Robert Greene disappeared in 1592, from a surfeit of Rhenish wine and pickled herrings : [1] George Peele, whose overflowing spirits were the joy of the convivial, died still more lamentably before he was thirty. [2]

In these unorthodox gatherings at " The Mermaid " or elsewhere amid the communicative warmth of wine and talk, daring and even forbidden subjects were tackled without the disputants suspecting the presence of an informer.   Yet Anthony Munday, Topcliffe's secret agent, held his sessions there, as much to keep watch over Papists and Atheists as to prove his own wit.   Remembering the fate which awaited several of his friends, the thought that Shakespeare must often have rubbed elbows with this implacable pursuivant produces a retrospective shudder.

On May 18th, 1593, Thomas Kyd was arrested and taken to Bridewell prison.   A document in opposition to the teaching in the Protestant Prayer Book was found in his pocket.   Under interrogation he admitted that he obtained this paper from Marlowe.   Thomas Kyd was never seen again. [3] As for the author of *Faustus*, he was arrested, interrogated by the Star

---

[1] " Robert Greene died of a surfet taken at Pickeld Herrings, and Rhenish wine, as witnesseth Thomas Nash, who was at the fatall banquet." (Francis Meres, *Palladis Tamia*, 1598, p. 286v.)

[2] " As Anacreon died by the pot, so George Peele by the pox." (*Ibid.*).

[3] The confirmation of Thomas Kyd's death does not appear in any official document ; on the other hand, his parents, Francis and Anna, gave up the administration of his property on December 30th, 1594.

Kyd's works were edited by F. S. Boas in 1901.   The popularity of the *Spanish Tragedy*, is shown by the sale of seven editions and of a ballad, to the tune of " Queen Dido " based on the play entitled, *The Spanish Tragedy*, containing the lamentable murders of Horatio and Balemperia with the pitiful death of old Hieronimo.

Chamber, then set at liberty, but twelve days later, he fell into an ambush laid by a government agent, Ingram Fryser, who, on the pretext of a quarrel, stabbed him to death in the eye with his dagger.[1]   Their common friend, Mathew Royden, scenting peril, left for Scotland,[2] while Penry who belonged to the same coterie, was quietly hanged.   Raleigh himself would not have escaped the prosecution which awaited any imprudent talker who expressed opinions contrary to the Act of Uniformity, if he had not enjoyed powerful protection.

But danger does not silence tongues in a period when every day saw the birth of a new idea.   Nothing could prevent discussions and thanks to these animated controversies, the art of conversation began to flourish in England. A letter in verse by Francis Beaumont recalls the brilliance of these oratorical tourneys.

> what things have we seen
> Done at the Mermaid ? heard words that have been
> So nimble, and so full of subtle flame,
> As if that every one from whence they came
> Had meant to put his whole wit in a jest,
> And had resolved to live a fool the rest
> Of his dull life. . . .[3]

Thomas Fuller,[4] who later became familiar with these haunts, often had the opportunity of hearing echoes of certain " heroic contests, whose setting was 'The Mermaid'".   Through him we know which was the more prompt in repartee : Ben Jonson or Will Shakespeare :

Many were the *wit combates* betwixt him and *Ben Johnson*, which two I behold like a *Spanish* great Gallion, and an *English Man of War ; Master Johnson* (like the former) was built for higher in Learning ; *Solid*, but *Slow* in his performance. *Shake-spear* with the *English-man* of War, lesser in *bulk*, but lighter in sailing, could turn with all tides, tack about and take advantage of all winds, by the quickness of his Wit and Invention.   He died anno Domini 16—and was buried at *Stratford* upon *Avon*, the Town of his Nativity.

Fuller might have added that the frigate which was able to manoeuvre in every sort of water, did not often cast anchor in the purlieus of London, as sometimes happened with the great galleon, Jonson.   An actor, Christopher Beeston, who joined Heminge and Condell's troupe when Shakespeare's memory was still alive, told the biographer Aubrey that the poet was " the more to be admired that he was not a company keeper, lived in Shoreditch and, if he was invited to, writ he was in pain ".

---

[1] J. Leslie Hotson (1925).
[2] Thomas Lodge left the country, but for other reasons : his zeal for the Catholic faith rendered his stay in England dangerous.   He embarked with the explorer Cavendish who intended to sail round the world.
[3] The British Muse (1738).
[4] Thomas Fuller (1608-61), nephew of John Davenant, began to collect documents for his publication *Worthies of England* in 1643.   The book was not published until after his death.

Jonson, on the other hand, practised every kind of excess; he was a Gargantua in the world of taverns and theatres. Vain, coarse, realist and humourist, he possessed great gifts of observation and satire; finesse was unknown to him; but beneath his rough and ugly exterior, he hid a sentimental side to his nature. His life was a long series of varied adventures and experiences. He was engaged in plying the trade of mason, when a man of letters, intrigued at hearing an apprentice at work with his trowel reciting Greek poetry, addressed some words to him. This encounter obtained for young Ben a place at Westminster school where the learned Camden noticed him and recommended him for a university scholarship. Next he fought in the Flanders' war where legends about him, ran rife. On his return to London, he applied his talent to the stage, but, a mediocre actor, he found it difficult to make a living, and was no more successful when he tried to have his plays acted. During these difficult years, he quarrelled with an actor of Henslowe's company, whom he killed in a duel, although his adversary presented himself on the scene with a sword six inches longer than his own. Henslowe, in a letter to his son-in-law, Edward Alleyn,[1] recounts

how troubled he is at having lost a man of his company, Gabriel Spencer, killed by the hand of Benjamin Jonson, brick-layer.

Evidently, Henslowe did not wish to gratify this " assassin " with the title of man of letters, and yet it was as a " clerk " in this instance that Ben Jonson saved his life. At the trial, he had the presence of mind to evoke the " Benefit of Clergy " clause, asked for a bible and read in Latin the verses of the fifty-first psalm. This proof of erudition reduced his punishment.

Nevertheless his thumb was branded with the infamous " T " signifying Tyburn, his property confiscated, and he then began to look for an impresario.

During his imprisonment he was converted, and embraced catholicism with ardour. Influenced by the priest who devoted himself to the prisoners of Newgate and Marshalsea, he wrote his best poems, but declared that he would have given them all for Robert Southwell's *Burning Babe*. In 1605, his name was on the list of Catholic suspects with twenty other recusants.[2]

When he left Newgate, fortune at last began to smile on him. His play, *Every Man in His Humour*, was presented by the Lord Chamberlain's company with Shakespeare himself playing the part of Knowell Senior. Shakespeare and Jonson passed for the best of friends; however, when their mutual dealings are studied, the comment of Nicolas Rowe, that Jonson never repaid all this kindness and loyalty, appears justified. Their natures were too dissimilar. Ben was haughty and insolent; even at the height of his fame, he was jealous of any who could threaten his glory. He believed

---

[1] This letter is dated December 24th, 1598.

[2] Beniamus Johnson nuper de pred' parochia Sancte Anne infra pred' precinctu' nuper fratru' predicatoru' jamdudu' dissolut' vulgo vocat' le Blackfryers . . . infra London pred' gener'. *London Sessions Record* (vol. xxxv, p. 7). Sessions File, Catholic Record Society.

it impossible for anyone but himself to attain the noblest thoughts and to express them in better style without the erudition which he had acquired with so much trouble, and derided the blind admiration of Shakespeare's companions for their idol. Even in his declaration of posthumous friendship, Jonson manifested his jealousy as an author and contempt as a scholar for the grammar school student.[1]

I lov'd the man (he says), and do honour his memory on this side Idolatry as much as any. He was indeed honest and of open and free nature : hed an excellent phantasie ; brave notions and gentle expressions ; wherein he flow'd with that facility, that sometime it was necessary he should be stopt'd.[2]

After this panegyric gives place to diatribe, and Ben reveals what he calls the faults of his deceased friend : the most serious in his eyes was his natural exuberance which, according to him led him into absurdity, as in this line given to Caesar :

> Caesar never did wrong but with just cause.

Now, as Rowe has remarked, this line does not figure in the printed text. The folio of 1623 reproduces the passage thus :

> Caesar did never wrong, nor without cause will he be satisfied.
>
> (*Julius Caesar*, Act III, Sc. 1)

which indicates that the author, ever disposed to listen to a just criticism, had modified the offending line before the printing.

The former mason laughed now and then at the dramatist's pretensions to the rank of " gentleman ". In his satire which appeared the year a coat of arms was accorded to Shakespeare's father, he took the opportunity of parodying the " falcon brandishing a spear " and the device " Non sans droict ", giving to one of his characters, the parvenu Sogliardo, armorial bearings which he described in language filled with technical terms from the noble science :

> . . . Gyrony, of eight peeces. Azure and Gules, betweene three plates ; a Chevron, engrailed checkey, Or, Vert, and Ermines ; on a cheefe Argent betweene two Ann'lets, sables ; a Bores head, Proper. . . . Let the word bee, Not without mustard.[3]

The author of *Bartholomew Fair* and of the *Humours* always seemed to be preoccupied with proving to the public that he knew how to write better

---

[1] John Lacy the actor provided information on Ben Jonson's personality of which Aubrey made use in giving a detailed portrait of the almost albino giant :
" He was (or rather had been) of a clear and faire skin ; his habit was very plaine. I have heard Mr. Lacy, the player, say that he was wont to weare a coate like a coachman's coate, with slitts under the arme-pitts. He would many times exceed in drink (Canarie was his beloved liquor) ; then he would tumble home to bed, and, when he had thoroughly perspired, then to studie. I have seen his studyeing chaire, which was of strawe, such as old woemen used, and as Aulus Gellius is drawen in." (Aubrey's *Brief Lives*, vol. II, p. 12.)
[2] Ben Jonson, *Timber and Discoveries out of Daily Readings*, 1641.
[3] *Every Man out of His Humour* (Act III, Sc. 4).

than the man from Stratford, and that he more legitimately deserved success. Those which his rival reaped seemed to him to have been too easily acquired.

I would not (he says), with three rusty swords and help of some few foot and half foot words, fight over York and Lancaster's long jars.[1]

Again with a mixture of bitterness and contempt, he notes that critics are still convinced that *Titus Andronicus* is " our best play yet ".[2]

But if Jonson taxed his rival with lacking classical culture and of presenting Romans with the features of Renaissance Englishmen, the poet's friends retorted that he did not translate whole scenes from Greek and Latin, a thing about which Ben had no scruples.   An echo of these literary bickerings is found in *Parnassus* the satirical Cambridge reviews already quoted, when Kempe, one of the actors supporting Shakespeare's cause, speaks thus of Jonson :

Why here's our fellow Shakespeare puts them all down ; Ay and Ben Jonson too.   O that Ben Jonson is a pestalent fellow, he brought up Horace giving the Poets a pill but our fellow Shakespeare hath given him a purge that made him bewray his Credit.

Meanwhile, Jonson was not a negligible enemy.   He had his school and his disciples, who were called the " Tribe of Benjamin ", and served as permanent " claque ".   Many of his contemporaries preferred him to his rivals : if others did not go as far as rating him above Shakespeare, they at least placed him on the same level ; witness that humorous author who, describing some literary love-feast,[3] represents " Eloquence ", the mistress of the house as waited upon by Shakespeare as majordomo, by Ben Jonson as Cook assisted by Aretino and an assembly of ballad-mongers, actors and supernumeraries.

The gentle Shakespeare sometimes used language which ranged the scoffers on his side.   Nicholas Lestrange, in a collection of jokes, recounts that when Shakespeare agreed to be godfather to a natural son of old Ben, he remarked that it was useless to offer the conventional present expected, namely, twelve gold spoons, for the poet is reported to have remarked,

Faith Ben, I will give a dozen lattin and thou shalt translate them.

(This jest turns on the fact that pewter in those days was commonly called " lattin ".) [4]

What is impossible to doubt from the various anecdotes, is that Ben accepted with bad grace the success of his illustrious colleague.   In his desire to do better than the actor-poet, he vainly set himself to write an impeccable Roman play, which would attract attention to the faults in Shakespeare's dramas, and enhance his own " industrious erudition ".

---

[1] Prologue (*Every Man out of His Humour*).
[2] Prologue (*Bartholomew Fair*).
[3] *A Hermeticall Banquet, Drest by a Spagiricall Cook : for the better Preservation of the Microcosme* (London, 1651).
[4] Sir Nicholas l'Estrange, *Passages and Jests*.   Harleian MSS. 6395.

His *Cataline* and his *Sejanus* were never as much to the public taste as *Julius Caesar* and *Coriolanus*. It was only in the comedy of manners, with his vigorous and satirical *Alchemist*, *Volpone*, and *The Silent Woman*, the *Humours* and *Bartholomew Fair* that he showed himself superior to his adversary.

When death put an end to all rivalry, Jonson offered a magnificent tribute to his departed friend. In the ode placed as heading to the folio of 1623, he acknowledged that Shakespeare should be ranked above Chaucer and Spenser as the poet " not of an age, but of all times ".

Jonson himself had the satisfaction of being able to review and correct his own works before leaving them to posterity.[1] He also had the misfortune, after his appointment as Poet Laureate in 1638, to survive his great reputation. He became poor, and was only rescued thence by a generous pension accorded by Charles I. Gerard Langbaine, comparing the works of two hundred and thirty authors from Elizabeth's reign to the Restoration, does not hesitate to give the palm to the *Swan of Avon*.[2]

Dryden, called upon to judge the respective talents of Shakespeare and his contemporaries, considers that these had little influence on the literary development of their fellow-writer ; it was he, on the contrary, who influenced them. In the prologue which he wrote on the occasion of a revival of *The Tempest*, he defined Shakespeare's true relation to his contemporaries :

> Shakespeare who, (taught by none), didst first impart
> To Fletcher Wit, to labouring Johnson Art.
> He Monarch-like gave those his subjects law,
> And is that Nature that they paint and draw.
> Fletcher reach'd that which on his heights did grow,
> Whilst Johnson crept and gather'd all below.
> This did his Love, and that his Mirth digest
> One imitates him most, the other best.
> If they have since out-writ all other men
> Tis with the drops that fell from Shakespeare's Pen.[3]

Certainly Dryden was not mistaken when estimating the relative value

---

[1] *The Workes of Benjamin Jonson* (London : printed by Richard Bishop are to be sold by Andrew Crooke in St. Paul's Churchyard). The volume contains a superb frontispiece engraved by Hole, and the portrait of the author crowned with laurels with this couplet beneath :
> " O could there be an art found out that might
> Produce his shape so lively as to write."
William Fulman points out in a distich that the public was not yet used to seeing the title " Works " given to a dramatic collection :
> Me thinks, in this, a mysterie there lurks
> That Jonson's players are now called Jonson's workes.
>   (MSS. Corpus Christi College, 309.)

[2] " I esteeme his plays beyond any that have been published in our language and tho' I extreamly admire Jonson and Fletcher ; yet I must still aver that when in competition with Shakespeare I must apply to them what Julius Lipsius writ in his letter to Andreas Schottus, concerning Terence and Plautus, ' Terentium amo admiror sed Plautum magis '." (Gerard Langbaine, *An Account of the English dramatic poets*, Oxford, 1691, p. 450.)

[3] John Dryden, Prologue written for *The Tempest* (1669).

of Shakespeare's rivals ; his remarks about Fletcher in particular are judicious and pertinent.

John Fletcher, this last-minute collaborator, is known above all for " the gentle familiarity of his style and the elegant grace of his dialogue ". In the two plays where his name is linked as author with that of Shakespeare, *Henry VIII* and *The Two Noble Kinsmen* [1] it is easy enough to distinguish the part written by each. These plays will be analysed in their place, but it may be said here that Fletcher, sixteen years younger than Shakespeare owed his presence beside the great dramatist because of his ready pen. He was useful at a time of fatigue and overwork, but this collaboration can hardly be said to have augmented his celebrity. He had shown his capacity, either working with Beaumont, or in a dozen comedies of his own.

Quite different was the case of Thomas Heywood, a friend and fellow worker from the beginning, for as we have seen he had his part in the unpublished drama of *Sir Thomas More*. A real comradeship linked this prolific author to the great poet. Heywood's whole work is full of allusions to Shakespeare's ability. We have observed with what veneration he spoke of him when he reproached the editor Jaggard for making use of Shakespeare's name to cover his own verses. One of his most popular plays *The Fayre Mayde of the Exchange* shows how a comic lover attempts to win the heart of his lady by phrases borrowed from *Venus and Adonis ;* maintaining that he could do no better than gain inspiration from a poem recognized as " the true quintessence of love ".[2] It was Heywood, one of the masters of occult science, who suggested Ariel as the name of the Tempest's airy being, and it was he who described the attributes of Prospero's " trickery spirit ".[3] Thomas Heywood wrote in 1608 an eloquent defence of players against puritans. Every line bears evidence of his desire to plead the cause of his friends of the " Globe ", both living and dead.

Michael Drayton [4] of Hartshill near Stratford, should also be counted among those who from birth were closely associated with the greatest of poets. Some of his sonnets have an almost Shakespearean depth. His hopeless worship of Lady Anne Rainsford prevented him from marrying. Later he is again found at Stratford at the home of the Rainsfords, themselves linked with Shakespeare's family. His *England's Heroicall Epistles* and his magnum opus in thirty volumes, *Polyolbion*, have made his fame. In his panegyric of *Lucrece* in 1596, he recalls the literary successes of his friend.

---

[1] *The Two Noble Kinsmen :* Presented at the Blackfriers by the Kings Majesties' servants, with great applause : Written by the memorable Worthies of their time ; Mr. John Fletcher and Mr. William Shakespeare Gent. 1634.

[2] *The Fayre Mayde of the Exchange* ; With the pleasant humours of the *Cripple of Fanchurch.* Very delectable, and full of mirth. Henry Rocket, 1607.

[3] *The Hierarchie of the blessed Angells*, their Names, orders and Offices. Written by Thomas Heywood (London, 1635).

[4] Michael Drayton (1562-1631). He served as equerry to Sir Walter Aston at the time of the coronation of James I, in 1603. He died in his Fleet Street lodging, not rich, but so well loved that all the students of the four Inns of Court and all the notables of the city followed his coffin to Westminster in a double line which extended as far as the Strand Bridge. (MSS. Corpus Christi College. Fulman MSS. 309.)

The admiration which he expressed for Shakespeare as an actor has already been mentioned.

Samuel Daniel [1] may also be placed among the poet's early associates. Of about the same age as Shakespeare and, like him, a close friend of Lord Southampton, he did not lack lyric inspiration although his contemporaries and posterity represent him rather as Shakespeare's imitator than a friend or rival.   His sonnets " To Delia ", border on plagiarism ; they are almost translations from the French Pléiade.   His borrowings from Shakespeare are so flagrant that in the academic revue already referred to, the " character " who declaims a few stanzas from *Venus and Adonis* is interrupted by this remark : " So we are going to hear a whole book by Samuel Daniel ! "

As for Edmund Spenser, he was, on account of his official duties more in Ireland than in London.   However, the author of *The Fairie Queene* and the creator of *Falstaff* could not but have met at the time when both gravitated round the Earl of Essex.   Towards the end of the century one represented the new inspiration, realism in drama and even in poetry, while the other whose constant cult for allegory, revived the past in archaic form, a fashion which was already overdone.   Shakespeare alludes in *A Midsummer Night's Dream* to the *Teares of the Muses* [2] which Spenser had recently dedicated to Lady Essex, when he himself was presenting his charming fairy play at the private celebrations of the wedding of the hosts of Essex House.   Spenser, for his part in a long poem, " Colin Clout's come home again ", published in 1595, reviews the merits of various poets, but reserves to " the last, but not the least of the gentle shepherds, Aetion "—who could not be anyone but Shakespeare—a very special eulogy, saying that this " eagle " has nowhere his superior.[3]

To these names should be added those of John Lyly, Thomas Dekker, William Alabaster, John Doune and John Webster to complete this galaxy of talent and wit.   But, except for the players with whom Shakespeare lived and for whom he wrote particular parts, none of those who were closely or remotely connected with him exerted much influence upon his writings ; that of Marlowe, although undeniable, was fleeting.   As Shakespeare himself declares, Henry Wriothesley, Earl of Southampton, alone exercised lasting dominion over his pupil's pen.   This pure friendship like that of Montaigne for Etienne de La Boetie, was exclusive.   The young lord enjoyed a widespread prestige which made him an arbiter and leader in the world of art.   This brilliant patron inspired and shed his light on the poet's work, who for his part preferred his counsels to those of men with riper

[1] Samuel Daniel (1562-1619).   Author of a play *Philotas*, in which the Essex rebellion is defended.   He was born and buried at Hartshill.
[2] See *Lives and letters of the Devereux Earles of Essex* by Walter Devereux Captain of the Royal Navy (John Murray, 1853).
[3] And there though last not least is Aetion,
   A gentler Shepheard may no where be found :
   Whose Muse full of high thoughts invention,
   Doth like himself Heroically sound.
(Spenser, *Colin Clouts come home againe*, p. C 2.   Printed for William Ponsonbie, London, 1595.)

experience. From Southampton, Shakespeare accepted suggestions and criticisms ; he even allowed himself to be guided in the paths of the Renaissance by his Italian master ; and it is this learned grammarian [1] who furnishes the missing link in the chain binding the English poet who came to London with Ovid, Holinshed and Plutarch as his sole literary baggage.

[1] Longworth Chambrun, *Un apôtre de la Renaissance en Angleterre* (*Giovanni Florio*), Payot, 1921. (Doctor's thesis sustained at the Sorbonne). G. Gargano, *Scapigliatura Italiana a Londra sotto Elisabetha e Giocomo I* (Florence, 1923). See also *The Life of an Italian in Shakespeare's England*, by Frances Yates (Cambridge University Press, 1934), and A. Koszul and Louis Cazamian, *Offering of a translator* (*Anglo-American Review*, 1938).

CHAPTER IX

ITALIAN INFLUENCE IN SHAKESPEARE'S WORK

Giovanni Florio—His family and his life—Influence of his writings on Shakespeare—Borrowings by the poet from the grammarian's " First " and " Second Fruits "—Florio's translation of Montaigne—Shakespeare finds a new inspiration in the " Essays "—He caricatures the Italian pedagogue—Florio's retort—The different characters of poet and pedant.

SHAKESPEARE'S debt to the grammarian Giovanni Florio was only finally established within the last hundred years. Yet it was well known to his contemporaries and his first biographers. Malone suspected it, and well before him Gerald Langbaine remarked as early as 1691 :

I am apt to believe that his [Shakespeare's] skill in the French and Italian tongues exceeded his knowledge in the Roman. For we find him not only beholding to Cynthio, Giraldi and Bandello, for his plots but likewise a scene in *Henry V* written in French between princess Catherine and her governante : besides Italian proverbs scattered up and down in his writings.[1]

Florio, who generally added the epithet " resolute " to his signature with the help of a stubborn will, constant industry and a gift for intrigue, won for himself an enviable position in the English university world, among the intellectuals of London, and finally at court. Indeed, on the accession of the Stuarts, his name figures in the Lord Chamberlain's accounts as Gentleman of the Chamber, and Reader in Italian to Queen Anne of Denmark. But at the outset of his career, he was far from the steps of a throne.

This son of Italian refugee parents was born about 1554 under the roof of Archbishop Cranmer in somewhat equivocal circumstances. His father, Michelangelo Florio of Florence, peculiar product of those strange times, was of Jewish ancestry.[2] He entered the Franciscan order, was quickly unfrocked, and for a long time kept prisoner in Rome. Converted to Calvinism, he went over to England, where, thanks to the protection of

---

[1] *An Account of the English Dramatick Poets,* or Some observations and remarks On the Lives and Writings of all those that have Publish'd either Comedies, Tragedies, Tragicomedies, Pastorals, Masques, Interludes, Farces or Opera in the English tongue, by Gerard Langbaine (Oxford, 1691).

[2] " I was never a Jew, nor the son of a Jew, for my parents were baptised as papists as I was myself. . . ." declares Michelangelo to defend himself against the attacks of Bernardino Spada, but he adds : " If you said that my forefathers were Jewish before baptism, I would not be able to deny that." *Apologia di Michel Agnolo, fiorentino, ne la quale si tratta de la vera e falsé chiesa, de l'essere e qualita de la messa . . . (Scritta contro un' Heretico . . .* Chamogosko, 1557).

highly placed Protestants, he became Lady Jane Grey's tutor, wrote the history of her life and described her death with sympathetic emotion.[1] Forced to leave England with his wife and unborn child by the edict of February 1559, which forbade foreigners to stay in the country after this date, Michelangelo Florio took refuge in the Grisons, where he finished his life as pastor at Soglio.   His son Giovanni was educated under the direction of the scholar Vergerio at Tubingen. He travelled through Italy and returned to England about 1576. There he made a living from private lessons, taught at Oxford and was authorized to wear the gown of Magdalen College. This encouraged him to dedicate to the Earl of Leicester an excellent manual of Italian-English conversation augmented by a summary of grammar.[2] His first book conveys a vivid impression of a curious personality, vain and susceptible but of incontestable erudition and culture.

At Oxford, he allied himself with Samuel Daniel and married his sister Rosalind.   The geographer Hakluyt suggested that he translate the account of the first two voyages of Jacques Cartier [3] from the Italian text of Ramutius and, thanks to his knowledge of French, he entered the service of Michel de Castelnau, lord of Mauvissière and French ambassador to Elizabeth's court, as tutor to his daughter, Marie-Catherine, god-daughter of Mary Stuart.[4]

Thus Florio took part in the animated life of an embassy in constant touch with the captive queen and closely watched by Walsingham's agents. Several times a hostile crowd broke the windows and roughly handled the servants of France's representative.[5]

It is more than likely that Florio played the part of secret-agent on behalf of Burleigh in this employment, but without arousing the slightest suspicion on the part of the ambassador who, at his departure gave him full authority to finish up his business in London. He even recommended him to his successor, Baron de Châteaubeuf.

Then it was that at the instigation of Walsingham, Lord Burleigh confirmed Florio's appointment as resident tutor to his ward Southampton, whose former tutor, a Catholic, Swithin Welles, had recently been hanged for his faith.   It seemed prudent to keep an eye on the young lord, and the

[1] *Historia de la vita e de la morte de l'Illustriss.   Signora Giovanna Graia . . . Michelangelo Florio Fiorentino, gia predicatore famoso del Sant Evangelo in piu citta d'Italia e in Londra* (Ricardo Pittore, Venetia, 1607).

[2] Florio, *His First Fruts ;* whiche yielde familiar speech, merie proverbes, wittie sentences and golden sayinges ; also a perfect Introduction to the Italian and English Tongues as in the table appeareth (London, Thomas Dawson for Thomas Woodecocke, 1578).

[3] *A shorte and briefe narration of the two Navigations and Discoveries to the northwest partes called New France.*   First translated out of the French into Italian by that learned man Geo. Bapt. Ramatius and now turned into English by Iohn Florio (Bynneman, London, 1580).

[4] The Queen of Scots added to one of her important letters to the ambassador this charming note to little Catherine : " Ma filleule, ma mie, j'ay esté très aise de voir par vos lettres la preuve des perfections dont j'ay entendu que Dieu vous a donée en si grande jeunesse."

If Florio can be believed, his remarkable pupil played several instruments and spoke English and Italian like her mother tongue at the age of six.

[5] Another Italian refugee, Giordano Bruno, had sought protection in England under the same roof. The celebrated martyr of the Campo de Fiore describes an evening spent with Florio in his *Cena di Ceneri*.

presence of a zealous protestant like Florio who had already proved his loyalty to the crown, provided Walsingham with an astute political observer in the heart of this Romanist citadel.[1] This fixes the date of Giovanni Florio's entry upon his duties as tutor to Henry Wriothesley, Earl of Southampton, as 1591. It was precisely the moment when Shakespeare was beginning that monumental work more durable than bronze or stone, the immortal sonnets, dedicated to Florio's new pupil.

This strange collaboration between a rich dilettante, a poet eager to learn and a teacher eager to instruct, was to have fruitful results. Southampton, always attracted by romance, wished to see the characters and places of Italian fiction transported to the English stage ; Lombardy, the garden of the world, Venice, the indescribable city of which Florio boasted. For his part, the grammar school-pupil perceived an original method of triumphing over the hostile academicians by substituting for their eternal evocations of the classics the colourful Italy of the Renaissance. As for the pedagogue, he was content and happy to have found both a powerful nobleman and a poet of genius as propagandists of the culture he personified.[2] At the beginning of the last decade of the sixteenth century, this inseparable trio was much talked of. Two satires of the time—the only ones to come down to us—are full of the doings of the actor-poet and the young aristocrat followed like his shadow by an Italian.[3]

When the satirist Nashe joined Robert Greene in belittling the young dramatist he jeered at the author of *Hamlet* and accused him of delving for plots into Italian sources although ignorant of the rudiments of the language—an undeserved reproach, for Shakespeare had learned from Florio enough to suffice for his art.

[1] The learned Italian quickly gained the confidence of his young master, since he figures among the fourteen loyal servants to whom Southampton confided the lives of his two best friends, Sir Charles and Sir Henry Danvers. The Danvers brothers had been involved in a quarrel of the Capulet-Montague kind with Sir Harry Long, and had killed their man. The Earl of Southampton, in order to save them from justice, organized under the guise of hunting parties, their escape to the coast where they could embark for France. They were almost arrested at the ferry over the Itchin, when the sheriff recognized them. Among the young Earl's men, four distinguished themselves by their bravery, " the barber ", " the valet ", " the equerry " and M. Florio, the Italian master, and were denounced to the county justices (Lansdowne MSS. 827-5).

[2] We read in *First Fruits*, p. 51, an amusing dialogue on English culture and courtesy. " Towards whom are Englishmen ill mannered ? Towards strangers. When I arrived first in London I could not speak English and I met above five hundred persons afore I could find one that could tell me in Italian or French where the post dwelt—What would you have them do ; Learn languages ?—Yes Sir, and bring up their children well and have them taught to read, write and speak divers languages. . . . I see certain gentlemen, rather lowns to tell the truth, that begin to learn to speak Italian, French and Spanish and when they have learned two words of Spanish, three of French and four of Italian they think they have enough. . . ."

Shakespeare's Portia echoes this idea in giving the portrait of her English suitor. " I say nothing to him for he understands me not—nor I him—He hath neither Latin, French nor Italian. I have but a poor penny worth of English. He is a proper man's picture but who can converse with a dumb show. How oddly he is suited I think he bought his doublet in Italy, his round-hose in France, his bonnet in Germany and his behaviour everywhere."

[3] These two parodies are : *Willobie his Avisa*, a libel by an anonymous author (see Chapter VI) and *Histrio-Mastix* by Marston (see Chapter X).

Florio's library, to which Shakespeare had easy access, contained more than three hundred volumes, including some thirty old-style comedies. In this precious collection, the source of nearly all the Stratford dramatist's early plays, might be found the *Novelle* of Cinthio, Luigi da Porto, Boccaccio, and Bandello, the works of Machiavelli, Ariosto, Ser Giovanni, Florio Fiorentino, Petrarch, Aretino, and Dante. Many of these Italian works, plays and tales proudly listed by Florio were not yet translated : but with such an interpreter at his side, the writer from Stratford was able to learn their plots and their contents. Numerous proverbs quoted by him first appeared in Florio's publications. The title itself of *Love's Labour's Lost* is a saying in Florio's *First Fruits*—it were labour lost to speak of love.[1]

The manuals written by Florio and the dramatist's personal contact with their author sufficed for the rapid and convincing impressions of Italy to be found in the plays ; by imagination depending on a few descriptive features, he created the atmosphere of his trans-Alpine comedies and dramas. His impressionist brush-strokes are disconcerting in their simplicity. By means of a few proper names, Padua, Mantua, Verona, Milan and Venice, a proverb or two, scraps of phrases, in the " dolce lingua ", such as " con tutto il cuore ", " mi perdonate ", " ben trovato ", " molto honorato signor mio ", " fortuna della guerra ", together with the words " Madonna ", and " Signor " carelessly thrown in from time to time, he succeeded in creating an environment which seems essentially Italian. This facility has often deceived critics. Some think that, to evoke the peninsula with the strength of vision of a Titian or a Veronese, Shakespeare would have had to steep himself in Italian art, forgetting, however, that no artist is mentioned in his whole work, except in one of his latest plays, *The Winter's Tale*, where he praises a painter of the decadence, whom he takes furthermore for a sculptor.[2] A loggia under moonlight, a grove of sycamores, these are the background he uses to transmit an impression of a whole landscape. In *A Midsummer Night's Dream*, Titania's court is described with quite as much realism as that of Navarre in *Love's Labour's Lost*, or the Louvre in *All's Well that Ends Well*. From contact with Florio, Shakespeare became sufficiently familiar with Italian masterpieces to recognize the fame of Petrarch, to comprehend the geography of Dante's hell purgatory and paradise, and to comment on Machiavelli's political theories.

In *Romeo and Juliet*, when Mercutio mocks at his friend's lyrical passion, he compares it to Petrarch's devotion to Laura.

Now is he for the numbers that Petrarch flowed in : Laura to his lady was but a kitchen-wench ; marry she had a better love to be-rime her. . . .[3]

---

[1] " We r. ede not speak so much of love ; al books are ful of love, with so many authours, that it were labour lost to speake of love " (*First Fruits*, p. 71).

[2] The Princess hearing of her mother's statue—a piece many years in the doing and now newly performed by that rare Italian master Julio Romano, who, had he himself eternity and could put breath into his work, would beguile Nature of her custom, so perfectly he is her ape . . . (*The Winter's Tale*, Act v, Sc. 2).

[3] This same scene contains a passage inspired by Florio where Mercutio exclaims : " A duelist, a duelist ; a gentleman of the first house and second cause. Ah the immortal

It is by a reference to Dante's purgatory that Shakespeare excuses the libertinism of young Prince Hal in *Henry IV* :

> Most subject is the fattest soil to weeds
> And he, the noble image of my youth,
> Is overspread with them. . . .[1]
>
> (*Henry IV*, Part II, Act IV, Sc. 4)

The first direct allusion to the *Inferno* is in *Richard III* where Clarence tells the gaoler of the nightmare prophetic of his approaching death :

> O ! then began the tempest to my soul.
> I pass'd methought, the melancholy flood,
> With that grim ferry man which poets write of,
> Unto the kingdom of perpetual night.
>
> (*Richard III*, Act I, Sc. 4)

In speaking of the poets who give us glimpses of hell, Clarence was not thinking only of Virgil, but of Dante also.   In *Measure for Measure*, there is a more substantial indication that Shakespeare remembered the fifth Canto of the *Inferno* when he described Claudio's terror at the chastizement inflicted upon those who have sinned like him through love.   Claudio evokes, after the great Florentine, the vast expanse of ice and the circle of eternal winds, carrying on their invisible current the tormented souls of the illicit lovers Paolo and Francesca.[2]   Shakespeare's prisoner cries :

> Ay, but to die, and go we know not where ;
> To lie in cold obstruction and to rot ;
> This sensible warm motion to become
> A kneaded clod ; and the delighted spirit
> To bathe in fiery floods, or to reside
> In thrilling region of thick-ribbed ice ;
> To be imprison'd in the viewless winds,
> And blown with restless violence round about
> The pendant world.
>
> (*Measure for Measure*, Act III, Sc. 1)

Shakespeare alludes to Machiavelli three times.   In *The Merry Wives*

---

passado ! the punto reverso ! the Hay . . . a pox on such antick, lisping, affected fantasticoes these tuners of accents, these pardonnez mois. . . ."

Florio had described the celebrated Vincentio Saviolo, who " lookes like Mars himself ", fencing master to Essex and Southampton, thus : " He will hit any man be it with a thrust or imbrocada, a stoccada or a charging blow, a right or reverse blow with edge, back or with the flat." (*Second Fruits*, p. 117.)

[1] Ma tante pio maligno e piu silvestre
Si da il terren col mal seme e non colte
Quant egli ha piu del buon vigor terrestre.
(*Purgatorio*, Canto XXX, 118)

[2] Io venni in luogo d'ogni luce muto
Che mugglia come fa mar per tempesta
Se da contrari venti e combatuto.
La bufera infernal che mai non resta
Men gli spiriti con la sua rapina
Voltando e percitendo li molesto.
(*Inferno*, Canto V)

of Windsor, the host of the " Garter ", proud of his diplomacy and astuteness cries : " Am I politic ? am I subtle ? am I a Machiavel ? " [1]   And in the first part of *Henry VI* the Duke of York exclaims : " Alencon that notorious Machiavel ! " [2] and later in the third part of the same drama, Gloucester declares :

> I can add colours to the chameleon,
> Change shapes with Proteus for advantages,
> And set the murd'rous Machiavel to school.
> (*Third Part of Henry VI*, Act III, Sc. 2)

There is still another mention of the *Prince* in *The London Prodigal*,[3] often considered apocryphal, but full of originality.   There we find the young prodigal saying :

I have been reading over Nick Machiavel ; I find him good to be known not to be followed ; a pestilent human fellow, I have made certain annotations of him such as they be.

Among the three hundred proverbs which Florio boasted of having introduced into England, Shakespeare uses over thirty : there are a few quoted by the poet more than ten times.   The grammarian had declared that an Italian proverb translated into English " could not have the same grace or salt as in its original tongue ".   It is true that he hastened to add : " What matter if the sense is there ; it is still a delight to the hearer."   The linguist was right ; certain of his sayings, " chi non fa non falla ", for example, sound better in Italian than when translated, as : " He who makes not, mars not."   But both poet and pedant agreed in making frequent use of proverbs.   It is interesting to observe the manner in which Shakespeare incorporates Florio's " golden sentences " in his dialogue or fits them into his verse.

> All that glistereth is not gold . . .
> (Florio, *First Fruits*, p. 32)

> All that glisters is not gold
> Golden tombs do dust enfold . . .
> (*The Merchant of Venice*, Act II, Sc. 5)

> More water flows by the mill than the miller knows . . .
> (Florio, *First Fruits*, p. 34)

> More water glideth by the mill than wots the miller of.
> (*Titus Andronicus*, Act II, Sc. 1)

> When the cat is abroade the mise play . . .
> (Florio, *First Fruits*, p. 33)

---

[1] *The Merry Wives of Windsor*, Act III, Sc. 2.

[2] First part of *Henry VI*, Act v, Sc. 4.

[3] Although this play is generally labelled apocryphal, I believe Shakespeare had a hand in it, if only for the following reason : even in its author's lifetime, after having been played with great success at " The Globe ", it appeared in his name after being entered officially with the Stationers' Company.   Its authenticity is therefore otherwise established than that of *Locrine* and other plays signed " W.S.", which were not acted at " The Globe ".

Playing the mouse in absence of the cat . . .
>(*Henry V*, Act I, Sc. 2)

He that maketh not, marreth not . . .
>(Florio, *First Fruits*, p. 26)

What make you ?   Nothing ?   What mar you then ?
>(*As You Like It*, Act I, Sc. 1)

An ill weed groweth apace . . .
>(Florio, *First Fruits*, p. 31)

Small herbs have grace ;   great weeds do grow apace.
>(*Richard III*, Act II, Sc. 4)

Give losers leave to speak . . .
>(Florio, *Second Fruits*, p. 69)

But I can give the loser leave to chide,
And well such losers may have leave to speak.
>(*Henry VI*, Part II, Act III, Sc. 1)

Necessity hath no law . . .
>(Florio, *First Fruits*, p. 32)

Nature must obey necessity . . .
>(*Julius Caesar*, Act IV, Sc. 3)

The end maketh all men equal . . .
>(Florio, *First Fruits*, p. 31)

One touch of nature makes the whole world kin . . .
>(*Troilus and Cressida*, Act III, Sc. 3)

That is quickly done, that is done well . . .
>(Florio, *First Fruits*, p. 27)

If it were done when 'tis done, then 'twere well it were
    done quickly . . .
>(*Macbeth*, Act I, Sc. 7)

Fast binde, fast finde . . .
>(Florio, *Second Fruits*, p. 15)

Fast bind, Fast Find, A proverb never stale in thrifty mind.
>(*The Merchant of Venice*, Act II, Sc. 5)

In *Love's Labour's Lost* a title borrowed, as has been seen, from the Italian-English manual, Shakespeare makes Holofernes say :

Ah ! good old Mantuan.   I may speak of thee as the traveller doth of Venice : —Venetia, Venetia,
>Chi non te vede, non te pretia.

Florio had written :

Venetia qui non ti vedi non ti pretia ; ma chi ti vede ben gli costa ! [1]

---

[1] The discovery of this saying by Richard Farmer in 1767 caused critics to fix the date of *Love's Labour's Lost* as subsequent to 1591 when Florio's *Second Fruits* was written. This deduction is erroneous, Florio having already set down the proverb in Italian in his *First Fruits* which bears the date : London. August 10th, 1578. Thus on the almost unique occasion when a modern commentator acknowledges that Shakespeare did owe something to Southampton's tutor, he draws from a correct premise a false conclusion.

The author of *King John* certainly borrows another passage from the *First Fruits,* when describing the arrival of a foreigner in an English home. His ideas, sentences and words are all quoted ; there is even the tooth-pick which Florio considered the mark of elegance.

> Now your traveller,
> He and his toothpick at my worship's mess,
> And when my knightly stomach is suffic'd,
> Why then I suck my teeth, and catechize
> My picked man of countries : ' My dear sir,'
> Thus leaning on mine elbow, I begin,
> ' I shall beseech you,'—that is question now ;
> And then comes answer like an absey-book :
> ' O sir,' says answer, ' at your best command;
> At your employment, at your service, sir ' :
> ' No sir,' says question, ' I, sweet sir, at yours ' :
> And so, ere answer knows what question would,
> Saving in dialogue of compliment,
> And talking of the Alps and Appennines,
> The Pyrenean and the river Po,
> It draws toward supper in conclusion so . . .
>   (*King John*, Act 1, Sc. 1)

How many times has it been objected that Shakespeare could not have been the author of *The Merchant of Venice*, since he never went to Italy, and that in this play, not only are Venetian customs mentioned, but the Rialto is described as a quarter where merchants congregate to transact business. " An uncultured man like Shakespeare ", it is averred, " would only have used ' the Rialto ' to refer to the bridge of that name."

Such critics forget that the pedant Florio, once settled in London, found a real vocation in instructing those who never travelled ; but his stay-at-home pupil could easily learn about the Rialto from his dictionary :

Rialto—An eminent place in Venice where merchants commonly meet, as on the Exchange in London.

In his second conversation manual published in 1591, and entitled *Second Fruits to be gathered of twelve trees of divers but delightsome tastes to the tongues of Italians and Englishmen*, Florio shows some aptitude for versification. The Spondaic form was practically non-existent at this time in English poetry ; yet Florio used this metre to enumerate the physical qualities which a woman must possess to be considered perfectly beautiful.

> In choyse of faire, are thirtie things required
> For which (they say) faire Hellen was admired . . .
> White teeth, white hands and neck as yvorie white.
> Black eyes, black browes, black heares that hide delight.
> Red lippes, red cheekes, and tops of nipples red,
> Long leggs, long fingers, long locks of her head.
> Short feete, shorte eares and teeth in measure short,
> Broad front, broade brest, broad hippes in seemely sort.

> Streight leggs, streight nose and streight her pleasure place,
> Full thighes, full buttocks, full her bellies space,
> Thin lipps, thin eylids, and heare thin and fine
> Smale mouth, smale waist, smale pupil of her eyne,
> Of these who want, so much of fairest wants,
> And who hath all, her beautie perfect vauntes.[1]

Shakespeare, in his turn, uses the spondee to describe the perfect horse.[2]

> So did this horse excel a common one
> In shape, in courage, colour, pace and bone.
> Round hoofed, short jointed, fetlocks shag and long
> Broad breast, full eye, small head and nostril wide.
> High crest, short ears, straight leggs and passing strong
> Thin mane, thick tail, broad buttock, tender hide
> Look what a horse should have he did not lack
> Save a proud rider on so proud a back.

The author, in his *Second Fruits*, proposes to inculcate his own opinions on art and morals. The puritanism he affected in 1578 appears much attenuated in the dialogues of the second miscellany. The subject of love was omitted from the First. In the Second he devotes sixty pages of discussion to the tender passion, quoting Ovid constantly; it would seem that he already felt Shakespeare's influence, for he concludes that love is as indispensable to mankind as eating or lying and that these major needs led to the invention of Rhetoric.

All the subjects or rather hobbies which were dear to Southampton: cards, dice, primero, riding, fencing, falconry, hunting, the theatre and tennis, are constantly referred to in *Second Fruits*. The tennis match played by Thomas and Henry where Master John acts as umpire but refuses to make a wager because he does not like to see his money take wings, is amusing, we might almost say up to date. Rules and scoring are practically the same; the balls are expensive and extremely fragile—three-and-a-half dozen were put out of commission in six sets. This is how the game is led up to.

> Let us make a match at tenis.
> Agreed, this coole morning calls for it,
> And afterwards we will dine together;
> Then after dinner we will goe see a plaic.
> The plaies they plaie in England are not right comedies;
> Yet they doo nothing else but plaie every daye.
> Yea but they are neither right comedies, nor right tragedies.
> How would you name them then ?
> Representations of histories without any decorum.[3]

This remark might be taken as a hit at Shakespeare, already reputed for his trilogy *King Henry VI* and *King John*. But this is improbable, for the

---

[1] Florio's *Second Fruits*, p. 131.   [2] Shakespeare's *Venus and Adonis*, line 292.
[3] Florio's *Second Fruits*, p. 23.

linguist makes his meaning clear on the Italian side of the dialogue where the words are " Senz'alcun decoro " (without any scenery). However this may be, it was only after 1598, when the dramatist caricatured Florio on the stage, that the Florentine reacted with a series of attacks not only on his production but upon the author himself.

Florio's manuals of conversation were followed in 1598 by his copious Italian-English dictionary entitled *Woorlde of Words*.[1]

This publication, dedicated to his best pupils, presented a serious problem to the super snob : how to compose a dedicatory epistle so as to honour his patron Southampton, without offending Lord Rutland, who was of higher rank, but to whom the author was less beholden ?

Florio found a way out of the difficulty by inscribing the names of the two Earls side by side, and in his most pompous style asked them to take each others' hands as " peers of equal parity " without disparagement and settle their order of precedence between themselves, remarking that for the philosopher there exists neither right nor left, for Plato considered the man who was not ambidexterous an imperfect being. As for himself, Florio, if he followed his " heart and his duty ", he might " commit the error of giving the place of honour to the patron to whom he owed all ", whereas custom and etiquette designated Lord Rutland to " preside at the baptism of this brain babe ", whose appointed godmother was Lucy, Countess of Bedford, one of the most notable literary patronesses in the Queen's court.

The compliments which he addressed to the Earl of Southampton on this occasion look as if they were inspired by Shakespeare's dedication of *Lucrece*. Doubtless Florio hoped that with a text imitated from Shakespeare's, he might reap a similar success. It was a good deal to ask.

In truth I acknowledge an entyre debt, not onely of my best knowledge, but of all, yea of more then I know or can, to your bounteous Lordship, most noble, most vertuous, and most Honorable Earle of Southampton in whose paye, and patronage I have lived some yeeres ; to whom I owe and vowe the yeeres I have to live.

But Florio's star had begun to wane. Though merchants might continue to buy dictionaries and conversation manuals, men of letters were turning away from an Italy which in 1597 had ceased to be productive. The publication of Montaigne's Essays at Bordeaux was to discriminating readers a literary event. The robust philosophy of Montaigne replaced the complex opportunism of Machiavelli. Many were anxious to read his essays ; some wished to imitate them, among them Francis Bacon and Southampton's uncle, Cornwallis ; but what the public asked for was above all the real text, or else a good translation. Florio, who had observed, not without bitterness, the influence of French thought increase around him to the

---

[1] *Worlde of Words*, Or Most copious and exact Dictionnarie in Italian and English collected by Iohn Florio ; Printed at London by Arnold Hatfield for Edward Blount (1598). Thirteen years later, he published a second edition of his dictionary, much amplified and under more flattering auspices : *Queen Anna's New World of Words*, etc., collected . . . by Iohn Florio, Reader of the Italian unto the Sovereigne Maiestie of Anna . . . London, printed by Melch Bradwood for Edward Blount and Wm. Barret (anno 1611).

detriment of his Italian idols, pressed by his friends and pupils, agreed to translate the Essays into English. He describes himself in his preface, struggling with difficulties of every sort ; but faithful to his designation of " resolute " he pursued his labour :

I with one Chapter found myselfe over-charged, . . . your Honor having dayned to read it, without pitty of my failing, my fainting, my labouring, my langishing, my gasping for some breath. . . . Yet commaunded me on . . . I must needes say while this was in doing, to put and keepe mee in hart like a captived Canniball fattend against my death, you often cryed *Coraggio*, and called Cà Cà, and applauded as I passt, . . . I sweat, I wept and I went on, til now I stand at bay :

The printing licence was not requested until 1600 and the book did not appear until 1603 ; but Florio succeeded in interesting patrons in his work from the commencement.   The enterprise was encouraged by Southampton and his kindred.   His uncle Cornwallis, struck as much by the intelligence as by the ugliness of the Italian translator, wrote in 1598 : [1]

Montaigne now speaks good English. The work has been done by a man to whom nature has given more wit then fortune, yet more fortune than pleasant aspect.[2]

Once embarked, Florio gave himself over to his task.   If he had not a very high opinion of the English language, it must be admitted that on this occasion, he showed ability in handling it.

It doth not like me at al, because it is a language confused, bepeesed with many tongues : it taketh many words of the latine, mo from the French, & mo from the Italian, and many mo from the Duitch, some also from the Greeke, & from the Britaine, so that if every language had his owne wordes againe, there woulde but fewe remaine for English men, and yet every day they adde. (*First Tributes*, p. 50.)

For him, a translation, even in prose, could not adequately render a masterpiece ; it could give the sense of the original text, but to the detriment of form :

every language hath it's *Genius* and inseperable fame, without *Pythagoras* his Metempsychosis it can not rightly be translated. The Tuscan altiloquence, the *Venus* of the French, the sharpe state of the Spanish, the strong significancy of the Dutch cannot from hcere be drawne to life.   The sense may keepe forme ;

---

[1] Florio does not seem to have shared the unfavourable opinion of Cornwallis on his physiognomy, since he had included his portrait, engraved by the celebrated Hole, in his edition of the *Dictionary* and also in his translation of the *Essays*.

[2] The *Essays* of Montaigne in English were printed in a fine folio edition, embellished by a frontispiece representing three altars : on each of which was written either First, Second or Third book of the *Essays*, and under these titles, two women's names under whose aegis he flatteringly placed his work.   The names of the Duchess of Bedford and Lady Harrington figure on the first altar ; Penelope Devereux, Lady Rich and the Countess of Rutland adorned the second, Lady Elizabeth Grey and Lady Mary Beville, the third. Addressing these pupils, Florio declares his love for the languages by which he makes his living, but that he never loves them so well as when he hears these fair ladies speak them.

the sentence is disfigured ; the finenesse, fitnesse, featenesse diminished : as much as artes nature is short of natures arte, a picture of the body, shadow of a substance. . . . Why then belike I have done by *Montaigne*, as Terence by Menander. . . . His horse I set before yow, perhaps without his trappings : and his meate without sause.

But he finishes this apology on a note of customary defiance :

In summe, if any thinke that he could do better, let him trie : then will he better thinke of what is done. Seven or eight of great wit and worth have assayed, but found these Essayes no attempt for French apprentises or Littletonians. If thus donne it may please you, as I wish it may, and hope it shall, I with you shall be pleased : though not, yet still I am the same resolute.

Iohn Florio.

It would be hard to praise this translation of the *Essays* too highly. The fault of Florio's style is preciosity ; but when he limits himself to transposing Montaigne's phrases from French into English, his qualities as linguist, grammarian and scholar find their proper sphere. Florio selects the best word, the felicitous expression, and his inclination to pedantry disappears before Montaigne's simplicity. Some passages, notably those from the chapter entitled *That to philosophize, is to learn how to die* could be termed models of English style ; the translations of the *Apologia of Raymond Sebond* and the *Essay on Etienne de la Boétie* compared favourably with the originals. It has often been said that Florio made use of a Shakespearean English in his translations. Like Montaigne himself, he charms and fascinates his reader ; by a happy turn of phrase he compensates for occasional infidelity to the text. In short, he has achieved a second masterpiece. He did not completely follow either of the two contemporary French editions, but took from one or the other the expression best suited to his translation. He retains the famous preface which begins : " C'est ici un livre de bonne foi, lecteur ", which Mlle. de Gournay had suppressed in the Paris edition, but he renders due homage to Montaigne's adopted daughter by adding to the " Préface au lecteur " of the second edition the author's own words : " Que t'en semble donc, lecteur ? " He preserves the passage on Mary Stuart [1] of the second French edition and returns to the first to render the curious phrase : " Les plus mortes morts sont les plus saines " by " The deadest deaths are best ".[2]

The success of the *Essays* in England was enormous, and Shakespeare, conforming once again to contemporary fashion, lost no time in acquainting himself with the ideas which they expressed. About forty allusions or quotations from Montaigne's work can be found in the plays written during the years when Florio was translating the *Essays*.[3]

---

[1] " La plus belle royne veufve du plus grand roy de la chrétienté vient-elle pas de mourir par main de boureau, indigne et barbare cruanté."

[2] This reflection is omitted from the copy corrected by Montaigne in 1590 (Book I, Chapter XIX).

[3] Only thirty years elapsed before the book reached three editions (1603, 1613, and 1632). The folio of 1613, with its frontispiece designed and drawn by Martin Droeshout, sold at a price equal to that of Shakespeare's.

The quotations which follow bring out not only a similarity established by Capell nearly two centuries ago, but also demonstrate how much Shakespeare had absorbed of the true spirit of the *Essays*.

The great writer of Bordeaux had thus described his ideal republic :

. . . what in these nations wee see by expericece, doth not only exceede all the pictures wherewith licentious Poesie hath prowdly embellished the golden age, and all hir quaint inventions to faine a happy condition of men, but also the conception and desire of Philosophie. . . . It is a nation, would I answere Plato, that hath no kinde of traffike, no knowledge of letters, no intelligence of numbers, no name of magistrate, nor of politike superioritie ; no use of service, of riches, or of poverty ; no contracts, no successions, no dividences, no occupation but idle ; no respect of kinred but common, no apparell but naturell, no manuring of lands, no use of wine, corne, or mettle. The very words that import lying, falshood, treason, dissimulation, covetousnes, envie, detraction and pardon, were never heard of amongst them. How dissonant would hee finde his imaginary common-wealth from this perfection ?

> (*Essays*, Book I, Chapter XXX, " Of the cannibals ", Florio's translation)

Shakespeare's corresponding text is found in *The Tempest :*

Gonzalo :	I' the commonwealth I would by contraries
	Execute all things ; for no kind of traffic
	Would I admit ; no name of magistrate ;
	Letters should not be known ; riches, poverty,
	And use of service, none : contract, succession,
	Bourn, bound of land, tilth, vineyard, none ;
	No use of metal, corn or wine or oil ;
	No occupation ; all men idle, all ;
	And women too, but innocent and pure ;
	No sovereignty.
Sebastian :	Yet he would be king on't.
Antonio :	The latter end of his commonwealth forgets the beginning.
Gonzalo :	All things in common nature should produce
	Without sweat or endeavour : treason, felony,
	Sword, pike, knife, gun, or need of any engine,
	Would I not have ; but nature should bring forth,
	Of its own kind, all foison, all abundance,
	To feed my innocent people.
Sebastian :	No marrying 'mong his subjects ?
Antonio :	None, man ; all idle ; whores and knaves.
Gonzalo :	I would with such perfection govern, sir,
	To excel the golden age.

When Shakespeare puts into the mouth of the noble Edgar this reflection :

> Men must endure their going hence, even as their coming hither ;
> Ripeness is all.
>
> (*King Lear*, Act v, Sc. 2)

The English poet recalled Montaigne who, in his chapter " That to philosophize, is to learne how to die ", wrote : " Nature compels us to it. Depart (saith she,) out of this world, even as you came into it. . . . If you have profited by life, you have also beene fed thereby, depart then satisfied." (*Essays*, Book I, Chapter XIX.)

More striking than the number of Shakespeare's borrowings from Montaigne is the similarity of thought between the great humanist and the humanitarian. This intellectual affinity can be detected in the English poet from the moment he became acquainted with the *Essays*. That Montaigne's ideas greatly impressed Shakespeare, may be seen in the introspective modifications made in *Hamlet*, a play which, before its alteration, was shown as a melodrama. The sympathy felt by Shakespeare for the thought of Montaigne is evident in all his seventeenth-century work ; particularly in *King Lear, Macbeth, The Winter's Tale, Measure for Measure* and *Othello*. In the earlier plays, Shakespeare was simply preoccupied with the action. It was the spectator's part to understand why the characters behaved thus and thus. Henceforth his heroes begin to think, doubt and analyse their feelings, attempting to discover the motives behind decision. The unseen drama thenceforth takes place in Hamlet's or Macbeth's mind rather than in the play's visible development. It is therefore not surprising to find Shakespeare's signature followed by the words " Mors Incerta ", in the copy of the *Essays* preserved at the British Museum. The handwriting certainly appears to be that of the poet, who must have possessed Florio's translation, and the reference to the *Essay* on death, where he found so many of the thoughts repeated in his plays, is not surprising. This volume has been in the British Museum since 1780 ; it would have taken a clever forger to choose a translation of the *Essays* in which to write an apocryphal signature at a date when nobody recognized Montaigne's influence upon Shakespeare nor the link which united the English poet and the Italian pedant.

According to local tradition the two mulberry trees which graced the gardens of Shakespeare and his daughter at Stratford [1] were imported from Italy by Florio, and if probabilities can be accepted without proof, how tempting to believe that Southampton had brought about a real friendship between his poet and his Italian tutor ? Unfortunately Shakespeare's works and Florio's writings lead to quite another conclusion. Far from being a connecting link between his protégés, Southampton was a subject of continual discord, caused by a rivalry almost bitter on the part of the tutor, moderated in the poet by good sense and kindliness.

In *Love's Labour's Lost*, Shakespeare drew, with much humour and little malice, the portrait of an Italian schoolmaster resembling Florio like a brother. It is even said that when altering his comedy for the first time, the author accentuated the resemblance between his burlesque character and its model. The name " Holofernes " taken from Rabelais was chosen

---

[1] The tree planted by Shakespeare in his garden was cut down in the eighteenth century by one F. Gasterall, tenant of New Place, on the pretext that this souvenir of the poet attracted too many visitors. In their indignation, the inhabitants of Stratford forced the vandal to leave the town. The mulberry in Susanna Hall's garden is still in existence.

because it constituted an anagram of " Iohn-Florio ", transparent enough to be universally recognized.[1]   In those days a vowel more or less was permissible in this fashionable literary game.   It cannot be objected that the anagram is only approximate, since Florio himself accepts and publishes—in the preface to his *Dictionary* of 1611—one which is no better : " Ihonnes Florio—Orifons Alieno."

The similarity between Holofernes' speech and that of the grammarian in the *First Fruits* is remarkable.   Admittedly the habit of quoting latin on every occasion is common to pedants in general, but it is not the abuse of latin, however, which attracts attention toward Holofernes ; on the contrary it is the use he makes of Italian and French expressions.   Obviously the character alluded to is a teacher of languages.

Florio's exaggerated taste for alliteration is sufficiently shown in these quotations :

Good partes imparted are not impaired.

Proverbs are the pith, the proprieties, the proofes, the purities, the elegancies, as the commonest so the commendablest phrases of a language.   To use them is a grace, to understand them a good, but to gather them a paine to me, but a gaine to thee.[2]

Holofernes affects alliteration quite as much as the grammarian, and boasts of his excellence therein.   When reciting his verse on the death of the deer, he announces his intention :

I will something affect the letter ; for it argues facility.
The preyful princess pierc'd and prick'd a pretty pleasing pricket ;
Some say a sore ; but not a sore, till now made sore with shooting.
                    (*Love's Labour's Lost*, Act IV, Sc. 2)

It would be hard to achieve a more striking imitation of Florio.   Again Holofernes declares his taste for apostrophes.   He says that they avoid hiatus and that, slipped in suitably, they replace the caesura with happy effect, allowing the reader to stress the important syllable.   When his interlocutor reads, the pedant objects : " But you find not the apostrophes, and so miss the accent."   Had not Florio written in the *First Fruits :*

The addition of the apostrophe is a good method of pleasantly continuing the word by a sort of delectation, not only for him who speaks but for those who listen.

Holofernes is pastmaster in the art of choosing recondite terms : " phantasm ", " epitheton ", " insanie ", figure in his repertoire ; like Florio he uses the word " peregrinate " as an adjective.   " He is too picked, too spruce, too affected, too odd, as it were to peregrinate as I may call it."

---

[1] *The Italian Dictionary* by Florio contains the following definitions : Coelo—heaven, the sky or welkin.   Terra—earth, land, soil.   These two definitions are repeated literally by Holofernes.   Shakespeare here aims his epigrams directly at the English Vadius. (Francois-Victor Hugo, notes on the translation of the *Comedies de l'amour*.)

[2] *Second Fruits :* Epistle to the reader.

(*Love's Labour's Lost*, Act v, Sc. 2.)   He delights in selecting rare epithets :
" Congruent ", " Thrasonical ", and " point-devise " so that Costard the
rustic, who is listening, exclaims to the small page :

O ! they have lived long on the alms basket of words.   I marvel thy master
hath not eaten thee for a word ; for thou art not so long by the head as " honorificabilitudinitatibus ".[1]

(*Love's Labour's Lost*, Act v, Sc. 1)

As for the argument which maintains that a poet who had dedicated two
works to Lord Southampton would never have dared make fun of his tutor,
this objection betrays a lack of knowledge both of the psychology of literary
jealousy and also of the mentality of youth.[2]

In Shakespeare's time, young people were not less fond of jokes and
ridicule than they are today : " the prosperity of a jest " was to them an
important matter.   Several of Shakespeare's comedies have as their principal
theme the success of a practical joke at some victim's expense, as proved by
The Merry Wives of Windsor, *Twelfth Night* and *All's Well That Ends Well*.
These plays evidence the taste for farcical situations.   The pleasantries
perpetrated especially amused their victim's friends and patrons.   Besides,
has it ever been observed that the profession of teacher—however popular—
protects the master from his pupils' mirth ?

If it is true that the poet's intention was to make an amusing caricature
of Florio, it was doubtless with the desire to entertain Lord Southampton.
The caricature is witty, gay and well-observed ; in no way is it cruel or
malevolent.   The pedant is represented as a somewhat boastful egoist, a
lover of definitions who is for ever quoting Italian ; but he is full of good

---

[1] Under the title, *Offering of a Translator :* Notes on the English of John Florio, translator of Montaigne, Mr. A. Koszul published in the *Anglo-American Review* a very well-
documented article where he enumerates the new terms, the neologisms and archaisms
introduced into the English language by John Florio.

Mention should be made of *l'Etude sur la grammaire et le vocabulaire de Montaigne*, by
Joseph Coppin (Lille, 1925), and a little dissertation by Fritz Dieckow : *Englische Ueber-
setzung der Essais von Montaigne*.

Florio was the first in England to criticize the use of words of ten or twelve syllables,
and gives as examples :

" Misericordiosissimamente " and " Constantinopolotanissimo ".   " Such words ", he
says, " disfigure prose and are intolerable in poetry."

Written in the margin of the parish register of Pillerton in Warwickshire are the two
words : " Constantinopolotanissimo " and " Honorificabilitatitudinibus " ; on the other
hand, on the Northumberland manuscript one finds among numerous inscriptions and
signatures of Shakespeare, the word " Honorificabilitudine " written in the same hand,
probably that of the poet.

[2] The question : did Shakespeare intend to caricature Florio in the character of Holofernes, has been the subject of controversies since 1776 when Ricjard Farmer published his
Essay on Shakespeare's erudition.   On one side there are those who, in accordance with
tradition, hold that the Italian did indeed serve as model for the pedantic schoolmaster,
and on the other, those who believe that Shakespeare would never have dared to attack
any member of Southampton's entourage.   Warburton, Hanmer, Steevens and Acheson
agree with Farmer and traditional belief.   The other group consists of Hunter, Furness,
Saintsbury, the German Franz Horn and several writers of the " Shakespeare did not
write Shakespeare " school of thought, among others, Abel Lefranc.

intentions, and he acquits himself in his part of Judas Maccabeus in the *Nine Worthies* a little less absurdly than his colleagues.

The caricature does not seem to have overstepped permissible bounds. It was considered extremely funny ; the habitués of Rutland and Southampton's world must have been amused at the entrance of the stage pedant, made up, as tradition asserts, to resemble Florio. They must have laughed again when Shakespeare, stimulated by this success, drew on his imagination for another caricature of the Italian linguist. The vain, self-satisfied steward of *Twelfth Night* is named Malvolio (the ill-intentioned). His precise speech, his absurd pretensions and exaggerated puritanism recall salient traits of both Florio and Holofernes. Once again the audience sided with the poet and laughed at his irreverent wit directed against the irate grammarian.

Perhaps Shakespeare went too far when he maliciously mocked the doctrine of Pythagoras, so dear to Florio and his friend Giordano Bruno.[1] This theory was almost a religion to the linguist, and Bruno died a martyr to this belief.

While theatrical enthusiasts easily recognized Florio in Malvolio and Holofernes, it is certain that the learned Italian also understood that he was the subject of the joke, and did not temper his vengeance. In reply to Shakespeare's lightly drawn portrait, he wrote violent diatribes and declared war upon the actor-dramatist who laughed at erudition and took liberties with his name.

In the *Epistle to the reader* of his 1598 *Dictionary* Florio heaps invective on the enemy calling him " Sowgelder " or " swine's head ", in Italian " hypocrito simulatore " and " hedara sequace ". He compares him with a " crow " who has stolen a sage's golden harvest.

Let Aristophanus, he exclaims, and his comedians, write their plays and scour their mouths on Socrates. Their mouthings will become a means of exalting his virtues.

And the new Socrates continues :

For I have a whole faction of good authors to bandy with me.

We can perhaps identify the friends whom Florio calls to his rescue as John Marston [2] and Joseph Hall.[3]

[1] *Clown :* What is the opinion of Pythagoras concerning wild fowl ?
Mal. : That the soul of our grandma might haply inhabit a bird . . . etc.
(*Twelfth Night*, Act IV, Sc. 2)
Shakespeare again alludes to the Pythagorean theory in *As You Like It* and *The Merchant of Venice*.
Rosalind :   I was never so be-rimed since Pythagoras' time,
that I was an Irish rat, which I can hardly remember.
(*As You Like It*, Act III, Sc. 2)
Gratiano :   Thou almost mak'st me waver in my faith
To hold opinion with Pythagoras,
That souls of animals infuse themselves
Into the trunks of men. . . .
(*The Merchant of Venice*, Act IV, Sc. 1)
[2] *Scourge of villanie* (London, 1598).   [3] *Virgidemiarum* (London, 1597).

Marston, after quoting some lines from *Venus and Adonis*, twice parodied the famous passage in *Richard III :* " A horse, a horse, my kingdom for a horse " with " A man, a man, my kingdom for a man " and also " A fool, a fool, my cockscomb for a fool ", adding :

> I set thy lips abroach, from whence doth flow
> Naught but pure *Juliat* and *Romio.*
> Say, who acts best ?   *Drufus,* or *Roscio ?*
> Now I have him, that nere of ought did speake
> But when of playes or Plaiers he did treate.
> H'ath made a common-place booke out of plaies,
> And speakes in print, at least what ere he sayes
> Is warranted by Curtaine *plaudeties.* . . .

Joseph Hall also joined the chorus of detractors who attack the dramatist for daring to place vulgar clowns beside great kings and to represent on the stage taverns of ill repute such as were described by " wicked Rabelais ".

It would indeed have been hard for such dissimilar natures as those of Shakespeare and Florio to understand or admire one another.   Naturally frank, generous and kindly, the poet had a marked taste for persiflage ; his satire was often biting enough to offend the susceptible grammarian, especially when he ridiculed his person and his gods.   From the day when Southampton brought the two men together at Holborn House to that upon, which, under James's patronage, they found themselves side by side at court, the one wearing the livery of the King's Privy Chamber, the other exercising the duties of secretary to the Queen, they had many opportunities of meeting.

In literary and printing circles, their associates were the same, Ben Jonson, so closely linked to Shakespeare, addressed a fine copy of his *Volpone* to Giovanni Florio, accompanied by a dedication thanking the erudite Italian for having provided examples of local colour which enabled him to present convincing scenes of Venetian life, which Jonson no more than Shakespeare had ever seen in reality.

To his loving father and worthy friend, Mr. John Florio, ayde of his muses, Ben Jonson seals this testimony of Friendship and Love.[1]

Florio for his part thanked Jonson in some preliminary lines included in a series of epigraphs praising the author of *Volpone*.   James Mabbe was an admirer of both protagonists, covering each with praise in dithyrambic stanzas.   Samuel Daniel, Florio's brother-in-law, was also probably a friend of Shakespeare.[2]

Thomas Thorpe, publisher of the Sonnets in 1609, dedicated his translation of *Epictetus* to Florio in the same year.   Edward Blount published several volumes of both writers.   Martin Droeshout, who designed the

---

[1] The copy of *Volpone* containing the dedication belongs to the British Museum.

[2] Daniel dedicated one of his works as follows : To my deare friend and brother, Mr. John Florio, one of the gentlemen of her Majesties Royall Privie Chamber.

excellent frontispiece of Florio's translation of Montaigne's *Essays*, engraved the mediocre portrait of Shakespeare reproduced in the folio of 1623.

When Shakespeare and his Troupe passed into the service of King James, they found themselves under the direct orders of the Earl of Pembroke, who had been created Lord Chamberlain. Florio enjoyed the same patronage and thus could display at the very beak of Shakespeare's Falcon his " Marygold proper in chief a sun in splendour proper ".[1]

But Florio's good fortune came to an end with Queen Anne's death in 1618. His last years were spent in the vain struggle to get his later manuscripts printed, in fighting poverty, in vain bickerings with his daughter Aurelia and his son-in-law, Doctor Mollins. He died of the plague at Fulham, 1625, leaving three or four hundred rare volumes in Spanish, Italian and French, to Lord Pembroke adjuring him to care charitably for his wife Rose Spicer " than whom no man ever had a more painful nurse nor comfortable consort ".

Of the misunderstandings between poet and pedant, there remains today only a distant echo. But scholars will only remember that Florio enriched the English language by hundreds of words, and that by his writings and conversation, he revealed new horizons to Shakespeare, gave him the means of impregnating his Italian comedies with an atmosphere of reality, and introduced his muse to the genius of Montaigne.

---

[1] This blazon of which the British Museum has the design (Harleian MSS. 6140, fol. 9) was accorded by Sir W. M. Seegar, August 23rd, 1614.

CHAPTER X

DRAMATIC PRODUCTION, 1592-1596

The plays written in this period—Date of production—*Richard III*—*All's Well That Ends Well*—*The Two Gentlemen of Verona*—*Romeo and Juliet*—*The Merchant of Venice*—Moroccan portrait—*Richard II*—*Henry IV*—*Troilus and Cressida*—Marston's attacks : *Histrio-Mastix*—Death of Lord Hunsdon ; Lord Cobham succeeds him as Chamberlain—Closing of the theatres—The actors on tour—Death of Hamlet Shakespeare.

SHAKESPEARE'S dramatic writing at this time, like his lyric poetry, reflects the influence of Southampton. The varied tastes and pre-occupations of his patron account for the dramatist's wide choice of subjects and the originality of their treatment. With astonishing facility, Shakespeare turns from a drama of violent death and the powers of darkness to an idyllic world ; then, as though to reconcile the two muses, he embarks upon a genre of his own invention—tragi-comedy.[1]

In his *Treasures of the Mind* (Paladis Tamia) Francis Meres, an admirer of the sonnets, mentions the plays acted during his stay in London (1593-98).[2]

As Plautus and Seneca are accounted the best for comedy and tragedy among the Latins so Shakespeare among the English is the most excellent in both kinds for the stage ; for Comedy, witness his *Gentlemen of Verona*, his *Errors*, his *Love's Labour's Lost*, his *Love's Labour's Won*, his *Midsummer Night's Dream* and his *Merchant of Venice ;* for tragedy his *Richard II, Richard III, Henry IV, King John, Titus Andronicus* and his *Romeo and Juliet.*

Titus Andronicus, King John and the farces or fairy plays mentioned by Meres were studied in Chapter V ; three new comedies therefore remain—*Love's Labour's Won, The Two Gentlemen of Verona, The Merchant of Venice,* and four tragedies—*Richard III, Romeo and Juliet, Richard II, Henry IV*—which made their first appearance on the stage after 1592 and before 1598,

---

[1] Nicholas Rowe in excusing Shakespeare's tragedies for not conforming to Aristotle's rules says : " But as Shakespear liv'd under a kind of mere Light of Nature, and had never been made acquainted with the Regularity of those written Precepts, so it would be hard to judge him by a Law he knew nothing of. We are to consider him as a Man that liv'd in a State of almost universal License and Ignorance : There was no establish'd Judge, but every one took the liberty to Write according to the Dictates of his own Fancy. When one considers that there is not one Play before him of a Reputation good enough to entitle it to an Appearance on the present Stage, it cannot but be a Matter of great Wonder that he should advance Dramatick Poetry so far as he did." (Nicholas Rowe, 1709, p. 26.)

[2] Meres' book appeared in 1598. At this date the author, graduate of Oxford and Cambridge, lodged in the narrow St. Botolph Street, in Eastcheap. In 1602, he was at Wing as preacher in the church, and master at the school.

the date at which Meres' book was written. By taking into account the topical allusions, it is possible to establish the chronological order of the plays.

Richard III should be considered as the complement of the vast tripartite tragedy of *Henry VI*. The subject of this historical drama is described in its title :

The Tragedie of King Richard the Third. Containing his treacherous plots against his brother Clarence : the pitiful murder of his innocent nephews ; his tyrannical usurpation : with the whole course of his detestable life, and well deserved death. As it hath been latley acted by the Right Honourable the Lord Chamberlain his servants. By William Shakespeare.

This play was therefore the continuation of the trilogy of *Henry VI*. It brought to a bloody conclusion the desperate struggles between the houses of York and Lancaster. The last scenes of the previous play showed Richard of York boasting that he knew neither pity, love nor fear as he stabbed pious King Henry.

He has other crimes in preparation. Every obstacle between him and the throne must be removed. His brother Clarence is the first victim of his informers ; then it is the turn of the informers themselves. He hopes that by wedding the widow of the Prince of Wales, he will efface the stigma of her husband's murder, for which he is held responsible by public opinion. The courtship which he is unscrupulous enough to pay to Lady Anne when she is following the coffin of good King Henry, is an outrage against propriety, but one which the author has rendered plausible by his success in presenting this horrible being, as cynical as he is powerful. With hypocritical but convincing eloquence Richard manages to seduce the weak and tender hearted widow to the astonishment of an hypnotized audience. Scarcely is this feat accomplished when, contemplating a better match with King Edward's daughter, he gets rid of the unfortunate Lady Anne. The spectator's natural reprobation gives place to an almost morbid curiosity. He watches the machinations of this bloodthirsty Machiavel, as he would a spider spinning its web and awaiting its predestined victim.

With *King John*, Shakespeare had presented an untutored mediaeval savage, punished for his crimes by a tragic end ; but in the dramatist's opinion Richard III is more guilty than John, since his atrocities are cloaked by hypocrisy and flattery calculated to obtain popular favour. Many are the famous actors who have shone in this part, which requires infinite versatility !

Curiously enough, the vogue of *Richard III* after publication almost equalled its success on the stage.[1] The triumph of this melodrama was not one to add to Shakespeare's fame as a master of poetic expression ; but this is excusable, the English public relished this kind of play—it still demands it—and, at the time the drama was written, Henslowe and Alleyn

---

[1] Numerous reprintings followed the first impression of Vallentyne Sims and Andrew Wyse in 1597. They are dated 1598, 1602, 1603, 1605, 1612, 1622, 1623, 1629 and 1634.

were rivals to be equalled, if not surpassed. This play, a windfall for the servants of the Lord Chamberlain, added to the author's renown, and covered Burbage, who played the name part, with new laurels.

Love's Labour's Won is probably the play which, adapted and developed, became *All's Well That Ends Well*. It forms, in a sense, a pendant to *Love's Labour's Lost*, and must have closely followed it in date of composition. Like its elder-sister, this comedy takes place at the French court ; but the story is directly borrowed from one of Boccaccio's, whose plot is scrupulously followed. The choice of the subject and manner of treatment correspond to the tastes and occupations of the Earl of Southampton, a great lover of Italian tales.

The argument of the ninth story on the third day of the *Decameron* is as follows :

Gilette de Narbonne, who inherited from her father a medicinal secret, cures the French King of a fistula. As reward she asks for the hand of Bertrand de Roussillon in marriage, whom she has loved since childhood. The chevalier unwillingly weds her, but at once departs for Florence. There he woos a young girl, but at the rendez-vous he finds Gilette whom he does not recognize. They have two sons and he gives her all due honour as his wife.

The improbability of this plot is diminished in Shakespeare's comedy, by the naturalness of the characters and the brilliant animation of the dialogue. The action, which commences at the castle of Roussillon and the Louvre, is continued on the Italian battlefields in the time of Henry II of France. It serves to bring into relief three characters drawn in masterly fashion. The old Countess of Roussillon, together with her witty gentleman in waiting, Lafeu, represents the most attractive qualities of the France of that time : good sense, good manners, good heart and good humour. Her son is what one would call today a complete snob. To extenuate his behaviour, the author is careful to give him as confidant a despicable flatterer, Parolles, who plays on his weaknesses. In the person of Helen of Narbonne —her name is no longer Gilette as in Boccaccio's tale—Shakespeare introduces a type of young girl unknown before in literature, who may be classed with Portia, Rosalind, Marina and Beatrice. Helen of Narbonne proves that a woman may be intelligent and cultured without being pedantic, virtuous and not prudish, honest without becoming a bore, and that she may be light-hearted without diminishing her strength of mind. It required a woman of this temper to bring back a man like Count de Roussillon without sacrificing her dignity. Her character explains the transformation which takes place in that of her husband.

No quarto edition of this play under its first title is in existence. *All's Well That Ends Well* appeared for the first time in the great collection of 1623.

The Two Gentlemen of Verona, like *All's Well That Ends Well*, is based upon an Italian novel.[1] There is even an episode suggested by the *Diana*

---

[1] *Apolonius and Sylla* by Bandello.

of George de Montemayor,[1] for which Giovanni Florio must be responsible for from 1578 on he tried to encourage English interest in Spanish letters.[2]

Valentine leaves Verona to undertake the traditional tour with a view to completing his education, while his friend Proteus, betrothed to the charming Julia, remains behind. But the descriptions of the Milanese court in his letters decide Proteus to join him. No sooner has he arrived in this town than the faithless lover finds his friend secretly betrothed to the Duke of Milan's daughter, Silvia, with whom he himself falls desperately in love. She repulses him, and in a fit of jealousy, he reveals Valentine's temerity to the Duke who immediately banishes him. The Two Gentlemen of Verona meet again in a forest, but before they can engage their swords, Silvia appears with her page ; this page is none other than Julia, who, has come in disguise to seek her fickle lover. Instead of a tragic outcome, the play ends with a general reconciliation—rather too sudden to be probable.

There is not a trace of any publication of this sentimental comedy during its author's lifetime[3] ; however, the play does not lack good qualities ; it even has moments which presage Shakespeare's highest achievements. Its faults are essentially those of youth. The author is dealing with a subject too far removed from real life. Nevertheless in *The Two Gentlemen of Verona* are to be found passages of exquisite poetry. When Valentine, banished on pain of death from the Milanese court describes the miseries of exile, he gives a foretaste of Romeo's lamentations, and when he is forced to seek refuge with brigands whose chief he becomes, his speeches on the benefits of open-air freedom as opposed to the artificial life of the court contain in embryo the beautiful scenes of *As You Like It*, situated not in the imaginary woods between Verona and Milan, but in the depths of the Forest of Arden, so familiar to the poet. Similarly Julia, the tender and loving abandoned fiancée who follows Proteus disguised as a page, is an earnest of Shakespeare's most delightful heroines. The episode in which the friars Laurence and Patrick protect the lovers is re-enacted more tragically in the very different drama which Shakespeare was about to begin at scarcely thirty years of age.

In *Romeo and Juliet*, the poet of love found a subject worthy of his talents. Deriving his inspiration from two Italian stories, the one by Luigi da Porto, the other by Mateo Bandello,[4] he presented a burning passion hindered but

[1] " *Les Sept Livres de la Diane* de George de Montemayor esquelz par plusieurs pleasantes histoires . . . sont décrites les variables et estranges effects de l'honneste amour " (trad. de l'espagnol en francais, Jean de Fogny, Rheims, 1578).

[2] Florio has incorporated numerous passages of the *Marc Aurèle* and the *Mépris de la Cour* by Antonio Guévara in his *First Fruits*.

[3] It appeared for the first time in the folio of 1623, between *The Tempest* and *The Merry Wives of Windsor*.

[4] Luigi da Porto's conte of 1535 has for its title " Istoria novellamente introvata de due nobile amanti con la loro Pietosa Morte ; Intervenuta gia nella città di Verona Nel Tempio del Signor Bartholomeo Scala." In 1554, Bandello, in a novel published at Lucca, uses the same subject, which he claimed to have heard from a certain Peregrino, an archer, also responsible for da Porto's story. Bandello's version was put into French by Pierre Boisteau, who amplified it, and introduced the character of the apothecary. It was this version which was translated into English by Arthur Brookes, with the title : *The Tragicall History*

[OVER

not prevented by the age-old feud of two principal Verona families.   This hymn of youthful love is sung in the midst of warring factions.   The prologue which announces the argument of the play is in sonnet form and archaic language.

> Two households, both alike in dignity,
> In fair Verona where we lay our scene,
> From ancient grudge break to new mutiny,
> Where civil blood makes civil hands unclean.
> From forth the fatal loins of these two foes
> A pair of star-crossed lovers take their life ;
> Whose misadventured piteous overthrows
> Do with their death bury their parents strife.
> The fearful passage of their death-marked love,
> And the continuance of their parents rage
> Which, but their children's end naught could remove,
> Is now the two hours traffic of our stage . . .

No superfluous incident mars the implacable march of events.   Rising above complications and forced contrasts Shakespeare establishes that harmony and unity of sentiment which is the mark of his special genius.

Verona, which appeared flat and characterless when Valentine and Proteus quitted it for Milan, now springs to life seething with movement and colour, imbued with poetry and enlivened with music—a typical city of the glorious Renaissance.   Streets and Piazzas glisten in the torrid heat of midday June.   The air is charged with electricity and threat of storm, the natural setting for the excitation of conflict or the spur of ecstatic passion.

The quarrel between the servants of the rival houses contrasts with the splendour of the masked ball given by the Capulets, to which the élite of the city are bidden and where hundreds of torches illumine the blossoming of an immortal idyll.   But hardly have the lovers confessed their mutual passion when the hereditary feud rears its ugly head.   A Montagu has been recognized among the guests.   Three tableaux follow : each perfect of its kind—the garden—the hermits' chapel—the family tomb.   These in turn charm, move and terrify the spectator.

The spell of Juliet's balcony bathed in moonlight is reflected in all romantic poetry from Goethe, Musset and Rostand to our own day, without ever having been equalled.

The poet seems to have attained the very summit of art in the lover's exchange of vows ; and yet when the grey dawn makes the stars grow pale and the lark's song silences the nightingale, this same garden will be the silent witness to the married lovers' heart rending adieux.   Through a fatal error in the heat of combat, Romeo has killed a nephew of old Capulet ; he

---

of Romeus and Juliet (1562).   Another writer, Paynter, in a collection *Palace of Pleasure*, gives another account of the same story which was very close to that of Boisteau.

The historical incident on which the drama is founded, took place in Verona in 130 3, when the turbulent town was ruled by the Prince Bartolome della Scala.   Dante, in the Sixth Book of the *Purgatorio* mentions the Capiletti and the Mantecchi as among the families who upset Italy by their quarrels.

knows that immediate death or exile awaits him nor can Juliet doubt longer of their tragic destiny.

Between first vows and last farewells the spectator is introduced to the worthy franciscan with his basket of herbs and simples. This benevolent priest and philosopher, Friar Laurence, is learned in the laws of nature. He even comprehends the language of human passion sufficiently to admit that if God permits such love as this to his earthly children the wisdom of old folks must accept it as a divine gift. The friar is the more willing to consecrate a union between Montagu and Capulet because he believes that this marriage will bring a happy termination to the bloody strife which for so long has lacerated Verona.

But instead of the happy ending he foresees in giving his blessing on their nuptials, it is the family tomb of the Capulets which opens to receive the fair bride. To escape from the sacrilegious marriage which her father insists upon, Juliet appeals to the franciscan. He consents to give her an opiate powerful enough to suspend animation until he can summon Romeo to be there when she wakes and take her back with him to his place of exile. But before there is time for Romeo to receive the friar's message of hope, the news of Juliet's sudden death, which has shocked the town, is brought by his own page, so that Romeo, determined to die with her, sets forth at once for her tomb. The poor friar who arrives at the hour appointed for Juliet's awakening finds her husband already dead at her side. But Romeo's arrival was not unnoticed ; aroused from their sleep, Capulets, Montagues, and the Duke himself, all gather at the tomb. To them Friar Laurence recounts with noble simplicity how by a sublime paradox these tragic deaths have proved that a moment's love is stronger than centuries of hate and that this sacrifice must open the way to reconciliation.

Theatrical producers who bring down the curtain at Juliet's death, commit a grave error. Shakespeare's drama forms a whole and the final scene may not be arbitrarily curtailed. A mere catastrophe did not provide the right dénouement for Shakespeare's art. Friar Laurence's recital is necessary that such an overflowing of passions may conclude upon a note of serenity and reconciliation. The tomb must not close upon the immortal lovers of Verona until their parents have buried their inveterate feud.

The play is inimitable. Perhaps others describe more violent passion but never in any work has the author, without overstepping that reticence and moderation inseparable from art, depicted the pure and sincere flame of a youthful idyll with such mastery. In *Romeo and Juliet*, Shakespeare reveals himself as the veritable poet of the love which binds two hearts in eternity, and that without a single equivocal allusion on the lovers' lips. The author of *Romeo and Juliet* has shown himself a great interpreter of passion, but he does so with good taste. His drama deserves the predilection given it by each successive generation. As Flaubert says : " Virgile a fait la femme amoureuse, Shakespeare, la jeune fille amoureuse, toutes les autres sont la copie plus ou moins éloignée de Didon et de Juliette."

In this play Shakespeare has given proof of the richest and most contrasting gifts ; he has even interspersed his most pathetic scenes with an entertaining humour ; the secondary personages contribute to the achievement of the whole. It is by effects of contrast that the lovers gain the hearer's sympathy. Their parents' age is exaggerated to place a deeper gulf between them and their children ; the selfishness of old Capulet, angry and vociferous, contrasts with the benevolent wisdom of his daughter's confessor ; the opposition of Benvolio's cold correctness and the frank joie de vivre of Mercutio, that truculent Rabelaisian, enhances the idealism of their friend Romeo.

Mercutio does not appear in the Italian tale whence the story of the play is taken, but he is necessary to Shakespeare's drama. Dryden recalls that the contemporary public were so fond of this character, that many spectators complained to the author for having made away with him in the third act. Shakespeare would reply that if he had not sacrificed Mercutio at this precise moment, Mercutio would have killed him.

As for the nurse, that " good Angelica ", so esteemed by her master and mistress, with her ample proportions, her noisy vulgarity, fondness for the bottle, loud laughter and equivocal meanings, she could at first be taken for a good old soul devoted to her young mistress, but, when the tragic test comes she joins the other camp, and Juliet, revolted by her treachery, is strengthened by this desertion. Knowing that henceforth she can rely only on herself and the help of the good Franciscan, she becomes heroic.

The rapidity of the action holds the spectator breathless from the prologue to the end of the drama. In Bandello's story three months elapse between the lovers' wedding night and the fatal climax. With sure dramatic instinct, Shakespeare has condensed this whole period between the Sunday and the Thursday of the same week. He thus intensifies emotion, establishes unity of sentiment, and arouses in the spectator an artificial exaltation, like that which, in Greece, formed a part of the worship of the god of the theatre, Dionysius.

In this extraordinary achievement, the quality of the poetry has its part. If the text bristles with the " concetti " dear to the times, they are but one of the means employed by the author to create the climate he sought. They are abandoned when this atmosphere changes. Conscious of his ability to raise or lower the " temperature " merely by the virtuosity of his language, he adapts it to each change of emotion. Romeo, like Petrarch, rejoices in florid and far-fetched rhetoric during the early scenes, but as tragedy deepens, his expressions become concise, his meter broken and staccato. Exiled, Romeo has developed into a man of few words and determined action.

Similarly Juliet's characteristic language betrays her state of mind. Naïvely divided between modesty and passion, between fear and impatience to know the heart of love, she greets the dawn in an aubade overflowing with lyric ecstasy ; adjuring the steeds of Phoebus' chariot to hasten the approach of night, and with it her Romeo. Her almost delirious anguish when the nurse, entering with the rope ladder, brutally recounts how her cousin Tybalt has been killed and Romeo condemned to immediate death or perpetual banishment, could not be better conveyed. Then, in a torrent of words which scintillate like pyrotechnics, she expresses her despairing passion, a real test for Juliet's interpreter.

The poet was still so much under the domination of the sonnet form, that he has employed it to describe the lovers' first meeting at the Capulets' ball. Romeo, in the garb of a pilgrim, exchanges with Juliet half jestingly the devout language appropriate to his costume, which brings about their mutual confession of love at first sight.

Romeo : If I profane with my unworthiest hand
This holy shrine, the gentle sin is this ;
My lips, two blushing pilgrims, ready stand
To smooth that rough touch with a tender kiss.

Juliet : Good pilgrim, you do wrong your hand too much,
Which mannerly devotion shows in this ;
For saints have hands that pilgrims hands do touch,
And palm to palm is holy palmer's kiss.

Romeo : Have not saints lips, and holy palmers too ?

Juliet : Ay, pilgrim, lips that they must use in prayer.

Romeo : O ! then, dear saint, let lips do what hands do . . .

Juliet : Saints do not move, though grant for prayers' sake.

Romeo : Then move not, while my prayers' effect I take,
Thus from my lips, by thine, my sin is purg'd.

Juliet : Then have my lips the sin that they have took.

Romeo : Sin from my lips ? O trespass sweetly urg'd !
Give me my sin again.

Juliet : You kiss by the book.

In short, meter, rhymes, ornate style, and even the " concetti " of *Romeo and Juliet* are characteristic of the romantic comedies and the poems which Shakespeare wrote under the direct influence of his young and generous patron.

According to a firmly-rooted tradition at Tichfield, the village a few miles from Southampton, where stands the Abbey Castle of Shakespeare's protector, now in ruins, the first representation of *Romeo and Juliet* took place in the immense tithe barn there on October 6th, 1594, when Southampton attained his majority. His sister, Lady Arundel, had arrived with her cook and household staff to help wait on the numerous guests. The Danvers' brothers took part in the celebrations on the eve of their departure for France. Florio [1] was also on hand, and for once must have been able to praise a play of Shakespeare's unreservedly, since it came direct from Italy, and was steeped in the atmosphere of Italy. *Romeo and Juliet* therefore belongs to the same year as *The Rape of Lucrece* and the fine sonnet written in celebration of Southampton's majority.

The drama's success was considerable. An unscrupulous publisher,

---

[1] In a complaint written by the sheriff of Southampton, in the same week, Florio is mentioned as having aided the Danvers in their flight.

John Danter, brought out in 1597 a small quarto text of the play ostensibly due to short-hand copy, entitled :

An excellent conceited Tragedie of Romeo and Juliet. As it hath been often (with great applause) plaid publiquely, by the right Honourable, the Lord of Hunsdon his Servants.[1]

The stenographer was not able to transcribe the complicated dialogue which precede and follows the duel ; instead he substitutes stage directions : They draw their swords—Tybalt enters—They fight—The prince enters, followed by old Montague and his wife, old Capulet, his wife and other citizens who separate them ; and so forth.

In 1599 the theatre itself issued an authorized text, thus entitled :

The most excellent and Lamentable Tragedie, of Romeo and Juliet. Newly corrected, augmented, and amended : As it hath bene sundry times publiquely acted, by the right Honourable the Lord Chamberlaine his Servants.

It was re-printed in 1607, 1609, 1623 and 1627. In the quarto of 1609 it is noted that the play has been given several times at the " Globe " by the servants of His Majesty the King.

The Merchant of Venice is a play about current politics ; the date of its composition is even easier to fix than that of *Romeo and Juliet*.

In the first days of the year 1592, a sensational arrest was made at Burleigh's order for an alleged plot against the Queen. Her principal doctor, Roderigo Lopez, was accused of consenting to poison his august patient, " attracted by the promise of fifty thousand crowns and of many honours for his children ".

The Queen never believed in the guilt of Lopez [2] who, for many years, had been the accredited physician of her favourite, Leicester ; but the doom of this Portuguese Jew was already sealed by her ministers. After an interminable trial, he was executed on June 7th, 1594. An anti-semitic wave swept the country. Henslowe at once revived the *Jew of Malta*, and Alleyn triumphed again in the terrible part of Barabbas. The Lord Chamberlain's company could not let slip an opportunity of entering the lists. They were confident that Shakespeare's pen and Burbage's talent could beat the Lord Admiral's company on its own ground : author and actor did not hesitate to launch quite a new kind of play ; that same year they presented to the public their first tragi-comedy. The play was parodied in two theatrical revues of 1596, proving that it was then well known. There is therefore no doubt about the date of its presentation. The first quarto, printed by James Roberts, carries this descriptive title :

The most excellent Historie of *the Merchant of Venice*, With the Extreame crueltie of Shylocke the Jewe towards the sayd Merchant in cutting a just pound

---

[1] London, John Danter, 1597.

[2] Martin Hume, who for his study *Treason and Plot* had access to the Spanish archives, considers with Professor G. B. Harrison that Lopez never intended to harm Elizabeth. But he had received gifts from Philip of Spain and had instructed Leicester in the use of poisons.

of his flesh : and the obtayning of Portia, by the choyse of three Chests, as it hath been divers times acted by the Lord Chamberlaine his Servants.[1]

The whole plot of *The Merchant of Venice*, even the most romantic scenes, turns upon greed of gold and covetousness ; but the drama closes upon a note of comedy. Three Renaissance stories have provided the plot of *The Merchant of Venice*. The principal episode, the story of the Jew, is taken from *Il Pecorone* of Ser Giovanni Fiorentino ; [2] the casket fable is borrowed from the *Gesta Romanorum ;* Jessica's elopement after having robbed her father of his ducats comes from a story by Massuccio da Salerno.[3]

The author has cleverly woven a coherent web from these heterogeneous sources. It is interesting to note that the clown Gobbo's peculiar name actually belonged to one of Lord Southampton's servants, once again showing that his patron's influence was never far from the poet. The parish registers of St. Peter's church at Tichfield mention the burial of Augustine Gobbo, December 23rd, 1593, and the marriage of Wm. Gobbo, in 1631.

A stage tradition dating from Burbage, who knew Lopez well, ordains that the actor of Shylock's part should be made up to resemble that unfortunate Israelite ; even today, Shylock is generally represented as red-haired rather than dark. Shakespeare's portrait differs essentially from Marlowe's Barabbas by its realism, he gives to Shylock the cynical humour which was characteristic of Lopez, who declared at his trial [4] that he " loved the Queen quite as much as he did Jesus Christ ".

The historian Camden remarks :

This declaration was interpreted as a mockery on the lips of a bigoted Jew.[5]

Some producers, basing their theory on Nerissa's remarks to her mistress concerning the strange parental manner of disposing of his daughter's hand as it were by chance, make this astute confidant a conscious instrument of destiny. Accordingly she drops a rose upon the lead casket when Bassanio approaches to make his choice—so that Portia's suitor is no longer guided by chance alone.

It may be interesting to reproduce the first critical study made on *The Merchant of Venice* by Nicholas Rowe :

I believe, Thersites in *Troilus and Cressida*, and Apemantus in *Timon*, will be

---

[1] To avoid the clandestine publication of an unauthorized text such as had been issued of *Romeo and Juliet*, the request for a printer's licence is entered in the registers in these terms : " For James Roberts, the 2nd July, 1598, the book of *The Merchant of Venice*, otherwise called the *Jew of Venice*, on condition that the play must not be disseminated by the above-mentioned or other persons whatsoever without the express consent of the honourable the lord Chamberlain." Four re-impressions, 1619, 1623, 1637 and 1685 attest the success of this play with its readers.

[2] *Il Pecorone nel quale si contengono cinquanta novelle antiche* (Milano, 1558).

[3] *Cinquante Novelle intitolate il Novellino* (Venise, 1484).

[4] Lopez' reputation as a savant was considerable ; he was one of the first to establish clinics ; he inaugurated the system of house-surgeons at St. Bartholomew's hospital, and was one of the founders of the Royal College of Physicians.

[5] *Annales rerum Anglicarum . . . regnante Elizabetha*, autore Guil. Camdeno, 1625.

allow'd to be Master-Pieces of ill Nature, and satyrical Snarling. To those I might add, that incomparable Character of Shylock the Jew, in *The Merchant of Venice ;* but tho' we have seen that Play Receiv'd and Acted as a Comedy, and the Part of the Jew perform'd by an Excellent Comedian, yet I cannot but think it was design'd Tragically by the Author. There appears in it such a deadly Spirit of Revenge, such a savage Fierceness and Fellness, and such a bloody designation of Cruelty and Mischief, as cannot agree either with the Stile or Characters of Comedy. The Play it self, take it all together, seems to me to be one of the most finish'd of any of Shakespear's. . . . There is something in the Friendship of Antonio to Bassanio very Great, Generous and Tender. The whole fourth Act, supposing, as I said, the Fact to be probable, is extremely Fine. But there are two Passages that deserve a particular Notice. The first is, what Portia says in praise of Mercy ; and the other on the Power of Musick. . . .[1]

Rowe's judgement is that of posterity. Today, when the mixed genre of tragi-comedy is more easily accepted, *The Merchant of Venice* has not aged. Its brilliance, the sparkling dialogue, the dizzy speed of certain scenes, the unity of feeling produced by the constant preoccupation with gain, the clownish talk mingled with sober sense, make this drama one of the favourites of the theatre.

At the time *The Merchant of Venice* was written, Morocco was one of the topics of the day as much among the royal courtiers as with the city merchants. Political and commercial interests turned towards this country exploited by the merchant adventurers, who were organized by Leicester under the name of the " Barbary Company ". The general public was also interested in these distant lands where sugar cane [2] was cultivated and where there was an abundance of saltpetre. Elizabeth, hoping to reach her peninsular enemies by way of Morocco, encouraged the smuggling of arms and munitions. It was on the pretext of trade negotiations that a settlement was reached between the English Queen, and the Sultan of Morocco. Such a cordial understanding was established that at Marrakesh great rejoicings took place after the destruction of the " Invincible Armada ". James Roberts, brother of the printer Henry Roberts, who published *The Merchant of Venice* and many other Shakespearean plays, was at this time English minister plenipotentiary in the " Fortunate Empire ". This explains why Shakespeare's work includes sixty allusions to Barbary and why *The Merchant of Venice* brings us face to face for the first time with one of its princes.

If the discourse of the Prince of Morocco is full of anachronisms, it is imaginative and picturesque ; the author had probably heard that Arab conversation was refined, and that the great sheikhs employed language ornamented with flowery rhetoric. He expressed this in the Italian fashion, with many mythological allusions, which in his eyes represented patrician taste combined with an exotic form of expression. The method is simple: many poets have since made use of it.

---

[1] Nicholas Rowe (1709), p. 19.
[2] The cases of sugar from which the Queen's table and the court were supplied were imported directly from the refineries at Sousse.

By mentioning Padua, Verona and Venice, he was certain to please those who had seen his first comedies. The gilded youth which frequented the theatres had visited Tuscany or intended to go there one day, and the merchant adventurer who came for amusement to the theatre between two voyages, was pleased to find that the capital showed some interest in the scenes of his exploits.[1]

The Tragedy of Richard II which closely followed *The Merchant of Venice*, is equally easy to date. A letter of December 7th, 1595, from Sir Edward Hoby, the Lord Chamberlain's son-in-law, invites Sir Robert Cecil to sup at his house in Cannon Row where he " will see King Richard ". A private showing of the play was to be given by Lord Hunsdon's company. This time Shakespeare broke away from the melodramatic style dear to Burbage to undertake a deep psychological study almost in the manner of *Hamlet*, combined with a lyrical element sometimes recalling *Romeo and Juliet*. The action is rapid and the portrait of young Richard, brave and handsome but poisoned by the flattery of his ambitious and rapacious courtiers, is historically convincing.

The author has succeeded in transferring the sympathy of the audience from one camp to the other as the story proceeds, with sure dramatic sense. Richard, weak and despicable in prosperity, increases in grandeur under the blows of misfortune. In the last act he defends himself like a hero.

At the end of the century, when Elizabeth was criticized for having abdicated many of her powers in favour of Cecil and Raleigh, this tragedy was revived and exercised a profound influence on Shakespeare's career. It featured in the trial of Essex and Southampton : its political aspects will be examined in Chapter XII which deals with the conspiracy against the Queen.

From its first presentation in 1595, this original drama was very successful. Andrew Wyse was roused to publish it surreptitiously in 1597.[2] Next year, the play was twice reprinted, and for the first time the name of William Shakespeare figured on the title page of one of his plays. The success of *Richard II* was such that the dramatist continued to develop the riches of an historical vein.

Henry IV is the logical continuation of *Richard II*. For his basic material, Shakespeare again had recourse to Holinshed's Chronicles and listened to anecdotes told by " Hotspur's " family. Sir Charles and Sir Jocelyn Percy, closely connected with Southampton, were able to provide

---

[1] Unpublished sources of *l'Histoire du Maroc* by Comte Henri de Castries (Leroux, Paris, 1918). See also " Shakespeare et le Maroc ", by Longworth Chambrun, *Revue de Paris*, June 15th, 1925.

[2] *The Tragedie of King Richard the second*. As it hath beene publikely acted by the Right honourable the Lord Chamberlaine his servants (London, printed by Valentine Simmes for Andrew Wise . . . 1597).

Two other editions were printed the following year under the same title with one difference : the author's name was added in each case : by William Shakespeare. From this moment his works were assured of successful sales, and quarto editions multiplied with or without the consent of the actors, who remained the sole proprietors of the printing rights.

these at first hand. This drama is a kind of philosophical commentary on *Richard II* to which it is closely allied. In the first part the author contrasts the dark figure of the king tortured by remorse and fear with the genial character of Sir John Falstaff, the jovial companion of his prodigal son. The fat knight, brilliantly witty, boastful, and a shameless liar, yet persuades the dullest to share in his joy of life. By his inexhaustible spirits, Falstaff obliges the audience to excuse his total lack of morals.

The First Part of Henry IV concludes with the king's victory at Shrewsbury where Prince Hal kills the heroic Hotspur with his own hand, while the ineffable Falstaff claims the glory, though he has distinguished himself only by his cowardice. He decides to amend his life, " to leave sack, and live cleanly as a nobleman should " but his good resolutions are short-lived ; he returns to the stage, more amusing, more shameless and more inimitable than ever.

In *The Second Part of Henry IV*, the reconciliation between the king and his irresponsible son, in whom he sees the punishment of his own misdeeds, is one of the finest scenes in all the historical dramas. The Prince of Wales announces his intention of becoming a model king and of ridding himself of all his evil counsellors. Accordingly when Falstaff thrusts himself forward at his coronation, certain of obtaining for himself and his merry band the particular favour of the new sovereign, he and his companions are placed under arrest. Here the author seems to have followed history almost with regret. Certainly it was necessary to underline the profound change in Prince Hal after his accession, but was it indispensable to follow Holinshed's writings so exactly and to humiliate Falstaff so completely ? The spectator had learned to love the fat knight, " not only witty himself, but the cause of wit in others ".[1] He is the real hero of *The Second Part of Henry IV*. The audience is eager for his entries and regrets his exits. This character has evidently taken possession of the author in spite of himself and occasionally becomes his spokesman. When he is at loggerheads with Justice Shallow, we are vividly reminded of Sir Thomas Lucy of Charlecote, the author's former persecutor. This revenge upon the man who caused Shakespeare to leave Stratford must have greatly amused the spectators of those days, but perhaps not as much as it amused the author himself while composing the scenes where the malicious Falstaff insists on recalling certain discreditable episodes in the self-sufficient proprietor's early life.

The name of Falstaff, now universally renowned, was substituted for

---

[1] ' Falstaff is recognised as Shakespeare's masterpiece. This character is remarkably sustained although he appears throughout three plays. Even the account of his death given by his old hostess, Mrs. Quickly, in the first act of *Henry V*, is as diverting as every other incident of his life, although perfectly straightforward and natural. If one fault can be found in the painting of this old rascal, it is that while Shakespeare describes Falstaff as a thief, a liar, a coward and braggart, in fact vicious in all his ways, he has at the same time made him so agreeable that I believe many people, grateful for the amusement they have derived from Sir John, regret the prince's callous treatment of his old friend.' (Nicholas Rowe, 1709.)

that of Sir John Oldcastle. It must be admitted that Shakespeare was audacious in presenting his braggart under a name dear to the British Protestants, who saw in Sir John Oldcastle, hanged for heresy by Henry VI, one of their first martyrs. Some members of this family were still living, including the influential Lord Cobham, who was little inclined to favour the theatre as he was soon to prove. When the authorities required the suppression of Oldcastle's name Shakespeare was not ready to admit defeat ; with sly pleasure he found in Holinshed's chronicles a certain Sir John Fastolfe, a knight accused of cowardice in the retreat of Patay ; with only a slight change the name became Falstaff.[1] The text of the play still contains an allusion to the name of Oldcastle. When Prince Hal summons Sir John, he apostrophizes him thus : " What, my old lad of the castle ! " Again, in the epilogue, the author refers to the change of name imposed upon him :

If you be not too much cloyed with fat meat, our humble author will continue the story, with Sir John in it, and make you merry with fair Katharine of France ; where, for anything I know, Falstaff shall die of a sweat, unless already a' be killed with your hard opinions ; for Oldcastle died a martyr, and this is not the man.

At the rival theatre of the Lord Admiral, the chance of entering the fray against the Lord Chamberlain's company was not lost. They were only too pleased to fire a protestant broadside at Shakespeare's dramatic success. Anthony Munday and his fellows, who knew " from what Roman purse this bad piece had come ", asked no better than to administer a lesson " to petulant poets and the malicious papists ". It was not long before they presented on the stage their own version of the life and death of Sir John Oldcastle.[2]

The prologue to this drama contains the statement that their play's chief character was quite the reverse of Falstaff.

It is no pamperd glutton we present,
Nor aged Councellor to youthfule sinne,
But one whose vertue shone above the rest,
A valiant Martyr and a vertuous peere,
In whose true faith and loyaltie exprest
Unto his soveraigne, and his countrie's weale :
We strive to pay that tribute of our Love,
Your favours merite, let faire Truth be gracte
Since forg'de invention former time defac'te.

[1] Thomas Fuller in his book *Worthies of England*, disapproves the choice of the name of Falstaff as much as that of Oldcastle.

" Much as I am relieved that the name of Sir John Oldcastle has been suppressed, I nevertheless regret that the author should have chosen that of Sir John Fastolfe to serve as anvil for the blows of the public. Our actor is not excusable considering he has only slightly changed the spelling of the name ; he has left enough resemblance to damage the reputation of an honourable knight . . ." (p. 253).

[2] Sir John Oldcastle, the good lord Cobham, as it hath been lately acted by the right honourable, the earl of Nottingham, lord high Admirall of England, his servants, 1600.

In the name of " gracing fair truth ", Henslowe's company presented, with *Sir John Oldcastle*, a similar adventure to that of Prince Hal and his amateur robbers ; but what a difference in the matter and in the manner! The highwayman invented by Munday is a priest who, with " Doll, his mistress ", robs travellers, cheats at dice when playing with King Henry and is finally condemned to be hanged.

Although *Henry IV* was a great success [1] and *Sir John Oldcastle* only exists now as a title for reference, political and religious passion in 1596 was so strong that it was the Lord Admiral's company who, on this occasion, won the theatrical rubber.

Between *The First Part of Henry IV* and *The Second Part of Henry IV* we must place *Troilus and Cressida*, a curious experiment in quite a new style, which Shakespeare lost no time in abandoning. This parody is about the demi-gods of ancient Greece. Achilles is made to play the coward and the heroism of Hector is seriously brought in question. The author seems conscious of having gone astray, for in the epilogue to *The Second Part of Henry IV* [2] spoken probably by Kempe the clown, an allusion is made to the failure of a preceding play, most probably *Troilus and Cressida*.[3]

Be it known to you,—as it is very well,—I was lately here in the end of a displeasing play, to pray your patience for it and to promise you a better. I did mean indeed to pay you with this ; which, if like an ill venture it come unluckily home, I break, and you, my gentle creditors, lose.

Troilus and Cressida undoubtedly leaves a painful impression when read.

---

[1] The popularity of Falstaff was such that Shakespeare consented to make him the sole subject of a play, which was acted by a group of amateurs at the court of James I. Shakespeare recast the two parts of *Henry IV* to bring into relief the scenes concerning the fat knight, suppressing those which were too long or too sad in his historical play. The contemporary manuscript arranged by Sir Charles Deering belongs today to the Folger library at Washington ; it shows Shakespeare's flexibility, for he willingly assured fresh success to a play which had already become immortal.

[2] In *Troilus and Cressida*, Kempe played the part of Pandarus and spoke the epilogue. In spite of his comic ability, he was unable to dispel the audience's discontent by his dancing.

[3] *The Historie of Troylus and Cresseida.* As it was acted by the King's Majesties Servants at the Globe. Written by William Shakespeare. (London, imprinted by G. Eld, 1609.) The play was reprinted there in the same year. The late date of its first publication need not cause surprise. Its failure on the stage must have led the author to delay the printing. However, on February 7th, 1603, James Roberts asked for a licence to print Shakespeare's drama, " such as it has been played by the servants of the lord Chamberlain and as soon as he should obtain authorisation ". Evidently, this authorization was refused.

There is other evidence that the play was given well before these dates. In 1603, the Jesuit priest, Joseph Cresswell, who was rector of the English college in Rome and, like Father Southwell, was interested in Shakespeare's writings, refers in his *Conversion of Saint Mary Magdalene*, to *The Rape of Lucrece, Troilus and Cressida* and *King Richard* which he groups as if these works belonged to the same epoch.

> Of *Helens* rape and *Troyes* beseiged *Towne*,
> Of *Troylus* faith, and *Cressids* falsitie,
> Of *Rychards* stratagems for the english crowne,
> Of *Tarquins* lust and lucrece chastitie,
> Of these, of none of these my muse nowe treates,
> Of greater conquests, warres, and loves she speakes.
>
> (*Saint Marie Magdalens Conversion*, by I. C., 1603.)

Several speeches of great beauty, especially those of Ulysses, need not fear comparison with other masterpieces of the poet's : but they do not redeem the drama's weaknesses ; on the contrary they appear misplaced in this bitter satire, where Pandarus, prototype of the character to whom his name has passed, instructs his niece, the cunning Cressida, in the art of handling false sentiment with all the skill of an Emma Bovary.   The detestable Thersites employs such gross language as to discomfit his chiefs ; it suggests the twentieth century rather than the end of the sixteenth.   The disequilibrium between the subject and the characters, the sublimity of some lines and the coarseness of others, leave the reader perplexed.   Is he in the presence of a parody of the *Iliad*, which Chapman had just popularized, an early comedy on the Belle Hélène theme ?   Or is it a tragedy of sincere love in which the spectator is intended to sympathize with the misfortunes of Troilus and suffer with him as he did with Romeo ?   To ask this question is to admit that, for once, Shakespeare had made a false start.   His enemies, still numerous, seized this chance of attack.   Two satires which survive to the present day seem to be aimed, in part, at Shakespeare.

In his *Poetaster*, Ben Jonson caricatures Shakespeare's company setting forth on tour.   Less known is John Marston's burlesque *Histrio-Mastix*, often witty and always well observed.[1]   This parody has all the qualities of an amusing and caustic revue ; it is full of life and movement.   If, as is probable, Giovanni Florio counted on Marston to defend him and turn his wit against Shakespeare's, the Italian pedagogue made a happy choice.[2]

The avowed object of this pretended morality play was to correct the eccentricities of the time, especially the passion for the theatre which then raged alike among nobility, gentry and middle class, and from which commoners were not exempt.   The author shows how pride and ambition, the fruits of idleness, engender war ; war brings in its train poverty and famine; an impoverished nation becomes humble, and humility is the sister of peace. With peace idleness returns and is accompanied by all the vices ; so the fatal cycle continues.   To show England's decadence, a company of players is introduced with their author, who has to provide all their plays.   The latter's name is Post Haste, an allusion to the rapidity of his work ; it is easy on first appearance to recognize Shakespeare as seen by his rivals. " Post-Haste " is always eager to offer his services to the great, and glad to

---

[1] *Histrio-Mastix or the Player whipt* (London, Thomas Thorpe, 1610).

In 1875, the scholar Richard Simpson wrote a serious study of this volume, and came to the conclusion that the character named Post-Haste who comes with his actors to present *Troilus and Cressida* before a noble lord and his Italian friend was certainly intended to ridicule Shakespeare and his latest play while imitating his style, Richard Simpson did not know the date of production of *Troilus and Cressida* nor of the presence of Florio with the Earl of Southampton, and was insufficiently aware of the ties which bound the young lord to Shakespeare ; otherwise he would also have identified the patron of letters and his Italian master before whom Post-Haste presented his play.   See *The School of Shakespeare* by Richard Simpson, B.A. (New York, 1878, pp. 18-89).

[2] See Chapter IX.

give a performance in exchange for a good dinner and bed at his Lordship's house.   His repertoire is varied :

> The Lascivious Knight and Lady Nature.
> The Devil and Dives (A comedy).
> A Russet Coat and a Knave's Cap (An infernal).
> A Proud Heart and a Beggar's Purse (A pastoral).
> The Widow's Apron Stringes (A nocturnal).
> Mother Gurton's Needle (A tragedy).[1]

He also has in preparation an entirely new morality play which he is finishing and intends to stage without delay.

When Post Haste appears his companions bow low for they count on his talent for their future shows.   He consents to give the actors a fore-taste of his new play, *The Prodigal Son*,[2] but his voice is so broken with sobs that he cannot continue reading.   He declares, however, that he is always equal to improvising a prologue appropriate to every occasion, a universal prologue [3] and also an epilogue.

The example he chooses satisfies him completely ; he has never been so pleased with his genius ; his rhymes have flowed with extreme facility ; the director and the company are amazed, and exclaim : " What a pity Post Haste is not engaged upon affairs of state ! "   Meanwhile the majordomo invites the troupe to present themselves to his master and perform.   He has previously ascertained the quality of the itinerant players : " The best who have ever trod the boards."   As for Post Haste, he calls himself a " gentleman ", for " whoever, like him, possesses a little learning and always wears a clean shirt, has a right to this title ".   All are introduced into the great hall where Lord Mavortius awaits them, surrounded by beautiful ladies, knights and guests amongst whom appears an erudite Italian, named Landulpho.

Post Haste announces in a prologue of archaic style the subject of *Troilus and Cressida*.[4]   At the sixth line the Italian protests : the matter is vile ;

---

[1] This enumeration parodies the passage in *Hamlet* where Polonius praises the itinerant players : " The best actors in the world, either for tragedy, comedy, history, pastoral, comical historical-pastoral, tragical-historical, tragical-comical-historical-pastoral, scene indivisible, or poem unlimited . . ." (*Hamlet*, Act II, Sc. 2).

[2] Shakespeare's play about the prodigal son in entitled : *The London Prodigal*.

[3] Here is the prologue :
> " Lords we are here to show you what we are ;
> Lords we are here although our clothes be bare
> Instead of flowers in season
> Ye shall gather Rime and Reason."

This is the epilogue :
> " The glass is run, Our play is done :
> Hence : Time doth call, we thank you all."

These lines recall the simplicity of the conclusion of *Twelfth Night* (*Histrio-Mastix*, Act II).

[4] Phillida was a fair maid—I know one fairer than she
Troylus was a true lover—I know one truer than he
And Cressida, that dainty dame, whose beauty fair and sweet
Was clear as is the crystal streame that runs along the street
How Troylus, he, that noble knight, was drunk in love and bade good night
So bending leg-wise, do you not us despise.

it is criminal thus to abuse divine poetry.[1] To this the lord of the manor
replies : " Be patient ; for perhaps the play will mend." [2]

With the entrance of the principal characters, the imitation of the scene
where, in Shakespeare's play, Cressida bestows her colours on the Trojan
champion is all the more evident because Troilus is careful to introduce a
pun on Shakespeare's own name :

> When he shakes his furious speare,
> The foe in shivery fearful sort
> May lay him down in death to snort.[3]

The dialogue is so ridiculous that the Earl stops the performance. But
Post-Haste, not so easily discouraged, offers to compose an impromptu on
no matter what subject. The Italian at once suggests as a theme :

> Your Poetts and your Pottes
> Are knit in true-Love knots.
> (*Histrio-Mastix*, Act II)

Post-Haste thereupon sings a bacchanale not lacking in merit. Its
vivacious swing recalls the malicious ballad ridiculing the master of
Charlecote :

> Give your Scholar degrees
> And your lawyer his fees
> And some dice for Sir Petronell Flash.
> Give your courtier grace,
> And your knight a new case
> And empty their purses for cash.
> Give your play-gull a stool

---

[1] *Landulpho :* Most ugly lines and base brown paper stuffe
Thus to abuse our heavenly poesie.
That sacred offspring from the braine of Jove
Thus to be mangled with prophane absurds
Strangled and choked with lawless bastard words.
(*Histrio-Mastix*, Act II)

[2] *Mavortius :* I see my lord ! This home-spun country stuffe
Brings little liking to your curious eare
Be patient, for perhaps the play will mend.
Enter Troylus and Cressida.
(*Histrio-Mastix*, Act II)

[3] *Troylus :* Come Cressida, my cresset light
Thy face doth shine both day and night
Behold, behold thy garter blue
(Which as a proof that he is true)
Thy knight on's valiant elbow wears,
That when he *shakes* his furious *speare*
The foe in shivering fearful sort
May lay him down in death to snort.

Cressida : O knight with valour in thy face
Here take my skreene, wear it for grace
Within thy helmet put the same
Therewith to make thy enemies tame. . . .

Mavortius : No more, no more, unlesse 'twere better. . . .
(*Histrio-Mastix*, Act II)

And my lady her fool
And her usher potatoes and marrow
But your poet were he dead
Set a pot to his head
And he rises as pert as a sparrow.
Oh delicate wine,
With thy power so divine,
Full of ravishing sweet inspiration
Yet a verse may run clear
That is tapped out of beer
Especially in the vacation.
But when the term comes
That with trumpets and drums
Our playhouses ring in confusion,
Then Bacchus we murder, but rime we no further,
Some sack now, upon the conclusion. . . .

Those present applaud Post-Haste, except Landulpho who proclaims that Italy would blush to hear such poor twaddle, while Lord Mavortius dismisses the troupe with forty pence, declaring that the song was good and that the Italian lord is only an ass.[1]

The actors' tour ends in a seaside hostelry where at the landlady's instigation they are arrested for non-payment. A recruiting sergeant, who enrols them by force, seizes their fine costumes to equip his officers, and this concludes the Post-Haste episode in Marston's burlesque.[2]

This skit shows both wit and talent. The parody of *Troilus and Cressida* is amusing without being too bitter ; some passages indicate an acute critical sense, and Shakespeare's portrait in the likeness of Post-Haste is well observed. Post-Haste has a fertile imagination ; thanks to this gift, the company is well supplied with plays. Though an actor himself, he prefers to be considered a poet and insists on being treated as a gentleman. He is at ease with the great and likes to be received at their table. His manners are good, his power of persuasion strong, and his ascendancy over his companions considerable. He possesses imagination, humour, richness of language—" Plenty of Old England's mother words "—repartee of the most prompt description, and to crown all, an extreme facility, precisely that gift of which Ben Jonson complained in Shakespeare—in a word, everything which both friends and enemies recognized in the poet of Stratford.

Having thus sharpened his sarcastic wit against Shakespeare himself, Marston attacks the whole company of the " Globe " Theatre in another satire written later in collaboration with Webster. This time he parodies

---

[1]   *Mavortius :*   Give them forty pence and let them go ! . . .
The Italian lord is an asse,
The song is a good song.
                    (*Histrio-Mastix*, Act II)

[2] It is interesting to note in Post-Haste's song an evident allusion to *Twelfth Night* : " Give my lady her fool and her usher potatoes and marrow." The marrow and potato pasties recommended for the amorous Malvolio were supposed at the time to contain aphrodisiac properties.

Measure for Measure and precedes it by a prologue in which Sly, Burbage, Lowen and Condell take part.[1]

In *The Malcontent*, William Sly first enters : he is accompanied by a prompter carrying a stool, and is soon joined by his friends ; the conversation which follows is crammed with allusions to current plays. The custom of the introduction of music in the theatre is criticized on the pretext that it is not permitted at the " Globe ". The dialogue contains references to *Henry IV*, *Love's Labour's Lost*, *Hamlet*, and *Twelfth Night ;* the conclusion is a virtual paraphrase of the epilogue spoken by Rosalind at the end of *As You Like It*. Then Burbage makes his excuses and leaves to dress for his part. When he reappears on the stage, it is in the rôle of Malevole, the chief character of the play.[2]

Satires and parodies of this sort have never damaged an author's reputation, nor that of his interpreters : they rather establish it. Falstaff was the talk of the town, the popularity of *The Second Part of Henry IV* soon effaced the unfavourable impression made by the failure of *Troilus and Cressida*, and it may be said that the superiority of Shakespeare's art was never in doubt either at that time or afterwards.

The magistrates of the city of London were little concerned with the encouragement of dramatic art. On the contrary, towards the end of 1595, they decided to close the theatres of the north bank of the river and forbid performances in innyards.[3] The order affected all the established companies except Henslowe's, which was already installed on the Surrey side at the " Rose " theatre in Southwark.

The servants of the Lord Chamberlain, thanks to the stubbornness of their protector, found a way out of this difficulty. Henry Carey, Lord Hunsdon, ably pleaded their cause against their city fathers. He maintained that Her Majesty counted on this company for the festivals of Christmas, Easter and Whitsuntide. To fulfil such august desires, it was necessary for the actors to rehearse, and to earn their living ; he obtained for them the privilege of playing at the " Cross-Keys " until further notice, on condition that the performance was given outside the hours of religious services, that neither trumpet nor drum was to be used to attract the crowd, and that part of the receipts was to go to the poor of the parish. The actors maintained themselves as best they could during the first months of 1596, playing either in the innyards, or in the halls and palaces of the great. But a harder blow awaited them.

[1] *The Malcontent* augmented by Marston with the additions played by the King's Majesties Servants written by John Webster (At London : printed by V.S. for William Aspley and are to be sold at his shop in Paules church-yard, 1604).

[2] The fact that this play was acted by the King's players must have accentuated the effects of the satire. If Sly, Burbage, Lowen and Condell were represented on the stage in their own characters, the success of the play must have been great. It shows also that " The Globe " company could not have doubted that the rough pleasantries of Webster and Marston were aimed at them.

[3] Now the players are pitifully persecuted by the lord Mayor and the aldermen, and however in their old lord's time they thought their state settled, it is now so uncertain that they cannot build upon it. (Letter from Nash to Cotton, September, 1596.)

On July 22nd, 1596, their official protector suddenly died, and without even waiting until after Lord Hunsdon's funeral, the puritans obtained from the Lord Mayor an order forbidding all plays in London and its suburbs, on the pretext that large assemblies would create a public danger by increasing the risk of infection. Yet at this time, there was no plague in or near the capital.[1]

The new Chamberlain, an ardent reformer, was none other than Henry Cobham, inveterate enemy of the theatre, who had forced Shakespeare to suppress the name of his ancestor, Oldcastle, in *Henry IV*. He was not the man to allow his livery badge to be worn by the company of his predecessor. Shakespeare and his fellow-actors were obliged to renounce official protection, and departed much sooner than usual for their tour in the provinces.

Ben Jonson describes the discomfited troupe setting out on their journey, old Phillips with his viol da gamba on his back, Hemings the former grocer munching cloves, and the rest following with their shoes full of gravel, leading an old blind nag laden with baskets, bales and accessories. A mounted herald precedes the procession, posts the programme of the show in those villages that are worth the trouble, and, to the blast of a trumpet which Jonson imagines to be cracked, acts as crier in the market-place.[2] Their itinerary is recorded in every town where the mayor authorized the performance.

On the first of August they arrived at Faversham, where the municipality gave them sixteen pounds ; at Rye, a few days later, the remuneration was better : their funds were increased by twenty pounds ; Dover was less generous, Bristol more so. At Bath they again took in twenty pounds. After Marlborough, where they received the disastrous sum of five and sixpence, the troupe disbanded.

They were quite close to Stratford when they separated. Phillips could return to his family at Mortlake and Shakespeare to his home in Henley Street ; but he did so only to find the family in tears.

> Grief fills the room up of my absent child, . . .
> Puts on his pretty looks, repeats his words,
> Remembers me of all his gracious parts,
> Stuffs out his vacant garments with his form.
> (*King John*, Act III, Sc. 4)

His son Hamlet had died on August 11th, on the threshold of his twelfth year. However, Hamlet Shakespeare will always live in his father's works, where we feel that he is recalled in each portrait of a delicate, charming and intelligent boy destined to a premature death. In *Titus Andronicus*, he is the child danced on his grandfather's knee who listens to stories suited to his age until he goes to school with Ovid's *Metamorphoses* under his arm ; then, in *King John* he is Arthur, whose moving language charms kings and softens murderers ; again in *Richard III* he is the model for Edward's two children, the elder, who wants to know all about Julius Caesar, and the other,

---

[1] Dassent, *Acts of the Privy Council*, XXVI, p. 38.   [2] *Poetaster*, Act III, Sc. 1.

more carefree, who laughs at his hunchback uncle ; he is the son of Caius
Martius, whose proud language arrests Coriolanus's arm when the women's
prayers have been vain ; finally, he is Mamilius in *The Winter's Tale*, the
sensitive boy overcome with grief at the announcement of his mother's
condemnation.

In the same play are the moving lines reflecting the father's feelings on
those rare days he spends with the child :

> . . . if at home, sir,
> He's all my exercise, my mirth, my matter,
> Now my sworn friend and then mine enemy :
> My parasite, my soldier, statesman, all :
> He makes a July's day short as December,
> And with his varying childness cures in me
> Thoughts that would thick my blood.
>   (*The Winter's Tale*, Act I, Sc. 2)

It was at the time when the only male heir of the eldest branch of the
Shakespeares had just died, that, by a curious irony of fate, the college of
arms at last decided to grant the mayor of Stratford's request, and on
October 2nd, 1596, assigned to John Shakespeare and his descendants the
armorial bearings of a gentleman, as specified in his original request.   Today,
the falcon with the spear and the proud device " Non sans Droict " are
known throughout the world ; but the line which might have prided itself
in this coat of arms became extinct with the poet's grandchildren.

CHAPTER XI

THE TURN OF THE CENTURY

The actors regain London; they utilize the " Swan " theatre—Shakespeare's quarrel with the Justice of the Peace in Southwark—*Twelfth Night*—Death of Lord Chamberlain Cobham ; Sir George Carey, second Lord Hunsdon, takes his place—*The Merry Wives of Windsor*—Shakespeare's financial success ; he buys the Cloptons' house at Stratford and assists his native town, ravaged by two fires—After the production of *The Isle of Dogs*, the theatres are again menaced —The " Globe " is built—*Henry V*—*As You Like It*—*Much Ado About Nothing* —*Julius Caesar*—Death of Edmund Spenser.

AT the end of their tour, the actors found that the precarious state of affairs, cause of their departure, still prevailed in London. No hope of playing at the " Theatre " or at the " Curtain ". Their only course was to look for a site at Southwark, where in time James Burbage, after dismantling the old Holywell Theatre, would transport beams, flooring and rafters to the other side of the river and erect the famous " Globe ".[1] This time fortune favoured the company. There was a new theatre on the south bank, recently built, which had never been used. A certain Francis Langley, formerly member of the rich companies of clothiers and goldsmiths utilized his capital to embark upon a bold speculation. In Paris Garden he made a vast enclosure reaching to the river's edge where an impressive building rose among the trees. To increase the value of this land, he had hit upon the idea of constructing a large play house for the use of different groups of actors who had no regular theatre at their disposal. The " Swan ", according to a Dutch traveller, Johannes de Wytt, was the finest theatre of all. This stone construction could seat three thousand spectators. The columns which flanked the stage were so well painted that the most experienced eye might take them for marble.[2]

At first, Langley encountered the same difficulties as had hindered the proprietors of the " Blackfriars " theatre. The Lord Mayor wrote to Burleigh that it would be better to close all places of entertainment in Middlesex and Surrey rather than allow the erection of any new theatres

[1] James Burbage, who had successfully concluded the negotiations for this undertaking, did not live long enough to see the building completed.
[2] This theatre built by Francis Langley, is thus described by the traveller de Wytt, who also made a drawing of it :
" Omnium praestantissimum et amplissimum quippe quod tres miles homines in sedilitas admittat, constructum concervato lapide puritide ligneis sulfatum columnis quae ob ille tum marmoreum colorem quoque fallire possent."

on either side of the Thames.[1]   But, in spite of opposition, Langley realized his project and in 1596 placed his stage at the disposal of Shakespeare and his company, at least for the time being.   This explains why Shakespeare transferred his dwelling from Bishopsgate to the other side of the river, near the scene of his future activities.[2]   Edmund Malone drew attention to this change of residence in 1700 when he wrote that the poet went to live at Southwark in the neighbourhood of the Bear Garden, where Sackerson the gigantic bear from the Ural Mountains used to fight.   This animal was so well known for its ferocity that to touch its chain was proof of bravery.

In *The Merry Wives of Windsor* the coward Slender boasts of this exploit, and also of having often seen the bear at liberty.

> *Slender :* I love sport well ; I have seen Sackerson loose,
> twenty times and have taken by the chain.
> *(The Merry Wives of Windsor*, Act I, Sc. 1)

When the harassed players crossed the river to establish themselves in Surrey, they were not yet at the end of their troubles.   Who would have thought that in Southwark Shakespeare was to find himself, as in his native county, again in the toils and threatened by the heraldic pike of the Lucy family !

On November 3rd, 1596, a strange adventure befell him, of which the echo reaches us from the Queen's Bench thanks to the discovery made by Leslie Hotson in 1931.[3]   He records a fine exacted from Shakespeare, Langley and two women, Dorothy Soer and Anne Lee, for having treated William Wayte in a manner that made him believe that his life was endangered. The document is drawn up in these terms :

Anglia scire silicet Willelmus Wayte petit securitates pacis versus Willelmum Shakspere, Franciscum Langley, Dorotheam Soer, uxorem Johannis Soer, & Annam Lee ob metum mortis &c.[4]
Attachiamentum vicecomiti Surreie retornabile XVIII Martini.

which may be thus rendered :

England.   Be it known that William Wayte seeks sureties of peace against William Shakespeare, Francis Langley, Dorothy Soer, wife of John Soer, and Anne Lee, for fear of death, etc.

---

[1] " I understand that one Francis Langley intendeth to erect a nieu stage or Theator (as they call it) for the exercising of players upon the Banckside and foreasmuch as we find by dailly experience the great inconvenience that groweth to this citie and the government thereof by the sayd players . . . let us rather suppresse all such places built for that kinde of exercise than to erect any more of the same sort. . . ." (November 3).

[2] " From a paper now before me which formerly belonged to Edward Alleyn the player, our poet appears to have lived in Southwark near the Bear Garden." Edmund Malone, *The Plays of William Shakespeare.* Two other members of the company, William Sly and Alexander Cooke, also went to live in the same parish.

[3] See his *Shakespeare versus Shallow* (London, 1931).   As will be seen, I do not agree with the whole of Mr. Hotson's reconstruction.

[4] This same formula is written several times in the list, many words are abbreviated.

Order of seizure sent to the Sheriff of Surrey, who must reply by the 18th day of Saint Martin (November 29th, 1596).[1]

The incident may be reconstituted when the identity of each person is ascertained, which is by no means hard.[2] Langley is none other than the proprietor-director of the " Swan ", which Shakespeare's company had lately hired for the winter season. Anne Lee is the wife of the notable recusant Roger Lee, in whose house many proscribed priests took refuge.

In 1595, we find Lady Anne Lee denounced as having attended Mass in company with Lady Gray and Margaret Neville, close friends of Southampton ; she distinguished herself by her presence of mind when a search was in progress. Barring the way to the pursuivants on the narrow stair she gave Father Gerard time to gain his hiding place while his faithful servant John Lilly donned a cassock and got himself arrested in his master's place.[3]

Dorothy Soer belonged to a modest family of Paris Garden, one of whose members was a constable ; she was probably in Langley's service. Shakespeare after all was not in such bad company. On the other hand the plaintiff, William Wayte, who was in terror of his life, was far from being respectable. The records describe him as involved in blackmail, extortions and prevarications,[4] which fill the Southwark archives, where he is thus set down : " entirely dominated and ruled by the Southwark Justice of the Peace, William Gardiner ", to whom he was related. In fact, William Wayte's mother, Frances Lucy, had married Justice Gardiner as her second husband. After this marriage, the magistrate proudly quartered his heraldic griffon with the Lucy's three white pikes,[5] and, in imitation of his relative by alliance, Sir Thomas of Charlecote, he specialized in conducting searches of recusant homes, and raids in the neighbourhood of theatres ; like Lucy, he amassed a considerable fortune from fines and confiscations of which

[1] The fact that Shakespeare came under the jurisdiction of a Southwark court, shows that Malone was not mistaken in saying that the poet was living in this district at the time.

[2] When these lines came to light, the finder thought they alluded to one of those incidents so common in London's underworld. The discoverer, forgetting that women were not permitted on the stage in Elizabeth's England, thought that Shakespeare and Langley together with two actresses must have had some bone to pick with the Southwark police.

[3] This priest hunt, described by Father Gerard himself, deserves our attention because he mentions, among the women present in Anne Lee's parlour, another woman named Anne Lyne, whose tragic fate inspired one of the most beautiful of Shakespeare's poems. John Lilly, who saved his master had already distinguished himself by his courage in rescuing Father Gerard and Francis Arden from the Tower.

[4] The files of the Southwark court show that even before this incident, Langley had crossed swords with Justice Gardiner and his stepson, Wayte. The owner of the " Swan " had called Gardiner in public a rascal, a liar, and a perjurer, and Wayte a " loose person, of no reckoning or value ", and entirely under Gardiner's domination. (See *Shakespeare versus Shallow*.)

[5] The arms of William Gardiner, quartered with the Lucy family's, are reproduced in the Stowe Manuscript at the British Museum (587, fol. 1).

the Catholics were victims.[1] It appears that it was Shakespeare who won the day in this affair, as no more was heard of William Wayte, while the poet's fame grew daily.

Langley's theatre in Paris Garden must have been a godsend to the players, deprived as they then were of any hall or theatre. It was without doubt on this stage that, among other plays from his repertory, Shakespeare revived his *Hamlet*. It will be remembered that the tragedy had already been presented before 1589, and again in 1594, when, as Thomas Lodge put it, the ghost cried like an oyster-wife : " Hamlet, revenge ! "

This time, Thomas Dekker, author of *Satiro-Mastix*, announces the event in the words of one of his characters :

My name is Hamlet—Revenge ; hast been to Paris Garden, hast not ?

Dekker's question is doubly interesting. It associates the first version of *Hamlet* with the exact place where Shakespeare's troupe were playing in 1596, and confirms that this grandiloquent version was used by the Lord Chamberlain's players before the careful alterations which resulted in the text of 1623.

The fact that *Hamlet* was given at the " Swan " lends added interest to the Dutch traveller's sketch of the theatre, for in his well-known drawing, he has shown not only the interior and its proscenium, but also an episode of the play which he saw there. A woman may be seen sitting on a bench, over which another woman leans, while a bearded man strides before them holding a long stick, evidently Malvolio with his staff of office, attitudinizing before Olivia and Maria. If this be true, then *Twelfth Night* must have been written at an earlier date than most critics assign to it, a supposition all the more plausible as John Marston alludes to the play in *Histrio-Mastix ;* Ben Jonson also in 1598. It is therefore safe to fix 1596-97 as the date of the first performance of *Twelfth Night*, that is to say, at the time de Wytt made his drawing of the " Swan Theatre ".[2]

---

[1] A report from Edward Soer a constable of Paris Garden and of another constable working under Gardiner's orders reads thus :

Imprimis : . . . about Christmas last they came to the house of one Hewghe Katlyne, there to search for a papist, and found certain suspected persons within the house. The which Hewghe Katlyne would not suffer them to come in, neither to search his house, but kept the door having his weapon in hand. . . . they watched the house with a strong watch, and afterward upon a new search, they came into the house, and there found John Worrall, a notorious person of papistry o and . . . divers suspected persons . . . and 8 papists' books hid in sundry places. . . . aforesaid Katlyne . . . stale away in the night for fear he should be taken ; . . . one crucifix ; . . . books and pictures remains in Mr. Recorder's hands.

[signed] Willyam Gardiner (*Shakespeare versus Shallow*, p. 214).

[2] Leslie Hotson's discoveries at the Record Office show that Lord Pembroke's servants, a newly-founded company of actors, had rented the " Swan " for a year from February 1596. These actors testified in a lawsuit, that before they took possession, another company played in Langley's theatre. The identity of these first tenants was never established until the day when Shakespeare's name, linked to that of Langley, the proprietor, was found by Hotson. Thenceforward, it was legitimate to assume that author and manager were in professional association at the time and Dekker's allusion could be given its full significance. (*Shakespeare versus Shallow*, p. 19.)

John Manningham, the law student who saw this play when it was given at the celebrations in the Middle Temple in 1601, and whose enjoyment of the comic scenes seems to have been greater than his appreciation of its many exquisite and delicate qualities, probably refers to a revival when he writes :

At our feast we had a play called *Twelfth Night*, or *What You Will*, much like *The Comedy of Errors*, or *Menaechmi* in Plautus but most like and near to that in Italian called *Inganni*.

A good practise in it to make the steward believe his lady widow was in love with him by counterfeiting a letter as from his lady, in general terms telling him what she liked best in him, and prescribing his gesture in smiling, his apparel, etc., and then when he came to practise making him believe they took him to be mad.

Twelfth Night was never published in quarto nor given a proper title. The festive atmosphere which pervades the play made it specially suited to the joyful festivities with which England of old celebrated Epiphany. To the actors naturally it was only known as " our Twelfth Night play ". In the folio of 1623, it appears under the title *Twelfth Night*, or *What You Will*.[1]

This comedy belongs to his first manner ; Shakespeare again found in *Gli Ingannati* and in Bandello's *Novelle* inspiration for its improbable situations, mystifications and misunderstandings. Upon a double theme of unrequited love he has grafted a parallel comic episode, and deftly leaps from tender sentiment and poetic melancholy to the merry scenes with Sir Toby and his companions. The transitions from one atmosphere to another are natural and effective ; they add to rather than detract from the comedy's great charm.

It has been said that contemporary audiences recognized in Malvolio a caricature of Giovanni Florio. Those who had seen an earlier caricature of Southampton's Italian master in Holofernes were amused to meet him again in a different costume but still with the same eccentricities and the same characteristic expressions. Furthermore, it was just at this time that the butt of these caricatures was taking up arms and invoking his friends' help against the poet in the preface to his first *Dictionary*.

Let Aristophanes and his comedians make plaies and scowre their mouthes on Socrates ; those very mouthes they make to vilifie, shall be the meanes to amplifie his vertue. . . . It may be Socrates would not kicke againe, if an asse did kicke at him, yet some that cannot be so wise, and will not be so patient as Socrates, will for such jadish tricks give the asse his due burthen of bastonadas. . . . I have a great faction of good writers to bandie with me.

> Thinke they to set their teeth on tender stuffe ?
> But they shall marre their teeth, and finde me tough.

The ever-increasing success of the *Second Part of Henry IV* with Falstaff

[1] *Twelfth Night*, or *What You Will*, is the thirteenth comedy in the folio. Charles I who greatly appreciated Shakespeare wrote the name of Malvolio beside the title of the play.

and his jolly companions, the new play, *Twelfth Night*, and some dramas of the old repertory such as *Hamlet* and *The Merchant of Venice*, sufficed to bridge that period when Shakespeare, after the death of Lord Hunsdon, had almost fallen anew into the clutches of the Lucys. Fortunately the company was not to remain long without official support.

Towards the end of March 1597, Henry Cobham died, and the Queen, perhaps for the last time, imposed her own choice on the Council. The troupe immediately found a patron whose name was already dear to them. George Carey, Lord Hunsdon's heir, undertook, in spite of his youth, the important functions of Lord Chamberlain. Great-nephew to Anne Boleyn, he was one of Elizabeth's nearest relatives and the letters which the Queen addressed to him show an unaccustomed affection. While he was taking a cure in Bath, he received these lines from " his most affectionate and loving Sovereign " :

Good George I cannot but wonder, considering the great number of pails of water that I hear have been poured upon you, that you are not rather drowned than otherwise ; but I trust that all shall be for your better means to health— Your most affectionate and loving Sovereign, Elizabeth R.[1]

In view of these sentiments, Elizabeth naturally did not hesitate to confer upon her young cousin the Order of the Garter and to include him among the four knights whom she created on April 23rd, 1597. No nomination in this order had been made for upwards of four years. Now at the palace of Westminster preparations were hastened to celebrate the traditional banquet of St. George with due solemnity. It was customary to enhance the enjoyment of such a festival by a dramatic performance ; and Queen Elizabeth who had been much amused by Falstaff, commanded the poet to write a play showing Sir John in love.

The Merry Wives of Windsor [2] was composed in response to this royal command. Writing against time, Shakespeare turned out this middle-class comedy in less than three weeks.[3] The two more or less jealous husbands and their handsome wives encounter the fat knight, who imagines he is going to make a brace of easy conquests ; but beautiful Mistress Page and gay Mistress Ford, faithful to the maxim : " Wives may be merry and honest too ", boldly thwart Falstaff's schemes. The would-be seducer,

---

[1] *Shakespeare versus Shallow*, p. 116.

[2] The first quarto and unauthorized edition of this play appeared with this title :

A / Most pleasaunt and excellent conseited Co / medie of Syr John Falstaffe, and the merrie Wives of Windsor. Entermixed with sundrie / variable and pleasing humors, of syr Hugh / the Welch Knight, Justice Shallow and his wise Cousin M. Slender. With the swaggering vaine of Auncient Pistoll and Corporall Nym. By William Shakespeare. As it hath bene divers times Acted by the right Honorable my Lord Chamberlaines servants Both before her Majestie, and elsewhere (London, 1602).

[3] Most commentators have insisted upon the rapidity with which Shakespeare wrote this play : the 1710 editor of *The Works of Mr. William Shakespeare* (*Remarks* in *Volume the Seventh*) notes that the Queen obliged Shakespeare to write a play about Sir John Falstaff in love, and this was composed in a fortnight, a prodigious achievement when everything is so well thought out, and put into action without the slightest confusion. This tradition is confirmed by John Dennis in 1702 and 1703. See Chambers, *William Shakespeare*, vol. ii, pp. 262-263.

caught in his own snare, becomes the laughing-stock of the whole town of Windsor, while Mistress Page's pretty daughter chooses a husband for herself with more attractions than the French Doctor Caius, or the absurd Slender.

To strengthen his comedy and increase the number of burlesque scenes, Shakespeare resuscitated another character from *Henry IV*, who had shared the laughter of the audience with Falstaff. Justice Shallow, caricature of Sir Thomas Lucy still bewailing the poaching incident in his Fulbrooke demesne, comes to Windsor, and as soon as he appears airs his griefs which he intends to bring to the attention of the Star Chamber. The author wished perhaps to carry the spirit of good-humoured revenge further still when he causes the Justice to be accompanied by an equally ridiculous follower, his cousin Slender. This character in his attitude and affectation strongly resembles William Wayte, stepson of Justice Gardiner who had attempted to prosecute the actor-poet in the Paris Garden affair. Even the name of Slender, who was also anxious to adorn his coat of arms with three white Luces, reminds us by contrariety of Wayte=(weight).

The very individual English used by Doctor Caius in *The Merry Wives of Windsor* shows that the creator of this comic Frenchman already employed the curious idiom known today as " English as she is spoke "—

> Vat is you sing ?   I do not like dese toys.
> Pray you, go and vetch me in my closet une
> boitine verde ; a box, a green-a box ; do you
> intend vat I speak ?   A green-a box . . . Fé, fé
> fé, fé ! ma foi. il fait forte chaud.   Je m'en
> vais à la cour—la grande affaire.

Mrs. Quickly : Is it this Sir ?

Doctor Caius : Oui ; mettez le au mon pocket : dépêchez,
> quickly . . . by my trot I tarry too long.—
> od's me !   Qu'ay j'oublié ?   Dere is some simples
> in my closet, dat I vill not for de varld I
> shall leave behind. . . . O diable ! diable ! Vat
> is in my closet ?   Villain ! larron ! . . . Baillez
> me some paper.

To turn a French expression into English, Shakespeare chooses an English word with the same assonance as the French ; for instance : " Do you *intend* vat I speak ? " for " Do you hear what I say ? "   Bearing in mind the French form, " Entendez-vous ce que je dis ? " the author finds it natural for the Frenchman to say " intend " for " entendre ".

Two things are noticeable about this jargon : first, the English seems to have been concocted by an author who has observed the way some foreigners express themselves : and secondly, the choice of words and phrases appears rather to be that of an Italian trying to speak English than that of a Frenchman.   " Green-a box ", " Tell-a me ", these and many expressions with superfluous vowels are really those of an Italian for whom the pronunciation of words divided by consonants is difficult.   Perhaps the explanation of this is that maybe Giovanni Florio taught his pupils French as well as Italian.

Shakespeare and his company must have put all their energies into the performance of *The Merry Wives of Windsor*, and have entered whole-heartedly into the gaiety of this play, so overflowing with laughter. They had been too near ruin when Cobham became Lord Chamberlain and the puritans prevailed in the Council, not to rejoice at the distinction accorded to the son of their former protector, who had now in his turn become their patron. They must therefore have made fine preparations for the ceremonial procession to Windsor, a month after the St. George's day banquet. Even Francis Bacon expressed his admiration for the way in which " the Lord Chamberlain flaunted it gallantly " at the head of a cavalcade " three hundred strong and all gentlemen ".[1] When the procession riding four abreast entered Windsor for the Garter celebrations the populace admired Sir Henry Lee's suite, Lord Mountjoy's or that of Sir Thomas Howard. But none could compare with George Carey, Lord Hunsdon, the old Queen's young Chamberlain. At the head of all his actors, he made a brilliant entry. Shakespeare, Burbage, Heminge, Condell and all the others wore wide-brimmed felt hats ornamented with orange feathers which swept so low on their shoulders that they almost covered the escutcheon of their patron and the device " Honi soit qui mal y pense ". Their cloaks were blue in honour of the Garter which their master was about to receive. One of the new Knights was missing from the cavalcade, Frederick, Duke of Würtemberg. He had made great efforts to obtain this high distinction, and was nominated to receive the Order, but the Queen neglected to inform him of it, and post-poned *sine die* the investiture of the costly insignia. This explains Doctor Caius' allusion to the absence of the German Duke (cousin Garmombles) whom the court no longer awaits.

Before the performance at Windsor, Shakespeare added a few passages to the text of the play as it was written for the banquet of St. George at Westminster. There is, for example, the one where the " Fairy Queen " commands her elves to prepare everything for the forthcoming solemnities ; they are to furnish up the royal castle of Windsor, pinch the lazy servants, and polish the stalls and armorial bearings in the chapel ; while the lawns must be garnished with fairy rings reminiscent of the Garter's form and colours.

> . . . " Honi soit qui mal y pense " write
> In emerald tufts, flowers purple, blue and white ;
> Like sapphire, pearl, and rich embroidery,
> Buckled below fair Knighthood's bending knee :
> Fairies use flowers for their charactery.
> (*The Merry Wives of Windsor*, Act v, Sc. 5)

Shakespeare was not yet thirty-four, and he had already produced eight

[1] See Bodley Ashmole Collection (MS. 112, fol. 16ᵛ). There is another in the Stowe Collection 595, fol. 45ᵛ.

comedies, twelve tragedies, published two poems and adapted a dozen old plays. Besides his income as author, he drew his regular portion of the theatrical profits due to him as an original shareholder. At Stratford he was considered a rich man, when on May 4th, 1597, he bought the Clopton's old town house for one hundred and twenty pounds, and set about renovating it with a view to installing his family there. The former Maecenas had been obliged to sell it to William Underhill. The agreement between the latter and Shakespeare was concluded and a first instalment paid, when Underhill was poisoned—by his elder son, it was said. Shakespeare had therefore to wait until the younger son's majority before entering into possession of the much coveted domain, which made the poet third in importance among Stratford's landed proprietors. The very old house and its dependencies required extensive repairs. One façade had to be entirely rebuilt. The moment had come for Shakespeare to experience the worries of the new proprietor described in *The Second Part of Henry IV* :

> . . . When we mean to build,
> We first survey the plot, then draw the model ;
> And when we see the figure of the house,
> Then must we rate the cost of the erection ;
> Which if we find outweighs ability,
> What do we then but draw anew the model
> In fewer offices, or at last desist
> To build at all ?
>
> (*The Second Part of Henry IV*, Act 1, Sc. 3)

Meanwhile his parents tried to lift the mortgage upon their Asbies domain, feeling themselves once more in a position to take their old place in the community as " people of good figure and fashion ".

When Stratford neighbours saw men working busily round the Clopton manor house and cartloads of stone unloaded [1] on Chapel Street, they must have realized that Sir Thomas's one-time victim was now favoured by fortune. All desired to be on good terms with him, particularly as the town had greatly suffered in the fires of 1594 and 1595,[2] when more than a third of the houses had disappeared. The Shakespeares' home in Henley Street was only saved by the family's presence of mind. Without hesitation they sacrificed the barn where their wool was stored, thus separating the house from that of their neighbour Richard Badger which was already in flames like most of the buildings in that part of town. The traces left by the fire can still be seen on the western gable-end of the house and also the marks of the irons used to isolate it from the condemned buildings.[3] After these

---

[1] The following spring Shakespeare sold what was left of this building material to repair the great bridge over the Avon.

[2] As a result of these two conflagrations, a hundred and twenty dwelling houses, eighty buildings of various kinds, and merchandise to the value of twelve thousand pounds were destroyed. Four hundred persons were rendered homeless.

[3] John Shakespeare ceded a strip of ground to one of his neighbours, George Badger, and to another, Edward Willis, some square yards so that they could rebuild their houses. (Stratford Corporation Records.)

conflagrations Stratford was on the verge of bankruptcy. The council appealed to John Combe, the capitalist, who consented to a loan guaranteed by the municipal plate and, after the custom of those times, the surrounding counties were asked to come to the municipality's assistance. The mayor, Richard Quinney, collected funds in Oxford and Cambridge, then proceeded Londonwards in an attempt to obtain reduction of the taxes levied on the sorely stricken town. From the subsequent correspondence, it appears that Shakespeare, always responsive to the claims of his home town, was more than once petitioned by his fellow Stratfordians. In a first missive from Adrian Quinney to his son in London we find :

If you bargain with William Shakespeare, or receive money there, bring your money home.[1]

A letter dated January 24th, 1598, from Abraham Sturley, the Stratford treasurer, to his mayor delayed in London, contains this edifying passage :

This is one special remembrance from your father's motion : It seemeth by him that our countryman, Master Shakespeare, is willing to disburse some money upon some odd yardland or other at Shottery or near about us. He thinketh it a very fit pattern to move him to deal in the matter of our Tithes. By the instructions you can give him thereof, and by the friends he can make therefor, we think it a fair mark for him to shoot at, and not impossible to hit. If obtained, would advance him indeed, and would do us much good. Hoc movere et quantum in te est permovere ne negligas, hoc enim et sibi et nobis maximi erit momenti. Hic labor, hoc opus esset eximie et gloriae et laudis sibi.[1]

On November 4th, the same Sturley returned to the attack and wrote to Mayor Quinney :

Your letter which imported that our countryman, master William Shakespeare would procure us money, which I shall like of as I shall hear when and where and how, and I pray, let not go that occasion. . . . [1]

Evidently the petty intrigue cherished by the Stratford town council came to naught at this time ; but a few years later on July 24th, 1605, Shakespeare redeemed for the sum of four hundred and forty pounds, a large part of the tithes paid by the town ; this, among other advantages, gave all his family the right to be buried in the choir of the parish church, and to occupy a place in the Clopton family pew, privileges to which no Stratford resident was insensible.

There is also extant Richard Quinney's letter to Shakespeare in which the mayor of Stratford asks his old school fellow for financial assistance. Among the numerous missives which the poet must have received, this is the only one remaining. It is preserved in the birthplace Museum at Stratford.

[1] Stratford Birthplace Museum.

Loving Countrymen I am bold of you as of a friend, craving your help wite thirty pounds upon Mr. Bushell's and my securities or Mr. Mytton's [1] with me. Mr. Rosswell is not come to London as yet and I have special cause, you shall friend me much in helping me out of all the debts I owe in London. . . . I thank God and much quiet my mind which would not be indebted. I am now towards the Court in hope of answer for the dispatch of my business. You shall neither lose credit nor money by me the lord willing. And now but persuade yourself so as I hope and you shall not need to fear but with all hearty thankfulness I will hold my time and content your friend and if we bargain farther you shall be the paymaster yourself. My time bids me hasten to an end and so I commit this to your care and hope of your help. I fear I shall not be back this night from the Court. Haste. The lord be with you and with us all amen.

Yours in all kindness

Ryc Quyney

From the Bell inn Carter Lane the 25 October 1598.
To my loving good friend and countryman
Mr. Wm. Shackespere deliver these.

That the writer of this letter obtained the thirty pounds of which he had such pressing need, there is no doubt ; it is even probable that it was Shake-speare's influence, aided perhaps by Essex, that persuaded Her Majesty to grant Stratford's petition for remittance of taxation, ravaged as it was by two destructive fires.

Decidedly the former refugee had won for himself the influential place in his native town which the Knight of the Shire had wrested from his family. His old father, so fond of honours, was to experience another great satisfaction before his death. The heralds at arms, William Dethicke and William Camden, who had granted him his armorial bearings three years before, authorized him in 1599 to quarter them with those of the Arden family.

This is recorded in the register of the college of arms for 1599 :

We have assigned, granted, and confirmed, and by those presents exemplified, unto the said John Shakespeare and to his posterity, that shield and coat of arms (heretofore assigned to him) and we have likewise upon one other escutcheon impaled the same with the ancient coat of arms of the said Ardens of Wellingcote signifying thereby that it may and shall be lawful for the said John Shakespeare, gentleman, to bear and use the same single or impaled during his natural life, and for his children, issue and posterity to bear, use, and quarter and show forth the same.[2]

It should be mentioned that the heralds were careful not to reproduce the coat of arms belonging to the Ardens of Park Hall—a bar with four ermines—and had substituted the martin and the three crosses of Lorraine appertaining to the branch of the Ardens who lived at Longcroft in Stafford-

---

[1] Mr. Mytton, mentioned in the letter, was Paymaster General to the Earl of Essex' troops. The fact that Quinney proposes him as guarantor is proof of the close relations which existed between Shakespeare's family and that of the Viceroy of Ireland.

[2] MS. Coll. of Arms, R. 21. Shakespeare evidently did not take advantage of the privilege of quartering his arms.

shire, and whose escutcheon had not been tarnished by the " treason " of Edward Arden.

Langley, proprietor of the " Swan ", was more unlucky with Lord Pembroke's players than he had been with Shakespeare and his troupe. The new tenants had signed a year's lease but hardly were they in possession of the theatre when they had the unfortunate idea of presenting a satire by Nashe entitled *The Isle of Dogs*,[1] in which, apparently England was the " Isle " and the government the " dogs ". Essex had already termed the cabal which had grown up against him in the government, " the pack ", and there is no doubt that Nashe, whom Thomas Lodge called an English Aretino, had this time produced a work more virulent and more subversive in tone than any previously conceived. The reaction was immediate : both innocent and guilty were given exemplary punishments. The Privy Council decided that, because this " seditious and obscene " play had been publicly acted, all the theatres of the capital and within a radius of three miles must not only close their doors, but must be dismantled. Every actor was forbidden to play in public for three months.[2] Nashe, responsible for the play, was confined in Fleet prison. Ben Jonson, Robert Shaw and Gabriel Spenser were sent to the Marshalsea. Nashe's lodging was searched and Topcliffe ordered to examine all his papers. The magistrate William Gardiner was given the task of seeing that the new decree was carried out in the theatrical quarter. Francis Meres, who had so eloquently sung Shakespeare's praises, then wrote in Nashe's defence, in spite of the severe sentence which condemned Nashe to six months' imprisonment and forbade his residence in London.

As Acteon was wooried of his owne hounds : so is Tom Nash of his *Ile of Dogs*. Dogges were the death of Euripedes, but bee not disconsolate gallant young Juvenall, Linus, the sonne of Apollo died the same death. Yet God forbid that so brave a witte should so basely perish, thine are but paper dogges, neither is thy banishment like Ovids, eternally to converse with the barborous Getes. Therefore comfort thy selfe sweete Tom. . . .[3]

The council's order that every copy of the play must be suppressed was so well executed that it is impossible today to find any trace but the title accompanied by the inscription : " By Thomas Nashe and inferior players." These words may be read in a manuscript list of documents preserved at Alnwick Castle which the present author was enabled to study *in situ* thanks to the courtesy of the Duchess of Northumberland.[4] This first page or cover on which the index is written deserves attention, for the name of William Shakespeare appears there several times.

Beside the *Isle of Dogs*, near the right-hand margin there is a list of works of which many could pass for subversive, such as the *Letter to the Queen* by

---

[1] This performance took place on July 27th, 1597.
[2] Chambers' *The Elizabethan Stage* (vol. iv, pp. 322 ff.).
[3] Meres, *Palladis Tamia*, f. 286v.
[4] This document is known today as the " Northumberland Manuscript ". Mr. Frank J. Bourgoyne published it with numerous facsimiles (Longmans Green, 1904).

Sir Philip Sidney, in which the author reproaches Her Majesty for her project of marriage with the French King's brother ; Philip, Earl of Arundel's *Letter to the Queen* explaining his conversion to the Catholic faith ; *Leicester's commonwealth*, whose circulation Elizabeth had suppressed, and Shakespeare's *Richard II* and *Richard III*, two plays which were open to criticism from the political point of view.

The rest of the page is covered with notes and scribblings. It is easy to decipher the name of Anthony Fitzherbert, at that time secretary to Cardinal Allen, founder of the English overseas college, and that of Henry Neville, Ambassador in Paris, who left his post to take part in the Essex conspiracy, and was sent to the Tower. Near his name is the twice repeated pun : " Ne vile velis " and this appreciation of the perfect diplomat :

> Multis annis jam transactis
> Nulla fides est in pactis
> Mel in ore gerba lactis
> Fel in corde Fraus in factis.[1]

The name of William Shakespeare, written in full or abbreviated, appears about ten times. The word " Honorificabilitudine " attracts attention on account of its resemblance to the celebrated polysyllable, " honorificabilitudinitatibus " used by Shakespeare in *Love's Labour's Lost*. This unfinished phrase is also to be found in the manuscript page : " Revealing day through every cranny peeps and see . . ."

In *The Rape of Lucrece*, Shakespeare had written :

> Revealing day through every cranny spies
> And seems to point her out where she sits weeping. . . .

It is logical to suppose that this document was once in Shakespeare's hands, or at least in those of some literary friends not in favour with the Government, one of the Percy brothers for example. This is plausible since the famous manuscript is preserved in the library of their family castle at Alnwick.

Fortunately for the players, the Privy Council's decision to close and dismantle the theatres of the capital, remained a dead letter. Once again Shakespeare and his fellows were free to take the road and perform in country towns, and when at the end of their tour they returned to London, the storm had blown over. Their new patron, the second Lord Hunsdon, threw the doors of the court wide open. They entertained the Queen on December 28th, 1598, at the palace of Westminster, and two months later (February 20th, 1599), they took part in the royal festivities at Richmond.

Between these two dates, the company were engaged in quite a different occupation, the business of recovering the material of the old " Theatre ", when the landlord of the site upon which it was built claimed that the building belonged to him because the rent was not paid in full.

---

[1] Francis Bacon's name is written twice in this document as author of several essays and a discourse at Gray's Inn.

The players turned up their sleeves and, directed by a carpenter, Peter Street, armed with axes, poignards, swords and billhooks, assisted in the demolition and transport of the materials across the Thames. On January 20th, they repeated their exploit and took possession of what remained of the old structure, not without protests from the guardians of their former play house.[1] Everyone worked with such a will, that in three months the task was accomplished. At the end of April 1599, the " Globe ", above whose stage figured the noble device : " Totus mundus agit histrionem ", opened its doors.

An amusing tradition has it that Ben Jonson, reading the inscription, composed this impromptu couplet :

> If all the world the Actor plays
> Who are the spectators of its plays ?

To which Shakespeare is said to have replied :

> Little or much of what we see we do
> We are both actors and Spectators too.

The rent of the ground upon which the " Globe " was built, was fixed at fourteen pounds ten shillings for twenty-one years. Although Shakespeare possessed only a tenth of the shares in the theatre, he is the only member of his company mentioned by name in an inventory of the premises dated May 16th, 1599.[2]

Even if the enterprise did not completely fulfil the hopes of the Burbages,[3] posterity must rejoice at its conclusion. The building was only of wood, and its roof, from which the troupe's silken flag proudly fluttered, was thatched, but nevertheless, the " Globe " was accounted the finest theatre of the day. Like all the others, it was open to the sky : but the stage was sheltered by a projecting roof which prevented the actors' voices being lost in space, and turned to advantage the resonance of this vast " wooden O ", as Shakespeare himself called his " Globe ". Another peculiarity was that the proscenium was placed in such a way that the actor could easily be seen by all the three thousand spectators whether seated in the galleries or standing in the pit.

A year later, when Henslowe and Alleyn decided in their turn to construct a new theatre the " Fortune ", they found that they could do no better than apply to the same builder, Peter Street, and contract for a " building on the same lines " as the " Globe " at all points.

This stage, henceforth celebrated, witnessed the production of masterpieces

---

[1] Street spent several days in prison as a result of these incidents.

[2] Cf. Chambers, *The Elizabethan Stage*, vol. ii, p. 415.

[3] " Wee at like expence built the Globe, with more summes of money taken up at interest, which lay heavy on us many yeres ; and to ourselves wee joyned those deserveing men, Shakspere, Hemings, Condall, Philips, and others, partners in the profittes of that they call the House, but makeing the leases for twenty-one yeeres hath beene the destruction of ourselves and others, for they dyeing at the expiration of three or four yeeres of their lease, the subsequent yeeres became dissolved to strangers, as by marrying with their widdowes and the like by their children." *Ibid*. p. 417.

by Webster, Beaumont and Fletcher, the eighteen still unpublished plays of Shakespeare, and many of Ben Jonson's comedies, recommended to the company by Shakespeare, according to a tradition, against the opinion of his seniors. It will be remembered that it was Shakespeare himself, who in 1598, had created the part of Father Knowell in *Every Man in his Humour*,[1] while Richard Burbage played that of his son with much success. The popularity of the *Humours* was so great that five years later, when Ben Jonson tried his hand at Roman tragedy with *Sejanus* [2] he asked the same actors to interpret his play.

While Henslowe and Alleyn contented themselves at the " Rose " with a programme where novelty was certainly not the attraction—they presented Kyd's *Spanish Tragedie*, Marlowe's *Doctor Faustus* and an old play of Chapman's, *An Humorous Day's Mirth*—the " Globe " opened its doors with a repertory both brilliant and varied. The heroic *Henry V* inaugurated the new theatre.

Shakespeare had promised the public to continue Falstaff's story and to show him playing the soldier in France ; but after *The Merry Wives of Windsor*, he had doubtless exhausted the subject, so that the presence of the fat knight in a patriotic epic such as *Henry V* would have been an error of taste. Hence Falstaff disappears and is only recalled in the first act when Mistress Quickly describes his death in a lugubrious but involuntarily comic manner.[3]

In *Henry V*, Shakespeare returns to English history at the exact point where he left it in the last act of *Henry IV*. The epilogue of the new play contains a very interesting feature. It reveals an author bent over his work and wishing to show that his historical dramas form a true whole. Not only is *Henry V* the continuation of *Henry IV*, but both are closely linked with his grandiloquent trilogy of *Henry VI* and the episodes of the Wars of the Roses.

> Thus far, with rough and all unable pen,
> Our bending author hath pursu'd the story ;
> In little room confining mighty men,
> Mangling by starts the full course of their glory.
> Small time, but in that small most greatly liv'd
> This star of England : Fortune made his sword,
> By which the world's best garden he achieved,
> And of it left his son imperial lord.
> Harry the Sixth, in infant bands crown'd King
> Of France and England, did this King succeed ;

[1] *Every Man to his humour*. A comedie. Acted in the yeare 1598 by the then Lord Chamberlayne his Servants. The author B. J. London, printed for Richard Bishop. MDCXI. Shakespeare is listed amongst the Actors.

[2] *Seianus His Fall*. A Tragedie. First Acted in the yeare 1605 by the Kings Majesties Servants with the allowance of the Master of the Revels. The author B. J. London, Printed by Richard Bishop MDCXI. Shakespeare is on the Actors' list.

[3] " His nose was as sharp as a pen and a' babled of green fields . . ." (*King Henry V*, Act II, Sc. 3).

Whose state so many had the managing,
That they lost France and made his England bleed :
Which oft our stage hath shown ; and, for their sake,
In your fair minds let this acceptance take.
(*Henry V*, Epilogue)

Shakespeare thus emphasizes that his was the lion's share in the writing of *Henry VI* where the influence of Marlowe is often perceptible, and he shows that with *Richard II, Richard III*, the three parts of *Henry VI*, the two parts of *Henry IV* and *Henry V*, he had presented on the stage more than a century of English history in sequence.

Henry V was certain to capture the attention of the audience and provoke applause. At that time England's mood was warlike. The public was especially interested in recital of past victories. Shakespeare could satisfy this taste with little trouble, he had only to reopen the Chronicles of his friend and master, Holinshed. Never did he follow him more faithfully, borrowing from him ideas and often whole passages. *Henry V* is the triumphant amalgamation of Holinshed's narrative with Shakespeare's imaginative blank verse, bringing to life the persons and events of this troubled epoch. In order to increase the importance of his hero and to make him worthy of the spectator's sympathy from the beginning of the play, Shakespeare with much skill chooses from Holinshed exactly what is required to create a flattering portrait. Henry realizes the gravity of the decision which he is about to make (the invasion of France), and if the situation does not permit of either peace or compromise, he wishes to learn his exact legal position. To this end he summons the most learned statesmen of the realm, and discusses the legality of his claims to certain French duchies. A comparison of Holinshed's and Shakespeare's texts where the Salic Law is set forth (*Henry V*, Act I, Sc. 2) is very instructive to anyone who wishes to see how faithfully Shakespeare follows his sources.[1]

Holinshed : *In terram salicam mulieres ne succedant*, that is to saye, lette not women succeede in the land Salique, which the Frenche glosers expounde to bee the Realme of Fraunce, and that this law was made by K. Pharamond, whereas yet their owne authors affirme, that the land Salique is in Germanie, betweene the rivers of Elbe and Sala, and that when Charles the great had overcome the Saxons, hee placed there certaine Frenchmen, which having in disdeine the onhonest maners of the Germain women, made a lawe, that the females shoulde not succeede to anye inheritance within that lande, which at this day is called Meisen. . . .

Shakespeare : In terram Salicam mulieres ne succedant,
No woman shall succeed in Salique land :
Which Salique land the French unjustly gloze
To be the realm of France, and Pharamond
The founder of this law and female bar.
Yet their own authors, faithfully affirm,

[1] *Chronicles of England, Scotlande and Irelande faithfully gathered and compiled by Raphael Hollinshed* (London, 1577, p. 1168).

8

That the land Salique is in Germany,
Between the floods of Sala and the Elbe :
Where Charles the Great, having subdued the Saxons
There left behind . . . and settled certain French
Who holding . . . in disdain the German women,
For some dishonest manners of their life,
Established then this law,—to wit no female
Should be inheritrix in Salique land.
Which Salike (as I said) 'twixt Elbe and Sala
Is at this day in Germany called Meisen.

This erudite discussion is interrupted by the French Ambassadors bringing with them a gift and a piece of advice ; namely, to make use of their present and cease to meddle with affairs of state-craft.   When opened, the barrel they have brought is found to contain a large number of tennis balls.   This insulting allusion to the young king's frivolous past allows the sovereign to define the spirit of this historical epic.

And tell the pleasant prince this mock of his
Hath turn'd his balls to gun-stones : and his soul
Shall stand more charged for the wasteful vengeance
That shall fly with them : for many a thousand widows
Shall this his mock mock out of their dear husbands ;
Mock mothers from their sons, mock castles down
And some are yet ungotten and unborn
That shall have cause to curse the Dauphin's scorn.

                                        (*Henry V*, Act I, Sc. 2)

With great realism, he conducts us step by step to the fields of Agincourt. The changing fortunes of the battle are described with the technique of a Froissart, yet Henry V is all the time the centre of the spectator's interest. His bravery, his modesty, his sympathy for the common soldier, make him a romantic figure, and explain his marriage with the French princess.

This play shows the extent of Shakespeare's acquaintance with the French tongue.   In his previous dramatic works, scraps of phrases, curses, · interjections and proverbs already demonstrated that he had some knowledge of it.   But here a more extensive vocabulary permits a better appreciation of his proficiency : Rowe was right in affirming that the poet " certainly understood French ".

One of the Princess Katharine's phrases in her conversation with King Henry, is especially interesting, since it sheds some light on Shakespeare's methods :

Les dames, et demoiselles, pour estre baisées devant leur noces, il n'est pas la coutume de France.   (Act v, Sc. 2)

This is literally translated from the English :

For ladies and young girls, to be kissed before marriage, is not customary in France.

Nevertheless, the author who employed French in this naïve manner was capable of appreciating its shadings as another intentionally mediocre passage shows. The scene commences with a misunderstanding :

A French prisoner takes the miserable Pistol for a powerful lord, and asks for mercy. Pistol thinks that the prisoner's " Ayes pitié de moi " is an offer of ransom, and claims " forty moys ". Pistol explains to the little ragamuffin who has presented himself as interpreter that he will dispatch the prisoner if he does not provide this ransom, and uses a few French words pronounced English fashion to make the audience laugh. The interpreter speaks slightly better French, and the prisoner uses expressions which demonstrate the author's efforts to write correctly :

Boy : Il me commande à vous dire que vous faites vous prest ; car ce soldat icy est disposé tout à cette heure de couper vostre gorge.

Pistole : Ouy, cuppele gorge, parmafoy, peasant, unless thou give me crowns, brave crowns ; or mangled shalt thou be by this my sword.

Fr. Sol : O ! je vous supplie pour l'amour de Dieu, me pardonner ! Je suis gentilhomme de bonne maison : gardez ma vie, et je vous donneray deux cents escus.

Pistol : What are his words ?

Boy : He prays you to save his life : he is a gentleman of a good house ; and, for his ransom he will give you two hundred crowns.

Pistol : Tell him—my fury shall abate, and I the crowns will take.

Fr. Sol : Petit monscieur, que dit-il ?

Boy : Encore qu'il est contre son jurement de pardonner aucun prisonnier ; neant-moins, pour les ascus que vous l'avez promis, il est content de vous donner la liberté, le franchisement.

Fr. Sol : Sur mes genoux je vous donne mille remerciemens ; et je m'estime heureux que je suis tombé entre les mains d'un chevalier, je pense le plus brave, valiant, et très distingué seigneur d'Angleterre :

(*Henry V*, Act IV, Sc. 4)

Henry V was first printed in 1600, and re-printed posthumously. In spite of its success, the play is not on a level with *Henry IV*. When writing it, Shakespeare was bowing to circumstances. He was too anxious to make the Irish war, then about to begin, more acceptable. He wished to enlist public opinion in support of Essex, his idol, and Southampton his patron, who were to devise and lead the expedition. In this play the atmosphere of propaganda is too obvious.

He was better inspired when he returned to his characteristic vein of romantic comedy, derived not from the Italian novelists this time but from the work of a friend. The idyllic subject of *As You Like It* is borrowed from the *Roselynde* [1] of Thomas Lodge, who, in 1598, came back to London to practise medicine. [2]

[1] *Roselynde, Euphues his Golden Legacie* . . . Fetcht from the Canaries by T. L. gent. (London, 1590).

[2] Thomas Lodge (1558-1625) having finished at Trinity College, Oxford, read law at Lincoln's Inn and launched himself into literary circles ; denounced as a recusant, he was obliged to go abroad, but returned to London to bring out *Roselynde* written during his long sea voyage, and then abandoned letters for the practice of medicine. He had studied and obtained his diploma at Avignon ; he established himself as practitioner in London

As You Like It [1] is a pastoral whose title alone indicates that the author meant to please the taste of the young lord who adored such improbable and romantic tales. As in many other plays of this period, Shakespeare's art is constantly subordinated to his patron's liking; human existence is not depicted as it is, unjust and illogical and sad, but such as the enthusiastic young man wished to find it: amusing, delicate, full of optimism, where all comes to a happy conclusion.

The beautiful forest of Arden, dear and familiar to the author who had spent his childhood under its " melancholy boughs ", is planted in a pseudo-French duchy to form an appropriate Arcadian setting for the exiled duke and his court.

An atmosphere of friendship and love permeates these woods. Names, hearts and ballads are carved on the bark of the trees. Though the forest is immense, the spectator does not doubt that the loving errants, whether disguised or not, will soon meet and pursue their amorous romance. The idyll of Rosalind and Orlando is the most beautiful symphony of the theme of love ever orchestrated by Shakespeare. It ends like that of Celia and Oliver in a marriage. But in this fairy-land dream and reality are brought together by the introduction of three characters, three kinds of materialist philosophers whose minds and thoughts are of the earth earthy. Coreir, the shepherd—perhaps a memory of old Whittington who tended Richard Hathaway's sheep—always states the honest truth with simple good sense. Touchstone, the optimist clown, never fails to point out the plain and pleasant side of things, people and events while Jaques, the pessimist, reminds the audience that:

> . . . All the world's a stage,
> And all the men and all the women merely players.

That Shakespeare had recently become acquainted with the works of Rabelais, *As You Like It* bears witness: Rosalind having besieged her cousin with questions, calls on her to answer in a single word. Celia replies:

> You must borrow me Gargantua's mouth first: 'tis a word too great for any
> mouth of this age's size.   (Act III, Sc. 2)

The dramatist had already alluded to Rabelais' work in *Love's Labour's Lost*, where he gave his pedant the name of Holofernes, teacher of the young Gargantua who could read his alphabet backwards. In *Twelfth Night* Sir Andrew tells of " Pigrogromitus, of the Vapians passing the equinoctial of Queuebus ". The critics Swinburne and Staunton see in this text an allusion to Pantagruel's voyage. After all, why should Shakespeare not

---

in 1598, and, according to Anthony à Wood, had a large practice among Catholics and made as great a reputation for himself as a doctor as previously as poet. (*Athenae Oxonienses* London, 1691, p. 424.)

[1] *As You Like It* was not published until the folio of 1623 where the play is given the sixth place among the comedies; but a request for a printing licence had been made on August 4th, 1600. This request is accompanied by a comment " not to be granted " inscribed on the Stationer's Register.

have known Rabelais, since his friend Nashe had translated *la Pantagrueline Prognostication* and had sought, though without obtaining, permission to print all the French writer's works. The creator of the gigantic Falstaff was severely taken to task, as we have seen, for having imitated the drunken revellings of "wicked Rabelais". Nevertheless in *As You Like It* the dramatist has lost much of his gay spontaneity. His Pastoral muse is given over to contemplative melancholy. The characters become more human because they seem aware that they must play their future parts in a hard world after this Arcadian interlude comes to an end.

Much Ado About Nothing, for which permission to print was asked at the same time as for *As You Like It, Every Man in His Humour* and *Henry V*, like the rest received no licence ; an indication at least that all these plays belong to the period when the Lord Chamberlain's men were out of government favour.[1]

Much Ado About Nothing takes place in an aristocratic setting. The author has drawn admirable portraits of the three lords : Leonato, governor of Messina, his old friend Antonio, and Don Pedro of Aragon. An atmosphere of grandeur pervades the first act, where Claudio and his betrothed propose to bring about the marriage of two unwilling candidates for matrimony, Beatrice and Benedick.

These two are the counterparts of Biron and Rosaline in *Love's Labour's Lost ;* if their minds are higher, they arrive none the less at the same conclusion as the pair in the earlier comedy.

Rosaline had considered that the perpetual merry-making in which her flirtation with Biron took place was not an atmosphere conducive to a lifelong contract durable even beyond the grave. She therefore required her lover to pass a year in contact with human suffering, caring for the sick in hospitals, before renewing his marriage proposal. Beatrice, for her part, submits Benedick to a different kind of ordeal, making him challenge his best friend Claudio, who in her eyes is guilty of disgracing her cousin.

In the printed editions of *Much Ado About Nothing* we occasionally find the names of the actors substituted for those of the characters represented ; instead of Dogberry the night watchman and his lieutenant Verges, the names of Kempe the clown, and his foil, Cowley, appear in the quarto. Similarly where music occurs the entry of Jack Wilson with a song is noted. This well-known musician later became Master of the Chapel Royal to Charles I.

The public always appreciated this comedy. Forty years after its first performance, the poet Leonard Digges wrote of it :

> . . . let but Beatrice
> And Benedicke be seene, loe, in a trice
> The cock-pitt, galleries, boxes, are all full,

[1] This request of August 4th, 1600, carries, as previously mentioned, the marginal note, " Not to be granted ". The same remark figures on the demand for permission to print *Hamlet* in 1602. It is impossible to discover whether this prohibition came from the actors, the owners of publication rights, who wished to preserve them, or on the contrary from the censor who at that time, viewed the activities of the lord Chamberlain's servants, with disfavour.

This tribute of Leonard Digges' applies equally to *Julius Caesar* which was billed soon after *Much Ado About Nothing*.

The first description of a performance in the new " Globe " is given by a notability from Basle, who made this report of his afternoon at that theatre on September 21st, 1599, when *Julius Caesar* was presented :

After dinner on the 21st of September at about two o'clock, I went with my companions over the water and in a thatched roof house saw the tragedy of the first Emperor Julius with at least fifteen characters very well acted. At the end of the comedy they danced according to their custom with extreme elegance. Two in men's clothes two in women's gave this performance in wonderful accord with each other.

Shakespeare's *Julius Caesar* breaks with the universally accepted tradition which saw in the great Roman the quintessence of military glory and the highest expression of political genius. The spectator expects the entry of some super-man, with words of wisdom on his lips. The character presented by the actor-poet is quite different. The imperator, when he appears, is in his decline and no longer possesses many traces of former greatness. His glorious days are recalled by hearsay ; Caesar has outlived himself, and can only reconquer fame through the sacrifice of death, when he is ennobled by the eloquent words of Mark Antony, the only being who really loved him. How was it that the politicians behind the scenes in that troubled epoch never recognized a parallel between the senile Caesar of the drama and the superannuated queen whose succession was under discussion ? Caesar advises his mature wife to touch the shoulder of the young athlete in the race, in order to partake of the divine spark with a view to curing her sterility. When he opens his lips again amid a hushed silence and everyone awaits the inspiring words which should fall from his august lips, what do they hear ? Simply a desire to be surrounded by men who are fat, well nourished and comfortably lodged : such do not bother their heads about politics : who read and think little, but sleep much. There is hardly a word which suggests a dazzling past career. The contrasting idealism of Brutus the thinker has been observed as an allusion to that of Essex.

In dramatizing the vast subject of imperial Rome, Shakespeare went far beyond his insular horizon. The manner in which he makes use of Plutarch is unlike his approach to and treatment of Holinshed. He relies solely on the intrinsic interest of his subject to captivate the spectator. This play is the most virile of his whole production. No need for love stories or comic interludes ; the marital affection which unites Brutus and Cato's daughter is grave and solemn ; Shakespeare no longer excuses as in *Henry V* the shortcomings of his stage. The shock of opposing interests, the clash of passions and adverse natures, suffice to depict the man essentially virtuous who kills his friend, not from hate but for the public good. Brutus' case is unique ; it differs profoundly from that of the other self-seeking conspirators. He sincerely believes that he has purified a corrupt world

by removing Caesar.   He piously signs himself with the victim's blood when
Cassius declares :

> . . . How many ages hence
> Shall this our lofty scene be acted o'er,
> In states unborn and accents yet unknown !
> . . . So oft as that shall be
> So often shall the knot of us be called
> The men that gave their country liberty.
> (*Julius Caesar*, Act III, Sc. 1)

But the revelation of the futility of his deed opens the idealist's eyes.
The other conspirators have acted from motives far less pure than his own
love of justice and liberty.   Hatred and above all envy of Caesar's power
and material possessions directed the weapons of the assassins.

When Brutus realizes their greed and corruption, he revolts against his
fellow plotters.

> . . . What ! shall one of us,
> That struck the foremost man of all this world
> But for supporting robbers, shall we now
> Contaminate our fingers with base bribes,
> And sell the mighty space of our large honours
> For so much trash as may be grasped thus ?
> I had rather be a dog and bay the moon,
> Than such a Roman.
> (*Julius Caesar*, Act IV, Sc. 3)

Then, distracted, disillusioned, defeated at Philippi, where the ghost of
his victim shows him that Caesar's death has only added to his fame, he
takes his own life by the sword, with better will than ever he had turned it
against the great Consul.

It is with this tragedy that Shakespeare reached the end of the century
whose last years were saddened for the world of letters by the tragic death
of the author of *The Faerie Queene*.

Edmund Spenser after an unlucky attempt at protestant colonization in
Ireland, had been driven out by the peasants who set fire to his house.   He
lost one of his sons in the conflagration : and came with his wife and three
remaining children, to seek refuge in London, where he died in extreme
poverty.   The Earl of Essex undertook his funeral expenses, as the Queen
preferred not to be associated with a miserable end which reflected adversely
upon her policy, for rebellion grew in Ireland from day to day.

On January 20th, 1599, the poets gathered at the modest house where
their illustrious colleague lay dead.   They carried his coffin in procession
to Westminster Abbey near at hand, and deposited it in the chapel reserved
for famous men of letters.   His tomb was placed next to that of Chaucer,[1]

---

[1] Edmund Spenser of London, nurseling of the University of Cambridge, and so much
favoured by the Muses at his birth, that he excelled all the English poets of the preceding
century, not even excepting Chaucer.   Scarcely had he found the means to retire there
into private life, than he was driven from his home and deprived of his goods by the rebels,

and each poet with head inclined dropped on it a symbolic scroll to which a quill was attached. The historian William Camden wrote an account of the funeral.

The identity of the eight poets who carried Spenser's coffin to his burial in Westminster Abbey, is revealed by the historian, who was an eye-witness of the ceremony. Camden, moreover, declares that they are the most distinguished authors of his time and those whom future Sages will be compelled to admire : " Samuel Daniel, Hugh Holland, Ben Jonson, Tho. Campion, Mich Drayton, George Chapman, John Marston and William Shakespeare."[1]

A few years later, Sir Francis Beaumont was interred beside Spenser.

At the time when Shakespeare took part in Spenser's funeral ceremony, his works already excelled Spenser's in fame. An anthology which appeared in 1600, *England's Parnassus*,[2] contains sixty-three extracts from *Venus and Adonis* and *The Rape of Lucrece*, thirteen from *Romeo and Juliet*, a dozen from *Richard II*, *Richard III* and *Love's Labour's Lost ;* another collection, *Belvedere, the Garden of the Muses*,[3] includes more passages of Shakespeare's than of any other poet. Two hundred and thirteen quotations are taken from his plays and poems and only eighty from the works of Spenser.

Thus, as the last decade of the century drew to a close, Shakespeare was recognized as England's greatest poet.

---

and obliged to return a poor man to England where he died shortly after and was buried at Westminster, beside Chaucer, at the expense of the Earl of Essex, the poets accompanying his body to the earth, and throwing verses and other mourning writings upon his tomb. (*Annales rerum Anglicarum . . . regnante Elizabetha*, autore Guil. Camdeno, Lug. Batavorum, 1625.   French translation by—Paul de Bellegent, 1627).

[1] The Bacon Society, headed by the Dean of Westminster, decided that the best way to find out whether Bacon signed Shakespeare was to dig up the corpse of Edmund Spenser, buried, it was believed, near the north wall between Chaucer and Francis Beaumont.   Work started at midnight, November 1938.   For forty hours the Dean dug under the north wall and was rewarded by the discovery of the bones of Mathew Prior.   The diggers forgot that even had they found Spenser's coffin they would have been no wiser, for according to William Camden who was present at the burial ceremonies the symbolic scrolls and pens were laid on the grave, not in it.

Report of Frederick Wellstood, official representative of the Stratford Birthplace Trust on this occasion.   (*Stratford-on-Avon Herald*, November 18th, 1938.)

[2] *England's Parnassus, or The Choicest Flowers of our Modern Poets*, edited by R. A. (1600).

[3] *Belvedere, the Garden of the Muses* (London by F. K. for Hugh Astely dwelling at St. Magnus' Corner, 1601).

CHAPTER XII

THE ESSEX CONSPIRACY

Essex is appointed to suppress the Irish rebellion—Shakespeare undertakes propaganda on his behalf—Disgrace of Essex—The Drury House conspiracy—Southampton's activities—Trial of the conspirators ; *Richard II* is cited as proof of premeditation—Repression—Shakespeare writes an elegy on the execution of two victims—" The Phoenix and the Turtle "—*Timon of Athens.*

EARLY in 1599, Essex was so popular and the disorders in Ireland so disquieting, that his appointment as leader of the expedition organized to pacify the island was unanimously approved. The hero of Cadiz, acclaimed by public opinion, was the obvious choice. Who could be found better qualified to conduct the operations against Tyrone ?

Even his faults endeared Essex to the multitude ; his ideas were in advance of the time. In an age when such conceptions were rare, he aspired to the benefits of individual liberty, and advocated wide religious tolerance. In politics he favoured alliance with France and ardently desired the union of the crowns of England and Scotland ; he wished, however, to come to terms with Ireland, and that at a moment when a gentle poet like Spenser had said that the sole manner of preserving peace in this " Commonwealth of common woe " was to exterminate the inhabitants.

A scholar and an occasional poet, Essex expressed himself in vigorous prose. His English style was pure and original, his French and Latin fluent. It was in the latter language that he maintained a correspondence with Antonio Perez, and exchanged ideas with de Thou. The learned William Camden, the Queen's historian, thus describes him :

Robert Devereux, Earl of Essex, was a personage gifted with all the virtues worthy of a noble family of ancient extraction which took its name from the town of d'Evreux in Normandy. Certainly he did not seem suited to the court for he was slow in committing crimes, easily offended and forgetting offences with difficulty, so open (as Cuff, his secretary, was accustomed to complain to me) that one could easily see in his face both love and hatred, and so frank that he could conceal nothing.[1]

In fine, he had those qualities of heart, mind and person certain to attract an enthusiastic nature like Southampton's. Another circumstance drew

---

[1] *Annales rerum Anglicarum . . . regnante Elizabetha,* autore Guil. Camdeno, Lug. Batavorum, 1625.

them together. By his marriage with Elizabeth Vernon, cousin and ward to Essex, Southampton tightened the bonds which affinity of temperament had created between them; but if this romantic marriage, counselled by Shakespeare in *A Lover's Complaint*, was welcomed among the recusants, it helped to increase government hostility toward these favourites of fortune. The Queen's displeasure at this union, for which she held Essex largely responsible, forbade them the Court and from that day the man whom she had never ceased to love became an object of fear and suspicion. The Cecils and the Raleighs—that band whom Essex himself termed the " pack " —keen on the scent played on this situation. They put no obstacle in the way of Essex' departure for Ireland. By removing this powerful rival, they hoped to be in a better position to undermine his influence and prepare his downfall.

Warned of the Council's opposition and conscious of the slanders of which he was the object, Essex wrote a very curious document, partly historical, partly political. This defence of his point of view was launched in the form of an open letter addressed to Anthony Bacon,[1] who occupied a post similar to that of a present-day under-secretary of state in the Foreign Office. The letter is headed:

An Apologie of the Earle of Essex against those wich falselie and malitiouslie taxe him to be the onely hynderer of the peace and quiett of his country.

Thanks to the devotion of friends and partisans the document was copied later in large numbers and widely distributed. It is reckoned that hundreds of copies of this tract were made. Several still exist. One bears the date 1600, and the copyist's initials: " W.S." It was discovered a hundred years ago in Shakespeare's birthplace, and sold by the last descendant of Joanne Harte, the poet's sister.[2]

But, at the beginning of March, universal interest turned towards the preparations for the expedition. London alone furnished five hundred and fifty soldiers trained at the citizens' expense. Six thousand were levied in the shires. Five hundred gentlemen volunteers, well armed and equipped, ornamented with rich laces and nodding plumes formed the bodyguard of the Earl of Essex, Lord Admiral, Commander-in-chief of the armies and governor-general of Ireland. Such was the nucleus around which the twenty thousand troops of the expeditionary force gathered. Lord Southampton, who had distinguished himself in a bold landing in the course of the operations against Spain, accompanied his cousin Essex as master of his cavalry with the title: General of the horse.

The country rejoiced. The Queen, people said, has at last freed herself

---

[1] Anthony Bacon, unlike his brother Francis, remained loyally devoted to his benefactor Essex, and died of sorrow, it is said, after the trial in which his brother pleaded for the Crown.

[2] A copy is in the possession of the author of this volume. In 1640 the *Apologie of the Earle of Essex* was printed. Only one copy of this now remains. It is preserved at the British Museum.

from corrupt counsellors. Leaders tried and proved who have shed their blood for their country at last occupy high positions ! Essex in his optimism cried : " By the Lord ! Now that I have conquered mine enemies in the council, I shall certainly beat Tyrone in the field ! "

The departure from London was impressive ; the chronicler Stowe, whose descriptions were usually sober, states that compact masses were drawn up, on both sides of the road for four miles to see the contingent march past. On the way to Chester, the crowd followed the soldiers many hours simply for the pleasure of gazing at Essex.

Those who traduced the Lord Lieutenant at court, could but resign themselves to this popularity. They knew, however, that the hero of the day would soon encounter insurmountable difficulties in the execution of his task. They certainly were ready to increase them by systematic obstruction.

Essex disembarked at Dublin on April 14th, and Southampton distinguished himself from the beginning of the campaign. In the work of pacification, the cavalry commander proved himself, according to his contemporaries, an able diplomat and a good general. He was the chief instrument in quieting the troubled region of Munster, restoring order and obedience to this rich province.

The friends of Essex who remained in England, eagerly followed Irish events, and maintained a lively interest in London. Shakespeare took this opportunity to place his talents at the service of his friends. The patriotic drama of *Henry V* is a striking example of discreet theatrical propaganda. Gerald Langbaine notes the service which Shakespeare rendered to his " patrons " when he wrote *Henry V :* [1]

This Play was writ during the time that Essex was General in Ireland, as you may see in the beginning of the first Act ; where our Poet by a pretty Turn, compliments Essex, and seems to foretell Victory to Her Majesties forces against the Rebels.

Throughout the whole play, Shakespeare's desire to interest his public in the Irish campaign is evident. For the first and last time, as playwright, he stresses his own personality and uses the pronoun : " I ". He offers himself as a guide to those who are ignorant of the facts ; to those acquainted with history he tenders apologies for the twists given chronological sequence.

> Vouchsafe to those that have not read the story,
> That I may prompt them : and of such as have,
> I humbly pray them to admit the excuse
> Of time, of numbers, and due course of things,
> Which cannot in their huge and proper life
> Be here presented.
>
> (*Henry V*, Act v, prologue)

Shakespeare well knew that speeches of patriotic fervour always please the crowd, and that the victories of Henry V might serve to glorify the

---

[1] Gerard Langbaine, *An Account of the English Dramatick Poets* (Oxford, 1691, p. 457.)

adventurous captains who had undertaken a hardly less heroic task in Ireland.
Again in the prologue to Act V he predicts his friends' triumphant return :

> . . . But now behold,
> In the quick forge and working-house of thought,
> How London doth pour out her citizens.
> The mayor and all his brethren in best sort,
> Like to the senators of the antique Rome,
> With the plebians swarming at their heels,
> Go forth and fetch their conquering Caesar in :
> As, by a lower but loving likelihood,
> Were now the general of our gracious empress—,
> As in good time he may—from Ireland coming,
> Bringing rebellion broached on his sword,
> How many would the peaceful city quit
> To welcome him ! . . .

This return was not what the poet foresaw : Essex did not " bring
rebellion broached on his sword ". Making use of the extensive powers
conferred on him by his commission, he decided after the conquest of
Munster, to negotiate rather than fight with the Earl of Tyrone, head of the
insurrection in Ulster. Although he succeeded in imposing conditions
which were on the whole advantageous to the Crown—later, the same
conditions were accepted by Elizabeth after years of costly war—he was
accused of having intelligence with the enemy.

However, long before his policy in Ireland had had time to bear fruit,
he became the victim of the chicanery and ill-will of the government in
London. They even contested his right to nominate the officers serving
under his command. Southampton's success as general of the horse caused
a bitter dispute to which the commander's despatches bear witness.

Was it treason in my Lord of Southampton to marry my poor kinswoman,
that neither long imprisonment nor no punishment beside that have been usual
in like cases, can satisfy or appease ? Or will no kind of punishment be fit for
him, but that which punisheth not him, but me, this Army and poor country of
Ireland ? Shall I keep this country when the army breaks, or shall the army
stand when all our voluntaries leave it ? . . . I dare not, whilst I am her Majesty's
minister in this great action, do that which will overthrow me and it.[1]

To these arguments the Queen drily replied that she could with difficulty
believe that the army attached so much importance to serving this or that
officer when it was, after all, only a matter of serving her person.[2]

Deprived of his command, Southampton remained with Essex as an

---

[1] *Calendar of the Carew MSS.*, vol. 621, p. 141.

[2] " For the matter of Southampton, it is strange to us that his continuance or displacing
should work so great an alteration either in yourself—valuing our commands as you ought
—or in the disposition of the army. . . .

" We cannot as yet be persuaded that the love of our service and the duty which they
owe us, have not been as strong motives to these their travials as any affection to the Earl
of Southampton or any other which we will not so much wrong ourselves as to suspect. . . ."
(*State Papers, Ireland*, vol. 205, no. 113.)

ordinary captain, and the former's secretary, Sir Gelly Merrick, wrote in August 1599 :

The vexations which have reached us from England this year have caused to Her Majesty's services here injuries which no money could ever repair.[1]

The Governor-General, as much in order to reply to his accusers as to obtain confirmation for his appointments, hastened to London on September 24th with a handful of friends, resolved to lay before the Queen a situation which he knew had been presented to her by ministers bent on frustrating his plan of campaign.

Still confident in the ascendancy he had possessed over Elizabeth's heart, he was convinced that he would gain his cause if he managed to speak to her alone.

On the way, Essex and his little band caught up with a deserter from the expeditionary force, Lord Gray, also hurrying Londonwards, but for quite a different motive. This officer, who had been reprimanded by Southampton for a flagrant breach of discipline, had sworn to be revenged and was carrying a report incriminating his superior officers, certain that such action would not displease Cecil and the other ministers.

Sir Christopher St. Laurence, always a believer in violent methods, offered to stab the informer ; but Essex contented himself with a courteous request to let him pass. Gray's answer was to spur his horse forward, and a race began with the royal residence as goal. The two parties arrived at Nonesuch simultaneously. Lord Gray rushed to see Robert Cecil, Essex went straight up to the Queen's apartments, where he found Elizabeth at her toilet with her sparse hair about her shoulders.

As she advanced in age, the Queen became fearful and suspicious. She saw around her plots and machinations, and considered it a crime even to discuss the succession. She had recently read a panegyric of Essex where it was suggested that his royal blood placed him near the throne ; accordingly, when the Viceroy of Ireland presented himself, he was ill received, although less violently than at the time of Southampton's marriage (she had slapped her former favourite and told him : " Go and be hanged ! "). Her anger now, though better controlled, was the more dangerous. Essex left the royal mansion under arrest.

Egerton the chancellor, who was sincerely attached to him, wrote beseeching him to ask his offended sovereign's pardon. Essex' reply is characteristic of his indomitable pride :

When the vilest of all indignities are done unto me, doth religion enforce me to sue ? Cannot princes err ? Cannot subjects receive wrong ? Is an earthly power infinite ? Pardon me, pardon me, my Lord ! I can never subscribe to these principles. Let Solomon's fool laugh when he is struck. Let those that mean to make their profit of Princes, show no sense of Princes' injuries.

As for me I ' have received wrong. My cause is good and whatever comes

---

[1] *Hist. MSS. Com. Salisbury Papers*, IX, 343.

all the powers on earth can never show more constancy in oppressing than I can show in suffering whatsoever can or shall be put upon me.[1]

Essex was arraigned before the Star Chamber, which refused to maintain the accusation of lèse-majesté, but declared him guilty of " error of judgment and of lack of respect towards the royal authority ".   This new offence was called " contempt ".

Placed in the custody of Lord Chancellor Egerton, he was continually attacked by his enemies.   Sir Walter Raleigh wrote to Cecil who did not require to be encouraged in arousing Elizabeth to rigorous action :

. . . if you take it for a good counsel to relent towards this tyrant you will repent it when it shall be too late.   His malice is fixed, and will not evaporate by any your mild courses, for he will ascribe the alteration to her Majesty's pusillanimity and not to your good nature, knowing that you work but upon her humour.   For after revenges, fear them not ; for your own father that was esteemed to be the contriver of Norfolk's ruin, yet his son followeth your father's son. . . . Look to the present and you do wisely.   His son shall be the youngest Earl of England but one, and if his father be now kept down, Will Cecil shall be able to keep as many men at his heels as he, and more too.   He may also match in a better house than his, and so that fear is not worth fearing.   But if the father continue, he will be able to break the brances and pull up the tree ; root and all.   Lose not your advantage.   If you do, I read your destiny.   Yours to the end W. R.

[*P.S.*]—Let the Queen hold Bothwell while she hath him.   He Will ever be the canker of her estate and safety.   Princes are lost by security and preserved by prevention.   I have seen the last of her good days and all ours after his liberty.[2]

Eight months elapsed during which Essex, under close surveillance was shorn of his possessions and privileges.   The zealous correspondent of the Sidney family noted in his news letter that it was a lamentable and pitiful spectacle to see him " that was mignon of fortune reduced to such misery " as though unworthy of the least honour.

Events moved rapidly.   On January 9th, 1600, Lord Gray, accompanied by partisans attacked Southampton in the street.   The latter defended himself with the skill of a d'Artagnan and succeeded in fighting his way out. Essex, on his side, had been the object of a double attempt at assassination. Henceforward, all those who had espoused their cause believed it would be lost if they did not free the Queen from the influence of " the caterpillars of the commonwealth ".   The ministers especially aimed at were Gray, Raleigh and Robert Cecil, who, when his father Lord Burleigh died, hoped to succeed him, but who, merely with the rank of secretary to the Queen and Council, finished by ruling the country at his will.

Christopher Blount, Essex' stepfather—he had lately married Leicester's widow—thought, like Southampton, that it was high time to force the Queen to hear reason, and name her heir, instead of continuing to repeat that " raising the question of the royal succession was an act of high treason ".

---

[1] To this argument, Bacon replied : " Far be it from me to attribute divine qualities to mortal princes ; yet this truly may I say, that by the common law of England, a Prince can do no wrong."   [2] *Salisbyur MSS.*, vol. X, p. 439.

The malcontents—this was the term given to the ministers' opponents —met at Drury House, home of the Danvers, where the plot against established authority was fomented, Essex being the leading spirit, and Southampton the right arm.   All were certain that Robert Cecil was corresponding with King Philip and was in his pay ; they were anxious to deliver the country from the fear of a Spanish succession by proclaiming James of Scotland the rightful heir to the throne.

The Venetian ambassador in London, an apparently disinterested witness, reported that, " following an agreement signed by the six principal conspirators, none but secretary Cecil and councillor Raleigh were to be removed as responsible for the Earl's disgrace ; then all were to cry ' Long live the Queen and after her, long live King James of Scotland, only legitimate heir to the English throne ' a declaration which the Queen had hitherto refused to make ".[1]

The partisans believed they might count upon the sympathy of the London crowd, whose idol Essex had often been ; and the better to prepare public opinion they turned once again to a theatrical appeal.   Sir Gelly Merrick and Richard Cuffe, Essex' secretaries, acted as intermediaries, and invited Shakespeare's company to revive *Richard II*, a play much appreciated by their master.   This tragic story of a sovereign in the clutches of evil counsellors was undoubtedly of topical interest.   Each actor's pay was doubled for that special performance ; the manager received forty shillings in gold ; a fact which is important, as these gratuities were brought up at the trial of Essex' partisans as proof of premeditation.

Richard II even more than *Henry V* was likely to arouse the spectators' enthusiasm.   Bolingbroke's eloquent tirades created indignation against the unworthy ministers of the weak Richard.

> The caterpillars of the commonwealth
> Which I have sworn to weed and pluck away
> (*Richard II*, Act II, Sc. 3)

were personified in the counsellors of Elizabeth.

The scene where the gardener laments the fate of the country which, left to the sovereign's care, had become neglected and unpruned was such an evident allusion to the conditions of Elizabethan England, that the wonder is how the censor ever permitted its presentation.

> Why should we in the compass of a pale
> Keep law and form and due proportion,
> Showing, as in a model, our firm estate,
> When our sea-walled garden, the whole land,
> Is full of weeds, her fairest flowers chok'd up,
> Her fruit-trees all unprun'd, her hedges ruined,
> Her knots disorder'd, and her wholesome herbs
> Swarming with caterpillars ?
> (*Richard II*, Act III, Sc. 4.)

[1] *Calendar S.P. Venice*, 1603-1607, p. 25.   Ambassador's letter (May 15th, 1603).

Another striking example of how skilful propaganda can open the eyes of simple citizens to the abuses which they daily see around them is provided by John of Gaunt's magnificent patriotic speech, where England's interior hurts are exposed with a force which matches its poetry.

> This royal throne of Kings, this scepter'd isle . . .
> Is now leas'd out,—I die pronouncing it,—
> Like to a tenement, or pelting farm :
> England, bound in with the triumphant sea,
> Whose rocky shore beats back the envious siege
> Of watery Neptune, is now bound in with shame,
> With inky blots, and rotten parchment bonds :
> That England, that was wont to conquer others,
> Hath made a shameful conquest of itself.
> Ah ! would the scandal vanish with my life,
> How happy then were my ensuing death.
> (*Richard II*, Act II, Sc. 1)

Or this eloquent charge against an unworthy sovereign :

> Landlord of England art thou now, not King :
> Thy state of law is bond-slave to the law.
> (*Richard II*, Act II, Sc. 1)

These lines spoken by John of Gaunt are often quoted as if they were the hymn of praise of a man actuated only by patriotic fervour ; but this estimate leaves out of account that their whole object is to lament the sorry state into which the country had fallen. It is easy to imagine the reaction of an audience listening to Burbage in the part of Henry Bolingbroke, the welcome liberator, and to Shakespeare himself perhaps in that of John of Gaunt.

In fact, the 7th of February, at three o'clock in the afternoon, the " Globe Theatre ", capable of accommodating three thousand spectators, was crowded to overflowing and the atmosphere was such that the heads of the conspiracy—with the exception of Essex all present at the performance—carried away with enthusiasm arranged their revolt for the following day.

Next morning London awoke to an atmosphere of rebellion. At dawn, Southampton at the head of his supporters, made his way to Essex House, freed the Earl and left in his place as hostages Lord Chief Justice Popham, Keeper of the Seals, the Earl of Worcester and Sir William Knollys, under the guard of Captain Owen Salisbury and Sir John Davies. The conspirators, whose numbers continually grew, marched with Essex and Southampton at their head through the armourers' quarter requisitioning guns and lances as they went, and proceeded towards Westminster.

But instead of finding the entries to the palace in friendly hands, Essex and his partisans ran into a defence prepared the day before, and reinforced by cannon. Blount and the Danvers, who were to open the gates, had been arrested. Ferdinand Gorges, one of the chief instigators of the revolt, had the day before gone over to the enemy and revealed their plan to Sir Walter Raleigh, captain of the royal guard.

The conspirators, seeing how their plot had miscarried, were forced to retreat and barricade themselves in Essex House. There a defence was hastily organized. While Essex' wife, daughter of old Walsingham and widow of Sir Philip Sidney, wept with her mother-in-law Lady Blount, Essex' sister, the romantic Penelope Rich, of a different temper, encouraged the defenders weapons in hand. Young Lady Southampton, an expectant mother, had been sent to the country. The siege lasted a whole day ; the conspirators, in this improvised fortress, suffered grave casualties. Regular forces had succeeded in establishing their marksmen on the neighbouring belfry of St. Clement Danes, and musket fire directed from this dominating position raked the rebels ensconced behind a bulwark of books in guise of sandbags. Captain Owen Salisbury was the first to fall, then came the turn of Lord Southampton's young page ; finally, Sir Christopher Blount was wounded. At nightfall cannon from the Tower were drawn up, and powerful charges of powder laid at the foot of the walls. It was high time for a parley. Southampton, torch in hand, appeared on the leads to discuss terms of capitulation. He recognized below the features of his own cousin, Sir Robert Sidney, with whom it was agreed that the women should be allowed to depart in safety and that the conspirators should be judged by an impartial court. The claims of the two earls would be dispassionately examined. A storm was raging. High tide rendered it impossible to reach the Tower by way of the Thames, accordingly the idea of taking Essex and Southampton through the traitors' gate was abandoned ; they were incarcerated instead in Lambeth Palace. The Queen, who had sworn not to sleep until her enemies were under lock and key, was able to rest quietly that night.

From his temporary prison Southampton wrote a letter to his wife which, because of its seizure, is today among the Cecil papers :

To my Bess ;
Sweet heart, I doubt not but you shall hear ere this my letter come to you of the misfortunes of your friends. Be not too apprehensive of it, God's will must be done and what is allotted by destiny cannot be avoided. Believe that . . . there is nothing can so much comfort me as to think you are well and take patiently what has happened. . . . Doubt not but that I shall do well, and . . . remain ever your affectionate husband.[1]

London was seething and these internal dissensions soon echoed beyond the frontiers of England. Essex had supporters on the continent and even in Morocco. Sir Henry Neville at the Louvre, Sir Henry Wotton in Venice and Sir Anthony Shirley at Marrakesh acted as his ambassadors. Inversely, the French plenipotentiaries at the Court in Greenwich found themselves doubled by an official representative accredited to the man who looked forward to becoming regent, if not successor to the Queen. Thus Hercule de Rohan close to Southampton, represented Henry IV at Essex' unofficial Foreign Office.

Knowing that serious events were about to take place, many foreign

---

[1] *Hist. Mss. Com.* Salisbury, MSS. xi, p. 35.

delegates were naturally assembled in London at the beginning of the year 1601. They had even been present at the performance of *Twelfth Night*, Shakespeare's gay and charming comedy in which a leading rôle is given to Duke Orsino of Illyria, an undisguised compliment to Don Virginio Oesino, Duke of Bracciano.

But the spectators' thoughts were elsewhere ; the noble visitors were preoccupied as to the outcome of the political situation which confronted them. In France especially, private correspondence and newsletters disseminated by the merchants were avidly read. Sir Ralph Winwood, chargé d'affaires, learned of the disturbances from Henry IV himself. He thus reported his interview with the king, to his ambassador on leave in London.

Upon Sunday being at the Louvre, the King tooke me asyde, and asked me what newes I hard of England. I answered I had not lately receaved any. He then tolde me, of a strange commotion which lately should be in London, which he compared to the Barricades at Paris, intended as he sayd, by thearles of Essex, and Southampton, followed with divers knightes, and men of other qualletie, to the nomber of tow thousand. I asked him, yf he had receeved these advertise-mentes from his Ambassador. He sayd noe, but by Monsieur de Rohan, who freshly came out of England, and arryved that morning in post.[1]

This letter naturally failed to reach its destination. Sir Henry Neville had been arrested with the ringleaders. However, Winwood received a few terse lines from the hand of Sir Robert Cecil himself, informing him that " unforeseen events had compromised the fortune of ambassador Neville ".

On February 19th, the House of Lords assembled with great pomp in the sinister hall of Westminster to try the conspirators. Lord Buckhurst, Burleigh's successor as lord treasurer, seated on a canopied throne, presided over the High Court between the lawyers and clerks on one side, and the peers on the other. The solicitor-general, Sir Edward Coke, spoke for the Crown ; assisting him was Francis Bacon, who had formerly been an adherent and supporter of Essex and had received many favours from him. Robert Cecil, the moving spirit of the trial, alone appeared to be absent. In reality, he had stationed himself behind a tapestry and could not help peeping from his hiding place to reply each time that the Earl's defence placed him in a bad light. When Essex saw Lord Gray among the jurors, he invoked the right of every English citizen to protest against the presence in the jury of a personal enemy.

By a curious coincidence, this trial brought together four persons to whom certain commentators attribute, according to individual taste, the works of Shakespeare : the future chancellor Bacon, William Stanley, Earl of Derby, Edward Vere, Earl of Oxford, and Roger Manners, Earl of Rutland. The first sought and obtained Lord Southampton's head, and the next two by their votes accorded it. How then can *Richard II* be logically attributed

---

[1] S.P. France, vol. 45 f. 19ª.

to any one of them ?—Shakespeare's play had been presented to influence the conspirators and encourage their revolt ! As for the Earl of Rutland whose sympathies lay with the accused and with Shakespeare's friends, he shared the bench of those on trial. Though he might have been glad to have written such a fine tragedy, the court considered him " too young, flighty and talkative to have been admitted to the counsels of Drury House ".

In the accusation which he printed to crush his victims still further, Bacon insisted that the performance of *Richard II* established premeditation of murder.

The afternoone before the Rebellion, Merricke, with a great company of others, that afterwards were all in the Action, had procured to bee played before them, the Play of deposing King Richard the second.

Neither was it casuall, but a play bespoken by Merrick.

And not so onely, but when it was told him by one of the Players, that the Play was olde, and they should have losse in playing it, because fewe would come to it : there was fourty shillings extraordinarie given to play it, and so thereupon playd it was.

So earnest hee was to satisfie his eyes with the sight of that Tragedie, which hee thought soone after his Lord should bring from the Stage to the State, but that God turned it upon their owne heads.[1]

One of the principal accusations brought against the conspirators there-fore was to have commanded a performance of Shakespeare's *Richard II*, so as to arouse the public against the Queen's ministers ; and when South-ampton, after Essex, came to defend himself this special performance [2] was again cited. In firm deliberate tones, the young Earl declared that he had neither drawn his sword during the riot, nor armed his servants.

That was a ruse (replied Bacon). A ruse fit for traitors ! Like the duc de Guise in Paris, you placed your faith in the citizens, so that they might arm you and your men.

Southampton gave his oath that the life of the Queen was never in question; his prosecutor again retorted :

It was the custom of traitors to strike at their princes indirectly through their ministers. Besides, had he not caused to be acted at the theatre with malice aforethought, the tragedy of *Richard II* ?

Turning towards the solicitor-general, Southampton asked calmly if anyone could really believe that he had meditated using violence towards Her Majesty. Lord Coke replied :

Upon my soul and conscience, I believe the Queen would not have lived long

[1] Francis Bacon's *Declaration of the Practises and Treasons attempted and committed by Robert late Earle of Essex and his complices*. At London, Robert Baker, 1601, p. K 2v.

Camden, a more objective witness, affirms that the presentation at the " Globe " of *Richard II* was the sole proof of premeditation possessed by the prosecuting party. " Quod ab eo factum interpretati sunt juris consulti quasi illud pridie in scena agi spectarent quod postridie in Elizabetha abdicanda agendum " (*Camden's Annals*, 1625, p. 810).

[2] The Earl of Essex himself was often present when this tragedy was played and showed his approval by loud applause. (*An Abstract of Essex his Treasons*. S.P. Dom. Eliz., vol. 275, no. 33.)

if she had fallen into your power. Think of historical examples. How long did Richard II survive when he was surprised in the same way ? Then the same excuses were made, that certain councillors were to be removed, but soon he himself was also deprived of life.

These debates are reported in detail by the historian Camden [1] who was present.

A more colourful and lively account has come down to us through another spectator, M. Boissize de Thumery. Writing to the duc de Rohan, the French Ambassador to Elizabeth's court gives free rein to sarcasm in this letter :

London March 4th 1601

Monsieur,

I am convinced that the evil which overtook the Earl of Essex when you were in England enabled you to foresee the issue of a tragedy which from the beginning was accompanied with much misfortune and disgrace. The end followed naturally by what was feared : cruelty and despair, to wit : a sentence of death against the Earl of Essex and the Earl of Southampton. I being present through a desire to witness such strange things and also to observe what countenance their enemies who had little by little driven them to this pass, would put upon it. I considered it my duty to write to you privately all that took place at this judgment.

On February 17th, the Earl of Essex having surrendered to the Admiral at about eleven o'clock at night with promises that all would be treated with infinite courtesy, was taken next day to the Tower ; and soon afterwards the Earls of Southampton and of Rutland, the Knight Christopher Blount, step father of the said Earl, Ferdinand Gorges, Charles Danvers and some other gentlemen, who were imprisoned elsewhere. The Queen commanded those of her Council to examine the Earl of Essex and the Earl of Southampton and judge them without delay. These, not wishing such an examination, asked to be judged by their peers. This was accordingly done rather to give weight to the proceedings and make the people believe that the accused were traitors than to comply with the prisoners' wish. They were conducted to the great hall of Westminster the first day of March to answer the accusation.

Their judges were nine earls and sixteen barons. The Chief Justice was the Lord Treasurer (very unsuitable for this office) ; there were also eight councillors of the parliament, who were seated a little lower than the peers.

These were : the Earl of Oxford (near relative of the secretary) the Earl of Shrewsbury (notoriously enemy to the Earl of Essex), the Earl of Derby, the Earl of Sussex, the Earl of Hereford, the Earl of Nottingham (who is High Admiral), the Earl of Cumberland and the Earl of Lincoln.

The accusers were ; a sergeant-at-law and an advocate of the Queen whom they call Mr. Attorney Bacon.

Essex, before replying to the accusations prayed his judges to permit him one thing never refused to the lowest persons, which was not to be judged by his personal enemies and to be allowed to challenge those whom he saw fit. He was

[1] " I have faithfully and shortly reported these events at which I myself was present, and have not voluntarily omitted any worthy of remembrance." *Annales rerum Anglicarum . . . regnante Elizabetha*, autore Guil. Camdeno, Lug. Batavorum, 1625.

answered maliciously that it was not possible that his enemies, men of quality when they had sworn an oath " on my honor " as they say, that they should break an oath which would be a hundred times more dear to them than life.

This request having been iniquitously denied, he replied to everything by word with such assurance and bearing that he astonished his enemies who were reduced to silence or spoke shamefacedly with stammering accents indicating their fear and hatred. He declared that he came with no hope of saving his life but merely to defend his honour too long tarnished since his enemies desire to see him there so that with their chicanery and tortuous inventions they might obtain his head.

Then appeared the man most involved in the tragedy Secretary Cecil. He had not that day forgotten to bring his little hump [1] which never showed so handsome and, having for more than two years carefully rehearsed what he would say, he thundered a torrent of harsh words against the Earl of Essex.

When the Secretary had finished his insults the lawyers concluded their indictment and their Lordships attacked their beer and preserves ; for, while the debates still continued, these worthies fed as though they had not seen food for a fortnight, puffing tobacco the while ; then they retired to another room where well soused and drunk on tobacco fumes they gave their votes condemning the two Earls to the same punishment as Captain Lee [2] calling them rebels and traitors.

The Earl of Essex hearing his sentence looked as calm and contented as though invited to dance with the Queen. The trial lasted from eight in the morning until seven at night ; many gentlemen and ladies were there ; the latter having given vent to their tears wept and lamented so that if the judges had not possessed tigers' hearts which only seek blood, they would, without doubt, have revoked their sentence.

This is all I have been able to witness or find out concerning this misfortune which involving as it does the Englishman endowed with so many virtues and who above all others cherished France, cannot fail to cause immense regret to all especially to you who being extremely virtuous yourself and knowing the merits of these gallant gentlemen must realise better than an other this inestimable loss. I will there bring this sad story to an end, contenting myself with the honour if you will allow it to remain your humble and very obedient servant : [3]

de Thumeri.

When Essex heard that his body was to be quartered and displayed like that of a traitor, he exclaimed : " This poor body was capable of rendering a better service than that to her Majesty ! " And when he saw the head of the fatal axe turned towards Southampton, he made an eloquent appeal to Robert Cecil, in which he repeated that he alone was responsible for this revolt, besought the peers to reconsider their verdict and spare his young friend who, if allowed to live, was capable of honourably serving his country. When the court rose, Raleigh had the satisfaction of escorting the condemned

---

[1] Allusion to the deformity of Robert Cecil, who was a hunchback.

[2] Captain Lee was executed a few days before the trial of the two earls. He had tried to penetrate to the Queen to plead for his beloved chief, Essex. Thumeri says : " His body was opened, the heart and the entrails torn out, and when they were consumed by the fire, several quarters of his body were made which they put on parade. (They are accustomed to punish thus those whom they call traitors.)"

[3] Foundation Godefroy (Library of The Institut), Paris.

to the Tower. The only concession shown by the Queen towards her one-time favourite was that the sentence of hanging and quartering should be changed to decapitation, and that his body, instead of being exposed at the four corners of London, should be buried in the Tower chapel.

Essex expressed gratitude for this small favour. Perhaps he still hoped to obtain the pardon which the Queen had promised. On the appointed day, he mounted the scaffold clothed in a long robe of embossed velvet, over a suit of black satin with a small white collar, and a black felt hat. He was accompanied by the Earls of Cumberland and Hereford, and by Sir John Payton, lieutenant of the Tower. The chaplain exhorted the Earl in moving terms to repent if he had ever favoured popery in the realm, an accusation made because of his friendship with Blount, Catesby, Danvers and Southampton. Essex calmly replied that he was neither atheist nor papist, unless to hope for salvation through the mercy of Our Saviour Jesus Christ were to be either. He had already declared in the course of his interrogation that no free citizen should suffer because of faith or conscience. When asked to pray for the Queen, he simply said : " May God give her an understanding heart " and then repeated the fourth psalm. Then, kneeling, he placed his head on the block. The executioner was clumsy and struck aslant ; terrified, he redoubled his blows turning away his face. . . . At the time of his death, Essex was no more than thirty-three years of age.

He had written Southampton a farewell letter full of solicitude and affection for one from whom " no cause on earth was capable of separating him ". He wished to hope for the Queen's clemency and continued : " It would be an unspeakable comfort to me to think that by sparing your life the country and your friends will find their happiness."

A few days later, Sir Christopher Blount, Sir Charles Danvers, and Essex' secretaries Sir Gelly Merrick and Richard Cuffe, the latter one of the most learned Hellenists of the day, were similarly executed ; and, to show the people that the Papists were not strangers to the conspiracy, several previously condemned Catholics were also brought to the scaffold.

The newsletters of the continent commented unfavourably upon these blood-thirsty reprisals. Essex' execution almost cost the headsman his life. Raleigh and Bacon found it prudent to go into hiding for fear of being roughly handled by the crowd which paraded the streets affirming the innocence of the victims. Danvers, before he was beheaded, swore that the Queen's person had never been threatened. According to him, the conspirators had only followed Southampton to whom they were all bound through gratitude. For his part, he was happy to die in such a cause. This declaration daily gained credence, and Elizabeth finally agreed with the citizens of London that too much blood had been shed. But the treasury, always short of money, intervened and turned the situation to its own profit. The list of fines imposed upon those imprudent enough to have taken part in the insurrection shows that none of them were spared. Even Lord Rutland, considered by the judges as too irresponsible to pay for his fault with his life, found that his delinquency was estimated at thirty thousand pounds ; the Earl of Bedford was fined twenty thousand pounds ; Baron Sandys six, Baron Cromwell five and Lord Monteagle eight. Sir Jocelyn and Sir Charles Percy were each forced to pay five thousand pounds. Sir Henry Carey, Sir Robert Vernon, Sir William Constable, Sir Robert Catesby, Francis Tresham, Francis Manners, Sir George Manners, Sir Thomas West, Sir Edward Middleton, Thomas Crofton, Walter Walsh and Grey Bridges [1] were sentenced to fines ranging between four hundred pounds and one thousand marks. The same document recalls that " the persons condemned but still in captivity, are the Earl of Southampton, Sir John Davies, Sir Edward Bainham and John Littleton ".[2] The latter died in prison ; Southampton almost did the same ; for two years he endured such rigorous incarceration that the lieutenant of the Tower, still Sir John Payton, refused to be responsible for the consequences if " more air, more exercise and spiritual comfort " were not granted him.[3]

A tragic event which took place three days after the execution of Robert Devereux, Earl of Essex, left a singular trace on the literature of those times. Later in 1601 there appeared an Octavo volume entitled *Love's Martyr*, more generally spoken of as the Phoenix and the Turtle, of which one sole copy now exists in private hands.[4] Though a second edition was launched in 1611, there is again but one copy surviving, in the British Museum.

In 1878, Alexander B. Grosart was moved to make the original text accessible to subscribers of the New Shakespeare Society. The volume is an exact reprint of what was denounced as " seditious ". Never inscribed on the Stationer's Register, it was clandestinely printed, sold and distributed.

The first hundred and sixty pages are far from suggesting any aggressive intent on the part of author or printer against the safety of the State.

LOVE'S MARTYR
OR,
ROSALIN'S COMPLAINT.
ALLEGORICALLY SHADOWING THE TRUTH OF LOVE,
IN THE CONSTANT FATE OF THE PHOENIX
AND TURTLE

A Poeme enterlaced with much varietie and raritie

Now first translated out of the venerable Italian Torquato Caeliano, by Robert Chester.

With the true legend of famous King Arthur, the past of the nine worthies being the first essay of a new British poet collected out of Diverse Authenticall Records

---

[1] This brave partisan of Essex', raised to the peerage with the title of Lord Chandos, was, with Sir Charles Percy, one of the large landed proprietors of the Stratford neighbourhood. He was the owner of Sudeley Castle, kept a large number of servants and a famous pack of hounds. He seems to have served as Shakespeare's model in many hunting scenes such as that in *The Taming of the Shrew* (see Chap. I).

Bridges' son was killed under his father's eyes at the time of the Essex revolt. See E. Barnard, *New Links with Shakespeare* (Cambridge Univ. Press, 1930, p. 67).

[2] *S.P. Dom. Eliz.*, vol. 291, 67. [3] C. C. Stopes, *The Life of Southampton*, p. 224.

[4] Christie Miller's Library at Britwell.

To these are added some new compositions, of severall moderne
writers whose names are subscribed to their several workes
upon the first subject : viz. The Phoenix and Turtle
Mar : Mutare dominum non potest liber motus

London
Imprinted for E.B.
1611

On opening the volume the reader enters into a maze of mystification.
The alleged author, Robert Chester, is totally unknown to the world of
English letters. As to the venerable Torquato Caeliano, from whom the
translation claims to be made, he is equally apocryphal : the name never
existed in Italy ; the text is utter nonsense, the versification beneath contempt.   Here is a sample :

> Where two hearts are united all in one,
> Love like a King, a Lord, a Souveraigne,
> Enjoyes the throne of blisse to sit upon,
> Each sad heart craving aid, by Cupid slaine :
> Lovers be merrie, Love being dignified,
> Wish what you will, it shall not be denied.
> Finis quoth R. Chester.

Alexander Grosart managed to wade through this labyrinth of ineptitude,
studying, comparing and annotating, in order to arrive, with Sir Israel
Gollancz, at a nebulous conclusion that Elizabeth, though still alive, could
be identified with the dead Phoenix and that the turtle dove typifies " the
brilliant but impetuous, greatly dowered but rash, illustrious but unhappy
Essex ".   Sir Sydney Lee is relieved by the thought that Shakespeare wrote
nothing else of this kind.   However, any reader who finds courage to go so
far as Robert Chester's finis is rewarded by a strange surprise : a new
title-page.

HEREAFTER
FOLLOW DIVERSE

Poeticall Essaies on the former Subject ;
viz : the Turtle and Phoenix

Done by the best and chiefest of our
modern writers, with their names subscribed
to their particular workes ;
never before extant

And (now first) consecrated by them all
generally
to the love and merite of the true-noble Knight,
Sir John Salisburie

Dignum laude virum Musa vetat mori

And here, as though to underline the fact that from this moment we are
confronted with a most important document from Shakespeare's pen, we

see the printer's device of Richard Field : an Anchor surrounded by laurels and accompanied by the ancient motto ANCHORA SPEI which had become the trade mark of the Stratford Tanner's son, who first made the world acquainted with his school fellow's poems by printing *Venus and Adonis* (1593) and following it up by *The Rape of Lucrece* (1594).

Immediately after an anonymous invocation, we reach the poem signed William Shakespeare which precedes the inferior elucubrations announced as by our best and chiefest hands, to wit : George Chapman, John Marston and Ben Jonson.

This poem of Shakespeare's consists of thirteen four line stanzas with the rhymes disposed in a manner followed by Tennyson in his famous *In Memoriam.* The ode or self-styled " requiem " is concluded by a threnos composed of five three line rhyming stanzas which might be designated as terza rima of which no contemporary parallel exists. The whole is so rich linguistically, so pure, intense and profound in sentiment, so passionately eloquent, that modern readers who fail to grasp the inner meaning or historical allusions, are carried away by the verbal harmony and complete sincerity of the writer. They cannot avoid being emotionally moved.

Though the poet's meaning may at first appear obscure to the uninitiated, to those who are ignorant of the source from which his inspiration was drawn, such was not the case with his contemporaries who, necessarily conversant with the drama depicted, eagerly bought up the two editions, both of which were sold out in the author's life time. The " tragic scene " to which he acted as " Chorus " was a striking historical event and its " Dramatis Personae ", treated allegorically, were real persons who lived, moved and finally died in the poet's familiar world.

Ralph Waldo Emerson, one of America's most subtle and sensitive critics, an extravagant admirer of Shakespeare's *Phoenix and Turtle*, wrote :

I would like to have an academy of letters propose a prize for an essay on Shakespeare's poem : " Let the bird of loudest lay . . . and the threnos with which it closes : the aim being to explain by historical research the frame and allusions of the poem.

When forty years ago, I printed my first study of the great dramatist's lyric work *New Light and Old Evidence on Shakespeare's Sonnets*, I came across an item in John Stowe's *Day-by-Day Chronicle of Notable Happenings in England*, I was struck by a notice of the simultaneous hanging at Tyburn of two priests, T. Silcox and Mark Bosworth, a woman, Mistress Anne Line, Sir Gelly Merrick and Richard Cuffe, distinguished scholars and secretaries in the Earl of Essex' household, also a gentleman from Norfolk who took part in the rioting. I felt convinced then that the key to the mystery of Shakespeare's poem might be found in this event, but it required years of plodding along ways untrodden by any biographer of Shakespeare before I reached a conclusion which now seems to me incontrovertible.

The field of historical research was limited. Though fully informed on the conspirators in the Earl's household, I had no data whatever on the two missionary priests nor the woman for whom the poet asks those present at their death and burial to "sigh a prayer". However, there could be no doubt as to the identity of the female victim for there was but one woman hanged at this time and she was clearly defined in the chronicle as "a gentlewoman, a widow, Mistress Anne Line".

Through Father Thurston, S.J., with whom I had studied the spiritual testament of John Shakespeare, I obtained an introduction to Father Newdigate, historian of the Elizabethan martyrs, and learned at once that the Church of Rome had beatified Anne Line with her fellow martyrs. Such honours are not conferred without thorough investigation into evidence drawn from contemporary sources, and thus I was soon able to learn all that it was necessary to know about Shakespeare's Phoenix.

Anne Line's parents, William Higham of Dunmow in Essex and Anne Allen his wife, having profited by the spoils of a convent, naturally brought up their children as strict Protestants. Their daughter, Anne, was highly educated and lived in London with a lady attached to the Court: her brother, William, was well versed in Latin and played the harp admirably. Both, when their parents learned that they had embraced Catholicism, were turned out of doors. Anne married a Catholic, Roger Line, but immediately after having left the altar where Mass had been said, her husband and brother were arrested. William Higham was consigned to Bridewell treadmill where he toiled under the lash. Roger Line remained long at Newgate refusing the fine estate of Ringwood offered him on condition of his recantation. Remaining obstinate, he was deported and died in Flanders. His widow, left destitute, consecrated her life to the oppressed clergy and was denounced as being present at Masses in the Earl of Worcester's house. Her services were engaged by Father John Gerard as hostess in the London house he kept as a clandestine refuge for priests. He says of her:

When I decided to establish the house mentioned above I could think of no better person to put in charge of it. She was able to manage the finances, do all the house-keeping, look after the guests and deal with inquiries of strangers. She was full of kindness, very discreet and possessed her soul in great peace. She was however a chronic invalid—always suffering from one ailment or another. Often she would say to me: "I naturally want more than anything to die for Christ. But it is too much to hope that it will be by the executioner's hand. Possibly Our Lord will let me be taken one day with a priest and be put in some cold filthy dungeon where I won't be able to live very long in this wretched life." So she said and indeed her delight was in the Lord and the Lord granted the petitions of her heart.[1]

Bishop Challoner further says:

On Candlemas day the pursuivants having some intelligence or suspecting that Mrs. Line entertained a priest, beset her house at the very moment Mass

---

[1] *John Gerard, Autobiography of an Elizabethan*, translated from the latin (Longman's Green and Co., London). By special permission of editor and translator.

was actually beginning. However, as the door was strongly barred and fastened, they were forced to wait some time before they could come in ; and in the meantime the priest Mr. Page had leisure to unvest himself and make his escape. After they broke in they searched every corner of the house, and seized upon everything that they imagined to savour of popery, but could find no priest. However they hurried away Mrs. Line to prison, and with her Mrs. Gage (daughter to Baron Copley) whom they found in the house. Mrs. Gage, by the interest of a certain nobleman, was soon set at liberty ; but Mrs. Line was brought upon her trial at the *Old Bailey* before the Lord Chief Justice Popham—a bitter enemy to the Catholics. She was carried to her trial on a chair, being at the time so weak and ill that she could not walk. The evidence against her was very slender, . . . one Marriot, who deposed that he saw a man in her house dressed in white, who, as he would have it, was certainly a priest. However, any proof it seems was strong enough with Mr. Popham against a Papist, and the jury, by him directed, brought in Mrs. Line guilty of the indictment, viz. of having harboured or entertained a Seminary priest. According to which verdict the judge pronounced sentence of death upon the prisoner, and sent her back to *Newgate* to prepare for her execution. . . . When the keeper acquainted her with the death-warrant being signed, and when afterwards she was carried out to execution she shewed not the least commotion or change in her countenance. At *Tyburn*, when she was just ready to die, she declared to the standers by, with a loud voice, " I am sentenced to die for harbouring a Catholic priest, and so far I am from repenting for having done so, that I wish, with all my soul, that where I have entertained one, I could have entertained a thousand." . . . Mr. Barkworth, whose combat came next, embraced her dead body whilst it was yet hanging, saying : " O blessed Mrs. Line, who hast now happily received thy reward! Thou art gone before us, but we shall quickly follow thee to bliss, if it please the Almighty."

She was executed February 27, 1601.[1]

Mark Barkworth (or Bosworth) has a place among the martyrs as heroic and devoted as Anne Line. At Douay, Rheims and at Valladolid where he joined the Benedictine order, he was considered as one of the most intellectual in these universities. Brought up a Protestant in Lincolnshire he was converted at twenty-two and had scarcely joined the English mission when he was arrested.

Ordered to hold up his hand at the Old Bailey he inquired for what crime, and was informed by Justice Popham " for the crime of priesthood and treason ". He replied, " was not our Saviour a priest according to the order of Melchisedek, and will anyone say that he was a traitor ? Though should he be judged by this tribunal he would meet with a like treatment as I look for." " Barkworth, by whom wouldst thou be tried ? " " By God, the Apostles and Evangelists and all the blessed martyrs and saints in heaven." " Nay not so, you must say By God and my country." " What my Lord, mean you these poor men of the jury ? I will never let my blood

---

[1] Roger Silcox (or Filcock), executed after witnessing the deaths of his comrade Barkworth and Anne Line, showed no sign of terror, only prayed that he too might be quickly dissolved in Christ. Born in Sandwich, Kent, his studies were performed at Douay and Rheims. He made his vows at Valladolid and came on the English mission together with Barkworth by whom he was described as " a man exceedingly humble and of extraordinary patience, piety and charity ". (*Douay Records*, quoted by Challoner, p. 256.)

lie at their door for you will oblige them to bring in their verdict against
me right or wrong, or lay so heavy a fine upon them in the Star Chamber
that they will scarcely be able to pay it in their whole lives." " I see that
thou art a priest." [1] " Prove it and I am a dead man.   Your laws stand
against me and I ask no favour at your hands.   Neither do I fear death,
trusting in the grace of God, and would suffer willingly to lay down ten
lives if I had them, for Him who suffered so many torments and so cruel a
death for my sins."   " If thou wilt not confess thyself a priest what art
thou ? "   " A Catholic, but if I were worthy to be a priest I would be
placed in a dignity not inferior to angels ; for priests have power to remit
sins in God's name, a power never given to angels."   At this all the company
laughed and the same question was asked as before " By whom would ye
be tried ", and he replied as before, adding " Not by these unlearned men.
Let learned men judge my cause for I have taken degrees among the learned
and have spent among them seven years."   " Wilt thou then be judged by
a jury of ministers ? "   " If I were, hell fire would try them."   " You wish
then to be tried by priests ? "   " Call in a jury of them."   " Your Lordship
knows that a complete jury of them can be found at Wisbeach Castle."   At
this the Lord Chief Justice withdrew and the recorder without more ceremony, neglecting to take the depositions of witnesses nor waiting for the
verdict, pronounced sentence upon the prisoner as in cases of high treason,
which, as soon as Mr. Barkworth heard lifting up his eyes to heaven he said
" Thanks be to God ".   He was sent back to Newgate and walked through
the streets fettered as he was with such an air of magnanimity that the crowd
enquired whether he was not one of the ring-leaders of the Earl of Essex'
riot.   " No ", said Mr. Barkworth, " But a soldier of Christ who am to
die for his faith."   He chose to be taken to Tyburn in the Benedictine
habit.

The day was bitterly cold ; it seemed for a time that Anne Line might
" cheat the gallows ".   But, to the amazement of those in the cart waiting
for their turn to come, she knelt, kissed the gallows and remained so absorbed
in prayer as to appear unconscious of the hangman's hand on her throat.
A bystander observed that she was so emaciated that her limbs were smaller
than the rope about her neck.   Then the tragic scene recorded in the Douay
dossier took place.   Mark Bosworth, pushing aside the executioner, embraced the dead body before it was cut down, apostrophized the martyr and
the ghastly work went on.

Instead of setting up the heads on London Bridge according to common
practice, Bosworth's was purchased from the hangman by Father Garnet
whose dangerous duty required him to be present at every catholic execution.[2]

---

[1] Obedience constrained the Jesuit missionaries never to confess under torture or
examination that they had been ordained priests.   Witnesses were required to bring proof
of the assertion.   They were ordered, on the other hand, always to proclaim their Catholic
faith.

[2] Father Garnet's letter sent to Rome asking for Anne Line the palms of a blessed martyr
shows her the very emblem of selfless abnegation :

" She was indeed a holy woman and for the last fourteen years had to bear most patiently

He found means to have it secretly transported to the Benedictine convent at Douay where it remained until the chapel was destroyed by the fanatical crowds in the French Revolution. While the onlookers eagerly sought scraps of Anne's sleeves as relics, her body, acquired by the same method, was carried off by her friends in solemn procession under the falling snow and dark winter skies to some place of burial in a cellar situated near a chapel or church where, according to Father Gerard, catholic burials were always held at midnight.

This was the event which inspired Shakespeare's immortal allegory. Although pronounced enigmatic it is in reality simplicity itself. The legend of the phoenix, that bird that nests above the world cut off from all association with beings of a lower sphere, who sprang from the ashes of its home and whose burnt cinders give birth to another lonely being destined to live the same life and constrained by fatality to die the same death, is mentioned by the poet in many other works.[1]

Here, in the present poem, five stanzas suffice to set the scene where the emblems of Faith and Constancy have just met a violent death, to summon those who must be present at their funeral rites, to warn their enemies to remain afar and describe the ceremony which takes place.

First the summons :

> Let the bird of loudest lay,
> On the far Arabian tree,
> Herald sad and trumpet be
> To whose sound chaste wings obey.

But before asking the beings of a higher sphere to assemble, the poet warns the ill-omened screech-owl or nocturnal birds of prey not to interrupt these ceremonies :

> But thou shrieking harbinger,
> Foul precursor of the fiend,
> Augur of the fever's end,
> To this troop come thou not near.

---

the persecution of former friends, great poverty and extreme sickness. Those who knew her carefully can testify that she lived as though dying daily. She had made a vow of chastity and poverty, and, I believe also, of obedience although no one was found willing to receive her vows."

[1] Shakespeare always had a special predilection for the legend of the Phoenix. He speaks of it in the Sonnets, in *As You Like It, Henry VI, Henry VIII, Antony and Cleopatra* and *Cymbeline*.

In *The Comedy of Errors* it is given as the name of an inn ; in *Twelfth Night* it is the name of a ship.

In *The Tempest*, Sebastian in face of a prodigy exclaims :

" I'll believe that there are unicorns, that in Arabia there is one tree, the Phoenix' throne, one Phoenix at this hour reigning there " (Act III, Sc. 3).

" When the bird of wonder dies, the maiden phoenix,
  her ashes new create another heir . . . (*Henry VIII*, Act v, Sc. 5).

" Burn the long yeared phoenix in her blood " (Sonnet 19).

" From their ashes shall be rear'd a Phoenix that shell make all France afeared " (*First Part of Henry VI*, Act IV, Sc. 7).

" Rare as Phoenix " (*As You Like It*, Act IV, Sc. 3).

For Shakespeare this bird of wonder was essentially feminine and virginal.

The accursed messenger of danger and death may well represent the notorious Richard Topcliffe who mercilessly tracked down Catholics and handed them over to a tribunal from whose net none might hope to escape. It could also indicate Chief Justice Popham, who liked to pronounce judgement without consulting the jury or interrogating witnesses and who was especially active in the case now before us.

Not only are these enemies forbidden to show themselves, but every tyrant or servitor of Tyranny is thrust aside, exception being made for the Royal Eagle who is specially bidden to present himself and follow the procession.

> From this session interdict
> Every fowl of tyrant wing,
> Save the eagle feathered king,
> Keep the obsequie so strict.

This stanza recalls that when the Essex conspirators plotted to place James Stewart on the throne he had already promised full religious liberty to his future subjects who looked forward to his advent as to that of a young Fortinbras prepared to sweep corruption from the State. Disillusion came later and under circumstances totally unforeseen, when James achieved the Crown, not as a result of the Essex rebellion but through regular succession and with the aid of the all-powerful Robert Cecil who obliged the young sovereign to temporize.

As to the ceremony : two words prove that it was conducted according to Catholic ritual. It is called a requiem for which the service of a Catholic priest is required.[1]

> Let the Priest in surplice white,
> That defunctive music can,
> Be the death-divining Swan,
> Lest the requiem lack his right.

Not only is an exception made for the Northern Eagle, but an aged and jet black crow is invited to join the mourners. This probably refers to the venerable Archbishop of Canterbury whom Elizabeth playfully called her " Little black husband ".

> And thou treble dated crow,
> That thy sable gender makest,
> With the breath thou giv'st and takest,
> 'Mongst our mourners shalt thou go.

According to the Elizabethan Prayer Book, only a man with bishop's

---

[1] In Sonnet no. 31 the Poet alludes to his practice of praying for the dead :
How many a holy and obsequious tear
Hath dear religious love stolen from mine eye
As interest to the dead. . . .

rank is empowered to transmit the divine spirit he holds from above to the vicar, curate or deacon whom he is ordaining.[1]

Among the high prelates thus empowered to perpetuate by breath from above the divine spirit, John Whitgift aged seventy-one, seems to be the one alluded to. This is not surprising. He was obviously well known to Shakespeare. His nomination to the Bishopric of Worcester in 1577 was made by Burleigh against the will of Leicester and in spite of the opposition of the powerful Dudleys. In this capacity he issued the licence of William Shakespeare and Anne Hathaway's clandestine marriage and that of three other catholic unions. In 1583 he was promoted to the see of Canterbury where in 1594 he authorized the publication of *Venus and Adonis*, Shakespeare's first poem which, by strict ecclesiastical standards, must have been deemed " most lascivious ". The year before he had given the imprimatur to Robert Southwell's *Magdalen's Tears* at a time when the young Jesuit priest was hiding in peril of his life.[2]

Both volumes were among the best sellers of those days which shows John Whitgift's good taste for high literature and explains why the historian John Stowe dedicated to the Archbishop of Canterbury his annals and mentioned in his preface " the great love and the entire affection to all good letters " of the prelate.

Moreover, in the numerous documents relative to the arrests, trials, tortures and executions of Catholic martyrs recently published by the Catholic Record Society where Richard Topcliffe appears to be the drastic foe of the recusants, taking pleasure in torturing his captives and assisting to their execution, we find no criticism addressed to the see of Canterbury. The full name of John Whitgift appears but once and that time the accuser of the Archbishop is no other than Richard Topcliffe himself. For this curious text brought before the council, Topcliffe offers to liberate a prisoner, the priest Thomas Pormort if he consents to say that he is a bastard of the Archbishop of Canterbury, adding that " the Archbishop of Canterbury was a fitter counselor [in] the kitchen among wenches than in a Prince's courte ". The paper further reads thus " and to Justice Young the said Topcliffe said that he would hang th[e] Archbishop and 500 more yf they were in his hands ".[3]

All these remarks bring us to the conclusion that John Whitgift can well be the treble-dated crow admitted among the mourners of two of Topcliffe's victims.[4]

Eight stanzas follow ; the poet initiates his reader into a new metaphysical

---

[1] In the Elizabethan Prayer Book we read : Then said Jesus . . . As my Father sent me even so I send you also, and when he had said these words he breathed upon them and said unto them " Receive ye the Holy Ghost ". (*The Ordering of Priests. Prayer Book of Queen Elizabeth, 1559.* Reprint by Griffith, Farran, Okeden & Welsh (London, 1890), p. 150.)

[2] He was executed in 1594, the year after his book appeared.

[3] *Publications of the Catholic Record Society,* vol. v, p. 210.

[4] The life of Archbishop John Whitgift has been written by Stripe and by Sir George Paule.

expression and tries to make him comprehend what language never rendered before, to understand what seems incomprehensible. Shakespeare's mastery of paradox, instead of confusing, clarifies a simple truth : the possibility of complete union between two creatures of different essence, different sex and different species. Through divine love opposites are transmuted. Reason is confounded when obliged to acknowledge the miracle of spiritual communion and the elimination of self.

> Here the Antheme doth commence :
> Love and Constancy is dead ;
> *Phoenix* and the *Turtle* fled
> In a mutual flame from hence.
>
> So they loved, as love in twain
> Had the essence but of one ;
> Two distincts, division none :
> Number there in love was slain.
>
> Hearts remote, yet not asunder ;
> Distance, and no space was seen
> Twixt the *Turtle* and his Queen ;
> But in them it was a wonder.
>
> So between them love did shine
> That the *Turtle* saw his right
> Flaming in the *Phoenix*' sight ;
> Either was the other's mine.
>
> Property was thus appalled,
> That the self was not the same ;
> Single nature's double name
> Neither two nor one was called.
>
> Reason, in itself confounded,
> Saw division grow together,
> To themselves yet either neither
> Simple was so well compounded ;
>
> That it cried, ' How true a twain
> Seemeth this concordant one !
> Love hath Reason, Reason none,
> If what parts can so remain.'
>
> Whereupon it made this *Threne*,
> To the *Phoenix* and the *Dove*,
> Co-supremes and stars of love,
> As chorus to their tragic scene.

At this point, the emotional climax having been reached, Shakespeare suddenly changes his method of prosody, and embarks on a funeral hymn unique of its kind which carries the reader into the very spirit of loss, where he is constrained to repeat sadly : " We ne'er shall look upon their like again." This is expressed in a Dantesque terza rima never met with before in Shakespeare or any of his contemporaries. The third stanza clearly indicates the mystic marriage in which the victims have been united.

Beauty, Truth and Rarity,
Grace in all simplicity,
Here enclosed in cinders lie.

Death is now the *Phoenix*' nest ;
And the *Turtle's* loyal breast
To eternity doth rest.

Leaving no posterity ;
'Twas not their infirmity,
It was married Chastity.

Truth may seem, but cannot be ;
Beauty brag, but 'tis not she ;
Truth and beauty buried be.

To this urn let those repair,
That are either true or fair ;
For these dead birds sigh a prayer.

With this poem Shakespeare's lyric period practically concludes. The days when he wrote joyous comedy are also left behind. From this time forth his heroes, however generous, noble and high minded, will be punished by destiny in proportion to their virtues.

Timon of Athens, an unfinished tragedy, bears no indication of ever having been staged in its author's lifetime. It appears to have been sketched during a phase of morbid depression as though the poet were attempting to give voice to a misanthropic mood which, until then, was foreign to his nature. If, for once, he left his canvas abandoned on its frame, doubtless he realized that his chief character had not the qualities to conquer and retain the sympathies of an audience. The attitude of Alcibiades toward the ungrateful Athenians lacked soldierly dignity, and perhaps he was tempted to reserve the powerful episodes where he hurls the disdainful sarcasm against the " many headed multitude " ready to profit equally by peace or war as a more appropriate background to set off a more striking figure—such as Coriolanus.

I believe that Shakespeare did not go further in building his Timon because he lost interest in the character he was creating. Even the social and political satire he had in mind lacked substance when he started to mould it into shape. If so, we may be grateful to Shakespeare's fellows for not having left *Timon of Athens* out of their 1623 Folio. For, it in no way diminishes his glory, and sheds considerable light on his method of composition. It shows us an author hastening to sketch some general ideas and throwing his material pell-mell on the anvil, confident that his mastery of dramatic technique would suffice, when the time came, to co-ordinate and weld plot and characters into a homogeneous whole.

As it stands, the drama is practically without action : yet it contains elements of extraordinary force. Some passages are scarcely inferior to the poet's best manner. Certain scenes are well begun and finished, but lack vital substance in the middle as though the author was postponing his efforts. This it is which leads us to suppose that the *Timon of Athens* we possess represents only a first draft.

Those familiar with *Coriolanus* will find in that magnificent tragedy all the qualities and intrinsic merit of the best part of *Timon of Athens*. Shakespeare seemingly has fitted more interesting characters into an argument worthier of a great theme. We may suspect that Timon, the misanthropist, would never have become an appropriate hero for this impassioned drama; whereas Coriolanus forces us to admit that what appeared impossible has been triumphantly achieved.

Two magnificent scenes detach themselves from the confusion of the Athenian drama. The banquet offered by Timon to his false friends is served on sumptuous dishes of gold and silver, but the choice of fruits and delicate pastries are but sculptured stones skilfully painted so as to deceive the greedy profiteers of the host's former riches. No sooner is the trick played, than Timon drives his guests from the board with a volley of the very missiles that they had hoped to feed on and the climax of the masterfully composed scene is reached when Timon, after working himself into a fury, suddenly passes from bitter sarcasm to tragic insanity.

In the final act, hidden in a cavern near the seashore, he subsists on a meagre diet of roots refusing to hold converse with any living creature, but with his bare hands prepares the grave where he expects to lie down and die, letting the waves cover him while he pronounces curses on all mankind. Even here he is importuned by adventurous Athenians who believe that a treasure has been buried in Timon's cave. Alcibiades too, who has been ostracized by his townsmen, presents himself at the head of a troop of conscripts offering to avenge Timon's wrongs and his own as well. The hermit replies only with a torrent of insults to which, in comparison, his unbridled curses at the banquet appear mild. The greedy courtesans and camp-followers are castigated with a violence surpassing anything till then expressed in the English tongue. The maniac inveighs without measure against the two worst evils which afflict mankind and which this human tide is bringing to his shore: Lust for gold and prostitution kill more men than do a million swords, declares Timon. This diatribe contains a veritable dictionary of invective which, according to Schlegel exhausts the language of hate.

The inequality of this sombre drama has led certain critics to believe that Shakespeare might have sought aid from an inferior hand, such as Chapman, Heywood, Middleton or Cyril Tourneur; if not, they suggest some posthumous attempt at retouching. I rather agree with Sir E. K. Chambers and Ulrici that *Timon of Athens* is Shakespeare's alone and that, as he had left it unfinished, his editors preferred to respect the integrity of the manuscript.

The story of " Cynic Timon " had already been told in Painter's *Palace of Pleasure*: but the dramatist does not follow the character of Timon as described there. Instead of a violent and brutal being, Shakespeare's Timon is a cultivated Athenian who is generous to a fault and never becomes brutal until his legitimate anger degenerates into madness.

The subject, as usual when Shakespeare selects a classic theme, is borrowed from Plutarch but he also had access to an Italian version of Lucian's dialogues the mark of which is left on one of the stage directions which reads : *Enter the Bandetti.*

Julius Caesar, with its bitter allusions to contemporary events, was already risky ; the political climax which followed without doubt forced the author to absent himself from London. During these months—whether long or short—the poet conceived and perfected a new version of his great melodrama, *Hamlet's Revenge*, and transformed it into a tragedy of quite a different kind. The young and virile Prince who had commanded circumstance and mastered occasion, grew into an entirely different personage. In the *Tragical History of Hamlet*, the Prince's character suffers a complete alteration and the drama, instead of taking place externally, develops within his mind and heart. This new process is utilized by the dramatist from that hour. It revolutionized his future work as will be seen. It is repeated in *Coriolanus*, *Othello*, *King Lear* and *Macbeth*, all those tragedies of ripened middle age in which we can follow the author's gradual transformation from the most sensitive of poets to the wisest of philosophers.

CHAPTER XIII

HAMLET

The play's origins : Saxo Grammaticus and François de Belleforest—Shakespeare's personal experiences introduced into the story—Commentaries—Date of performance of successive versions.

TO understand the whole depth of this tragic story which Shakespeare carried in his head and heart throughout life, its evolution must be followed from the first melodrama presented at the Shoreditch theatre which earned Lodge's jealous gibe about the ghost crying like an oyster wife, to the ultimate version, a mature poet's masterly philosophical study, whose thought was close to that of Montaigne. *Hamlet* did not spring fully armed from the brain of its creator. To understand the evolution of Shakespeare's conception its different phases must be recognized. It is also indispensable to consult the primitive and pagan sources whence he derived his original inspiration if the reader is to appreciate the power of the artist who endowed his hero with a super-civilized mind and intelligence joined to a Christian habit of thought. Three centuries before the presentation on the stage of William Shakespeare's drama, an obscure monk, Saxo Grammaticus, had set down for posterity the story of young Amleth,[1] an ancient legend from Jutland which had passed into the folklore of the peninsula, because of its appeal to popular imagination. The parchment of this pious Danish chronicler who, like Herodotus, knew how to mix the real with the fantastic, reached the presses of Josse Bade, a Parisian printer, in 1514. The amateur of ancient texts, may therefore read today, in medieval latin and gothic characters, the first version of the tragedy of *Hamlet*, interesting to study, even if it was not the direct source of Shakespeare's drama.

The facts are related with clumsy brutality ; the supernatural enters nowhere into the story ; the feminine element is negligible ; Amleth is assailed neither by doubt nor scruple. He feigns madness solely for self-protection. He lacks means not will to avenge his father's murder.

Saxo Grammaticus' tale may thus be summarized :

Horwindille, renowned for his bravery and brilliant deeds on land and sea was a noted pirate ; he made war on the King of Norway whom he slew with his own hand. After this victory, he brought back to his country rich booty, became a popular hero, obtained in marriage Geruth, daughter of the King of Denmark, and had a son by her called Amleth. So much prosperity aroused the envy and

---

[1] The poet Snaebjorn (*c.* 980) recited the " Legend of Amlodi " in his Icelandic saga.

jealousy of his brother Fengon, who by ruse and treachery, succeeded in getting rid of Horwindille and, his crime accomplished, found no difficulty in convincing Geruth that he had only acted to save her from an unworthy husband.

Geruth allows herself to be persuaded, and becomes his wife. Henceforward Amleth thinks only of avenging his father. To accomplish his object, he feigns madness which permits him to conceal his plans, and to live unmolested. His insanity is treated as a joke at court. Perhaps love will restore his reason ? The king discovers a young woman to effect a cure ; but this stratagem succeeds no better than the exhortations of his friend and foster-brother in extracting Amleth's secret. As a last resort, Fengon decides to absent himself, and give Amleth the opportunity of opening his heart to his mother, while one of her confidants hides under a bed to overhear the interview.

Amleth, suspecting the presence of an eavesdropper behaves as though stark mad, crows like a cock, jumps on the bed, with his foot detects a man hidden under the cushions, kills him, and has his remains cooked and given as food to the swine. He then confides his plans of vengeance to his mother, whose repentance he achieves.

On his return, Fengon looks in vain for his accomplice, and suspects that Amleth has caused his disappearance. He resolves to remove his nephew, but dares not strike him directly. He therefore banishes him from the realm and charges the King of England, his vassal, to carry out his wishes.

During the voyage, Amleth steals their instructions from his guards, and substitutes the order to kill those who were to betray him ; more than this, during his exile, he wins the favour of the English king and obtains his daughter in marriage. He returns to Denmark, where the news of his death has preceded him. In fact he arrives just as his own funeral is being celebrated. Profiting by the general drunkenness—in Denmark at this time, all ceremonies were followed by libations—he seizes a torch, sets fire to the castle and rushing to Fengon's chamber, pierces him with his sword. He justifies his act before a council of notables who proclaim him King, and reigns to the great good of his people until the day when he loses his life in a war undertaken to extend the frontiers of his country.

Such is, according to the Danish chronicler, the story of the Prince of Jutland, raised to the throne by his prowess in love and war. This version cannot be considered the direct source of the English playwright's inspiration. Shakespeare, who always sought subjects of present interest, would hardly have used a volume published nearly a hundred years before, difficult to decipher, inordinately long, and hard to find, when he had near at hand a contemporary and widely circulated book dealing with the same subject in less obscure language.

In 1572, the novelist François de Belleforest of Comminges printed a collection of stories in the Italian style, where Saxo Grammaticus' narration is followed closely. He entitles his fifth tragic tale :

Avec quelle ruse Amleth, qui depuis fut roy de Danemark, vengea la mort de son père. Horwendille, occis par Fengon, son frère, et autre occurrence de son histoire.

Belleforest does not substantially change the account given by Grammaticus ; however, he suggests some thoughts which contain the germ of a new psychology whose resources Shakespeare was fully to exploit. The variations introduced by the French author are interesting since they confirm the opinion that Shakespeare derived his inspiration directly from his version. A comparison of the texts shows that a simple rhetorical figure borrowed from that of 1572, enabled the English dramatist to create a whole vivid scene. In Belleforest, the king, troubled by Amleth's ambiguous answers, concludes that he is " either mad to the highest note (fol jusqu'à la haute gamme), or that he is one of the wisest of his time ". This musical illustration of madness impressed Shakespeare, who places the famous recorder in his hero's hand with the words :

You would sound me from my lowest note to the top of my compass ; and there is much music, excellent voice, in this little organ, yet cannot you make it speak.

For Saxo Grammaticus, Hamlet by his prowess " rivalled the gods and accomplished deeds greater than those of Hercules ",[1] but at best, he was only a brave and crafty warrior to whom the idea of vengeance was inseparable from his ambitious schemes.

According to Belleforest, Prince Hamlet had " vanquished the malice of fate by the strength of his constancy, leaving a notable example of greatness and courage ". The French writer gave the pagan and barbarous hero of the legend, moderation and an inflexible sense of duty. According to him, Hamlet remained " sober at banquets, and instead of accumulating riches, was content to amass honour and virtue ". It was by a sort of clairvoyance " possessed by exceptional minds " that he avoided the traps set by his uncle. His melancholy endowed him with a kind of extra-lucidity.

The supernatural element which Shakespeare utilized was therefore already suggested. The Stratford poet fully realized the dramatic possibilities of such a subject. Under his pen Hamlet is christianized and humanized ; he becomes the agent of a spiritual world, a victim of the sacred duty of punishing the guilty and purifying the State. Shakespeare's first care was to transform his hero's character. To win the sympathy of the audience, there had to be a nobler motive than the mere ambition of a prince deprived of his heritage. Hence the dramatist stresses the moral and even patriotic reasons which prompt Hamlet's actions. He has given him psychical powers which enable him to converse directly with the invisible world. The soldier on watch before the silent spectre of the murdered king says unhesitatingly : " Upon my life, this spirit dumb to us, will speak to him."

It is his father's ghost armed as in the time of his victories who comes to enlighten Hamlet upon the subject of his death.

Ophelia's character is also much enhanced. In the Danish story, a courtesan is chosen by the king on account of her beauty to charm Hamlet

---

[1] Hic Amlethi exitus fuit : qui si parem naturae atque fortunae indulgentiam expertus fuisset, aequasset fulgore superos : Herculea virtutibus opera transsendisset. (Gollancz, *The Sources of Hamlet*, Oxford University Press, London, 1926, p. 162.)

and draw his secret from him ; with Belleforest, she is a chaste young girl who loves the prince " more than her own life " and who would have been sorry if he had fallen into the clumsy snare she was obliged to set for him in obedience to the king. The Danish chronicler had presented a wholly superficial character ; the French story-teller introduced the idea of sentiment in the young girl, and Shakespeare, elaborating his emendation, created the part of the touching Ophelia, so necessary to the construction of his drama.

Belleforest's version of the story is therefore a link between Saxo Grammaticus's barbarous tale, and Shakespeare's searching analysis of an ultra-civilized mentality.

Fundamentally *Hamlet* resembles the poet's other tragedies ; the same method of composition is found in all. The subject is derived from an outside source, freed from useless or vulgar incidents, and transplanted to a sphere where the author, guided by his own experience of places, things and people, creates a convincing reality, all the diverse elements being harmonized and unified by Shakespeare's powerful and individual imagination.[1]

It is necessary to emphasize the dramatist's debt to Italy and France which, though previously recognized, has since the Victorian era been questioned by nationalist commentators following the lead of Professor Tyler and Sir Sidney Lee. This school of critics maintains that the actor-poet always worked on a text translated and printed in English. He did not dramatize Belleforest's story, but did not scruple to plagiarize a play of Kyd's or some other writer. Rather than recognize the French story as the source of *Hamlet*, they prefer to support the theory that it must have been imitated from an old English play now lost. Nevertheless, Malone, the first protagonist of this idea, ceased to uphold it in his second edition of *Shakespeare's Plays.* Certainly it is inadmissible to base an argument upon documents imagined for the sake of that argument and of which no trace whatever can be found.

The mistake of which Sir Sidney Lee was the principal propagator, in attributing to Thomas Kyd the first drama concerning the Prince of Denmark, has been repeated in our day by Dover Wilson and Granville Barker. Accordingly it is necessary to give here *in extenso* the passage in the single document upon which this theory is based. Its perusal leads to quite another conclusion than the one they exploit. This document is a preface to Robert Greene's *Menaphon* written by Thomas Nashe in 1589. Bearing in mind Shakespeare's difficulty in finding work in London, the hostility he

---

[1] According to Pierre Le Tourneur (1736-83), one of Shakespeare's first French commentators, " this play, which has made the deepest impression upon English minds, and which is the one most often played, is almost continually moral. It is a chain of profound reflections, the thoughts of one person concerning a single tragic event which arouses terror and pity. It can be said that it has only one character, one principal rôle. No insipid flattery of women, no impious maxims against heaven, no exaggerated heroism : there is none of that artificial mixture of art and nature, the usual basis of modern tragedy, which confines itself to vacillating between the two delicate subjects of love and honour."

encountered from the university men, the opposition of Henslowe's faction, the jealousy of his rivals, a violent diatribe from opponents like Nashe and Greene is only to be expected.

For what was he chiefly criticized ? His origin, his friends in the recusant world, his sympathy with the literature of the Jesuit college of Douai, the boldness with which he gained inspiration from the works of the Italian Renaissance. Here we are in the presence of a text where all these reproaches are made against the author of *Hamlet*.

It is a comon practise now a daies amongst a sort of shifting companions that runne through every arte and thrive by none, to leave the trade of *Noverint* whereto they were borne, and busie themselves with the indevors of Art, that could scarcelie latinize their necke-verse if they should have neede, yet English *Seneca* read by candle light yeeldes manie good sentences as *Bloud is a begger* [1] and so foorth ; and if you intreate him faire in a frostie morning, he will affoord you whole ' Hamlets ',[2] I should say handfulls of tragicall speaches.   But o griefe ! ' tempus edax rerum ', what's that will last alwayes ?   The Sea exhaled by droppes will in continuance bee drie, and ' Seneca ' let bloud line by line and page by page, at length must needes due to our Stage ; which makes his famished followers to imitate the Kidde in ' Aesop ', who, enamored with the Foxes new fangles, forsooke all hopes of life to leape into a newe occupation ; and these men renouncing all possibilities of credite or estimation, to intermeddle with Italian Translations wherein how poorely they have plodded, (as those that are neither provenzall men, nor are able to distinguish of Articles,) let all indifferent Gentlemen that have travailed in that tongue, discerne by their two-pennie pamphlets : & no marvell though their home borne mediocritie bee such in this matter ; for what can bee hoped of those, that thrust ' Elisium ' into hell, and have not learned, so long as they have lived in the Spheyres, the just measure of the Horizon without an hexameter ?   Sufficeth them to bodge up a blanke verse with ifs and ands, and other while for recreation after their Candle stuffe, having starched their beardes most curiously, to make a peripaticall path into the inner parts of the Citie, and spend two or three howers in turning over French ' Doudie ',[3] where they attract more infection in one minute, than they can do eloquence all daies of their life, by conversing with any Authors of like argument. . . .[4]

What is striking about this long passage is that it has but one theme. The young Juvenal's animosity is directed against the same person throughout, whom it is always easy to identify with Shakespeare and impossible, on the other hand, to connect with Thomas Kyd, an atheist living in the

---

[1] In Sonnet 67 Shakespeare uses the expression " Beggar'd of blood ".

[2] It is the proximity of " Hamlets " to the word Kidde which gives rise to the mistake of those who consider that there is an allusion here to Thomas Kyd.   Some commentators, who have refrained from reproducing the text *in extenso*, see in the capital K of Kidde proof that this is a proper name—that of the author of *Hamlet*—without observing that Nashe's introduction bristles with capital letters, and that the word Fox which closely follows Kidde, has also a capital letter.

[3] In his learned thesis on Robert Greene and his novels, M. René Provost, Professor of literature at Algiers deals with this controversial passage of Nashe's preface.   Commendably he quotes the whole text, but he prefers to interpret the words " French Doudie", an evident allusion to the publications of the college at Douai, as " dissolute morals ".

[4] Preface to Greene's *Menaphon*.   Epistle to the Gentlemen students of both Universities, by Thomas Nashe.   (Stationer's Register, 1589.)

company of Marlowe, Royden and Raleigh.   Certainly he was not the man to delve in the backs of shops running through the proscribed publications of Douai.

When the sources of *Othello* and *Measure for Measure* are discussed by the school above referred to, the similarities noted between these plays and the Italian tales are explained away by the hypothetical existence of two old English plays of which naturally there remains no trace !   To acknowledge Shakespeare's debt—which is not enormous—to Belleforest and the Italian novelists does not belittle his talent ; but it would seriously discredit him to pretend that he had copied *Hamlet, Othello* and *Measure for Measure* from English dramas already in existence, as certain over-zealous admirers affirm.   Is it more praiseworthy to plagiarize a compatriot's work than to create a drama based upon an ancient theme ?

Shakespeare acknowledges the origin of Hamlet in the very title given to his first version :   *The Tragical History of Hamlet, Prince of Denmark.*   In the Danish chronicle the story of Amleth figures as a simple narrative, with a happy ending ;   Belleforest on the contrary incorporates it in a volume he calls :   *Histoires tragiques.*

Is it astonishing that Shakespeare made use of a French tale ?   He knew the language sufficiently well to introduce French quotations and even puns into his dialogue.   To read and understand a text like Belleforest's *Histoires tragiques* requires less competence than is shown in *Henry V* and *The Merry Wives of Windsor.*

We have no reason to doubt that the assertion made by Nicholas Rowe, who after having reproached Ben Jonson for borrowing whole scenes from the classic theatre, adds :

Our Shakespeare owed no man anything, except the fable which he took from the novelists, but in which he made notable modifications.[1]

In another place he dwells at length on the dramatist's knowledge of French.

If we return to Stratford and look into the surroundings where the poet lived guided by Belleforest's story, we can follow the evolution of the tragedy in its author's own mind.

All the elements of this drama, which were absent from the Franco-Danish account, appear when certain youthful impressions are invoked. Let us give ear to the thousand echoes of the little Warwickshire town where Shakespeare was born and bred.   Even the name " Hamlet ", today universally famous, emanates from Stratford.   And perhaps its similarity with " Amleth " of Jutland explains why Shakespeare chose among Belleforest's numerous stories this particular one.

Hamlet [2] was the unusual name of Sadler, his intimate friend from school days, and throughout life.   This comrade remained beside Shakespeare to the last and gave his name to the child whom he lost.   Again it was the family name of that young Katherine, model for Ophelia, whose

---

[1] In all his repertoire, Shakespeare can be reproached for his indebtedness to other dramatic works only in two comedies, *The Comedy of Errors* and *The Taming of the Shrew.*
[2] This name is spelled Hamlet, Hamlett or Hamnet.

drowning is recounted with poetical sympathy and substituted in his drama
for the sudden end of the abandoned girl in the *Histoires tragiques*.

It is easy to imagine the feelings of William Shakespeare, then a boy of
sixteen, as he took part in the discussions which ensued after the Hamlett
family's tragedy.   His sensitive nature could not remain indifferent to the
grief of parents who after suffering the loss of a child became victims of the
malevolent gossip of the townsfolk, anxious to put a sensational construction
upon a death which friends and kindred believed accidental.   The truth
was never discovered, and the mystery surrounding Katherine's death
envelops Ophelia's also.

The drama which stirred Stratford is faithfully reconstructed by Shakespeare.   In Queen Gertrude's moving recital, the incident is seen once more
in all its details ; the feelings of the little circle of friends outraged by official
cruelty is well conveyed by Laertes' argument with the priest ; only the
popular commentary is missing, and this is soon provided by the gravediggers.

The report of the inquest on Katherine Hamlett was preserved in the
Stratford archives until the last century.   It is echoed in the gravediggers'
discussion on whether a suicide should be allowed burial in consecrated
ground.   The resemblance between the terms usually employed in such a
case, and the language of the actors in this lugubrious scene is remarkable,
especially if the primitive text of *Hamlet* be consulted.

First Gravedigger :   I say no, she ought not to be buried in christian buriall.
Second Gravedigger : Why sir ?
First :   Marry because shee's drownd.
Second :   But she did not drowne her selfe.
First :   No, that's certaine, the water drown'd her.
Second :   Yea but it was against her will.
First :   No, I deny that, for looke you sir, I stand here,
              If the water come to me, I drowne not my selfe :
              But if I goe to the water, and am there drown'd,
              Ergo I am guiltie of my owne death :
              Y'are gone, goe y'are gone sir.
Second :   I but see, she hath christian buriall
              Because she is a great woman.
First :   Marry more's the pitty, that great folke
              Should have more authoritie to hang or drowne
              Themselves, more than other people. . . .

The conversation is interrupted by the arrival of Hamlet and Horatio.
Then in the confidences exchanged between the two friends, the poet
develops another thought which recurs not only in his plays and sonnets
but in his last will, where he asks to be buried under the choir of his parish
church, at a depth of sixteen feet, safe from any profanation and leaving a
curse upon whomsoever disturb his resting place.   According to an old
Stratford tradition the cemetery scene would have been written in a house
next to the church which overlooks the charnel where, according to local
regulations, the corpses after ten years were removed to the potters field.

Like most of his contemporaries, Shakespeare well knew of an incident which occurred in the course of a provincial tour when, to the great astonishment of audience and actors alike, the old and popular drama of *Friar Francis* was interrupted. A murderess who had killed her husband, moved by the appearance on the stage of the ghost of a man who had met a like fate, rose and confessed publicly that seven years before she had poisoned her life companion.

This occurrence explains Hamlet's words :

> I have heard, that guilty creatures sitting at a play
> Have by the very cunning of the scene
> Been struck so to the soul that presently
> They have proclaimed their malefactions. . . .[1]

In consequence, following this idea he set the mouse trap for his uncle :

> . . . The play's the thing
> Wherein I'll catch the conscience of the King.

When he came to describe Elsinore and the reception of the itinerant players, Shakespeare was fortunate. Three actors belonging to his company, Kempe, Pope and Bryan, returned in 1585 from a tour in Denmark where they had had the privilege of acting before the King and Queen. They brought back with them names such as Rosencrantz and Guildenstern used by Shakespeare for his courtiers.

The players had been scandalized by the prevailing intemperance ; so that Shakespeare is authorized in making Hamlet say :

> This heavy-headed revel east and west
> Makes us traduc'd and tax'd of other nations ;
> They clepe us drunkards, and with swinish phrase
> Soil our addition. . . .[2]

They had been struck by the prestige enjoyed by the French in Denmark, where they were admired for their good taste, their dress and their dexterity with the foils. Polonius therefore sends his son to Paris to complete his education, that he may learn good manners, how to dress well and expecially how to perfect his fencing.

The actors had also noted that in Denmark the English were regarded as eccentric if not crazy, and this gives rise to the gravediggers' question :

> Why was he sent into England ?
> Why, because he was mad : he shall recover his wits there :
>   or, if he do not, tis no great matter there.
> Why ?
> 'Twill not be seen in him there ; there the men are as mad as he.

---

[1] Thomas Heywood, recalls the incident to which Shakespeare alludes in his *An Apology for Actors : Their Antiquity, Their ancient Dignity ; The true use of their quality* (London, 1612).

[2] These adverse criticisms of Denmark do not appear in the folio of 1623 ; the reason is that *Hamlet* was modified for representation before Queen Anne, a Danish princess, who was twice visited by her brother, the King of Denmark.

Nevertheless when it came to local colour Shakespeare disregards minor geographical accuracy. He situates Elsinore, where the terrace is almost level with the sea, upon the summit of an overhanging cliff; dramatic effect is more important to a poet than flat reality. Shakespeare needed this dangerous background to intensify his characters' irrational fear of imaginary peril at the approach of the spectre.

> What if it tempt you toward the flood, my lord,
> Or to the dreadful summit of the cliff
> That beetles o'er his base into the sea, . . .
> The very place puts toys of desperation,
> Without more motive, into every brain
> That looks so many fathoms to the sea
> And hears it roar beneath.

Even in dealing with the ghost, and everything touching the supernatural in his drama, Shakespeare had not far to go to find documentation. His schoolfellow, Robert Dibdale, was one of the most renowned spiritualistic experts among the Catholics. Later in London, Marlowe and Thomas Heywood,[1] both students of magic, could continue his initiation. The poet followed the best authorities of his time in his presentation of psychic phenomena.[2] Visions, ghosts, maledictions and incantations are described according to the formulae traced by Virgil and Dante, codified by Cornelius Agrippa[3] and described by his contemporaries Reginald Scot,[4] Lavater[5] and James Stuart.[6]

Thus Shakespeare, without leaving Stratford, could glean in the field of his own experience enough incidents, anecdotes and impressions to clothe and dramatize the story of Belleforest's which provided the basis of his great masterpiece.

[1] Cf. Thomas Heywood, *The Hierarchie of the Blessed Angells Their Names, orders and Offices* (London, Adam Islip, 1635).

[2] It has been asked why, when the ghost disappears, Hamlet swears by Saint Patrick. The explanation is simple : Saint Patrick, in medieval legends, held the keys of Purgatory. An account by Edmund Campion is given in Holinshed's *Chronicles*.

[3] Henrici Cornelii Agrippae, *De occulta philosophia* (Paris, C. Wechet, 1531).

[4] Reginald Scot, *The Discoverie of witchcraft*, wherein the lewde dealing of witches and wichmongers is notablie detected, the knaverie of conjurors, the impietie of inchantors, the follie of soothsayers . . . lately written by Reginald Scot esq. (London, Wm. Brome, 1584).

Scot's book is extremely rare. King James who quotes it in his *Demonology* caused almost every copy of this edition to be destroyed, but the best Shakespearean commentators are agreed in admitting that the poet was acquainted with Reginald Scot's work, and M. Cambillard has established that the episode in *A Midsummer Night's Dream* where by Puck's spells Bottom is given an ass's head is suggested by his book.

[5] Lewes Lavater, *Of ghostes and spirites walking by nyght, and of strange noyses crackes, and sundry forewarnynges, whiche commonly happen before the death of menne, great slaughters ane alterations of kyngdomes written by Lewes Lavaterius of Tigurine and translated into english by R.H.* (London, Henry Benneyman for Richard Walkins, 1572.)

[6] King James is the author of the learned work : *Daemonologieen, in forme of a dialogue*, Edinburgh, Robert Waldegrave, 1579, and of *Newes from Scotland*, Declaring the Damnable life and death of Doctor Fian, a notable Sorcerer, who was burned at Edenbrough in January last 1591. . . . With the true examinations of the saide Doctor and Witches, as they uttered them in the presence of the Scottish King. (London, Wm. Wright.)

From the point of view of composition, *Hamlet* is not faultless. It is a philosophical monologue, interspersed with scenes of action or of topical interest, and the final holocaust in which all the chief characters perish appears excessive. The order of several scenes may be changed without harming the whole ; certain personages may be suppressed without affecting the argument of the play. Nevertheless *Hamlet* is generally considered Shakespeare's masterpiece. All the qualities scattered in the other works, tragedies, comedies, histories and pastorals are to be found in *Hamlet* and more besides.

The astonishing youth and freshness of the early poems is here displayed ; the strength of style and the lyric fire characteristic of Shakespeare's first manner are allied to the startling simplicity of his middle period : the play's rapid development is punctuated by a commentary worthy of the great dramatist's maturity, when his thought reached beyond the horizon of his island to communicate with the thought of the continent.

Between the first and last *Hamlet*, Shakespeare had been profoundly impressed by Montaigne. Passages of deep meditation introduced in a wild and sanguinary drama constitute one of those daring literary innovations which render a work immortal without either reader or spectator knowing why.

Hamlet suits all tastes and all ages. It pleases the young, the mature, and those entering into the twilight of life. It charms the romantic and captivates the disillusioned ; it appeals to the believer and interests the sceptic ; it encourages heroism and teaches the prudent discretion. In this play those who swear by love only see their sentiment upheld, while the cynical smile at the sight of treachery grimacing under the mask of friendship. To the best qualities of the classic stage it adds the quintessential spirit of the Renaissance, always of topical interest, it makes more modern works seem out of date.

These reasons, sufficient to endear *Hamlet* to some, are not the only ones which make it appreciated. As the young prince himself says, the heart of his mystery cannot be plucked out ; elusive, intangible, unique, he arouses perpetual curiosity, and yet, whatever be said, he remains eternally misunderstood.

Hamlet will never be satisfactorily analysed, for he carries a paradox in his personality. If his brain is that of a man of forty, his heart is less than half that age. It seems as if, having matured with his creator, he none-the-less retains the deep imprint of youthful feeling. His torments are those of the simple hearted. Many have suffered in like manner and for the same cause. Hamlet is not the only child deprived of a dearly loved father, who, with rebellious melancholy watches his mother console herself in a second marriage. This filial susceptibility is natural and common. Many feel it, attributing to their widowed mothers a faithlessness which often exists solely in their imagination. As to friendship, what sincere minded adolescent who encounters duplicity in a comrade has not, like Hamlet, lamented the shattering of an illusion ? And what man, having idealized the object of his first love, is not invaded by cynical bitterness when he perceives that traps and intrigues replace candour and loyalty ?

Some critics, and not the least gifted, have even reproached the author for making Hamlet too human. . . . Le Tourneur maintains that the Prince of Denmark does not always express himself according to his royal status.   He is of the opinion that the cruelty of existence, the insolence of officialdom, the delays of justice, tyrannical oppression, and the pains of unrequited love are troubles of which princes know nothing.   " It is William Shakespeare and not Hamlet who speaks of these grievances ", he declares.

Shakespeare has used the most daring devices in creating his masterpiece. Who else ever brought together such varied material with such audacity ? Not content with developing a difficult and complicated situation and creating strongly marked characters, the poet found room in his dialogue for totally unconnected subjects without unduly delaying the action.   Thus he introduces a discourse on dramatic art, and considerations upon the comparative positions of actor and playwright and the relation of each to the public.   He criticizes contemporary extravagances and his rivals' eccentricities.   He finds an opportunity to boast of the " Globe " and its troupe to the detriment of the " Children of the Chapel Royal " who had recently established themselves as a theatrical company.   He even raises the question of the actor's legitimate share in the benefits of the association.

He raises from oblivion an old tragedy in which he had collaborated, and has a whole scene of it recited as a model of dramatic description.   What is the use of all this, wonders the spectator in the midst of a tirade which causes the actor who speaks it to weep and change colour ?   What is Hecuba doing here ?   The answer is that, though the audience may be unaware of it, this scene is one of the most striking in literature.   The artificial emotion of a professional player is the means of awaking in Hamlet the realization of his own inaction.   If a common actor sheds torrents of tears over the lot of a Trojan Queen long since lost in the mists of time, how can he, Hamlet, remain inert in the presence of a foul crime of which his beloved father has been the victim ?   All these secondary episodes, grafted upon the central plot, all these excursions into contemporary topics, are Shakespeare's method of applying realism to an archaic subject and of capturing the spectators' attention while the inexorable drama is unfolded.

Numerous references to the tragedy of *Hamlet* made before there was any thought of printing it are still in existence.   The earliest is dated 1589, the last 1598.   The first as usual reflects hostile criticism.   In 1589, Nashe called the author of *Hamlet* a jack of all trades and decried his play because it abounded in tragical speeches borrowed from Seneca.[1]   In 1594, Lodge and Greene in their *Looking-glass for London*,[2] parody the ghost scene, while

---

[1] Nashe's preface to *Menaphon.*

[2] Alas Sir, your father, why Sir mee-thinks I see the Gentleman stil, a proper youth he was faith aged some foure & ten, his beard rats colour, halfe blacke, halfe white, his nose was in the highest degree of noses. (*A Looking-glass for London and England.* Made by Thomas Lodge gentleman and Robert Greene gentleman in Artibus Magister. Thomas Creede, 1598.)

Henslowe [1] records in the same year that the Lord Chamberlain's players received eight shillings for a performance of their *Hamlet*. In 1596, Lodge in his pamphlet *Wit's Miserie*, described a fiend as :

Pale as the vizard of the ghost which cried so miserably at the theater, like an oysterwife, Hamlet—Revenge.

and Dekker makes one of the characters of his revue, *Satiro-Mastix*, say :

My name's Hamlet—Revenge ; thou hast been at Paris Garden, hast not ? [2]

Finally, Gabriel Harvey, writing possibly as early as 1598, gives the impression that the drama was already well known, remarking that :

The younger set take much delight in Shakespeare's *Venus and Adonis* but his *Lucrece* and his *Tragedy of Hamlet prince of Danemark* have it in them to please the wiser sort.[3]

Is it necessary to find fault with Shakespeare if his first version of *Hamlet* was melodramatic ? The taste of the day demanded that sort of play ; the public enjoyed exaggerated performances, it applauded the declamations of Richard Burbage in *Hieronimo ;* and it was this " juvenile lead ", idol of the public, who was invariably given the part of Hamlet as long as he lived. It must be remembered that *Titus Andronicus*, the most brutal of all the Shakespearean repertory, judged severely by Ben Jonson, was welcomed at this time with much enthusiasm.

In spite of academic diatribes, *Hamlet* has brilliantly held its own from that day to this, and in every country.[4]

---

[1] Henslowe's Diary Dulwich MS. Beginning at Newington my lord Admirall's men & lord Chamberlen men As Followeth : *The Jewe of Malta*, X. S., *Andronicus*, XI. S., *Hamlet*, VIII, S.

[2] *Satiro-Mastix* or The untrussing of the Humorous Poet. As it hath been presented publikely, by the Right Honorable the Lord Chamberlaine his Servants ; and privately, by the Children of Paules, by Thomas Dekker for Edward White, 1602.

[3] Contemporary allusions to Shakespeare's *Hamlet* are innumerable. Many refer to the first version and the name Hamlet is always accompanied by the word " revenge ". Here are some examples :

" when light Wives make heavy husbands, let these husbands play mad Hamlet ; and crie revenge " (*Westward Hoe*, As it hath beene divers times Acted by the Children of Paules T. Dekker and J. Webster.)

" Hamlet, are you madde ? whether run you now . . . put on your blew cote and waite upon Mistriss Toochstone " (*Eastward Hoe*, Act III, Sc. 2, by Geo. Chapman, Ben Jonson and J. Marston).

" Government, [in Russia] was but as the Poeticall Furie in a Stage-action, . . . no second to any Hamlet ; and that now Revenge, iust Revenge was comming with his Sworde." (Sir Thomas Smithes *Voiage and Entertainment in Rushia With the tragicall ends of two Emperors and one Empresse, within one Moneth during his being there*. London, 1605.)

I will not crie " Hamlet revenge my greeves ".
But I will call " Hangman revenge on theeves ".
(*The Night Raven*, Samuel Rowlands)

[4] Even in the author's lifetime, *Hamlet* was one of the most frequently acted plays. A captain on an African voyage says in his diary that on September 1607, the crew of the *Dragon* gave a performance of *Hamlet* on the coast of Sierra Leone, in honour of the visit of the king's brother, Boera. (*Narratives of voyages towards the North-West*, Hakluyt Soc. 1849.)

On July 26th, 1602, the publisher James Roberts entered in the Stationers' Register a manuscript work entitled.

the Revenge of Hamlet, prince of Denmarke, as yt was lateli Acted by the lord Chamberleyne his servantes . . . VI d.[1]

This request for a printing licence had no result ; publication was not authorized, and for a good reason.   Both company and author shared the Queen's disfavour.   Southampton, the great patron, was languishing in the Tower.   Lord Essex had died not long since beneath the axe.   Many were those both friends and enemies who distinguished some traits of the Queen's ex-favourite in Hamlet's introspective character.   Author and actors were associated with the recent plot and all these factors rendered it impossible to obtain official permission to print.   But in the provinces and at the universities, *Hamlet* was acted.   At the Scottish court it was naturally well received by the King, who flattered himself on being a poet, and by the Queen, who was a Danish princess.

In 1603, the political situation had completely changed.   James I occupied Elizabeth's throne ;   Shakespeare and his comrades had become the " King's players ".

In this year, the first quarto edition of *Hamlet* appeared.   One copy is in the British Museum ;   it was bought in Dublin in 1856 by a student who gave a shilling for it, and was afterwards acquired for the sum of seventy pounds ;   a second copy is in the possession of the Huntington Library, California, discovered by Sir Herbert Bunbury in 1823.   Luckily these two volumes complete one another, as a different page is missing from each.

The title reads :

THE
Tragicall Historie of
HAMLET
Prince of Denmarke
By William Shake-speare.
As it hath beene diverse times acted by his Highnesse
seruants in the Cittie of London : as also in the two
Vniuersities of Cambridge and Oxford, and else-where.
At London printed for N.L. and John Trundell, 1603.

This text, divided neither into acts nor scenes is much abbreviated (two thousand one hundred and forty-three lines).   The second version printed a year later contains three thousand seven hundred and nine lines.

This version is more emphatic and less polished than the later ones. There is little psychology throughout and no outstanding study of character. Queen Gertrude is represented as ignorant of her second husband's crime and when she learns from Hamlet of this deed she consents to aid his project of revenge.   On this point Shakespeare followed the story as related by both Saxo Grammaticus and Belleforest.

[1] 26 julii James Robertes. Entred for his Copie under the handes of master Pasefeild and master Waterson, warden.   A booke called *The Revenge of Hamlett, etc.*

Unfortunately this text is full of misprints and even mistakes in the transcription of whole sentences, which indicates that it was taken down by a scribe who had difficulty in following the rapid dialogue. The spelling of some words makes it evident that he was guided mainly by ear. The scenes of quick action and vehement language are more faulty than those that move slowly.

It is only by comparison with the quarto edition which appeared the following year that these textual errors can be rectified. Thus one reads

Invelmorable	*for invulnerable*
Plate	*for Plautus*
Guyana	*for Vienna*
Capapea	*for Cap-à-pied*
Rosencraft	*for Rosencrantz*
Gilderstone	*for Guildenstern*

Some proper names are completely altered. Ophelia's father appears as Corambis instead of Polonius, his servant as Montano instead of Reynaldo.

It has been suggested that the text of 1603 was due to one of those numerous literary piracies of which authors and serious publishers continually complained at this time. This is a possibility. Heywood affirms that a few of his own plays reached the press without his knowledge and were passed on to the public in such a mutilated condition as to be hardly recognizable.

In the edition of 1603, the stage directions are very complete, showing that the transcriber was present at a performance. Not only are the names of the characters given as they enter or leave the stage but their description, and sometimes their attitude is defined. For example:

Enter Ofelia playing on a Lute, and her haire downe, singing.

In the duel scene, the action may be followed in the margin : the moment when the foils engage, the first hit and the next bout ; then : " They catch one another's Rapiers and both are wounded, Laertes falles downe, the Queene Falles downe and dies."

In short, when corrected of its glaring faults, the text of 1603 remains as a skilful and artistic play not far inferior to that of 1604. It was well adapted to the exigencies of the time, to the primitive stages rigged up on trestles with which the company had to content themselves when on tour.

Eight actors sufficed to the whole play. The sentinels of the first episode could reappear later as Rosencrantz and Guildenstern. These courtiers in their turn were available to take over the gravediggers' parts. The ghost and Laertes were free when the troupe of players arrived at Elsinore. Four actors with no other part at that point could re-enter as the soldiers of Fortinbras in the final scene : the youth who played Ophelia might also take the part of the effeminate and pretentious Osric.

The performance of *Hamlet* at the " Globe " was quite different, judging by the stage directions of the quarto of 1604. Here in this relatively well

equipped theatre the difficulties were attenuated. The proscenium could
be transformed with the help of properties into the castle ramparts, Polonius'
apartment or the throne-room. A plain or a cemetery in Denmark could
be represented with equal ease. The recess with its curtain provided the
king and Polonius with a hiding place. The touring actors found there a
small stage for their play, later the same alcove served as an oratory for
Claudius. The pantomime which precedes the murder of Gonzago was
acted on the balcony, thus explaining why the royal couple did not stop the
performance of the *Mouse-trap* during the dumb-show, which to them
remained invisible.

A comparison between the texts of 1603 and 1604 would lead to this
conclusion : the first version contains the dominant thoughts which are
developed and commented upon in the second. What the first loses in
philosophic depth, it sometimes gains in vigour. The first is within everyone's reach, the second sometimes borders on preciosity. It seems fair to
give the famous soliloquy in both texts for the sake of comparison :

Text of 1603 :

> To be, or not to be, I there's the point,
> To Die, to sleepe, is that all ?   I all :
> No, to sleepe, to dreame, I mary there it goes,
> For in that dreame of death, when we awake,
> And borne before an everlasting Judge,
> From whence no passenger ever return'd,
> The undiscovered country, at whose sight
> The happy smile, and the accursed damn'd.
> But for this, the joyfull hope of this,
> Whol'd beare the scornes and flattery of the world,
> Scorned by the right rich, the rich curssed of the poore ?
> The widow being oppressed, the orphan wrong'd,
> The taste of hunger, or a tirants raigne,
> And thousand more calamities besides,
> To grunt and sweate under this weary life,
> When that he may his full Quietus make
> With a bare bodkin, who would this indure,
> But for a hope of something after death ?
> Which pusles the braine, and doth confound the sence
> Which makes us rather beare those evilles we have,
> Than flie to others that we know not of.
> I that, O this conscience makes cowardes of us all. . . .

Text of 1604 :

> To be, or not to be, that is the question,
> Whether tis nobler in the minde to suffer
> The slings and arrowes of outragious fortune,
> Or to take Armes against a sea of troubles,
> And by opposing, end them, to die to sleepe
> No more, and by a sleepe, to say we end
> The hart-ake, and the thousand naturall shocks

That flesh is heire to ; tis a consumation
Devoutly to be wisht to die to sleepe,
To sleepe, perchance to dreame, I there's the rub,
For in that sleepe of death what dreames may come
When we have shuffled off this mortall coyle
Must give us pause, there's the respect
That makes calamitie of so long life :
For who would beare the whips and scornes of time,
Th' oppressors wrong, the proude mans contumely,
The pangs of despiz'd love, the lawes delay,
The insolence of office, and the spurnes
That patient merrit of th' unworthy takes
When he himselfe might his quietas make
With a bare bodkin ; who would fardels beare,
To grunt and sweat under a wearie life,
But that the dread of something after death,
The undiscover'd country, from whose bourne
No traviler returnes, puzzels the will,
And makes us rather beare those ills we have
Than flie to others that we know not of,
Thus conscience dooes make cowards,
And thus the native hiew of resolution
Is sickled ore with the pale cast of thought,
And enterprises of great pitch and moment,
With this regard theyr currents turne awry,
And loose the name of action. . . .[1]

The Quarto of 1604 contains a complete version of the tragedy of *Hamlet*. Even from the typographic point of view, it contains few faults. The title, identical with that of 1603, continues thus :

By William Shakespeare.
Newly imprinted and enlarged to almost as much againe
as it was, according to the true and perfect Coppie.[2]

Such an announcement to the reader made with the author's approval, when the dramatist enjoyed popular favour and the full confidence of a literary king, is proof that this volume contained a text sanctioned by Shakespeare himself. It reappeared unchanged the next year, 1605, and remained the sole authorized version until the edition of 1623.

The Quarto of 1604 is therefore the first text which can be called complete. It is perhaps too complete, and I am inclined to believe that the author

---

[1] It will be noticed that the first version conforms to the teaching of the Roman Catholic Church. The second influenced by a more abstract philosophy, verges on free thought.

[2] At London printed by I.R. for N.L. and are to be sold at his shoppe under St. Dunstan's Church in Fleet Street, 1604.
The quarto of 1605 and that of 1607 have the same title ; in 1611 publication rights were legally acquired by John Smethwick and the quarto edition of this date appeared under the name and sign of this firm. In the Folio of 1623, the play appeared in the index simply under the title : *The Tragedie of Hamlet ;* it occupies seventh place between the tragedies of *Macbeth* and *King Lear*.

himself, after mature reflection agreed to the abridgements applied to the 1623 folio, wisely concluding that the quarto texts of 1604 and 1605 were immoderately long.

These variations, however, have always troubled the critics : if one text is good, the other must necessarily be bad. They would like to think that Shakespeare never made any rough sketches of his work, or that he carefully destroyed them after successive improvements. On the contrary we ought to take the view that all these modifications indicate his desire to seek perfection and make continual improvements.

Many volumes have been written about the acting of *Hamlet*, just as the true rendering of Molière's Alceste has also been much discussed. To present the man with green ribbons as a misanthropist so bitter that he is incapable of love, and the Prince of Denmark so melancholy in his solemn black as to be incapable of action, is to transform eccentricities arising from virtues into irremediable defects. Like a well cut diamond, Hamlet has so many façets that the actor who undertakes this rôle is sometimes tempted to shine in one aspect to the detriment of others. Woe to him who allows himself to stress a single side of this complex and subtly presented character. To exaggerate the melancholy for example, or to permit the pretended madness to dominate a fine intelligence, would ruin the drama as a whole.

Fortunately for posterity the author of *Hamlet* left behind him an approved text and also a tradition. His hero is depicted as the very flower of civilization, a man morally sane and physically sound, a model for his contemporaries. He has a soldier's courage and probity, the brain of a statesman, the heart of a Christian. In short he stands as the final expression, the *Nec plus ultra*, of his creator's ideal of manhood.[1]

Besides an impeccable text passed three or four times through the mills of criticism, Shakespeare has bequeathed to us a precious stage tradition in which no link is lacking. He himself kindled the flame which passed unextinguished from Burbage, Lowen, Betterton, Harte, Garrick, Kemble, Kean, Booth, Macready, Forest, Irving and Forbes Robertson to those few of our own day who possess enough intelligence, literary integrity and artistic conscience to keep the torch burning.

---

[1] The Romantic school, in adopting Hamlet, was inspired neither by his wise speeches nor his noble sentiments, but retained mainly the paradoxes he utters when feigning madness. A breath of Hell seems to have passed over him and robbed him of his true nature to produce such perversions of the real Hamlet as Manfred, Werther and Lorenzaccio.

CHAPTER XIV

THE RISING SUN

Consequences of Essex' death—Shakespeare and his company disappear from London, and twelve English actors under the management of Lawrence Fletcher are mentioned as being in Scotland—King James and the witches—*Macbeth*— The players return to London.

THE death sentence pronounced against Southampton was not carried out, but the young lord remained a prisoner in the Tower, cut off from his family and from the world of letters. His former tutor, Giovanni Florio, was one of the first to seek new patronage outside the kingdom. Even before the political storm burst, Florio, prudent as he was " resolute ", broke all ties with " the malcontents " and set off for Scotland.[1]

There exists among the State Papers a letter addressed to him by Niccolo Molino dated August 10th, 1600, wherein it is hinted that Robert Cecil desires to have his receipt for documents sent by post into Scotland. Does this prove as Arthur Acheson [2] and Miss Yates suggest that Southampton's former professor was profiting by his visit to Edinburgh to inform Cecil of what the Essex party was fomenting in the Scottish Court ? Not necessarily ; since the day of the Earl's disgrace, there were many satellites who, having revolved round the deputy Lieutenant's orb, felt drawn towards the rising sun. Thanks to his initiative Florio obtained an excellent post as reader, secretary and Gentleman of the Chamber to Queen Anne, who greatly prided herself upon her taste for the Tuscan language.

Shakespeare and his company, however, fell under suspicion for their connection with Essex, Southampton and the rebels. On February 18th, 1601, at the conclusion of the trial of no less than ninety accused persons, including five earls, three lords and sixteen knights, Augustine Phillips was

---

[1] It is interesting to read in the dictionary dedicated to " the Imperiall Maiestie of the Highest-borne Princes, Anna of Denmarke, by God's permission, Crowned Queene of England ; Scotland, France & Ireland ", the definition which Florio gives of the unusual word Ecniphia : a kind of prodigious storme comming in Summer with furious flashings the firmament seeming to open and burne, as happned when the Earle of Essex departed from London to goe to Ireland.

[2] Arthur Acheson, *Shakespeare's Sonnet Story* (London, Bernard Quaritch, p. 528) ; the future Venetian ambassador's letter is thus worded : " molto magnifico signor mio, Mandai a vostra la settimana passata li reposti si come facio al presente por la posta poi inviati inscotia conforme all' ordine lasciatomi dal sign. Secretario dalla Majesta della regina, mi sara caro e intender la recevuta." (S.P. Dom. Eliz. vol. 275, no. 46.)

summoned before the Privy Council to answer an accusation brought against his troupe and the author of *Richard II*.[1]

No trace remains of measures taken to punish the servants of the Lord Chamberlain, but in view of the severity of the authorities towards the theatre, probably the players suffered a penalty at least as severe as that inflicted on Nashe and Jonson when the *Isle of Dogs* was interdicted. Six months prohibition from playing was in those days too light a punishment for a company considered guilty of a serious misdemeanour.

Whatever the sentence, Shakespeare and his fellows disappeared from the theatrical world and from London on the morrow of these tragic events. No trace of them can be found in the capital or anywhere else in England. Yet Shakespeare's father died on September 8th at Stratford, and this event normally should have brought his eldest son back to his family. The absence of the poet seems more curious still when on May 1st, 1602, he bought from William and John Combe " one hundred and seven acres of arable land near Stratford " for the considerable sum of three hundred and twenty pounds. The local archives mention that the act of transfer was sealed and handed to his brother Gilbert " acting on behalf of the said within-named William Shakespeare ".[2]

If the author of *Richard II* was neither in London, Stratford nor on tour in the provinces where there is no record of his passage, it is logical to seek him in a situation which might explain the signal favours he was soon to receive from King James. It would also explain why the name of Lawrence Fletcher suddenly appears before Shakespeare's as heading the list of the King's Players incorporated at the very beginning of the new régime. Lorentio Fletcher was slated in Scotland as " comediane serviture " of his Majesty and the twelve English players who suddenly appeared at the Scottish court were placed under his direction.

The prestige enjoyed by this actor in his master's eyes must have been great, since, as soon as the rumour that he had been hanged in England reached Edinburgh, King James sent for Roger Aston, Elizabeth's envoy, and told him, " If this be true, I will have you hanged also ".[3] The monarch looked upon the theatre as the best possible means of propaganda and did not object to the appearance of Queen Anne in the private performances of plays at court. He even defied his clergy on this point and obliged the Edinburgh pastors to cease their fulminations against the stage.

---

[1] The report of Augustine Phillips' interrogation is as follows : " He sayeth that on Friday last was sennyght on Thursday Sir Charles Percy, Sir Joscelyne Percy and the Lord Monteagle with some three more spake to some of the players in the presens of thys Examinate to have the play of the deposyng and kyllyng of King Richard the second, to be played the Saterday next promysing to geve them xls more then their ordynary to play yt. When this Examinate and his fellowes were determyned to have play'd some other play, holdyng that the play of King Richard to be so old and so long out of use as that they shold have small or no Company at it. But at their request this Examinate and his fellowes were Content to play yt the Saterday and had their xls more then their ordinary for yt and so played yt accordingly."

[2] Stratford Archives, Birthplace Museum.

[3] Aston and Nicholson, *State Papers, Eliz.*, Scotch series, lv, 59.

Fletcher had enlisted in London in 1599 a young English actor, Martin Slaughter, who had once played the part of the page in *Romeo and Juliet*. In 1601, he returned to Scotland accompanied this time not by Slaughter, but by a dozen English actors whose names are unknown. After the troupe had entertained the public in Edinburgh it was sent by royal orders to Dunfermline [1] to play before the Queen, afterwards to Aberdeen, where many traces of its visit are extant, then to Inverness.

The journey at that time between Edinburgh and Inverness, by way of Glamis, Aberdeen, Cawdor, Birnam and Dunsinane was deemed perilous ; it was prudent to travel in large numbers. Accordingly the king synchronized the players' expedition [2] with the arrival of an important visitor, the noble gentleman François de l'Hôpital,[3] who desired to see the wild beauties of the kingdom. The Aberdeen registers show that the suite included thirty persons. The French chevalier was accompanied by MM. de Scheyne and La Bone [sic.] ; by three Scotsmen, Sir Claude Hamilton, Sir John Grahame and Sir John Ramsay, escorted by their servants, several arquebusiers and the king's trumpeter, Archibald Sym. At Aberdeen, one of Scotland's richest towns, the visitors were received in great pomp by provost William Cullen and the local notabilities. They sojourned there from October 9th until the end of the month. A personal letter from King James recommending the actors assured them of a warm welcome. A special performance was given in the town hall and the troupe was offered a supper [4] by the municipality.

The historian William Guthrie declared in 1767, that he had serious reasons for thinking that Shakespeare was one of these actors. Charles

---

[1] In the Edinburgh municipal archives one finds the royal order to dispatch twelve feather beds to Dunfermline for the English actors. The fine palace of Linlithgow at Dunfermline, situated by a romantic lake, had been sumptuously furnished by James V for Princess Madeleine of France, daughter of François 1st, then for Marie de Lorraine, who became the mother of his only legitimate child, Mary Stuart. Linlithgow, much improved by Queen Anne, whose favourite residence it was during her fourteen years as queen in Scotland, received visits several times from the players.

[2] This fashion of making use of the actors' services and employing them as guards of honour was personal to King James. Later when the Constable of Castile came to London, His Majesty's Players, then Lawrence Fletcher, William Shakespeare, Richard Burbage and the rest of the troupe, fulfilled the duties of grooms waiting and attending upon the Spanish grandee in the scarlet livery of His Majesty's Chamber.

[3] 1601, Oct. 23. The Quhilk day Sir Francis Hospitall of Haulzie knycht frencheman being recommendit be his majestie to the provest Baillies and counsall of this burt to be favourablie Intertenit, with the gentilmen his majesties servandis efterspect, quha war direct to this burt be his Majestie to accompanie the saie frenchman, being ane noble man of France Cuming onlie to this burt to sie the town and countrie the said frenchemen with the knightis and gentilmen following wer all reesavit and admittit Burghesses of gild of this burt quha gave aythis in commun form. (Extract from the *Aberdeen Council Register* vol. xl.)

[4] The payment made on the occasion of this supper is thus entered in the municipal account book :

   Discharge. Item, to the stage playeris, Inglischmen, XXXII lib.
           Item, for the stage playaris supper that nicht thaye plaiid to the towne.
       iii lib.

(*Aberdeen Council Register*, vol. xl, fol. 210.)

Knight supported this opinion, held also by George Wyndham,[1] Carmichael Stopes [2] and Felix Schelling.[3]

The piece of direct evidence which would finally have solved the mystery is missing, like so many untraceable documents of the " Shakespeare dossier ". The letter addressed by King James to the municipality of Aberdeen is no longer in the town archives.[4] The poet's godson William d'Avenant possessed another letter to Shakespeare signed by the King of Scots, but this document, said to have been very complimentary, has also disappeared.[5]

If the principal members of the " Globe " company were not among the actors associated with Fletcher, it is difficult to explain Shakespeare's presence at his side when they returned to London ; the privilege granted them by the new sovereign upon his arrival in his new capital (May 19th, 1603), would also be inexplicable. The document places Fletcher and Shakespeare on an equal footing and its wording implies that these players' services had been already appreciated by James of Scotland.[6]

Patent Roll, 1 Jas. I, part II.

James by the grace of god &c To all Justices Maiors Sheriffes Constables hedborowes and other our Officers and lovinge Subiectes greetinge knowe yee that wee of our speciall grace certeine knoweledge & mere motion have licenced and aucthorized . . . theise our servauntes Lawrence Fletcher William Shake-

---

[1] This commentator thought he saw in *Hamlet* an allusion to the Shakespeare troupe's journey outside the kingdom. His remarks have some value. When the prince asks why the city tragedians travel when they must be able to earn more at home, he is told that perhaps " their inhibition comes by the means of the late innovation ", from the fact that the boy actors carry all before them even Hercules and his load. This passage was slightly altered in the *Hamlet* editions of 1603, 1604 and in the final version. " The late innovation " is an evident allusion to the rival company, the Children of the Chapel Royal, who played Ben Jonson's *Cynthia's Revels*, and who had dispossessed Shakespeare and his fellows from Blackfriars theatre. The inhibition referred to and the tour undertaken by the Load of Hercules, otherwise the " Globe " troupe, could very well be applied to the actors' enforced departure from London, and all the more as this prohibition is not mentioned in the first text of *Hamlet*, which is the only version printed before the probable journey to Scotland.

[2] In a paper read on February 24th, 1897, before the Royal Society of Literature, this conscientious critic gave numerous reasons in support of her thesis.

[3] Nothing could have been more natural or more consonant with the worldly thrift that we know to have been Shakespeare's than for him to have arranged thus cleverly to anticipate the patronage of the Sovereign " to come " and nothing could have been more natural than that Lawrence Fletcher, already experienced in Scotland and personally known to King James, should have been selected to lead the troupe thither rather than an old sharer. (Felix Schelling, *Elizabethan Drama*, Houghton Mifflin, 1908.)

[4] An Ordinance of the Dean of Gild of Aberdeen dated October 9th, 1601, orders that " threttie twa merkis to be gevin to the Kingis Seruances presently in this burcht quha playes comedeis and staige playes Be reasoun they are recommendit be his majesties speciall letter. . . ."

[5] Bernard L. Lintot, editor of Shakespeare's poems in 1710, affirms that King James wrote a friendly letter to Shakespeare in his own hand. It long remained in the possession of Sir William Davenant where it was seen by a trustworthy person who was still alive. Oldys supposes that this personage was the Duke of Buckingham, who died in 1721.

[6] This document is in a glass case in the Museum of the Public Record Office. Fletcher has first place, probably because the King had known him for many years. But it is noticeable that in the eyes of the troupe he was not the leader. When Augustine Phillips died in 1605, he left to his " Fellowe William Shakespeare a thirtie shillings in gould ", and to his " fellowe Lawrence Fletcher twenty shillings ", an indication that Shakespeare, in his view, remained the most important personage of the company.

speare Richard Burbage Agustyne Phillippes, Johm Hemings Henrie Condell William Sly Robert Armyn Richard Cowly and the rest of theire Associates freely to use and exercise the Arte and faculty of playinge Commedies Tragedies histories Enterludes moralls pastoralls Stageplaies and suche others like as theie have alreadie studied or hereafter shall use or studie aswell for the recreation of our lovinge Subiectes as for our Solace and pleasure when wee shall thincke good to see them duringe our pleasure And the said Commedies tragedies histories Enterludes Morrall Pastoralls Stageplayes and suche like to shewe and exercise publiquely to theire best Commoditie when the infection of the plague shall decrease aswell within theire nowe usuall howse called the Globe within our County of Surrey as alsoe within anie towne halls or moute halls or other conveniente places within the liberties and freedome of anie other Cittie Universitie towne or Boroughe whatsoever within our said Realme and Domynions.

Willing and Commanding you and everie of you as you tender our Pleasure, not onlie to permit and suffer them herein, without anie your letts, Hindrances or Molestations during our saied Pleasure but also to be aiding and assistinge to them of anie Wrong be to them offered and to allow them such former Curtesies as hath been given to men of their place and qualitie ; and also what further favour you shall shewe to theise our servaunts for our sake wee shall take kindly at our landes. Witnesse ourselfe at Westminster the nynetenth day of Maye, *Per breve de privato sigillo.* Jacobus R.[1]

It is remarkable that James did not even wait to be sovereign of England to accord to his troupe the title of the King's Players, for on May 30th, 1602, the actors, doubtless returning from Scotland, gave a performance at Ipswich where their payment is thus entered in the municipal register :

To His Majesty's Players, as gratification, twenty-five shillings eightpence.

The whole tragedy of *Macbeth* seems to bear the imprint of this adventurous journey. Shakespeare would not have been able to construct his drama or collect his detailed documentation without having visited the localities in which its action takes place. From beginning to end, *Macbeth* is soaked in the atmosphere of Scotland. The forbidding heather-covered mountains, the " blasted heath " the harsh pine forests and the grey stone castles haunted by the ghosts of murdered guests contrast with the soft climate of Inverness looking towards the south, sheltered from the wind, where the delicate air invites the martlet to build his nest on the castle walls. *Macbeth* presents the spectator with a realistic landscape. There is nothing second-hand here in the author's strongly felt impressions. His characters are true Scots, at home in this rough and bleak countryside. The inhabitants of these mountains, woods, heaths and caves are no longer the good people of Stratford nor the citizens of London, as in Shakespeare's previous plays where his practice was to transport his familiar friends to Rome, Athens, Paris or Verona.

Banquo's first question : " How far is't called to Forres ? " is an essentially Scottish idiom. " Quell " for murder, " skirr " for search, " latch "

[1] Patent Roll, 1 Ja. I.

instead of catch, "gruel" for soup, "slab" for sticky, "cribbed" for enclosed, are northern words which Shakespeare uses only in *Macbeth*. The extent to which he discards his usual vocabulary in writing this drama is remarkable for here there are two hundred and forty-four words or expressions which he uses nowhere else in the same sense ; [1] the proper names chosen for the notables of the country are precisely those of James's court : Ross, Lennox, Menteith, Angus, Caithness and Seyton.

The story of *Macbeth* which the poet had read in Holinshed was not this time the principal source of his argument.   It was the *Chronicles* of William Stewart,[2] read on the spot, which enabled him to develop his tragedy in the political direction desired.   For it must not be forgotten that this play was intended first of all as propaganda in favour of James's claim to the throne of England.   The popular mind had been prepared by *Richard II* for Elizabeth's abdication ; now, with *Macbeth*, Shakespeare was advocating the union of both crowns.

The dramatist's treatment of Banquo's character is completely different from the tradition established by Holinshed who makes the Scottish lord an accomplice in Duncan's murder.   Drawing on Stewart's account, Shakespeare idealized this Scottish chief.   Macbeth, conscious of his own inferiority, admits that his genius is dominated by that of Banquo, just as Mark Antony's was by Caesar's.   The innate nobility of Banquo's personality is shown upon his first appearance.   Seeing that Macbeth dares not raise his eyes and question the weird sisters, he summons them in the name of truth, to reveal the future to a man who is able to hear good or evil fortune with equal serenity.

> If you can look into the seeds of time,
> And say which grains will grow and which will not,
> Speak then to me, who neither beg nor fear
> Your favours nor your hate.[3]
>
> (*Macbeth*, Act 1, Sc. 3)

Stewart's work, written with the intention of flattering the line to which James belonged, that is to say Banquo and his descendants, to the detriment of Macbeth, was most valuable to Shakespeare and was unknown in England at that time.   It was not printed until 1858, and then by a learned society ; [4] but the Scottish King, "apprentice in the divine art of poesy", possessed the book and used to comment upon it.

---

[1] *The Henry Irving Shakespeare*, vol. v, p. 429.

[2] William Stewart, poet, "magister in artibus" of the University of Saint Andrews, and cousin of the King of Scotland, was commissioned by the dowager Queen Margaret Tudor, eldest sister of Henry VIII to translate the latin *Chronicles* of Boece into verse for her son, the future James VI.   Begun on April 18th, 1551, the work was finished at the end of September 1558.   About the same time, Archdeacon John Bellenden translated the *Chronicles* of Boece, the principal source of Holinshed's own *Chronicles*, into Scots prose.

[3] The accusation against one of the Aberdeen witches, affirms that by walking through a field of corn she could recognize the crops which would yield good or bad harvests.

[4] Rolls Series.

A glance at Stewart's text shows that the encounter with the witches is taken from the Scotch chronicle, not from Holinshed.

> In Forres town where that this King Duncan
> Happened to be with many noblemen,
> Where Macobey and Banquo one ane day
> Passeth at morne right early for to play
> The hand-for-hand until a forest green,
> Three women met, that wisely were beseen
> In their clothing which was of eldritch hue
> And what they were was none of them that knew
> The first of them that Macobey came to
> " The Thane of Glames, good morn to him " said she
> The second said, withouten any scorn
> " The Thane of Cawdor, sir, give you good morn."
> The hindmost, with a pleasant voice benyng
> " God save you, sir, of Scotland shall be King ! "
> Then Banquo said : " Abide a little wee ;
> Ye give him all, what ordain ye for me ? " . . .
> " Thou, Banquo, take good tent unto this thing :
> Thou thine own self shalt ne'er be prince or King
> But of thy seed shall lineally descend
> Shall wear the crown until the world is end."
> When this was said, they bade all three good night
> Syne suddenly they vanished out of sight,
> And where away ? Whether to heaven or hell
> Of what they were, was no man yet can tell.[1]

This excerpt shows that Shakespeare followed the narration closely ; but in his description of the supernatural beings who foretell the future it is evident that the poet does not give us Stewart's well-dressed and well-spoken damsels clad in fairy green, still less the sybils of the antique world described by Holinshed, but something much more like the bearded hags with whose persons and gruesome practices King James was so familiar and whom he considered the devil's agents and enemies of mankind.

James Stewart was the man best versed of his time in the occult sciences. His study of *Daemonology* [2] is remarkable as the product of long experience of sorcerers.[3] He had been present in person at many trials of sorcerers

---

[1] Stewart, *Chronicles of Scotland*, vol. ii.

[2] *Daemonologie* in form of a dialogue printed by Robert Waldegrave, Edinburgh, 1597.

[3] The King of Scots had published in 1592 a book founded upon his own experiences, *Newes from Scotland* (William Wright, London). In this little volume, he describes " the atrocious life of the notable sorcerer, Dr. Fian ", whose trial he followed, and whose interrogation he conducted. Fian was burned at Edinburgh. The king was present at many other trials of this sort. In 1596 he set up a commission including the provost of Aberdeen and its town council, to judge witches and sorcerers ; in the course of one year, twenty-three women and one man found guilty of sorcery, were put to death, and a quantity of others were banished or severely punished. The reports of these trials were published in 1841 by the Spalding Society.

and witches [1] and held this tribe responsible for having raised a storm which had almost cost him his life and had caused the loss of the ship carrying his wedding presents to the Princess Anne.   He believed that Satan always found his most artful proselytes among old women.   Having himself experienced their malignity, he warns his readers against frequenting magicians and fortune-tellers.   This royal warning against all commerce with the "evil spirit" is repeated not without bitterness by Macbeth, who had only too often disregarded it:

> And be these juggling fiends no more believ'd,
> That palter with us in a double sense ;
> That keep the word of promise to our ear,
> And break it to our hope.
>
> *(Macbeth*, Act v, Sc. 8)

The witches conjured up by Shakespeare before Macbeth and Banquo recite their infernal misdeeds.   They tell of their nocturnal voyages in sieves, of how they command the wind to raise storms, of their spells causing animals to die, men to waste away and harvests to fail.   Their language reveals their sinister practices.   They speak of noxious herbs, gathered at midnight beneath gibbets or in cemeteries, poisoned entrails, venomous toads, lizard's leg, dragon's scale, hemlock root, newborn baby's finger. It is upon a windswept heath amidst rolling thunder and lightning flashes that they conduct their mysterious rites.

The desolate country between Nairn and Forres where they first appear to the travellers, is characteristic of Scottish folklore.   The three ragged bearded and skinny witches call to mind Agnes Thomson, Janet Wishart and Violet Leys, the unfortunate victims of the cruel Inquisition at Aberdeen described by King James in his *Newes from Scotland*.[2]

[1] King James was present at the trial of Agnes Thomson and other witches who boasted of having raised a storm while his Majesty was on a voyage.   She was sent to sea with a whole concourse of sister-witches, each one riding in a riddle or sieve very substantially, to " Riddle or Ciue " to the Kirk of North Berwick.   There they took hands and danced singing all in one voice while the sorcerer, Giles Duncan, played upon a jew's trump.   At the trial this strange scene was re-enacted to the great satisfaction of the king.   Agnes Thomson confessed " that she took a black toade and did hang the same up by the heels three days and gathered the venome as it dropped and fell from it in an oister shell . . .". She took a cat and christened it which caused such a tempest that the vessel " wherein was sundrye Jewelles and rich gifts which should have been presented to the now Queen of Scotland " perished.   The ship in which James sailed would have met the same fate if the king's " faith had not prevailed above their intentions ".   See James's own book, *Newes from Scotland.*

[2] Discussing the nature of the three witches, Holinshed writes : " The common opinion was, that these women were eyther the weird sisters, that is (as ye would say) goddesses of destinie, or els some Nimphes or feeries, endewed with knowledge of prophesie by their nicromanticall science, because everything came to passe as they had spoken."   The Thane of Cawdor having been condemned for treason at Forres, his lands, duties and dependencies passed through the King's liberality to Macbeth.   Now, that very night, after supper, Banquo joked with him and said : " Now Macbeth thou haste obtayned those things which the two former sisters prophesied, there remayneth onely for thee to purchaseth at which the third sayd should come to passe."   Thereupon, Macbeth, turning over the matter in his mind, began to imagine how he could reach the kingdom. . . . At last, communicating his intentions to his most faithful friends chief among whom was Banquo, and trusting in their support, he murdered the king at Inverness in the sixth year of his reign.   (*Chronicles of England, Scotland and Ireland,* faithfully gathered and set forth by Ralph Holinshed (London, 1577), vol. i, p. 243.)

Shakespeare's witches interrupt their dances and lugubrious incantations to announce by their prophecy the subject of the drama. Macbeth, victor in a battle in which he has saved the kingdom, hears that he will be Thane of Glamis, Thane of Cawdor and later king ; his lieutenant Banquo will never be king, but his heirs will rule Scotland. Macbeth hastens to announce these tidings in a letter to his wife saying at the same time that King Duncan intends to honour them with a visit. This is enough to inflame the imagination of Lady Macbeth, whose criminal ambition becomes the mainspring of the tragedy.

Holinshed had barely sketched her portrait saying :

His wife lay sore upon him to attempt the thing as she that was very ambitious burning in unquenchable desire to bear the name of Queen.

On the other hand, Stewart's *Chronicle of Scotland* recalls her past and is more precise about her dominating character. Heiress in her own right to the throne of Scotland, she had seen her first husband perish in a fire kindled by enemy hands which destroyed her home and all her family, except for one son whom she carried into safety through the snow.[1] Macbeth gave her hospitable shelter and then married her in order to strengthen his right of succession to the throne of the aged King Duncan, whose son was too young to reign. The chief obstacle to Lady Macbeth's designs was the natural disposition of her husband, " too full of the milk of human kindness ". But by her subtle insinuations, taunts, and accusations of cowardice, she dispels his hesitation : " Only look up clear, . . . Leave all the rest to me ",[2] she says according to both Stewart and Shakespeare. The Scottish chronicler also suggests the charming welcome which she gives to King Duncan, at a time when the ravens themselves have filled the air with sinister forebodings.

Such are the sources on which the poet has drawn to build his subtle psychological study of a couple perfectly united in love as in crime. Danger, remorse, isolation from every human contact will never break the bonds which passion forged. Husband and wife go hand in hand into darkness. Responsibility for the first murder rests particularly on Lady Macbeth. The initial crime and its preparations are her work ; she would have struck the fatal blow herself if the sleeping Duncan had not reminded her of her father ; and it is she who thinks of returning to the scene of the crime to place the dagger near the prostrate guards so as to attract suspicion upon them.

With profound knowledge of the forces of the human heart, Shakespeare then develops the different effects of remorse and fear in these two dissimilar

[1] The allusion in *Macbeth* (Act I, Sc. 7) to this son : " I know how tender 'tis to love the babe that milks me ", is an indication that Shakespeare has followed Stewart's *Chronicle*, the only historian to mention Lady Macbeth's first marriage.

[2] Stewart's words are : " Only look up clear and leave the rest to me." The same thought and almost the same words are repeated by Lady Macbeth :

Only look up clear,
To alter favour ever is to fear ;
Leave all the rest to me.

(*Macbeth*, Act I, Sc. 5)

natures.   The rash and unscrupulous wife is stricken with fright and horror ;
she is haunted by nightmares ; she is unable to sleep ; madness lies in wait
for her.   All the perfumes of Arabia cannot remove the scent of blood from
her hand.   Macbeth, on the contrary, tender and imaginative by nature,
becomes, once his first crime is committed, a hardened assassin ready to
eliminate all who stand in his way.

Much of this sinister epic remains invisible to the spectators.   Shakespeare uses the same method here as in his dramatic poem, the *Rape of
Lucrece*, where, at dead of night, in the sudden glimmer of a wavering torch,
a few whispered words, footsteps in the stone corridors, the far-off screech
of an owl, the terrified exclamation of a semi-drunken watchman sustain the
impression of fear.

The weird sisters have early divulged the theme of the drama ; it is they
also who foretell its conclusion.   The usurper learns that no man of woman
born shall harm Macbeth.   But, greedy for power, he yearns to know all the
secrets of the future.   Unluckily for him, the ghost of Banquo, which had
already appeared at the coronation feast, comes again at the witches' summons
and proudly displays to his murderer a long line of kings of which he is the
progenitor.   All wear the crown of Scotland, and in the distance they carry
the triple sceptre of the three kingdoms.   The vision of this endless procession is nearer Stewart's text than that of Holinshed :

> But of thy seed sall linealie descend,
> Sall wear the crown until the world is end.
>
> (*Chronicles of Scotland*)

Shakespeare again closely follows Stewart when he describes Macbeth's
wonder at the news that the impossible has happened : Birnam Wood is
marching towards Dunsinane.   He then comprehends that he has been
merely a toy in the hands of occult powers and has sold his soul to win a
barren crown.

This drama, the shortest Shakespeare ever wrote, is also the least complicated ; no secondary action distracts attention from this epic of tragic
ambition.   Aeschylus himself never combined more power with such
simplicity.

Macbeth was not printed until 1623, where it occupies twenty pages of
the great folio, and is correctly placed between *Julius Caesar* and *Hamlet*.
The first publishers, who classified this magnificent play among the tragedies
of this period, were better inspired than some modern editors who class it
with the historical plays and assign too late a date to its composition.
Saturated as it is in the misty atmosphere of Scotland, it probably first
appeared under those skies inevitably associated with superstition and
folklore.

Whether the play was written in Scotland or in London, it was a work
imagined and realized with the intention of winning the favour of James
Stuart.   Not only was Banquo's line honoured, but the union of the two
crowns was foretold, and demonology, a subject very dear to James, was

dealt with in full conformity with his theories.   The first statute after his accession punished with death everyone who stole corpses from tombs or gallows for sorcery or similar purposes.   The struggle against necromancy, in which he saw Satan's triumph over the Christian world, was to him a divine mission ; and in *Macbeth* he saw the ideal propaganda play.

A reference to the meeting between the witches and the ancestor of his house was certain to please him ; when, on August 20th, 1605, the University of Oxford ceremoniously received the new king, Giovanni Florio's alter ego, Mathias Gwinne composed a Latin interlude performed by the best amateur actors among the students of St. John's.   Upon a stage erected at the northern entrance to the city, the initial episode was presented before the court.[1]   Three sibyls greeted King James as they were said to have welcomed his ancestor.   Then, kneeling before Queen Anne, they apostrophized her as " daughter, spouse and mother of kings ".   The two princes shared in the compliment, but the prophecy concerning them was not fulfilled.   Henry was to die before his parents ; the unfortunate Charles was destined to perish by the hands of his own subjects.

Some plays given in 1606 [2] or possibly before this date, contain allusions to *Macbeth*, notably John Marston's *Sophonisba*, and *The Puritaine* (author unknown), in which the chief character, Sir Godfrey Over Plus, recalls the apparition of Banquo's ghost at the feast, when he exclaims :

Instead of a clown we will have the ghost sitting in a white sheet at the end of the table.

A later date has sometimes been assigned to this tragedy on the grounds that Simon Forman describes in detail a performance at the " Globe ", which he saw on April 20th, 1610, observing that the appearance of the spectre provided a very striking dramatic effect.   He implied that Macbeth and Banquo entered the stage of the " Globe " on horseback.[3]

There are so many indications which point to an earlier date for the first performance of *Macbeth*, that it is evident that the spectacular performance recalled by Forman must have been a revival of the play, after the modern appliances which were to amaze, and sometimes shock the " Globe " spectators, had been perfected.

At midsummer 1602, Shakespeare's and Fletcher's company journeyed

[1] *Vertumnus* or the Oxonian Anniversary.   Enacted on the stage before King James, prince Henry, the nobles and the Johnsmen.   M.G. (London, Edward Blount, 1607).

[2] Many commentators have based their theory that the date of composition of *Macbeth* was 1606 upon the monologue of the porter (Act III, Sc. 3).   They see in his mention of a man ready to swear as loudly for one cause as another, an allusion to Father Garnett, sentenced and executed at the time of the Gunpowder Plot.   In the same comic character's remark about the suicide of a farmer after a bad harvest, they see a reference to the poor season of 1606.   Other deductions, but less reasonable, have been made from this speech.   However, I do not see any necessary link between the tragic drama of which Father Garnett was a victim and the porter's words about those who practise equivocation ; and as Malone has remarked, the price of corn in 1606, was not very different from the prices of 1605 and 1607.

[3] Simon Forman's *Booke of Playes* (MS. Bodley Ashmole 208).

through Bath, Shrewsbury, Coventry and Ipswich [1] where the troupe performed under the denomination of " His Majesty's players ".   Two payments made to the senior actor, Heminge, entered in the accounts of the " Queen's Chamber ", indicate that all restrictions upon their movements had then been removed.   But that the rash company ever returned to favour with Queen Elizabeth seems more than doubtful.   There is no indication that she ever saw them again.   However, it is known from the correspondence of Dudley Carleton,[2] that on December 29th, 1602, she attended a theatrical performance after dining with her cousin the Lord Chamberlain, and what she saw then was not a Shakespearean play but *Cynthia's Revels*, a much-praised work by Ben Jonson.

[1] The King's Players received 30 shillings at Bath, 20 shillings at Shrewsbury, 40 shillings at Coventry, 25 shillings, 8 pence at Ipswich.

[2] The Q. dined this day privatly at my Lord Chamberlaines ; I came even now from the blackfriers where I saw her at the play with all her candidae auditrices.   (Dudley Carleton to John Chamberlaine, December 29th, 1602.   S.P. Dom. Eliz. 282, 48.)

CHAPTER XV

A ROYAL PATRON

Death of Elizabeth ; accession of James I—Liberation of Southampton—Fletcher, Shakespeare and their company take part in the coronation—Shakespeare moves to the right bank of the Thames—*The Tragedy of Gowry*—*The London Prodigall*— *A Yorkshire Tragedy*—*Measure for Measure*—King James and Shakespeare.

IN the spring of 1603, James of Scotland still believed that the crown of England was a far distant dream. He declared that Elizabeth " would last as long as the sun and moon ", adding with dry humour : As long as there is an old woman in England whom they can deck out in ruff, jewels and farthingale, the ministers will go on telling us that the Queen still lives. Elizabeth herself took malicious pleasure in trying his patience and never lost an opportunity of appearing active and frisky every time she thought James Stuart's representative was observing her. Feigning to ignore his presence in the room, but certain that he would not omit to report the exploit to his royal master, she would proceed to dance to a violin accompaniment. But Christophe de Harley, Lord of Beaumont, the French ambassador, saw the Queen under quite another aspect. To him she complained of having never felt a moment's happiness nor the least satisfaction since the death of Essex. She left her palace for the last time to visit the bedside of the Countess of Nottingham, where she learnt, it is said, that this lady had retained the ring which Essex had confided to her that she might send it to the Queen as a token of his repentance.[1] It is said that Henry VIII's daughter dealt the dying woman a blow which hastened her demise. Nor did Elizabeth recover from the shock of this interview ; she returned to Richmond, and henceforward declined from day to day. She could neither eat nor sleep and refused to go to bed, crying out that under the heavy state canopy she had been visited by strange and terrible apparitions.[2] Cushions were piled up for her in the throne room where on March 27th, 1603, she died, worn out by remorse rather than by any specific malady. However, knowing that the end was near, she decided to

[1] According to the tradition which Thomas Corneille, before Schiller, followed when writing of this scene, Elizabeth had given Essex a ring promising to grant any wish or pardon no matter what offence at the sight of this jewel. After the sentence of the House of Lords, she vainly awaited some sign from her former lover then, furious at this evidence of pride, she affixed her seal to the death sentence. The whole tradition is, however, very questionable.

[2] *The Court and Character of K. James*, written and taken by Sir A. W. (Anthony Weldon) being an eye and ear witness (London, 1650).

adopt the policy which Essex had advocated, asserting to the Archbishop of Canterbury that her throne was that of kings and a king must occupy it. The ring, sign of royal power, was sawn off her swollen finger, and, at three in the morning, Robert Carey, brother of the Lord Chamberlain, rode northwards to present Mary Stuart's son with the symbol of his new authority. He traversed the distance between London and Edinburgh in sixty hours,[1] certain of finding a warmer welcome than he had received fifteen years before when he carried Elizabeth's letter announcing the execution of James's mother.[2]

In London consternation was general. The masses foresaw civil war. When the royal barge, draped in a black pall, appeared on the Thames, every stroke of the oars, said Thomas Dekker in his *Wonderful Yeare*, was accompanied by tears and sobs. The people's joy only burst forth when they learned that James " the pacific " had announced in his proclamation a general amnesty, and was about to set out for his new capital. Dekker, who described the dismay caused by Elizabeth's death, notes this sudden change in the mind of the crowd.

Upon Thursday it was treason to cry God save King James of England, and uppon Fryy hgh treason not to cry so. In the morning no voice heard but murmures and lamentation, at noone nothing but shoutes of gladnes and triumphe. S. George and S. Andrew that many yeares had defied one another, were now sworne brothers. . . .

While official lamentations continued and Elizabeth entered into the glory of deceased monarchs, amidst public tears and eulogies, Henry Chettle expressed his surprise at Shakespeare's silence. He would have liked the " silver tongued poet to compose an elegy on the rape of Elizabeth done by that Tarquin death ",[3] and invited him to commemorate the mournful

---

[1] Agnes Strickland, *Lives of the Queens of England* vol. vii, p. 287.

[2] Here is the gist of the letter which Robert Carey was sent to give to the king. It is dated February 14th, 1587. Elizabeth had signed the death sentence on February 1st ; the execution took place on the 7th at Fotheringay.

I should like you to know without experiencing it, the extreme pain which the miserable accident just taken place, quite contrary to my intentions, causes me. I send to you my cousin to tell you the truth. God and man know that I am innocent. If I had ordered it, I should have defended it. No mortal could make me order an injustice or deny what I have done. If I had had the intention of committing this act I should not have placed the blame upon another. I do not wish to blame myself either, since I am innocent. As for yourself, be well assured that you do not possess in the whole universe a more affectionate relative nor a more trustworthy friend than myself.

King James refused to give the messenger audience or to receive the letter he brought. Carey had to describe it in a written report. (*Warrendor Papers*, Series III, vol. ii, Scottish History Society, Edinburgh University Press, 1932.)

[3] Nor doth the silver tongued Melicert
Drop from his honied muse one sable tear
To mourne her death that graced his desert,
And to his laies opened her Royall ear.
Shepheard, remember our Elizabeth
And sing her Rape, done by that Tarquin death.

England's Mourning Garment, S.R., April 28th, 1603.) An anonymous poet echoes this sentiment : " A mournefull Dittie, entituled Elizabeth's Losse together with A Welcome for King James." (*Shakespeare Allusion Book*, 1676.)

event. In view of the feelings of the Essex faction in regard to the " chaste Cynthia " the silence of the great poet is comprehensible.

From the moment that he was invested with royal authority, James showed particular zeal in recompensing the victims of the old régime. Before leaving Edinburgh, he signed the order for the release of Lord Southampton, who left prison on April 10th and immediately rode north to meet the king.[1] He found the new sovereign at Huntingdon, was appointed to carry the sword of State and precede the monarch in the towns through which the procession passed.   King James, in spite of his impatience to reign over England, had the good taste not to show undue haste ; it took him five weeks to reach London. Hunting parties, banquets, visits to noblemen whose estates lay along the route, marked his progress, which ended on May 7th.

In spite of the prediction that Elizabeth's death would lead to civil war, the accession of James Stuart to the throne of the Tudors was effected in absolute tranquillity.   Even nature seemed to participate in the general joy and the exceptional profusion of the spring was taken as a happy omen.

It was at this time that Shakespeare addressed his joyful sonnet to Southampton, which celebrates the liberation of that friend whose life was " suppos'd as forfeit to a confin'd doom ".   The allusion to the eclipse of the mortal moon evidently refers to the Queen's death.

> Not mine own fears, nor the prophetic soul
> Of the wide world dreaming on things to come,
> Can yet the lease of my true love control,
> Supposed as forfeit to a confin'd doom,
> The mortal moon hath her eclipse endur'd,
> And the sad augurs mock their own presage ;
> Incertainties now crown themselves assur'd,
> And peace proclaims olives of endless age.
> Now with the drops of this most balmy time
> My love looks fresh, and Death to me subscribes,
> Since, spite of him, I'll live in this poor rhyme,
> While he insults o'er dull and speechless tribes :
> And thou in this shalt find they monument,
> When tyrant's crests and tombs of brass are spent.
>
> (Sonnet 107)

As soon as he arrived in London, James restored to Southampton his titles and properties. He granted him a post at court with a revenue of six thousand crowns.

The Venetian ambassador, describing this sudden change of fortune, remarks :

On his journey his Majesty meantime, has destined to great rewards the Earl of Southampton and Sir Henry Neville . . . and also others, and has received the twelve-year-old son of the Earl of Essex and taken him in his arms and kissed

[1] C. C. Stopes, *The Third Earl of Southampton* p. 265

him, openly and loudly declaring him the son of the most noble knight that English land has ever begotten.[1]

Among the strange documents of this period when everyone executed a skilful right-about, there is one deserving of attention.

Addressed to Southampton, the following letter emanates from the man who, with Robert Cecil, had worked hardest to bring about his downfall. The letter is to this effect :

I would have been very glad to have presented my humble service to your Lordship by my attendance, if I could have foreseen that it should not have been unpleasing to you.   And therefore as I would commit no error, I choose to write, assuring your Lordship (how credible soever it may seem to you at first) yet it is as true a thing that God knoweth, that this great change hath wrought in me no other change towards your Lordship than this, that I my be safely nowe that which I was truely before.   And so, craving no other pardon than for troubling you with this letter, I do not now begin, but continue to be your Lordship's humble and much devoted.   Francis Bacon.[2]

Twenty years later, when sitting in his turn as judge in the council which condemned Bacon for malpractice and abuse of his high office, Southampton proposed that the penalties of banishment and deletion from the peerage should be added to that of dismissal from the Chancellorship.

The official coronation ceremony did not take place until July 25th. The King explained the lateness of the date assigned by the desire to spare his subjects the expenses of two coronations.   As a politic and prudent man, he wished to sound out his English people, and, above all the old ministers whose loyalty he intended to prove before sending for the queen and the princes.[3]   It was lucky that he took this cautious attitude, for he was thus enabled to discover a plot hatched by the famous " diabolical triplicity " for whom he entertained an understandable distrust.

He regulated the Queen's journey in all its details.   She was to be joined in Edinburgh by the Countess of Bedford and Lady Harrington, and then set off with Prince Henry, Princess Elizabeth and Lady Arabella Stuart, the King's near relative.   Anne of Denmark arrived on June 3rd at Berwick where ladies-in-waiting, dresses and jewels were ready for her to complete the meagre trousseau with which she had left Scotland.   The cortège appointed to accompany her to London started south.   At Althorpe, the Earl of Cumberland gave her not only a royal but a poetic welcome.   As soon as she was inside the gate, a faun bounded from a bush followed by a band of fairies who came dancing to meet her.   Queen Mab waved her wand, and this bevy of beauties presented Ben Jonson's *Satyr* [4] in a verdant natural theatre.   Her Majesty was enchanted to hear herself addressed as

---

[1] *Cal. S.P. Venice*, vol. x, p. 25, May 15th, 1603.
[2] Additional MSS. 5 503, fol. 24.   [3] *Nichols' State Progresses*, vol. i, p. 414.
[4] *A Particular Entertainment of the Queene and Prince Their Highnesse* at Althrope at The Right Honourable the Lord Spencers, on Satturday, being the 25 of June, 1603, as they came first into the Kingdome. (The author B.J., London, V.S. for Edward Blount, MDCXL.)

Oriana, " she who surpasses in glory our late Diana ", and immediately adopted the author of *Volpone* as her official poet. She later commissioned his long series of *Masques*.

At Grafton, where the King met her, the Danish princess scandalized the old dowagers by reserving her sweetest smiles for young women of her own age, and at Windsor, the last halting-place, initial court ceremonies were held and the Garter was conferred upon Prince Henry, the Duke of Lennox, and the Earls of Mar, Southampton and Pembroke. The harmony of these three days of rejoicing was disturbed by a violent quarrel between the Earl of Southampton and Lord Gray. Shakespeare's patron defended the memory of the Earl of Essex, called the councillor a traitor, and challenged him to a duel.

Three days later, Gray, Raleigh and Cobham were involved in a conspiracy against the monarch and his " cubs ". They intended to assassinate father and children, then to set Arabella Stuart on the throne, counting on finding this young woman of royal descent a still more docile tool in their hands than Elizabeth had been. The pardon which the king granted the three Privy Councillors when they were already on the scaffold [1] was considered a sign of weakness rather than of magnanimity. It was also found strange that he took no measures against his own cousin, who continued after this event to occupy the position of first lady in waiting on the queen.

On June 23rd, the cortège at last arrived at the Palace of Whitehall. The plague was still raging so furiously that their sojourn at the Tower was cancelled, and the procession from that fortress to the Abbey, which formed part of the traditional coronation ceremonies, was postponed. The King and Queen made the short journey between Whitehall landing-stage to that of Westminster by barge. There, according to an eye witness, the Queen made a great impression, her beautiful fair hair falling round her shoulders encircled by a slender golden crown : she greeted her new subjects so graciously that the women present were touched and cried with one accord : " God bless the Queen, may she be welcome to England." [2]

During the ceremony, she caused a sensation by refusing the sacraments of the Established Church, which inevitably caused her to be suspected of " affection towards the papacy ". The King, however, made his communion fervently, subscribing to the same oath which had been administered to Elizabeth at her coronation. By a strange irony, James swore as she had

---

[1] The wily Robert Cecil, with a skill worthy of his father succeeded in confusing the evidence in two plots which he called the main plot and the bye plot, and was thus able to compromise and eliminate all his rivals. Cobham, Gray and Raleigh, condemned to death, were reprieved in December 1603. The first died in captivity, the second in exile. The third, imprisoned at first in the Tower, where he finished his famous *History of the World*, was at last liberated and departed in search of gold. But in the course of his voyage his sailors burned the town of Saint Thomaz, in spite of his solemn promise to respect Spanish possessions. On his return the Spanish ambassador insisted that Raleigh should be punished in exemplary fashion, and he was executed in 1618 on the charge of high treason, which had been pronounced against him fifteen years before.

[2] *Nichols' State Progresses*, vol. i, pp. 414 ff.

" to maintain the purity of religion in his Estates according to the practices of Edward the Confessor ".[1]

The day after the ceremony, all those who had means deserted London to avoid infection. The players went on tour. The court removed to the Palace of Woodstock and received the foreign representatives there. The Spanish ambassador distributed embroidered gloves among the ladies and perfumed waistcoats to the courtiers. This made him far more popular than Henry IV's envoy, the illustrious Sully, who, on this occasion, brought only fine words. Ulric, Duke of Holstein, came from Denmark to congratulate his sister, and lost his heart to Lady Arabella.

Early in the autumn, the Queen stayed for more than six weeks at Wilton House, the beautiful residence of the Earl and Countess of Pembroke. Thence it was that Lady Pembroke wrote to her son, who was with the King at Salisbury, asking him to come with His Majesty to a performance of *As You Like It*, adding, " We have the man Shakespeare here in person ".[2]

The presence of the actor-poet is confirmed by the payment entered in the Lord Chamberlain's accounts :

Dec 2nd, John Heminge, one of His Majesty's players, for the paynes and expenses of himself and rest of his company in coming from Mortlake in the county of Surrey unto the court (at Wilton) and then presenting before His Majesty one play : thirty pounds.

The inscriptions which follow, dated December 26th, 27th, 28th and 30th, January 1st and February 2nd, mention that payments totalling fifty-three pounds were made to the actors as remuneration for the spectacles given at Hampton Court, where their Majesties repaired before returning to London. Among the plays given in the old palace built by Wolsey in the days of his greatness, Dudley Carleton, in his correspondence with Chamberlain, mentions *A Midsummer Night's Dream*, which he calls Robin Goodfellow.[3] Shakespeare's company received as the king's personal gift at the time the sum of thirty pounds, sent to Burbage as compensation to him and his fellows for being obliged to renounce their season in London owing to the closure of the theatres on account of the persistence of the epidemic.

In February 1604, the court returned to London, and on the 15th of the same month, the talents of the King's Players were again in request. In the course of this year and the first months of the next, they played a dozen times before the royal family. The following comedies were given in their almost exclusively Shakespearean repertory : *The Merry Wives of Windsor*, *The Comedy of Errors*, *Henry V*, *The Merchant of Venice*, which pleased the

[1] A. Strickland, the historian who draws attention to this paradox, remarks that the Privy Council and the lords were obliged to modify the oath to make it conform to that sworn by Edward VI, and to warn James of this before his entry into the kingdom so that he might accommodate his lords better to Protestant practices. But it is a fact that from the time of William the Conqueror until 1688 the same formula was retained. (*Strickland's Queens*, vol. vii, p. 308.)

[2] This letter was still in the possession of the Pembroke family in 1865. (F. W. Cornish, *Extracts from the Letters and Journals of William Cory* (1897), p. 168, August 5th, 1865.)

[3] *S.P. Dom.* Jac. I, vol. vi, p. 21.

King so much that he commanded a second performance, Ben Jonson's *Every Man in his Humour* and its counterpart *Every Man Out of His Humour*, lastly Shakespeare's two most recent creations : *Measure for Measure* and *Othello*.[1]

On the occasion of the visit of the Queen's brother, the Duke of Holstein, another Shakespeare play was given in the presence of the Queen at Holborn House, *Love's Labour's Lost*.

The circumstances which determined this choice are mentioned in an amusing letter from Sir Walter Cope to Robert Cecil. Sir Walter who had undertaken to prepare a theatrical entertainment for Her Majesty's arrival which would be worthy of her, had vainly hunted everywhere for actors, musicians and jugglers. When at last he discovered Burbage,[2] it was to learn that his company had no recent play that the queen did not already know.[3] He proposed, however, to revive for this occasion an old comedy, *Love's Labour's Lost*, certain to please because of its gaiety and wit. This was arranged and Burbage himself carried the order to prepare the performance at Holborn House where it was given on 12th January, 1604.[4]

As may be seen, Shakespeare and his colleagues had no cause to regret their enforced departure from London at the time of the political disorders which resulted in the sentence of their patrons. The extraordinary favour extended to them by James amply compensated for past sacrifices. They received sums totalling a hundred and sixty pounds from the Lord Chamberlain for the year 1604 alone. Between James's accession and Shakespeare's death, they earned one thousand six hundred and thirty-five pounds and gave not less than a hundred and fifty performances. What a contrast to the lean times under Queen Elizabeth, when they were struggling with unequal odds against Henslowe and his Admiral's troupe, continually favoured by the all-powerful ministers ! In the last twelve years of her reign they played only forty times at court and were paid three hundred and ninety pounds.

In London the citizens impatiently awaited the promised festivities which should have accompanied the coronation the previous year. At last, on March 15th, the royal procession left the Tower and passed under the seven triumphal arches [5] erected in the principal quarters of the capital. At every halt, pantomimes, poems and speeches composed by Thomas Dekker, a

---

[1] *Revels accounts* for the year 1604-5.

[2] " Burbage ys come & sayes ther ys no new playe that the Quene hath not seene, but that they have revyved an olde one, cawled *Loves Labore Lost*, which for wytte and mirthe he sayes will please her excedingly." (Hatfield MSS. 159 95.)

[3] That Queen Anne should have known a large part of the Shakespearean repertory before her arrival in London is yet another indication added to many others of the presence of Shakespeare and his troupe in Scotland.

[4] " It seems we shall have Christmas all the yeare. . . . last night's revels were kept at my Lord of Cranborn's where the Q with the Duke of Holst with a great part of the court were feasted, and the like two nights before at my Lord of Southamptons." (Letter from Dudley Carleton to John Chamberlain, *State Papers*, Dom. Jac. I, XII. 19.)

[5] *The Arches of Triumph Erected in honor of the High and mighty prince James, King of England, and the Sixt of Scotland, at his Majesties Entrance and passage through his Honorable citty and chamber of London upon the* 15*th day of March* 1603. Invented and published by Stephen Harrison Joyner and Architect and graven by William Kip (London, 1604).

specialist in this line, greeted the royal couple.[1]   Wine and ale gushed from the fountains.   The Queen, although exhausted, was gracious.   Their Majesties were surrounded that day by guards of honour who carried the great canopy over their heads.   The eight new grooms of the Chamber, who had the privilege of taking part in the ceremony were none other than Shakespeare, Phillips, Fletcher, Heminge, Burbage, Sly, Armin, Condell and Cowley, principal players of the " Globe " company.   They wore the handsome red and black royal livery with scarlet cloak, and walked bare-headed.   The special allowance for their costume is set down in the accounts kept by Sir George Holmes, Master of the Wardrobe, where we learn that four yards of red cloth, were distributed to each of the grooms of the Chamber " against His Majesty's royal proceedings through the city of London ". The list of actors who were to benefit by the distribution is headed by Shakespeare, Phillips and Fletcher.[2]

In one of his last sonnets Shakespeare alludes to this ceremony, declaring that exterior honours such as carrying the canopy leave him indifferent ; these are not the favours he seeks.   All his gratitude goes to his patron, Lord Southampton to whom his homage and devotion have always been offered exclusively.

The same year, when the King received the ambassador extraordinary from Spain, who had come with seven dignitaries to sign a peace treaty, he chose Somerset House as residence for these distinguished strangers, and " to serve and assist the constable of Castile, Juan Fernandez de Velasco, Duke of Frias, head of the mission during their stay of three weeks " he appointed the same troupe of actors whose noble presence and good manners he had already appreciated at the coronation ceremonies.   He sent them twenty-one pounds twelve shillings for this service, and the constable of Castile himself presented each actor with a personal souvenir.[3]

The more than benevolent protection shown by the king to the players is noted by Gilbert Dugdale.

King James gave not only to those worthy of honour, but to the mean gave grace as taking unto himself the Lord Chamberlains servants now the King's actors. The Queen taking to her the Earl of Worcester's servants that are not her actors, and their son Henry took to him the Earl of Nottingham's servants.[4]

[1] *The Magnificent Entertainment Given to King James, Queene Anne his wife, and Henry Frederick the Prince*, upon the day of his Majesties Tryumphant Passage (from the Tower) through his Honourable Citie (and Chamber) of London, being the 15 of March 1603. . . . With the speeches and Songes, delivered in the severall Pageants.   (Imprinted at London by Thomas Dekker, T. Creed, for Thomas Man, the yonger 1604.)

[2] Red Cloth bought of sondrie persons and given by his Majestie to diverse persons against his Majesties sayd royale proceeding through the Citie of London . . . Viz the chamber
Red Cloth . . . Faukeners, etc. William Shakespeare, Augustine Phillipps
. . . ells.   Laurence Fletcher, John Hemminge, Richard Cowley.
Account of Sir George Home, Master of the Great Wardrobe, for the proceeding of King James through London on March 15th, 1604, *Record Office*, Lord Chamberlain's books, IX, 4.

[3] *Relacion de la Jornada del Excellentissimo Condestable di Castilla.*   Valencia Molino di Rovella 1604 (impresa in Valencia).

[4] *The Time Triumphant*, declaring in Briefe the arival of our Soveraigne—Leidge Lord King James of England (Gilbert Dugdale, 1604).

On his return to the capital, Shakespeare did not go back to his house in Southwark, but elected to stay with a Huguenot wigmaker, Christopher Montjoye, who lived with his wife, daughter and brother at the corner of Silver and Monkswell Streets, in a well-to-do quarter of the town where, according to the historian Stowe, the houses were handsome. The distance from there to the " Globe " was not great. Shakespeare had only to walk down Wood Street, where his friend Richard Field the publisher lived, cross Cheapside, pass through Bread Street, pass " The Mermaid ", and place himself in the hands of one of the numerous boatmen who plied to and fro on the river and whose cries of " Eastward Ho ! " or " Westward Ho ! " enlivened this water highway. His friends Heminge and Condell also lived near Cheapside in the parish of Saint Mary (Aldermanbury) and could attain their theatrical destination with the same facility.

In Montjoye's family, Shakespeare had a good opportunity to improve his French. He also interested himself in the future of young Marie, the daughter of the house. From the deposition of the maid-servant Jeanne before the court where a financial dispute about the dowry was settled, we know that Master Shakespeare used his influence to persuade the young apprentice Bellot, whom he considered an excellent servant, moved by the best intentions and a sincere affection, to marry his employer's daughter.

Shakespeare who supported the efforts of Mme. Montjoye in this affair, succeeded in bringing about the match, and no doubt accompanied the pair to the church of Saint Olave where the wedding took place on November 19th, 1604.[1]

It was at this time that Shakespeare wrote *Measure for Measure*, a new kind of comedy reflecting the character and interests of the new king, and his tragic masterpiece *Othello*, which will be studied in the next chapter.

But before giving a sketch of *Measure for Measure*, mention must be made of three short plays that could more appropriately be called interludes, presented at the " Globe " by Shakespeare's company when King James and especially Queen Anne [2] were showing such interest in theatrical events and when the public, following their sovereign's example, demanded new plays, reserving their applause to the old popular actors.

The fact that these interludes, *The Tragedy of Gowry*, *The London Prodigall* and *The Yorkshire Tragedy* were played at the " Globe " and that the two latter bear Shakespeare's signature does not necessarily imply that they were written by the actor-poet himself and that they should be considered as belonging to his " repertoire ". We can probably consider that Shakespeare took only part in correcting and perhaps rewriting certain passages.

The *Tragedy of Gowry*, founded on an episode in the life of the King,

---

[1] The Bellot-Montjoye affair was discovered in the *Archives* of the Court of Requests by Professor Wallace, who published his findings in *Harper's Magazine* (March 1910). Shakespeare was the chief witness, and his name appears twenty-eight times in numerous depositions.

[2] See Fripp, *Shakespeare, Man and Artist*, pp. 629-630.

was only played twice and the text is lost.   It was perhaps suppressed by
the order which interrupted the performances.   Yet the play seems to have
been written to please the sovereign whose part in the story as he liked to
tell it was not unheroic.   James I had left Falkland at dawn to take part in
a hunt, and had promised to visit the Earl of Gowry at Perth, where a mysterious Jesuit with a sack of gold, was detained.   The Earl counted, he said,
on the monarch's assistance to discover the intentions of the priest.   In
order to keep his visit secret, James rode ahead of the horsemen of his suite
and went alone to the castle of the Ruthvens.   There he was thrown into
a Tower and owed his life only to his presence of mind and to the opportune
arrival of his escort who, hearing his shouts, were in time to free their
master.   In the skirmish the Earl of Gowry and his brother Alexander
Ruthven met their death.   They intended, according to general belief, to
avenge their father who had been executed during James' minority.   A
more romantic version brings the Queen's name into this affair.   According
to this the King invented the tale of the Jesuit as an excuse to punish the
Ruthven brothers whom Anne of Denmark was protecting because of their
sister Beatrice, her favourite lady-in-waiting.   Such a subject [1] was evidently
objectionable, and the decision to suppress its performance is perfectly
comprehensible.   The only document which today recalls the drama twice
presented at the " Globe " by His Majesty's players is a news letter written
by John Chamberlain to Ralph Winwood, secretary at the Paris embassy,
dated December 18th, 1604 :

The Tragedy of Gowry, with all the action and actors hath been twice represented by the King's Players with exceeding concourse of all sorts of people ; but
whether the matter or manner be not well handled, or that it be thought unfit
that princes should be played on the stage in their life-time, I hear that some
great counc'llors are much displeased with it, and so it is thought shall be forbidden.

It is understandable that the public should have rushed to the Playhouse
to see enacted such a sensational episode in their new sovereign's life and
great must have been the players' disappointment when they learned of the
suppression of the work.   In the programme of court entertainments in
1604, there is mention of a play which was to have been acted on February
3rd, but which was withdrawn and compensation given to the troupe.   There
is therefore every reason to believe that this was the *Tragedy of Gowry*.
The fact that a week later, *The Merchant of Venice* was given before the
court shows that the King at least bore no grudge against Shakespeare or his
company for the recent incident.

The London Prodigall, a comedy of manners in Ben Jonson's style, whose
qualities appear better when acted than when read, is a hastily composed
piece perhaps intended to fill the breach created by the suppression of
the play they had counted upon.   A young prodigal, a typical libertine of
his time is left by his father, a wealthy English merchant established in

[1] Publications of the Scottish History Society, *Third Series, Warrender Papers* (vol. ii,
Edinburgh University Press, 1932).

Venice, to the care of an uncle incapable of checking his inclination to debauchery. When the prodigal's fate seems desperate, the father returns home, bringing the boy's last chance of salvation. But the rich merchant's educational principles—sympathy and comprehension—are opposed by his brother's stern severity. The merchant has left his son as a small child; not being recognized the traveller appears as a friend, not as father. However he has no more success than the boy's uncle. When the prodigal's mercenary schemes are about to result in a rich marriage, his father reveals himself, and creates a scene at the very door of the church, confounding his son, and driving him into still deeper straits. However, the test succeeds at last, and it is a repentant and regenerated being who comes to seek pardon of the woman he has insulted and the father he has misunderstood.[1]

Shakespeare wrote parts of this play; his touch may be seen in the masterly presentation of the rich merchant experienced in the school of life and the contrast of this with his brother's stern puritanism. The scene in which he takes under his protection the woman whom his son has abandoned is of great beauty. If divine grace comes rather suddenly to save the prodigal, it is not sufficient reason to deny Shakespeare's authorship, for the same fault may be found several times in his uncontested work.

The comic element is achieved in *The London Prodigall* by a procedure already proved successful. Shakespeare was on solid ground in introducing a military humbug and a Welshman who expresses himself, like Fluellen in *Henry V*, with a strong accent.

The constant use of proverbs and aphorisms borrowed from the manuals of Florio, the reference to Macchiavelli, whom the prodigal is annotating, are indications that Shakespeare himself had a hand in the writing of this play.[2]

The London Prodigall was printed in quarto in 1605, the year following its presentation at the " Globe ", under Shakespeare's name; but the play was not included in his complete works until the publication of the third and fourth folio editions.

A Yorkshire Tragedy is the third interlude to be staged at this time. *Not so new as lamentable and true*, proclaimed the descriptive title.[3]

---

[1] *The London Prodigall*. As it was plaide by the Kings Majesties servaunts. By William Shakespeare (London, printed by T. C. for Nathaniel Butler, 1605). It is included in the third and fourth editions of the folio (1664 and 1685). It also figures in the editions of Rowe, Malone and Steevens.

[2] " None knows the danger of a fire more than he that falls into it " (Act I, Sc. 1).

" I have bene reading over Nick Marchivill : I find him good to be knowne not to be followed a pestilent humane fellow. I have made certain annotations upon him such as they be . . ." (Act III, Sc. 1).

" The Italian hath a pretie saying, *Questo*.—I have forgotten it too, 'tis out of my head, but in my translation it holds thus thou hast a friend keep him, if a foe trip him " (Act III, Sc. 2).

" Where naught is, the King doth lose his due " (Act III, Sc. 3).

[3] *A Yorkshire Tragedy*. Not so New as Lamentable and true. Acted by his Majesties Players at the Globe. Written by William Shakespeare. (At London, printed by R.B. for Thomas Pavier and are to be sold at his shop on Comhill, neare to the Exchange, 1608.)

This time, as with *Arden of Faversham*, the author has simply dramatized a contemporary murder case which had aroused universal interest. Stowe tells us that :

Walter Calverly, of Calverly Hall in Yorkshire, Esq., murdered his two young children, stabbed his wife into the body with full purpose to have murdered her and instantly went from his house to have slain his youngest child at nurse. At his trial he stood mute and was judged to be pressed to death.

The only valid motive of this crime is presented as a frantic passion for gambling of which an almost pathological study is made in ten rapid scenes. The violent and morbid language of Walter Calverley is only equalled in force and brutality in *Timon of Athens* and *King Lear*. The weaknesses of this lightning-like tragedy could be attributable to haste. If Shakespeare took part in the writing or staging of this play this part must have been very small and if he worked with a collaborator it might well have been with George Wilkins a fellow-lodger with the Montjoyes, who was involved in the affairs of Bellot the apprentice and himself published in 1607 *The Miseries of inforst marriage*, a play based on a similar theme.[1]

A Yorkshire Tragedy was published in quarto in 1608 and, like *The London Prodigall*, was not included in Shakespeare's complete works until the third and fourth folios.[2] Many commentators hesitate to attribute these two interludes to the pen of the great genius ; but who can expect that such an author should always be equal to his own best achievement ? The comedy and the tragedy which they refuse to assign to Shakespeare possess many passages worthy of his inspiration and, if it was natural that his friends Heminge and Condell in their first collections of his works, found it best not to include these inferior interludes, which are mere sketches, it was logical that thirty years later, the editors of the folios of 1664 and 1685 should incorporate therein these plays which appeared under Shakespeare's name, and which he presented himself at the " Globe ".

The dramatist was more in his element when he embarked upon what was for him a new kind of comedy, a true psychological study reflecting the thought and character of the new sovereign.

Measure for Measure is a commentary on theoretical and practical justice. The theme of this social study is the inability of harsh laws to control moral corruption. In this respect, the play is related to *Pericles* and *Timon of Athens*. The subject is taken directly from the *Epitia* of Giraldo Cinthio who also wrote it as a story in *Gli Heccatommithi*. But, as was his custom, Shakespeare modified the Italian author's version, in which passion and cruelty vie with one another and the heroine surrenders herself to save her brother's life. The English poet, diverting the plot at the critical moment,

---

[1] *The Miseries of inforst mariage* as it is now playd by his Majesties Servaunts. (By George Wilkins for George Vincent, 1607.)

[2] Steevens and Ulrici recognize Shakespeare as the author of this drama ; Malone, Knight, Swinburne and Tucker Brooke classify it among his apocryphal works, and very few more recent scholars allow Shakespeare any share in it.

has succeeded in giving the play an elevated moral tone and a tragic dignity ; but the general argument remains sordid, because the author, in order to save Claudio's life and his sister's virtue, resorts to the same subterfuge that he had previously employed in *All's Well That Ends Well*, when he makes the villainous minister of justice who thinks that he has met the object of his desires, find that he has in fact slept with the woman whom long before he had promised to marry and abandoned.

Angelo, Duke Vincentio's deputy, an example of narrow and repressive puritanism, sees in sensuality the worst of vices and proposes to pull down the " houses of resort " in the Viennese suburbs, put a stop to youthful irregularity, and in short impose a reign of terror. His edicts provide the author with the opportunity to draw inimitable portraits of the disreputable Mistress Overdone, her chief assistant Pompey Bum and some of her regular clients.

Isabella belongs to the race of Shakespearean heroines, a sister to Portia and Helen of Narbonne. But unlike these two her heart aspires only to divine love. At the convent of St. Clare she obtains permission to plead the cause of her unhappy brother Claudio, imprisoned under Angelo's new laws.

The scene where Isabella visits her brother in prison to tell him the result of her mission to Angelo is masterly : Claudio in a frenzy of terror, cannot believe that Isabella will not accept Angelo's infamous proposal and urges her to reconsider her decision.

In this dialogue, the abyss between two natures is revealed. Human weakness which clings at all costs to life in this world, is broken against the rock of uncompromising virtue.

In the last act, Vincentio resumes his ducal powers, and his identity with the supposed friar is avowed. Knowing all the threads of the plot, he judges the characters' various problems with practical wisdom. That of Claudio and his mistress Juliet, and that of Angelo and Mariana are resolved by marriage. Angelo, in the Duke's opinion, really deserves the death to which he had condemned Claudio, but Mariana in her turn eloquently pleads pardon for her future husband.

All the secondary characters reappear before a judge, more human than Angelo who had condemned them. Instead of their well merited punishments, procurers and go-betweens are given good advice. The only personage who is not pardoned is the cynic Lucio, the libertine who has slandered virtue and mocked divine love.

Many critics have noticed allusions to King James in certain of the Duke's speeches. This rôle contains more than allusions, it is a psychological portrait of the new sovereign.

James, whom Henry IV of France was fond of ridiculing as " the new Solomon " and of whom Sully said, " He is the wisest fool in Christendom ", had very personal theories on the art of government. It was a point of honour with him to be the most learned man in his kingdom ; in conversation he was very witty, but his Scotch accent and his natural good nature inevitably raised a satirical smile at court. Sincerely convinced of his divine right to

reign, he claimed by his own methods to be able always to discover the truth
and loved to investigate his subjects' private affairs. Equally at ease in
the courts of law and in the universities, he had a horror of the mob and did
not hide an aversion which was only too obvious. When the English
populace pressed around their new monarch and frightened his horse, he
almost fainted.

In *Measure for Measure*, Vincentio declares as King James would have done:

> . . . I love the people,
> But do not like to stage me to their eyes.
> Though it do well, I do not relish well
> Their loud applause and aves vehement,
> Nor do I think the man of safe discretion
> That does affect it. . . .

(Act I, Sc. 1)

But Shakespeare is careful to supply the Duke, that is to say James, with
a good reason for this weakness, recalling how the well-meaning crowd
often harms instead of helping the object of its solicitude.

> So play the foolish throngs with one that swounds :
> Come all to help him, and so stop the air
> By which he should revive : and even so
> The general, subject to a well-wished King,
> Quit their own part, and in obsequious fondness
> Crowd to his presence, where their untaught love
> Must needs appear offence.

(Act II, Sc. 4)

The king's ideas could not have been better conveyed nor could he
have been better satisfied than by the fifth act of *Measure for Measure*,
where by his personal intervention and psychological knowledge the Duke
of Vienna resolves apparently inextricable situations to the benefit of all
and establishes a régime of tolerance and equity. This was one of James's
chief ambitions, set forth in his book on the art of government which,
published in 1603, had just reached its third edition.

In *Henry VIII*, Shakespeare makes Archbishop Cranmer prophesy that,
after Elizabeth, a new sovereign

> Shall star-like rise, as great in fame as she was,
> And so stand fixed : peace, plenty, love, truth, terror . . .
> Shall then be his, and like a vine grow to him :
> Wherever the bright sun of heaven shall shine,
> His honour and the greatness of his name
> Shall be, and make new nations : [1] he shall flourish
> And, like a mountain cedar, reach his branches
> To all the plains about him :—our children's children
> Shall see this, and bless Heaven.[2]

---

[1] This allusion to the founding of new nations refers to the colonizing activities in which
the king was seconded by Southampton who, in his capacity of secretary to the Virginia
Company, equipped the ships for departure to the new world.

[2] *Henry VIII* (Act v, Sc. 5).

If the allusions contained in *Macbeth*, *Measure for Measure* and *Henry VIII* indeed refer to King James, the logical conclusion is that Shakespeare who in Elizabeth's reign refused to flatter the sovereign's enormous vanity, must have felt sincere sympathy for her successor, a learned and timid man, but inflexible in his principles. If he cultivated philosophical comedy to please James, he was not acting against his own inclination. On the contrary, he was entirely in his element when entering so thoroughly into the thought of an intellectual ruler.

At this time, the King finally separated from the puritans and became the champion of a sane tolerance which Shakespeare, recent disciple of Montaigne, could only welcome. In order to understand the mentality of James I, it is necessary to discount the opinion of his subjects, who were apt to laugh at his best qualities and never forgave the haste with which he negotiated peace with Spain or the marriage of his son Charles with a Catholic French princess.

Some of his letters to the Queen and the princes are models of natural and playful familiarity. His secret correspondence with Robert Cecil [1] and his magnum opus *Basilikon Doron* attest his political wisdom. His translation of Tasso, of psalms and biblical commentaries show his exceptional erudition. Two collections of his sayings bear witness to an original and finely ironical wit, and his taste for puns and *concetti* was as marked as Shakespeare's own. [2]

His policy of tolerance prevented him from profiting by his accession to punish those responsible for the death of his mother, but he respected her memory and never forgot her best friends. He gave the name Mary to the princess born to him on April 7th, 1607, and on the day of the christening commissioned the fine monument to the Queen of Scots which faces Elizabeth's in Westminster choir. For his mother's confidential friend, Ambassador Melville, whose wife, Katherine Kennedy, had completely devoted herself to the unhappy queen, he never ceased to express warm affection. He restored titles and possessions to the Earl of Arundel's family, loaded

---

[1] *The Secret Correspondence of Sir Robert Cecil with James VI, King of Scotland* (Edinburgh, MDCCLXVI).

[2] Anthony Weldon, in his *Court and Character of King James* (1675) attests that the king was very witty and used to make many impromptu jokes keeping a straight face and not laughing himself. When a certain Lumley boasted unreasonably of his ancestors, the king exclaimed : " Now I am convinced that Adam's name was Lumley."

At the first meeting with the English, whose enthusiasm touched upon delirium, he slyly said : " These brave people are trying to spoil a good King."

Among his aphorisms may be quoted :

" I love not one who will never be angry, for as he that is without sorrow is without gladness even so he that is without anger is without love."

" It is likely that the people will imitate the king in good, but it is sure that they will follow him in evil."

" Parents may forbid their children an unfit marriage but they may not force their consent to a fit one."

" I wonder not so much that women paint themselves as that when they are painted men can love them."

" No man gains by war but he that hath not where withal to live in peace."

" Much money makes a country poor for it sets a high price on everything."

" I intend to govern for the Common-well not according to the Common will."

(*King James, His Apophthegmes*)

Essex' heirs with favours, and showered many benefits upon Southampton's family.   He held the heir to the title in his arms as godfather at his christening.   His generosity to this godson and his nurse may still be read in the register of the Chapel Royal.[1]   He would even have made Southampton his intimate counsellor, if Robert Cecil had not distrusted all Essex' former partisans.   The Machiavellian minister took care to whisper in the King's ear that the handsome young man danced " brandos " and " corantos " too often with Queen Anne.[2]

If James's emotionality occasionally made him flinch at the sight of a naked sword, if he preferred to carry an empty scabbard at his belt, he could also defend himself very well when the occasion demanded.   At the age of sixteen he escaped, thanks to his courage and presence of mind, from a trap laid by the rebellious nobles ; at twenty-two he rushed to the rescue of the sixteen-year-old princess whom he had married by proxy, and whom the storm had cast upon the inhospitable shores of Norway.   His part in the Gowry affair has been related ; Shakespeare considered him perfectly worthy of the heroic stage.

At the beginning of his reign, King James had not yet succumbed to the vice of alcoholism inherited from his father, Lord Darnley ; the Stratford poet could see in him a monarch determined to keep his country out of war, inclined to encourage arts and sports and resolved to favour the colonial enterprises so dear to Southampton.   He knew that with this royal patron, his career would meet with no further shackles ; under his benevolent influence he could at last give his spirit free rein.

At forty-two years, anyone other than Shakespeare, would have been intoxicated by such success.   But the equipoise of his character drew him away from the turbulence of London.   Far from having his head turned by his court employment, he says in Sonnet 125, as has been noted, that the exterior marks of royal favour mean nothing to him.   What he appreciated were the joys of perfect and unmaterial friendship.   He also valued the simple pleasure to be found with his own family.

His father was dead.   Thomas Lucy, the powerful enemy, was no more. He was wanted back in the country, which had always haunted him and where he had recently increased his domain by the acquisition of a cottage, garden and orchard adjoining his property of New Place.   No doubt he had early thought of this peaceful retreat, where he could enjoy those amenities and honours which in *Macbeth* he describes as the greatest satisfaction of mature years.

---

[1] " To the nurse and midwife at the Christening of the Earles child being a sonne to whom his Majestie himself was Godfather in person in his Highness chapple at Greenwich, 26 March 1605 " (*Cheque book of the Chapel Royal*, fol. 71).

[2] " And now doth the King return to Windsor, where there was an apparition of Southamptons being a Favourite to his Majesty, by that privacy and dearnesse presented to the Court view, but Salisbury liking not that any of Essex his faction should come into play, made that apparition appeare as it were in transitu, and so vanished, by putting some jealousies into the Kings head. . . ." (Anthony Weldon, *The Court And Character of King James*, London, 1650, p. 41.)

CHAPTER XVI

TOWARDS THE SUMMIT

The sources of *Othello*—Origin of the names of the chief characters—Morocco in Shakespeare's time ; the Barbary Company—First text of the play—The poet among his own people—Marriage of Susanna Shakespeare to Doctor John Hall.

IT is often said that prosperity prejudices artistic production, but this dictum cannot be applied to Shakespeare ; each stage of his existence was productive ; his mind remained continually alert, and he modified his work to some extent with the march of events. Until the end of Elizabeth's reign, wishing above all to please a patron ten years younger and still more romantic than himself, the author of *Love's Labour's Lost* was perhaps too faithful a follower of the idyllic muse. In order to please James, he devoted attention to more serious comedy or to tragedies of the human soul. With *Othello* he reaches the summit of his art ; this masterpiece represents a peak whence the streams of his inspiration flowed into new channels, a work of prodigious imagination, and at the same time of deep philosophy. It is remarkable for combining characteristics of his first manner with the qualities of his later Promethean production.

From the point of view of dramatic composition, *Hamlet* is not faultless ; in compensation *Othello* is an impeccable drama, a work where the characters live, love and suffer with an intensity which Shakespeare himself had never before attained. Not a superfluous word, not a gesture is made without reason ; each incident is the logical consequence of these words and gestures. They succeed one another as though controlled by clockwork, each personage entering at his appointed time to prepare the fatal dénouement.

Shakespeare found his inspiration for this play in a novel of Giraldo Cinthio's concerning infidelity in men and women.[1] There was no English translation of this story at the time of the composition of *Othello ;* but, as has already been remarked, the author could have heard a commentary on the text from Southampton, if not from his tutor Florio. He might also have read it himself in the excellent French version of Gabriel Chappuys, published in 1584, which like Belleforest's *Histoires tragiques* was widely circulated in England.

Nevertheless, on comparing the English drama with the Italian tale, it becomes apparent that there are more differences than similarities between the two. According to Cinthio, the wicked ensign vainly tried to seduce

---

[1] *Hecatommitti*, seventh story of the third decade.

his superior's wife ; repulsed with scorn, he imagines a horrible vengeance and succeeds in convincing the Moor that he is being deceived. His wife's supposed lover is a corporal who has boasted of the possession of the lady's handkerchief as a love token. The master's honour must be avenged. The ensign volunteers to aid the wronged husband and the two men unite to kill the Moor's innocent wife. This is brutally done by battering their victim's head with sacks of sand ; then, to give the impression that her death was accidental, they bring down the heavy oak tester of the bed the unhappy woman sleeps on. Their crime committed, the murderers decamp and the truth is only discovered by the revelations of the ensign's abandoned wife.

Before dealing with this unpleasing subject, the dramatist transformed the unsavoury setting and ennobled the characters ; he then modified the story to fit its new social sphere. He was also obliged to provide names for his personages who, in the Italian story, are known only by their military grades, except the heroine, Disdemona, which Shakespeare altered into Desdemona.

In naming the villainous ensign, he fell back on a memory of childhood recalling a rough woodcut with the title in capital letters, IAGO, which by an indelible impression was linked with the idea of malignity. It figures on page 27 of the first volume of Holinshed's *Chronicles*. The features of this king, with no story, but with a particularly sinister aspect, are engraved opposite a picture of Cordelia, Lear's daughter, which he had often contemplated, while reading of this princess whom he was later to immortalize. Evidently the sound of the name Iago had impressed the poet, since later in *Cymbeline* he slightly changed it, and adopted for his new villain, whose character was almost as atrocious as the cunning Venetian, the name of Iachimo. Gratiano had already figured in *The Merchant of Venice*, and Bianca in *The Taming of the Shrew*, Lodovick is used in *Measure for Measure*. As for the name Othello, it came probably from Moghrib: Hawth Allāh.

Besides these Italian sources, Shakespeare possessed a vast quantity of documentation already touched upon in connection with *The Merchant of Venice* and *Titus Andronicus*, quite enough to furnish his *Othello*. The Barbary Company agents did not fail to inform Londoners of the military and political relations between the Fortunate Empire and Elizabeth's government. Henry Roberts, for example, brother of the printer of repute who published, besides other Shakespearean plays, the Quarto edition of *The Merchant of Venice*, represented the interests of the Company and those of his country for more than two years with the Sultan of Morocco, and would naturally relate his adventures to his family and to the author who, for the first time, was presenting Barbary and its inhabitants on the London stage.

The Record Office Archives contain a series of letters exchanged between the Portuguese ambassador and Elizabeth's ministers showing the plenipotentiary's indignation on the subject of arms smuggling and the export of Bibles in Hebrew for the conversion of Moroccan Jews.

Elizabeth repudiated the accusation, but declared herself quite ready to administer severe punishment if the ambassador would furnish her with explicit proofs of contraband activities, asserting that when the English landed upon the African shores they only carried arms in self-defence not with the intention of selling them.

As for the " Hebrew Bibles ", Her Majesty was astonished to find that her subjects possessed them in such quantities, when it was so difficult to find them in her own country.   Moreover, she did not understand why she must not provide Bibles for the Saracens and the Jews since these books contained the true commandments of God.   More subtle than the ambassador, the Queen evaded the question ; her adversary was obliged to content himself with replying that he had not come to England to dispute if it were reasonable or not that Christians should bring Bibles to the Jews in Barbary, but only to make this remonstrance and return incontinent to his embassy at the court of France.

Contraband of arms continued, and was carried on not only by English traders, but by the Sultan's agents travelling under a British safe conduct,[1] and as political rivalry grew between England and Spain, the rôle of Morocco increased accordingly.   The Queen was justified in seeking some agent among the merchant adventurers capable of representing her officially or un-officiously in a country where trade with England rested upon three thousand lengths of dark blue English cloth for making burnouses, against three thousand cases of sugar. leather, copper, spices, olives or saltpetre.   When one remembers the small capacity of the ships of those days, there is no doubt that the merchant fleet was a large one.[2]

The choice of her first representative to the Emperor of Morocco, " King of Fez and Sus ", was unfortunate.   James Hogan, unaccustomed to the habits and ways of barbarian countries, returned to London without having obtained the cargo of saltpetre which was the principal object of his mission. His failure was keenly felt, especially as the Sultan, at every threat of a rupture in diplomatic relations, replied by a popular saying characteristic of Mussulman philosophy : " If your dogs leave, other dogs will come."

National interests required to be defended by individuals better qualified to thwart the competition of French and Flemish merchants.   In 1585, the enterprising Henry Roberts, a close friend of Leicester, left London with three tall ships for the port of Safi, where the local official furnished an escort and mules which enabled him and his suite to reach the Sultan's capital.

After a stay of several years, he was summoned to the fairy gardens which

---

[1] Moulay Abdallah el Ghalib writing to Queen Elizabeth on behalf of his Sultan in order to obtain safe conducts for merchants and vessels begins his letter thus :

" From the servant of the Almighty, chief of the believers upheld by the certainty of Victory, the help of God and brilliant conquests . . . to the Queen of England and Ireland, the respectable, illustrious and excellent Elizabeth, daughter of king Henri, may God direct her steps in the straight and salutary path and, by his benevolent protection, keep her in good health."   *State Papers Foreign, royal letters,* vol. II, no. 52.

[2] Elizabeth's Charter gave forty merchants for twelve years the exclusive right to trade in the Sultan's territories ; no other English subject could do business without authorization on pain of imprisonment and confiscation of his merchandise, half of the goods thus confiscated to revert to the Queen, the other half to the Company.

he calls *Shersbonare*, meaning Sheridj-el-Menara, where he was " honourably and often welcomed by His Majesty himself ".   Roberts received, when his mission was over, the usual presents and returned accompanied by a captain named Merzouk-el-Rhais, appointed by the commander of the Faithful to sign an offensive and defensive alliance, in which the two powers proposed to set Don Antonio on the Spanish throne.[1]

The representatives of England and Morocco met at St. Ives on January 1st, 1589, and journeyed on together.   Before reaching London they met a delegation of the City Corporations joined by fifty representatives of the Barbary Company, all well mounted and equipped.   A magnificent coach awaited the two emissaries at London Bridge so that they could make a solemn entry together surrounded by horsemen with flaming torches, a spectacle likely to impress the Stratford poet not yet blasé from too many years in the metropolis.

Speaking of the reception of Merzouk-el-Rhais at court, the correspondent John Chamberlain expressed his satisfaction that England's glory should be shown to persons who had come from so far ; but he admits that these friendly receptions offended the feelings of ordinary mortals.[2]

On his master's behalf, the plenipotentiary proposed that if Elizabeth would furnish arms, money and provisions, they in their turn would open all Moroccan harbours to the English and even support Don Antonio in his enterprise.   He invited the queen to add her squadron to some Moroccan galleys, to force Spain to face a double threat and thus facilitate the claimant's march on Lisbon.   These negotiations excited public opinion and left profound traces upon the circle frequented by Shakespeare which explain his interest in North Africa.

A few impressionist touches add an exotic element to his Moroccan pictures.   Deserts and mountains where the sun shines with violence, where the horses are fine, the men warlike, Guinea fowl, bears and lions numerous. He does not seem to have known of the presence in Rabat of storks, so dear to descriptive writers of the present day.

No error, however, can be found in the two portraits drawn in 1589 and 1593.   In 1604 he was better informed as relations between Morocco and England were closer.   Hardy travellers, tempted either by the attraction of the unknown or by the lure of gain, had explored far into the country and their tales were retold throughout London.   A Scottish explorer, William Lithgow [3] related how he had reached Fez the Mysterious and endured hardships in Spain, where, on his return journey, he was arrested and racked by the Inquisition.   He exhibited his tortured limbs in public to

---

[1] *Sources inédites de l'Histoire du Maroc* (Paris, 1918).

[2] " Our merchants and mariners thinck it a matter odious and scandalous to be too freindly or familiar with infidells.   But yet it is no small honour to us that nations so far remote and every way different should meet here to admire the glory and magnificence of our Quene of Saba." (*Letter from John Chamberlain to Dudley Carleton.   Sources inédites de l'Histoire du Maroc*, English Archives, vol. ii, p. 192.)

[3] Lithgow was accompanied to Morocco by a French jeweller in search of King Solomon's Emerald Mines.

show that the wild inhabitants of Barbary were less cruel than the civilized Spaniards. This experience made him popular in his own country, and ended by becoming profitable. James I sent him to the waters of Bath at his own expense, and he found sympathizers in every level of society. It was even said that the story of his strange adventures won the heart of some English Desdemona. The account of his journey in Morocco, a very rare work, is in the library at Rabat.

The exploits of a more aristocratic adventurer were already legendary in England at the end of the sixteenth century. Sir Anthony Shirley, one of three Catholic brothers who specialized in Oriental knowledge, was successively the Earl of Essex' agent at the courts of Henry IV, Boris Godownov and Rudolph II. As Ambassador in Morocco he held open house for six months at Marrakesh, while he tried to negotiate with the Sultan El-Mansour for the sale of a diamond belonging to the treasure of St. Denis. A near neighbour of the Shakespeares in Warwickshire, Sir Anthony, after matriculating at Hart Hall, Oxford, served in the Low Countries, and with Essex in Normandy, where he was knighted by Henry of Navarre. He explored Jamaica, returned to England by way of New-foundland, then again served with Essex whom he followed in the campaign of 1597, and who sent him to Venice, to Persia on a politics-commercial mission, and finally to Morocco. He undertook an expedition against the Turks for the King of Spain, and died a poor man in Madrid, having pub-lished in 1609 an account of his travels in Persia where he was accompanied by his brother, Sir Robert Shirley, who entered the Shah's service and married a noble Circassian woman.[1]

Shakespeare evidently made use of these various accounts to lend colour and life to his plays. The merchants who had witnessed the sufferings of chained slaves at the time of the early incursions on Moroccan shores, had enabled the author of *Titus Andronicus* to present on the stage the villainous Aaron, half semitic, half negro, cunning, spiteful and arrogant, who em-phasizes his acts of revenge with sinister jokes. We know exactly how the Roman Empress's Moorish lover appeared on the Shakespearean stage, as a manuscript has been preserved at Longleat containing a pencil drawing by Henry Peacham, where the liberated slave is shown with the coarse features of a woolly negro, black as ebony.

How much this conception differs from that of the Prince who comes to Belmont to seek the hand of Portia ! This Moor presents himself with the luxurious magnificence proper to the heir of an Arab prince.

> Mislike me not for my complexion,
> The shadow'd livery of the burnish'd sun,
> To whom I am a neighbour and near bred.
> Bring me the fairest creature northward born,

[1] A third brother had a no less adventurous career : incarcerated by the Turks for piracy, he was also imprisoned by Elizabeth for having contracted a secret marriage. Under the title, *The Shirley Brothers*, a namesake, Evelyn Philip Shirley published in 1848 the history of the three adventurers.

Where Phoebus' fire scarce thaws the icicles,
And let us make incision for your love,
To prove whose blood is reddest, his or mine. . . .
(*The Merchant of Venice*, Act II, Sc. 1)

Thanks to the quarto edition of *The Merchant of Venice* (1600), so valuable because of the stage directions, we know the exact complexion of the Prince of Morocco.

" Enter Morochus, a tawny Moor, all in white."

Thus ten years before writing the drama of *Othello*, the author distinguished between two types ; the prince as proud as he was noble, and the vilest of slaves, as different from one another as the mountain and the plain, but both he calls Moors.   This was the fashion of his time, when no ethnological difference was made between the inhabitants of the coast and the warriors of the mountains.   The names, however, do not matter ; the genius who wrote *Othello* realized the abyss which separates Aaron from the Moor of Venice.

Not one of Othello's words or gestures contradicts his origin.   He springs from the warlike rulers of the Atlas :

I fetch my life and being
From men of royal siege, and my demerits
May speak unbonetted to as proud a fortune
As this that I have reached.

he declares when the Venetian Senate hesitates to confide to a foreign adventurer the hand of the patrician Desdemona.   He has the dignity and simplicity of heart which distinguishes the men of the Atlas region ; [1] but once betrayed or when his suspicions are aroused, he is capable of tragic ferocity.   Superstitious like his kind he believes in omens.   He seeks proof of his wife's fidelity in the lines of her hand and torments himself accordingly. Desdemona's hand shows candour and generosity, but is it not perhaps too warm and moist ?   The first gage of his love is a fetish irrevocably intertwined with their mutual destiny.

This handkerchief did an Egyptian to my mother give . . .
She dying gave it me and bid me, when my fate would have me wive
To give it to her.   I did so, and take heed on't . . .
To lose or giv't away were such perdition
As nothing else could match.

It is the Moor's characteristic qualities, his sincerity, his total inexperience of the world and of women, his simple credulity, that bring about his ruin. Outside the frame of his soldier's life the great man is ignorant of everything.

---

[1] The intellectual and moral superiority of *Othello* is intimately linked with the very idea of the drama.   This fact is not only essential to the development of the action, but to the exposition of the characters.   It explains the furious hatred of Iago, and the unbounded love of Desdemona. . . . (François Victor Hugo, *Oeuvres complètes de Shakespeare*, vol. 5, p. 64.)

He admires Iago for his worldly knowledge, which he himself lacks. Temperamentally he is slow to distrust. All the cleverness and baseness of a devilish genius are needed to raise the monster of jealousy in such a simple heart.

Like most of his enlightened contemporaries Shakespeare respected the Moorish race. The Moors had helped to found the first and foremost seat of learning at Salerno, had unlocked the secrets of Algebra and introduced the Arabic system of numerals, and had produced an architecture from which gothic art derived much inspiration. He knew something of the history of the crusades with their knightly paladins, worthy adversaries of European chivalry who, in the intervals of truce, courteously offered Charlemagne the relics of Christian saints.

In Shakespeare's day Venice was far from despising Granada, and in the opinion of her senate Othello possessed an incontestible superiority over his European rivals. Even Iago admits that there is no other man in Venice capable of conducting the war against the Turks, adding :

> The Moor how be it that I endure him not,
> Is of a constant, loving noble nature.

Only the eyes of hate and envy succeed in piercing the secret of his sensibility and capacity for suffering. To those who love and admire him—especially to his wife—Othello remains a mystery ; and it might be added that most of his Anglo-Saxon commentators—Coleridge excepted—fail to understand his character. As for theatrical directors and producers, ignorant or out of touch with ethnographical and psychological truth, they persist in representing the heroic Condottiere with the features and complexion of a stout nubian.

Shakespeare in creating Iago departs completely from the Italian source. According to Cinthio's tale the ensign's revengeful hatred is directed against his master's wife whom he loves desperately but who has repulsed him with scorn ; whereas Shakespeare's villain never thought of loving any human creature save himself. Iago has nothing but contempt for love. Desdemona's spiritual and mystic passion for her husband seems to him a sign of depravity. Should she succumb in the holocaust he is preparing, so much the worse for her. He seeks nobler game ; his general and his lieutenant who have cheated him out of his due rank.

The ensign of the story is a base wretch who can only turn circumstances to best advantage ; Iago is the far-seeing evil doer who prepares all in advance, dominates circumstances and never allows chance to interfere with his deep laid designs. This is why he must have an agent docile enough to obey, and sufficiently trusting to furnish the sinews of war to a gambler perpetually in quest of money. Hence Shakespeare creates a personage who does not exist in Cinthio's tale. Roderigo, the dupe, is the result of the new proportions the dramatist needs for his super villain Iago.

The first victim of the ensign's jealous spite, pursued under the guise of intimate and sympathetic friendship, is naturally the young lieutenant whose place Iago covets though he is totally unfit for it, Michael Cassio, an expert strategist, devoted to his profession and to his great commander ; his military superiority is enough to arouse a fierce hatred which thus finds words :

> He hath a daily beauty in his life
> which makes me ugly.

That is enough to set in motion the implacable clockwork which is never allowed to slacken nor run down.   The ensign manoeuvres all the characters of the drama without ever arousing the least suspicion that this " Deus ex machina " has taken command of what each believes to be his or her destiny.

Shakespeare's magic pen raises Cinthio's sordid novel to a higher plane by the same formula which he had so brilliantly employed in *Romeo and Juliet* : that is he contrasts a beautiful setting with the suffering and despair of the drama's chief personages.   After Mantua and Verona he now portrays Venice and Cyprus.

The initial action takes place in the wondrous city described by Florio as the impossible within the impossible.   Venice is revealed under the ruddy glare of flaring torches where the majestic sweep of the Grand Canal is intersected near the Bridge of Sighs by the canaletto, the very point made famous by tradition and art, where stands " Desdemona's house " that charming palazzo with its graceful torsades and balcony which local guides still show as the actual site where this child of the poet's imagination possessed a local habitation and a name !

From this balcony, Senator Brabantio, awakened during his midnight sleep listens unwillingly to the gross account of his daughter's nocturnal flight in the " foul embracements of a lascivious moor " under no better escort than a public gondolier.   It is told with calumnious skill under cover of darkness by Roderigo, who repeats parrot-like Iago's poisonous inventions against his own general.   No more is necessary for the enraged father, though he has been the first to admire Othello and entertain him as an honoured guest, to rush forth calling on kindred, neighbours and the Venetian night-watch to help chastise the ravisher.

Othello having left his newly-made bride in his lodgings at the Arsenal [1] encounters Brabantio's well-armed band on his way to the council's secret session.   His calm attitude and soldierly prestige lend force to his remonstrance.

> Put up your bright swords, for the dew will rust them ;
> Good Signior, you will more command with years
>   Than with your weapons.

Hastening on to the Doge's palace he finds the council in an uproar, suddenly reduced to silence as one messenger after another from the galleys

---

[1] The Sagittary which Shakespeare mentions as the residence where *Othello* had taken his young wife, was the block of buildings connected with the great arsenal of Venice, reserved as lodging for heads of land and sea services.   The sculptured figure of an archer ornamented the entrance to this edifice.

assails their ears with tales of innumerable Turkish fleets menacing Cyprus. Immediately the Senators invest the great soldier with full command over land and sea forces, when Brabantio bursts in with his story and protests loudly against this nomination crying out that the Moor is a practiser of the forbidden art of black magic and should be burned forthwith in accordance with the strict Venetian statutes. His passionate accusations come to naught before the Moor's manly defence ; not only is Othello ordered to sail that very night, but permission is given to his bride, escorted by Iago and his wife Emilia, to join him in Cyprus as soon as due preparations for their embarkment can be made. Brabantio suddenly leaps to his feet and solemnly addresses to Othello these words steeped in gall. They are destined to haunt the Moor's subconsciousness ; they will also furnish Iago with a perpetual spur to doubt and suspicion.

> Look to her Moor, if thou hast eyes to see ;
> She has deceived her father and may Thee.

What are we to think of Desdemona, of whom as yet we have seen little ? Her character from the start has been sharply defined. Essentially romantic, nurtured on tales of heroic adventure and the glory of the Venetian Republic, she dreams of the love of a hero, and finds her ideal in the Condottiere who has devoted his sword and talents to the service of her country.

Before leaving Venice all these personages have been made known to the spectator ; so that he is prepared to watch how each will contribute to the building up of the drama according to the natural reaction of his or her special character.

The scene shifts to Cyprus where the Governor Montano and his officers await in anguish of mind the attack of their adversaries. A violent tempest lashes the coast which we are soon to learn had dispersed and destroyed the greater part of the Turkish fleet, thus rendering Othello's victory easy and complete.

Suddenly the storm ceases and, under a brilliant sunset, a Venetian caravel enters the port, which modern research defines as Famagusta, capital of the island but which Shakespeare, in his stage-directions denominates : " A Seaport in Cyprus."

Montano hastens to greet Desdemona and her suite. The islanders recognize in this beautiful Venetian their tutelary Goddess, the Divine Kypris.

During the pause which naturally ensues, for as yet no news has been heard as to the outcome of the seafight, Shakespeare, with great dramatic skill, takes occasion to establish his characters more completely in a scintillating dialogue. In spite of her anxiety Desdemona, great lady that she is, consents to take part in conventional pleasantries, while Iago dissembles his hatred and malice under the mask of servile devotion. The rough life of camp and field serves as an excuse for audacious vulgarity. He knows that this trait brings with it privileges and that often an excess of frankness, though bordering on brutality, may pass for bluff honesty. In fact, for a

long time, Iago has stood for the personification of that virtue ; the epithet
" Honest " has become inseparable from his name.   His wife Emilia adores
her husband blindly without in the least understanding or resenting his rude
treatment, for a kind word or rare caress she obeys his smallest whim, little
thinking that her docility may lead her to commit a grave fault, even a crime.

A thunder of salvo shots announces that the Admiral ship is entering
the harbour and the great captain sets foot on shore amidst wild enthusiasm,
greeting his bride with ecstasy and telling the massed crowds to make all
ready for a festive night to celebrate at once his victory and his happy nuptials.
The generous Cassio who has shared in the honour of victory is ready to
rejoice in Othello's present happiness.   Only Iago is left gnashing his teeth
and exclaiming under his breath :

> Oh you are well tuned now
> But I'll set down the pegs that make this music.

His first care is to persuade his superior officer Cassio that he cannot
without discourtesy refuse to toast his fellow officers belonging to the Cypriot
garrison.   The lieutenant is a man of sober habits and has neither taste nor
head for libations.   But like Othello, he believes in Iago's knowledge of
the world and military traditions and is easily persuaded to drink more than
is good for him.   Whereupon Roderigo following Iago's orders draws
Cassio into a quarrel which soon becomes a broil, then a free fight.   The
Governor attempts to make peace and is wounded.   By Iago's instructions
the tocsin is rung and all is riot and confusion when Othello descends from
the citadel, enters the piazza and cries indignantly.

> What in a town of war yet wild
> The people's hearts brimful of fear
> To manage private and domestic quarrel
> And on the Court of guard and safety
> 'Tis monstrous ; say Iago who began it ?

Thus adjured as an impartial witness, the ensign makes a report, pretending
to be in Cassio's favour but in truth blackening his action and placing upon
him full responsibility for the fray.   The General falls into the trap and
pronounces judgement.

> I know Iago,
> Thy honesty and love doth mince this matter,
> Making it light to Cassio . . . . Cassio I love thee.
> But nevermore be officer of mine.

Thence there is but a step to suggest to the broken hearted Cassio to intercede
with Desdemona that she may plead with her husband in the Lieutenant's
favour.   Generous Desdemona does not hesitate an instant to place her
charm and eloquence at a friend's service.

Never surely was such apparently disinterested advice so venomous and
fatal !   While the warm-hearted girl cannot understand such harsh discipline

and continues to weary Othello with her pleas for clemency, Iago manages
to make her natural interest in Cassio's fate appear like a guilty partiality,
manoeuvring his unsuspicious victims with such skill that the spectator longs
to intervene in order to put a stop to Desdemona's prayers.

> What Michael Cassio,
> That came a wooing with you and so many a time
> When I have spoke dispraisingly of you
> Hath ta'en your part.

Half convinced Othello consents to listen to the excuses and explanations
of his discharged lieutenant. A deft lie from Iago prevents the meeting and
the poison which has already begun to work goes on ruthlessly.

It is easy to undermine Othello's confidence in his right to be loved for
himself alone by one who has been courted by all the gilded youth of Venice.
He is a man of ripe age, of another race, without fortune, lacking the social
amenities which a cultured woman has a right to expect from her husband—
why then did she choose him ? He has but a weak defence against Iago's
skilful insinuations. At length the Moor will listen no longer without proof.
Alas, proof is never lacking for such as Iago. With fiendish cunning he
prepares the heart-rending scene in the course of which each time poor
Desdemona recommences her praise of Cassio, she is answered by two words
spoken in the most varied tones ranging from despair and rage to madness,
" The Handkerchief ? "

But to follow the story step by step, the reader would need Shakespeare's
own pen.

The climax is finally provoked almost without warning, by the sudden
arrival of a deputation from Venice charged to remove Othello from command
and transfer his title to Cassio. This blow convinces Desdemona that the
new policy must be the work of her father Brabantio which partially explains
her husband's changed attitude. She appeals to Iago for advice and this
allows him to give her hypocritical comfort with assurance. Othello will
soon be himself ; his bad humour is a passing phase, his character is too
strong, his nature too magnanimous for even this disappointment to affect
him longer. If only Desdemona will calmly preside at the banquet which
custom demands should be offered to the Doges' envoy, all will yet be well.
So the poor child does her best to conceal the rift and when her task is
accomplished finds herself roughly ordered to bed while Othello, as in duty
bound, escorts his guests to their lodgings outside the citadel.

Here Shakespeare places an exquisite interlude, a peaceful oasis in a
desert over which hovers unseen the wings of death. Emilia while preparing
her mistress' night toilet indulges in worldly prattle which brings into strong
relief the candour and purity of Desdemona who, while setting aside her
pearls and laces, tries to conjure away the vague apprehensions which oppress
her mind. She hums the air of an ancient ballad learned in her childhood
from a love-crazed servant Barbara. So before lying down to rest and
perhaps feigning sleep, while awaiting Othello's return, she soothes herself

with the willow song made famous now the world over by the music of Rossini and Verdi.

Meanwhile, on his homeward way under the stars Othello pauses before the house where Iago and Roderigo lie in ambush prepared to kill Cassio the instant he emerges from supper.   Suddenly the Moor's ears are assailed by desperate cries for help ; then complete silence.   Assured that " Honest Iago " has avenged his tarnished honour a strange spirit of calm invades his heated brain.   His personal wrongs seem to melt away, and give place to stern determination, for he now sees his duty clearly.   The shameless woman who through her fatal beauty and feminine craft is capable of ensnaring men's souls and driving them to destruction and death must not live longer.   Entering the chamber softly he extinguishes the candle burning beside the bed and parts the curtains. . . .

Hardly is the horrible deed accomplished when the Venetian lords enter, summoned by Emilia's calls for help, and Othello is obliged to answer their interrogations by declaring himself :

> An honourable murderer if you will
> for all was done for honour not in hatred.

Finally, enlightened by Emilia's confession that her husband had stolen the fatal handkerchief in order to lay it in Cassio's room, when Iago has cut short her explanations by a swift dagger stroke, Othello at length awakes to his monstrous error.   With one farewell look at his ill-starred victim he consigns himself to eternal flames.

> Whip me ye devils from the possession of this heavenly sight
> Blow me about in winds, roast me in sulphur,
> Wash me in steep-down gulfs of liquid fire
> Oh Desdemona ! Desdemona dead.

But while calling down condign punishment and devoting himself to the just wrath of God, he refuses to accept judgement at the hands of the Venetian Republic that he has so often saved and brings the tragedy to a close by diverting their attention to his narration which he suddenly interrupts by plunging a concealed poignard in his heart.

> I pray you in your letters,
> When you shall these unlucky deeds relate
> Speak of me as I am, nothing extenuate
> Nor set down aught in malice.   Then must you speak
> Of one that loved not wisely but too well :
> Of one not easily jealous, but being wrought
> Perplexed in the extreme : of one whose hand
> Like the base Judean threw a pearl away
> Richer than all his tribe.

Many critics join with Professor Furness in expressing regret that this *too* moving and too cruel tragedy ever saw the light.   Others on the contrary claim that its reading ought to be compulsory, as being a most eloquent sermon on the consequences of jealousy and calumnious reports. Without taking sides in this debate I may remark that the suppression of such a masterpiece of dramatic construction and exalted language would deprive the world of one of its greatest literary treasures.

One word more on the mystery of the poet's meaning in drawing Iago as he does. I am not of those who claim to be able to sound the poet's *mind*, but I do believe that three score years of study have taught me a good deal about his *methods*. When the Moor comes to his senses and is brought face to face with his Ensign I believe that Shakespeare meant his readers and spectators to think that Othello saw in his tormentor the Prince of Darkness himself. He cannot bear to look on his face or ask him a direct question, he only gazes at his feet in search of the cloven hoof which even when Satan assumed human form was his indispensable attribute. Thus the tragedy represents in greater dimensions the Morality play of the Coventry pageants. We remember Othello's bitter cry, " If thou art the devil I cannot kill thee ". In spite of the Moor's mastery of his blade, Iago exclaims triumphantly, " I'm hurt sirs but not killed ". Though we have the council's assurance that he will be tortured to death they are aware that Satan cannot be killed by human agency.

Performed for the first time on November 1st, 1604, in the presence of King James, Anne of Denmark and her brother Prince Frederik of Wurtemberg, *Othello* or *The Moor of Venice* had an unprecedented success. This play was revived more often than any other tragedy given in England up to the death of Charles I. At the Restoration it reappeared triumphantly and, since then, on every stage and in every country, it has earned an uninterrupted acclamation.

At forty-eight, Burbage was too old for the young prince of Denmark, but he could play the Moor with the same success until his last breath : and the fact that no quarto edition was published at this time indicates that the tragedy was continually acted. It was only later, in October 1621, that Thomas Walkeley sought and obtained the Lord Chamberlain's consent to publish the text of *Othello*.[1] The Stationer's register has this inscription :

The tragedy of *Othello, the Moore of Venice*. As it hath beene diverse times acted at the " Globe " and at the " Black-Friars ", by his Majesties servants. Written by William Shakespeare, London, printed by N.O. (Nicholas Okes) for Thomas Walkeley and are to be sold at his shop, at the Eagle and Childe in Brittans Bursse, 1622.

This text is interesting on account of the extreme vigour of the language. It contains all the oaths, curses, blasphemies and invocations of the name of God which a law passed in 1606 prohibited on the stage or in print. It is therefore evident that this text is the original version of the tragedy as it was played before the King at the Palace of Whitehall, and appears to have been

---

[1] The Stationer's register for October 6th, 1621, inscribes : " Thomas Walkley. Entred for his copie under the handes of Sir George Buck and Martin Swinhowe warden, *the Tragedie of Othello, the moore of Venice*. VI pence."

that of the prompter reproduced by the printer without alteration, while the 1623 version seems to have been reviewed and corrected to comply with censorship requirements. But, if expressions thought to be blasphemous were suppressed, certain emendations and re-arrangements evidence the author's desire to perfect his work before giving it to posterity. One hundred and sixty lines are added which do not appear in the quarto, and these changes are undoubtedly improvements. It should also be mentioned that the text of *Othello* in the complete works, contains a list of the chief characters in the drama with their names and occupations.[1]

The first reference to the play of *Othello* is an indirect proof of the impression it made. The register of St. Leonard of Shoreditch, the parish of Burbage and many other actors, contains the record of a christening. A certain William Bishoppe, touched by the poetic grace of the charming Venetian, gave to his newly-born daughter the name of Desdemona, hitherto unknown in England, which Shakespeare had just rendered famous.[2]

Of the numerous performances of *Othello*, some have left their trace in the news letters or archives of the time. For example, in April 1610, His Excellency the Duke of Wurtemberg " went to the ' Globe ' where comedies are ordinarily played to attend the representation of the *History of the Moor of Venice* ". At court, *Othello* was chosen among fourteen plays given in honour of the Elector Palatine on the occasion of his marriage to James's daughter, the beautiful Princess Elizabeth. It was also acted before Henry, Prince of Wales, and his brother, the unfortunate Charles I.[3] On the public stage *Othello* was always profitable. On November 22nd, 1629, its performance brought in the considerable sum for those days of nine pounds, sixteen shillings, a figure reported by Sir Henry Herbert himself.[4] But the record receipts were reached by the celebrated Betterton, interpreter of all the heroic Shakespearean rôles, when he played Othello for his farewell to the stage and found himself the recipient of the incredible sum of five hundred and twenty-six pounds.[5]

---

[1] The folio of 1623 has no indications of place : only the entrances and exits of the characters are noted at the beginning of each scene. The " Dramatis Personae " is thus reproduced at the end of the play :
Othello : the Moore. Brabantio : father of Desdemona.
Cassio : an honourable lieutenant. Iago : a villain.
Roderigo : a duped gentleman. The Doge of Venice. Senators.
Montano : a governor of Cyprus. Gentlemen of Cyprus.
Ludovico and Gratiano : Venetian nobles. Sailors. The Clown.
Desdemona : wife of Othello. Emilia : wife of Iago.
Bianca : a courtesan.
[2] Halliwell Phillips, *Outlines* (5th edn., p. 177).
[3] A first critical mention has been found in the *Memoranda* written before 1637 by a certain Abraham Wright : *Othello* by Shakespeare, a very good play, as much in its versification as in its plot. The rôles of Iago, the villain, and of Othello the jealous husband are masterly written. The scene between these characters in the third act and the first scene of the fourth act, show admirably the character of the wretch Iago when he persuades Othello and leads him into the road of jealousy.
[4] From King's company being brought to me by Blagrave, upon the play of *The Moor of Venice* (9L. XVI S).
[5] *Annales of the English Stage* (Dr. Doran, F.S.A. London, 1887).

A pamphlet published in 1605, provides an unexpected commentary on Shakespeare's visits to Stratford. It is the story of an actor held up by the celebrated highwayman Ratsey and his band. By way of forfeit for his lack of cash they forced him to declaim a scene from his stage repertory. The young actor acquitted himself with such brio that the chief, moved to enthusiasm, gave the player this timely advice :

Get thee to London, for if one man were dead, they will have much need of such a one as thou art. There would be none in my opinion fitter than thyselfe to play his parts : My conceipt is such of thee, that I durst venture all the mony in my purse on thy head, to play *Hamlet* with him for a wager. There thou shalt learne to be frugall (for Players were never so thriftie as they are now about London) and to feed upon all men, to let none feede upon thee ; to make thy hand a stranger to thy pocket, thy hart slow to performe thy tongues promise : and when thou feelest thy purse well lined, buy thee some place of Lordship in the Country, that growing weary of playing, thy mony may there bring thee to dignitie and reputation. . . .

Sir, I thank you (quoth the Player) for this good counsel. I promise you I will make use of it, for I have heard indeede of some that have gone to London very meanly, and have come in time to be exceeding wealthy.

Shakespeare was certainly then in Stratford for he was present at the christening of his sister, Johanne Harte's, son, July 24th, 1605—the day when he bought half of the tithes of his parish for the large sum of four hundred and forty pounds.[1] The whole family were also assembled on June 5th, 1607, for the marriage of Susanna, the poet's favourite daughter, to Doctor John Hall.

Susanna Shakespeare, who became her father's sole legatee, was endowed with excellent qualities of heart and head, knew how to soften the lot of the unfortunate, and was considered by her contemporaries an exceptionally gifted woman. " Her mind she inherited from her father Shakespeare ; but her virtues came from her Father in heaven ", says her epitaph. She had herself written in Latin verse, the inscription on her mother's tomb.[2] The

---

[1] In this official act, Shakespeare is mentioned thus : " William Shakespeare of Stratforde-upon-Avon in the said countie of Warr. Gent."

[2] Ubera, tu mater, tu lac, vitamque dedisti
Vae mihi : pro tanto munere saxa dabo ?
Quam mallem, amoveat lapidem, bonus angelus orem
Exuat ut Christi corpus, imago tua—
Sed nil vota valent ; venias cito Christe ; resurget
Clausa jacet tumulo mater et astra petit.

This epitaph may still be read on the Hall tomb, thanks to the historian Dugdale, who preserved the text. The original inscription on copper, surmounted by the Shakespeare and Hall arms, had been scratched out to make room for the epitaph of a certain Richard Watts. In 1844, the original inscription was restored.

The inscription " Ubera Tu mater . . . ", etc., is that on the monument of Anne Shakespeare, the poet's wife, and not on that of Susanna Hall, his daughter. The lines do in fact record Susanna's grief.

Dugdale reproduces Anne's epitaph in his *Antiquities of Warwickshire* :
Here lyeth interred the body of Anne wife of William Shakespeare, who departed this life the 6 day of August 1623 being of the age of 67 years.
Ubera mater, etc. [OVER

prosody is not impeccable, but the sentiments which it expresses have none of the characteristic coldness of elegies of this kind. There is even the echo of one of the poet's ideas found in *Hamlet* and *Romeo and Juliet*.

O thou, my mother who hast given me life with thy breast, must I, alas! for all your kindness, reward you only with a stone? Since these regrets are vain, let us pray that this flagstone may quickly be set aside by the good angel and that thou mayest appear as I have known thee.

Come quickly, O Christ, so that she who is in this tomb may rise and mount to the stars.

Three generations were grouped around the young couple. Mary Arden, the grandmother, was still alive and was even to see the birth the following year of her great-grand-daughter. The poet, his wife, his two brothers, Gilbert and Richard, his sister Johanne Harte, and his daughter Judith, completed the immediate family.

The union could only have pleased William Shakespeare who found in this son-in-law, then aged thirty-two, a friend, an excellent fellow and a doctor of undisputed reputation. His company explains why Shakespeare's work bears evidence of such a profound knowledge of physiology, psychiatry and the empirical cures for the nervous system and for cerebral troubles. Technical terms of medicine and surgery abound in his plays, in which, unlike the works of Molière, medical art is treated with the highest respect.

John Hall, a precocious boy, matriculated at Queens' College, Cambridge, with his eldest brother in 1589. Like many Catholics he left England for France where he was a brilliant student of medicine. These qualifications permitted him to occupy an influential position in Warwickshire after having established himself at Stratford. To the books which he inherited from his father, comprising works on astrology, astronomy and the occult sciences, he added his own personal collection.

He left two manuscript volumes, written in Latin with a few French quotations, on the pathological cases he had studied. One of these volumes was luckily saved by a young practitioner who, during the civil war, mounted guard with the royalist army at Stratford bridge. This militiaman visited New-Place with a member of the Hall family. He bought one of the manuscripts, translated it into English and published it in 1657, under the title:

The Inscription on Susanna Hall's tomb in Stratford parish church is
Heere Lyeth the body of Susanna wife of John Hall. Gent: the daughter of William Shakespeare. Gent: she deceased the 13th of July Anno 1649, aged 66.
Witty above her sex, but that's not all,
Wise to salvation was good Mistris Hall
Something of Shakespeare was in that, but this
Wholy of him with whom she's now in blisse.
Then, Passenger, hast here a teare,
To weepe with her that wept with all;
That wept, yet set her self to chere
Them up with comforts cordiall.
Her love shall live, her mercy spread,
When thou hast ner'e a teare to shed.
R. Lewis, vol. 2, p. 608.

Select Observations on English Bodies or Cures both Empericall and Historicall performed upon very eminent Persons in desperate Diseases. First, written in Latine by Mr. John Hall Physician, living at Stratford upon Avon in Warwickshire, where he was very famous, as also in the Counties adjacent, as appeares by these Observations drawn out of severall hundreds of his, as choysest. Now put into English for common benefit by James Cooke Practitioner in Physick and Chirurgery.

Unfortunately Susanna Hall refused to part with the second manuscript which perhaps included the case of her famous father whom her husband was unable to cure.[1]

It was in a house contiguous to his own that Shakespeare installed the Hall couple. This house remains today as Hallscroft. The building and lovely garden over which the giant mulberry tree—twin brother of the one planted by Shakespeare at New Place—have been scrupulously respected. The former proprietor had already undertaken the reconstitution of the consulting room and laboratory in which the learned doctor pursued his researches. Today the domain has been taken over by the Shakespeare Birthplace Trust and under the enlightened direction of Mr. Levy Fox everything possible is being done to restore to Hallscroft the atmosphere of former days.

---

[1] The surviving manuscript is now in the British Museum. The text is almost effaced, and the Latin includes numerous abbreviations which makes it very difficult to decipher. The present author is in possession of an examplar of the printed text.

CHAPTER XVII

THE APEX

Visit of King Christian IV to the English Court ; Shakespeare takes part in the festivities—*King Lear*—The troupe rejuvenated—*Coriolanus*—Death of Mary Shakespeare—Death of the actors William Sly and Lawrence Fletcher—Revival of *Pericles* : numerous editions—*Antony and Cleopatra*.

AFTER the marriage of his daughter Susanna and the installation of the young couple at Hallscroft, Shakespeare was again obliged to leave his family and resume harness. Besides professional obligations, there were the duties attached to his new office of Groom of the Chamber. The troupe went first to Greenwich, then to Hampton Court to take part in the festivities organized in honour of Christian IV, King of Denmark, the brother of the Queen. These official celebrations, which lasted from July 10th until August 9th, included a large number of theatrical performances. In view of the personality of the distinguished guest, it is certain that *Hamlet* figured on the programme. Perhaps it was for this occasion that Shakespeare deleted from the text of 1604 the passage where the young prince speaks of Danish excesses at banquets in unflattering terms.[1] These cuts are kept in the final version of 1623.

A witness of this royal visit, forgetting that Mahomedans never touch alcohol, declared that King Christian, far from having left his customs behind in Copenhagen, succeeded in transforming the places he visited into " Mahomet's paradis ".

Sir John Harrington describes in detail the famous reception offered by Robert Cecil to the Danish sovereign and his brother-in-law King James.[2] This ambitious minister, created Viscount Cranborne on the morrow of the Coronation, had recently risen a step higher, and it was under his new title of Marquis of Salisbury that he invited their Majesties to his beautiful residence of Theobalds near London. Profiting by the absence of the Queen, who had just given birth to a seventh child, the Princess Sophie, he organized as the climax of the feast, a masque with songs and dances entitled : *Solomon and the Queen of Sheba*. In Harrington's account which is here

---

[1] This heavy headed reveale east and west
Makes us tradust, and taxed of other nations,
They clip us drunkards, and with Swinish phrase
Soyle our addition . . .

(Quarto of 1604, D)

[2] Harrington's letter is quoted in *The Elizabethan Stage*, E. K. Chambers, vol. i, p. 172.

summarized allowance should be made for an exaggeration natural in the godson of Elizabeth.

The lady who played the part of the Queen of Sheba was delegated to bring precious gifts to their Majesties but, tripping over the steps of the platform, she upset her tray over his Danish Majesty and fell at his feet. Towels and cloths were quickly fetched to repair the devastation. The King then rose to dance with the " Queen of Sheba ", but fell in his turn and " humbled himself before her ". He was then carried to a closed room and laid under a canopy. The bed suffered greatly from the gifts which the " Queen of Sheba " had just thrown over his person, wines, creams, cakes, spices and other delicacies. The spectacle nevertheless continued ; but most of the actors " went backward or fell down ", befuddled with wine. Suddenly, Faith, Hope and Charity appeared, sumptuously attired. Hope wished to speak, but wine prevented her. Faith then presented herself alone ; she was not accompanied by any good works and left the room stumbling. Then Charity threw herself at the feet of the King, in an effort to efface the faults of her sisters. She had intended to bring gifts, but alleged, curtseying, that His Majesty already possessed all that the gods could give and incontinently joined her sisters. Victory followed in shining armour to pay court with a jumble of incomprehensible prose and verse. She offered a beautiful sword which His Majesty put aside with his hand. Victory's triumph was short. She was led away like a feeble captive and laid on the steps of the landing with the theological virtues.

The series of feasts and banquets ended with a great review of the fleet at Chatham. At the farewell dinner on the Danish flagship, trumpet and cannon saluted each time one of the sovereigns raised his glass after the custom described in *Hamlet*,[1] and when the last salvoes were fired and the vessel raised anchor, a fireworks display more magnificent than any given before astonished the shore dwellers, especially as the departure took place at two o'clock in the afternoon.

The King and Queen returned to Windsor for the hunting season, while the actors went on tour playing at Leicester, Marlborough and Dover, where they arrived on October 4th. The troupe's visit to Dover provided Shakespeare with material for one of his most imposing scenes in the tragedy which he was then writing—*King Lear*. Like a modern tourist he climbed the high cliff now called Shakespeare's Cliff. It suffices to read the passage which he gives to Edgar to realize the profound impression felt by the poet as he stood on the edge of this precipitous height.

> Come on, Sir ; here's the place : stand still.
> How fearful and dizzy 'tis to cast one's eyes so low !
> The crows and choughs that wing the midway air
> Show scarce so gross as beetles ; half way down

[1] And there's no health the King shall drinke to day
But the great Canon to the clowdes shall tell
The rowse the King shall drinke unto Prince Hamlet.
(Quarto of 1603, B3)

Hangs one that gathers samphire, dreadful trade !
Methinks he seems no bigger than his head.
The fishermen that walk upon the beach
Appear like mice, and yond tall anchoring bark
Diminish'd to her cock, her cock a buoy
Almost too small for sight.   The murmuring surge,
That on the unnumber'd idle pebbles chafes,
Cannot be heard so high.   I'll look no more,
Lest my brain turn, and the deficient sight
Topple down headlong.

(King Lear, Act IV, Sc. 6)

Three months later, at Christmas time, Shakespeare presented before the royal family and the court his tragedy *King Lear*—the most perfect specimen of " dramatic art ", according to Shelley—" a painting imagined by Dante, executed by Michelangelo ", as Coleridge put it.

No sooner was authority obtained to publish the history of *King Lear*, " as it was played before the King at Whitehall, on St. Stephen's night ",[1] than three editions were exhausted in less than a year.   The slight variations in the texts reflect the modifications made in the course of performance. The final version, which appeared in the folio of 1623 [2] is shorter, but seems, like the corresponding *Hamlet* version, to be the one which Shakespeare wished to leave to posterity.

The first of the quarto editions carries the following descriptive title :

M. William Shak-speare : His True Chronicle Historie of the life and death of King Lear and his three Daughters With the unfortunate life of Edgar, sonne and heire to the Earle of Gloster, and his sullen and assumed humor of Tom of Bedlam : As it was played before the Kings Majestie at Whitehall upon S. Stephans night in Christmas Holidayes.   By his Majesties servants playing usually at the Gloabe in the Bancke-side.[3]

The story of *King Lear* had been told in 1130 by Geoffrey of Monmouth. It figures in *Albion's England*, a book which Shakespeare possessed and which contains his signature.   It may also be read in Holinshed's *Chronicles*, the poet's unfailing resource.   The story of the Celtic King Leire son of Baldud, who reigned in Britain (*c.* 800 B.C.) " at the time when Joas still governed Judea ", is told by all these chroniclers in much the same manner.   In Elizabeth's day it was popularized by *The Mirour for magistrates*,[4] a collection

---

[1] 26 Novembris. Nathaniel Butler John Busby.   Entred for their copie under the handes of Sir George Buck knight, and The wardens A booke called Master William Shakespeare his historye of *Kinge Lear*, as yt was played before the kinges majestie at Whitehall upon Sainct Stephens night at Christmas Last by his majesties servantes playinge usually at the " Globe " on the Banksyde.

[2] In the folio of 1623, the Tragedie of *King Lear* is placed between *Hamlet* and *Othello*.

[3] London, printed for Nathaniel Butler, and are to be sold at his shop in Paules Churchyard at the signe of the pide bull near St. Austin's gate (1608).

[4] *The Mirour for magistrates*.   New Edition, collated with various editions with historical notes by Joseph Haslewood (London, 1815).   *The Ballad of King Lear* contained in *Percies reliques* is of later date than Shakespeare's play.

of tragic legends in verse printed in 1558, wherein " is shown the fragility of happiness of those who appear most fortunate ".

In 1594, an author unknown, but almost certainly belonging to the coterie of Henslowe's theatre used this ancient legend for a play entitled : *The True chronicle history of King Lear and his three daughters Gonerill, Ragan and Cordells.*[1] The author of this drama diverges from the old sources on one essential point : he transports the action to Christian times, which allows him to cram his text with biblical quotations and to give Cordelia the aspect of a Puritan blue-stocking, so self-satisfied that her sisters' animosity and the old king's anger seem partly justified. It would show ignorance of the Stratford poet to think for one moment that he drew his inspiration from this childish and pretentious text written for a rival theatre, especially as he took care in treating the same theme to maintain the action in the pagan setting described by the original chroniclers. As usual, confident in his art and his methods, he created out of the monstrous characters and the extravagant plot of the primitive legend, living and moving beings, so that this unlikely material is transformed into one of the most realistic of his dramas.

Here is a summary of the story according to the old chronicler :

To lighten the burdens of government, King Leire, vain, selfish and naïve, decides to give to the one of his daughters who best expresses filial sentiments towards him, the greater part of his vast inheritance, since his sway extended over Albany (Scotland), Cornwall and Kent. He is convinced that his favourite daughter, Cordelia, will be the winner. When he asks Gonneril, his eldest child to declare the extent of her love, she answers : " I take the sky as witness that I love you more than my soul ". To the same question, Regan, the second daughter swears upon oath that she " prefers her father to every other creature ". At this, the credulous king authorises both to choose a husband and gives each of them a third of his kingdom. Cordelia, seeing how easily her father is satisfied with flattering protestation, proves her affection in quite different terms. " I love you ", says she, " according to the dictates of filial affection." Furious at this answer Leire excludes her from a share in the kingdom ; he authorises her to marry, however, if she can find a man who will wed her without a dowry. Thus Gonneril and Regan respectively wed the Dukes of Cornwall and Albany, and divide the country between them, while Cordelia accepts the suit of the French king's son who loves her for herself alone.

Time passes, Goneril and Regan, backed by their husbands, cannot bear to see the King continuing to administer wisely the small portion of territory reserved to him. Daughters and sons-in-law sap his authority and undermine his credit to such purpose that, abandoned by all, enfeebled with age, he is driven to leave his palace and seek shelter now with Gonneril, now with Regan. One reproaches him for his extravagance and reduces his sixty knights to thirty : the other refuses to receive him unless attended by a single servant only. Dispossessed, unhappy and infirm, Leire sees that Cordelia's sole fault was sincerity, and resigns himself to seek shelter with her. He departs for France, arrives at Karitia (Calais), learns that the daughter he has misunderstood has come to meet him, but, ashamed of

[1] As it hath bene divers and sundry times lately acted (London). Printed for Simon Stafford for John Wright and are to bee sold at his shop at Christes Church dore next Newgate market, 1605.

his rags he remains under the walls of the town. With as much pity as tact Cordelia does not welcome him until he is provided with garments which befit his rank. After listening to his woes, the King of the French and Cordelia raise an army, cross the straits and attack the forces gathered by the angry English sons-in-law, who are killed in this action. Leire is restored to power, reigns for two more years and leaves the crown to Cordelia. She governs England for five years, but her nephews, who do not admit that a woman may succeed to the throne, depose her and throw her into prison. This queen who had a man's heart, seeing that all hope was denied her, put an end to her life.

Guided by this austere account, Shakespeare constructed a great tragedy with complex ramifications. He grafts on to this tale of a credulous father, two ungrateful daughters and a third misunderstood, a secondary theme inspired by a story from Sir Philip Sidney's *Arcadia*,[1] which tells of an unjust sovereign who drives away his devoted son and reserves his gifts for a shameless bastard, greedy to secure his father's inheritance.

Here again the dramatist's debt to his predecessors is slight. Everything which makes for dramatic interest and gives his tragedy poetic and moral value is his own contribution, beginning with the chief character. To him, Lear is a symbol. Father and king, he belongs to no time or country. His passion and imaginative power dominate and awe the spectator. But when he descends from the heights his simple and familiar language is even more striking. This ostracized king, against whom the entire forces of nature are in league with his cruel daughters, commands our sympathies by the simplicity with which he recounts his grievances. The little dogs who bark at the sight of him are the supreme proof of the malevolence of this world.

In the very different characters of Lear's elder daughters, the author shows his originality and avoids facile exaggeration of their hardness and cruelty. The reproaches which they make to the king about his extravagance are sometimes just and reasonable, criticisms such as might be made by young people of the present day who have little patience with parents and grand-parents. Goneril and Regan inherit their faults from a proud and selfish father ; they reveal the worst part of their natures only when they are stirred to reciprocal jealousy by their love for Edmund.

Cordelia too takes essentially after her father. But in her pride is noble, and inflexible will becomes a virtue. Her contempt for falsehood, her disdain of flattery, are proofs of character. The traits which drive her sisters into unnatural viciousness bring her into the ways of righteousness.

The juxtaposition of two distinct family dramas is original to Shakespeare, as are the guilty loves of Goneril and Regan for Edmund the bastard, Lear's madness, the tempest, Gloster's terrible ordeal and the final disaster to Lear and Cordelia. All these are Shakespeare's own creation, along with the new characters of Gloster, Edgar, Edmund, the Fool, Kent, Oswald and Albany.

---

[1] *The pitifull state, and storie of the Paphalgonian unkinde King, and his kind sonne, first related by the son, then by the blind father.* (The Countesse of Pembrokes *Arcadia*, 1590, Lib. 2, Chap. 10.)

Gloster,[1] a vain and sensual courtier, boasts shamelessly of his feminine conquests. He puts aside his legitimate son Edgar, endowed with the highest qualities, in favour of his natural child Edmund, a sort of Iago for whom Shakespeare has furnished if not excuses, at least certain attenuating circumstances. He must calmly endure wounding allusions, listen without protest to paternal comments on his mother's partiality, hear repeated continually that his father's possessions must go to his legitimate heir Edgar, whom he has learned to hate even before knowing him.

Edgar is a strange mixture of knight errant and penitent Christian before his time, a redresser of wrongs by sacrifice and unselfish devotion. His disguise as Tom of Bedlam, one of the unfortunate lunatics turned out of the asylum, is a curious idea. It permits Shakespeare to contrast the true insanity of Lear with the feigned madness of Edgar, just as he had contrasted Ophelia's real insanity with Hamlet's pretended madness. Faithful to the law of contrasts, Shakespeare adds to the cast a poor fool, simple-minded but of innate good sense, who, faithfully following the unhappy king, brings home to him the hardest truths under the mask of irony and thus marks each step of the degradation into which he is falling.

Three more personages are introduced : the honest and stoical councillor Kent, with his forty-eight years of experience and plain dealing—Kent is as useful as the fool in bringing into relief the king's character ; the courteous Albany, whose better feelings are opposed to the brutality of the Duke of Cornwall, Goneril and his own wife Regan ; as for Oswald, the infamous major-domo, he is but a convenient instrument in the hands of the flinty-hearted Goneril.

All these men and women are animated by a Promethean breath. Each plays an essential part in this vast assemblage of words and thoughts which demanded the utmost of Shakespeare's moral and intellectual powers. All his experience, his mastery of language, his knowledge of theatrical technique were required when he undertook this strange adventure. A mad undertaking some might have declared, little knowing the immense success which awaited *King Lear ;* " a spring of spontaneous genius ; an impetuous torrent in which the author, freed from human personality, intervenes only to transmit the breath of life ", say certain commentators !

When attentively examined, however, the mechanism of the drama, shows that in writing it, Shakespeare remained perfectly lucid and master of his material ; he never expressed himself more clearly. The management of climax and crescendo, the control over the most extreme and varied effects of language, is so masterly that what at first might appear as a desperate gamble, reveals itself on better acquaintance as a logical literary triumph— natural result of the most inspired labour, a work of immortal art combining the spirit of Dante with that of Aeschylus.

The stupendous scene after Lear is turned out of his daughter's palace into a storm such as no man has ever experienced is a daring vision of the

---

[1] In writing *Gloucester*, Gloster, the spelling of the First Quarto texts is followed.

Inferno. Torrents of ice-cold rain pour down upon the old man's bare and defenceless head and make the poor fool tremble as he shivers under his master's cloak, trying to comfort him the while with hollow sounding jests and infantile snatches of song. Deafening thunder seems ready to shake our planet to pieces. Lightning flashes like sword thrusts that inflame the firmament. But this unleashing of the elemental forces of nature is a symbol of the tempest that tossed the brain of the king ; he becomes one with the storm which bows his defenceless head. However, the force of its fury seems to him no louder than the unnatural invectives of his daughters. His lyrical passion mounts higher than the winds and whirls down with them into the valley's depths until the clown begs for reprieve :

O Nuncle, court Holy water in a dry house is better than this rain water out o'door. Good Nuncle, in, and ask thy daughter's blessing ; here's a night pities neither wise man nor fool.

At this Lear's fury knows no bounds but rises into a paroxysm. Then suddenly some thought—an unforeseen reaction of conscience—makes him fall to his knees and lose himself in long unpractised prayer.

This act of contrition brings with it a sense of relief, the tortured elements grow suddenly calmer ; but this is only a pause arranged with consummate art by an author who knows that there is a limit to receptivity and that the tragedian cannot maintain himself longer at such a pitch.

There is no abatement in the tempest ; in a scene no less harrowing the action returns again to the storm-swept heath where in the shelter of a tiny cabin Lear sets up a tribunal to judge between his heartless daughters and himself. And what a tribunal ! Edgar, disguised as Tom of Bedlam, the Earl of Kent, exiled by Lear on pain of death and unable to make himself known, and the poor Fool sit together in judgement. The criminals, Regan and Goneril are represented by two joint stools which the king carefully disposed side by side. Here is " pure drama ".[1]

To attain its full effect every theatrical resource must be utilized—scenery, costume, gesture and spoken word with both sound and meaning used to the full. To read is not enough, it must be both seen and heard. These poor outlaws in their rags and royal robes must appear visible and audible. The Fool's songs must alternate with the wild ramblings of Poor Tom, the solemn voice of Kent contrast with the agonised tones of the aged monarch. This is a strange quartet to which Gloster can only listen in silence, wondering how poor Lear can have been driven to such a pass, never dreaming that a still worse fate awaits him.

For scarcely has he seen King Lear safely on the road to Dover when

---

[1] " Pure drama as one speaks of pure mathematics or pure music—in the sense that it cannot be rendered into other terms but its own. . . . Poor Tom and the Fool chant antiphonally ; Kent's deep kindly tones tell against the high agonized voice of Lear, melodious in verse or turning to the hard certitude of prose. . . . Pure drama in that its effect can only be gained by due combination of sound, sight and meaning, acting directly on the sensibility of the audience." (Granville Barker, Prefaces to Shakespeare, London, first series, 1927, p. 178.)

he is arrested as a traitor to their Majesties and dragged before the two queens. "Hang him", cried Regan, "Pluck out his eyes", shouts Goneril. The last named punishment is selected, which Gloster endures with stoical fortitude at the hands of the brutal Duke of Cornwall. But the horror and barbarity of the scene is offset by an act of heroism. A servant, oblivious of his own danger, leaps up to defend his master and mortally wounds Cornwall. The classic tragedians never depicted their scenes of horror against such a luminous background of compassionate pity. The terrified servants hasten at their own risk to bring homely remedies to staunch Gloster's bleeding sockets. Gloster sets off for Dover under the guidance of a poor mad beggar, in fact his disguised son Edgar. On the way they fall in with the king.

> As flies to wanton boys are we to the Gods.
> They kill us for their sport
> But worse is still to come.

At Dover where the French forces have landed, Cordelia in a scene full of tenderness and pity attempts to restore her father and gradually nurses him back to strength and reason ; but the island army gain a victory over the French invaders and take the king and his daughter prisoner.

Vainly the old king tries to save Cordelia, he only succeeds in killing the wretched hangman and enters with his daughter dead in his arms. He tries vainly with looking glass and feather to detect a sign of life. The feather only wavers because his poor hand trembles and the mirror remains unmisted crystal clear.

> . . . No no no life
> Why should a dog, a cat, a rat have life
> And thou no breath at all ? Thou l't come no more
> Never, Never, Never never never . . .

With this despairing cry Lear's old heart breaks ; Edgar attempts to revive him, but Kent more understanding knows that death alone is merciful.

> Vex not his ghost, O let him pass : he hates him
> That would upon the rack of this tough world
> Stretch him out longer

Inevitable and sublime conclusion. As near to the Christian ideal as was possible, considering that this drama is set in distant pagan times. We feel that the drama of *King Lear* does not finish with the fall of the curtain. Cordelia though dead is clearly destined for the realm of the blessed, where her father, after so much suffering, may join her, for the old man has refound the childlike faith and simplicity of those who, according to the Gospel, may enter the Kingdom of Heaven. Cordelia's rôle contains only some hundred lines, forty in the first act, sixty in the last, but her influence is felt throughout the drama ; hers are the "tears of holy water" and the angelic compassion capable of redeeming others' faults, has the sacrifice "upon which the gods

II*

themselves throw incense ", which gives to the conclusion of this tragedy a spiritual atmosphere rarely felt in the theatre.

The drama has not received unmixed enthusiasm. Dr. Johnson blamed the dramatist for having made virtue perish in a righteous cause contrary to natural ideas of justice, to the hopes of the reader, and, what is most singular, to the account of the chroniclers.

Charles Lamb declares that *King Lear* is a work too vast for the theatre. Swinburne considers it a drama too cruel for the human heart. Murray opines that the physical and moral sufferings described are of an artificial and unbearable violence. According to Sir E. K. Chambers, the disaster which overtakes Lear and Cordelia shows the gods deaf to men's righteous prayers. Ernest Hello regrets that " the landscape in *King Lear* has no sky and that the author remains the man of darkness whose mystical knowledge is only the mysticism of hell ". Such commentaries seem to justify David Garrick, who, in spite of his Shakespearean cult, adopted for the stage of the " Dukes Theatre ", a *King Lear* arranged by Naham Tate.[1] In this version, the part of the fool is suppressed ; Cordelia marries Edgar and restores the throne to her father, after triumphing over her sisters. Curiously enough, this mutilation pleased the eighteenth-century English public so well that the play's popularity revived, and this adaptation was even printed in certain editions of the poet's works. But the protests of Addison, Coleridge and Shelley were so eloquent that the so-called improvement was discarded and the English theatre returned to Shakespeare's original text.

At the court of King James, as at the " Globe " the play was unreservedly applauded. The king could not fail to grasp the subject's magnitude, and to see in Albany,[2] the Scottish prince who eventually reigns over the British Isles, an allusion to his own career. *King Lear* was presented in a guise sure to interest this devoted student of the art of government. The belated admission of an aged sovereign, recognizing past injustices towards the humble, the unfortunate, was certain to arouse sympathy in a still youthful monarch who aspired to learn his duties from direct and familiar contact with the people. James was too self-confident, too convinced of his intellectual superiority, to be offended by the presentation of a sovereign stricken with insanity. His family so far was exempt from this affliction. He could not foresee that one of his direct descendants[3] would forbid the play and that one day a great French admirer of Shakespeare would hesitate to translate this tragedy on the pretext that such a representation might appear a crime of *lèse-majesté*.[4]

---

[1] *The History of King Lear*, acted at the Dukes Theater. Reviv'd with alterations by Naham Tait (London, 1681).

[2] The eldest son of the King of Scotland had borne from time immemorial the title of Duke of Rothesay, the second son, that of Duke of Albany. This latter title belonged at the time to Charles, James' second son.

[3] *King Lear* was forbidden by the Regent during the last years of George III.

[4] " I have trembled more than once when trying to translate *King Lear* at the idea of presenting on the French stage, a King who has lost his reason." (J. F. Ducis, *Works*, Paris, Ledentu, 1839, p. 84.)

The acting of *King Lear* had a large part in the play's success ; troupe like author had attained their artistic apex. Richard Burbage, after a masterly rendering of *Othello*, interpreted *King Lear* with no less inspiration. " *King Lear* " and " *The grieved Moor* " are mentioned together in the *Elegy* on Burbage's death (1618).[1] How easy to imagine Shakespeare in the congenial part of Kent.[2]

John Davies, who in 1603, had already expressed his high opinion of Shakespeare and Burbage, now praised the talent of two of their fellow-actors : William Ostler and Robert Armin, who distinguished themselves in *King Lear*.

Davies calls Ostler the only *Roscius of our time :*

> To the Roscius of these times, Mr. W. Ostler.
> But if thou plaist thy dying Part as well
> As thy Stage-parts, thou hast no Part in hell.
> . (*Scourge of Folly*, p. 98.)

The second, Robert Armin, succeeded Kempe, and by his more refined and delicate mentality modified the interpretation of Shakespeare's clowns. The anonymous rôle of King Lear's fool seems to have been written especially for this subtle spirit. Davies addressed a long ode to him with the title :

> To honest—gamesome Robin Armin,
> That tickles the spleene like an harmeles vermin.

The lines conclude :

> So thou, in sport, the happiest men dost schoole
> To do as thou dost ; *wisely play the foole.*
> (*Scourge of Folly*, p. 228.)

John Lowin and Joseph Taylor, who in Jonson's *Volpone* had brilliantly played the respective rôles of Volpone and of Mosca, found themselves once again opposite each other in the parts of Edmund and Edgar. Heminge was cut out for the difficult and moving part of Gloster, and it is natural to suppose that young Edmund Shakespeare, who had recently joined the company, had been chosen with Nathan Field and Robert Gough to play one of the king's three daughters, as women's parts were reserved for youthful newcomers.

This brother was seventeen years younger than William. Of his short life few traces remain. Three entries in official documents : his baptism at Stratford, the funeral in London of a natural child whom he recognized, his own death in December 1607, one year after the first performance of *King Lear*, that is all. The great bell of St. Saviour's Church in Southwark,

---

[1] *King Lear*, the grieved moor and more beside
    that lived in thee,
    Have now forever died.
[2] The part of Kent corresponded perfectly to Shakespeare's scope (see Chapter VII) and would permit him to be frequently in the wings directing the performance.

where he had come to live near the " Globe ", solemnly tolled for him on the morning of December 31st.[1] His mortal remains were buried in the church itself, as was the custom with "important persons ". This fact, together with the inscription in the sexton's book, where the name is spelled in the form adopted by William Shakespeare and his publishers, indicate that his great brother himself took the responsibility of the obsequies.

An actor's life consists of contrasts. In the morning, Shakespeare attended the sad ceremony, in the afternoon of the same day he was obliged to present before the court *The Merry Wives of Windsor*, the gayest of his comedies and one of King James's favourites.

That winter was particularly rigorous ; the sky darkened and the air froze to an exceptional degree. The Thames, covered with drift ice, suddenly froze over. To the boatmen's despair, the river above the bridge transformed itself into a highway. People crossed it on foot, and even in coaches, on their way to the theatre. The urchins organized slides, and great fires were lit on the ice where vendors sold mulled wine.

The general opinion of critics is that *Coriolanus* was presented at this time. Perhaps the reference to "the coal of fire upon the ice " in the first scene is a recollection of what the poet saw that winter as he crossed the Thames. Apart from this incident, there is nothing in contemporary writings nor in the tragedy itself which could fix the precise date at which *Coriolanus* was written and performed.

The story of the hero of ancient Rome whom circumstances transformed into an enemy of his state is broadly followed by Shakespeare as Plutarch related it. If he had read Livy's version of the death of Caius Martius, published in English by Philemon Holland in 1600, he set it aside without hesitation, thinking that the calm ending was inappropriate as a climax to his drama. As with his other Roman tragedies, he found Plutarch's account sufficient, but did not refrain from embellishing it after his own fashion, adding incidents of daily life, traits of character or personal recollections to the original narrative. The fable which he used with such effect in the forum scene—the revolt of the members of the body against the stomach—is taken almost word for word from a recently published book by his friend Camden. Each time he departs from the Greek historian he has reasons of art and sentiment, and here again the reader may perceive Shakespeare's technique by noting the differences between the history and his drama.

His Caius Martius possesses all the qualities accorded to him by Plutarch, but there are others, notably those which the Earl of Essex' admirers recognized in their hero. In him Shakespeare has found the character which had escaped him when he wrote *Timon of Athens* in justification of misanthropy and even treachery when caused by a people's ingratitude.

The man who aroused so much hatred, whom the plebeian populace held responsible for increased prices, and whom they would willingly have put to death, belongs to one of the great senatorial families. He has fought

[1] 1607, December 31. Edmund Shakespeare a player buried in the church with a forenoon knell of the great bell. 20 shillings (Sexton's accounts).

in seventeen battles and brought Tarquin the proud to his knees. He is disinterested and brave, frank and magnanimous. Indomitable in arms, he is gentle and charming in private life. Plutarch describes this hero as a disagreeable acquaintance unfit for the commerce of his fellows.

Shakespeare, on the contrary, endows his hero with all the social qualities of a great lord.

In the play, Caius Martius treats his wife Virgilia,[1] "his gracious silence", with tender solicitude; he kneels before his mother Volumnia with a spontaneity which leaves the spectator in no doubt as to his filial devotion; he gives his dear friend Menenius the frank accolade of true comradeship and embraces his young son with sincere paternal warmth.

There is, however, a flaw in this noble character—a fault important enough for Shakespeare to use it as the basis of his tragedy. Dominated by his headstrong pride, Martius was led to disaster. While insisting upon this fatal weakness, the poet provides extenuating circumstances. Volumnia has inculcated in this only son all her own caste prejudices; she has fortified his innate pride with her feminine vanity and taught him a horror of the multitude. The people become, for him, the "monster with a thousand heads", a rabble without heart or reason. He replies to the insults which greet his arrival in the forum with abuse and threats. He stands up with indignation against the pusillanimity of the Senate who, fearing rebellion, consent to treat with the crowd; vain weakness, for disorders continue, and the watchful Volsci threaten the city of Romulus. None but Caius Martius is able to rally the Roman centuries. The great soldier, not waiting to be attacked, falls upon the enemy before Corioli, defeats Tullus Anfidius, and leaves to his fellow officers the easy task of collecting the spoils. In this epic battle, the author gives his personage the gigantic stature of a mythical hero. Martius before Corioli is not merely a Roman general at the head of his legions, he is more like Achilles leading his bands of myrmidons in the assault of Troy.

Shakespeare introduces an exquisite scene not to be found in Plutarch. It comes directly from his Stratford home. While awaiting the triumphal return of Caius Martius now surnamed Coriolanus, his mother and her daughter-in-law "set them down on two low stools and sew", according to the stage direction. These low stools for sewing, with their cushions, are mentioned in all the inventories of the Stratford houses in contrast to the high stools used at meals round the table. The ladies receive a visit from a neighbour who tries to entice them out to meet the victors. She rallies Virgilia on her industry and remarks teasingly that all the wool spun by Penelope "did but fill Ithaca full of moths". They talk over various items of gossip: the health of a friend lying in, Caius Martius' young son chasing a golden butterfly, and the news of war. Many other Stratford reminiscences may be found in the dialogue: the fruit of the mulberry tree which is too

---

[1] Shakespeare has changed the feminine names from those handed down by history. That of Virgilia seemed too gracious for the formidable matron, whom he called Volumnia, reserving for the tender and ideal wife that of Virgilia.

soft to stand touching, rabbits emerging from their burrows after rain,[1] tradesmen singing in their shops, or going cheerily about their business,[2] the player who tumbles farther than his bowl on slippery ground [3] are pictures evocative of Shakespeare's life in the country.

When the victor returns, his mother claims for him a consul's toga. Coriolanus would prefer to serve the Romans in his own way rather than rule them in theirs; nevertheless, he obeys and presents himself to the Senate. The city fathers proclaim him consul, but custom demands that he also seek the plebeian voices. He must beg for votes, by showing publicly the wounds he had received in the defence of Rome. Coriolanus can never conform to this degrading custom. Here again, the drama departs from Plutarch's account which expressly says, " Martius complied without resistance, publicly showed several of his scars, and was elected ".

The Coriolanus of Shakespeare, instead of soliciting votes, claims them as his right with insolence and sarcasm. " It was never my desire yet to trouble the poor with begging ", says he, defying instead of flattering the citizens; and they, taken unawares by such an attitude, accord him their votes. Again, when Coriolanus is banished, his fall is due to his provocative bearing and not, as in Plutarch, to the caprice of the multitude.

The conflict betwixt democracy represented by the tribunes and aristo-cracy in the person of Coriolanus ends in a violent crisis. The plebs insist that the conqueror of the Volsci be thrown from the Tarpeian rock, but Menenius Agrippa intervenes to change the death sentence into exile. In a magnificent scene due to the author's imagination and not to history, Coriolanus challenges the jurisdiction of the plebeian tribunal, casts back their own sentence in the people's teeth and, escorted by his tearful family with a few dismayed patricians, the exile shakes the dust of Rome from his feet.

Sombre, haggard, athirst for vengeance, Coriolanus directs his steps towards Antium where Tullus Anfidius is preparing to exterminate the Romans. Actuated by wounded pride, he no longer knows family, friend nor country. Deaf to the appeals of conscience, this Roman joins forces with the enemies of Rome.

Beneath the walls of the city, his compatriots await to plead with him for peace, but even the prayers of Menenius are vain. Rome will suffer tomorrow the fate of Troy. The pride of Coriolanus will change the course of history.

At this last moment, a small procession approaches. His mother, wife and son have come as suppliants. Coriolanus vows to remain unmoved. Suddenly Volumnia abandons her eloquent entreaties as recorded in Plutarch, to speak in the words purely Shakespeare's of a woman outraged. Her

---

[1] " They will out of their burrows like conies after rain." (Act IV, Sc. 5.)

[2] " Our tradesmen singing in their shops and going about their functions friendly." (Act IV, Sc. 6.)

[3] " Sometimes like to a bowl on subtle ground I have tumbled past the throw." (Act V, Sc. 2.)

daughter-in-law echoes them in vain. Coriolanus remains unflinching until his little boy clenching his small fist and frowning exclaims " 'a shall not tread on me ". Then Coriolanus comprehends that in avenging his wrongs on the ungrateful city, his mother, wife and child, this son whose audacious language recalls his own, would perish horribly. In sparing Rome, he well knows that he signs his death warrant, but he will meet death fearlessly.

> . . . O my mother ! mother ! O !
> You have won a happy victory to Rome ;
> But for your son, believe it, O ! believe it,
> Most dangerously you have with him prevail'd,
> If not most mortal to him. But let it come.
> . . . ladies you deserve
> To have a temple built you . . .
>
> (*Coriolanus*, Act v, Sc. 3)

Coriolanus braves the death which awaits him with such dignity that the Volscian officers and soldiers, an instant after having executed him, salute the Roman's body with respect and bear it to the tomb with full honours. " Trail your steel pikes " orders Tullus Anfidius. Evidently the general of antiquity wished to mark the obsequies with the same ceremonial as the English author had observed at official funerals in his own country, where the custom was for the Halberdiers to trail their pikes in sign of mourning. Those who take pleasure in discovering anachronisms, will note that the names Dick and Hob are hardly Roman, that the mention of a holy church and cemetery is not appropriate in a drama which takes place five centuries before the Christian era, that Cato, Alexander and the physician Galen, all mentioned by Coriolanus, lived after his time. It is more pertinent to point out that in spite of all the difficulties of his task, Shakespeare has been able to retain for his hero the sympathy and understanding of the spectator. He must have thought more than once of Essex, who despite his nobility of mind and true patriotism, received from his peers and his sovereign the condemnation of a traitor. The drama is so living, the conflict of the social classes so realistic and applies so strikingly to every age that its presentation in France has produced political upheaval.

Although the principal part gave Richard Burbage a magnificent opportunity to display his talents, Coriolanus is not mentioned among his triumphs. Nor could the play have enjoyed a theatrical success comparable with the poet's other dramas. No request for a printing licence is traceable in the registers, no contemporary student boasted of having been present at its first night ; nor was it printed until the publication of Shakespeare's complete works. There it appears in the 1623 folio at the head of the tragedies regularly divided into acts and scenes.

Not long afterwards Mary Arden died in Stratford.[1] Her son was certainly present at her funeral and was obliged to prolong his stay at Stratford in order to attend the christening of his sister Johanne Hart's first child.

---

[1] 1608 Sept. 9. Burial. Mary Shakespeare widow.

He probably remained with his family until October 16th to stand godfather to the son of Henry Walker, his old schoolfellow, three time mayor of Stratford,[1] before rejoining his troupe at Coventry where they gave a performance on their way back to London.

Two of the actors had died during the summer. William Sly,[2] shareholder of a seventh part in the Blackfriars theatre, was interred on August 16th at St. Leonard's Shoreditch, "the old players' church".[3] A month later, the bell of St. Saviour's near the "Globe" tolled in its turn. Lawrence Fletcher, probably a victim of the fatal plague, was buried on September 12th, 1608, in the churchyard, near Edmund Shakespeare. It is curious that so few details are available concerning this actor who played such an important part in the company's fortunes. Was he related to the dramatist John Fletcher? The question has never been seriously examined, but the fact that shortly after his death Shakespeare collaborated with this John Fletcher in the composition of three plays (*Henry VIII*, the *Two Noble Kinsmen* and *Cardenio*) leads one to think that possibly ties of kindred existed between John and Lawrence, that Lawrence who had come to his assistance in perilous times and to whom he owed the enjoyment of royal favour.

The year 1608 concluded with a facile success. The immense popularity of *Measure for Measure* in spite of, or perhaps because of, its sordid underworld scenes between Mistress Overdone and Pompey Bum her pandar, caused the directors of the troupe to seek a like attraction. It took little imaginative effort for Shakespeare to revive,

The Late, And much admired Play called Pericles, Prince of Tyre. With the true Relation of the whole Historie, adventures, and fortunes of the said Prince: As also: The no lesse strange, and worthy accidents, in the Birth and Life of his Daughter Marina. As it hath been divers and sundry times acted by his Majesties Servants, at the Globe on the Banck-side by William Shakespeare. Imprinted for Henry Gosson London: and are to be sold at the signe of the Sunne in Paternoster row 1609.

Pericles, renovated at little cost, fully satisfied public taste, always avid for melodrama. Six editions were exhausted in a relatively short time. Better still, the same year, George Wilkins, Shakespeare's fellow-lodger with the Montjoye family, obtained from the theatre the authorization to adapt the scenario of *Pericles* as a novel.

The distant source of *Pericles* may be found in an old story of the first or second century, concerning the adventures of the legendary King Apollonius of Tyre. More than a hundred Latin manuscripts of this popular story still exist in continental libraries, one of them dating from

---

[1] 1608 Oct 16. Baptism William sonne to Henry Walker aldermanus.

[2] Sly left his sword and his plumed hat to Cuthbert Burbage, and forty pounds to James Sands, his musician friend.

[3] A marble tablet placed in the choir by the Shakespeare Society of London, recalls the considerable number of artists musicians and other members of the theatrical world interred in this place, notably: James Burbage, 1597; Cuthbert Burbage, 1599; William Somers, 1560; Richard Tarleton, 1588; Gabriel Spencer, 1598; William Sly, 1608 and Richard Cowley, 1619.

the ninth century. It has been translated into Italian, Spanish, Provençal, German, Danish, Swedish, Dutch and medieval Greek. The French version is included in the collection of *Histoires tragiques* of François de Belleforest whence *Hamlet* was taken. But without doubt, the fourteenth-century English version, put into verse by John Gower and included in his *Confessio Amantis*, is the direct source of Shakespeare's play.

The first liberty taken with Gower's ancient text was to change the name of the principal characters. Apollonius became Pericles whose terse syllables sound better on the stage than the heavy Latin name. Princess Thaïsa becomes Marina, a happy choice for her who was born during a storm at sea, and was to discover her father on shipboard. When retouching this old melodrama, the author apparently did not consider it necessary to alter the first two acts, dealing with the extravagant adventures of a prince looking for an ideal wife who, like Oedipus, does not hesitate to place his life in jeopardy in order to solve a riddle. Their archaic tone is emphasized by the introduction in guise of a chorus of old Gower [1] himself, who explains or excuses all improbabilities and unravels the tangled sequence of events.

The three last acts bear the stamp of genius, especially the scene of Pericles' anguish when his wife lies apparently dead after a child-birth precipitated by their tempest tossed voyage.

The scenes which follow Marina's kidnapping by pirates, who sell her to the proprietress of a house of ill-fame at Mytilene, provide Shakespeare with the opportunity to describe her establishment with the utmost boldness. Neither Aretine nor Rojas ever painted scenes coarser, more realistic, more humourous and more replete with philosophy. Against this background Marina's essential purity shines flamelike. Her gentleness and innocence, the charm of her persuasive eloquence, the strength of her youthful character work wonders among the wretched creatures of the brothel. She is rescued from their midst through the good offices of the Governor of Mytilene, Lysimachus. Struck by her accomplishments and gift of song, he takes her on board a ship which has just cast anchor in the harbour. It carries the rich King Pericles who, victim of profound melancholia, pursues an endless voyage in search of news of his lost daughter. Hope is renewed when he sees her, his wife's living image, and this leads to a conclusion that seems to herald the final act of *The Winter's Tale*.

Father and daughter undertake a thanksgiving pilgrimage to the Temple of Diana at Ephesus where the Priestess is none other than the long lamented wife and mother. To reward virtue it only remains for Marina to become the wife of her rescuer, whom she loved at first sight and who on his part never doubted the girl's celestial purity.

It cannot be denied that *Pericles* obtained an immense theatrical success.

---

[1] Shakespeare must have known Gower's tomb in St. Saviour's Church well. The effigy of the learned poet is still visible, robed in a toga and a university cap. His head reposes upon three fat volumes, representing his Latin, French and English works : *Vox Clamantis, Speculum Meditantis* and *Confessio Amantis*.

A revue of 1609 entitled *Pimlyco* or *Runne Red Cap*, enviously mentions this success :

> . . . all the Roomes
> Did swarme with *Gentiles* mix'd with *Groomes*,
> So that I truly thought all These
> Came to see *Shore* or *Pericles*.[1]

In 1614, Robert Tailer could wish nothing better for his play *The Hogge Hath Lost His Pearle*, than a reception equal to that of *Pericles*.

> And if it prove so happy as to please,
> Weele say tis fortunate like *Pericles*.

Ben Jonson, not without bitterness, declares twenty-five years later that *Pericles* still holds the scene to the detriment of his *New Inn* which, however, so disgusted the public that they left the theatre empty before the end of the performance.

> No doubt some mouldy tale,
> Like Pericles ; and stale
> As the Shrieues crusts, and nasty as his fish-
> Scraps, out every Dish,
> Throwne forth, and rak't into the common tub.
> May keepe up the Play-club : [2]

Samuel Sheppard, that faithful admirer of the Stratford writer, quotes *Pericles, Prince of Tyre* in his *Times displayed* as the drama which made great Shakespeare the equal of Euripides, of Sophocles, and of Aristophanes.[3]

In 1618, *Pericles* was acted at the great feast held at court in honour of the Marquis de La Trémoille, the new French ambassador. The play was revived at the " Globe " on June 21st of the same year when the theatre, celebrating the end of the plague, was packed to overflowing. Its popularity continued, and, at the Restoration, Betterton, Burbage's successor, constantly performed it. As to the text, it is worth noting that seventy-four copies of the six editions published before 1635 are still extant.[4]

In the eighteenth century, George Lillo who staged the three last acts with the title of *Marina* remarks in his prologue that it would be bold to claim that the whole play is by Shakespeare, but that his brilliant and inimitable lines are as easy to distinguish as is gold from base metal.[5]

Langbaine in 1690, Rowe in 1709 and Farmer in 1766 supported this opinion. Thenceforward, serious critics have taken it for granted.

---

[1] *Jane Shore* was a play of Heywood's which had great success.
[2] Jonson, *Ode to Himselfe, The New Inne*, 1631, p. H2.
[3] Samuel Sheppard, *The times Displayed in six Sestyads* (1646).
[4] The Clarendon Press published a facsimile of Malone's copy of the first edition of *Pericles*. The same publishers discovered the proprietors of seventy-four copies which appeared before 1635, and were in existence in 1901. One of these was sold for sixty-six pounds at Sotheby's, while a copy of the first edition reached the sum of one hundred and seventy-one pounds.
[5] This play was given at Covent Garden, April 1st, 1738.

Coleridge even chose *Pericles* to show how Shakespeare set about altering a play, working at first with indifference, then throwing into the text a new thought or a new image, and finishing by becoming so interested in his subject that he almost entirely refashioned the last three acts.

A request entered in the printers' register enables an approximate date to be assigned to the composition of *Antony and Cleopatra*, which with *Coriolanus* and *Julius Caesar*, forms Shakespeare's Roman trilogy.

While asking permission to print *Pericles* in 1608 Edward Blount applied at the same time for the rights of *Antony and Cleopatra*.

20 Maii Edward Blount. Entred for his copie under thandes of Sir George Buck Knight, and Master Warden Seton A Booke called *the Booke of Pericles, prynce of Tyre* (VId).

Edward Blount. Entred for his coppie by the like auctocritie a Booke called *Anthony and Cleopatra* (VId).

It must be noted that this same Blount, one of the five members of the syndicate which published under the direction of the senior members of the troupe the Folio of 1623, hastened to cede his rights on *Pericles* to a second-rate publisher, Henry Gosson, retaining those which he had acquired for *Antony and Cleopatra*. The obvious conclusion is that Blount, in agreement with the author, was already interested in the publication of Shakespeare's complete works, and decided that *Pericles* even with alterations, was not worthy to take its place in the precious collection. This is likely, for *Pericles* was only incorporated among the poet's plays sixty-two years later in 1685, when the folio was reprinted for the fourth time.

In the great Folio, *Antony and Cleopatra* occupies its rightful place among the tragedies between *Othello* and *Cymbeline*. From the excellence of the text, it may be inferred that the author had carefully revised his manuscript, as is observable in *The Tempest ;* misprints and errors are rare. One peculiarity, however, differentiates it from the other plays published by Heminge and Condell : there is no division into acts or scenes ; [1] the drama is presented like a long pageant without pause or stop. [2] The magnificent language, the rich costumes and the plastic beauty of the action made it a spectacular show, especially suited to court festivities.

Antony and Cleopatra provides another illustration of the dramatic genius and the consummate art with which Shakespeare adapted history to the stage. The poet drew from Plutarch's account the elements of a spectacular tragedy, while omitting the details which would have weighed down or disfigured this epic of love and war. The classical studies of his childhood were probably insufficient to permit his use of the Graeco-Latin Renaissance

---

[1] A century later, Nicholas Rowe divided the drama into five acts, and eighteen scenes, meeting thus the exigencies of his time without spoiling the charm of the spectacle.

[2] The first performance of a " newsreel " comparable to a film took place in Shakespeare's time ; John Aubrey tells of a representation he had seen of the obsequies of Sir Philip Sidney. Two revolving reels unrolled huge canvases upon which were painted life-size figures which by this device marched in order. (Aubrey's *Brief Lives*, manuscript at the Bodleian Library.)

text published by H. Estienne, later by Cruserius ; but he knew enough Latin not to be over-influenced by the florid style of Sir Thomas North, whose translation more nearly approaches Amyot's version than the text of Plutarch. Dealing with a Roman subject, he instinctively sought moderation and adopted the concise and laconic construction of the Latin tongue. Unhesitatingly, he suppressed unnecessary adjectives and sometimes even verbs when they were not essential. Perhaps this rather dry precision has always made *Antony and Cleopatra* more appreciated by the elite than by the mass. Certainly the rapidity of a dialogue where superfluous words have been eliminated has caused many translators to embroider on the English text, without ever reaching the majestic clarity of the Shakespearean vocabulary.[1]

In *Antony and Cleopatra*, the dramatist demonstrates his absolute mastery of that rhythmic prose which he used to perfection in *Othello*, *Macbeth* and *King Lear*. In these dramas he no longer plays with words, there are no concetti or Italian turns of phrase so characteristic of his first manner. His Roman trilogy is equally exempt from that affectation bordering on preciosity which reappears in his three last works : *Cymbeline*, *The Winter's Tale* and *The Tempest*. Led by his love of poetry, the author formerly often gave his personages a language which was too noble for their station. Here the speech of each and all is the exact reflection of character.

It is unnecessary to be alarmed at the considerable length of the " Dramatis Personae ". Most are supernumeraries intended merely to swell the ranks of the conflicting forces. Throughout the action, whether in Athens, Alexandria, Rome, Sicily, in the plains of Syria, on the battlefields, on board the galleys or in the tomb of the Ptolemys, Shakespeare has created and maintained an emotional unity with which he replaced Aristotle's classical rules. Here political ambition seizes and corrupts all the protagonists, so that in this drama of love, love itself becomes subordinate to the imperious desire for power. The action is woven round the triumvirs' dreams of glory. Each aspires to be sole emperor, but all are obliged to ally themselves closely against the common enemy, Sextus Pompey, now becoming the people's idol. Over these machinations brood the shades of the great Julius, and of Pompey the elder, rivals in Rome as they had been in Egypt.

The triumvir Octavius Caesar cleverly gains his ambitious ends ; devoid of military talent, he enjoys the prestige conferred by his birth and takes full advantage of Antony's mistakes ; his austere morals preserve him from the seductions of Cleopatra. His words are imperious and resounding.

Lepidus, his colleague, is a poor creature, swollen with pretentions. An incorrigible drunkard, he plays in the drama the part of the fool indispensable in Shakespeare's time, asks absurd questions, or utters platitudes to amuse the audience. His language is invariably flat and banal.

---

[1] " What the gods defer they not deny."
" Caesar through Syria intends his journey."
" Now the fleeting moon no planet is of mine."
are sentences closer to Latin than to English.

Pompey appears late in the play ; he is young, audacious and loyal ; but disarmed by trickery he falls into the trap set by the wily Caesar. The scene in which he invites his rivals to feast and carouse aboard his galley where all affairs of state are forthwith forgotten is one of the most biting satires ever written upon the great ones of the earth.

Personal and political rivalries, the violent clash of opposing natures are brought into relief by an essentially Shakespearean character owing nothing to Plutarch, a kind of antique chorus whose intentionally brutal commentaries clarify the situations and lighten the dialogue : this is Domitius Enobarbus, Mark Antony's comrade in arms. Trusted by Romans and Egyptians alike, he has the soldier's bluntness of speech which he abuses on occasion to provide the author with language trivial and crude enough to contrast with the nobility of the ensemble. The meanness of Enobarbus is necessary to reveal Antony's magnanimity. On the night of his defeat, when sadness invades the battlefield, he abandons his master and goes over to the enemy camp with such precipitation that he leaves behind all the gold he has amassed. Here is the opportunity for Antony, betrayed, to show the generosity of his nature. He asks and obtains of the victorious Caesar a safe-conduct for the pack mules returning the renegade's treasure.

The number of persons in the play is matched by the diversity of scenes in which the action takes place. No theatre ever exhibited a scene so vast. The action begun on the morrow of Philippi finishes after the battle of Actium. It embraces ten years. Of the ninety-five chapters of Plutarch, Shakespeare uses only a third, but with what originality he treats this ill-assorted material ! Among the thirty-six tableaux presented without interruption, the most beautiful and most convincing is that which remains invisible, brought before the eyes of imagination with such art that the spectator almost sees Cleopatra's fabulous barge slowly sailing down the Cydnus when he hears Enobarbus's eloquent description.[1]

Of the triumvirs, Mark Antony is the true warrior and real chief. With Plutarch, Shakespeare sees in him the son of Hercules, nonchalent, debonair, grey-headed, matured in the toil and carousings of war, a soldier hardened to every excess. During the crossing of the Alps, he has astonished the army by prodigious feats of endurance ; he could exact from his body every privation and enjoy every pleasure. Spartan and sybarite, he would leap to the forefront of battle after a night of orgy. It is only Cleopatra's lips that give him the taste of the infinite, and yet this illicit love is dominated by a restless ambition : to become Augustus Caesar's ally, he leaves Cleopatra, abandons Egypt, and rushes to Rome where he is persuaded to marry his colleague's sister, the gentle Octavia. Never, however, will he be capable of rising to the dignity of this new existence. The bewitching queen has only to send an astute messenger, and at once, his desire and jealousy reawaken. To this versatile being, Shakespeare gives now the nervous, short and authoritative language of the great leader, now the more polished

---

[1] *Antony and Cleopatra*, Act II, Sc. 2.

speech of a citizen of Rome.   Antony also expresses himself with the lyricism
of a man passionately in love, or with the anger of a jealous lover.   Antony's
love, fatal passion which destroys empires, is comparable with that which
made the poet the slave of a woman whom his reason showed as cruel,
deceitful, hard, ambitious, unscrupulous and no longer young.   In Sonnet
150 he thus wrote to the " dark lady " :

> O ! from what power hast thou this powerful night,
> With insufficiency my heart to sway ?
> To make me give the lie to my true sight,
> And swear that brightness does not grace the day ?
> Whence hast thou this becoming of things ill,
> That in the very refuse of thy deeds,
> There is such strength and warrantise of skill,
> That in my mind, thy worst all best exceeds ?
> Who taught thee how to make me love thee more,
> The more I hear and see just cause of hate ? . . .

Is not this sentence of Enobarbus's an echo of this sonnet :

> . . . For vilest things
> Become themselves in her, that the holy priests
> Bless her when she is riggish.
>
> (*Antony and Cleopatra*, Act II, Sc. 2)

Antony is forty-five, just Shakespeare's age when he wrote the drama, and
it is not surprising that Shakespeare should give one of his heroes his own
emotions, hopes and disillusions.   Linked by a passion similar to the poet's,
the Roman laments his weakness in the same terms as Shakespeare in the
Sonnets ; he abuses his haughty mistress in the stinging syllables which
all the Cleopatras of the world forgive ; because, athirst for power, they find
that hatred and contempt overcome by desire is the most complete and
intoxicating homage they can receive from their lovers.   Antony heaps the
worst insults upon Cleopatra, accusing her of cowardice, lying and treachery,
but a few minutes afterwards he is in her arms.   How could she help being
flattered by such proof of her power ?

Cleopatra is certainly the most original creation of all in this varied
assembly.   Shakespeare has boldly made a great light-o'-love at the decline
of her passionate life the heroine of his play.   She is thirty-six at its opening :
silver threads mingle with her chestnut hair : twenty years have passed since
she subdued Caesar, and now it is already ten years that Antony has been
" caught in her strong toil of grace ".   Age cannot wither her : expert and
wheedling, violent and tragic, Cleopatra is always seductive and human
through the infinite variety assumed by " those that trade in love ".   The
secret of that moving charm with which the poet has endowed her was not
found in Plutarch.

To create the personality of the fascinating Egyptian sorceress there was
no need to have recourse either to documents, or to imagination ; she was
for him reality.   Cleopatra possessed all the characteristics of the " dark

lady " of the Sonnets. But as Raphael borrowed the features of la Fornarina to paint the Queen of Heaven, Shakespeare transformed the heroine of his poems into a Queen of Egypt. He gave her a royal dignity such as the hostess of the Oxford inn most surely did not possess.

At the end of the play, Cleopatra finds herself exposed to the cruellest vengeance of fate : that of seeing her superb rôle unworthily played. According to Shakespeare, it is not Antony's death nor the crumbling of her empire which drives her to suicide ; the author shows her as having decided to survive her lover and already preoccupied with recovering from the Roman treasury the little hoard which she has saved for a rainy day—it is the news that she is to be paraded in Caesar's triumph which prompts her sudden resolution.

> . . . the quick comedians
> Extemporally will stage us, and present
> Our Alexandrian revels. Antony
> Shall be brought drunken forth, and I shall see
> Some squeaking Cleopatra boy my greatness
> I' the posture of a whore.

This is what the haughty queen will never accept. She is too great an actress not to demand a fine part to play. She will create a catastrophe to bring about a scene worthy of her. She will find a way to " die in beauty ". Intoxicated by the nobility of her act, she entirely enters into her new character ; she believes at last in the sincerity of her passion. She thinks she loves Mark Antony, she thinks she is dying for him.

Corneille saw in Cleopatra the essentially amorous woman, whose essence is to love nobody. " She is ", he says, " ambitious and without love, using the influence of her beauty for political ends." He emphasizes the artifices she displays to subjugate Octavius Caesar as she has previously conquered Julius Caesar and Mark Antony, and concludes severely : " Since she only gave herself to the great of the world, she must have attached herself less to the person of her last lover than to his worldly power."

Shakespeare, more sentimental than Corneille, casts no doubt on the sincerity of his heroine. Rather than allow herself to be dragged from Egypt to serve the triumph of Rome, Cleopatra chooses a royal end to rob great Caesar of his final victory. But while she wishes to preserve her royal and feminine prestige, she is not insensible to Antony's last appeal who " after the high Roman fashion " has taught her the way to liberty. Her lover, ennobled by misfortune, has proved himself a hero worthy of her, a being " greater than Caesar, greater even than Rome " ; at least she feels for him a love which is genuine. She will in her turn be worthy of him. This liaison which has kept them enchained for twelve years, ceases to be merely a political union or a sensual attachment and becomes through sacrifice, a marriage in eternity :

> Husband I come !
> Now to that name my courage prove my title !

as if the author had wished to close this pagan drama with a Christian thought.

CHAPTER XVIII

RETIREMENT

Shakespeare takes up residence in New Place—Contemporary Stratford—*The Tempest*, conceived in serenity—Influence of the great French prose writers upon Shakespeare—*The Winter's Tale*—*Cymbeline*.

BEFORE settling down in Stratford, Shakespeare, like many another English gentleman, seems to have had his portrait painted.[1] The artist of his choice, Martin Droeshout, a Dutchman, had acquired some renown in the little group of foreigners from whom he separated in 1608 to become a British subject. This painter of mediocre talent had the advantage of working from life, and the merit of sincerity. At the top left-hand corner of the canvas, he wrote the name of his sitter and the date of his work : Willm. Shakespeare, 1609.

The face, framed in a starched muslin collar is noble in expression and correctly drawn, but the doublet is faulty and out of perspective. This painting was evidently considered a good likeness : Heminge and Condell made use of it in preference to the " Chandos " canvas for the frontispiece in the folio edition [2] which inspired Ben Jonson's somewhat excessive eulogy.

Droeshout's painting is life size. Comparison between his portrait and the bust, modelled from a death mask, in the choir of the church at Stratford, leaves no doubt concerning its resemblance to the poet.

Stone and canvas bring out his most characteristic features : the high and wide forehead, arched eyebrows, finely drawn but well marked beneath which the light brown eyes seem to say :

> I am that I am and they that level
> At my abuses reckon up their own,
> I may be straight although themselves are bevel
> By their base thought my deeds must not be shown.[3]

The nose is strong and straight ; the well defined mouth is faintly smiling. It was this portrait which probably adorned the great chimney-piece of

---

[1] E. I. Fripp in his *Shakespeare, Man and Artist*, p. 726, suggests that Shakespeare's fellow-actors may have had the portrait painted in anticipation of the poet's departure.

[2] This engraving much inferior to the portrait was made by the painter's nephew, son of Michel Droeshout and Suzannah von Ersbeck. He was baptized April 20th, 1601, in the Dutch church in London. Thus he was scarcely of age when he undertook this drawing. In 1632 he was far more expert when he engraved the frontispiece of Montaigne's Essays, third edition.

[3] Sonnet 121.

Shakespeare's new home before it took its place in the " Memorial Gallery " of the theatre at Stratford.

From the journal of Thomas Green, a lawyer who never separated his own interests from those in his keeping, but who loved to recall his ties of kinship with the poet's family, it is possible to fix Shakespeare's definite return to his native town in the spring of 1610. Thomas Green had been left on the spot to supervize the improvements at New Place which he dragged out until the day when he himself became the purchaser of a handsome property next to the cemetery known as St. Mary's House for which he claimed to have given more than four hundred pounds.[1]

In 1610, therefore, Shakespeare entered into the full enjoyment of his domain, which after the recent costly work must have looked very satisfactory. Thirty yards long, and thirty feet high, the main façade with its wide bay windows, columned doorway and three ornamented gables stood imposingly in Chapel Street. This house with its considerable additions contained, apart from the central hall, ten rooms and cellars. A staircase of carved oak led to the upper floor, the large room with the best bed reserved for distinguished visitors, and the owner's room furnished with the four-poster, which Anne Hathaway had received as dowry was to be left to her in her husband's will as a special legacy.

The house was reached through a garden gate opening on Chapel Lane, the muddy countrified road which separated New Place from the land belonging to the ancient Guild. Facing the Shakespeares' gate was the playground of the grammar school with its fountain and its bowling-green ; a picturesque neighbourhood if ever there was one, full of happy memories and dominated by the square tower of the ancient Guild chapel. Family and friends entered by a path paved with large irregular stones, to reach the Clopton's hospitable porch. The lawn with closely cut grass, the formal garden, the kitchen-garden, the orchards and meadows sloping gently down to the banks of the Avon, bordered with willows and poplars, all this was reminiscent of those idyllic scenes described by Rosalind's creator.[2]

This property with everything else which belonged to Shakespeare is today part of the national heritage ; but the administrators have had the good sense to plant it with flowers, hedges and the bushes dear to the garden-loving poet. The visitor may still see the borders of rosemary, thyme and lavender, the old sun-dial, the remains of the mulberry tree and the shady arbour similar to the one where the master took his ease in a large rustic arm chair surrounded by his family and friends.

His brother Gilbert, then thirty-eight, still enjoyed his confidence ; his other brother, Richard, was thirty-four and lived in the old house in Henley Street with his sister Johanna, the wife of Harte the hatter, who had, according

[1] " A pratty neat, gentlemanlike house with a pratty garden and little orchard standing very sweet and quiet " according to the purchaser's description.

[2] New Place remained intact until 1653, when it was bought by F. Gastrell. Angry at the appearance of so many tourists he cut down the mulberry tree and under pretext of diminishing his taxes tore down the new building and rented the old dependencies. Today what is left is called New Place Museum and belongs to the National Trust.

to E. I. Fripp, succeeded John Shakespeare in the glove trade. Without leaving the lawns of her garden of Hallscroft, contiguous with the grounds of New Place, Susanna could show the little Elizabeth to her grandfather and her Harte cousins, who had hardly more distance to traverse when coming from the old Henley Street home.

The little that is known of Shakespeare's wife is all to her credit. That she must have suffered during the hard years which followed Will's departure, that she had difficulty in feeding and clothing her little family, and that she shared the prosperity which accompanied her illustrious husband's returr is certain. Certain also that she was loved by her children and respected by her servants. Her father's shepherd left her his savings, to be distributed amongst the poor of the parish. Thomas Whittington's will, dated March 25th, 1601, reads :

Thomas Whittington bequeathed to the poor of Stratford what is in the hand of Anne Shaxspere wyfe unto Mr. William Shakespeare.

The testator is described in Anne's father's will as " my Sheepherd ". Her conjugal devotion is shown by the desire expressed to the old sexton, William Castle, to share her husband's tomb.[1] Her wishes were piously fulfilled. The poet's wife died at the age of sixty-seven, having had the satisfaction of seeing the publication of her husband's complete works, and sleeps at his side in the choir of the old church,[2] under the Latin inscription by her daughter Susanna.[3]

Many near or immediate neighbours eager to admire if not to understand the poet swelled the circle of friends. Among these were William Reynolds and his wife. This rich farmer, wool merchant and confirmed Papist, lived in Chapel Street, a few steps from New Place, where he had a beautiful house, today part of the Shakespeare Hotel. He had twenty-two persons in his service including his hidden chaplain. Also very near, in Sheep Street, lived Richard Tyler always a close friend of John Shakespeare. Hamlet and Judith Sadler, godparents of the poet's twins, were established at the corner of Sheep Street and High Street only a few yards away from the house of their celebrated friend. Anthony Nash, whose son Thomas was to marry Shakespeare's grand-daughter lived in Henley Street and also belonged to the circle, as did Thomas Russell, who had retired to the nearby manor of Alderminster. Francis Collins, although then resident in Warwick, came almost every day to Stratford before deciding to live there ; this old schoolfellow was still Shakespeare's friend and lawyer. All are mentioned in the dramatist's will.

Clifford-Chambers near Stratford was the home of Sir Henry and Lady Rainsford with whom lived the poet Michael Drayton. These were probably among the numerous visitors to New Place, all three being patients of Dr.

---

[1] Letter, April 10th, 1623, published as Preface to *Traditionary anecdotes of Shakespeare* (T. Robb, 1838).

[2] Here lyeth interred the body of Anne wife of William Shakespeare who departed this life the 6th day of August 1625 being of the age of 67 years.

[3] See chapter XVI.

Hall. John Thornborough, Bishop of Worcester also had his gout and nightmares treated by the poet's son-in-law and must have visited the companion of so many youthful adventures. Was it not said that both had been among the carefree poachers of Sir Thomas Lucy's game ? William Somerville, brother of the unhappy John who was condemned as a traitor, had been re-established at Edreston in the family lands restored by James's favour, and naturally renewed the ties formerly existing between Somervilles, Ardens and Shakespeares. This Somerville possessed a miniature by Nicholas Hilliard, believed to represent the poet, which passed directly to his grandson and is today in the Folger Shakespeare Library.

It is therefore not extraordinary that Nicholas Rowe qualifies the Shakespeares as :

People of good figure and fashion mentioned as gentlemen in the register and public writings relating to that town.

and states that :

The latter Part of his Life was spent, as all Men of good Sense will wish theirs may be, in Ease, Retirement, and the Conversation of his Friends. . . . His pleasurable Wit, and good Nature, engag'd him in the Acquiantance, and entitled him to the Friendship of the Gentlemen of the Neighbourhood.

This declaration of Rowe's on the Shakespeares' social status at Stratford has sometimes been quoted as conflicting with that of Aubrey. Yet the two appreciations are in no way contradictory. Aubrey had invoked the witness of a Henley Street neighbour who knew the family at the time of their financial troubles ; he stated that the father had been a butcher, and that William was apprenticed in this trade for a certain time. Far from contesting these facts, Rowe describes the family's impoverishment, noting that the son had been taken from school to help his father ; but when he writes that the Shakespeares " cut a good figure " in Warwickshire, he speaks of their circumstances after the poet had left the theatre and returned to his own people loaded with riches and laurels. Aubrey's information, on the other hand, referred to the state of affairs twenty years before : hence the two texts are not incompatible.

It was in the beautiful manor of New Place, surrounded by gardens and orchards that Shakespeare wrote three plays in a new style : a pastoral tragedy, a romantic comedy and an allegorical fantasy, profound and philosophical, an exquisite fairy play, which remains unequalled. These last literary productions reflect the serenity of his new mode of life. *The Tempest*, *Cymbeline* and *The Winter's Tale* are works apart marking a final phase in the poet's evolution. From each is derived an impression of moral serenity ; even *Cymbeline*, which the author denominates " tragedy ", ends in reconciliation.

The three heroines drawn during the years of his retirement, bear little resemblance to the other feminine figures of his plays, and this suggests that the poet was influenced by his two daughters whose future happiness he was anxious to secure. The memory of the son he had lost lives again in the moving portrait of young Mamilius in *The Winter's Tale*.

Imogen, Perdita and Miranda are children of the country. Less clever than Portia, Helena, Rosalind or Beatrice, less " women of the world " than the gracious Desdemona and the gentle Ophelia, they have a characteristic freshness, a simple gaiety, a more naïve sweetness ; they are field wild flowers not garden roses.

The author now had more leisure and lingered longer over his manuscript, not only with the idea of perfecting his play for theatrical representation, but for the prospective publication of all his works.

This explains why his editors gave *The Tempest* first place in the Folio. The comedy had no need of revision and could be printed as it stood. It was completed towards the end of 1610.

Faithful to the memory of old friendships, and always seeking subjects of topical interest, the poet found his theme as often before in Southampton's world. The former lover of Italian tales had for several years been absorbed in colonial expansion. After the unfortunate setback to Raleigh's venture and the massacre of the last English settlers in Virginia, he undertook the cherished project once more and brought it to a successful conclusion.

Thanks to William Strachey we know the extent of Southampton's efforts to infuse new life into the moribund colony and create what became known as Virginia Britanica. He began by organizing shipping and equipped a large vessel, the *Concorde*.

Under the command of Captain Bartholomew Gosnell, accompanied by various gentlemen, the bark departed from Dartmouth for North Virginia. There they found rich territory and a navigable river which they named the James, and took possession of the country in the name of the king, who accorded them a patent on April 10th, 1605. This was not enough to satisfy a spirit as ardent and ambitious as that of the Earl of Southampton ; he had to continue the work and assure its future, giving himself up to the re-organization of this colony. Not content with dispatching the *Concorde* to the shores of America, in May 1609 he equipped an entire fleet. Eight vessels and a little sloop were sent after her.[1] There was much rivalry as to which of them would arrive first. To settle the dispute between Lord Delaware, Thomas Gates and Sir George Summers, it was decided for them to sail together aboard the *Sea Venture*. The main flotilla arrived safe and sound in Virginia, but the ship bearing the three leaders was separated from the convoy by a furious tempest and the rumour circulated in London that she was lost with all hands. While this tragic story disturbed the capital, a circumstantial report reached Lord Southampton, secretary of the company. The *Sea Venture* had been wrecked in a small sandy bay of the Bermudas.

---

[1] The convoys sent to the new Colony carried carpenters, metal workers, wine growers, hunters, woodsmen and glass makers to furnish windows on the spot for the houses under construction. King James wished to avoid costs of transportation and disapproved the importation of tobacco but wished to encourage the manufacture of silk and velvet by planting Mulberry trees and breeding silk worms.

Crustaceans and molluscs were found in abundance. Inland, the forest teemed with game ; pea-nuts, valuable as food, were there in plenty. The adventurers were able not only to subsist for several months, but under the direction of Lord Summers, who gave his name to the island, even constructed two boats from the wreckage of the *Sea Venture* permitting them to rejoin the other colonists in Virginia. This odyssey became legendary. According to some of the sailors Summers Island was inhabited by invisible beings, and the sounds of mysterious music accompanied the voices of the spirits who were masters of the place. Unquestionably these tales suggested the subject of *The Tempest* and led Shakespeare once more to adapt his muse to the taste for current affairs. Just as formerly, when Barbary was the topic of the day, he showed one of its princes arriving at Belmont, now that Virginia was on the lips of high and low, his mind and pen turned to the " still vexed Bermoothes ". The play itself recalls how the citizens of London, when they visited the fair, willingly gave a shilling to look at a dead Indian or to gaze at a strange fish.[1] Crowds pressed round the " beautiful Savage " Pocahontas, the Indian princess, who after saving the life of the settlers' leader, married James Rolfe and came to England with her young husband. Under Southampton's auspices, the Rolfes were presented at Court and introduced to society. The King himself, won over to the colonial cult, hinted that he would be happy to receive some souvenir from those unknown parts, and Southampton, aware of James' love of natural history, undertook to search for a flying squirrel for the King's zoological garden. Shakespeare's former patron describes this animal as smaller than a rat, and having a membrane joining its shoulders to its feet like a bat's wing which enabled it to jump thirty yards from tree to tree. In these days *The Tempest* would have been excellent propaganda in favour of colonial enterprise in Virginia, yet those who were financially interested in developing the Bermudas and the neighbouring coast feared that such ideas would discourage prospective colonists. It was thought opportune to order William Barrett to print a little work affirming that the rumour that the Bermudas were tempest-tossed and peopled by devils and evil spirits, was utterly false and there was nothing in this tragic comedy to discourage settlers, an evident allusion to *The Tempest*.[2] But nothing could deflect the current drawing the peoples of Europe towards a new world whose riches were disputed by French, English and Spaniards. Vainly did William Crashaw fulminate in his sermons against Papists and actors who, according to him, were the colonists' true enemies.[3] America continued to grow and *The Tempest* pursued its brilliant career on both sides of the Atlantic.

[1] A strange fish ! were I in England now as I once was, and had but this fish painted, not a holiday fool there but would give his piece of silver when they will not pay out a doit to relieve a lame beggar they will lay out ten to see a Dead Indian. (*The Tempest*, Act II, Sc. 2.)

[2] *A true declaration on the Estate of the Colonie of Virginia*, published by advice and direction of the Council of Virginia.

[3] A sermon preached by Master Crashaw intituled a New Years' gift to Virginia, March 19th, 1610.

Rowe's sober judgement on this play nearly two hundred and fifty years ago has lost nothing of its authority :

It seems to me as perfect in its Kind, as almost anything we have of his. One may observe, that the Unities are kept here with an Exactness uncommon to the Liberties of his Writing. . . . His Magick has something in it very Solemn and very Poetical : And that extravagant Character of Caliban is mighty well sustain'd, shews a wonderful Invention in the Author, who could strike out such a particular wild Image, and is certainly one of the finest and most uncommon Grotesques that was ever seen. The Observation, which I have been inform'd [1] three very great Men concurr'd in making upon this Part, was extremely just. That Shake-spear had not only found out a new Character in his Caliban, but had also devis'd and adopted a new manner of Language for that Character.

On a rock-bound coast a hurricane raised by the genii of the island endangers a ship in distress ; she has on board Alonzo king of Naples, usurper of Prospero his elder brother's realm, and his son Ferdinand. Passengers and crew are cast ashore on the very same spot where twelve years before Prospero with his little daughter Miranda found refuge. There, thanks to his studies in astronomical science and the black arts, the passion for which of old made him neglect his subjects and lose his crown, he has brought up the girl to be the marvel of her sex. While he himself subdues through his magic the occult forces of the island.

In the beginning Caliban the evil genius welcomed the castaways, showed them hidden springs, found them fruits and sea-birds eggs, dug pea-nuts for them with his claw-like nails and, in order to provoke Miranda's laughter, caught young monkeys for her amusement. In turn the maiden taught him human speech and the songs of far off Italy. But all this time the monster dreamed of killing Prospero and carrying Miranda to his underground lair. It was only through perpetual vigilance that the magician kept him tame and in servitude.

He had better luck with the other spirit of the island, Ariel,[2] the delicate winged being through whom the sinister forces of the air were set in motion. He brought the ship wrecked passengers toward the magician's cave. But when Alonzo had collected his scattered followers, he found to his horror that young Prince Ferdinand was not among them. This awakens the father's conscience and makes him regret his former villainy. His household is beset with other preoccupations. The drunken Butler with Trinculo his aid, thinks only of saving from the sea a few kegs of strong liquor. While

---

[1] Ld. Falkland, Ld. C. F. Vaughan, and Mr. Selden.

[2] Strachey's recital contains a description of the phenomenon called St. Elmo's fire " an apparition of a little round light like a faint star trembling, and streaming along with a sparkling blaze, half the height of the mainmast, and shooting sometime from shroud to shroud three or four hours together ".

In Shakespeare's *Tempest* it is Ariel who is responsible for the apparition. " I boarded the King's ship ; now on the beak, now in the waist, the deck, in every cabin, I flamed amazement : sometime I'd divide and burn in many places, on the topmast, the yards and bowsprit would I flame distinctly. . . ." (*The Tempest*, Act I, Sc. 2.)

the good councillor Gonzalo dreams of founding on this virgin soil an ideal Republic which will revive the Golden Age.

Prince Ferdinand, however, in spite of the sea-maid's knell and Ariel's elegy is too vigorous a swimmer to let himself drown weeping on the beach for the supposed loss of his father and comrades, he is taken in charge by the tricksy spirit and led to Prospero's cavern.

Miranda is dazzled by the sight of this, to her, unknown species and Ferdinand with all his knowledge of the world and of courts, has never encountered such sweetness, grace and beauty. Prospero, magician that he is, possesses enough worldly wisdom to throw all kinds of obstacles in the way of their intercourse and forces the young man to submit to many painful ordeals. Prospero the sage has put away ambition, so has his wicked brother in learning the ways of repentance. Everything is prepared for Miranda and Ferdinand to mount the throne of Naples. The royal vessel is discovered lying peacefully at anchor ready to set sail for Italy, with the betrothed prince and princess and all the other actors of the drama who among interludes of mirth, have been taught many profitable lessons. As for Ariel, that ethereal spirit who chafed at serving a human being however benevolent, liberated henceforth, he returns to the pure element from which he sprang.

Since Rowe's appreciation, *The Tempest*, shortest and simplest of Shakespeare's comedies, which takes place in a single day, has caused much ink to flow. The author must have possessed a deep knowledge of the occult to have portrayed a magician ; he must have learned Hebrew also because of the name Ariel. Finally, must he not have visited Patagonia, to have heard Setebos invoked, the god adored by Caliban ? And where must he not have travelled to find this name of Caliban ?

Here again simplest explanations are best. The name Ariel appears exactly as it stands in the popular rhymed description of the occult sciences : the *Hierarchie of Blessed Angels*. The spirit who commands the elements and governs tempests bears this name, and the author, Thomas Heywood, well versed in magic and sorcery, as has been already noted, was Shakespeare's life-long friend.

Nor did Shakespeare give proof in *The Tempest* of great technical knowledge in dealing with magic. His presentation of fairies, spirits, sorcerers and magicians is more " impressionist " than realistic, and Prospero's invocation is paraphrased from that of Medea in Ovid's *Metamorphoses*.

The name Setebos printed for the first time in Thevet's *Cosmographie* also figures in such popular books as Eden's *History of Travayle* (1577), a volume well within Shakespeare's reach. As for Caliban, his name is simply the phonetic anagram of *cannibal* used by Montaigne : it perfectly suits the wild and bestial creature who bears it.

To sum up, *The Tempest*, like all Shakespeare's other works demonstrates an acute sensibility to natural impressions and an innate poetic sense. Still more than his other works, it proves his vocation for dramatic art and his deep knowledge of theatrical craft, acquired by long apprenticeship as producer.

It is not the knowledge, erudition, polish or execution which most distinguish *The Tempest*, but the perfect mastery of technique and art, together with the mature reflections of a man approaching fifty, who, like Prospero, obeys Montaigne's counsel in preparing " a good end " by meditating on the life to come.

Nor is it strange that commentators have seen in Prospero the author's own likeness. When Shakespeare left the stage he undoubtedly broke a powerful magic wand, and we would fain know whether he also reaped the reward of his renunciation. He firmly believed that children are the source of moral education in their parents. This seemingly modern idea constantly reappears in his writings, but nowhere so clearly as in *The Tempest*. Through Miranda, Prospero is softened and humanized. While educating his daughter the sage perfects his own education.

> O ! a cherubin
> Thou wast, that did preserve me. Thou didst smile
> Infused with a fortitude from heaven . . .
> Here on this island we arrived : and here
> Have I thy schoolmaster made thee more profit
> Than other Princess' can, that have more time
> for vainer hours and tutors not so careful.
>
> (*The Tempest*, Act 1, Sc. 2)

New influences had been at work in the development of Shakespeare's genius after those of Ovid, Plutarch and Boccaccio, as has been shown in Chapter IX. But Montaigne is not the sole French prose writer to have left his impress on Shakespeare's work. *The Tempest* shows him well acquainted with the creator of Gargantua and Panurge.

It is difficult to measure the degree of Shakespeare's admiration for Rabelais, but we must admit that the power with which that master of laughter managed his own tongue was likely to arouse enthusiasm in a verbal artist like Shakespeare. Certain dominating thoughts of the French writer, his lofty conception of the infinity of worlds, of celestial harmony and of the immortality of " intellective souls " must have found a ready response. Doubtless some aspects of Rabelais' work may have displeased Shakespeare's idealism. Often the clear-sighted doctor's analysis of our poor humanity must have appeared cruel. Perhaps it is because Shakespeare did not adopt all the grossness found in Rabelais' work that no comparison between them has been made, though the first scene of *The Tempest* presents striking resemblances to the incident of the hurricane in the *Quart Livre*.

When the storm drives the King of Naples' ship aground on an unknown island, the realism of the action is astounding.

How describe so powerfully what happens on board a ship in such danger, if one has not had such an experience ? It would require, they say, the travels of a Rutland, the science of a Bacon, the heaven knows what of a Stanley, to succeed. Critics forget Shakespeare's profound understanding of stagecraft. It would be natural that he should have sought his model for a storm at sea from the great realist of the time, who painted an unforgettable picture of a tempest. Only, like a true artist, he did not make a servile copy but contented himself with extracting a sort of quintessence from the original.

Rabelais recounts how Pantagruel and his suite, already prey to the depression which precedes sea-sickness, remain " afflicted—and half dead " while the pilot foreseeing trouble, orders all hands on deck with officers, cabin boys and passengers to assist the crew. Suddenly the sea begins to swell and rage from the abyss, the squall whistles through the rigging, surely antique chaos had come again for never were fire, air, sea and land all the elements in such refractory confusion.

Then comes Pantagruel's dissertation on the moment of death, his fine appeal to courage in spite of man's natural horror of drowning which Rabelais calls " Chose grieve, abhorrente et dénaturêe ". All begin to pray, when Panurge makes his celebrated invocation to terra firma.

I wish to God I were comfortably on dry land. Oh thrice and four times blessed is he who plants cabbage ; for he has always one foot on the ground and the other is not far off ! Ah ! there is no such Godlike mansion than the Cows flooring. . . . Oh my friends this wave will carry us overboard. . . .

But the danger passed : all are astonished at having been so afraid, Brother John denounces the coward Panurge :

By the worthy frock I wear, Panurge, during the tempest thou wast afraid without cause and reason, for thy fatal destiny is not to perish in water ; thou shalt, high in air, certainly be hanged.

What Rabelais relates in several pages, Shakespeare indicates in a few lines, dramatizing the incident, but following the order of events. There is the same description of the troubled elements, the same activity in that manoeuvre called by sailors, " Tack about, wear ship ". Similar again in both authors are the passengers' nervousness and the instructions to the sailors for the preservation of the vessel.

Admitting that all this may be fortuitous, it is more difficult to accept that chance alone has given Gonzalo the same lugubrious jokes which Pantagruel makes on the seaman's inevitable destiny.

To Gonzalo's remonstrance : remember whom you have aboard, the Boatswain replies :

None that I love more than myself. You are a counsellor : if you can command these elements to silence, and mark the peace of the present, we will not handle rope more. . . . Cheerly, good hearts !—Out of our way, I say.

Gonzalo then makes a remark identical with Rabelais' Brother John :

I have great comfort from this fellow : methinks he hath no drowning mark upon him, his complexion is perfect gallows. Stand fast, good fate, to his hanging ! make the rope of his destiny our cable. . . . If he be not born to be hanged, our case is miserable.

Then having accepted fate, he apostrophizes the land in the same terms as Panurge :

Now would I give a thousand furlongs of sea for an acre of barren ground ;

long heath, brown furze, anything. The wills above be done! but I would fain die a dry death.

There is nothing surprising in this echo of the *Quart Livre*. Is it not, on the contrary, natural to suppose that Shakespeare, one of a group of literary celebrities interested in Italian and French thought, should have known the work of Rabelais, especially as the shipwreck episode of *The Tempest* is not the only allusion to the famous satirist which may be found in his work?

We have already noted allusions to Rabelais in *Love's Labour's Lost*, *As You Like It* and *Twelfth Night*. Iago too, when he wishes to shock his audience, borrows from Rabelais word for word the picture of the gross loves of Grandgousier and Gargamelle,[1] and a long passage of *Pericles*, where a giant who swallowed a whole church while the beadle was ringing the bells, recalls the episode of the first book where Gargantua seizes the bells of Notre-Dame to decorate the breast-strap of his mare.

Such comparisons do not diminish Shakespeare. His vision extended beyond his country's frontiers, and drawing as he did new thought from the springs of the Renaissance, he continually renewed his inspiration without sacrificing originality. Shakespeare was essentially a man of his time, a time when the cultivated Englishman did not limit his interest and information to his own island; and like others who look beyond national barriers, he was attracted first to the art of Italy then to the philosophy of France.

The Tempest inaugurated a new era in theatrical technique. A realistic rendering of storms was achieved; thunder and lightning, owing to pyrotechnic innovations, were sufficiently daring to provoke a sour attack by Ben Jonson. In the prologue to *Bartholomew Fair* he makes ironic excuses for not having sought applause by staging domesticated monsters (an allusion to Caliban), and for hesitating to unleash nature, like the author of *Tales and Tempests*.[2] The spectacular presentation of *Pericles* had had too much success with the public to permit a sudden return to simplicity in the theatre. Like other writers, Shakespeare was obliged to submit to the exigencies of fashion and to make use of everything which mechanical progress placed at his disposal; he even made overmuch use of theatrical devices. In *The Tempest* Juno's throne descended from the skies; Ariel appeared suspended in the air. At the revival of *Macbeth* at the " Globe ", the hero and Macduff appeared on horseback; in *The Winter's Tale*, which succeeded *The Tempest*, a ballet in which pretty milkmaids and disguised princes mingled with farmers and antique satyrs, entertained those who cared for such novelties. Perhaps it was the drama of *Henry VIII* which was accompanied by the boldest innovations. Real cannon were introduced on the stage to fire the royal salute when the King arrives at the York Place masquerade. The unheard of splendour with which this play was staged, was described by the

---

[1] See Chapter XI.
[2] If there bee never a Servant-monster i' the Fayre; who can helpe it? he sayes; nor a nest of Antiques? Hee (the author) is loth to make Nature afraid in his Playes, like those that beget Tales, Tempests. . . . (*Bartholomew Fayre*, Introduction).

ambassador to Venice, Sir Henry Wotton, who wrote that they even laid a carpet on the boards, that the supernumeraries who were Knights of the Garter wore their insignia, that the bodyguards' uniforms were richly embroidered and so on ; enough, said he " to render greatness and dignity very familiar, if not ridiculous ".[1]

The Winter's Tale, which Jonson in his sarcastic criticism linked with *The Tempest*, was another of the trio of tragi-comedies written after the poet's retirement to Stratford. The title was suggested by a passage of Marlowe's and the argument is taken from *Pandosto* [2] a story by Robert Greene. It was composed between 1610 and 1611, as is proved by an account given by Simon Forman, the same enthusiastic playgoer who had attended a performance of *Macbeth*.

Ignoring the tragic side of the drama, Forman jumps to the comic element which evidently pleased him. He remembers a rogue who reminded him of " Coll Pixci ".[3] who feigned to have been robbed and wounded ; then after cheating a poor shepherd of his money goes disguised to his sheep shearing and picks the pockets of the guests " Beware ", exclaims Forman, " Of those who have beggar's faces and the false tongues of flatterers."

The moral of *The Winter's Tale* is by no means so simple. Its wide scope Forman failed to grasp. The purpose of the play was not to put the spectator on guard against the tricks of some rascal but to preach the most eloquent of all sermons against egoism and jealousy.

Leontes is not like Othello the victim of circumstances and an adroit slanderer. A morbid imagination is the sole cause of his frenzy. No disquieting facts give ground for suspicion as in the Moor's case. Leontes the supposedly civilized husband cannot see his wife take a friend's arm without believing that both are betraying him. Not only is he ready to put his friend and guest to death against all rules of hospitality but he accuses his wife and drags her before the tribunals of their country. She is declared innocent too late, alas ! to prevent a tragedy.

To bridge the years which have elapsed between the day when Leontes gave orders to expose his new born daughter on a distant coast and the day when the young Perdita returns to Sicily as the bride of Prince Florizel of Bohemia, Time appears on the stage in person with scythe and hour glass. Nothing could be more daring and witty than this method of avoiding a major difficulty.

In sixteen years Time has transformed the abandoned infant into the loveliest shepherdess in all Bohemia, who has unwittingly kindled a profound

---

[1] Reliquiae Wottonianae, fol. 425.
[2] Pandosto, the Triumph of Time wherein is discovered by a pleasant history that although by the meanes of sinister fortune, truth may be concealed yet by Time, in spite of Fortune it is most manifestly revealed. Pleasant for age to avoid drowsy thoughts, Profitable for youth to eschew other wanton pastimes, and bringing to both a desired content by *The Delectable Tale of Dorastus & Fawnia 1607.* This was followed by fourteen more editions.
[3] This is said to refer to a low comedian who was popular at this time.

and pure passion in the heart of Prince Florizel ready to renounce his prospective throne to marry the unknown damsel. The sheep-shearing celebrations presided over by this " queen of curds and cream ", take place of course in the Forest of Arden ; the Bohemia whither the author transports it is none other than this Arcadia dear to his dreams. The old shepherd who finds Perdita by his sagacity recalls the Corin of *As You Like It*. The pastoral feast is interrupted, however, by the arrival of King Polixines and his minister, furious at discovering the heir to the throne in such company ; the young couple, fearing an enforced separation, hasten to make their escape and take ship happily bound for Sicily.

Up to this point, Shakespeare follows the plot of Greene's *Pandosto* as of old he clung to Holinshed or Plutarch. The modifications brought to the work of his former enemy are of small importance, but were necessary to bring about the surprising conclusion he gave to his *Winter's Tale*.

In Greene's story Queen Hermione dies of grief and the author complacently describes the incestuous love of the king for his newly found daughter, thus making his tragic suicide inevitable. By resurrecting Hermione and giving Perdita the husband of her choice, Shakespeare facilitates Leontes' repentance and his wife's pardon. To this end the dramatist is obliged to invent a means hitherto never employed ; if Hermione forgives Leontes, she must take up life again with him, and this necessitates the moral rejuvenation of her jealous husband. He must be forced to recognize in his wife other qualities than charm and beauty ; she is now sixteen years older and bears the marks of all that she has been through. While King Leontes is called upon to undergo a psychological ordeal, she too must be assured that love is still possible between them. Before revealing that she is still alive she must be exhibited to the king as a marble statue placed on a monument raised to her by the faithful Paulina, who as she draws aside its curtain explains the intentions of the supposed sculptor.

The artist has represented Hermione, not as she was sixteen years ago but as she would be now had she lived. Leontes gazes a long time at the lightly tinted statue. Then overcome by emotion he cries ; no matter though he appear mad, he must kiss her lips. For a moment the statue trembles then slowly and majestically the queen steps down from her pedestal, embraces Leontes and, with a maternal gesture, solemnly blesses her rediscovered Perdita.

Of all Shakespeare's heroines, Hermione is the one who combines tenderness of heart and the pathetic submission to unjust sufferings with the most moral greatness. Like Constance in *King John*, she is the synthesis of maternal love and it is easy to imagine the triumph of Sarah Siddons, named the " tragic muse ", in these two magnificent rôles.

Compared with Hermione, Paulina, intrepid champion of truth who prefers to risk her head rather than hold her tongue, and who devotes sixteen years of her life to the moral cure of the jealous king, possesses a completely original character. A great lady on occasion, she has the good sense of a daughter of the people. While courtiers bow down in deference to the sovereign, she scolds and abuses the king with a natural flow of vituperation which her husband in reality approves although he condemns its violence. The contrast between Hermione and her faithful Paulina is considered by many as one of Shakespeare's greatest achievements.

This pastoral play was a favourite at court, where it was often performed, notably on the occasion of the wedding of the Princess Elizabeth and the Elector Palatine then aged sixteen. The courtiers naturally compared the young couple to Florizel and Perdita. Later, in 1618 and 1619, after the Elector had been offered the crown of Bohemia, the play was revived and the audience could not help admiring Shakespeare's gift of divination in placing this gracious idyll in Bohemia, which had not been done by Greene. *The Winter's Tale* was again given at court on January 18th, 1624, but not without certain obstruction, for the official book of Sir Henry Herbert, Master of the Revels, contains this note :

For the king's players. An olde playe called *Winter's Tale*, formerly allowed by Sir George Buck, and likewyse by mee on Mr. Hemmings his worde that there was nothing profane added or reformed, thogh the allowed booke was missinge ; And therefore I returned it without a fee, this 19 day of August 1623.

The disappearance of the original manuscript may be explained by its having been entrusted to the publishers of the Folio then in preparation, where the play is placed last among the comedies. It was very popular on the stage and the text, which was never published in quarto, is almost free of faults, which would indicate that the author revised the manuscript minutely before publication as he did with that of *The Tempest* and *Coriolanus*. Although the list of " Dramatis Personae " is included, the text contains very few stage directions. The scene is never mentioned. It must be concluded that Shakespeare himself wished to remain indefinite in delivering to the public this piece of pure imagination strongly contrasting with the tragedy to follow. In *Cymbeline* the descriptions are vivid : the stage directions frequent and detailed ; it seems as if in this case Shakespeare wished to give body and realism to a plot which nevertheless is most improbable.

The story of Cymbeline, King of Britain, suggested once more by Holinshed's *Chronicles*, takes place when Britain was under Roman domination. Its king still paid to the Emperor Augustus the tribute imposed by Caesar. In this semi-classical, semi-barbaric frame, Shakespeare placed an intrigue of marital jealousy borrowed from the *Decameron*.[1] This unexpected fantasy gives to his play a curious Renaissance atmosphere accentuated by an artificial refinement of style. He also introduces a romantic theme of his own which gives him an opportunity to present the harsh and rough existence in the woods and caverns of the Welsh mountains in opposition to life at court.

It might appear impossible to achieve a harmonious whole with such heterogeneous material. Nevertheless the poet has done so by the creation

[1] Second day ; 9th Novello.

of characters who are convincingly alive and, above all, a heroine so captivating that the spectator never thinks of exercising his right of criticism. In writing *Cymbeline* the author adapted himself once more to the taste of the moment, and continued to make use of situations and theatrical effects which had already been tried and proved, dressing old ideas in new garments.

King Cymbeline, like Lear, is a noble and generous sovereign, but like him he is led to commit injustice. His evil genius is none other than his second wife, an unscrupulous widow who from the beginning attacks Bellarius, her husband's bravest soldier and wisest counsellor, whom she accuses of treachery. He escapes to the mountains with the king's two sons, whom all at court believe dead. Their sister, Imogen, becomes the prey of the scheming queen and her villainous son Cloten, but is deaf to threats and provocations ; this girl, who possesses Viola's grace, Juliet's generous passion, Desdemona's confident loyalty and the self control of Portia, has married her childhood friend, Posthumus Leonatus, an orphan whom the king had taken under special protection. This marriage upsets the queen's designs and Posthumus is exiled.

In Rome he falls in with an early model of Don Juan to whom Shakespeare gives the suggestive name of Iachimo so that the spectator, already acquainted with Iago, knows what may be expected from him. This subtle villain about to leave for Britain, hearing the praises of Princess Imogen's beauty and virtue wagers that he will on arriving at Cymbeline's court make an easy conquest of Leonatus' wife and bring back to her husband proof of his success.

On arriving in Britain Iachimo stealthily penetrates into Imogen's chamber where she has fallen asleep while reading Ovid's *Metamorphosis*. This the intruder carefully notes, then, while muttering to himself the exploit of Tarquin he proceeds to make an inventory of the furniture. Her room is hung with tapestry wrought in silk and silver where Cleopatra is portrayed on the river Cydnus which swells with pride under the weight of her triremes. *Tarquin ! The Rape of Lucrece, Antony and Cleopatra !* Decidedly Shakespeare while mentioning Ovid and Plutarch has not forgotten his own works. But to continue the exploration of the apartment : the richly sculptured chimney-piece represented the chaste Diana bathing ; the sculptor, nature's own brother, would have excelled her but that he omitted to give his figures breath and movement. The silver and irons were cupids, holding torches. The rich ceiling was fretted with golden cherubins. Lucrece's bedchamber as described by Shakespeare was not more evidently furnished in Renaissance style than Imogen's.

The Romans landing at Milford Haven invade Britain. In Cymbeline's tent, all the personages of the drama are now assembled, except the queen who has died of vexation. Having thus collected all the threads of his complicated web, Shakespeare uses each to produce that work of art—the denouement of his plot—before which criticism is disarmed. Departing from the ancient convention that a tragedy must finish with rivers of blood, he seeks a clever plan—too clever perhaps—to avert inexorable fate. The play ends with a joyful reunion of all the characters, and, so that peace between Rome and Britain may endure, Cymbeline majestically promises to pay his wonted tribute to Caesar.

Commentators have pronounced very various judgements upon this " tragedy ", which concludes as happily as *As You Like It*. While all admit the qualities of Imogen, the most perfect of Shakespeare's feminine creations, many make important reservations about the whole ; Granville Barker, for example, goes so far as to claim that the great dramatist's hand in it is small.

It must be remembered that this play, like *The Winter's Tale*, was written in view of the celebrations of a royal marriage. James I, a pacific sovereign must have applauded the happy conclusion of *Cymbeline*, and may even have commanded it. The play was one of King Charles' favourites.[1] There is no indication of a decline in the poet's lyrical qualities. What a pearl is the " aubade " sung under Imogen's window ! What more solemn than the requiem recited by the two princes over Fidele. Here again is shown the importance Shakespeare attached to time-honoured funereal conventions.

> Nay, Cadwal, we must lay his head to th' east ;
> My father hath a reason for't.

orders the elder of the two brothers before strewing flowers over their comrade's body.

Masterly too is the long *tête-à-tête* between Iachimo and Imogen, so revealing of the character of each, the young woman's charming cordiality towards her husband's supposed friend, followed by her cold dignity in response to his infamous proposals. The dialogue is one of Shakespeare's best conceptions. The mountain episodes also, strikingly contrasted with the court intrigues and the subtle villainy of Iachimo that sophisticated Roman, are in Shakespeare's best manner. This cannot be said of the innovation which brought Jupiter and his eagle down from the skies amid thunder and lightning to visit the imprisoned Posthumus ; but this spectacular interlude forms part of the scenery rather than of the play itself, and must often have been omitted.

For the fifth time, the green-eyed monster controls the drama ; but Shakespeare as he grew older showed less sympathy for those dominated by jealousy. Its pangs arouse amusement in the spectator of *The Comedy of Errors* and *The Merry Wives of Windsor*, pity and terror in *Othello*, anger in *The Winter's Tale* and simply disgust in *Cymbeline*.

Shakespeare's *Othello* presents a case where calumny and not nature was the cause of tragic passion. Devilish suggestion and almost conclusive evidence transform the noble Moor of Venice into his wife's assassin. *The Winter's Tale*, shows a man morbidly jealous by nature, who requires neither suggestion nor proof. Between these two examples of pathological jealousy

---

[1] A memorandum on the Revel's book notes a performance given before Charles I and Henrietta Maria which indicates the continued vogue of the play. " On Wednesday night the first of January 1633 *Cymbeline* was acted at Court by the King's Players—well lik't by the King."

stands that of Posthumus, who believes in his wife as long as none suggests that he might think otherwise.   This type is so common as to be uninteresting.   There is something shocking in the happy conclusion which constrains the charming Imogen to live the rest of her life with a husband who, when put to the test, has shown himself incapable of understanding her essential character.   Shakespeare in *The Winter's Tale* showed that sixteen years of repentance were necessary for Leontes to obtain the pardon of his wronged wife.   The over-rapid reconciliation that takes place between Imogen and Posthumus gives insufficient time between the husband's offence and the forgiveness he obtains from his consort.

Must we deduce from the imperfections noticed in *Cymbeline* that Shakespeare sought and found assistance from a writer of inferior talent as Granville Barker alleged ?   This seems to me unlikely ; for the style is homogeneous and no break in continuity can be found.   But there are certain passages which appear laborious and leave an impression that the drama was the fruit of hard work rather than of inspiration, so that those who link cause with effect are tempted to admit that Shakespeare, obliged to provide dramatic material for both " Globe " and " Blackfriars ", was only too glad to accept the co-operation of John Fletcher in composing and staging the new plays he had promised to furnish his two theatres.[1]

[1] John Ward, Vicar of Stratford from 1662 to 1681, notes in his journal, the sixteen volumes of which are preserved in the Folger Shakespeare Library, that the dramatist on his retirement, was pledged to furnish two plays a year to his company.

CHAPTER XIX

SWAN SONG

Journeys between Stratford and London—Borough affairs—Collaboration with Fletcher—*Cardenio* and *The Two Noble Kinsmen*—*Henry VIII*—Celebrations in honour of the royal wedding—Shakespeare buys a London house—Burning of the " Globe " ; its reconstruction—The poet's last stay in the capital.

AT the beginning of his retirement, Shakespeare's visits to the banks of Avon were frequent rather than prolonged. It is not surprising to find his name on a bill (September 11th, 1611) [1] concerning the necessity of repairing and improving the highways. How many times had he not travelled these roads. Three days' ride from Stratford to London ; three to return ! But as his fame grew, the journey took on the character of a triumphal progress. The days were long passed when, as an outcast he rode Londonwards to seek his fortune. His interest in horses was more than natural. He describes with equal sympathy the superb stallion of Adonis, Antony's proud steed, Richard II's roan Barbary and Petruchio's nag which exhibited every blemish known to veterinary science. [2] The actor poet could count now at each halt on a hospitable welcome first at the fine manor at Alderminster where Thomas Russell and his sons-in-law Sir Dudley and Leonard Digges, [3] were ever ready to greet him, then at Oxford where the Davenants reserved for him their best painted chamber—its walls are still decorated with Persian designs and biblical inscriptions encircling the monogram I.H.S.

The presence of Shakespeare in London is attested by his excuse for not being able to await the verdict of the tribunal in the Bellot-Montjoye affair which was rendered on June 19th, 1612, an indication that before this date he had returned to his native town where he entered by the great bridge recently repaired and repaved at the cost of twenty-seven pounds, nineteen shillings and five pence. [4]

No sooner had he arrived at New Place than he was caught in the whirl of petty borough affairs, and the gossip of the town where he had become a

---

[1] *Stratford Records* (Mis. Doc., vol. i, No. 4).

[2] Glanders, spavins, lampass, windgalls, yellows, staggers, sway-backed. *The Taming of the Shrew*, Act III, Sc. 2.

[3] All three lived together after the marriage of Sir Thomas Russell with the widow of Thomas Digges whose property and fortune, in danger of being seized by the Crown, were safeguarded by this union.

[4] Stratford's Chamberlains' account January 8th, 1612.

principal personage. A complicated difference of opinion absorbed his fellow townsmen. The question was whether a landowner had the right to fence a pasture which the inhabitants considered common land. This case was similar to that of the enclosure of Fulbrooke Park. Shakespeare's position must have been delicate : on the one side community interest was at stake, on the other that of the Combe family with which he was intimately connected. Certainly he fulfilled his conciliating mission with tact, since old Combe one of the promoters of the enclosure, known for avarice and called by the poet " ten percent " in a humorous epitaph [1] not only forgave both joke and intervention but bequeathed five pounds to his neighbour.

Even a Shakespeare was not strong enough to shield his family from malicious criticism. A private supper one evening assembled the Palmers of Compton Wynyates, eminently respectable folk, Doctor Hall and his wife Susanna, Robert Whatcott, whose name is among the witnesses of Shakespeare's will, Ralph Smith, son of former bailiff William Smith and nephew of Hamlet Sadler, and finally a young puritan aged twenty-three, by name John Lane. Although familiar gaiety was natural, and all had been acquainted since childhood, Lane left the house scandalized declaring that Susanna Hall had behaved disgracefully with Ralph Smith, and that her husband, was wrong to allow her so much rein. [2]

Robert Whatcott, angered by such aspersions against the honour of a matron of thirty, offered to act as witness in the libel suit at the Bishop of Worcester's court, where Doctor Hall obtained excommunication of the scandalmonger.

There is no evidence of Shakespeare's opinion on this affair. Perhaps he considered his son-in-law fully capable of defending his wife's reputation, but the incident suffices to prove that in this Arcadian retreat the serpent calumny sometimes reared its ugly head against the Shakespeares. It also indicates that ancient animosities were still alive, for the said John Lane belonged to a family long hostile to the poet's family. In the midst of their worst financial difficulties his father had procured old John Shakespeare's arrest for debt. William on his part did not hesitate, when necessary, to set in motion the forces of the law. He won a case against Philip Rogers the apothecary, also against John Addenbrooke and Thomas Hornby, son of the farrier whose forge was next his birthplace. Evidently the magnanimous Shakespeare did not always forgive his fellow townsmen's malevolence. [3]

About July 10th, 1612, he joined with Richard Lane and his cousin Green to ask and obtain from the government " a more equitable " arrange-

---

[1] Ten in the hundred lies here en-graved
Tis a hundred to ten that his soul is not saved
If any man asketh who lies in this tomb
" Oh ho " quoth the devil " tis my John a Combe."

[2] She has the running of the reins and had been nought with Rafe Smith at John Palmers. (Ecclesiastical Causes in Gloster and Worcester Act Book No. 9, Diocesan Register.)

[3] A summary of these affairs may be found in E. K. Chambers's *William Shakespeare*, vol. ii, pp. 113-118.

ment of the payment, too often deficient, of the parish tithes redeemed in 1605 for which all three were individually held responsible.

But literature held the chief place in that summer's work. For the writing of three new plays he was assured of John Fletcher's assistance.

A better choice could not have been made. This able but slightly effeminate writer whose lines flowed with extreme facility, is primarily known for his long association with Francis Beaumont. Together they gave the world a folio volume of dramas, comedies, parodies and farces, an immense production where they often seem to have skimmed the cream from Shakespeare's work. At the time of Beaumont's marriage, his friend temporarily resumed his independence and came to offer his pen to the King's Players. Fletcher's work shows considerable understanding of the stage, a gift for dialogue, and an undeniable elegance of style, bordering on decadence. Moreover, he had some knowledge of Spanish literature from which Shakespeare evidently profited in writing *Cardenio*.[1]

It is impossible to form any opinion upon this comedy, the first fruit of their collaboration, as the prompter's copy, the only manuscript, disappeared the year it was first acted in the fire at the " Globe ". But, given that *Don Quixote* provided the subject, it is probable that it enjoyed a success approaching that obtained a few years before by Beaumont and Fletcher's *Knight of the Burning Pestle*, in which a London grocer and his wife seek to imitate the noble deeds of Cervantes' hero.

On the second play in which Fletcher's name is linked with that of Shakespeare, the *Two Noble Kinsmen*, many commentators have expressed varied judgement, summarized in C. F. Tucker Brook's excellent study.[2] The probabilities are that we have a play of which the major part was written by Fletcher and which was only revised and corrected by Shakespeare.[3]

The plot is taken from one of *The Canterbury Tales*, and is concerned with the rivalry of Palamon and Arcite two friends united in heart and kinship, but changed into bitter enemies by their common passion for Emilia.

This subject enabled the authors to exploit afresh a situation which had never failed to please the theatrical public. It sufficed to transport to Thebes the story of betrayed friendships as shown in *The Two Gentlemen of Verona* and to renew the spectator's acquaintance with Theseus and Hippolyta, who had such an important place in *A Midsummer Night's Dream ;* but in this case, the amateur producer is not a " mechanical " like Peter Quince or Nick Bottom, but a pedantic schoolmaster reminiscent of Holofernes of

---

[1] *Cardenio* was presented at Court May 20th and again June 8th, 1613. But the manuscript was accidentally destroyed. Theobald, Shakespeare's commentator, in 1727 presented a play on the same subject called the *Double Falsehood* noting on the programme that Shakespeare and Fletcher had previously treated it.

[2] *Shakespeare Apocrypha*, Clarendon Press, Oxford, 1929.

[3] *The Two Noble Kinsmen :* Presented at the Blackfrirs by the Kings Majesties servants, with great applause : Written by the memorable Worthies of their time : Mr. John Fletcher and Mr. William Shakespeare, Gent. Printed at London by Tho. Cotes, for John Waterson; and are to be sold at the signe of the Crowne in Pauls Church-yard 1634.

Love's Labour's Lost. As a romantic touch a young girl whose love is unrequited appears. Her father is the gaoler, of the noble captive Palamon, with whom she is desperately in love. The liberation of the prisoner imperils her father's life and the unfortunate damsel becomes mad, a gentle madness, feeble echo of Ophelia's despair.

Shakespeare certainly gave his sanction to Fletcher's work, for it was produced and played by his troupe. No doubt he had some hand in its writing, especially in the first and third acts, but he must have acknowledged only partial responsibility because his editors did not feel authorized to include the " Kinsmen " in the master's complete works. It was regularly entered in the Stationers' register, April 8th, 1634, and though it appeared in quarto the same year, it was not until 1685 that it was classed among the poet's plays, that is to say in the fourth impression of the Folio.

The case was different with *Henry VIII*, which terminated the epic cycle devoted by Shakespeare to England and her kings. This time the editors of the first folio had no hesitation in including in their great volume this last historical drama, a play which, though made to order, was written with the author's whole heart.

James I had his reasons for once more affirming his divine right to the throne. He derived his claim not from Henry VIII, the English Bluebeard, but from Henry VII, a sovereign of a quite different temper. Shakespeare for his part, seized the proffered opportunity to close the long series of royal portraits with the triumph of the House of Lancaster and at the same time to applaud the victory of legitimacy, the indispensable apanage of royal power.

At the beginning of his career, with *King John*, he had given evidence of his superiority over his rivals. The thesis of a John Lackland, patriotic, respecter of true religion and castigator of vice, as supported by Bishop Bale and exploited by the Lord Admiral's Players, collapsed before the powerful tragedy of the Stratfordian who had the courage to attack official doctrine. With what satisfaction he must again have braved the same adversaries! At present it is no longer the country lad making his difficult way in the London literary world, but the foremost dramatist of the day, supported by the public and his king.

John Bale had already dealt with the first and second marriage of Henry VIII, siding with the prosecution against the victims. He was not alone in holding that the king by his marriage with Anne Boleyn had inaugurated an era of political and religious emancipation. After him the official chroniclers, from Speed to Baker, including John Foxe and Edward Herbert, made this Tudor King a national hero:

Henricus Magnus, solidae virtutis amator.

John Speed wrote of him as the most magnanimous, the most heroic of princes, the only morning star in the Western hemisphere at the time he ascended the throne. It required nothing less than the dissolution of his first marriage to pacify the scruples of his delicate conscience, so that the wrong done to Queen Catherine by this divorce was not as serious as her partisans pretend.[1]

John Foxe described Henry VIII as a prince pure, honest, truly evangelical, sent into the world by Divine Providence for the defence of the Gospel. It was only after having vainly demanded justice of the Pope, that he was forced to take his misunderstood cause into his own hands and, by the will of God, to play the noble rôle of Alexander and cut the Gordian knot. . . . No Christian prince was ever known to undertake so great a religious reform.[2]

The popular John Baker, after a pompous eulogy of the king, observed that his cruelty to women could be not only excused, but defended : if they were guilty, their treatment was just, and if they were not, the king's conscience could remain at rest because he thought he had good reasons to believe them guilty. By suppressing abbeys, far from showing cupidity, he proved his great piety and prudence.[3]

Edward Herbert, whose metaphysics were admired by Descartes, went further, saying that the most irregular actions of this prince represented a type of greatness analogous to broken lines stretched in different directions which though not as concentrated nor as direct as straight lines, seem to have in them more of infinity.[4]

He who wrote this incredible apology considers that royal prevarications are covered by a double privilege : the authorization of Parliament, whose judgement is infallible, and the natural rights of a temperament to which chastity was antipathetic. It is not only the divorce of Catherine that he justifies, but all the steps taken by this excellent King Henry to overcome by legislation or the axe all obstacles to the satisfaction of his alternatively voluptuous and sanguinary caprices.

According to these historians Henry's second wife was a sort of Esther, even a kind of St. Anne, whom she imitated in becoming the mother of a virgin ! It was true, observes Foxe, that like David, she had sinned ; yes, from fragility : but he hastens to add : " Who has never sinned ? " Speaking of the execution which ended her life, he observes that if God permitted the tragic end of this apostle of liberty it was in order that the freedom which she brought should not be attributed to human agency, and to spare this elect soul the misfortune of fixing her affections on the vain pomps of this world.

After such dithyrambic eulogy, with which the England of that day concurred, it is impossible not to admire the boldness of a Shakespeare who presented Henry VIII and Anne Boleyn [5] as they actually appeared to their court. This temerity is explicable : Elizabeth had been dead ten years when the play was given and for James Stuart there was nothing offensive in the sinister portrait of Henry VIII as drawn by Shakespeare. In the

---

[1] *History of Great Britain.*   [2] Foxe's *Martyrs* (edition 1562).
[3] Baker's *Chronicle of the Kings of England,* 1643.
[4] *Life of Henry the VIII,* Lord Herbert of Cherbury, 1649.
[5] In contemporary documents this name appears Boleyn or Boulogne or Bullen ; the latter is adopted in Shakespeare's play.

eyes of the new Sovereign and of his poet, *Great Harry* was, as has been said, Henry VII, who had given his name to the fine squadron launched in his reign, the conqueror of Richard III, who on the battlefield of Bosworth received the symbolical golden circlet which his defeated adversary wore on his helmet. Great Harry had the constant desire to increase his country's riches and prestige ; the vast sums he raised were never used for his own luxury. Parliament was rarely convoked in his reign ; he reduced the power of the nobility single-handed. Although absolute sovereign, he was no tyrant and rescued England from the state of anarchy into which she had been plunged by the long Wars of the Roses. His only entravagance was the construction of the central chapel of Westminster Abbey where Mary Stuart and Elizabeth were to lie side by side.

In depicting Henry VIII as he was in fact, cruel, voluptuous, hypocritical, cowardly, suspicious and bloodthirsty, Shakespeare was only presenting the truth, and in order to stress his disagreement with the historians and also with John Bale's drama, he chose for his play the descriptive title : *All is True*. The prologue underlines his meaning.

> I come no more to make you laugh : things now,
> That bear a weighty and a serious brow,
> Sad, high and working, full of state and woe,
> Such noble scenes as draw the eye to flow,
> We now present. Those that can pity, here
> May, if they think it well, let fall a tear ;
> The subject will deserve it. Such as give
> Their money out of hope they may believe,
> May here find truth too. . . .

Shakespeare confined himself to setting forth the truth, leaving the spectator to draw his own conclusion. Instead of criticizing Henry VIII directly, all of his victims heap his majesty with benedictions. First, the Duke of Buckingham, before his death, finds words which recall the tragic memory of the Earl of Essex. The splendid indignation which fulminates in *King John*, *Richard III* and *Macbeth* against tyrants, is not heard in Henry VIII. But the reprobation is none the less eloquent for being unexpressed. Each gesture of the king denounces him ; each act reveals his shameless egoism in spite of the exterior of frank geniality which earned him his nickname of Bluff King Hal.

In divorcing Katherine of Aragon and declaring illegitimate the princess Mary whom she had borne him, he inaugurated the new schism by despotic act. Four years later he arbitrarily affirmed that Anne Bullen's child was also a " bastard ". Shakespeare brings these paradoxical acts into clear daylight.

All is True or the *Famous History of Henry VIII* [1] begins by an execution, certainly a dramatic opening which strikes the key note of this sanguinary

---

[1] *All is True* appears in the Folio as *The Famous History of the Life of King Henry the Eighth*.

drama.   Upon mere suspicion Henry has Buckingham, the most loyal of his
subjects, arrested and condemned on the evidence of a witness paid by the
Duke's enemies.   But nothing can alter the royal " good pleasure " ! vainly
Queen Katherine intercedes for the guiltless Buckingham, Henry knits his
jove-like brows, refuses clemency and betakes himself to the Masquerade
offered by Cardinal Wolsey.   Disguised as a shepherd he mingles with the
pleasure-seeking throngs and takes part in a two hundred course banquet.
The kiss which before the public he places on the lips of Anne Bullen was
the beginning of the violent passion which was to upset European politics.

Elizabeth's future mother appeared at these festivities not as an individual
worthy to be queen but as a simple adventuress ; her conversation is a
mixture of arch-coquetry and immodest suggestiveness.   Under her im-
passive brows shoot provocative glances.   She encourages Lord Sands to
embrace her before welcoming the sovereign's kiss and participating with
him in the revelry until dawn.

When King Henry again appears he is sad and preoccupied.   Seated in
his oratory he is absorbed in his Prayer Book.   Since meeting Anne he is a
prey to conscientious scruples.   Twenty years of marriage with the Spanish
Infanta have been so many decades of sin.   How could he without sacrilege
thus have espoused his elder brother Arthur's betrothed ?   Had he not been
destined for a high ecclesiastical career before becoming heir to the throne ?
Had he not even taken his pen to fulminate against the heresy of Martin
Luther and received from the Pope the proud title " Defender of the Faith " ?
Yes, he prided himself on being an excellent theologian.   For such a devout
and enlightened mind the idea of continuing to live incestuously with
Katherine is repugnant and even intolerable.   He therefore sets the case
before Cardinal Wolsey, his Minister of State and explains the necessity of
a rupture with the present queen.

> Oh my Lord
> Would it not grieve an able man to leave
> So sweet a bedfellow ?   But : Conscience, Conscience !
> O 'tis a tender place, and I must leave her.
> (*King Henry VIII*, Act II, Sc. 2)

The Cardinal does not say no ; and the news spreads quickly among the
courtiers to whom the Lord Chamberlain confides :

> It seems the marriage with his brother's wife
> Has crept too near his conscience—

and Suffolk replies :

> . . . No, His conscience
> his conscience has crept too near another Lady.

After presenting the king in this hypocritical light, Shakespeare stages Anne
Bullen in a scene replete with irony.   She is painfully surprised and afflicted

by the king's decision—more deeply moved than any one at court by Katherine's hard lot.   She must open her heart to the person at her side :

> . . . By my life,
> She never knew harm-doing.   Oh ! now after
> So many courses of the sun enthroned
> To give her the avaunt it is a pity
> Would move a monster . . .
> By my troth and maidenhead
> I would not be a Queen.

The reply is unexpected :

> Beshrew me I would,
> And venture maidenhead for it and so would you
> For all this spice of your hypocrisy.
> (*King Henry VIII*, Act ii, Sc. 3)

exclaims the old lady who has been receiving her confidences.

After Anne's protestations that she cannot accept the king's offer of a thousand pounds annuity together with the title : Marchioness of Pembroke, the spectator is not surprised to find her on her knees declaring herself :

> A blushing handmaid to his highness
> Whose health and royalty I pray for.

To her old confidant she murmurs before parting that nothing of all this must be repeated to Queen Katherine.   This elicits a response which may be epitomized :

> Who the devil do you take me for ?

Then it is the turn of Cardinal Wolsey to be judged by hearsay.   Opinions are all unfavourable.   This great newly rich adventurer is presented as a master of intrigue.   The statesman who had planned the meeting of the two sovereigns on the field of the cloth of Gold and who, encouraged by Charles V, dreamed of attaining the papacy, is now attempting to consolidate an Anglo-French alliance by the marriage of Henry VIII with Francois I's sister.   He naturally agrees with King Henry that Queen Katherine must be gotten rid of, and is ready to do everything to free his master from her :

> That like a jewel, has hung twenty years
> And never lost her lustre
> Of her that loves him with that excellence
> That angels love good men with, even of her
> That, when the greatest stroke of fortune falls
> Will bless the King.

At Blackfriars Theatre the audience could hardly fail to be impressed by the evocation of a trial which had taken place in this very hall, then transformed into a high tribunal.   It was indeed on this very spot that eighty years before the Spanish Princess who had been for a score of years

Queen of England had been sacrificed by Wolsey for reasons of State, and by the King for a sensual caprice.

The crier calls out : " Katherine Queen of England come into court ", according to the stage directions. Without answering she rises, comes to the King's feet and kneels. She then begins her defence—forty odd lines— in which eloquence vies with simplicity, dignity with tenderness. Her powerfully reasoned speech shows the pride of the Infanta, the affection of the wife, and the mother's devotion to her child. Intuition was also needed to enter thus into a foreigner's mentality. On the other hand, the same qualities were required to sustain the insular point of view expressed by Cardinal Wolsey and that of Campeggio the Papal legate as well.

The Queen takes exception to a tribunal conducted exclusively by her enemies and rests her cause in the hands of the Pope. Then majestically, she leaves court protesting that she will never more appear before men who under pretence of representing cardinal virtues display naught but hollow hearts and cardinal sins.

Public trial having thus failed secret pressure is resorted to. The two Cardinals are charged with the task of extracting from the Queen the consent necessary for a legal divorce. With the arms of terror they possess this object is achieved. Henceforth Katherine will no longer be Queen of England but only Princess dowager, widow of Arthur Prince of Wales. With a mere handful of retainers she ends her days in the prison castle of Kimbolton.

Wolsey's triumph is short-lived. With stupefaction he realizes that if the divorce he has insisted on is pronounced, it is not the Catholic duchess of Alençon that the King intends to marry but a bigoted Lutheran. However, it is too late to unravel the tangled skein of his intrigues. His confidential letter to the Pope advising the Roman authority to defer pronouncing the King's divorce falls into the sovereign's own hands. Disgraced, degraded, bereft of all, his princely palace at Hampton Court is seized by the Crown, his London residence at Whitehall is taken also as a royal perquisite. Sir Thomas More succeeds him in the functions of Chancellor, while Cranmer his detested rival is named Archbishop of Canterbury. Hereupon a revolution takes place in this haughty mind. The hitherto unknown sensation of being no longer a man of national and international importance shatters his outrageous pride and brings with it an unexpected satisfaction which acts like a transfiguration.

The scene in which the fallen Cardinal defends himself against the insulting attacks of the noble Dukes of Surrey and Suffolk for the first time commands the spectators' sympathy :

If I blush it is to see a nobleman want manners.

The public must have admired the art with which the author puts into Wolsey's mouth the eulogy of Sir Thomas More to whom he gives the unstinted praise that posterity accords to England's great Chancellor.

Certainly the blessing he calls down upon his rival is the worst arraignement possible against the monarch who commanded his execution.

The Cardinal instead of criticizing his successor declares :

> But he's a learned man, may he continue
> Long in his highness' favour, and do justice
> for truth's sake and his conscience ; that his bones,
> When he has run his course and sleeps in blessings
> May have a tomb of orphan's tears wept on 'im !
> What more ? . . .

(King Henry VIII, Act III, Sc. 2)

It may be remembered that early in his career Shakespeare had joined with Munday and Heywood to write the drama of Sir Thomas More, the production of which was forbidden by the censor. He saw in this hero a blessed martyr without dreaming that centuries later he would be canonized, together with John Fisher, Cardinal Bishop of Rochester[1].

The following scenes give contrasting pictures of the two queens, the new having achieved her crown through seductive art, the old ennobled by misfortune.

Every sort of worldly pomp, all the sumptuous adornments of a rich kingdom are showered on Anne, on this parvenue escorted to her coronation by the greatest nobles of the realm ; Suffolk bears before her the wand of high Seneschal, the Duke of Norfolk that of Marshall. Two mitred archbishops precede her, and behind, the venerable Duchess of Norfolk, doyen of the English peeresses, staggers under the weight of a train she can hardly carry. Within the Abbey the guards brutally defend the entrance against the multitudes eager to force their way in to see the crown of Edward the Confessor placed upon that frail head.

Then suddenly the scene shifts from this ostentatious ceremony to the mournful silence of Kimbolton where the true queen is slowly dying. Murmured words are scarcely audible, her breath comes short. Two faithful servants, her gentleman usher Griffith and Patience her waiting woman, endeavour to console her last hours. They bring happy news, the death of her implacable enemy the Cardinal, but elicit only this magnanimous comment :

"May he rest in peace and his faults lie gently on him."

---

[1] After brilliant studies at Oxford Thomas More or Morus (1478-1535) was admitted to the bar, elected to Parliament and introduced by Wolsey became the King's privy counsellor, treasurer of the royal exchequer and made Lord Chancellor. He voluntarily gave up this post on learning the King's intention to place himself at the head of the Anglican Church, and refused to take the oath of Supremacy. Imprisoned in the Tower he was moved neither by the tears of his family nor yet by the King's threats, declared that the King's authority in spiritual affairs was contrary to English law and that of the Church as well. The celebrity of his book *Utopia* is world-wide. His daughter Margaret Roper risked her own life but gained her end by taking her father's head from the lance on the Tower. He was canonized in 1936.

Only words of forgiveness and generosity are on her lips. But she fain would hear melody and calls the musicians to play her knell. Hardly has she closed her eyes than a blessed vision appears. The sombre rafters give place to a dazzling light which illumines her pale features.

This contrast between the earthly but ephemeral pomp of one queen and the heavenly vision of the other brings the drama of the two queens to an end.

The final act cannot be considered to form an integral part of this strange tragedy. It is rather a political treatise on the transmission of the divine right to reign, as King James saw it. For this it was necessary to bring Wolsey's arch enemy Cranmer from the Tower in order that he might stand as sponsor at the christening of the infant Elizabeth. And having predicted the splendours of the reign of this maiden Phoenix, the former archbishop turns to her legitimate successor James Stuart, in whom her ashes create an heir as great in admiration as herself.

In the modest epilogue to the play as given at Blackfriars Shakespeare declares that he bases his hope of success on the favourable judgement of good women who love to see feminine virtues like those of the heroine depicted. The fears expressed by the author on the fate of his play were not justified.

An enthusiastic audience welcomed Henry VIII and went on applauding when it was transferred to the " Globe ". Unbroken success continued under Charles I and during the Restoration.

When the Ambassador from Savoy came to London (1628) the all-powerful Buckingham chose this spectacular drama [1] for his entertainment. In 1664 it was played at the Duke of York's theatre during fifteen consecutive days.[2]

Like his former historical dramas Henry VIII owed the psychology of his personages and the sequence of the argument to Holinshed's *Chronicles*. Thus toward the end of his literary career he returned to the old sage of Packwood. It is noteworthy that the portrait of Wolsey which Shakespeare follows was inserted in the *Chronicles* from the writings of Edmund Campion. The dramatist as usual introduces certain episodes which do not appear in Holinshed nor is he wrong—though the history describes the masquerade given by Cardinal Wolsey where the King in a shepherd's fleece jacket dances

---

[1] On Thursday his Grace was present at the acting of K. Hen. 8. at the Globe, a play bespoken of purpose by himself ; whereat he stayd till the Duke of Buckingham was beheaded and then departed. Some say he should rather have seen the fall of Cardinal Wolsey who was a more lively type of himself, having governed the Kingdom 18 years as he hath done 14. Robert Gell's letter dated August 1628.

[2] The part of the King [Henry VIII] was so right and justly done by Mr. Betterton, he being instructed in it by Sir William, who had it from old Mr. Lowen, that had his instructions from Mr. Shakespear himself, that I dare and will aver, none can, or will come near him in this Age, in the performance of that part : Mr. Harris's performance of Cardinal Wolsey, was little inferior to that, he doing it with such just State, Port and Mein. . . . Mrs. Betterton, Queen Catherine : Every part by the great Care of Sir William, being exactly perform'd ; it being all new Cloath'd and new Scenes ; it continu'd Acting 15 days. (*Roscius Anglicanus*, John Downes, p. 24.)

until morning, there is no mention of Anne Bullen being present.   Shakespeare, however, is artist enough to bring her in appropriately just at this point as if to show that the most important events, such as revolutionize the course of history, may spring from an accidental meeting during a midnight orgy.

Queen Katherine's personality is also suggested by Holinshed, but it is completed by details furnished by George Cavendish, Chamberlain to the Cardinal whose memoirs on his master's life and death were known to Shakespeare.   Again it is evident that the poet is largely indebted to himself. Had he not recently given a wonderful trial scene in *The Winter's Tale* in which the spectators' sympathies were powerfully worked upon in favour of a wronged queen ?   He was therefore quite at ease when he needed to use much of the same procedure in presenting an historical personage instead of a " Queen of fiction ".

On returning to London in the early autumn, Shakespeare took his place beside his fellows all busy rehearsing the old repertoire which Lord Chamberlain had selected to fill out the celebrations in honour of the first wedding in the Royal family.[1]   On October 26th, 1612, the ship bringing Prince Frederick Simmern, accompanied by some fifty nobles, gentlemen, pages and lacqueys, anchored at the Whitehall landing stage.   His Majesty's Players in their ceremonial dress were lined up on the shore while the Earl of Southampton, surrounded by the chief courtiers, advanced to welcome the sixteen-year-old bridegroom and lead him to the throne room.

An eye-witness gives this account of the interview.   Prince Frederick respectfully saluted his future father-in-law, kissed the Queen's hand and entered into friendly talk with Henry, Prince of Wales ;   then he knelt before the princess who up to this moment had not raised a lid veiling her lovely eyes.   The prince took the hem of her skirt and kissed it religiously, the princess dropped him a deep curtsey and with a graceful gesture helped him to his feet ;   at the same time she permitted him to kiss her cheek.[2]

The episode was pronounced charming even by the disillusioned courtiers. The groom was declared handsome, slim, and well made with a pleasant face which denoted intelligence, judgement and courage.   His dark complexion admirably set off the dazzling cream and roses of his future bride.

At court all was joy ;   banquets, tournaments and plays were everywhere discussed ;   then suddenly, a tragic event checked all festivities.   On October 25th Prince Henry was seized by a violent fever.   On the 29th his condition grew worse and the theatrical performance fixed for the evening of All Saints was cancelled.   Five days later he died and on November 7th, his

---

[1] Item.   Paid to John Heminges upon the Couwncells warrant dated at Whitehall XX die Maij, 1613 for presenting before the Prinsces highnes the Lady Elizabeth and the Prince Pallatyne Elector fowerteene severall playes. . . . (93 pounds six shillings 8 pence).

Item.   Paid to the said John Heminges upon the lyke warrant dated att whitehall XX die Maij 1613 for presentinge sixe severall playes. . . . All played within the tyme of this accompte (60 pounds) Lord Treasurer Stanhope.   Rawlinson MSS. 239.

[2] Fynnet to Trumbull, October 23rd, 1612.

burial took place at Westminster.   The country was in consternation, the
Court in deep mourning.

Naturally all entertainments were in abeyance during the proscribed
month.   It was only on December 27th, the betrothal day of the young
couple, at which the Archbishop of Canterbury officiated, that representations
were once more authorized.

The list of plays on the programme of the Revels office is most interesting.
It contains, besides three new productions today forgotten,[1] nine plays
written by Shakespeare,[2] six by Beaumont and Fletcher [3] and one by Ben
Jonson.[4]

St. Valentine's day was selected for the postponed espousal rites of the
young Elector Palatine with Princess Elizabeth.   A tournament also had
been arranged in their honour on March 24th.   On this occasion Shakespeare
and Burbage were called upon to adorn the shield carried in the joust by
Roger Manners, Earl of Rutland with an " impresa " a personal device—
not a heraldic blason—preferred by the youth of those days to the family
scutcheon.   King James for his part ordered three impresas.   A contemporary letter gives the names of the twenty competitors among whom is
that of Rutland.   Unfortunately the only shields described are those of
the Earl of Pembroke and his brother the Earl of Montgomery.   But a
book printed in London, 1618,[5] displays many emblems and gives a
precise idea of the sort of work undertaken by the two players.   In this
publication the impresa used by Lord Southampton appears—a rose on an
azure field between four sea gulls encircled by the garter and framed in a
set of verses—sometimes attributed to Shakespeare ; another seems both
in device and rhyme to apply to the Earl of Rutland who was attached
to both arms and letters.   The device consists of a personage divided in
half, the left side represents Mars fully armed, the right Mercury with
winged staff, helm and sandals ; a ten-lined stanza praises this union of
two Gods in one.[6]

Burbage for his painting and Shakespeare for his verses received in the

---

[1] *Knott of Fooles, Twins Tragedy, Love Lies a Bleeding.*

[2] *Much Ado About Nothing, The Tempest, Sir John Falstaff, The Winter's Tale,
Othello, Julius Caesar, All's Well that Ends Well, Cardenio* and *The Second Part of Henry
IV*.

[3] *Philaster, The Maid's Tragedy, A King and No King, The Nobleman, The Captain* and
The Merry Devil of Edmonton.

[4] *The Alchemist.*

[5] *The Mirrour of Majestie : Or Badges of Honnour emblazoned* (London, 1618).

[6] What coward Storc or blunt Captain will
Dislike this Union.   Or not labour still
To reconcile the Arts and Victory ?
Since in themselves Arts have this quality
To vanquish errours traine : What other than
Should love the Arts if not a valiant man ?
Or how can he resolve to execute,
That hath not first learned to be resolute.
If any shall oppose this or dispute
Your great example shall their spite confute.

newly minted coin called *Jacobus* 6 pounds 2 shillings. The gift is noted on the Rutland account book.[1]

A fortnight previously the poet invested the amount received for his dramatic contribution to the royal celebrations in acquiring a dwelling house situated close to Blackfriars. Probably since the litigation between Old Montjoye and his apprentice he no longer counted on lodging in Silver Street, and decided to acquire a two-storied building on the western slope of St. Andrew's hill. The location is today known as Iron Yard. The ground floor was let to a mercer, the second to John Robinson a London friend of the poet who witnessed his will in 1616 and was at his bedside on the day of his death.

The original owner of the property was William Walker designated as " minstrel of the city of London ". He received one hundred and forty pounds for this transaction which was terminated March 10th, 1613. The next day Shakespeare mortgaged the acquired property for the sum of sixty pounds. Both the purchase and the mortgage deed bear his abbreviated signature, the former is preserved in the London Guild Hall Library, the second at the British Museum.

Upon the departure of the royal couple Shakespeare and his company were free to resume public performances. During the rest of April their success continued and increased. At the Blackfriars, the attractive theatre which the King's Players had had so much difficulty in retrieving from the Children of the Chapel royal, *King Henry VIII* had a long run.

The prologue recalls the elegance and good taste of the audience at this theatre, who were considered far superior in tone to those of the " Rose " or the " Globe ", saying : " You are known as the first and happiest hearers of the town."

The immense success of the play incited authors and players to present it in Southwark hoping that the large public at the " Globe " would appreciate it as the King, the courtiers and an elect audience had done on the other side of the river. It was decided to begin on St. Peter's day with a Gala performance. Unhappily this enterprise ended in calamity. The fruit of so many years labour was in an instant destroyed on June 29th, 1613.

The first act was not quite concluded when the whole building became a prey to a roaring fire. A greater misfortune than this was the destruction of the troupe's papers despite the efforts of Condell and the clown Robert Armin to save them. This loss rendered difficult the publication of certain plays of which only the prompters' copy remained, and it is said that in order to reconstitute parts of the original text it was necessary to have recourse to each actor's memory.

On the morrow Thomas Lorkins [2] in a letter to Sir Thomas Puckering

---

[1] 31 Martii. To Mr. Shakespeare in gold about my Lordes Impres xliiij[s].
To Richard Burbage for paynting and making yt in gold xliiij[s].
Hist. MSS. Com. Rutland MSS. vol. iv, p. 494.
Steward's Account Duke of Rutland's household papers.
[2] Harleian MSS. 7002, fol. 268.

described the disaster. When the King entered Wolsey's palace amid a glittering procession, as a final touch of realism a salvo was fired from a small mortar. Unfortunately this was a fatal idea, the flaming powder ignited the thatched roof of the tiring room and the timber structure of the famous wooden O two hours later lay in ashes.

Sir Henry Wotten [1] Ambassador to Venice then on leave in London, gives vivid details in a letter written to Edmund Bacon, two days after the accident :

> Now, to let matters of State sleep, I will entertain you at the present with what hath happened this Week at the Banks side. The King's Players had a new Play called *All is True*, representing some principal pieces of the Reign of Henry the 8th which was set forth with many extraordinary Circumstances of Pomp and Majesty, even to the matting of the Stage, the Knights of the Order, with their Georges and Garters. . . .
> Now King Henry making a Masque at the Cardinal Wolsey's House, and certain Cannons being shot off at his entry, some of the Paper, or other stuff, wherewith one of them was stopped, did light on the Thatch, where being thought at first but an idle smoak, and their Eyes more attentive to the show, it kindled inwardly, and ran round like a train, consuming within less than an hour the whole House to the very ground.
> This was the fatal period of that virtuous Fabrique wherein yet nothing did perish but Wood and Straw, and a few forsaken Cloaks ; only one Man had his Breeches set on fire, that would perhaps have broyled him, if he had not by the benefit of a provident wit put it out with Bottle Ale. . . .

A ballad which had wide circulation gives an equally humorous description of the catastrophe which respected [2]

> . . . neither the Cardinals might.
> Nor the mighty face of Henry eight.
>
> Now sit thee down, Melpomene,
> Wrapt in a sea-coal robe
> And tell the doleful tragedy
> That late was played at Globe
> For no man that can sing and say
> Was seared upon St. Peter's day
> Oh sorrow pitiful sorrow
> And yet all this is true.
> Oh sorrow piteous sorrow etc. . . .
> Out run the knights, out run the lords
> And there was great ado
> Some lost their hats and some their swords
> Then out run Burbage too.
> The reprobates though drunk on Monday
> Prayed for the Fool and Henry Cundy . . .
> Then with swol'n lips like drunken Flemings
> Distressed stood old stuttering Hemings
> Oh sorrow piteous sorrow etc. . . .

---

[1] Reliquiae Wottonianae.   [2] F 125. (MSS. Oxford, Corpus Christi.)

Ben Jonson too, in his *Execration against Vulcan*, mentions the destruction of the famous theatre among the god's misdeeds :

> Against the Globe, the glory of the banke,
> Which though it were the Fort of the Whol parish,
> Fenc'd with a Ditch and forkt out of a Marish :
> I saw with two poore Chambers taken in,
> And rais'd ere thought could urge : this might have bin.
> See the worlds ruines, nothing but the piles.
> Left, and wit since to covet it with tiles. . . .[1]

The good sense which Jonson recommends was not lacking among those who suffered this loss. Director and shareholders were unanimous not only in the decision to raise the " Phoenix " from its ashes but also to deck it with more handsome plumage.

The pranks of Vulcan were not confined to London that summer. Stratford, already so afflicted, paid a new tribute to this divinity. In a few hours fanned by a strong south west wind fifty-four dwellings and numerous barns and stables stacked with hay, wood and fodder fell a prey to the flames.

Fortunately the Henley Street property and New Place were spared. While the ruins were still smoking old Combe died, it was said from the shock caused by the disaster which had fallen upon the town. Shakespeare could no longer tax him with avarice after his demise. The poet who mocked at him in lifetime was rewarded after his death. The Master of Welcombe in his will left, together with many bequests to his family, considerable gifts to the poor of the parish, and five pounds to his lifelong friend Shakespeare.

His stately tomb in the north-east corner of the choir of Holy Trinity was sculptured by Garret Jonson the Flemish artist who, three years later, undertook the mural monument dedicated to the Swan of Avon.

The fact that Shakespeare is not mentioned among the actors present at the " Globe " on the day of the fire indicates that he was absent from London. But he hastened to return there, as all the chief members of the company were on the spot when it was agreed to rebuild the popular theatre.

Neither author nor company lost prestige by the interruption ; on the contrary, Thomas Freeman devoted his ninety-second epigramme to Master William Shakespeare.

> Whose wit in plaies doth winde like to Meander
> When needy new composers borrow more
> Thence Terence doth from Plautus or Menander.
> But to praise thee aright I want thy store ;
> Then let thine owne works thine owne worth upraise,
> And help t' adorne thee with deserved Baies.[2]

Camden [3] repeats Richard Carew's appreciation which claimed that Shakespeare's poetry rivals Catullus.

---

[1] Ben Jonson, *Execration against Vulcan*, F.B. 3ᵛ.
[2] *Runne and a Great Cast*, 1614.
[3] Camden's *Remarks Concerning Britain*, pp. 43-44.

Edmund Howes, who continued Stow's *Annalls*, places William Shakespeare, gentleman, among the poets who flourish as much in their works as in the hearts of friends, among whom he is proud to count himself.[1]

Another admirer C.B. (Christopher Brooke) in his *Ghost of Richard III* makes the monarch invoke and give thanks to the author who revived his memory and made him famous in history.[2]

Shakespeare was again in London, March 16th, 1614, to raise capital for the cost of rebuilding the " Globe ". His part in the fourteen hundred pounds subscribed was one hundred pounds.

The work was executed rapidly. Contractors and builders were infused with enthusiasm and, exactly one year from the disaster, transformed the wooden O to an octagonal shape, opened its doors under a neatly tiled roof. Triple turret and silken banner dominated the neighbouring trees. The oft quoted John Chamberlain wrote to Lady Carleton then in Venice that he had failed to see her sister when he called because that lady had gone to the " newly erected Globe which according to common report is the finest in London ".[3]

The poet John Taylor also praised the new construction :

> As gold is better that's in fire tried
> So is the Bank-side Globe that was late burn'd ;
> For where before it had a thatchéd hide,
> Now to a stately theatre is turned.

Shakespeare was certainly present at the " Globe's " reopening. He came again to London November 16th, 1614, and spent Christmas there, according to the indefatigable Thomas Greene who patiently awaited him there, counting on his assistance to prevent the enclosure of the common lands at Welcombe by an appeal to the Central Powers. The eternal dispute among Stratford's inhabitants was still being fiercely waged. Since Combe's death this was a more burning topic for his young heir was bent on maintaining the barricades.

my Cosen Shakspeare commyng yesterday to towne I went to see him howe he did he told me that they assured him they ment to inclose noe further then to gospell bushe & so upp straight (leavyng out part of the dyngles to the ffield) to the gate in Clopton hedge & take in Salisburyes peece : and that they meane in Aprill to servey the Land & then to gyve satisfaccion & not before & he & Mr. Hall say they think there will be nothyng done at all.[4]

Back in Stratford, Greene, always preoccupied by the same affair, decided together with those specially interested that a petition should be dispatched

---

[1] Stowe's *Annals up to the Present Yeare* (Edmund Howes, London, 1615).
[2] *The Ghost of Richard III*. Unique copy at the Bodleian Library.
[3] Birch's *James I*, p. 229.
[4] Wheler, MSS., Stratford birthplace Museum. Thomas Greene's journal which has been conscientiously studied by E. I. Fripp. It may be found in large part in that author's *Shakespeare, Man and Artist*, vol. 2 (Oxford University Press).

to Lord Chancellor Ellesmere.   His journal contains under date December 23rd, this note :

I alsoe wrytte of myself to my Cosen Shakspeare the Coppyes of all our oathes mde (made ?) then alsoe a not of the Inconvenyences wold g(row) by the Inclosure.

But, if all these remarks bear witness to Shakespeare's presence in London they fail to enlighten us on his condition of health when his " Cousin" called.

It is certain, however, that what Shakespeare accomplished in favour of his Stratford neighbour's cause turned out successfully since the same Greene inscribed in his unfailing journal :

At night Master Replingham supped with me, and Master William Barnes was [there] to bear him company ; where he assured me, before Master Barnes, that I should be well dealt withal, confessing former promises by himself—Master Mannering and his agreement for me with my Cousin Shakespeare.

In September following Shakespeare was back in the midst of his family nor was he again seen in London.   The " Globe " company vainly waited for the return of their poet on whom were based so many past successes and future triumphs.

CHAPTER XX

THE END . . . AND AFTER

Marriage of Judith Shakespeare—The Poet's will—His death—Posthumous homage—Publication of the 1623 Folio—First biographers—Nicholas Rowe.

AFTER leaving London for the last time, Shakespeare spent the following Christmas at New Place among his family. This permitted him to strengthen his bonds with the notables of the Shire and enlarge his circle of acquaintance. The projected marriage of his younger daughter Judith to Thomas Quinney, brother of his old schoolfellow Richard, brought the Shakespeares in closer touch with the Grevilles, Sheldons, Catesbys, Treshams and Winters,[1] all related to the Quinneys and notable recusants. The future bridegroom had exchanged his small house on High Street for a larger one belonging to his brother-in-law, William Chandler, situated at the corner of High and Bridge Streets in which he installed his wife after the ceremony.

Since the death of Richard Quinney [2] while still mayor of Stratford (1601) this Thomas, a prosperous wine merchant, had become head of the family, enjoyed the esteem of his fellow citizens and was soon to be received as a member of the Town Council. The account book with a delicately traced monogram which he kept as treasurer is preserved by the municipality. Some lines from Octavien de Saint Gelais :

> Heureul celui qui pour devenir sage
> Du mal d'aultruy fait son apprentissage.

indicate that Judith Shakespeare's husband cultivated a taste for French literature.

Little is known about his betrothed. She was born twin to Hamlet Shakespeare in 1585 ; the fact that this boy died at eleven years of age leads to the supposition that she too may have been delicate and would explain her late marriage. She was thirty-one at the time and like her mother chose a husband more youthful than herself.[3] Her first-born received at his christening the name of Shakespeare Quinney, which might have proved

---

[1] Robert Catesby, Thomas Tresham together with the three brothers Winter, Robert, Thomas and John, suffered death for the gunpowder plot.

[2] Richard Quinney died a victim to duty in trying to make peace in a town riot ; he was wounded in the head, refused to accuse his aggressor and died a few days later.

[3] Thomas was four years younger than Judith.

difficult to live up to, but the child died six months after birth.   Two other sons, Richard and Thomas scarcely attained majority.[1]

Unlike her brilliant elder sister Susanna, she left no samples of writing for posterity to discuss.   Her tomb bears no epitaph ; but there is a life-sized portrait in which her features are shown and her tastes indicated.   She has her father's high and prominent forehead, hazel eyes and sanguine complexion.   To judge by the sumptuous brown velvet dress trimmed with venetian lace and richly embroidered, she was probably fond of fine clothes. Her left hand holds an enormous yellow pear of the Bartlett variety, her right caresses the head of a handsome black stag hound.

The marriage ceremony took place on February 10th, 1616, during a season prohibited by the Church of England which extended from Septua-gesima Sunday to Easter week.   Between these two dates it was necessary to obtain special diocesan license, which neither bride, groom nor parents thought of asking.   This omission was noticed by the clerk of the Consistory Court and the couple, twice summoned to appear for breach of established rules, were sentenced to a fine of seven shillings and excommunicated.[2]

A probable explanation of all this seems to be that the marriage was unexpectedly hastened and the rules of the diocese infringed because the bride's father was already suffering from the illness which caused his death. On January 25th, Shakespeare sent for his friend Francis Collins, recently appointed Stratford's Town Clerk, to make a first draft of his will.   Collins, a comrade at the Grammar School, had transferred his practice to Warwick where he became a barrister.   There, according to tradition, his eloquence had freed the young poet from gaol after the poaching incident.

The handwriting of this document strongly resembles that of Shakespeare. This is hardly surprising since all the scholars of that period conscientiously imitated their writing master.   The words " after my Death " inscribed with trembling hand have led some specialists to believe that the entire document was written by Shakespeare himself, but other wills drawn up by Collins, especially his own and that of John Combe, leave no doubt that it was Francis Collins who set down his friend's last wishes and executed the beautiful copy preserved with the rough draft at Somerset House.   It was natural that this boyhood comrade who returned to Stratford at the same time as Shakespeare did should have been deeply moved when taking down from dictation the phrase " after my death ".   It has been noted that, though still a young man, he survived his friend only by a twelve month.

Shakespeare did not sign immediately.   He probably postponed the apposition of his name until after his daughter Judith's wedding, which took place a fortnight later.   These three pages denote perfect lucidity of mind

[1] The Stratford Municipal Register records
   23 November 1616   Baptism Shakespeare Filius Thomae Quiney gent.
   8 May Burial Shakespeare filius Tho. Quiney, gent.
   9 Feb 1618 Baptism : Richard, filius Tho Quinse
   28 Feb 1619 Thomas Filius Thomae Quiney
[2] Quod Nupti fuerunt absque licentia vircitati per Nixon non comparuerunt in Con-sistorio excomunicati . . . Visitation book Kington Deanery, Worcester Diocesan register.

in the testator.   When dividing his estate his decisions are equitable, logical and generous.   Affection for old friends remains intact : the poor are not forgotten.   His chief preoccupation is to bequeath to his next of kin, according to British aristocratic tradition, the bulk of the considerable property which had come into his possession.   Such desire to transmit his large estate intact and according to the rules of primogeniture might be thought peculiar on the part of a simple burgher ; however, the family prided itself on its gentility and he perhaps foresaw that in a short time a higher title than Gentleman would be conferred to him as acting poet laureate.

Charles I at his accession offered knighthood to Doctor Hall sole heir to the Stratford estate and Blackfriars property.   The Doctor modestly refused this honour and paid to the treasury the ten pounds due from those who declined it.   But it is worthy of note that John Barnard who married Shakespeare's grand-daughter Elizabeth Hall became Sir John Barnard of Abingdon, while William Davenant, the poet's godson and literary executor, became Sir William d'Avenant.

The opening paragraph of Shakespeare's will follows the formula employed by Thomas Combe, Sir William Russell and in general all those who remained attached to the old faith.

In the name of God Amen I William Shackspeare of Stratford upon Avon in the countie Warr gent in perfect health and memorie god be praysed doe make & ordayne this my last will & testament in manner & forme followeing.   That ys to saye First I Comend my Soule into the handes of god my creator, hoping & assuredlie beleeving through thonelie merittes of Jesus Christe my Saviour to be made partaker of lyfe everlastinge, And my bodye to the Earth whereof yt ys made.

Being preoccupied with the marriage of his daughter Judith he first provides for her future.   She naturally receives what remains unpaid of her dowry, namely, one hundred pounds ; to which are added another fifty if she consents to renounce her rights on all Stratford property in favour of her sister Susanna ; and still another fifty pounds if, within three years after her marriage, she has children, this last sum to revert to her heirs.   In addition Judith receives a large silver gilt bowl, " my brod silver gilt boul ".

Shakespeare leaves twenty pounds and his entire wardrobe [1] to his sister Johanna Hart ; the house in Henley Street where she lives is to remain hers with all its out-buildings for her lifetime on condition that she pays an annual rent of eleven pence.   To each of Johanna's three sons five pounds are left.   To his grand-daughter, Elizabeth Hall, he bequeathes all his silver plate.

Then comes the enumeration of the gifts for those not belonging to his immediate family :

---

[1] Thomas Hart, a descendant of Shakespeare's sister, told the author of *The Warwickshire Avon* in 1790 that he well remembered how Shakespeare's theatrical wardrobe was the joy of the neighbouring boys who dressed up like scaramouches in the poet's theatrical effects.

Item. I gyve; bequeth unto the Poore of Stratford aforesaied tenn poundes, to Mr. Thomas Combe my Sword, to Thomas Russell Esquier fyve poundes & to Frauncis Collins of the Borough of Warr . . . gent. thirteene pounds Sixe shillinges and Eight pence to be paied within one yeare after my deceas. Item I gyve & bequeath to [this name is crossed out in the will] to Hamlett Sadler xxvjs viijd to buy him A Ringe; to William Reynold's Gent. twenty eight shillings and eight pence to buy him a ringe, to my godson William Walker xxs in gold, to Anthonye Nashe gent xxvjs viijd & to Mr. John Nashe xxvjs viijd & to my fellowes John Hemynge Rychard Burbage and Henry Cundell xxvjs viijd A peece to buy them Ringes.[1]

Finally he comes to the principal portion of his estate, which is to remain indivisible; namely, his house at New Place with its dependencies, his Henley Street house, all the gardens, orchards, barns, stables, landed property and buildings wherever situated in Stratford-upon-Avon, Bishopston and Welcombe in the county of Warwick and also the house and property inhabited by John Robinson in Blackfriars, London.[2]

These possessions, which may be valued at more than one thousand pounds, are left to his daughter Susanna, who with her husband is appointed executor. The inheritance was to pass by order of primogeniture to Susanna Hall's children; then to the children of his grand-daughter, Elisabeth Hall, then, in default of heirs of this line, to Judith Quinney's children, and in their default to those of the testator's sister Johanna Hart.

There was no need to mention his wife except for a personal bequest, as she had according to law her widow's thirds for life in all his property which brought in revenue. The phrase added between the lines of the testament does not suggest that there was any intention of irony attached to his bequest of the handsomely carved four post oaken bed with its furniture. Although described as " Second best ", it must have been brought by Anne from Shottery as part of her dowry and it was natural to restore it to its owner. In all gentlemen's homes, the second best room was that of the master while the best chamber was reserved for distinguished guests; hence Shakespeare's afterthought only meant that he acknowledged that the furniture of the bedroom they occupied was the personal property of Anne Shakespeare. After her death it was returned to her old home at Hewlands, where it is still to be seen.

The will was signed on March 25th,[3] scarcely a month before his death. The document was witnessed by childhood friends, Julian Shaw, who lived three doors from New Place, Hamlet Sadler, Robert Whatcote, the yeoman

---

[1] Augustine Phillips, a senior member of the Company, on dying left Shakespeare a gold ring.

[2] This house was destroyed in the Great Fire of London 1666.

[3] The will concludes : " In witness whereof I have hereunto put my seal hand the daie and yeare first above written." The word *seal* is erased and the word *hand* substituted. This indicates that the poet's gold ring had fallen with its " W.S." and true-lovers knot from his emaciated finger. It was found indeed in 1810 between the Mill house and the Cemetery. It was sold to Richard Bell Wheler for thirty-six shillings. He left it to the Stratford Birthplace Museum.

who had offered his testimony in the libel suit concerning Susanna Hall, and his Blackfriars tenant John Robinson.

The executors when it was registered attested " inventorium exhibitum " but unfortunately no inventory exists today.

Little is known about the poet's death, which perhaps was caused by an infectious illness from which he had been suffering for some time. The final signature " By me William Shakespeare " is firmly and beautifully finished and is reminiscent of the one in the Florio Montaigne ; but the inscriptions of the testator's name on each of the three pages indicate extreme weakness.

Yet he lived until April 23rd, which suggests perhaps that death was due to an unexpected relapse. An infectious sickness was prevalent in the neighbourhood, to which Thomas Harte his brother-in-law fell a victim a few days before. He was buried on the 17th. Did Shakespeare insist on attending this funeral ? Tradition, as recorded in John Ward's diary, gives another version which is far more characteristic of the poet's sociable nature and devotion to his friends.

While keeping in his bed he learned of the arrival in Stratford of Ben Jonson accompanied by Michael Drayton, and nothing could prevent their impulsive friend from rising to celebrate this reunion in a manner worthy of such old friends.[1] Their " merry meeting " was such that in spite of the famous elixir of violets which Dr. Hall declared saved Michael Drayton, the physician's more celebrated father-in-law succumbed on his fifty-second birthday.

He died a Papist,[2] affirms Richard Davies, Archdeacon of Coventry, reporting this occurrence in his brief biographical notice. His testimony must be taken very seriously for his good faith is not open to doubt. A zealous minister of the Anglican Church and " an inveterate enemy to that of Rome ", like William Fulman whose biographical notes on Shakespeare he completed, he was considered one of the ablest logicians of his time and known for eloquence in his defence of the Established Church. If Davies states that the dramatist died a Roman Catholic it was because this information seemed to him indisputable—not because he wished to have it so. Though not one to claim that the mystery of Shakespeare's religious thought can be sounded, I think that conscientious study of his work as a whole clarifies many points which are open to discussion if not to belief. The

---

[1] " Shakespear, Drayton and Ben Jonson, had a merry meeting and it seems drank too hard, for Shakespear died of a fevour there contracted." John Ward's *Diary*.

[2] The Rev. Alexander Dyce, knowing the text to be authentic was troubled enough by this testimony to try to reassure himself and his readers : " This is contradicted by the tenour of Shakespeare's writings and the history of his life." The tradition originated no doubt " from the fact that the poet who could hardly have avoided all discussion on the controverted religious topics of the day, may have incidentally let fall expressions unfavourable to Puritanism which were misrepresented as papistical ".

Halliwell-Philipps expresses a hope which is based on no grounds whatever that " The poet's last hours were soothed by some Puritan pastor of the Halls' acquaintance ". Thus is history made in the image of each historian

language he gives to his ecclesiastics, from the haughty Bishop of Carlisle to the humble Franciscan friars, Laurence, Patrick and their brothers, shows that the Roman doctrine, its liturgy and dogmas, were familiar to him, indicating that his youthful days had been passed among those who remained faithful to the ancient church.

All that he wrote bears evidence of respect for the feelings of the Catholic listener or reader. Scenes which might have offended his audience had he servilely followed the English or Italian sources from which he borrowed, were altered by him or suppressed in his production. He did not conceal the fact that his sympathies went to the persecuted, never to the persecutors, and that, at a time when courage was necessary not to dissimulate the horror inspired by tyranny, he wrote that :

> Mercy is an attribute of God himself
> And earthly power doth then show likest God's
> When Mercy season's Justice.[1]

Sir E. K. Chambers found in *Timon of Athens* reason for thinking that the poet was, toward the end of his life, converted to Catholicism. If this be true, as Davies declared in 1688, it is more logical to suppose that he was not " converted " but " reconciled " to the ancient faith which he had seen practised by all his family in a house where Domina Isabella Shakespeare came to seek refuge when her convent at Rowington was dissolved. Certainly the Southamptons, the Arundells and the Montagues would not have used their influence to modify such beliefs, still less his grammar school teachers Simon Hunt and Thomas Cottam, nor yet his declared admirer Robert Southwell.

In spite of all his precautions to secure his inheritance to his direct descendants, it was decreed that he would survive by his thought alone.

The line of Susanna Hall was soon to become extinct. Her only daughter, Elizabeth, married Thomas Nashe and lived at New Place with her mother, but on April 4th, 1647, Nashe died suddenly, childless. However, hope still remained for his grand-daughter, when she re-married on June 5th, 1649, and became Lady Barnard of Abington. Elizabeth, however, died in 1660 without leaving any direct heir. New Place was purchased by Sir Edward Walker in 1675, passed again into the Clopton's possession later and ultimately fell into the hands of Francis Gastrell, a vandal, who in order to diminish his taxes pulled down the entire structure.

The other branches also became extinct before long. Judith, who married Thomas Quinney, died in February 1661 having survived her three sons, who never married and died before reaching majority.

When in 1828 Sir Walter Scott made his pilgrimage to Stratford, an old mad woman, Mrs. Ormsby, remained guardian of the house where William and his brothers were born. She cherished the illusion that she was directly descended from the bard-of-Avon and did a prosperous trade in small

---

[1] *The Merchant of Venice*, Act IV, Sc. 1.

souvenirs, particularly pieces of the mulberry tree which still flourished on the New Place lawn.

A certain Peter Cunnington, September 1847, bought the house for which he offered the sum of three thousand pounds but the sale never went through. Later John Shakespeare of Worthington (Somersetshire) offered the sum of two thousand five hundred pounds to pay for necessary repairs. Though the promised money was not paid, a local committee entrusted the work to an architect, Edward Gibbs. Repairs began, but public subscription was necessary, until finally the nation became purchaser of the historic spot. Little by little all the property which had belonged to the poet came under national ownership. As for the personal objects in Shakespeare's possession, we know through Dr. Hall's will [1] and an interminable chancery suit instigated by his widow, what traces remain of them.

The Chancery Records contain the complaint of Susanna Hall against a tailor of Stratford, Baldwin Brooks, to whom her husband, when he died, owed seventy-nine pounds for garments furnished to him. This tailor, profiting by the absence from home of the Hall family, decided to pay himself and, with five friends, broke into New Place and carried off cash, books and portable property estimated by Mistress Hall at over a thousand pounds.[2]

Here then is an adequate answer to the frequent inquiries concerning the fate of Shakespeare's vanished library and personal effects. The robbery at New Place, following the losses caused by the " Globe " conflagration, amply suffices to explain why so little is left of the poet's " books, goods & chattels ". But if little remains of the material objects which surrounded and ministered to his daily life, his memory survived intact in the hearts and minds of his friends.

[1] The Nuncipative will of John Hall declared the 25th November 1635 :
Imprimis   I give unto my wife my house in London.
   Item   I give unto my daughter Nashe my house in Acton.
   Item   I give unto my daughter my meadow.
   Item   I give my goods and money unto my wife and my daughter Nashe to be divided betwixt them.
   Item   Concerning my study of books I leave them (said he) to you my son Nashe to dispose of them as you see good. As for my manuscripts I would have given them to Mr. Boles if he had been here But forasmuch as he is not here present You, my son Nashe, may burn them or do with them as you please.
[2] May it please your Good Lordships . . . Baldwin Brookes combining and confederating with one Edward Raynsford, late under-sheriff of said County of Warwick, William Harrison alias Cutler, Giles Thompson of the said borough, Yeoman Oliver and James Newell of Stratford-upon-Avon men of mean estate or worth, did in or about the month of August last, break into and enter forcibly into the house of your said oratrix in Stratford-upon-Avon aforesaid, and there did take and seize upon the ready money, books, goods & chattels of the said John Hall deceased then remaining and being in the custody of your said oratrix, to the value of one thousand pounds at the least, and have converted the same to their or some of their own uses without inventoring or appraising of the same. . . .
These Chancery proceedings were discovered and published with interesting facsimiles by Frank Marcham, *William Shakespeare and his daughter Susanna* (Grafton & Co., London, 1931).

The first lyric voice raised in elegy of the poet, it is said, was that of his little godson, William Davenant, then aged eleven :

> Beware (delighted Poets !) when you sing
> To welcome Nature in the early Spring ;
> Your num'rous Feet not tread
> The Banks of Avon ; for each Flowre
> (As it nere knew a Sunne or Showre)
> Hangs there, the pensive head.
>
> Each Tree, whose thick, and spreading growth hath made,
> Rather a Night beneath the Boughs, than Shade,
> (Unwilling now to grow)
> Lookes like the Plume a Captive weares,
> Whose rifled Falls are steept i'th teares
> Whith from his last rage flow.
>
> The Piteous River wept it selfe away
> Long since (Alas !) to such a swift decay ;
> That reach the Map ; and looke
> If you a River there can spie ;
> And for a River your mock'd Eie,
> Will finde a shallow Brooke.[1]

When the news of Shakespeare's death reached London a movement was instigated to bury him in Westminster Abbey near Chaucer, Spenser and Beaumont, as was later done for Ben Jonson and Sir William d'Avenant.

The poet William Basse claims this honour as a right in his elegiac verses :

> Renowned, Spenser, lie a thought more nigh
> To learned Chaucer, and rare Beaumont lie
> A little nearer Spenser to make room
> For Shakespeare in you threefold fourfold tomb.

then suddenly changing his mind he continues . . .

> If your precedency in death doth bar
> A fourth place in your sacred sepulcher
> Under this carved marble of thine own
> Sleep rare tragedian Shakespeare, sleep alone ;
> Thy unmolested peace unshared cave.
> Possess as Lord not Tenant of thy grave
> That unto us and others it may be
> Honour hereafter to be laid by thee.

Ben Jonson approved the dispositions of the family and declared :

> My Shakespeare Rise ! I will not lodge thee by
> Chaucer or Spenser, or bid Beaumont lie
> A little further, to make thee a room :

---

[1] *Madagascar, with other poems,* 1638, p. 37.

> Thou are a monument without a tomb
> And art alive still, while thy book doth live
> And we have wits to read and praise to give.

Samuel Shepherd proposed an annual pilgrimage to Stratford, as in ancient times Statius yearly visited the tomb of Virgil.

At Stratford the poet's last wishes were strictly obeyed. He had asked to be buried sixteen feet below ground. The sums expended for redeeming the tithes gave to him and his family the right to be buried in the chancel before the high altar. There lies his tombstone today, along with those of his wife, his daughter Susanna, his son-in-law Doctor Hall, and Thomas Nash who married his sole grand-daughter. Upon his tombstone the simple and moving lines are inscribed :

> Good friend for Jesus sake forbear
> To dig the dust enterred here
> Blest be the man that spares these stones
> And cursed be he that moves my bones.

This quatrain has bred much discussion ; but it hardly seems surprising. Hamlet had expressed horror for the profanation of graves. This thought constantly appears in the *Sonnets*. Whatever their authorship, these lines have miraculously served their purpose in preserving Shakespeare's tomb from the assaults of the curious, the piety of admirers who periodically advocate the transfer of his coffin to Westminster, as was contemplated at his tercentenary celebrations, and the repeated appeals of Miss Delia Bacon. Shakespeare still rests beneath this naïve prayer, while the mortal remains of many kings, and those of Cromwell and the regicides, have become in Homer's phrase " the prey of obscene birds and ravaging dogs ".

Shakespeare's widow and daughters also erected to his memory a rich mural monument chiselled by the sons of a Dutch artist named Janssen or Johnson, who had been already called upon to carve the effigies of such prominent Stratfordians as Thomas Combe and Sir Thomas Lucy.

Beneath two allegorical figures, Labour and Repose, which support the famous crest, the poet is represented life size and at half length. His right hand rests on a cushion and holds a golden quill. A Latin inscription tells how " He who united the wisdom of Nestor and the genius of Socrates to the Art of Virgil, on earth elicited the multitudes' admiration and has his place on Olympus ".

It has been frequently suggested that some London man of letters composed this inscription ; it seems safer to assume that Doctor Hall, head of the family and, with his wife, Shakespeare's residuary legatee, being financially responsible for the monument was responsible for the inscription also. He was an excellent Latinist and wrote fluently in that language. It is to be noticed that the family seem to recognize as the traits most admirable in Shakespeare his wisdom and his philosophy. Art and fame come afterwards.

The Latin epitaph is followed by these verses :

> Stay Passenger, why goest thou by so fast ?
> Read if thou canst, whom envious Death hath plast,
> Within this monument Shakespeare : with whome,
> Quick nature dide : whose name doth deck this Tombe,
> Far more than cost : sieh all, that He hath writt
> Leaves living art, but page, to serve his witt.

The dramatist's theatrical associates set to work to erect a monument more lasting than bronze or marble. This consisted in the volume of Shakespeare's complete works. The death of Burbage in 1618, following that of Augustus Phillipps, left Heminge and Condell in charge of the enterprise. Before they could collect the material it took months, probably years, to overcome difficulties of copyrights for all the published and un-published texts and to unite them in the hands of Edward Blount and Isaac Jaggard. In 1623, the great Folio was given to the world. An advance copy dated 1622 exists in America, perhaps one given by the actor-editors to Lord Pembroke, the Chamberlain, to whom it was dedicated.

Southampton, to whom of old the poet himself had consecrated his entire work, and " whose virtues showed ever more fresh and green when his grave head was gray ", was with the army in the Low Countries, and expired in the camp of Rosendael in 1624 while caring for his eighteen-year-old son. He caught a pernicious fever and only outlived his boy two days.

Lady Southampton survived for many years, distinguished by her devotion to the memory of her dear Lord and by her loyalty to King Charles, whom she concealed in her " noble seat of Tichfield " after his escape from Hampton Court in 1647. Possibly she was a factor in the monarch's love for Shakespeare ; for, as we know, Charles' captivity was consoled by constant reading of his dramas.

Lord Southampton being inaccessible, the choice of Pembroke was natural, and it was under the double auspices of this great nobleman and his brother, Lord Montgomery, that the Folio of 1623 appeared, accompanied by numerous dedicatory epistles and laudatory verses—a veritable chorus of praise not so much to the great work itself as to the actor's own personality. At each reprint the number of these verses was augmented.

Four members of the Stationers' company were financially responsible for this important enterprise. All had shown an interest in Shakespeare's works before. William Aspley had the sales rightsfor half Thorpes' *Sonnets* edition and had himself published *Henry IV* and *Much Ado About Nothing ;* John Smethwick had brought out reprints of *Hamlet* and *Romeo and Juliet ;* Edward Blount had acquired the rights of *Pericles ;* William Jaggard, who had printed the *Passionate Pilgrim* (1599), had also placed his trade mark on many Quarto reprints. He died before the completion of the great work, but his son Isaac succeeded him.

Shakespeare's sudden death was a hard blow for his publishers, as they themselves admit. All the more gratitude is owed them, for they not only provided a better text of the plays already printed in quarto, but provided also for posterity texts of all those plays which the contemporary public knew only from having seen them acted.

On opening the volume the first impression is one of admiration for the excellent set up and typography. The title page is arranged so that the words

Mr William

SHAKESPEARES

Comedies

Histories &

Tragedies

Published according to the True Originall Copies

London

Printed by Isaac Jaggard and Ed. Blount 1623

harmoniously frame the portrait of the poet engraved by Martin Droeshout.[1]

Opposite the title page, on a fly leaf, is printed Ben Jonson's lines in praise of the likeness. The title page is followed by the two editors Heminge's and Condell's " epistles dedicatorie ".

Right Honourable,

Whilst we study to be thankful in our particular for the many favours we have received from your L.L., we are fallen upon the ill fortune, to mingle two the most diverse things than can be, fear and rashness—rashness in the enterprise, and fear of the success. For when we value the places your H.H. sustain, we cannot but know their dignity greater than to descend to the reading of these trifles ; and while we name them trifles, we have deprived ourselves of the defence of our dedication. But since your L.L. have been pleased to think these trifles something heretofore, and have prosecuted both them and their author living with so much favour, we hope that (they outliving him, and he not having the fate, common with some, to be executor to his own writings) you will use the like indulgence toward them you have done unto their parent. There is a great difference whether any book choose his patrons, or find them : this hath done both. For so much were your L.L. likings of the several parts when they were acted, as before they were published, the volume asked to be yours. We have but collected them, and done an office to the dead, to procure his orphans' guardians ; without ambition either of self-profit or fame : only to keep the memory of so worthy a friend and fellow alive as was our Shakespeare, by humble offer of his plays to your most noble patronage. Wherein, as we have justly observed no

---

[1] An interesting document complimenting the editors of the Folio is now in the possession of the National Library of Wales. It reads, in modern spelling :

To my friends Mr. John Heminge and Henry Condell :

To you that jointly, with undaunted pains,

Vouchsafed to chant to us these noble strains,

How much you merit by it is not said,

But you have pleased the living, loved the dead

Raised from the womb of earth a richer mine

Than Cortes could with all his Casteline

Associates ; they did but dig for gold

But you for treasure much more manifold.

(MS. 5390 D, p. 141)

man to come near your L.L. but with a kind of religious address, it hath been
the height of our care, who are the presenters, to make the present worthy of your
H.H. by the perfection.   But there we must also crave our abilities to be considered,
my lords.   We cannot go beyond our own powers.   Country hands reach forth
milk, cream, fruits or what they have ;   and many nations, we have heard, that
had not gums and incense, obtained their requests with a leavened cake.   It was
no fault to approach their gods by what means they could :   and the most, though
meanest, of things are made more precious when they are dedicated to temples.
In that name, therefore, we most humbly consecrate to your H.H. these remains
of your servant Shakespeare, that what delight is in them may be ever your L.L.,
the reputation his, and the faults ours, if any be committed by a pair so careful
to show their gratitude both to the living and the dead as is

Your Lordships' most bounden,

John Heminge,
Henry Condell

The editors proclaim confidently in their address to the " great variety
of Readers " that :

These plays have had their trial already and stood out all appeals and do now
come forth quitted rather by a decree of Court. . . .

They note regretfully how detrimental the author's death has been to
the pursuit of their enterprise :

But since it hath been ordained otherwise and he by death departed from
that right, we pray you do not envy his friends the office of their care and pain
to have collected and published them ;   and so to have published them, as where
(before) you were abused with divers stolen and surreptitious copies, maimed and
deformed by the frauds and stealthes of injurious imposters that exposed them :
even those are now offered to your view cured and perfect in their limbs ;   and
all the rest absolute in their numbers as he conceived them.   Who as he was a
happy imitator of Nature was a most gentle expresser of it.   His mind and hand
went together ;   and what he thought he uttered with that easiness that we have
scarce received from him a blot in his papers. . . .

This epistle is followed by the grandiloquent Ode by Ben Jonson.   The
author of *Volpone* calls Shakespeare " Sweet Swan of Avon, sole of the age ".
He declares that his rival was Not for an age but for all time.   If he regrets
his lack of classic learning, saying that he knew " small Latin and less Greek ",
he adds that his art was the product of his experience of life and constant
study of language and rhythm.

. . . he

Who casts to write a living line, must sweat,
(Such as thine are) and strike the second heat
Upon the Muse's anvil : turn the same,
(And himself with it) that he thinks to frame
Or for the laurel he may gain a scorn,
For a good poet's made as well as born
And such wert thou.

Speaking of the actor and how his buskined tread could shake a stage he says :

> When thy socks were on
> Leave thee alone, for the comparison
> Of all that insolent Greece or haughty Rome
> Sent forth, or since did from their ashes come.
> Triumph, my Britain, thou hast one to show,
> To whom all scenes of Europe homage owe.

Then, when he wishes to show how much Shakespeare put himself into his works :

> Look how the father's face
> Lives in his issue, even so, the race
> Of Shakespeare's mind and manners brightly shines
> In his well turned, and true filed lines,
> In each of which, he seems to shake a lance
> As brandished at the eyes of ignorance.

Dryden finds no proof of real admiration in Jonson's ode but declares that this poem is parsimonious in praise and insidious in suggestion ; that Jonson's eulogy goes not to the work, which he envied, but to the charming personality of its author. If so the hymns of praise that follow express more generous and sincere admiration.

The erudite Hugh Holland, a lifelong friend, who made the pilgrimage to the Holy Sepulchre, but whose career in England was rendered impossible by some sayings against Queen Elizabeth, laments Shakespeare's untimely death in a sonnet :

> Those hands, which you so clapped, go now and wring
> You Britains brave ; for done are Shakespeare's days :
> His days are done that made the dainty plays,
> Which made the Globe of heaven and earth to ring :
> Dried is that vein, dried is the Thespian spring,
> Turn'd all to tears, and Phoebus clouds his rays :
> That corpse, that coffin, now bestick those bays,
> Which crown'd him poet first, then poets' king.
> If tragedies might any prologue have,
> All those he made would scarce make one to this ;
> Where fame, now that he gone is to the grave—
> Death's public tiring-house—the Nuntius is :
> For, though his line of life went soon about,
> The life yet of his lines shall never out.

The ode of Leonard Digges moves the reader by its personal note :

> Shake-speare, at length thy pious fellowes give
> The World thy workes : thy Workes by which, out-live
> Thy tombe, thy name must, when that stone is rent,
> And Time dissolves thy Stratford Monument,

> Here we alive shall view thee still. This Book,
> When brasse and marble fade, shall make the look
> Fresh to all ages : when posterity
> Shall loath what's new think all is prodigy
> That is not Shakespeare's ; every line, each verse
> Here shall revive, redeem thee from thy herse.
> Nor fire, nor cankring age, as Naso said,
> Of his, thy wit-fraught booke shall once invade.
> Nor shall I e're believe, or think thee dead
> (Though mist) until our bankrupt stage be sped
> (Impossible) with some new strain t'out-do
> Passions of Juliet, and her Romeo ;
> Or till I heare a scene more nobly take,
> Then when thy half-Sword parlying Romans spake.
> Till these, till any of thy volumes rest
> Shall with more fire, more feeling be exprest,
> Be sure, our Shake-speare, thou canst never die,
> But crown'd with laurel, live eternally.

Leonard Digges had some literary celebrity of his own. His translation of Claudian was published by Edward Blount the year following the appearance of the Shakespeare Folio. Through him the voice of Stratford comes to us directly.

The last homage is the moving apostrophe of James Mabbe, the translator of Cervantes, Rojas and some Spanish books of Catholic piety. After many years spent in the embassy at Madrid with Sir John Digby the British ambassador, Mabbe returned to England. There he succeeded in enrolling himself as prebendary at Wells cathedral, where—it is said—the Catholic liturgy was long continued.

> We wonder'd, Shakespeare, that thou went'st so soon
> From the world's stage to the grave's tiring-room :
> We thought thee dead ; but this thy printed worth
> Tells thy spectators that thou went'st but forth
> To enter with applause. An actor's art
> Can die, and live to act a second part :
> That's but an exit of mortality,
> This a re-entrance to a plaudite.

The seventh page of the Folio lists the twenty-six " Principall Actors in all these Playes ". Page 8 gives the " Catalog " of the Comedies, Histories and Tragedies contained in the volume.

The Folio edition of 1623 was quickly sold out. About a hundred and forty copies are still extant, proof that great care was exercised in their conservation. The Folger Library in Washington possesses seventy-nine of these precious volumes ; among them is the copy offered by the printer Jaggard to his friend Augustine Vincent, containing some corrections made by the proof reader, and the copy owned by Samuel Gilburne, an actor of the company.

The Bibliothèque Nationale in Paris acquired the curiously annotated text formerly belonging to Bishop Butler. The British Museum, the Bodleian Library, the Stratford Museum and a few privileged individuals possess one or two copies.

In 1632 the Folio was reprinted ; this edition hardly differs from the first, except that some new verses were added notably one signed I M S, believed by some to mean Jasper Mayne Student. Others that these initials stand for In Memoriam scriptoris, a far-fetched interpretation. Then follows the often quoted epitaph by John Milton.

The third Folio of 1664 has become nearly as rare as the first. The warehouse where the volumes were stored was destroyed in the Fire of London (1666). In this edition the publishers included not only *Pericles*, *The London Prodigal* and the *Yorkshire Tragedy* but even the *History of Thomas Lord Cromwell*, *Sir John Oldcastle, Lord Cobham*, the *Puritan Widow* and *The Tragedy of Locrine ;* these latter are certainly not Shakespeare's.

When the fourth and last edition of the Folio was printed (1685) the copper-plate of Droeshout's engraving, already retouched several times, was so worn that the last impressions grew indistinct. Moreover, the text of the successive editions became more and more corrupt.

Meanwhile six biographers, Thomas Fuller, Edward Phillips, William Fulman, John Aubrey, William Winstanley and Gerard Langbaine furnished critical and biographical notices during Shakespeare's own century. These documents complete one another without ever being in contradiction. Furthermore, they are in agreement with the numerous contemporary testimonies quoted in this volume.

The first printed document is that of Thomas Fuller written in 1643 and published by his son twenty years later.

Fuller's notes on the *Worthies of England* were grouped according to region and classed alphabetically. In order to find the article on Shakespeare it is not the letter S which must be consulted but the word Warwickshire. As few readers got so far, it was some time before a consensus of authorities agreed that Fuller's notice was the earliest in date. This once established, it is astonishing that no trouble was taken to see whether he was in a position to speak with authority on Shakespeare.

Thomas Fuller's competence is unquestionable. Not only did he frequent, as a familiar, the taverns which he describes, but his London associations were the poet's own. He was a nephew of John Davenant, Bishop of Salisbury, and probably related to John Davenant of Oxford, and had been intimately linked with the Danvers family, notably with Sir Henry, over whose tomb he pronounced the funeral eulogy.

Thomas Fuller is described in Aubrey's *Contemporary Lives* as a most agreeable and open-minded " bonus socius " or good fellow, endowed with such a phenomenal memory that he could recite all the tradesmen's signs between Ludgate Hill and Charing Cross. In his notice on Shakespeare he says :

William Shakespeare was born at *Stratford* on *Avon* in this county [Warwick-shire] in whom three eminent Poets may seem in some sort to be compounded, 1. *Martial* in the *warlike* sound of his Sur-name, (whence some may conjecture him of a *Military extraction*) *Hasti-vibrans* or Shake-speare. 2. Ovid, the most naturall and witty of all Poets. 3. Plautus, who was an exact Comedian, yet never any Scholar, as our Shake-speare (if alive) would confess himself. Adde to all these, that though his Genius generally was *jocular*, and inclining him to *festivity*, yet he could (when so disposed) be *solemn* and *serious*, as appears by his Tragedies, so that Heraclitus himself (I mean if secret and unseen) might afford to smile at his Comedies, they were so *merry*, and *Democritus* scarce forbear to sigh at his Tragedies they were so *mournfull*.

He was an eminent instance of the truth of that Rule, *Poeta non fit*, sed *nascitur*, one is not *made* but *born* a Poet. Indeed his Learning was very little, so that as Cornish diamonds are not polished by any Lapidary, but are pointed and smoothed even as they are taken out of the Earth, so nature it self was all that art which was used upon him . . .

He died Anno Domini 16—— and was buried at Stratford-upon Avon the town of his nativity.

An interesting point in the above lines is the comparison between Shakespeare and Ovid, first made in 1598 by Francis Meres. It is here referred to as though the analogy had become a literary formula.

Edward Phillips' production quickly made its mark, thanks to his kinship with Milton and his friendship with the renowned Diodatis. In 1675 he published some critical considerations on the poets of England or *Theatrum Poetarum*. The preface concluded with the declaration that the greatest of all poets was Shakespeare. An interesting comparison follows:

Let us observe Spencer with all his Rustie, obsolete words, with all his rough-hewn clowterly Verses; yet take him throughout, and we shall find him a gracefull and Poetic Majesty: in like manner Shakespear, in spight of all his unfiled expressions, his rambling and indigested Fancys, the laughter of the Critical, yet must be confess't a Poet above many that go beyond him in Literature some degrees.

Benjamin Johnson, the most learned, judicious and correct, generally so accounted, of our English Comedians, and the more to be admired for being so, for that neither the height of natural parts, for he was no Shakesphear, nor the cost of Extraordinary Education; for he is reported but a Bricklayer's Son, but his own proper Industry and Addiction to Books advanct him to this perfection. Christopher Marlow, a kind of second Shakesphear (whose contemporary he was) not only because like him he rose from an Actor to be a maker of Plays, though inferiour both in Fame and Merit; but also because in his begun Poem of Hero and Leander, he seems to have a resemblance of that clean and unsophisticated Wit, which is natural to that incomparable Poet;

John Fletcher, one of the happy Triumvirat . . . among whom there might be said to be a symmetry of perfection, while each excelled in his peculiar way: Ben Johnson in his elaborate pains and knowledge of Authors, Shakespear in his pure vein of wit, and naturall Poetic height; Fletcher in a courtly Elegance and gentile familiarity of style, and withal a wit and invention so overflowing, that the luxuriant branches thereof were frequently throught convenient to be lopt off by his almost inseparable companion Francis Beaumont.

William Shakespear, the Glory of the English stage ; whose nativity at Stratford upon Avon, is the highest honour that Town can boast of ; from an Actor of Tragedies and Comedies he became a *Maker ;* and such a Maker, that though some others may perhaps pretend to a more exact Decorum and ecconomie, especially in Tragedy ; never any expresst a more lofty and Tragic heighth ; never any represented nature more purely to the life, and where the polishments of Art are most wanting, as probably his Learning was not extraordinary, he pleaseth with a certain wild and native Elegance ; and in all his Writings hath an unvulgar style, as well in his *Venus and Adonis* and his *Rape of Lucrece* and other various Poems, as in his Dramatics.

A third testimony concerning Shakespeare belongs to Corpus Christi College, Oxford, where it has been since the author's death in 1688. It is included in a collection of twenty-five manuscript volumes in irregular octavo size. The author of this immense work was William Fulman, a man of humble origin but precocious and distinguished intelligence which developed into exceptional learning under the tutelage of Henry Hammond an erudite Anglican clergyman, one of the collaborators in the famous Eikon Basilikê, intimate in his youth with both the Pembroke and Southampton families. More than half a century of Fulman's life was passed in the compilation and annotation of documents and correspondence.

His first four volumes treat of civil and religious history. Numbers five and six are given over to monastical records, seven and eight contain data referring to Oxford University. Nine, ten and eleven special information concerning Corpus Christi—the author's beloved Alma Mater—twelve, thirteen, fourteen and fifteen contain brief biographical notices of celebrities, seventeen and eighteen are devoted to theological matters, nineteen to a transcription of verses, and the remainder—from twenty to twenty-five—contain memoranda of divers kinds.

Shakespeare's name figures three times in the volume concerning British poets. It is spelled according to the accepted official and court form and the details given on his productions are correct.

Fulman notes the date and place of publication of the *Passionate Pilgrim* and adds that a collection containing one hundred and fifty-four sonnets, together with the *Lover's Complaint*, were issued at London in 1609.

A short biographical notice follows :

William Shakespeare was born at Stratford upon Avon in Warwickshire, about 1563-4.
Much given to all unluckiness in stealing venison and rabbits particularly from Sir Lucy—who had him oft whipt and sometimes imprisoned and at last made him fly his native country to his great advancement. But his revenge was so great, that he is his Justice Clodpate and calls him a great man and in allusion to his name bore three louses rampant for his Arms.
From an Actor of plays be became a composer. He died April 23, 1616, Aetat 53, probably at Stratford for there he is buried and hath a monument. (See Dugdale, p. 520.)
On which he lays a heavy curse upon any one who shall remove his bones. He died a Papist.

This manuscript note is composed in two distinct writings, that of Fulman, small, exquisite and meticulous, the other—in italics—more rapid and straggling calligraphy, is that of Richard Davies, Archdeacon of Coventry and rector of Sapperton. Far from diminishing the value of Fulman's evidence the testimony of Davies strengthens his authority.

Both authors are equally entitled to respect and the value of the manuscript is further confirmed by the best contemporary historian—who has given us all the facts relating to its composition.

We read in the *Athenae Oxonienses* that when the learned William Fulman died, he left behind him the immense collection of notes, texts and documents which had constituted his life work, asking his friend Davies, for years a sharer in his studies, to " digest and classify " the papers, complete certain unfinished memoirs from the random notes set down on separate sheets, then turn the whole over to the Corpus Christi Archives. The work was completed before 1690, for at that date Anthony Wood declared that he often begged the college authorities to let him have a sight of Fulman's papers " so serviceable to the promotion of my work now almost ready for the press ". (*The Athenae Oxonienses*, was indeed published in the same year.)

Wood then continues :

But such is the humour of the men of this age, that rather than they'll act a part for the public good and honour of learning, they'll suffer choice things to be buried in oblivion.

Through the courtesy of Dr. Cowley, who consented to retain all the volumes at the Bodleian long enough for me to study and obtain photographs of the pages concerning Shakespeare, I was able to take full cognizance of this valuable collection which is practically unknown, for I learned that they had never been consulted since the days when Dr. Dyce first mentioned them in his edition in 1854.

The blanks filled out by Davies were left by Fulman himself who reserves space for the ulterior information to be consigned thereto.

One of the fullest and most interesting of the notices is undoubtedly that of John Aubrey, composed *c.* 1650. Born in 1626 John Aubrey, who was in direct touch with the men of letters immediately preceding him, furnishes, on his own time and theirs, notes of exceptional vivacity and interest. He prides himself on not wasting time over things which every one knows, preferring to select small forgotten details. Hence the argument so often used by critics, " Aubrey does not mention this so we need not believe it ", is of no value. His curiosity concerning the generation preceding his own led him from boyhood to seek the company of the aged, whom he calls " pages of living history ". He loved to collect curious data about the private lives of great men and women, and often threw in such a phrase as this in the midst of his notes, " Without an old gossip like me there would be no remembrance of this ".

Aubrey worked without much method, jotting down pell-mell what he had collected about the physical appearance, associations, family and marital ties of the subject in hand. In the margin he noted the source from which he had got his information, or if he was put on a new track, adds, for instance, " Told that Wm. Lacy is the man now living that knows the most about Shakespeare and B. Jonson, for his address query Mr. Beeston ". When he had found Mr. Beeston, procured the desired address and finally traced Lacy to his haunts, he set down the information obtained, not in the life of Shakespeare, but in a separate note marked Beeston-Lacy.

When he had too much material for his page he wrote in the margin or between the paragraphs, which makes his manuscript very difficult to decipher. His collection, *Brief Lives Chiefly of My Contemporaries*, comprises four hundred biographical notes on distinguished persons : writers, statesmen, astrologers, soldiers, gentlemen and personal friends. They cover eight reigns, from Henry VIII to James II, five of which passed during his own lifetime. Belonging to a family renowned for longevity, he profited by direct evidence on the past, " My aunt Deborah Aubrey ", " my great-uncle Danvers ", " my friend Mr. Hoskins ", " Mr. Mollins, John Florio's son-in-law ", and Isaak Walton are contributors to his data. Endymion Porter, Mr. Hales of Eton and Sir John Suckling, and many more authorities on the poet, lived far into Aubrey's day. As he says himself : " Rarely has such authority been found for work of the sort ". For many years, Aubrey, whose lawsuits constantly led him to be on the road, was familiar in every tavern, worked only for himself and according to his own taste and choice. But one day, he was introduced to a professional historian—the same Anthony à Wood of whom mention has several times been made, and who was then engaged on an immense history of Oxford University, with notes on the principal graduates. Of solitary and secluded tastes, Wood was overjoyed at meeting a man of the world capable of furnishing data about persons of whom the antiquary could learn only what was dryly set down on the University records. Aubrey, agreed to compile information for Wood's volume. This explains the carelessness with which he sets down dates and quotations. He counted on Wood himself to verify dates and look up texts.

Aubrey's very faults give to his work extraordinary vitality and sincerity. Many pages are devoted to Ben Jonson. Walter Raleigh he detested, and consequently pictures remarkably. Descartes meets with his admiration, " the greatest mathematical genius of the age ", says he, " far more distinguished therein than by his theology ". Francis Bacon is shown as possessing an extraordinary legal mind. In the life of Harvey, the great physician, to whom he nevertheless denies the discovery of circulation— which he took from an obscure colleague, Walter Warner by name—Aubrey throws in this amusing observation. " Harvey had been physician to Lord Chancellor Bacon and admired his wit and style, but would not allow him to be a great philosopher. ' Tush ', exclaimed the old doctor, speaking in derision, ' he writes philosophy like a Lord Chancellor '. " Aubrey also remarks, in speaking of Bacon, that he sometimes wrote verse and quotes to prove it the stanzas most admired by his friends. Both in style and matter the verses are less than mediocre, but it is upon this passage, which they quote without its context, that Baconian critics base the claim that they find in Aubrey the recognition of Bacon's poetical genius. Let the reader judge it himself.

> Domestic cares afflict the husband's bed
> Or pains his head ;
> Those that live single take it for a curse
> Or do things worse ;
> Some would have children ; those that have them moan
> Or wish them gone.
> What is it then to have or have no wife
> But single thraldom or a double strife ?
>
> Our own affections still at home to please
> Is a disease ;
> To cross the sea to any foreign soil,
> Perils and toil.
> Wars with their noise affright us ; when they cease
> We're worse in peace.
> What then remains ? But that we still should cry
> Not to be born, or being born, to die.[1]

Aubrey is more explicit when he affirms the genius of Shakespeare. The notice which concerns him is marked with a symbolical crown of laurel. After mentioning that Mr. William Shakespeare was born at Stratford he adds that his father was a butcher and that neighbours informed the biographer that when William, as a boy, had followed the trade, he killed a calf in tragic style ; but that being naturally inclined to poetry he came to London at about eighteen, where he was actor in one of the theatres and played extremely well. That Jonson, on the contrary, was poor in the profession although an excellent instructor. Shakespeare began early to make essays in the dramatic art, which at that time was very low ; his plays " took well ". He was a handsome, well-shaped man, of pleasant natural wit, he and Jonson were in the habit of noting the humours and extravagances which they met on their travels, and it was when touring and at the village of Grendon that he found the individual who suggested his comic constable. " This person was still living when I came down to Oxford in 1642 and Mr. Joseph Howe, of this parish, knew him." Aubrey then recalls the anecdote of the supper in a tavern at Stratford when Shakespeare made the mock epitaph on John Combe, but to make the story better, he added that the poet was never forgiven, whereas we know that Combe bequeathed to his constant friend, Mr. Shakespeare, the sum of five pounds. He continues literally :

He was wont to goe to his native countrey once a yeare I thinke I have been told that he left 2 or 300 li. per annum there and there about to a sister.   Vide his epitaph in Dugdale's *Warwickshire.*

[1] *Brief Lives*, vol. i, p. 73.

I have heard Sir William Davenant and Mr. Thomas Shadwell (who is counted the best comedian we have now) say that he had a most prodigious witt, and did admire his naturall parts beyond all other dramaticall writers (vol. 2. p. 226).

Aubrey then makes allusions to the praise of Shakespeare for " never having blotted out a line " (would that he had blotted out a thousand, said Jonson), and continues with a personal appreciation :

His comoedies will remaine witt as long as the English tongue is understood, for that he handles *mores hominum*. Now our present writers reflect so much upon particular persons and coxcombeities, that twenty yeares hence they will not be understood. Though, as Ben : Johnson sayes of him, that he had but little Latine and lesse Greek, he understood Latine pretty well, for he had been in his younger yeares a schoolmaster in the countrey. (vol. 2, p. 227).

This information, adds Aubrey, was obtained from Mr. Beeston.

Mr. Beeston, having managed one of the playhouses in Shakespeare's time, was an excellent authority on all pertaining to drama. Francis Kirkman, who dedicated to him a play translated from the French in 1662, recognizes in Beeston the best authority on all theatrical matters. Beeston sent Aubrey to Mr. Lacy to obtain certain supplementary information. Aubrey then completed his text on Shakespeare by the lines :

The more to be admired, quaere he was not a company keeper, lived at Shorditch ; would'nt be debauched ; and if invited to court he was in paine.

But, like a good chronicler, Aubrey never completely squeezed his subject dry on first handling. Scandal is seldom found under the name of the subject implicated, but in the biography of someone else. Thus, his remarks concerning Bacon's private life are to be found in a notice about Mr. Thomas Bushell, and the history of Shakespeare's Oxford love-affair is set down in the biographical notice of Sir William d'Avenant.

As a vain pretext for discrediting Aubrey's authority it has been said that there are so many gaps in the text, so much banal information omitted, that surely the author was very ill-informed.

Such criticism ignores Aubrey's own statement that he voluntarily omits general knowledge which has become commonplace ; his boast is to mention " singularities ". If, for instance, he does not dwell on the deer-stealing episode in referring to Shakespeare it is because this anecdote about Justice Shallow was very well known. It is also generally forgotten by those who quote Aubrey that through no fault of the author himself we are no longer in possession of his complete original manuscript.

When Aubrey turned over his collection to Anthony à Wood, political strife reigned at Oxford. A rumour spread through the college that the historian was in the possession of much subversive matter—enough to cut the author's throat. Wood was a prudent man and feared search-warrants. Consequently, without a word to the author (" And I who trusted him with my life ", exclaimed poor Aubrey), he burnt a third of the incriminating papers which had been confided to his safe keeping. The remaining papers were left "gelded and unindexed" to the Bodleian Library, since when they have been partially edited by Edmund Malone and more recently by Andrew Clarke.

A brief mention will suffice for the account of Shakespeare by William Winstanley, for this author merely repeats what had been said by his predecessors. He adds to the foregoing information the remark that "Shakespeare was one of the actors who had been led to dramatic composition, like Marlowe in his own day, and Mr. Lacy who has since become celebrated". He also recalls the fact that he formed, together with Daniel, Drayton, and Jonson a famous poetic "quaternion" and "by his conversing with jocular wits, whereto he was naturally inclined, he became so famously witty—or wittily famous—as, without learning he attained to an extraordinary height in the comic strain".

Gerard Langbaine devotes thirty pages to the same subject in his *Account of the Dramatic Poets*, 1691. His work, an excellent critical study of the plays and poems, includes a transcription of *The Rape of Lucrece*, which evidently was hard to come by. The only new matter introduced is a description of the poet's tomb together with that of his wife and daughter; he transcribes the various epitaphs. Langbaine alone seems to have observed the frequency with which Italian proverbs are to be found in the poet's works:

One of the most Eminent Poets of his Time: he was born at Stratford upon Avon in Warwickshire; and flourished in the Reigns of Queen Elizabeth, and King James the First. His Natural Genius to Poetry was so excellent, that like those Diamonds, which are found in Cornwall, Nature had little, or no occasion for the Assistance of Art to polish it. The Truth is, 'tis agreed on by most, that his Learning was not extraordinary; and I am apt to believe, that his Skill in the French and Italian Tongues, exceeded his Knowledge in the Roman Language: for we find him not only beholding to Cynthio Giraldi and Bandello, for his Plots, but likewise a Scene in Harry the Fifth, written in French, between the Princess Catherine and her Governante: Besides Italian Proverbs scatter'd up and down in his Writings. . . . it would be superfluous in me to endeavour to particularise what most deserves praise in him, after so many Great Men that have given him their several Testimonials of his Merit: so I should think I were guilty of an Injury beyond pardon to his Memory, should I so disparage it, as to bring his Wit in competition with any of our Age. . . . I shall . . . take the Liberty to speak my Opinion, as my predecessors have done, of his Works; which is this, That I esteem his Plays beyond any that have ever been published in our Language: and tho' I extreamly admire Johnson, and Fletcher; yet I must still aver, that when in competition with Shakespear; I must apply to them what Justus Lipsius writ . . . concerning Terence and Plautus . . . Terentium amo, admiror, sed Plautum magis.[1]

Before the century's end, all the Folio editions had been absorbed. This incited Nicholas Rowe, who became poet laureate in succession to Jonson, Davenant and Dryden, to make a new and critical eight-volume edition of Shakespeare's Dramatic works.

---

[1] Gerard Langbaine, vol. ii, p. 453.

He was a man of great acumen, culture and refinement.   As a biographer he began collecting material when the memory of the actor-poet was still alive in Stratford and London, and his work may therefore be justly classed as belonging to the seventeenth rather than the eighteenth century.   He was a precursor in the attempt to establish a better text by comparing and combining the Quarto and Folio editions.   His reading of contested passages is often excellent.   He added tables of " Dramatis Personae " to such plays as were printed without one, and arranged the separation into acts and scenes which modern editors are obliged to follow.

As a critic we have never had a better.   Each time Rowe hazards an original opinion concerning the date or sequence of the dramas, his reasoned solution has been proved correct.

Thus he refused to accept *The Tempest* as an early work although placed first of all by the original editors.   His critical sense detected the full maturity of this conception.   He declared with equal accuracy that the *Midsummer Night's Dream* could only belong to a very early period, and fixed the date of *Henry V* as infallibly as was done after the discovery of the Stationer's Register.

So, at the dawn of the eighteenth century it may be said without exaggeration that the world already possessed what it is essential to know of the life and work of its greatest dramatic genius.

THE END

INDEX OF PERSONS

INDEX OF THE WORKS OF SHAKESPEARE

INCLUDING THOSE CONJECTURED TO BE BY HIM

INDEX OF OTHER WORKS MENTIONED IN THE TEXT